Artificial Intelligence: Foundations, Theory, and Algorithms

Series Editors

Barry O'Sullivan, Cork, Ireland
Michael Wooldridge, Oxford, United Kingdom

More information about this series at http://www.springer.com/series/13900

Audun Jøsang

Subjective Logic

A Formalism for Reasoning Under Uncertainty

Springer

Audun Jøsang
Department of Informatics
University of Oslo
Oslo, Norway

ISSN 2365-3051 ISSN 2365-306X (electronic)
Artificial Intelligence: Foundations, Theory, and Algorithms
ISBN 978-3-319-82555-7 ISBN 978-3-319-42337-1 (eBook)
DOI 10.1007/978-3-319-42337-1

Printed on acid-free paper

This Springer imprint is published by Springer Nature
The registered company is Springer International Publishing AG
The registered company address is: Gewerbestrasse 11, 6330 Cham, Switzerland

SUBJECTIVE LOGIC

To my parents Astri and Tormod,
to my wife Frauke, and
to my children Maia, Benjamin and Johanna.

Foreword

Decision making is a pervasive part of life. Every day we are confronted with deciding between multiple choices, in both our personal and professional lives. Any decision, whether it is being made in the corporate board room, the situation room, or simply in our breakfast room, is mired in uncertainty. Only an omnipotent being has perfect knowledge to make optimal decisions. Everyone has to deal with uncertainty when choosing between options. For instance, when deciding to accept a job offer, there is always a chance that the job will turn out to be a poor fit, which could hurt your career. Therefore, it is important to perform a thorough benefit versus risk analysis that accommodates uncertainty into the decision-making process. The issue of uncertainty is exacerbated by the fact that one should not trust (in the absolute sense) anything one hears or reads, whether it comes from social media, a news outlet or even this book. We are all confronted with conflicting information, and these conflicts add more uncertainty to the decision-making process. This book introduces the formalism of subjective logic, which in my humble opinion will become a critical tool in understanding and incorporating uncertainty into decision making.

Subjective logic is an uncertain probabilistic logic that was initially introduced by Audun Jøsang to address formal representations of trust. The evaluation and exploitation of trust requires reasoning, and thus, subjective logic has blossomed into a principled method for probabilistic reasoning under uncertainty. This book is the first to provide a comprehensive view of subjective logic and all of its operations. The field of subjective logic is still evolving, and I expect that this book will not be the final word on the subject. The book presents a great opportunity to learn and eventually participate in this exciting research field.

Uncertain reasoning is not new. For over forty years, it has been recognized that first-order Bayesian reasoning is unable to accommodate conflicting information. A number of great minds have developed belief theories over the years that generalize Bayesian reasoning in the face of conflicts. Other great minds argue that Bayesian reasoning is actually suitable for reasoning in all situations, even when conflicting information exists. For the purposes of full disclosure, I happen to side with the Bayesian camp. This is partially due to my electrical engineering signal processing background, and my experience working on target-tracking problems. One nice thing about Bayesian approaches is that their performance can be verified. In as much as the models accurately represent the real-world environment, one can verify that the Bayesian techniques are performing as expected through Monte Carlo simulations. On the other hand, there has been no statistical verification of belief theories that I am aware of. A belief theory is typically justified by anecdotal examples, which is one reason why ideas within the theories are disputed.

I am personally intrigued by subjective logic because it provides a principled way to connect beliefs to Dirichlet distributions. Furthermore, subjective logic offers computationally efficient operators that approximate second-order Bayesian reasoning. In fact, I believe that there are ways to justify the use of subjective logic in a statistical (and not just an anecdotal) sense. It might be the case that some of the operation will need to be adjusted. After all, the field of subjective logic is very much alive and evolving. I think the evolution of subjective logic could eventually dispel the present-day disputes within the belief theory community. No one subjective logic operator will be appropriate for every decision-making task, but I do believe that subjective logic is evolving into a framework that will enable the decision maker to select the most appropriate operator for his/her particular decision task.

There are many avenues of research left to explore. For instance, much work is needed to further formalize the connection to second-order Bayesian reasoning, including understanding under what conditions the efficient operations within subjective logic do or do not provide a good approximation to exact second-order Bayesian reasoning. This area of exploration is necessary in the study and development of subjective Bayesian networks. The area of trust determination and revision via reputation systems is still evolving and must be connected to subjective Bayesian networks to eventually obtain rigorous methods for uncertain probabilistic reasoning in the face of conflicts. To this end, one must also understand how to decompose human-generated reports into a set of subjective opinions. These are just a sample of interesting ideas worthy of exploration. If you want to understand and explore these exciting topics of research, I strongly encourage you to study this book.

Adelphi, Maryland, March 2016 *Lance Kaplan*

Preface

The development of subjective logic has been a journey, on which this book represents a milestone.

The original idea of subjective logic came to my mind in 1996, while I was a Ph.D. student at NTNU in Norway, visiting Queensland University of Technology (QUT) in Australia. For my Ph.D. project I needed a formal representation of trust, but could not find any adequate models in the literature, so I had to define my own model, which became subjective logic.

The subtropical climate of southern Queensland is great for outdoor activities, and the fundamental ideas of subjective logic were inspired by the sounds, smells and colours of the Australian bush. This may seem strange to some, but I have repeatedly found that being out in nature can be a catalyst for scientific inspiration.

After completing my Ph.D. in 1997, I worked on computer networks research at Telenor for a couple of years, which was natural because of my previous job as a telecommunications engineer at Alcatel Telecom. During that time, little progress in the development of subjective logic was made, until I joined the Distributed Systems Technology Centre (DSTC) in Australia in 2000. DSTC was a collaborative research centre of excellence, mainly funded by the Australian Government. At DSTC, I had the time and freedom to focus on subjective logic in combination with security research, and also enjoyed an environment of highly skilled and inspiring colleagues with whom it was fun to work. Free research jobs like that do not grow on trees.

In 2005 I moved to QUT, where some of the staff and Ph.D. students shared my interest in reputation systems and subjective logic reasoning. While I was quite busy with teaching and research in information security, the research on reputation systems, trust modelling and subjective logic also progressed well in that period, and still continues at QUT.

Then, in 2008, I joined the University of Oslo (UiO), where I have time to work on subjective logic, in parallel with teaching duties and research on information security. For the first time I have colleagues who work with me full time to advance the theory and applications of subjective logic, thanks to generous funding from the US Army's Open Campus program, as well as from the Norwegian Research Council.

The process of bringing subjective logic to its present state of maturity has thus taken 20 years. I have been privileged to have time, and to have great collaboration partners in this endeavour, for which I am grateful.

The name 'subjective logic' is short and elegant, but what is the intention behind it? The adjective 'subjective' refers to the aspects: 1) that opinions are held by individuals, and in general do not represent collective beliefs, and 2) that opinions represent beliefs that can be affected by uncertainty. The noun 'logic' refers to the aspect that subjective logic operators generalise both binary logic operators and probabilistic logic operators.

The fundamental innovation of subjective logic is to generalise the aforementioned operators, by including second-order uncertainty in the form of uncertainty mass. Concepts that are already described in Bayesian theory and probabilistic logic must then be redefined in terms of subjective logic, by including the uncertainty dimension. Explicit representation of uncertainty also opens up the possibility of defining totally new formal reasoning concepts, such as trust fusion and transitivity.

The present book harmonises notations and formalisms of previously published papers and articles. This book also improves, and corrects whenever appropriate, descriptions of operators that have previously been published.

The advantages of using subjective logic are that real-world situations can be realistically modelled with regard to how those situations are perceived, and that conclusions more correctly reflect the ignorance and uncertainties that necessarily result from partially uncertain input arguments. It is my wish that researchers and practitioners will advance, improve and apply subjective logic to build powerful artificial reasoning models and tools for solving real-world problems.

Oslo, March 2016 *Audun Jøsang*

Acknowledgements

I would like to thank the following persons for providing inspiration and direct contributions to the development of subjective logic.

Tanja (Ažderska) Pavleska wrote her Ph.D. thesis on computational trust where she applied subjective logic and defined formal models for trust transitivity.

Touhid Bhuiyan wrote his Ph.D. thesis on applying subjective logic to trust and reputation modelling.

Erik Blasch and Paulo C.G. Costa assisted in defining criteria for selecting appropriate fusion operators.

Colin Boyd is a colleague from QUT, now at NTNU, and has provided advice on developing Bayesian reputation systems.

Jin-Hee Cho has undertaken comprehensive studies on computational trust in general and has developed models based on subjective logic for the propagation of opinions in social networks.

Clive Cox applied subjective logic to analyse the friends network in the online social network Rummble, and contributed to developing practical concepts for implementing subjective reputation systems.

Martin and Dave Culwick developed the prototype tool 'Cobelir' for medical reasoning based on subjective logic, around 2007.

Milan Daniel engaged in highly interesting discussions about belief theory, and assisted in improving the binomial deduction operator in subjective logic.

Matthew Davey developed the first demonstration Java applet for subjective logic operators, while we worked at DSTC around 2000. He also designed the logo for subjective logic, with the triangle, the dot and the rays of red, amber and green.

Javier Diaz assisted in defining cumulative fusion for multinomial and hypernomial opinions.

Zied Elouedi helped to analyse the concept of material implication within the framework of subjective logic.

Eric Faccer assisted in simulating Bayesian reputation systems, when we worked together at DSTC.

Jennifer Golbeck has been a great inspiration in reputation systems research, and helped to describe robustness characteristics for reputation systems.

Dieter Gollmann, who was supervisor for my Security Master's at Royal Holloway, helped to formalise access authorisation policies based on subjective logic.

Tyrone Grandison assisted in developing the operator for binomial deduction in subjective logic, and also visited me at DSTC around 2002.

Elizabeth Gray did her Ph.D. on trust propagation in 'small worlds' and contributed to formalising transitive trust networks.

Guibing Guo contributed to enhancements of Bayesian reputation systems.

Jochen Haller contributed to defining Dirichlet reputation systems.

Robin Hankin defined the hyper-Dirichlet PDF, and assisted in adapting that formalism to subjective logic.

Shane Hird assisted in developing Bayesian reputation systems, and in improving the demonstration operator for subjective logic operators, when he worked at DSTC.

Jadwiga Indulska assisted in developing robustness models for Bayesian reputation systems.

Roslan Ismail wrote his Ph.D. thesis on security for reputation systems, and assisted in developing Bayesian reputation systems.

Magdalena Ivanovska is a colleague at UiO, and a great discussion partner for theoretical and philosophical questions related to subjective Bayesian networks. She has developed elements of multinomial deduction, and has also been a great help in tightening up the formalism of subjective logic in general.

Lance Kaplan took the initiative to collaborate through the ARL Open Campus program, for which I am very grateful, because it has directed subjective logic research towards subjective Bayesian networks. During a workshop at the University of Padova in 2015 he coined the term 'subjective networks', which is the topic of the last chapter in this book. Lance has also contributed to the development of models for classifiers based on subjective logic.

Michael Kinateder assisted in developing formal models for trust transitivity.

Svein Knapskog, who was my Ph.D. supervisor at NTNU, wanted me to work on formal methods. Thanks to his liberal attitude, he let me pursue my own intuition to work on trust modelling with subjective logic.

Stephane Lo Presti assisted in defining risk models based on computational trust and subjective logic.

Xixi Luo contributed to developing the concept of continuous reputation ratings.

Sukanya Manna did her Ph.D. project on applying subjective logic to semantic document summarisation.

Stephen Marsh engaged in philosophical discussions about trust, often over a few beers, and contributed to defining formal models for trust transitivity.

David McAnally, who sadly passed away in 2005, did a very thorough analysis of the variance approximation of product opinions, when he worked at DSTC.

Tim Muller wrote his Ph.D. thesis on trust formalisms based on subjective logic, engaged in interesting discussions about how to model trust, and assisted in developing the concept of entropy for subjective opinions.

Kristi O'Grady and Stephen O'Hara assisted in analysing the base rate fallacy in belief reasoning.

Robert Peime contributed to the demonstration applet for subjective logic operators, when he did an internship at DSTC.

Maria Silvia Pini invited me to spend three months at the University of Padova in 2013, generously funded by their Bando Visiting Scientist program. We collaborated on reputation systems research.

Simon Pope became interested in subjective logic when he joined DSTC in 2004. He made significant theoretical contributions to subjective logic, greatly improved the demonstration Java applet for subjective logic operators, and developed the professional 'ShEBA' tool for intelligence analysis based on subjective logic.

Sebastian Ries did his Ph.D. on visualisation of opinions, and developed the alternative CertainLogic representation.

Maria Rifqi assisted in defining cumulative fusion for multinomial and hypernomial opinions.

Francesco Sambo worked at the University of Padova, where I spent three months in 2013. Francesco became interested in subjective logic, helped develop a procedure for the inversion of conditional opinions, and visited me at UiO in 2014.

Francesco Santini worked with me when I visited the University of Padova in 2013, and contributed to enhancing Bayesian reputation systems.

Murat Sensoy has been a great discussion partner, and has produced innovative methods and applications of subjective logic.

Helen Svensson helped to define a model for distributed intrusion detection based on subjective logic.

Rachel Taylor, on a camping trip to the Sunshine Coast in 1997, indirectly gave me the inspiration for the name 'subjective logic'.

Greg Timbrell and I started discussing in the printer room at QUT, where he had picked up a draft paper of mine on subjective logic. Greg encouraged me to apply subjective logic to medical reasoning, which with the software design skills of Martin and Dave Culwick became a simple prototype called 'Cobelir'.

Patrick Vannoorenberghe, who sadly passed away, assisted in developing belief fusion operators.

Dongxia Wang contributed to the formalisation of entropy concepts for subjective opinions.

Andrew Whitby developed a nice robustness filter for Bayesian reputation systems, when he was a Master's student doing an internship at DSTC.

Yue Xu is a colleague at QUT. She has contributed to the development of formal trust and reputation models.

Jie Zhang invited me several times to NTU in Singapore, where I worked with his group on trust and reputation systems.

Many others have provided inspiration and advice. I am also grateful to all researchers and practitioners who apply subjective logic in their own work, thereby contributing to making subjective logic useful for themselves and for others.

Finally I would like to thank the technical and editorial team at Springer in Heidelberg for their professional support. My editor Ronan Nugent has been a great advisor for this book project.

Contents

Chapter 1
Introduction

We can assume that an objective reality exists but our perception of it will always be subjective. This idea is articulated by the concept of *"das Ding an sich"* (the thing-in-itself) in the philosophy of Kant [64]. The duality between the assumed objective world and the perceived subjective world is also reflected by the various logic and probabilistic reasoning formalisms in use.

In binary logic a proposition about the state of the world must be either true or false, which fits well with an assumed objective world. Probability calculus takes argument probabilities in the range $[0,1]$, and hence to some extent reflects subjectivity by allowing propositions to be partially true. However, we are often unable to estimate probabilities with confidence because we lack the necessary evidence. A formalism for expressing degrees of uncertainty about beliefs is therefore needed in order to more faithfully reflect the perceived world in which we are all immersed. In addition, whenever a belief about a proposition is expressed, it is always done by an individual, and it can never be considered to represent a general and objective belief. It is therefore necessary that the formalism also includes belief ownership in order to reflect the fundamental subjectivity of all beliefs.

The expressiveness of reasoning frameworks depends on the richness in syntax and interpretation that the arguments can express. The opinion representation which is used to represent beliefs in subjective logic offers significantly greater expressiveness than Boolean truth values and probabilities. This is achieved by explicitly including degrees of uncertainty and vagueness, thereby allowing an analyst to specify for example *"I don't know"* or *"I'm indifferent"* as input arguments.

Definitions of operators used in a specific reasoning framework depend on the argument syntax. For example, the AND, OR and XOR operators in binary logic are traditionally defined by their respective truth tables, which have the status of being axioms. Other operators, such as MP (Modus Ponens), MT (Modus Tollens) and CP (contraposition) are defined in a similar way. Subjective logic and probabilistic logic generalise these operators as algebraic expressions, and thereby make truth tables obsolete.

The concept of *probabilistic logic* has multiple interpretations in the literature, see e.g. [78]. The general aim of a probabilistic logic is to combine the capacity of probability theory to handle likelihood with the capacity of binary logic to make inference from argument structures. The combination offers a more powerful formalism than either probability calculus or deductive logic can offer alone. The various probabilistic logics attempt to replace traditional logic truth tables, whereby results defined by them instead can be derived by algebraic methods in a general way.

In this book, probabilistic logic is interpreted as a direct extension of binary logic, in the sense that propositions get assigned probabilities, rather than just Boolean truth values, and formulas of probability calculus replace truth tables.

Assuming that Boolean TRUE in binary logic corresponds to probability $p = 1$, and that Boolean FALSE corresponds to probability $p = 0$, binary logic (BL) simply becomes an instance of probabilistic logic (PL), or equivalently, probabilistic logic becomes a generalisation of binary logic. More specifically there is a direct correspondence between many binary logic operators and probabilistic logic operator formulas, as specified in Table 1.1.

Table 1.1 Correspondence between binary logic and probabilistic logic operators

Binary Logic		**Probabilistic Logic**		
AND:	$x \wedge y$	Product:	$p(x \wedge y) = p(x)p(y)$	(I)
OR:	$x \vee y$	Coproduct:	$p(x \vee y) = p(x) + p(y) - p(x)p(y)$	(II)
XOR:	$x \not\equiv y$	Inequivalence:	$p(x \not\equiv y) = p(x)(1-p(y)) + (1-p(x))p(y)$	(III)
EQU:	$x \equiv y$	Equivalence:	$p(x \equiv y) = 1 - p(x \not\equiv y)$	(IV)
MP:	$\{(x \rightarrow y), x\} \vdash y$	Deduction:	$p(y\|x) = p(x)p(y\vert x) + p(\overline{x})p(y\vert \overline{x})$	(V)
MT:	$\{(x \rightarrow y), \overline{y}\} \vdash \overline{x}$	Abduction:	$p(x\vert y) = \dfrac{a(x)p(y\vert x)}{a(x)p(y\vert x) + a(\overline{x})p(y\vert \overline{x})}$	(VI)
			$p(x\vert \overline{y}) = \dfrac{a(x)p(\overline{y}\vert x)}{a(x)p(\overline{y}\vert x) + a(\overline{x})p(\overline{y}\vert \overline{x})}$	(VII)
			$p(x\widetilde{\|}y) = p(y)p(x\vert y) + p(\overline{y})p(x\vert \overline{y})$	(VIII)
CP:	$(x \rightarrow y) \Leftrightarrow (\overline{y} \rightarrow \overline{x})$	Bayes' theorem:	$p(\overline{x}\vert \overline{y}) = 1 - \dfrac{a(x)p(\overline{y}\vert x)}{a(x)p(\overline{y}\vert x) + a(\overline{x})p(\overline{y}\vert \overline{x})}$	(IX)

Some of the correspondences in Table 1.1 might not be obvious and therefore need some explanation for why they are valid. The parameter $a(x)$ represents the base rate of x, also called the prior probability of x. The negation, or complement value, of x is denoted $\overline{x}$.

For the CP (contraposition) equivalence, the term $(\overline{y} \rightarrow \overline{x})$ represents the *contrapositive* of the term $(x \rightarrow y)$. The CP equivalence of binary logic can be derived by the application of Bayes' theorem described in Section 9.2.1. To see how, first recall that $p(\overline{x}|\overline{y}) = 1 - p(x|\overline{y})$, where $p(x|\overline{y})$ can be expressed as in Eq.(VII) which is a form of Bayes' theorem given in Eq.(9.9) in Section 9.2.1. Now assume that $p(y|x) = 1$, then necessarily $p(\overline{y}|x) = 0$. By inserting the argument $p(\overline{y}|x) = 0$ into Eq.(IX) it follows that $p(\overline{x}|\overline{y}) = 1$, which thereby produces the CP equivalence. Said briefly, if $p(y|x) = 1$ then $p(\overline{x}|\overline{y}) = 1$, where the term $p(\overline{x}|\overline{y})$ is the contrapositive of $p(y|x)$. In other words, the CP equivalence in binary logic can be derived as a special case of the probabilistic expression of Eq.(IX). It can be shown that Eq.(IX) is a transformed version of Bayes' theorem. Note that $p(y|x) \neq p(\overline{x}|\overline{y})$ in general.

MP (Modus Ponens) corresponds to – and is a special case of – the probabilistic conditional deduction of Eq.(V) which expresses the law of total probability described in Section 9.2.3. MT (Modus Tollens) corresponds to – and is a special case of – probabilistic conditional abduction. MP and MT are described in Section 9.1. The notation $p(y\|x)$ means that the probability of child y is derived as a function of the conditionals $p(y|x)$ and $p(y|\overline{x})$, as well as of the evidence probability $p(x)$ on the parent x. Similarly, the notation $p(x\widetilde{\|}y)$ for conditional abduction denotes the derived probability of target x conditionally abduced from the input conditionals $p(y|x)$ and $p(y|\overline{x})$ as well as from the evidence probability $p(y)$ of the child y.

For example, consider the probabilistic operator for MT in Table 1.1. Assume that $(x \rightarrow y)$ is TRUE, and that y is FALSE, which translates into $p(y|x) = 1$ and $p(y) = 0$. Then it can be observed from Eq.(VI) that $p(x|y) \neq 0$ because $p(y|x) = 1$. From Eq.(VII) we see that $p(x|\overline{y}) = 0$ because $p(\overline{y}|x) = 1 - p(y|x) = 0$. From Eq.(VIII) it can finally be seen that $p(x\widetilde{\|}y) = 0$, because $p(y) = 0$ and $p(x|\overline{y}) = 0$. From the probabilistic expressions, we just abduced that $p(x) = 0$, which translates into x being FALSE, as MT dictates for this case.

EQU denoted with the symbol '$\equiv$' represents equivalence, i.e. that x and y have equal truth values. XOR denoted with the symbol '$\not\equiv$' represents inequivalence, i.e. that x and y have different truth values.

The power of probabilistic logic is its ability to derive logical conclusions without relying on axioms of logic in terms of truth tables, only on principles and axioms of probability calculus.

When logic operators can simply be defined as special cases of corresponding probabilistic operators, there is no need to define them in terms of truth tables. The truth values of traditional truth tables can be directly computed with probabilistic logic operators, which means that the truth-table axioms are superfluous. To have separate independent definitions for the same concept, i.e. both as a truth table and as a probability calculus operator, is problematic because of the possibility of inconsistency between definitions. In the defence of truth tables, one could say that it could be pedagogically instructive to use them as a look-up tool for Boolean cases, because a simple manual look-up can be quite fast. However, the truth tables should be defined as being generated by their corresponding probabilistic logic operators, and not as separate axioms.

A fundamental limitation of probabilistic logic (and of binary logic likewise) is the inability to take into account the analyst's levels of confidence in the probability arguments, and the inability to handle the situation when the analyst fails to produce probabilities for some of the input arguments.

An analyst might for example want to give the input argument *"I don't know"*, which expresses total ignorance and uncertainty about some statement. However, an argument like that can not be expressed if the formalism only allows input arguments in the form of Booleans or probabilities. The probability $p(x) = 0.5$ would not be a satisfactory argument because it would mean that x and $\overline{x}$ are exactly equally likely, which in fact is quite informative, and very different from ignorance. An analyst who has little or no evidence for providing input probabilities could be tempted or even encouraged to set probabilities with little or no confidence. This practice would generally lead to unreliable conclusions, often described as the problem of 'garbage in, garbage out'. What is needed is a way to express lack of confidence in probabilities. In subjective logic, the lack of confidence in probabilities is expressed as *uncertainty mass*.

Another limitation of logic and probability calculus is that these formalisms are not designed to handle situations where multiple agents have different beliefs about the same statement. In subjective logic, *subjective belief ownership* can be explicitly expressed, and different beliefs about the same statements can be combined through trust fusion and discounting whenever required.

The general idea of subjective logic is to extend probabilistic logic by explicitly including: 1) uncertainty about probabilities and 2) subjective belief ownership in the formalism, as illustrated in Figure 1.1.

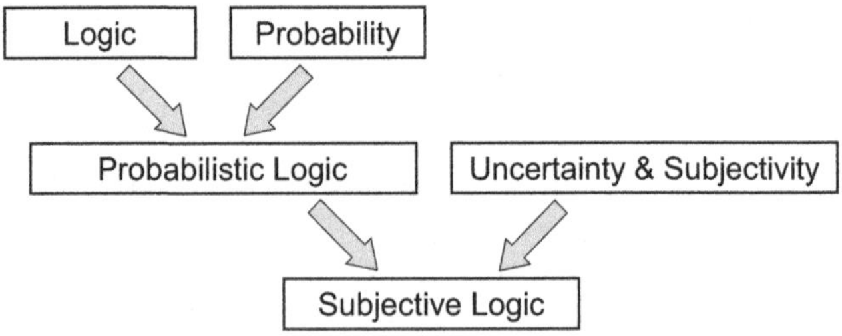

Fig. 1.1 The general idea of subjective logic

Arguments in subjective logic are called *subjective opinions*, or *opinions* for short. An opinion can contain uncertainty mass in the sense of *uncertainty about probabilities*. In the literature on statistics and economics, the type of uncertainty expressed by uncertainty mass in subjective logic is typically called *second-order probability* or *second-order uncertainty*. In that sense, traditional probability represents first-order uncertainty [31, 95]. More specifically, second-order uncertainty is represented in terms of a probability density function over first-order probabilities.

Probability density functions must have an integral of 1 to respect the additivity axiom of probability theory. Apart from this requirement, a probability density function can take any shape, and thereby represent arbitrary forms of second-order uncertainty. Uncertainty mass in subjective opinions represents second-order uncertainty which can be expressed in the form of Dirichlet PDFs (probability density functions).

A Dirichlet PDF naturally reflects random sampling of statistical events, which is the basis for the *aleatory* interpretation of opinions as statistical measures of likelihood. Uncertainty mass in the Dirichlet model reflects *vacuity* of evidence. Interpreting uncertainty mass as vacuity of evidence reflects the property that *"the fewer observations the more uncertainty mass"*.

Opinions can also reflect structural-knowledge evidence (i.e. non-statistical evidence), which is the basis for the *epistemic* interpretation of opinions as knowledge-based measures of likelihood. Uncertainty mass in epistemic opinions reflects vacuity of structural knowledge about a specific event or outcome which might only occur once, and which therefore can not be sampled statistically. The difference between aleatory and epistemic opinions is described in Section 3.3.

Subjective opinion ownership is closely related to trust, because when different agents have different opinions about the same statement, then an analyst needs to specify or derive levels of trust in the different agents/sources before their opinions can be integrated in a reasoning model.

In traditional Bayesian theory, the concept of base rate, also known as *prior probability*, is often not clearly distinguished from probability estimates. This confusion is partially due to the fact that in formalisms of Bayesian theory, base rates and probabilities are both denoted by the same mathematical symbol p. In contrast, subjective logic clearly distinguishes between probabilities and base rates, by using the symbol 'p' or 'P' for probabilities and the symbol 'a' for base rates.

The concept of *belief functions*, which is related to the concept of subjective opinions, has its origin in a model for upper and lower probabilities, proposed by Dempster in 1960. Shafer later proposed a model for expressing belief functions [90]. The main idea behind belief functions is to abandon the additivity principle of probability theory, i.e. that the sum of probabilities on all pairwise disjoint states must add up to one. Instead a belief function gives analysts the ability to assign belief mass to elements in the powerset of the state space. The main advantage of this approach is that ignorance, i.e. the lack of evidence about the truth of the state values, can be explicitly expressed by assigning belief mass to the whole state space. Vagueness can also be expressed by assigning belief mass to subsets of the powerset.

The subjective opinion model extends the traditional belief function model of belief theory in the sense that opinions take base rates into account, whereas belief functions ignore base rates. An essential characteristic of subjective logic is thus to include base rates, which also makes it possible to define a bijective mapping between subjective opinions and Dirichlet PDFs.

The definition of new operators for subjective opinions is normally quite simple, and consists of adding the dimension of uncertainty to traditional probabilistic operators. Many practical operators for subjective logic have already been defined. The set of operators offers a flexible framework for modelling a large variety of situations, in which input arguments can be affected by uncertainty. Subjective opinions are equivalent to Dirichlet and Beta PDFs. Through this equivalence, subjective logic also provides a calculus for reasoning with probability density functions.

Different but equivalent formal representations of subjective opinions can be defined, which allow uncertain probabilities to be seen from different perspectives. Analysts can then define models according to the formalisms and representations that they are most familiar with, and that most naturally can be used to represent a specific real-world situation. Subjective logic contains the same set of basic operators known from binary logic and classical probability calculus, but also contains some non-traditional operators which are specific to subjective logic.

The aim of this book is to provide a general introduction to subjective logic, to show how it supports decision making under vagueness and uncertainty, and to describe applications in subjective trust networks and subjective Bayesian networks which when combined form general subjective networks.

The advantage of subjective logic over traditional probability calculus and probabilistic logic is that uncertainty and vagueness can be explicitly expressed so that real-world situations can be modelled and analysed more realistically than is otherwise possible with purely probabilistic models. The analyst's partial ignorance and lack of evidence can be explicitly taken into account during the analysis, and explicitly expressed in the conclusion. When used for decision support, subjective logic allows decision makers to be better informed about the confidence in the assessment of specific situations and possible future events.

Readers who are new to subjective logic should first study Chapters 2 and 3 in order to get an understanding of the opinion representation. The sections describing Beta and Dirichlet PDFs in Chapter 3 can be skipped to save time. The remaining chapters do not have to be read in sequence. As long as the opinion representation is well understood, readers can jump to specific chapters or sections of interest.

Chapter 2
Elements of Subjective Opinions

This chapter defines fundamental elements in the formalism of subjective logic. It also introduces a terminology which is consistently used throughout this book.

2.1 Motivation for the Opinion Representation

Uncertainty comes in many flavours, where Smithson provides a good taxonomy in [94]. In subjective logic, confidence and uncertainty relate to probabilities. For example, let the probability of a future event x be estimated as $p(x) = 0.5$. In case this probability represents the long-term likelihood of obtaining heads when flipping a fair coin, then it would be natural to represent it as an opinion with a very high confidence (low uncertainty), which is interpreted as an aleatory opinion. In case the probability represents the perceived likelihood that a random person on the street has a specific medical condition, then before any relevant test has been taken it would be natural to represent it as a vacuous opinion (total uncertainty). The probability estimate of an event is thus distinguished from the confidence/uncertainty of the probability. With this explicit representation of confidence/uncertainty, subjective logic can be applied to analysing situations where events get assigned probabilities affected by uncertainty, i.e. where the analyst has relatively low confidence about the probabilities of possible events. This is done by including uncertainty mass as an explicit parameter in the input arguments. This uncertainty mass is then taken into account during the analysis, and is explicitly represented in the output conclusion. In other words, subjective logic allows levels of confidence in probabilities to propagate through the analysis all the way to the output conclusions.

For decision makers it can make a big difference whether probabilities are confident or uncertain. For example, it is risky to make important decisions based on probabilities with low confidence. Decision makers should instead request additional evidence so the analysts can produce more confident conclusion probabilities about hypotheses of interest.

2.2 Flexibility of Representation

There can be multiple equivalent formal representations of subjective opinions. The traditional opinion expression is a composite function consisting of belief masses, uncertainty mass and base rates, which are described separately below. An opinion applies to a variable which takes its values from a domain (i.e. from a state space). An opinion defines a sub-additive belief mass distribution over the variable, meaning that the sum of belief masses can be less than one. Opinions can also have an attribute that identifies the belief owner.

An important aspect of opinions is that they are equivalent to Beta or Dirichlet PDFs (probability density functions) under a specific mapping. This equivalence is based on natural assumptions about the correspondence between evidence and belief mass distributions. More specifically, an infinite amount of evidence leaves no room for uncertainty, and produces an additive belief mass distribution (i.e. the sum is equal to one). A finite amount of evidence gives room for uncertainty and produces a sub-additive belief mass distribution (i.e. the sum is less than one). In practical situations, the amount of evidence is always finite, so practical opinions should always have sub-additive belief mass that is complemented by some uncertainty. The basic features of subjective opinions are defined in the sections below.

2.3 Domains and Hyperdomains

In subjective logic, a *domain* is a state space consisting of a set of values which can also be called states, events, outcomes, hypotheses or propositions. A domain represents the possible states of a variable situation.

The values of the domain can be observable or hidden, just like in traditional Bayesian modelling. The different values of a domain are assumed to be exclusive and exhaustive, which means that the variable situation can only be in one state at any moment in time, and that all possible state values are included in the domain.

Domains can be binary (with exactly two values) or n-ary (with n values) where $n > 2$. A binary domain can e.g. be denoted $\mathbb{X} = \{x, \bar{x}\}$, where $\bar{x}$ is the complement (negation) of x, as illustrated in Figure 2.1.

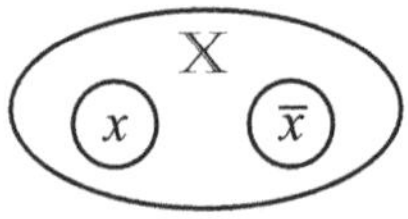

Fig. 2.1 Binary domain

Binary domains are typically used when modelling situations that have only two alternatives, such as a light switch which can be either on or off.

Situations with more than two alternatives have n-ary domains where $n > 2$. The example quaternary domain $\mathbb{Y} = \{y_1, y_2, y_3, y_4\}$ is illustrated in Figure 2.2.

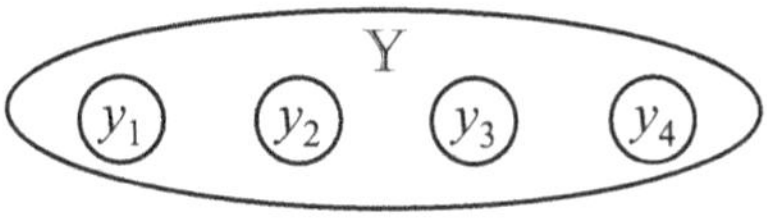

Fig. 2.2 Example quaternary domain

Domains are typically specified to reflect realistic situations for the purpose of being practically analysed in some way. The values of an n-ary domain are called *singletons*, i.e. they are considered to represent a single possible state or event. It is possible to combine singletons into composite values, as explained below.

Assume a ternary domain $\mathbb{X} = \{x_1, x_2, x_3\}$. The *hyperdomain* of $\mathbb{X}$ is the reduced powerset denoted $\mathscr{R}(\mathbb{X})$ illustrated in Figure 2.3, where the solid circles denoted x_1, x_2 and x_3 represent singleton values, and the dotted oval shapes denoted $(x_1 \cup x_2)$, $(x_1 \cup x_3)$ and $(x_2 \cup x_3)$ represent composite values.

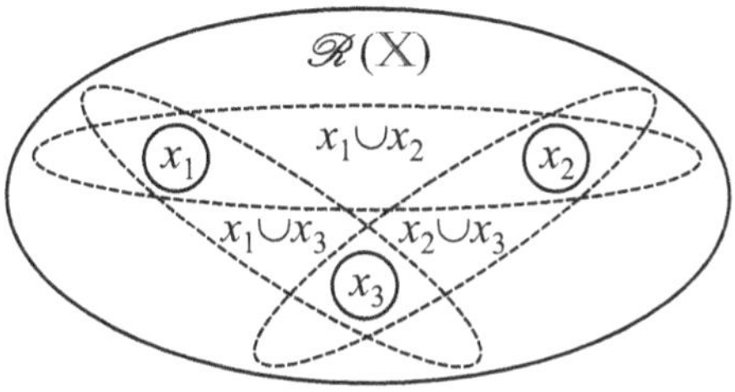

Fig. 2.3 Example hyperdomain

Definition 2.1 (Hyperdomain). Let $\mathbb{X}$ be a domain, and let $\mathscr{P}(\mathbb{X})$ denote the powerset of $\mathbb{X}$. The powerset contains all subsets of $\mathbb{X}$, including the empty set $\{\emptyset\}$, and the domain $\{\mathbb{X}\}$ itself. The *hyperdomain* denoted $\mathscr{R}(\mathbb{X})$ is the reduced powerset of $\mathbb{X}$, i.e. the powerset excluding the empty-set value $\{\emptyset\}$ and the domain value $\{\mathbb{X}\}$. The hyperdomain is expressed as

$$\text{Hyperdomain:} \quad \mathscr{R}(\mathbb{X}) = \mathscr{P}(\mathbb{X}) \setminus \{\{\mathbb{X}\}, \{\emptyset\}\}. \tag{2.1}$$

□

The composite set $\mathscr{C}(\mathbb{X})$ defined in Definition 2.2 can be expressed as $\mathscr{C}(\mathbb{X}) = \mathscr{R}(\mathbb{X}) \setminus \mathbb{X}$. A composite value $x \in \mathscr{C}(\mathbb{X})$ is the union of a set of singleton values from $\mathbb{X}$. The interpretation of a composite value being TRUE, is that one and only one of the constituent singletons is TRUE, and that it is unspecified which singleton is TRUE in particular.

Singletons represent real possible states in a situation to be analysed. A composite value on the other hand does not reflect a specific state in the real world, because otherwise we would have to assume that the world can be in multiple different states at the same time, which contradicts the assumption behind the original domain. Composites are only used as a synthetic artifact to allow belief mass to express that one of multiple singletons is TRUE, but not which singleton in particular is TRUE.

The property that all proper subsets of $\mathbb{X}$ are values of $\mathscr{R}(\mathbb{X})$, but not $\{\mathbb{X}\}$ or $\{\emptyset\}$, is in line with the hyper-Dirichlet model [33]. The cardinality of the hyperdomain is $\kappa = |\mathscr{R}(\mathbb{X})| = 2^k - 2$. Indexes can be used to identify specific values in a hyperdomain, and a natural question is how these values should be indexed.

One simple indexing method is to index each composite value as a function of the singleton values that it contains, as illustrated in Figure 2.3. While this is a very explicit indexing method, it can be complex to use in mathematical expressions.

A more compact indexing method is to use continuous indexing, where indexes in the range $[1,\ k]$ identify singleton values in $\mathbb{X}$, and indexes in the range $[k+1,\ \kappa]$ identify composites. The values contained in the hyperdomain $\mathscr{R}(\mathbb{X})$ are thus the singletons of $\mathbb{X}$ with index in the range $[1,\ k]$, as well as the composites with index in the range $[k+1,\ \kappa]$. The indexing according to this method is illustrated in Figure 2.4, which is equivalent to the indexing method illustrated in Figure 2.3

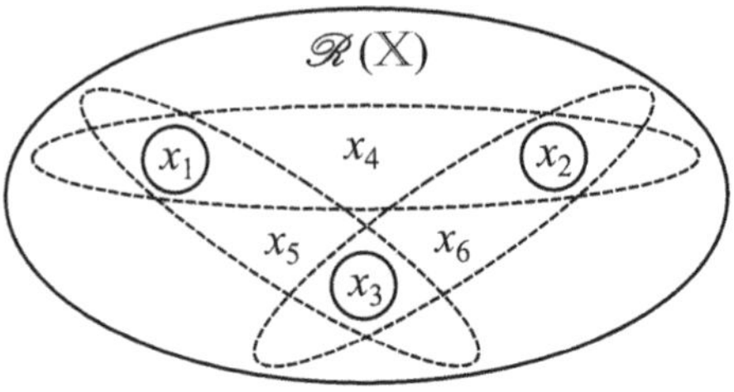

Fig. 2.4 Example of continuous indexing of composite values in a hyperdomain

The continuous indexing method is described next. Assume $\mathbb{X}$ to be a domain of cardinality k, and then consider how to index the values of the hyperdomain $\mathscr{R}(\mathbb{X})$ of cardinality κ. It is practical to define the first k values of $\mathscr{R}(\mathbb{X})$ as having the same index as the corresponding singletons of $\mathbb{X}$. The remaining values of $\mathscr{R}(\mathbb{X})$ can be indexed in a simple and intuitive way.

The values of $\mathscr{R}(\mathbb{X})$ can be grouped in *cardinality classes* according to the number of singletons from $\mathbb{X}$ that they contain. Let j denote the number of singleton values of a specific cardinality class, then call it 'cardinality class j'. By definition then, all values belonging to cardinality class j have cardinality j. The actual number of values belonging to each cardinality class is determined by the Choose Function $\mathrm{C}(\kappa, j)$ which determines the number of ways that j out of κ singletons can be chosen. The Choose Function, equivalent to the binomial coefficient, is defined as

$$C(\kappa, j) = \binom{\kappa}{j} = \frac{\kappa!}{(\kappa - j)!\, j!}\,. \tag{2.2}$$

Within a given hyperdomain, each value can be indexed according to the order of the lowest-indexed singletons from $\mathbb{X}$ that it contains. As an example, Figure 2.2 above illustrates domain $\mathbb{X}$ of cardinality $k = 4$. Let us consider the specific composite value $x_m = \{x_1, x_2, x_4\} \in \mathscr{R}(\mathbb{X})$.

The fact that x_m contains three singletons identifies it as a value of cardinality class 3. The two first singletons x_1 and x_2 have the lowest indexes that are possible to select, but the third singleton x_4 has the second lowest index that is possible to select. This particular value must therefore be assigned the second relative index in cardinality class 3. However, its absolute index depends on the number of values in the inferior cardinality classes. Table 2.1 specifies the number of values of cardinality classes 1 to 3, as determined by Eq.(2.2).

Table 2.1 Number of values per cardinality class

Cardinality class:	1	2	3
Number of values in each cardinality class:	4	6	4

In this example, cardinality class 1 has four values, and cardinality class 2 has six values, which together makes 10 values. Because y_m represents the second relative index in cardinality class 3, its absolute index is $10 + 2 = 12$. The solution is that $m = 12$, so we have $x_{12} = \{x_1, x_2, x_4\}$. To complete the example, Table 2.2 specifies the index and cardinality class of all the values of $\mathscr{R}(\mathbb{X})$ according to this scheme.

Table 2.2 Index and cardinality class of values of $\mathscr{R}(\mathbb{X})$ in case $|\mathbb{X}| = 4$.

	Singleton selection per value													
Singletons x_4				*			*		*	*		*	*	*
Singletons x_3			*			*		*		*	*		*	*
Singletons x_2		*			*			*	*		*	*		*
Singletons x_1	*				*	*	*				*	*	*	
Value index:	1	2	3	4	5	6	7	8	9	10	11	12	13	14
Cardinality class:	1				2						3			

By definition, the values of cardinality class 1 are singletons and are the original values from $\mathbb{X}$. The domain $\mathbb{X} = \{x_1, x_2, x_3, x_4\}$ does not figure as a value of $\mathscr{R}(\mathbb{X})$ in Table 2.2, because excluding $\mathbb{X}$ is precisely what makes $\mathscr{R}(\mathbb{X})$ a reduced powerset and a hyperdomain. A value of $\mathscr{R}(\mathbb{X})$ which contains multiple singletons is called a *composite value*, because it represents the combination of multiple singletons. In other words, when a value is a non-singleton, or equivalently is not a value in cardinality class 1, then it is a composite value in the composite set $\mathscr{R}(\mathbb{X})$. This is formally defined below.

Definition 2.2 (Composite Set). Let $\mathbb{X}$ be a domain of cardinality k, where $\mathscr{R}(\mathbb{X})$ is its hyperdomain of cardinality κ. Every proper subset $x \subset \mathbb{X}$ of cardinality $|x| \geq 2$ is a *composite value*. The set of composite values is the *composite set*, denoted $\mathscr{C}(\mathbb{X})$ and defined as:

$$\text{Composite set:} \quad \mathscr{C}(\mathbb{X}) = \{x \subset \mathbb{X} \text{ where } |x| \geq 2\} \,. \tag{2.3}$$

□

It is straightforward to prove the following equality:

$$\mathscr{C}(\mathbb{X}) = \mathscr{R}(\mathbb{X}) \setminus \mathbb{X} \,. \tag{2.4}$$

The cardinality of the composite set $\mathscr{C}(\mathbb{X})$ is expressed as:

$$|\mathscr{C}(\mathbb{X})| = \kappa - k \,. \tag{2.5}$$

Section 4.1.2 describes the degree of vagueness in an opinion as a function of the belief mass assigned to composite values, i.e. assigned to values in $\mathscr{C}(\mathbb{X})$.

2.4 Random Variables and Hypervariables

Let $\mathbb{X}$ denote a binary or an n-ary domain of cardinality k. Then we can define X to be a random variable which takes its values from $\mathbb{X}$. For example, if $\mathbb{X}$ is a ternary domain, then '$X = x_3$' means that the random variable X has value x_3, which is typically interpreted in the sense that x_3 is TRUE. Note our convention that domains are denoted by blackboard letters such as $\mathbb{X}$, $\mathbb{Y}$ or $\mathbb{Z}$, and that variables are denoted by italic capital letters such as X, Y or Z.

Let $\mathbb{X}$ be a ternary domain, and consider $\mathbb{X}$'s hyperdomain denoted $\mathscr{R}(\mathbb{X})$. The concept of hyperdomain calls for the possibility of assigning values of the hyperdomain to a variable. For example, it must be possible for a variable to take the composite value $\{x_1, x_3\} \in \mathscr{R}(\mathbb{X})$. This means that the real TRUE value is either x_1 or x_3, but that it is unspecified which value in particular it is. Variables that take their values from a hyperdomain are naturally called *hypervariables*, as defined below.

Definition 2.3 (Hypervariable). Let $\mathbb{X}$ be a domain with corresponding hyperdomain $\mathscr{R}(\mathbb{X})$. A variable X that takes its values from $\mathscr{R}(\mathbb{X})$ is a hypervariable. □

A hypervariable X can be constrained to a random variable by restricting it to only take values from the domain $\mathbb{X}$. For simplicity of notation we use the same notation for a random variable, and for the corresponding hypervariable, so that e.g. X can denote both a random variable and a hypervariable. When either meaning can be assumed, we simply use the term *variable*.

Now let X be a variable which can take its values from the ternary domain WEATHER $= \{rainy, sunny, overcast\}$ that contains the three possible weather types specified as $\{rainy\}$, $\{sunny\}$ and $\{overcast\}$. The hyperdomain denoted $\mathscr{R}$(WEATHER) contains the singletons of the original WEATHER domain, as well as all possible composites such as $\{rainy, overcast\}$. Remember that values in a domain are exclusive, meaning that it is assumed that only one value is TRUE at any one time. In case a composite value is considered TRUE, it must be interpreted in the sense that, in reality, only one of the contained singleton values is TRUE, but that it is unknown which value in particular it is.

So when a variable takes a composite value such as $X = \{rainy, sunny\}$ it means that the actual weather is either rainy or sunny, but not both at the same time. If the analyst wants to include the realistic possibility that there can be rain and sunshine simultaneously, then the domain would need to be extended with a corresponding singleton value such as $\{rainy\&sunny\}$. It is thus a question of interpretation how the analyst wants to distinguish between different types of weather, and thereby define an adequate domain of possible weather types.

2.5 Belief Mass Distribution and Uncertainty Mass

Subjective opinions are based on belief mass distributions over a domain $\mathbb{X}$, or over a hyperdomain $\mathscr{R}(\mathbb{X})$. In the case of multinomial opinions, the belief mass distribution is restricted to the domain $\mathbb{X}$. In the case of hyper-opinions, the belief mass distribution applies to the hyperdomain $\mathscr{R}(\mathbb{X})$. Belief mass assigned to a singleton value $x_i \in \mathbb{X}$ expresses support for x_i being TRUE. Belief mass assigned to a composite value $x_j \in \mathscr{C}(\mathbb{X})$ expresses support for one of the singleton values contained in x_j being TRUE, but says nothing about which of them in particular is TRUE.

Belief mass distributions are subadditive, meaning that that the sum of belief masses can be less than one. The sub-additivity of belief mass distributions is complemented by *uncertainty mass* denoted u_X. In general, the belief mass distribution $\boldsymbol{b}_X$ assigns belief masses to possible values of the variable $X \in \mathscr{R}(\mathbb{X})$ as a function of the evidence support for those values. The uncertainty mass u_X represents vacuity of evidence, i.e. the lack of support for the variable X to have any specific value. As explained in Chapter 1, uncertainty mass is interpreted as second-order uncertainty, where probability represents first-order uncertainty. The sub-additivity of the belief mass distribution and the complement property of the uncertainty mass are expressed by Eq.(2.6) and Eq.(2.7) below.

Definition 2.4 (Belief Mass Distribution). Let $\mathbb{X}$ be a domain with corresponding hyperdomain $\mathscr{R}(\mathbb{X})$, and let X be a variable over those domains. A belief mass distribution denoted $\boldsymbol{b}_X$ assigns belief mass to possible values of the variable X. In the case of a random variable $X \in \mathbb{X}$, the belief mass distribution applies to domain $\mathbb{X}$, and in the case of a hypervariable $X \in \mathscr{R}(\mathbb{X})$ the belief mass distribution applies to hyperdomain $\mathscr{R}(\mathbb{X})$. This is formally defined as follows.

$$\begin{aligned}&\text{Multinomial belief mass distribution: } \boldsymbol{b}_X : \mathbb{X} \rightarrow [0,1],\\ &\text{with the additivity requirement: } u_X + \sum_{x\in\mathbb{X}} \boldsymbol{b}_X(x) = 1.\end{aligned} \tag{2.6}$$

$$\begin{aligned}&\text{Hypernomial belief mass distribution: } \boldsymbol{b}_X : \mathscr{R}(\mathbb{X}) \rightarrow [0,1],\\ &\text{with the additivity requirement: } u_X + \sum_{x\in\mathscr{R}(\mathbb{X})} \boldsymbol{b}_X(x) = 1.\end{aligned} \tag{2.7}$$

□

The purpose of representing opinions with separate belief and uncertainty mass is to make the opinion model equivalent to the Beta and Dirichlet models [33, 59] as described in Chapter 3. It is assumed that initial vacuity of evidence exist *a priori*, as represented by uncertainty mass. Belief mass is then formed *a posteriori* as a function of collected evidence in accordance with the Beta and Dirichlet models.

Belief mass assigned to a singleton value $x_i \in \mathbb{X}$ represents *sharp belief* because it sharply supports the truth of that specific value only. Belief mass assigned to a composite value $x_j \in \mathscr{C}(\mathbb{X})$ represents *vague belief* because it supports the truth of a set of singleton values $x \in \{x_j\}$ but not which singleton value in particular. These aspects of belief mass distributions are described in more detail in Chapter 4.

2.6 Base Rate Distributions

The concept of base rates is central in the theory of probability. For example, base rates are needed for default reasoning, for Bayes' theorem, for abductive reasoning and for Bayesian updating. This section describes the concept of base rate distribution over variables, and shows how it can be used for probability projections.

Given a domain $\mathbb{X}$ of cardinality k, the default base rate of each singleton value in the domain is $1/k$, and the default base rate of a subset consisting of n singletons is n/k. In other words, the default base rate of a composite value is equal to the number of singletons in the composite value relative to the cardinality of the whole domain. Default base rate is sometimes called 'relative atomicity' in the literature. There also exist default *relative base rates* with respect to every other fully or partially overlapping value $x \subset \mathbb{X}$.

In contrast to default base rates, it is possible and useful to apply realistic base rates that reflect real background probabilities in practical situations. Realistic base rates are in general different from default base rates. For example, when considering the base rate of a particular infectious disease in a specific population, the domain can be defined as a set of two values {*'infected'*, *'not infected'*} with respect to a particular disease. Assuming that an unknown person enters a medical clinic, the physician would *a priori* be ignorant about whether that person is infected or not before having assessed any evidence. This ignorance should intuitively be expressed as uncertainty mass. The probability projection of a vacuous opinion using a default base rate of 0.5 would dictate the *a priori* probability of 0.5 that the person has the disease. However, the base rate of a disease is normally much lower than 0.5, and can typically be determined given relevant statistics from a given population.

Typically, statistical data about diseases is collected from hospitals, clinics and other sources where people diagnosed with the diseases are treated. The amount of data that is required to calculate a reliable base rate of a disease can be determined by guidelines, statistical analysis and expert opinion about whether the data is truly reflective of the actual number of infections – which is itself a subjective assessment. After the analysis of data and considering the guidelines, the base rate will be determined, and can then be used with medical tests to provide a better indication of the likelihood of specific patients having contracted the disease [35].

Base rates can also be dynamically updated as a function of observed evidence. For example, when an urn contains balls of red (x) and black ($\overline{x}$) balls of unknown proportion, the initial base rates of the two types of balls can be set to the default base rate $a(x) = a(\overline{x}) = 1/2$. Then, after having picked (with return) a number of balls the base rates can be set to the relative proportions of observed balls. This principle is applied for Bayesian reputation systems described in Section 16.3.5.

Integrating base rates with belief mass distributions enables a better and more intuitive interpretation of opinions, facilitates probability projections from opinions, and provides a basis for conditional reasoning. When using base rates for probability projections, the contribution from uncertainty mass is a function of the base rate distribution.

Base rates are expressed in the form of a base rate distribution denoted $\boldsymbol{a}_X$, so that $\boldsymbol{a}_X(x)$ represents the base rate of the value $x \in \mathbb{X}$. Base rate distribution is formally defined below.

Definition 2.5 (Base Rate Distribution). Let $\mathbb{X}$ be a domain, and let X be a random variable in $\mathbb{X}$. The base rate distribution $\boldsymbol{a}_X$ assigns base rate probability to possible values of $X \in \mathbb{X}$, and is an additive probability distribution, formally expressed as:

$$\begin{aligned}&\text{Base rate distribution: } \boldsymbol{a}_X : \mathbb{X} \rightarrow [0,1],\\ &\text{with the additivity requirement: } \sum_{x \in \mathbb{X}} \boldsymbol{a}_X(x) = 1\,. \end{aligned} \tag{2.8}$$

□

The base rate distribution is normally assumed to be common (i.e. not subjective) because it is based on general background information. So although different analysts can have different opinions on the same variable, they normally share the same base rate distribution over the domain of a particular situation. However, it is obvious that two different observers can assign different base rate distributions to the same random variable in case they do not share the same background information. Base rates can thus be partially objective and partially subjective.

This flexibility allows two different analysts to assign different belief masses as well as different base rates to the same variable. This naturally reflects different views, analyses and interpretations of the same situation by different observers.

Events that can be repeated many times are typically frequentist in nature, meaning that base rates for such events typically can be derived from statistical observations. For events that can only happen once, the analyst must often extract base rates from subjective intuition or from analysing the nature of the phenomenon at hand and any other relevant evidence. However, in many cases this can lead to considerable vagueness about base rates, and when nothing else is known, it is possible to use the default base rate distribution for a random variable. More specifically, when there are k singletons in the domain, the default base rate of each singleton is $1/k$.

The difference between the concepts of subjective and frequentist probabilities is that the former can be defined as subjective betting odds – and the latter as the relative frequency of empirically observed data, where the subjective probability normally converges toward the frequentist probability in the case where empirical data is available [16]. The concepts of *subjective* and *empirical* base rates can be interpreted in a similar manner, where they also converge and merge into a single base rate when empirical data about the population in question is available.

The usefulness of base rate distributions is to make possible the derivation of projected probability distributions from opinions. Projection from opinion space to probability space removes the uncertainty and base rate, to produce a probability distribution over a domain. The projected probability distribution depends partially on belief mass and partially on uncertainty mass, where the contribution from uncertainty is weighted as a function of base rate. It can be useful to project probability for composite values in a hyperdomain, and for that purpose it is necessary to first compute base rates for such values. The computation of base rates for values in a hyperdomain is defined below.

Definition 2.6 (Base Rate Distribution over Values in a Hyperdomain). Let $\mathbb{X}$ be a domain with corresponding hyperdomain $\mathscr{R}(\mathbb{X})$, and let X be a variable over those domains. Assume the base rate distribution $\boldsymbol{a}_X$ over the domain $\mathbb{X}$ according to Definition 2.5. The base rate $\boldsymbol{a}_X(x)$ for a composite value $x \in \mathscr{R}(\mathbb{X})$ can be computed as follows:

$$\text{Base rate over composite values: } \boldsymbol{a}_X(x_i) = \sum_{\substack{x_j \in \mathbb{X} \\ x_j \subseteq x_i}} \boldsymbol{a}_X(x_j)\ , \quad \forall x_i \in \mathscr{R}(\mathbb{X})\ . \tag{2.9}$$

□

Eq.(2.9) says that the base rate on a composite value $x_i \in \mathscr{R}(\mathbb{X})$ is the sum of the base rates on singletons x_j contained in x_i. Note that the this is not a base rate distribution, because base rates on singletons would be counted multiple times, and so would be super-additive.

Belief masses can be assigned to values in the hyperdomain that are fully or partially overlapping subsets of the hyperdomain. In order to take such belief masses into account for probability projections, it is necessary to also derive relative base rates for these values as a function of the degree of overlap with each other. This is defined below.

Definition 2.7 (Relative Base Rate). Assume a domain $\mathbb{X}$ of cardinality k, and the corresponding hyperdomain $\mathscr{R}(\mathbb{X})$. Let X be a hypervariable over $\mathscr{R}(\mathbb{X})$. Assume that a base rate distribution $\boldsymbol{a}_X$ is defined over $\mathbb{X}$ according to Definition 2.6. Then the base rate of a value x relative to a value x_i is expressed as the relative base rate $\boldsymbol{a}_X(x|x_i)$ defined below.

$$\boldsymbol{a}_X(x|x_i) = \frac{\boldsymbol{a}_X(x \cap x_i)}{\boldsymbol{a}_X(x_i)}, \quad \forall x, x_i \in \mathscr{R}(\mathbb{X}), \quad \text{where } \boldsymbol{a}_X(x_i) \neq 0\,. \tag{2.10}$$

In the case when $\boldsymbol{a}_X(x_i) = 0$, then $\boldsymbol{a}_X(x|x_i) = 0$. Alternatively it can simply be assumed that $a_X(x_i) > 0$, for every $x_i \in \mathbb{X}$, meaning that everything we include in the domain has a non-zero base rate of occurrence in general. □

From a technical point of view, base rates are simply probabilities. From a semantic point of view, base rates are non-informative prior probabilities estimated as a function of general background information for a class of variables. The term 'non-informative' is used to express that no specific evidence is available for determining the probability of a specific event other than the general background information for that class of events. Base rates make it possible to define a bijective mapping between opinions and Dirichlet PDFs (probability density functions), and are used for probability projections. The base rate concepts defined in this chapter are used for various computations with opinions, as described in the subsequent chapters.

2.7 Probability Distributions

A probability distribution assigns a probability to each value of a random variable. In case it distributes probability over a single random variable, it is a *univariate* probability distribution. A probability distribution can also be *multivariate*, in which case it distributes joint probability over two or more random variables taking on all possible combinations of values.

With a probability distribution denoted $\boldsymbol{p}_X$, the probability $\boldsymbol{a}_X(x)$ represents the probability of the value $x \in \mathbb{X}$. Probability distributions are formally defined below.

Definition 2.8 (Probability Distribution). Let $\mathbb{X}$ be a domain with corresponding hyperdomain $\mathscr{R}(\mathbb{X})$, and let X denote a variable in $\mathbb{X}$ or in $\mathscr{R}(\mathbb{X})$. The standard probability distribution $\boldsymbol{p}_X$ assigns probabilities to possible values of $X \in \mathbb{X}$. The hyper-probability distribution $\boldsymbol{p}_X^{\mathrm{H}}$ assigns probabilities to possible values of $X \in \mathscr{R}(\mathbb{X})$. These distributions are formally defined below:

$$\begin{aligned}&\text{Probability distribution: } \boldsymbol{p}_X : \mathbb{X} \rightarrow [0,1],\\ &\text{with the additivity requirement: } \sum_{x \in \mathbb{X}} \boldsymbol{p}_X(x) = 1\ .\end{aligned} \tag{2.11}$$

$$\begin{aligned}&\text{Hyper-probability distribution: } \boldsymbol{p}^{\mathrm{H}}_X : \mathscr{R}(\mathbb{X}) \rightarrow [0,1],\\ &\text{with the additivity requirement: } \sum_{x \in \mathscr{R}(\mathbb{X})} \boldsymbol{p}^{\mathrm{H}}_X(x) = 1\ .\end{aligned} \tag{2.12}$$

□

The hyper-probability distribution is not meaningful in the traditional sense, because hyper-probability is not restricted to exclusive values in the domain $\mathbb{X}$. The traditional assumption behind frequentist or subjective probability is that it is additive over values $x \in \mathbb{X}$, which in turn represent mutually exclusive real events. Probability distributed over the hyperdomain $\mathscr{R}(\mathbb{X})$ is still additive, but the values $x \in \mathscr{R}(\mathbb{X})$ no longer represent exclusive real events, because they can be composite and (partially) overlapping.

However, a hyper-probability distribution can be projected onto a traditional probability distribution according to Eq.(2.13) which uses the concept of relative base rates from Eq.(2.10).

$$\boldsymbol{p}_X(x) = \sum_{x_i \in \mathscr{R}(\mathbb{X})} \boldsymbol{a}_X(x|x_i)\, \boldsymbol{p}^{\mathrm{H}}_X(x_i), \quad \forall x \in \mathbb{X}\ . \tag{2.13}$$

Hyper-probability distributions are used when describing the Dirichlet model over hyperdomains in Section 3.6.3.

Chapter 3
Opinion Representations

Subjective opinions express beliefs about the truth of propositions under degrees of uncertainty, and can indicate ownership of an opinion whenever required. This chapter presents the various representations and notations for subjective opinions.

3.1 Belief and Trust Relationships

In general, the notation ω_X^A is used to denote opinions in subjective logic, where e.g. the subscript X indicates the target variable or proposition to which the opinion applies, and e.g. the superscript A indicates the subject agent who holds the opinion, i.e. the belief owner. Superscripts can be omitted when it is implicit or irrelevant who the belief owner is.

The principle that a subject agent A has an opinion about a target variable X means that there is a directed belief relationship from A to X, formally denoted $[A,X]$. Similarly, the principle that an agent A trusts an entity E means that there is a directed trust relationship from A to E, formally denoted $[A,E]$. These relationships can be considered as directed edges in a graph. This convention is summarised in Table 3.1. See also Table 14.1 on p.252 which in addition includes the concept of referral-trust relationship.

Table 3.1 Notation for belief and trust relationships

Relationship type	Formal notation	Graph edge notation	Interpretation
Belief	$[A,X]$	$A \longrightarrow X$	Agent A has an opinion about variable X
Trust	$[A,E]$	$A \longrightarrow E$	Agent A has a trust opinion about entity E

To believe and to trust are very similar concepts, the main difference being that trust assumes dependence and risk, which belief does not necessarily assume. So by abstracting away the dependence and risk aspects of trust relationships, subjective logic uses the same formal representation for both belief opinions and trust opinions. Trust opinions are described in detail in Chapter 14.

3.2 Opinion Classes

Opinions can be structurally different depending on the dimensionality of the domain they apply to, and on the amount of uncertainty they contain. This section describes how these aspects determine different classes of opinions.

Opinions apply to variables that take their values from domains. A domain is a state space which consists of values that are assumed to be exhaustive and mutually disjoint. The opinion itself is a composite function $\omega_X^A = (\boldsymbol{b}_X, u_X, \boldsymbol{a}_X)$, consisting of the belief mass distribution $\boldsymbol{b}_X$, the uncertainty mass u_X, and the base rate distribution $\boldsymbol{a}_X$, where the superscript A denotes the opinion owner, and the subscript X denotes the variable it applies to.

A few specific classes of opinions have been defined. In case the domain $\mathbb{X}$ is binary, then so is the variable X, and the opinion is *binomial*. In case the domain is larger than binary, and the variable is a random variable $X \in \mathbb{X}$, then the opinion is *multinomial*. In case the domain is larger than binary, and the variable is a hypervariable $X \in \mathscr{R}(\mathbb{X})$, then the opinion is *hypernomial*. These are the three main opinion classes.

Opinions can also be classified according to levels of confidence (inversely proportional to the uncertainty mass). In case $u_X = 1$, the opinion is *vacuous*; in case $0 < u_X < 1$, the opinion is relatively *uncertain*; and in case $u_X = 0$, the opinion is *dogmatic*. When a single value is considered TRUE by assigning belief mass 1 to that value, the opinion is *absolute*. The combination of three main opinion classes depending on the domain, and four subclasses depending on confidence produces 12 different opinion classes as listed in Table 3.2. These are further described in the next section.

The 12 entries in Table 3.2 also mention the equivalent probability representation of opinions, e.g. as Beta PDF, Dirichlet PDF or as a probability distribution over the variable X. This equivalence is explained in more detail below.

The intuition behind using the term ‘dogmatic’ is that a totally certain opinion (i.e. where $u = 0$) about a real-world proposition must be seen as an extreme opinion. From a philosophical viewpoint, no one can ever be totally certain about anything in this world. So when the formalism allows explicit expression of uncertainty, as opinions do, it is extreme, and even unrealistic, to express a dogmatic opinion. The rationale for this interpretation is that a dogmatic opinion has an equivalent Dirichlet probability density function in the form of a Dirac delta function which is infinitely high and infinitesimally thin. It would require an infinite amount of evidence to produce a Dirichlet PDF equal to a Dirac delta function, which in practice is impossible, and therefore can only be considered in the case of idealistic assumptions. This does not mean that traditional probabilities should be interpreted as dogmatic,

Table 3.2 Opinion classes and their equivalent probabilistic or logic representations

Class: Domain: Variable: **Confidence**	**Binomial** $\mathbb{X} = \{x, \overline{x}\},\ \lvert\mathbb{X}\rvert = 2$ Binomial variable $X = x$	**Multinomial** $\mathbb{X},\ \lvert\mathbb{X}\rvert > 2$ Random variable $X \in \mathbb{X}$	**Hyper** $\mathscr{R}(\mathbb{X}),\ \lvert\mathbb{X}\rvert > 2$ Hypervariable $X \in \mathscr{R}(\mathbb{X})$
Vacuous $(u_X = 1)$ Proba. equiv:	*Vacuous* *binomial opinion* Uniform Beta PDF on $p(x)$	*Vacuous* *multinomial opinion* Prior PDF on $\boldsymbol{p}_X$	*Vacuous* *hyper-opinion* Prior PDF on $\boldsymbol{p}_X$
Uncertain $(0 < u_X < 1)$ Proba. equiv:	*Uncertain* *binomial opinion* Beta PDF on $p(x)$	*Uncertain* *multinomial opinion* Dirichlet PDF on $\boldsymbol{p}_X$	*Uncertain and vague* *hyper-opinion* Dirichlet HPDF on $\boldsymbol{p}_X^{\mathrm{H}}$
Dogmatic $(u_X = 0)$ Proba. equiv:	*Dogmatic* *binomial opinion* Probability on x	*Dogmatic* *multinomial opinion* Proba. distribution over $\mathbb{X}$	*Dogmatic vague* *hyper-opinion* Proba. distr. over $\mathscr{R}(\mathbb{X})$
Absolute $(\boldsymbol{b}_X(x) = 1)$ Logic equiv:	*Absolute* *binomial opinion* Boolean TRUE/FALSE	*Absolute* *multinomial opinion* TRUE value in $\mathbb{X}$	*Absolute vague* *hyper-opinion* TRUE value in $\mathscr{R}(\mathbb{X})$

because the probability model does not include uncertainty in the way opinions do. Instead it can implicitly be assumed that there is some uncertainty associated with every probability estimate, but that it is invisible, because uncertainty is not included in the model. One advantage of subjective logic is precisely that it allows explicit expression of uncertainty.

A vacuous opinion represents belief about a random variable in case the observer or analyst has no specific evidence about the possible values of a random variable, except for the base rate distribution which represents general background information. It is thus always possible for an analyst to have opinions of varying confidence that genuinely represents the analyst's belief, so that analysts are never forced to invent belief where there is none. In case they are ignorant, they can simply produce a vacuous or highly uncertain opinion. The same can not be said when using probabilities, where analysts sometimes have to 'pull probabilities out of thin air' e.g. in case a specific input probability parameter to a model is needed in order to complete an analysis with the model.

Each opinion class from Table 3.2 has an equivalence mapping to a type of Dirichlet or Beta PDF (probability density function) under a specific mapping. This mapping then gives subjective opinions a firm basis in the domain of classical probability and statistics theory. The different opinion classes are described in more detail in the following sections.

3.3 Aleatory and Epistemic Opinions

Opinions can be semantically different, depending on the situation they apply to. This section describes the categories called *aleatory opinions* and *epistemic opinions*. Note that these categories are not the same as aleatory and epistemic uncertainty.

Epistemology is the study of knowledge and justified belief. It focuses on the nature of knowledge, how it can be acquired in general, and the extent to which knowledge pertinent to any given subject or entity can be acquired.

An important aspect of uncertainty quantification in the scientific literature is the distinction between aleatory and epistemic uncertainty, described below.

- *Aleatory Uncertainty*, which is the same as statistical uncertainty, expresses that we do not know the outcome each time we run the same experiment, we only know the long-term relative frequency of outcomes. For example, flipping a coin (which could be unfair) reflects aleatory uncertainty, because we can not predict the outcome of each flip, only the long-term probability. A person could e.g. estimate the probability of obtaining heads as $p = 0.6$, which expresses aleatory uncertainty.
- *Epistemic Uncertainty*, aka systematic uncertainty, expresses that we could in principle know the outcome of a specific or future or past event, but that we do not have enough evidence to know it exactly. For example, the assassination of President Kennedy in 1963 is believed by most people to have been committed by Lee Harvey Oswald, but there is considerable uncertainty around it. What is known with certainty is that Kennedy was shot. What is not known with certainty is who shot him. This is an event that only happened once, so talking about long-term relative frequency is not meaningful. A person could e.g. estimate the probability that Oswald shot Kennedy as $p = 0.6$, which expresses epistemic uncertainty.

Note that both aleatory and epistemic uncertainty represent first-order uncertainty, and therefore are not the same type of uncertainty as the uncertainty mass in opinions, which represents second-order uncertainty. Aleatory and epistemic uncertainties of a binary variable are greatest when $p = 1/2$. In contrast, when an opinion has projected probability $\mathbf{P}_X(x) = 1/2$ for some value x, it says nothing about the amount of uncertainty mass u_X in the opinion. The uncertainty mass could e.g. be zero ($u_X = 0$) in case the opinion is dogmatic, or it could be total ($u_X = 1$) in case the opinion is vacuous. In other words, high aleatory/epistemic uncertainty is consistent with both high and low uncertainty mass.

This distinction between aleatory and epistemic (first-order) uncertainty is also important in subjective logic as it puts constraints on the opinion classes that naturally apply to specific situations. The situation of flipping a coin and the situation of the assassination of President Kennedy are very different situations, not just from the point of view of their political and practical implications, but also from the point of view of how we can express opinions about them. The coin situation is clearly frequentist, whereas the Kennedy situation is not, which provides the basis for making a distinction between opinions about frequentist situations, called *aleatory opinions*, and opinions about non-frequentist situations, called *epistemic opinions*. These opinion categories are described next.

- **An aleatory opinion** applies to a variable governed by a frequentist process, and that represents the (uncertain) likelihood of values of the variable in any unknown past or future instance of the process. An aleatory opinion can naturally have an arbitrary uncertainty mass.
- **An epistemic opinion** applies to a variable that is assumed to be non-frequentist, and that represents the (uncertain) likelihood of values of the variable in a specific unknown past or future instance. An aleatory opinion is naturally constrained to be uncertainty-maximised, as described in Section 3.5.6.

The reason why epistemic opinions should be uncertainty-maximised is that epistemic evidence can not be accumulated in a statistical manner, which would reduce the uncertainty mass. Instead, different pieces of epistemic evidence that support opposite/different values should cancel each other out.

Because the Kennedy situation is non-frequentist, an opinion about *"Oswald killed Kennedy"* must therefore be an epistemic opinion, that e.g. can not be dogmatic, unless the opinion is absolute. If one person says: *"I saw Oswald shoot Kennedy"*, but another person says: *"I saw the security guard shoot Kennedy, so it wasn't Oswald"*, then these two testimonies can not be considered as statistical samplings that can be accumulated, because one of the testimonies is assumed to be wrong. It is of course possible that both Oswald and the security guard shot Kennedy, and including this possibility might require the addition of a corresponding value in the domain.

If the situation to be modelled and analysed is epistemic, such as the Kennedy case, then input arguments should also be epistemic. However, it can sometimes be unclear whether a situation is frequentist or non-frequentist, so distinguishing between aleatory and epistemic opinions is not always obvious. Output opinions from a reasoning model might not be uncertainty-maximised, even if the corresponding variables are considered to be epistemic. The analyst must therefore judge whether input arguments and output results should be considered as aleatory or epistemic. Especially for absolute opinions, the distinction between aleatory and epistemic is unclear, because uncertainty-maximisation is not applicable.

In traditional Bayesian theory, the difference between aleatory and epistemic uncertainty is mostly philosophical, and has no practical implication for modelling and analysing real situations, because the two types of opinions are formally and syntactically indistinguishable. In subjective logic however, the difference between aleatory and epistemic opinions is syntactically explicit, in the sense that epistemic opinions are uncertainty-maximised, whereas aleatory opinions can have arbitrary relative levels of uncertainty. The concepts of aleatory and epistemic opinions are important in subjective Bayesian networks, described in Section 17.5.

3.4 Binomial Opinions

3.4.1 Binomial Opinion Representation

A binary domain consists of only two values, and the variable is typically fixed to one of the two values. Formally, let a binary domain be specified as $\mathbb{X} = \{x, \bar{x}\}$, then a binomial random variable $X \in \mathbb{X}$ can be fixed to $X = x$. Opinions on a binomial variable are called binomial opinions, and a special notation is used for their mathematical representation. Note that a general n-ary domain $\mathbb{X}$ can be considered binary when seen as a binary partition consisting of a proper subset $x \subset \mathbb{X}$ and its complement $\bar{x}$, so that the corresponding multinomial random variable becomes a binomial random variable under the same partition.

Definition 3.1 (Binomial Opinion). Let $\mathbb{X} = \{x, \bar{x}\}$ be a binary domain with binomial random variable $X \in \mathbb{X}$. A binomial opinion about the truth/presence of value x is the ordered quadruplet $\omega_x = (b_x, d_x, u_x, a_x)$, where the additivity requirement

$$b_x + d_x + u_x = 1 \tag{3.1}$$

is satisfied, and where the respective parameters are defined as
b_x : *belief mass* in support of x being TRUE (i.e. $X = x$),
d_x : *disbelief mass* in support of x being FALSE (i.e. $X = \bar{x}$),
u_x : *uncertainty mass* representing the vacuity of evidence,
a_x : *base rate*, i.e. prior probability of x without any evidence.

□

Various types of binomial opinions are for example

1) $b_x = 1$ or $d_x = 1$: absolute opinion equivalent to Boolean TRUE or FALSE,
2) $b_x = 0$ or $d_x = 0$: uncertainty-maximised (epistemic) opinion $\ddot{\omega}_x$,
3) $u_x = 0$: dogmatic opinion $\underline{\omega}_x$, and a traditional probability,
4) $0 < u_x < 1$: a partially uncertain opinion,
5) $u_x = 1$: vacuous opinion $\widehat{\omega}_x$, i.e. with zero belief mass.

Uncertainty-maximised opinions correspond to epistemic opinions described in Section 3.3. Uncertainty-maximisation of opinions is described in Section 3.5.6.

The projected probability of a binomial opinion about value x is defined by Eq.(3.2):

$$\mathrm{P}(x) = b_x + a_x u_x \,. \tag{3.2}$$

The variance of binomial opinions is expressed as

$$\mathrm{Var}(x) = \frac{\mathrm{P}(x)\,(1 - \mathrm{P}(x))u_x}{W + u_x} \,, \tag{3.3}$$

where W denotes non-informative prior weight, which must be set to $W = 2$ as explained in Section 3.5.2. Binomial opinion variance is derived from the variance of the Beta PDF, as defined by Eq.(3.10) below.

Barycentric coordinate systems can be used to visualise opinions. In a barycentric coordinate system, the location of a point is specified as the centre of mass, or barycentre, of masses placed at its vertices [76]. A barycentric coordinate system with n axes is represented on a simplex with n vertices and with dimensionality $(n-1)$. A triangle is a 2D simplex which has three vertices, and is thus a barycentric system with three axes. A binomial opinion can be visualised as a point in a barycentric coordinate system of three axes represented by a 2D simplex, which is in fact an equilateral triangle, as illustrated in Figure 3.1. Here, the belief, disbelief and uncertainty axes go perpendicularly from each edge towards the respective opposite vertices denoted x, $\bar{x}$ and uncertainty. The base rate a_x is a point on the base line, and the projected probability $\mathrm{P}(x)$ is determined by projecting the opinion point onto the base line, parallel to the base rate director. The binomial opinion $\omega_x = (0.40, 0.20, 0.40, 0.90)$ with probability projection $\mathrm{P}(x) = 0.76$ is shown as an example.

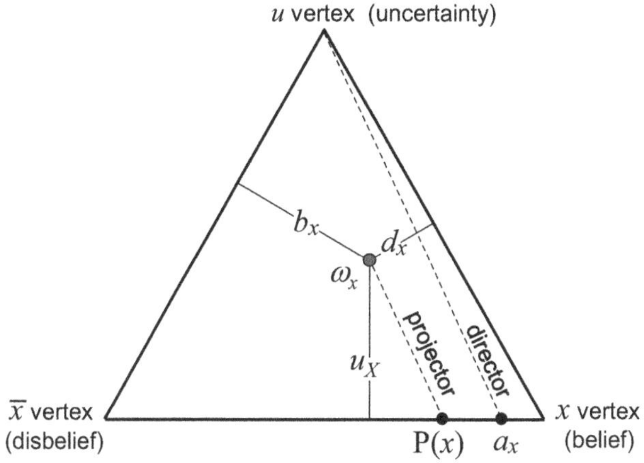

Fig. 3.1 Barycentric triangle visualisation of binomial opinion

With the opinion point located at the left or right vertex of the triangle, i.e. with $d_x = 1$ or $b_x = 1$ (and $u_x = 0$), then the opinion is equivalent to Boolean TRUE or FALSE, and subjective logic becomes equivalent to binary logic. With the opinion point located on the baseline of the triangle, i.e. with $u_x = 0$, then the opinion is equivalent to a traditional probability, and subjective logic becomes equivalent to probability calculus or – said more accurately – to probabilistic logic.

With an opinion point located at one of the three vertices in the triangle, i.e. with $b = 1$, $d = 1$ or $u = 1$, subjective logic becomes a form of three-valued logic that is comparable to – but not the same as – Kleene logic [25], where propositions can be 'TRUE', 'FALSE' or 'UNKNOWN'. Kleene logic does not include base rates. As a consequence, probability projections can not be derived from an 'UNKNOWN' argument in Kleene logic. See Section 5.1.4 for a more detailed explanation.

3.4.2 The Beta Binomial Model

A binomial opinion is equivalent to a Beta PDF (probability density function) under a specific bijective mapping. In general a probability density function, denoted $\mathrm{PDF}(p(x))$, is defined as

$$\mathrm{PDF}(p(x)) : [0,1] \rightarrow \mathbb{R}_{\geq 0}, \quad \text{where} \int_0^1 \mathrm{PDF}(p(x))\, \mathrm{d}p(x) = 1\,. \tag{3.4}$$

$\mathbb{R}_{\geq 0}$ is the set of positive real numbers including 0, which can also be denoted $[0,\infty>$. The variable of the PDF is thus the continuous probability $p(x) \in [0,1]$, and the image of the PDF is the density $\mathrm{PDF}(p(x)) \in \mathbb{R}_{\geq 0}$. When starting with the probability function $p(x) : \mathbb{X} \rightarrow [0,1]$, then the image of x is the probability $p(x)$ which in turn is the variable of $\mathrm{PDF}(p(x))$. In this way the functions $p(x)$ and $\mathrm{PDF}(p(x))$ are chained functions.

The density expresses where along the continuous interval $[0,1]$ the probability $p(x)$ is believed to be. At positions on the p-axis where the density is high, the corresponding probability is likely to be, and where the density is low the corresponding probability is unlikely to be. 'High confidence' in a specific probability means that there is high density at that specific position on the p-axis. A totally 'unconfident probability' means that any probability is equally likely, so the density is spread out uniformly over the whole interval $[0,1]$. The traditional interpretation of probability as likelihood of events gets a richer expression through probability density, which can be interpreted as second-order probability. This interpretation is the basis for mapping (high) probability density in Beta PDFs into (high) belief mass in opinions, through the bijective mapping described in Section 3.4.3. As a consequence, flat probability density in Beta PDFs is represented as uncertainty in opinions.

The Beta PDF is a probability density function denoted $\mathrm{Beta}(p(x),\alpha,\beta)$ with variable $p(x)$, and two 'strength parameters' α and β. The Beta PDF is defined below.

Definition 3.2 (Beta Probability Density Function). Assume a binary domain $\mathbb{X} = \{x,\bar{x}\}$ and a random variable $X \in \mathbb{X}$. Let p denote the continuous probability function $p : X \rightarrow [0,1]$ where $p(x)+p(\bar{x}) = 1$. For compactness of notation we define $p_x \equiv p(x)$ and $p_{\bar{x}} \equiv p(\bar{x})$.

The parameter α represents evidence/observations of $X = x$, and the parameter β represents evidence/observations of $X = \bar{x}$. With p_x as variable, the Beta probability density function $\mathrm{Beta}(p_x,\alpha,\beta)$ is the function expressed as

$$\mathrm{Beta}(p_x,\alpha,\beta) : [0,1] \rightarrow \mathbb{R}_{\geq 0}\,, \quad \text{where} \tag{3.5}$$

$$\mathrm{Beta}(p_x,\alpha,\beta) = \frac{\Gamma(\alpha+\beta)}{\Gamma(\alpha)\Gamma(\beta)}(p_x)^{\alpha-1}(1-p_x)^{\beta-1}, \quad \alpha > 0,\ \beta > 0, \tag{3.6}$$

with the restrictions that $p(x) \neq 0$ if $\alpha < 1$, and $p(x) \neq 1$ if $\beta < 1$. □

It can be shown that the additivity requirement $\int_0^1 \mathrm{Beta}(p_x, \alpha, \beta)\,\mathrm{d}p_x = 1$ holds, which in fact is a general requirement for all PDFs.

Assume that x represents a frequentist event, such as getting 'heads' when flipping a coin. Let r_x denote the number of observations of x (heads), and let s_x denote the number of observations of $\bar{x}$ (tails). The α and β parameters for this situation can be expressed as a function of the observations (r_x, s_x) and the base rate a_x:

$$\begin{cases} \alpha = r_x + a_x W\,, \\ \beta = s_x + (1 - a_x)W\,. \end{cases} \tag{3.7}$$

By expressing α and β parameters in terms of the evidence observations (r_x, s_x), the base rate a_x and the non-informative prior weight W, we get the evidence notation of the Beta PDF, denoted $\mathrm{Beta}^{\mathrm{e}}(p_x, r_x, s_x, a_x)$ which is expressed as

$$\begin{aligned} &\mathrm{Beta}^{\mathrm{e}}(p_x, r_x, s_x, a_x) \\ &= \frac{\Gamma(r_x+s_x+W)}{\Gamma(r_x+a_xW)\Gamma(s_x+(1-a_x)W)}(p_x)^{(r_x+a_xW-1)}(1-p_x)^{(s_x+(1-a_x)W-1)}, \\ &\text{where } (r_x + a_x W) > 0 \text{ and } (s_x + (1-a_x)W) > 0, \\ &\text{with the restrictions } \begin{cases} p_x \neq 0 & \text{if } (r_x + a_x W) < 1, \\ p_x \neq 1 & \text{if } (s_x + (1-a_x)W) < 1. \end{cases} \end{aligned} \tag{3.8}$$

The non-informative prior weight is set to $W = 2$, which ensures that the prior Beta PDF (i.e. when $r_x = s_x = 0$) with default base rate $a_x = 0.5$ is the uniform PDF.

The expected probability $\mathrm{E}(x)$ as a function of the Beta PDF parameters is

$$\mathrm{E}(x) = \frac{\alpha}{\alpha+\beta} = \frac{r_x + a_x W}{r_x + s_x + W}\,. \tag{3.9}$$

The variance $\mathrm{Var}(x)$ of the Beta PDF is defined by Eq.(3.10):

$$\begin{aligned} \mathrm{Var}(x) &= \frac{\alpha\beta}{(\alpha+\beta)^2(\alpha+\beta+1)} \\ &= \frac{(r_x + a_x W)(s_x + (1-a_x)W)}{(r_x + s_x + W)^2(r_x + s_x + W + 1)} \\ &= \frac{(b_x + a_x u_x)(d_x + (1-a_x)u_x)u_x}{W + u_x} \\ &= \frac{\mathrm{P}(x)\,(1-\mathrm{P}(x))u_x}{W + u_x}\,. \end{aligned} \tag{3.10}$$

The last two equalities in Eq.(3.10) emerge from the mapping of Eq.3.11 below.

The variance of the Beta PDF measures how widely the probability density is spread out over the interval $[0,1]$. Zero variance indicates that the probability density is concentrated in one point, which only happens for infinite α and/or β (or equivalently infinite r_x and/or s_x). The variance $\mathrm{Var}(x) = 1/12$ is that of the uniform Beta PDF (and of any uniform PDF), which results from $\alpha = \beta = 1$ (e.g. when $r_x = s_x = 0$, $a_x = 1/2$ and $W = 2$).

The Beta PDF is important in subjective logic, because a bijective mapping can be defined between the projected probability of a binomial opinion and the expected probability of a Beta PDF. This is described next.

3.4.3 Mapping Between a Binomial Opinion and a Beta PDF

The bijective mapping between a binomial opinion and a Beta PDF emerges from the intuitive requirement that $\mathrm{P}(x) = \mathrm{E}(x)$, i.e. that the projected probability of a binomial opinion must be equal to the expected probability of a Beta PDF. This can be generalised to a mapping between multinomial opinions and Dirichlet PDFs, as well as between hyper-opinions and hyper-Dirichlet PDFs. The detailed description for determining the mapping is described in Section 3.5.5.

The mapping from the parameters of a binomial opinion $\omega_x = (b_x, d_x, u_x, a_x)$ to the parameters of $\mathrm{Beta^e}(p_x, r_x, s_x, a_x)$ is defined below.

Definition 3.3 (Mapping: Binomial Opinion $\leftrightarrow$ Beta PDF).
Let $\omega_x = (b_x, d_x, u_x, a_x)$ be a binomial opinion, and let $p(x)$ be a probability distribution, both over the same binomial random variable X. Let $\mathrm{Beta^e}(p_x, r_x, s_x, a_x)$ be a Beta PDF over the probability variable p_x defined as a function of r_x, s_x and a_x according to Eq.(3.8). The opinion ω_x and the Beta PDF $\mathrm{Beta^e}(p_x, r_x, s_x, a_x)$ are equivalent through the following mapping:

$$\begin{cases} b_x = \dfrac{r_x}{W + r_x + s_x}, \\[2ex] d_x = \dfrac{s_x}{W + r_x + s_x}, \\[2ex] u_x = \dfrac{W}{W + r_x + s_x} \end{cases} \Leftrightarrow \left(\begin{array}{ll} \underline{\text{For } u \neq 0\text{:}} & \underline{\text{For } u_x = 0\text{:}} \\ \begin{cases} r_x = \dfrac{b_x W}{u_x}, \\[2ex] s_x = \dfrac{d_x W}{u_x}, \\[2ex] 1 = b_x + d_x + u_x \end{cases} & \begin{cases} r_x = b_x \cdot \infty, \\[1ex] s_x = d_x \cdot \infty, \\[1ex] 1 \;= b_x + d_x. \end{cases} \end{array} \right) \tag{3.11}$$

□

A generalisation of this mapping is provided in Definition 3.6 below. The default non-informative prior weight W is set to $W = 2$, because we require that a vacuous opinion is mapped to a uniform Beta PDF in the case of default base rate $a_x = 1/2$. It can be seen from Eq.(3.11) that the vacuous binomial opinion $\omega_x = (0, 0, 1, \frac{1}{2})$ corresponds to the uniform PDF $\mathrm{Beta}(p_x, 1, 1)$.

The example $\mathrm{Beta}(p_x, 3.8, 1.2) = \mathrm{Beta}^{\mathrm{e}}(p_x, 2.0, 1.0, 0.9)$ is illustrated in Figure 3.2. Through the equivalence defined by Eq.(3.11), this Beta PDF is equivalent to the example opinion $\omega_x = (0.4, 0.2, 0.4, 0.9)$ from Figure 3.1.

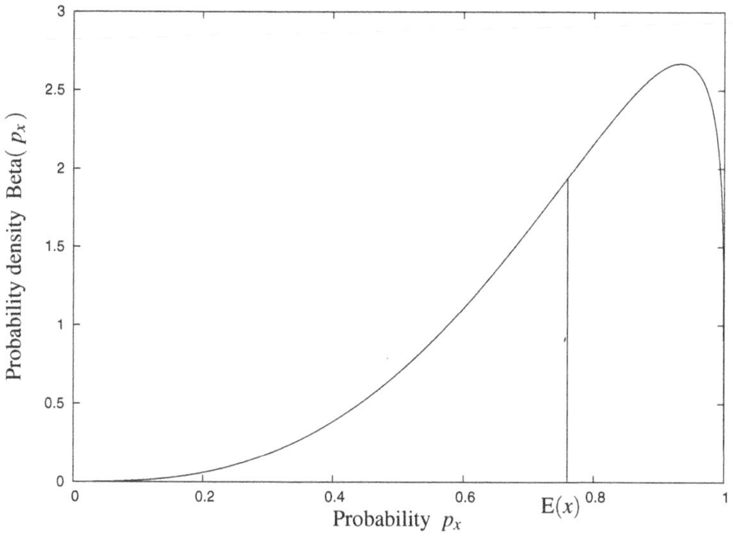

Fig. 3.2 Probability density function $\mathrm{Beta}(p_x, 3.8, 1.2) \equiv \omega_x = (0.4, 0.2, 0.4, 0.9)$

In the example of Figure 3.2 where $\alpha = 3.8$ and $\beta = 1.2$, the expected probability is $\mathrm{E}(x) = {}^{3.8}/_{5.0} = 0.76$, which is indicated with the vertical line. This expected probability is of course equal to the projected probability of Figure 3.1, because the Beta PDF is equivalent to the opinion through Eq.(3.11).

The equivalence between binomial opinions and Beta PDFs is very powerful, because subjective-logic operators (SL operators) can then be applied to Beta PDFs, and statistics operations for Beta PDFs can be applied to opinions. In addition, it makes it possible to determine binomial opinions from statistical observations.

Multinomial opinions, described next, are a generalisation of binomial opinions, in the same way as Dirichlet PDFs are a generalisation of Beta PDFs.

3.5 Multinomial Opinions

3.5.1 The Multinomial Opinion Representation

Multinomial opinions represent the natural generalisation of binomial opinions. Multinomial opinions apply to situations where a random variable $X \in \mathbb{X}$ can take one of multiple different values.

Definition 3.4 (Multinomial Opinion). Let $\mathbb{X}$ be a domain larger than binary, i.e. so that $k = |\mathbb{X}| > 2$. Let X be a random variable in $\mathbb{X}$. A multinomial opinion over the random variable X is the ordered triplet $\omega_X = (\boldsymbol{b}_X, u_X, \boldsymbol{a}_X)$ where

$\boldsymbol{b}_X$ is a *belief mass distribution* over $\mathbb{X}$,
u_X is the *uncertainty mass* which represents the vacuity of evidence,
$\boldsymbol{a}_X$ is a *base rate distribution* over $\mathbb{X}$,

and the multinomial additivity requirement of Eq.(2.6) is satisfied. □

In case $u_X = 1$, then ω_X is a vacuous multinomial opinion. In case $u_X = 0$, then ω_X is a dogmatic multinomial opinion. In case $0 < u_X < 1$, then ω_X is a relatively uncertain multinomial opinion. Finally, in the special case where for some $X = x$ all belief mass is assigned to a single value as $\boldsymbol{b}_X(x) = 1$, then ω_X is an absolute opinion, i.e. it is absolutely certain that a specific value $x \in \mathbb{X}$ is TRUE.

Multinomial opinions have the property that the belief mass distribution $\boldsymbol{b}_X$ and the base rate distribution $\boldsymbol{a}_X$ both have k parameters. The uncertainty mass u_X is a simple scalar. A multinomial opinion thus contains $(2k+1)$ parameters. However, given the belief and uncertainty mass additivity of Eq.(2.6), and the base rate additivity of Eq.(2.8), multinomial opinions only have $(2k-1)$ degrees of freedom.

The probability projection of multinomial opinions is relatively simple to calculate, compared to general opinions, because no belief mass applies to overlapping values in the domain $\mathbb{X}$. The expression for projected probability of multinomial opinions is in fact a special case of the general expression of Eq.(3.28). The projected probability distribution of multinomial opinions is defined by Eq.(3.12):

$$\mathbf{P}_X(x) = \boldsymbol{b}_X(x) + \boldsymbol{a}_X(x)\,u_X, \quad \forall\, x \in \mathbb{X}\,. \tag{3.12}$$

The variance of multinomial opinions is expressed as

$$\mathrm{Var}_X(x) = \frac{\mathbf{P}_X(x)(1-\mathbf{P}_X(x))\,u_X}{W + u_X}\,, \tag{3.13}$$

where W denotes non-informative prior weight, which must be set to $W = 2$. The multinomial opinion variance is derived from the variance of the Dirichlet PDF, as defined by Eq.(3.18) below.

The only type of multinomial opinions that can be easily visualised is trinomial, which can be represented as a point inside a tetrahedron (3D simplex), which in fact is a barycentric coordinate system of four axes, as shown in Figure 3.3.

In Figure 3.3, the vertical elevation of the opinion point inside the tetrahedron represents the uncertainty mass. The distances from each of the three triangular

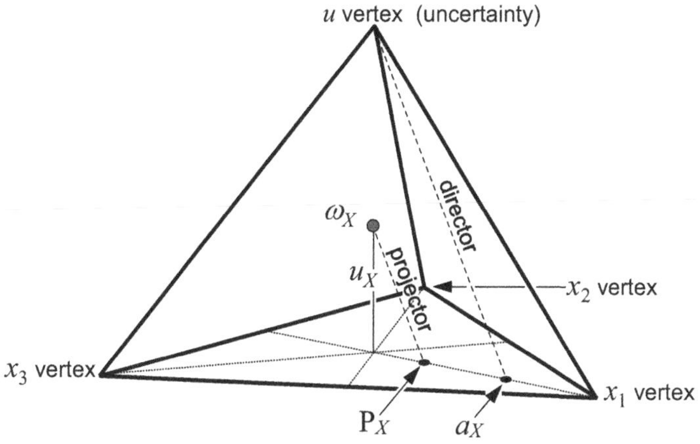

Fig. 3.3 Barycentric tetrahedron visualisation of trinomial opinion

side planes to the opinion point represent the respective belief masses. The base rate distribution $\boldsymbol{a}_X$ is indicated as a point on the base triangular plane. The line that joins the tetrahedron summit and the base rate distribution point represents the director. The projected probability distribution point is geometrically determined by tracing a projection from the opinion point, parallel to the director, onto the base plane.

Assume a ternary domain $\mathbb{X} = \{x_1, x_2, x_3\}$, and a corresponding random variable X. Figure 3.3 shows the tetrahedron with the example multinomial opinion ω_X that has belief mass distribution $\boldsymbol{b}_X = \{0.20, 0.20, 0.20\}$, uncertainty mass $u_X = 0.40$, and base rate distribution $\boldsymbol{a}_X = \{0.750, 0.125, 0.125\}$. Only the uncertainty axis is shown in Figure 3.3. The belief axes for x_1, x_2 and x_3 are not shown due to the difficulty of 3D visualisation on the 2D plane of the figure.

The triangle and tetrahedron belong to the *simplex* family of geometrical shapes. Multinomial opinions on domains of cardinality k can in general be represented as a point in a simplex of dimension k. For example, binomial opinions can be represented inside a triangle which is a 2D simplex, and trinomial opinions can be represented inside a tetrahedron which is a 3D simplex.

By applying Eq.(3.12) to the example of Figure 3.3, the projected probability distribution is $\mathbf{P}_X = \{0.50, 0.25, 0.25\}$.

Note that the multinomial probability projection, as expressed by Eq.(3.12), is a generalisation of the binomial probability projection, as expressed by Eq.(3.2).

3.5.2 The Dirichlet Multinomial Model

A multinomial opinion is equivalent to a Dirichlet PDF over $\mathbb{X}$, according to a specific bijective mapping described in Section 3.5.5. For self-containment, we briefly outline the Dirichlet multinomial model below, and refer to [32] for more details.

Multinomial probability density over a domain of cardinality k is expressed by the k-dimensional Dirichlet PDF, where the special case of a probability density over a binary domain (i.e. where $k = 2$) is expressed by the Beta PDF described in Section 3.4.2 above.

Assume a domain $\mathbb{X}$ of cardinality k, and a random variable $X \in \mathbb{X}$ with probability distribution $\boldsymbol{p}_X$. The Dirichlet PDF can be used to represent *probability density* over $\boldsymbol{p}_X$.

Because of the additivity requirement $\sum_{x\in\mathbb{X}} \boldsymbol{p}(x) = 1$, the Dirichlet PDF has only $(k-1)$ degrees of freedom. Hence, the knowledge of $(k-1)$ probability variables and their density determines the last probability variable and its density.

The Dirichlet PDF takes as variable the k-dimensional probability distribution $\boldsymbol{p}_X$. The strength parameters for the k possible outcomes are represented as k positive real numbers $\alpha_X(x)$, each corresponding to one of the possible values $x \in \mathbb{X}$. When starting from the probability distribution $\boldsymbol{p}_X$ which consists of k separate probability functions $\boldsymbol{p}_X(x) : \mathbb{X} \to [0,1]$, then the image of the variable X is the probability distribution $\boldsymbol{p}_X$ which in turn is the k-component variable of $\mathrm{Dir}(\boldsymbol{p}_X, \alpha_X)$. In this way, the functions $\boldsymbol{p}_X$ and $\mathrm{Dir}(\boldsymbol{p}_X, \alpha_X)$ are chained functions. Short notations for $\mathrm{Dir}(\boldsymbol{p}_X, \alpha_X)$ are e.g. $\mathrm{Dir}(\boldsymbol{p}_X)$ or Dir_X.

Definition 3.5 (Dirichlet Probability Density Function). Let $\mathbb{X}$ be a domain consisting of k mutually disjoint values. Let α_X represent the strength vector over the values of $\mathbb{X}$, and let $\boldsymbol{p}_X$ denote the probability distribution over $\mathbb{X}$. With $\boldsymbol{p}_X$ as a k-dimensional variable, the Dirichlet PDF denoted $\mathrm{Dir}(\boldsymbol{p}_X, \alpha_X)$ is expressed as:

$$\mathrm{Dir}(\boldsymbol{p}_X, \alpha_X) = \frac{\Gamma\left(\sum\limits_{x\in\mathbb{X}} \alpha_X(x)\right)}{\prod\limits_{x\in\mathbb{X}} \Gamma(\alpha_X(x))} \prod_{x\in\mathbb{X}} \boldsymbol{p}_X(x)^{(\alpha_X(x)-1)}, \text{ where } \alpha_X(x) \geq 0\,, \tag{3.14}$$

with the restrictions that $\boldsymbol{p}_X(x) \neq 0$ if $\alpha_X(x) < 1$. □

The strength vector α_X represents the prior, as well as the observation evidence. The non-informative prior weight is expressed as a constant W, and this weight is distributed over all the possible outcomes as a function of the base rate. As already mentioned, it is normally assumed that $W = 2$.

Singleton values in a domain of cardinality k can have a base rate different from the default value $1/k$, meaning that it is possible to define an arbitrary additive base rate distribution $\boldsymbol{a}_X$ over the domain $\mathbb{X}$. The total strength $\alpha_X(x)$ for each value $x \in \mathbb{X}$ can then be expressed as

$$\alpha_X(x) = \boldsymbol{r}_X(x) + \boldsymbol{a}_X(x)W\,, \text{ where } \boldsymbol{r}_X(x) \geq 0 \;\; \forall x \in \mathbb{X}\,. \tag{3.15}$$

This leads to the evidence representation of the Dirichlet probability density function denoted $\mathrm{Dir}^{\mathrm{e}}_X(\boldsymbol{p}_X, \boldsymbol{r}_X, \boldsymbol{a}_X)$ expressed in terms of the evidence vector $\boldsymbol{r}_X$, where $\boldsymbol{r}_X(x)$ is the evidence for outcome $x \in \mathbb{X}$. In addition, the base rate distribution $\boldsymbol{a}_X$ and the non-informative prior weight W are parameters in the expression for the evidence-Dirichlet PDF.

$$\text{Dir}^{\text{e}}_X(\boldsymbol{p}_X, \boldsymbol{r}_X, \boldsymbol{a}_X) = \frac{\Gamma\left(\sum\limits_{x\in\mathbb{X}}(\boldsymbol{r}_X(x)+\boldsymbol{a}_X(x)W)\right)}{\prod\limits_{x\in\mathbb{X}}\Gamma(\boldsymbol{r}_X(x)+\boldsymbol{a}_X(x)W)} \prod_{x\in\mathbb{X}} \boldsymbol{p}_X(x)^{(\boldsymbol{r}_X(x)+\boldsymbol{a}_X(x)W-1)}, \tag{3.16}$$

where $(\boldsymbol{r}_X(x)+\boldsymbol{a}_X(x)W) \geq 0$,

with the restrictions that $\boldsymbol{p}_X(x) \neq 0$ if $(\boldsymbol{r}_X(x)+\boldsymbol{a}_X(x)W) < 1$.

The notation of Eq.(3.16) is useful because it allows the determination of the probability densities over variables, where each value can have an arbitrary base rate. Given the Dirichlet PDF of Eq.(3.16), the expected probability distribution over $\mathbb{X}$ can be written as

$$\mathbf{E}_X(x) = \frac{\alpha_X(x)}{\sum\limits_{x_j\in\mathbb{X}}\alpha_X(x_j)} = \frac{\boldsymbol{r}_X(x)+\boldsymbol{a}_X(x)W}{W+\sum\limits_{x_j\in\mathbb{X}}\boldsymbol{r}_X(x_j)} \qquad \forall x\in\mathbb{X}, \tag{3.17}$$

which represents a generalisation of the projected probability of the Beta PDF expressed by Eq.(3.9).

The variance $\text{Var}_X(x)$ of the Dirichlet PDF is defined by Eq.(3.18).

$$\begin{aligned}
\text{Var}_X(x) &= \frac{\alpha_X(x)\left(\sum\limits_{x_j\in\mathbb{X}}\alpha_X(x_j)-\alpha_X(x)\right)}{\left(\sum\limits_{x_j\in\mathbb{X}}\alpha_X(x_j)\right)^2\left(\sum\limits_{x_j\in\mathbb{X}}\alpha_X(x_j)+1\right)} \\
&= \frac{(\boldsymbol{r}_X(x)+\boldsymbol{a}_X(x)W)(R_X+W-\boldsymbol{r}_X(x)-\boldsymbol{a}_X(x)W)}{(R_X+W)^2(R_X+W+1)}, \\
&= \frac{(\boldsymbol{b}_X(x)+\boldsymbol{a}_X(x)u_X)(1-\boldsymbol{b}_X(x)-\boldsymbol{a}_X(x)u_X)u_X}{W+u_X} \\
&= \frac{\mathbf{P}_X(x)(1-\mathbf{P}_X(x))u_X}{W+u_X}, \quad \text{where } R_X = \sum_{x_j\in\mathbb{X}}\boldsymbol{r}_X(x_j).
\end{aligned} \tag{3.18}$$

The last two equalities in Eq.(3.18) emerge from the mapping of Eq.3.23 below.

The variance of the Dirichlet PDF measures how widely the probability density is spread out over the interval $[0,1]$ for each dimension x. A variance of zero for some value x indicates that the probability density is concentrated in one point, which only happens in case the corresponding strength parameter $\alpha_X(x)$ is infinite, which is equivalent to the corresponding evidence parameter $\boldsymbol{r}_X(x)$ being infinite.

It is normally assumed that the prior probability density in case of a binary domain $\mathbb{X} = \{x,\overline{x}\}$ is uniform. This requires that $\alpha_X(x) = \alpha_X(\overline{x}) = 1$, which in turn dictates $W = 2$. Assuming a uniform prior probability density over a domain larger than binary would require a non-informative prior weight $W > 2$. In fact, W is always equal to the cardinality of the domain for which a uniform probability density is assumed.

Selecting $W > 2$ would result in new observation evidence having relatively less influence over the Dirichlet PDF, and over the projected probability distribution. Note that it would be unnatural to require a uniform probability density over arbitrarily large domains, because it would make the PDF insensitive to new observation evidence.

For example, requiring a uniform prior PDF over a domain of cardinality 100 would force $W = 100$. In case an event of interest has been observed 100 times, and no other event has been observed, then the projected probability of the event of interest would only be about $1/2$, which would be highly counter-intuitive. In contrast, when a uniform PDF is required in the binary case, meaning that $W = 2$, and assuming the positive outcome has been observed 100 times, and the negative outcome has not been observed, then the projected probability of the positive outcome is close to 1, as intuition would dictate.

3.5.3 Visualising Dirichlet Probability Density Functions

Visualising a Dirichlet PDF of large dimension is challenging, because it is a density function over $(k-1)$ dimensions, where k is the domain cardinality. For this reason, Dirichlet PDFs over ternary domains are the largest that can be practically visualised.

Let us consider the example of an urn containing balls of three different markings: x_1, x_2 and x_3. This situation can be modelled by a domain $\mathbb{X} = \{x_1, x_2, x_3\}$ of cardinality $k = 3$. Let us first assume that no other information than the cardinality is available, meaning that the number and relative proportion of balls marked x_1, x_2 and x_3 are unknown, and that the default base rate for any of the markings is $\boldsymbol{a}_X(x) = 1/k = 1/3$. Initially, before any balls are drawn, we have $\boldsymbol{r}_X(x_1) = \boldsymbol{r}_X(x_2) = \boldsymbol{r}_X(x_3) = 0$. Then Eq.(3.17) dictates that the prior projected probability of picking a ball of any specific marking is the default base rate probability $\boldsymbol{a}_X(x) = 1/3$. The non-informative prior Dirichlet PDF is illustrated in Figure 3.4.a.

Let us now assume that an observer has picked (with return) six balls marked x_1, one ball marked x_2, and one ball marked x_3, i.e. $\boldsymbol{r}(x_1) = 6$, $\boldsymbol{r}(x_2) = 1$, $\boldsymbol{r}(x_3) = 1$, then the *a posteriori* projected probability of picking a ball marked x_1 can be computed as $\mathbf{E}_X(x_1) = 2/3$. The Posterior Dirichlet PDF is illustrated in Figure 3.4.b.

3.5.4 Coarsening Example: From Ternary to Binary

We reuse the example of Section 3.5.3 where the urn contains three types of balls marked x_1, x_2 and x_3, but this time we consider a binary partition of the balls into the two types x_1 and $\bar{x}_1 = \{x_2, x_3\}$. The base rate of picking x_1 is set to the relative

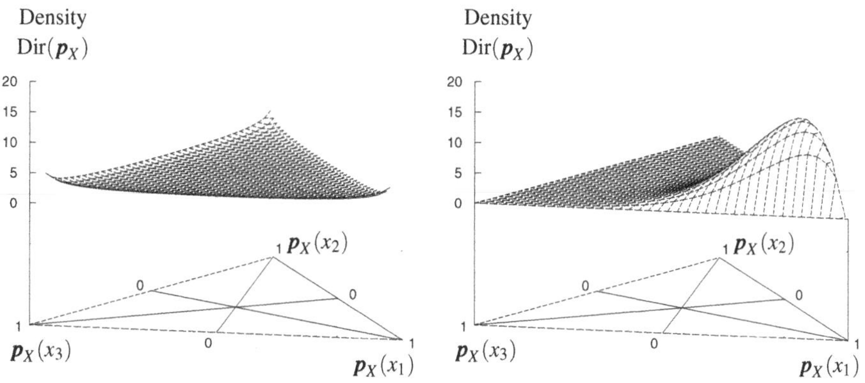

(a) Non-informative prior Dirichlet PDF (b) Posterior Dirichlet PDF

Fig. 3.4 Prior and posterior Dirichlet PDFs

atomicity of x_1, expressed as $\boldsymbol{a}_X(x_1) = 1/3$. Similarly, the base rate of picking $\bar{x}_1$ is $\boldsymbol{a}_X(\bar{x}_1) = \boldsymbol{a}_X(x_2) + \boldsymbol{a}_X(x_3) = 2/3$.

Let us again assume that an observer has picked (with return) six balls marked x_1, and two balls marked $\bar{x}_1$, i.e. marked x_2 or x_3. This translates into the observation vector $\boldsymbol{r}_X(x_1) = 6$, $\boldsymbol{r}_X(\bar{x}_1) = 2$.

Since the domain has been reduced to binary, the Dirichlet PDF is reduced to a Beta PDF which is simple to visualise. The prior and posterior probability density functions are illustrated in Figure 3.5.

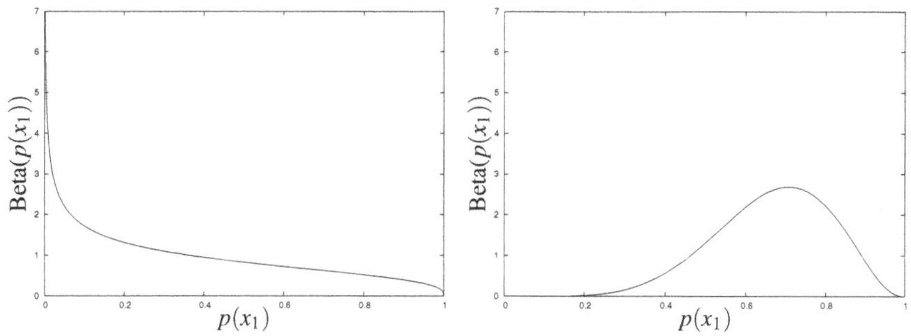

(a) Non-informative prior Beta PDF (b) After six balls marked x_1, and two balls marked x_2 or x_3

Fig. 3.5 Prior and posterior Beta PDF

Computing the posterior projected probability of picking ball marked x_1 with Eq.(3.17) produces $\mathbf{E}_X(x_1) = 2/3$, which is the same as before the coarsening, as illustrated in Section 3.5.3. This shows that the coarsening does not influence the projected probability of specific events.

3.5.5 Mapping Between Multinomial Opinion and Dirichlet PDF

The Dirichlet model translates observation evidence directly into a PDF over a k-component probability variable. The representation of the observation evidence, together with the base rate, can be used to determine subjective opinions. In other words, it is possible to define a bijective mapping between Dirichlet PDFs and multinomial opinions.

Let X be a random variable in domain $\mathbb{X}$ of cardinality k. Assume the multinomial opinion $\omega_X = (\boldsymbol{b}_X, u_X, \boldsymbol{a}_X)$, the probability distribution $\boldsymbol{p}_X$ over $X \in \mathbb{X}$, and $\mathrm{Dir}^{\mathrm{e}}_X(\boldsymbol{p}_X, \boldsymbol{r}_X, \boldsymbol{a}_X)$ over $\boldsymbol{p}_X$.

The bijective mapping between ω_X and $\mathrm{Dir}^{\mathrm{e}}_X(\boldsymbol{p}_X, \boldsymbol{r}_X, \boldsymbol{a}_X)$ is based on the requirement for equality between the projected probability distribution $\mathbf{P}_X$ derived from ω_X and the expected probability distribution $\mathbf{E}_X$ derived from $\mathrm{Dir}^{\mathrm{e}}_X(\boldsymbol{p}_X, \boldsymbol{r}_X, \boldsymbol{a}_X)$. This requirement is expressed as

$$\mathbf{P}_X = \mathbf{E}_X \tag{3.19}$$

$$\Updownarrow$$

$$\boldsymbol{b}_X(x) + \boldsymbol{a}_X(x)\, u_X = \frac{\boldsymbol{r}_X(x) + W \boldsymbol{a}_X(x)}{W + \sum_{x_j \in \mathbb{X}} \boldsymbol{r}_X(x_j)} \qquad \forall x \in \mathbb{X}\,. \tag{3.20}$$

We also require that each belief mass $\boldsymbol{b}_X(x)$ be an increasing function of the evidence $\boldsymbol{r}_X(x)$, and that u_X be a decreasing function of $\sum_{x \in \mathbb{X}} \boldsymbol{r}_X(x)$. In other words, the more evidence in favour of a particular outcome x, the greater the belief mass on that outcome. Furthermore, the more total evidence available, the less uncertainty mass. These requirements are expressed as:

$$\sum_{x \in \mathbb{X}} \boldsymbol{r}_X(x) \longrightarrow \infty \quad \Leftrightarrow \quad \sum_{x \in \mathbb{X}} \boldsymbol{b}_X(x) \longrightarrow 1 \tag{3.21}$$

$$\sum_{x \in \mathbb{X}} \boldsymbol{r}_X(x) \longrightarrow \infty \quad \Leftrightarrow \quad u_X \longrightarrow 0 \tag{3.22}$$

As already mentioned in Section 3.5.2, the non-informative prior weight is set to $W = 2$. These intuitive requirements, together with Eq.(3.20), provide the basis for the multinomial bijective mapping.

Definition 3.6 (Mapping: Multinomial Opinion $\leftrightarrow$ Dirichlet PDF). Let $\omega_X = (\boldsymbol{b}_X, u_X, \boldsymbol{a}_X)$ be a multinomial opinion, and let $\mathrm{Dir}^{\mathrm{e}}_X(\boldsymbol{p}_X, \boldsymbol{r}_X, \boldsymbol{a}_X)$ be a Dirichlet PDF, both over the same variable $X \in \mathbb{X}$. These are equivalent through the mapping:

$$\forall x \in \mathbb{X}$$

$$\left\{\begin{array}{lcl} \boldsymbol{b}_X(x) & = & \dfrac{\boldsymbol{r}_X(x)}{W + \sum\limits_{x_i \in \mathbb{X}} \boldsymbol{r}_X(x_i)}, \\ u_X & = & \dfrac{W}{W + \sum\limits_{x_i \in \mathbb{X}} \boldsymbol{r}_X(x_i)}, \end{array}\right. \Leftrightarrow \left(\begin{array}{c|c} \text{For } u_X \neq 0: & \text{For } u_X = 0: \\ \left\{\begin{array}{l} \boldsymbol{r}_X(x) = \dfrac{W \boldsymbol{b}_X(x)}{u_X}, \\ 1 = u_X + \sum\limits_{x_i \in \mathbb{X}} \boldsymbol{b}_X(x_i), \end{array}\right. & \left\{\begin{array}{l} \boldsymbol{r}_X(x) = \boldsymbol{b}_X(x) \cdot \infty, \\ 1 = \sum\limits_{x_i \in \mathbb{X}} \boldsymbol{b}_X(x_i). \end{array}\right. \end{array} \right) \tag{3.23}$$

□

The equivalence mapping of Eq.(3.23) is a generalisation of the binomial mapping from Eq.(3.11). The interpretation of Beta and Dirichlet PDFs is well established in the statistics literature, so the mapping of Definition 3.6 creates a direct mathematical and interpretation equivalence between Dirichlet PDFs and opinions, when both are expressed over the same domain $\mathbb{X}$.

This equivalence is very powerful. Primarily, statistics tools and methods, such as collecting statistical observation evidence, can now be applied to opinions. Secondly, the operators of subjective logic, such as conditional deduction and abduction, can be applied to statistical models that are based on Dirichlet PDFs.

Bayesian reputation systems, described in Chapter 16, offer practical methods to collect statistical evidence in the form of feedback ratings which represent observations in the evidence-Dirichlet model of Eq.3.16). The collected ratings can then be processed and represented in various ways, and can e.g. be translated into opinions with the mapping of Eq.(3.23).

3.5.6 Uncertainty-Maximisation

Given a specific multinomial opinion ω_X, with its projected probability distribution $\mathbf{P}_X$, it is often useful to know the theoretical maximum uncertainty mass that still preserves the same projected probability distribution. The corresponding uncertainty-maximised opinion is denoted $\ddot{\omega}_X = (\ddot{\boldsymbol{b}}_X, \ddot{u}_X, \boldsymbol{a}_X)$. Obviously, the base rate distribution $\boldsymbol{a}_X$ is not affected by uncertainty-maximisation.

The theoretical maximum uncertainty mass $\ddot{u}_X$ is determined by converting as much belief mass as possible into uncertainty mass, while preserving consistent projected probabilities. This process is illustrated in Figure 3.6 which shows an opinion ω_X as well as the corresponding uncertainty-maximised opinion $\ddot{\omega}_X$.

The projector line defined by the equations

$$\mathbf{P}_X(x_i) = \boldsymbol{b}_X(x_i) + \boldsymbol{a}_X(x_i) u_X\ , \quad i = 1, \ldots k, \tag{3.24}$$

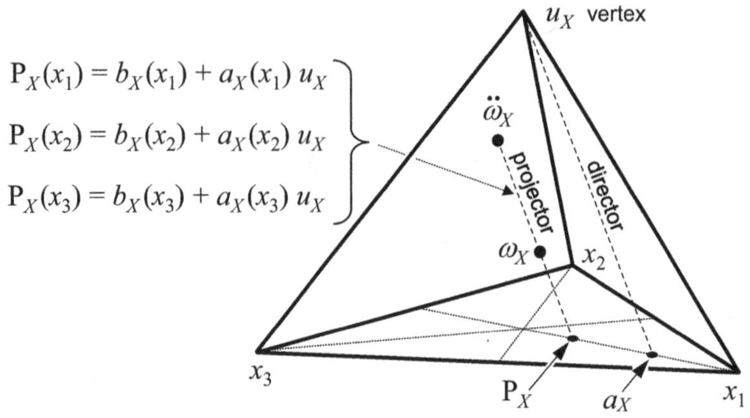

Fig. 3.6 Uncertainty-maximised opinion $\ddot{\omega}_X$ of multinomial opinion ω_X

which by definition is parallel to the base rate director line, and which joins $\mathbf{P}_X$ and $\ddot{\omega}_X$ in Figure 3.6, defines possible opinions ω_X for which the projected probability distribution is constant. As the illustration shows, an opinion $\ddot{\omega}_X$ is an uncertainty-maximised opinion when Eq.(3.24) is satisfied and at least one belief mass of $\ddot{\omega}_X$ is zero, since the corresponding point would lie on a side of the simplex. In general, not all belief masses can be zero simultaneously, except for vacuous opinions. The example of Figure 3.6 shows the case where $\ddot{\boldsymbol{b}}_X(x_1) = 0$.

The components of the uncertainty-maximised opinion $\ddot{\omega}_X$ should satisfy the following requirements:

$$\ddot{u}_X = \frac{\mathbf{P}_X(x_{i_0})}{\boldsymbol{a}_X(x_{i_0})}, \quad \text{for some } i_0 \in \{1,\ldots,k\}, \text{ and} \tag{3.25}$$

$$\mathbf{P}_X(x_i) \geq \boldsymbol{a}_X(x_i) u_X, \quad \text{for every } i \in \{1,\ldots,k\}\,. \tag{3.26}$$

Eq.(3.26) ensures that all the belief masses determined according to Eq.(3.12) are non-negative. These requirements lead to the theoretical uncertainty maximum:

$$\ddot{u}_X = \min_i \left[\frac{\mathbf{P}_X(x_i)}{\boldsymbol{a}_X(x_i)}\right], \quad \text{for } x_i \in \mathbb{X}\,. \tag{3.27}$$

Uncertainty-maximisation is a characteristic of epistemic opinions described in Section 3.3. Epistemic opinions apply to variables that are not governed by a frequentist process, so that statistical sampling is not possible or meaningful. This puts constraints on input opinion arguments to models for reasoning about epistemic situations. With reference to Figure 3.6, the opinion denoted ω_X should normally only be an aleatory opinion, whenever it is used as an input argument. The uncertainty-maximised opinion denoted $\ddot{\omega}_X$ could be either an aleatory or an epistemic opinion, when used as an input argument.

In the case of hyper-opinions described in the next section, there is no simple method for redistributing belief mass from singletons and composite values to form increased uncertainty mass in a consistent way. The simplest method is therefore to first project the hyper-opinion to a multinomial opinion according to Eq.(3.30) and then apply Eq.(3.27). It is not very meaningful to distinguish between aleatory and epistemic opinions in the case of hyper-opinions.

There is also no difference between aleatory and epistemic opinions in the limit case of absolute opinions, i.e. when one of the variable values x has assigned belief mass $\boldsymbol{b}_X(x) = 1$.

When analysing reasoning models based on input arguments, the resulting output opinions might not be uncertainty-maximised, even if the corresponding variables are considered to be epistemic. The analyst must apply judgment as to whether input arguments and output results should be considered as aleatory or epistemic, and in case they are considered epistemic, whether they should be uncertainty-maximised.

3.6 Hyper-opinions

In situations of multiple possible state values it is common that an observer/analyst can only express belief that some state value in specific set of values is TRUE, but can not identify a single value in particular which is believed to be TRUE. The concept of *hyper-opinions* allows belief mass to be assigned to a set of singleton values represented by a composite value $x \in \mathscr{C}(\mathbb{X})$. Belief mass assigned to composite values $x \in \mathscr{C}(\mathbb{X})$ represents *vagueness*, as described in Section 4.1.2. Hyper-opinions are equivalent to Dirichlet PDFs over hyperdomains, as well as to hyper-Dirichlet PDFs over n-ary domains. While the Dirichlet model is classical, the hyper-Dirichlet model was defined by Hankin in 2010 [33].

3.6.1 The Hyper-opinion Representation

Hyper-opinions naturally generalise multinomial opinions. In the case of a domain $\mathbb{X}$ with hyperdomain $\mathscr{R}(\mathbb{X})$, it is possible to obtain evidence for a composite value $x \in \mathscr{R}(\mathbb{X})$, which translates into assigning belief mass to that composite value.

Definition 3.7 (Hyper-opinion). Let $\mathbb{X}$ be a domain of cardinality $k > 2$, with corresponding hyperdomain $\mathscr{R}(\mathbb{X})$. Let X be a hypervariable in $\mathscr{R}(\mathbb{X})$. A hyper-opinion on the hypervariable X is the ordered triplet $\omega_X = (\boldsymbol{b}_X, u_X, \boldsymbol{a}_X)$ where

$\boldsymbol{b}_X$ is a *belief mass distribution* over $\mathscr{R}(\mathbb{X})$,
u_X is the *uncertainty mass* which represents the vacuity of evidence,
$\boldsymbol{a}_X$ is a *base rate distribution* over $\mathbb{X}$,

and the hypernomial additivity of Eq.(2.7) is satisfied. □

A subjective opinion ω_X^A indicates the target variable X as subscript and identifies the opinion owner A as superscript. Explicitly expressing subjective ownership of opinions makes it possible to formally express that different agents have different opinions on the same variable.

The belief mass distribution $\boldsymbol{b}_X$ over $\mathscr{R}(\mathbb{X})$ has $(2^k - 2)$ parameters, whereas the base rate distribution $\boldsymbol{a}_X$ over $\mathbb{X}$ only has k parameters. The uncertainty mass $u_X \in [0,1]$ is a simple scalar. A general opinion thus contains $(2^k + k - 1)$ parameters. However, given that Eq.(2.7) and Eq.(2.8) remove one degree of freedom each, hyper-opinions over a domain of cardinality k only have $(2^k + k - 3)$ degrees of freedom.

By using the concept of relative base rates from Eq.(2.10), the projected probability distribution $\mathbf{P}_X$ of hyper-opinions can be expressed as

$$\mathbf{P}_X(x) = \sum_{x_i \in \mathscr{R}(\mathbb{X})} \boldsymbol{a}_X(x|x_i)\, \boldsymbol{b}_X(x_i) + \boldsymbol{a}_X(x)\, u_X, \quad \forall x \in \mathbb{X}\,. \tag{3.28}$$

For $X \in \mathbb{X}$, it can be shown that the projected probability distribution $\mathbf{P}_X$ satisfies the probability additivity principle of Eq.(3.29.a). However, for hyper-probabilities over $X \in \mathscr{R}(\mathbb{X})$, the sum of projected probabilities is in general super-additive, as expressed in Eq.(3.29.b).

$$\text{(a):}\quad \overbrace{\sum_{x \in \mathbb{X}} \mathbf{P}_X(x) = 1}^{\text{Additivity}}\,, \qquad \text{(b):}\quad \overbrace{\sum_{x \in \mathscr{R}(\mathbb{X})} \mathbf{P}_X(x) \geq 1}^{\text{Super-additivity}}\,. \tag{3.29}$$

The super-additivity of Eq.(3.29.b) results from the fact that projected probabilities of partially overlapping composite values $x_j \in \mathscr{R}(\mathbb{X})$ are partially based on the same projected probability on their constituent singleton values $x_i \in \mathbb{X}$, so that probabilities are counted multiple times.

3.6.2 Projecting Hyper-opinions to Multinomial Opinions

Given a hyper-opinion, it can be useful to project it into a multinomial opinion. The procedure goes as follows.

If $\boldsymbol{b}'_X$ is a belief mass distribution defined by the sum in Eq.(3.28), i.e.

$$\boldsymbol{b}'_X(x) = \sum_{x' \in \mathscr{R}(\mathbb{X})} \boldsymbol{a}_X(x|x')\, \boldsymbol{b}_X(x')\,, \tag{3.30}$$

then it is easy to check that $\boldsymbol{b}'_X : \mathbb{X} \to [0,1]$, and that $\boldsymbol{b}'_X$ together with u_X satisfies the additivity property in Eq.(2.6), i.e. $\omega'_X = (\boldsymbol{b}'_X, u_X, \boldsymbol{a}_X)$ is a multinomial opinion. From Eq.(3.28) and Eq.(3.30) we obtain $\mathbf{P}(\omega_X) = \mathbf{P}(\omega'_X)$. This means that every hyper-opinion can be approximated with a multinomial opinion which has the same projected probability distribution as the initial hyper-opinion.

3.6.3 The Dirichlet Model Applied to Hyperdomains

The traditional Dirichlet model applies naturally to a multinomial domain $\mathbb{X}$ of cardinality k, and there is a simple bijective mapping between multinomial opinions and Dirichlet PDFs. Since opinions can also apply to a hyperdomain $\mathscr{R}(\mathbb{X})$ of cardinality $\kappa = 2^k - 2$, the question then is whether the Dirichlet model can also be applied to hyperdomains. This would be valuable for interpreting hyper-opinions in terms of traditional statistical theory. The apparent obstacle to this would be that two composite values $x_i, x_j \in \mathscr{R}(\mathbb{X})$ can be overlapping (i.e. non-exclusive) so that $x_i \cap x_j \neq \emptyset$, which is contrary to the assumption in the traditional Dirichlet model. However, there is a solution, as described below.

The approach that we follow is to artificially assume that hyperdomain $\mathscr{R}(\mathbb{X})$ is exclusive, i.e. to artificially assume that for every pair of values $x_i, x_j \in \mathscr{R}(\mathbb{X})$ it holds that $x_i \cap x_j = \emptyset$. Thus, we choose to ignore the fact that composite values $x_i, x_j \in \mathscr{R}(\mathbb{X})$ can be overlapping. In this way, the Dirichlet model can be applied to the artificially exclusive hyperdomain $\mathscr{R}(\mathbb{X})$. This Dirichlet model is then based on the κ-dimensional hyper-probability distribution $\boldsymbol{p}_X^{\mathrm{H}}$ from Eq.(2.12), where $X \in \mathscr{R}(\mathbb{X})$ is a hypervariable.

The set of input arguments to the Dirichlet PDF over $\mathscr{R}(\mathbb{X})$ then becomes a sequence of strength parameters of the κ possible values $x \in \mathscr{R}(\mathbb{X})$ represented as κ positive real numbers $\alpha_X(x_i)$, $i = 1 \ldots \kappa$, each corresponding to one of the possible values $x \in \mathscr{R}(\mathbb{X})$. Because this is a Dirichlet PDF over a hypervariable, it is called a Dirichlet Hyper-PDF, or Dirichlet HPDF for short.

Definition 3.8 (Dirichlet HPDF). Let $\mathbb{X}$ be a domain consisting of k mutually disjoint values, where the corresponding hyperdomain $\mathscr{R}(\mathbb{X})$ has cardinality $\kappa = (2^k - 2)$. Let α_X represent the strength vector over the κ values $x \in \mathscr{R}(\mathbb{X})$. The hyper-probability distribution $\boldsymbol{p}_X^{\mathrm{H}}$ and the strength vector α_X are both κ-dimensional. The Dirichlet hyper-probability density function over $\boldsymbol{p}_X^{\mathrm{H}}$, called Dirichlet HPDF for short, is denoted $\mathrm{Dir}_X^{\mathrm{H}}(\boldsymbol{p}_X^{\mathrm{H}}, \alpha_X)$, and is expressed as

$$\mathrm{Dir}_X^{\mathrm{H}}(\boldsymbol{p}_X^{\mathrm{H}}, \alpha_X) = \frac{\Gamma\left(\sum\limits_{x \in \mathscr{R}(\mathbb{X})} \alpha_X(x)\right)}{\prod\limits_{x \in \mathscr{R}(\mathbb{X})} \Gamma(\alpha_X(x))} \prod_{x \in \mathscr{R}(\mathbb{X})} \boldsymbol{p}_X^{\mathrm{H}}(x)^{(\alpha_X(x)-1)}, \text{ where } \alpha_X(x) \geq 0\,, \tag{3.31}$$

with the restrictions that $\boldsymbol{p}_X^{\mathrm{H}}(x) \neq 0$ if $\alpha_X(x) < 1$. □

The strength vector α_X represents the prior as well as the observation evidence, now assumed applicable to values $x \in \mathscr{R}(\mathbb{X})$.

Since the values of $\mathscr{R}(\mathbb{X})$ can contain multiple singletons from $\mathbb{X}$, a value of $\mathscr{R}(\mathbb{X})$ has a base rate equal to the sum of the base rates of the singletons it contains, as expressed by Eq.(2.9). The strength $\alpha_X(x)$ for each value $x \in \mathscr{R}(\mathbb{X})$ can then be expressed as

$$\alpha_X(x) = \boldsymbol{r}_X(x) + \boldsymbol{a}_X(x)W, \text{ where } \left\{ \begin{array}{l} \boldsymbol{r}_X(x) \geq 0\,, \\ \\ \boldsymbol{a}_X(x) = \sum\limits_{\substack{x_j \subseteq x \\ x_j \in X}} \boldsymbol{a}(x_j), \\ \\ W = 2\,, \end{array} \right\} \quad \forall x \in \mathscr{R}(\mathbb{X}). \tag{3.32}$$

The Dirichlet HPDF over a set of κ possible states $x_i \in \mathscr{R}(\mathbb{X})$ can thus be expressed as a function of the observation evidence $\boldsymbol{r}_X$ and the base rate distribution $\boldsymbol{a}_X(x)$, where $x \in \mathscr{R}(\mathbb{X})$. The superscript 'eH' in the notation $\mathrm{Dir}_X^{\mathrm{eH}}$ indicates that it is expressed as a function of the evidence parameter vector $\boldsymbol{r}_X$ (not of the strength parameter vector α_X), and that it is a Dirichlet HPDF (not PDF).

$$\mathrm{Dir}_X^{\mathrm{eH}}(\boldsymbol{p}_X^{\mathrm{H}}, \boldsymbol{r}_X, \boldsymbol{a}_X) = \frac{\Gamma\left(\sum\limits_{x \in \mathscr{R}(\mathbb{X})} (\boldsymbol{r}_X(x) + \boldsymbol{a}_X(x)W)\right)}{\prod\limits_{x \in \mathscr{R}(\mathbb{X})} \Gamma(\boldsymbol{r}_X(x) + \boldsymbol{a}_X(x)W)} \prod_{x \in \mathscr{R}(\mathbb{X})} \boldsymbol{p}_X^{\mathrm{H}}(x)^{(\boldsymbol{r}_X(x) + \boldsymbol{a}_X(x)W - 1)}, \tag{3.33}$$

where $(\boldsymbol{r}_X(x) + \boldsymbol{a}_X(x)W) \geq 0$,

with the restriction that $\boldsymbol{p}_X^{\mathrm{H}}(x) \neq 0$ if $(\boldsymbol{r}_X(x) + \boldsymbol{a}_X(x)W) < 1$.

The expression of Eq.(3.33) determines probability density over hyper-probability distributions p_X^{H}, where each value $x \in \mathscr{R}(\mathbb{X})$ has a base rate according to Eq.(2.9).

Because a value $x_j \in \mathscr{R}(\mathbb{X})$ can be composite, the expected probability of any value $x \in \mathbb{X}$ is not only a function of the direct probability density on x, but also of the probability density of all other values $x_j \in \mathscr{R}(\mathbb{X})$ that contain x. More formally, the expected probability of $x \in \mathbb{X}$ results from the probability density of each $x_j \in \mathscr{R}(\mathbb{X})$ where $x \cap x_j \neq \emptyset$.

Given the Dirichlet HPDF of Eq.(3.33), the expected probability of any of the k values $x \in \mathbb{X}$ can be written as

$$\mathbf{E}_X(x) = \frac{\sum\limits_{x_i \in \mathscr{R}(\mathbb{X})} \boldsymbol{a}_X(x|x_i)\boldsymbol{r}(x_i) + W\boldsymbol{a}_X(x)}{W + \sum\limits_{x_i \in \mathscr{R}(\mathbb{X})} \boldsymbol{r}(x_i)} \quad \forall x \in \mathbb{X}. \tag{3.34}$$

The expected probability distribution of a Dirichlet HPDF expressed by Eq.(3.34) is a generalisation of the expected probability distribution of a Dirichlet PDF expressed by Eq.(3.17).

3.6.4 Mapping Between a Hyper-opinion and a Dirichlet HPDF

A hyper-opinion is equivalent to a Dirichlet HPDF according to the mapping defined below. This mapping is simply an extension of the mapping between a multinomial opinion and a traditional Dirichlet PDF as described in Eq.(3.23).

Definition 3.9 (Mapping: Hyper-opinion $\leftrightarrow$ Dirichlet HPDF). Let $\mathbb{X}$ be a domain consisting of k mutually disjoint values, where the corresponding hyperdomain $\mathscr{R}(\mathbb{X})$ has cardinality $\kappa = (2^k - 2)$, and let X be a hypervariable in $\mathscr{R}(\mathbb{X})$. Let ω_X be a hyper-opinion on X, and let $\mathrm{Dir}^{\mathrm{eH}}_X(\boldsymbol{p}^{\mathrm{H}}_X, \boldsymbol{r}_X, \boldsymbol{a}_X)$ be a Dirichlet HPDF over the hyper-probability distribution $\boldsymbol{p}^{\mathrm{H}}_X$. The hyper-opinion ω_X and the Dirichlet HPDF $\mathrm{Dir}^{\mathrm{eH}}_X(\boldsymbol{p}^{\mathrm{H}}_X, \boldsymbol{r}_X, \boldsymbol{a}_X)$ are equivalent through the following mapping:

$$\forall x \in \mathscr{R}(\mathbb{X})$$

$$\begin{cases} \boldsymbol{b}_X(x) = \dfrac{\boldsymbol{r}_X(x)}{W + \sum\limits_{x_i \in \mathscr{R}(\mathbb{X})} \boldsymbol{r}_X(x_i)}, \\[2ex] u_X \quad = \dfrac{W}{W + \sum\limits_{x_i \in \mathscr{R}(\mathbb{X})} \boldsymbol{r}_X(x_i)}, \end{cases} \Leftrightarrow \left(\begin{array}{c|c} \text{For } u_X \neq 0\text{:} & \text{For } u_X = 0\text{:} \\ \begin{cases} \boldsymbol{r}_X(x) = \dfrac{W \boldsymbol{b}_X(x)}{u_X}, \\[2ex] 1 = u_X + \sum\limits_{x_i \in \mathscr{R}(\mathbb{X})} \boldsymbol{b}_X(x_i), \end{cases} & \begin{cases} \boldsymbol{r}_X(x) = \boldsymbol{b}_X(x) \cdot \infty, \\[2ex] 1 = \sum\limits_{x_i \in \mathscr{R}(\mathbb{X})} \boldsymbol{b}_X(x_i). \end{cases} \end{array} \right) \tag{3.35}$$

□

A Dirichlet HPDF is based on applying the Dirichlet model to values of the hyperdomain $\mathscr{R}(\mathbb{X})$, which in fact are partially overlapping values in the corresponding domain $\mathbb{X}$. A Dirichlet HPDF applied to $\mathscr{R}(\mathbb{X})$ can be projected into a PDF applied to $\mathbb{X}$, but this projected PDF is not a Dirichlet PDF in general. Only a few degenerate cases become Dirichlet PDFs through this projection, such as the non-informative prior Dirichlet, where $\boldsymbol{r}_X$ is the zero vector which corresponds to a vacuous opinion with $u = 1$, or the case where evidence only relates to singleton values $x \in \mathbb{X}$.

The advantage of the Dirichlet HPDF is to provide an interpretation and equivalent representation of hyper-opinions.

It would not be meaningful to try to visualise the Dirichlet HPDF over the hyper-probability distribution $\boldsymbol{p}^{\mathrm{H}}_X$ itself, because it would fail to visualise the important fact that probability is assigned to overlapping values $x \in \mathbb{X}$. This aspect would make it extremely difficult to see the probability on a specific value $x \in \mathbb{X}$, because in general, the probability is a function of multiple probabilities on overlapping hyper-values. A visualisation of probability density should therefore be done over the probability distribution $\boldsymbol{p}_X$, where probability on specific values $x \in \mathbb{X}$ can be seen or interpreted directly.

3.6.5 Hyper-Dirichlet PDF

The Dirichlet HPDF (hyper-probability density function) described in Section 3.6.3 above applies to hyperdomain $\mathscr{R}(\mathbb{X})$, and is not suitable for representing probability over the corresponding domain $\mathbb{X}$. What is needed is a PDF (probability density function) that somehow represents the parameters of the Dirichlet HPDF over the domain $\mathbb{X}$.

A PDF that does exactly that can be obtained by integrating the evidence parameters for the Dirichlet HPDF to produce evidence parameters for a PDF over the probability variable $\boldsymbol{p}_X$. In other words, the evidence on singleton values of the random variable must be computed as a function of the evidence on composite values of the hypervariable. A method for this task was defined by Hankin [33], where the resulting PDF is a *hyper-Dirichlet PDF*, which is a generalisation of the classical Dirichlet PDF. In addition to the factors consisting of the probability product of the probability variables, it requires a normalisation factor $B(\boldsymbol{r}_X, \boldsymbol{a}_X)$ that can be computed numerically. Hankin also has available a software package for producing visualisations of hyper-Dirichlet PDFs over ternary domains.

The hyper-Dirichlet PDF is denoted $\mathrm{HDir}_X^{\mathrm{e}}(\boldsymbol{p}_X, \boldsymbol{r}_X, \boldsymbol{a}_X)$. Its mathematical expression is given by Eq.(3.36) below.

$$\mathrm{HDir}_X^{\mathrm{e}}(\boldsymbol{p}_X, \boldsymbol{r}_X, \boldsymbol{a}_X) = B(\boldsymbol{r}_X, \boldsymbol{a}_X)^{-1} \left(\prod_{i=1}^{k} \boldsymbol{p}_X(x_i)^{(\boldsymbol{r}_X(x_i)+\boldsymbol{a}_X(x_i)W-1)} \prod_{j=(k+1)}^{\kappa} \boldsymbol{p}_X(x_j)^{\boldsymbol{r}_X(x_j)} \right) \tag{3.36}$$

$$= B(\boldsymbol{r}_X, \boldsymbol{a}_X)^{-1} \left(\prod_{i=1}^{k} \boldsymbol{p}_X(x_i)^{(\boldsymbol{a}_X(x_i)W-1)} \prod_{j=1}^{\kappa} \boldsymbol{p}_X(x_j)^{\boldsymbol{r}_X(x_j)} \right) \tag{3.37}$$

where

$$B(\boldsymbol{r}_X, \boldsymbol{a}_X) =$$

$$\int\limits_{\substack{\boldsymbol{p}_X(x)\geq 0 \\ \sum_{j=(k+1)}^{\kappa} \boldsymbol{p}_X(x_j)\leq 1}} \left(\prod_{i=1}^{k} \boldsymbol{p}_X(x_i)^{(\boldsymbol{r}_X(x_i)+\boldsymbol{a}_X(x_i)W-1)} \prod_{j=(k+1)}^{\kappa} \boldsymbol{p}_X(x_j)^{\boldsymbol{r}_X(x_j)} \right) d(\boldsymbol{p}_X(x_1), \ldots, \boldsymbol{p}_X(x_\kappa)). \tag{3.38}$$

A hyper-Dirichlet PDF produces probability density over a probability distribution $\boldsymbol{p}_X$, where $X \in \mathbb{X}$. Readers might therefore be surprised to see that Eq.(3.36) contains probability terms $\boldsymbol{p}_X(x_j)$, where x_j are composite values in $\mathscr{R}(\mathbb{X})$. However, the probability of a composite value is in fact the sum of a set of probabilities $\boldsymbol{p}_X(x_i)$, where $x_i \in \mathbb{X}$, as expressed by Eq.(3.39). This ensures that a hyper-Dirichlet PDF is really a PDF over a traditional probability distribution $\boldsymbol{p}_X$.

The expression for the hyper-Dirichlet PDF in Eq.(3.36) strictly distinguishes between the singleton value terms and the composite value terms. To this end, the k singleton state values $x \in \mathscr{R}(\mathbb{X})$ (i.e. values $x \in \mathbb{X}$) are denoted x_i, $i \in [1, k]$, and the $(\kappa - k)$ composite state values $x \in \mathscr{R}(\mathbb{X})$ are denoted x_j, $j \in [(k+1), \kappa]$.

The notation is more compact in Eq.(3.37), where the index j covers the whole range $[1, \kappa]$. This simplification results from interpreting the term $\boldsymbol{p}_X(x_j)$ according to Eq.(3.39), so that for $j = i \leq k$, we automatically have $\boldsymbol{p}_X(x_j) = \boldsymbol{p}_X(x_i)$:

$$\mathbf{p}_X(x_j) = \sum_{x_i \subseteq x_j} \mathbf{p}_X(x_i), \quad \text{for } j \in [1, \kappa] . \tag{3.39}$$

Unfortunately, the normalisation factor $B(\boldsymbol{r}_X, \boldsymbol{a}_X)$ is not given by a closed expression, so numerical computation is needed to determine its value for each set of parameters $\boldsymbol{r}_X$ and $\boldsymbol{a}_X$.

The ability to represent (vague) statistical observations in terms of hyper-Dirichlet PDFs is useful, because a PDF on a probability distribution $\boldsymbol{p}_X$ is intuitively meaningful, in contrast to a PDF on a hyper-probability distribution $\boldsymbol{p}_X^{\mathrm{H}}$.

Let us consider an example where a genetic engineering process produces eggs of three different mutations. The mutations are denoted by x_1, x_2 and x_3 respectively, which form the domain $\mathbb{X} = \{x_1, x_2, x_3\}$. The specific mutation of each egg can not be controlled by the process, so a sensor is used to determine the mutation that each egg has. Assume that the sensor is not always able to determine the mutation exactly, so that it sometimes can only exclude one out of the three possibilities. Hence, the sensor observes values of the hyperdomain $\mathscr{R}(\mathbb{X})$. We consider two separate scenarios of 100 observations. In scenario A, mutation x_3 has been observed 20 times, and mutation x_1 or x_2 (i.e. the value $\{x_1,x_2\}$) has been observed 80 times. In scenario B, mutation x_2 has been observed 20 times, the mutations x_1 or x_3 (i.e. the value $\{x_1,x_3\}$) have been observed 40 times, and the mutations x_2 or x_3 (i.e. the value $\{x_2,x_3\}$) have also been observed 40 times. Table 3.3 summarises the two scenarios. The base rate is set to the default value 1/3 for each mutation.

Table 3.3 Number of observations per mutation type

	Scenario A						Scenario B					
Mutation:	x_1	x_2	x_3	$\{x_1,x_2\}$	$\{x_1,x_3\}$	$\{x_2,x_3\}$	x_1	x_2	x_3	$\{x_1,x_2\}$	$\{x_1,x_3\}$	$\{x_2,x_3\}$
Count:	0	0	20	80	0	0	0	20	0	0	40	40

Because the domain $\mathbb{X}$ is ternary, it is possible to visualise the corresponding hyper-Dirichlet PDFs, as shown in Figure 3.7.

Readers who are familiar with the typical shapes of Dirichlet PDFs will immediately notice that the plots of Figure 3.7 are clearly not Dirichlet. The hyper-Dirichlet model [33] represents a generalisation of the classical Dirichlet model, and provides a nice interpretation of hyper-opinions that can be useful for better understanding their nature.

An interesting aspect of hyper-opinions is that they can express vagueness, in the sense that evidence can support multiple values in the domain simultaneously. Vague belief is defined in Section 4.1.2.

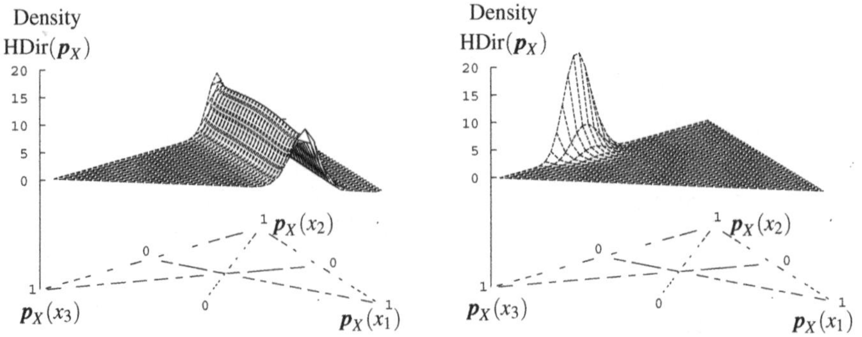

(a) Hyper-Dirichlet PDF of scenario A (b) Hyper-Dirichlet PDF of scenario B

Fig. 3.7 Example hyper-Dirichlet probability density functions

3.7 Alternative Opinion Representations

The previous sections have presented two equivalent opinion representations, which are the belief representation of opinions, typically denoted ω_X, as well as the evidence representation of opinions in the form of Dirichlet PDFs, typically denoted $\mathrm{Dir}^{\mathrm{e}}_X(\boldsymbol{p}_X, \boldsymbol{r}_X, \boldsymbol{a}_X)$. In addition, a probabilistic representation of opinions is described in Section 3.7.1 and a qualitative representation of opinions is described in Section 3.7.2. These can be useful in specific situations.

Without providing any details here it can also be mentioned that an equivalent representation of binomial opinions has been defined in *CertainLogic* [87].

3.7.1 Probabilistic Notation of Opinions

People with a basic training in the foundations probability calculus are able to intuitively interpret probabilities relatively well. The classical probability representation is used in all areas of science, so people are primarily interested in probability distributions when assessing situations that include various possible and uncertain events. It can therefore be seen as a disadvantage that the traditional opinion representation described in the previous sections does not explicitly express projected probability.

Although the projected probability distribution of an opinion can easily be derived with Eq.(3.28), the lack of explicit representation of projected probability might still create a mental barrier for direct intuitive understanding of opinions.

This barrier could be removed by designing an alternative representation of opinions that consists of explicit projected probability distributions, together with the degree of uncertainty and base rate distributions. This representation is called the *probabilistic opinion notation* and is formally defined below.

Definition 3.10 (Probabilistic Opinion Notation). Assume domain $\mathbb{X}$ with random variable X, and let $\omega_X = (\boldsymbol{b}_X, u_X, \boldsymbol{a}_X)$ be a binomial or multinomial opinion on X. Let $\mathbf{P}_X$ be the corresponding projected probability distribution over X defined according to Eq.(3.12). The probabilistic notation for multinomial opinions is given below.

$$\text{Probabilistic opinion:} \quad \pi_X = (\mathbf{P}_X, u_X, \boldsymbol{a}_X),$$

$$\text{Constraints:} \begin{cases} \boldsymbol{a}_X(x)\, u_X \leq \mathbf{P}_X(x) \leq (\boldsymbol{a}_X(x)\, u_X + 1 - u_X), \\ \\ \sum_{x \in \mathbb{X}} \mathbf{P}_X(x) = 1, \end{cases} \quad \forall x \in \mathbb{X}. \tag{3.40}$$

□

The uncertainty mass u_X is the same for both the belief notation and for the probabilistic notation of opinions. The base rate distribution $\boldsymbol{a}_X$ is also the same for both notations. The equivalence between the two notations is simply based on the expression for the projected probability distribution as a function of the belief distribution in Eq.(3.12). This leads to the bijective mapping defined below.

Definition 3.11 (Mapping: Belief Opinion ↔ Probabilistic Opinion).

Let $\omega_X = (\boldsymbol{b}_X, u_X, \boldsymbol{a}_X)$ be a multinomial belief opinion, and let $\pi_X = (\mathbf{P}_X, u_X, \boldsymbol{a}_X)$ be a multinomial probabilistic opinion, both over the same variable $X \in \mathbb{X}$. The multinomial opinions ω_X and π_X are equivalent because the belief mass distribution $\boldsymbol{b}_X$ is uniquely determined through Eq.(3.12) which is rearranged in Eq.(3.41):

$$\boldsymbol{b}_X(x) = \mathbf{P}_X(x) - \boldsymbol{a}_X(x)\, u_X \,. \tag{3.41}$$

□

In case $u_X = 0$, then $\mathbf{P}_X$ is a traditional discrete probability distribution without uncertainty. In case $u_X = 1$, then no evidence has been received and $\mathbf{P}_X = \boldsymbol{a}_X$, so the probability distribution $\mathbf{P}_X$ is totally uncertain.

Assume a domain $\mathbb{X}$ with cardinality k. Then both the base rate distribution $\boldsymbol{a}_X$ as well as the projected probability distribution $\mathbf{P}_X$ have $(k-1)$ degrees of freedom due to the additivity property of Eq.(2.8) and Eq.(3.29.a). With the addition of the independent uncertainty parameter u_X, the probabilistic notation of opinions has $(2k-1)$ degrees of freedom, as do the belief notation and the evidence notation of multinomial opinions.

In case of a binary domain $\mathbb{X} = \{x, \bar{x}\}$ a special notation for binomial opinions can be used. Eq.(3.42) shows the probabilistic notation for binomial opinions, which has three parameters and also has three degrees of freedom:

$$\pi_x = (\mathrm{P}(x), u_x, a_x)\,, \quad \text{where} \quad \begin{cases} \mathrm{P}(x) & \text{is the projected probability of } x, \\ u_x & \text{is the uncertainty mass,} \\ a_x & \text{is the base rate of } x, \end{cases} \tag{3.42}$$

under the constraint: $a_x u_x \leq \mathrm{P}(x) \leq 1$.

The advantage of the probabilistic opinion notation is precisely that the probability distribution is explicit. Most people are familiar with the concept of probability, therefore some people might get a better intuitive understanding of opinions with an explicit probability distribution than with the belief mass distribution.

The main limitation of the probabilistic opinion notation is that it does not cover hyper-opinions, it only covers binomial and multinomial opinions. However, in case only a binomial or multinomial opinion representation is required, this limitation might not be a problem.

The second, and more serious, disadvantage of the probabilistic opinion notation is that the algebraic expressions for operators often become unnecessarily complex. It turns out that the belief notation of opinions, as specified in Definitions 3.1, 3.4 and 3.7, offers the simplest algebraic representation of opinion operators. For this reason, we do not use the notation for probabilistic opinion operators here, but use the belief notation instead.

3.7.2 Qualitative Opinion Representation

Human language provides various terms that are commonly used to express different levels of likelihood and confidence. It is possible to express binomial opinions approximately in terms of qualitative levels, which can simplify the elicitation of opinions from observers, experts and analysts. The set of qualitative levels can be specified according to the needs and context of a particular application, where Table 3.4 shows one example.

The combinations of qualitative likelihood and confidence levels can be mapped to areas in the opinion triangle, as illustrated in Figure 3.8. The mapping must be defined for combinations of ranges of projected probability and uncertainty mass. As a result, the mapping between a specific combination of qualitative levels from Table 3.4 and specific geometric area in the opinion triangle depends on the base rate. Without specifying the exact underlying ranges, the visualisation of Figure 3.8 indicates the ranges approximately. The edge ranges are deliberately made narrow in order to have levels for near-dogmatic opinions, near-vacuous opinions, as well as near-absolute opinions. The number of likelihood levels and confidence levels, as well as the exact ranges for each, must be determined according to the needs of the application, so that the qualitative levels defined here must be seen as an example. An example of practical levels is described in Sherman Kent's *Words of Estimated Probability* [65]; based on the *Admiralty Scale* as used within the UK Na-

Table 3.4 Qualitative levels of likelihood and confidence

Likelihood levels:		Absolutely not	Very unlikely	Unlikely	Somewhat unlikely	Chances about even	Somewhat likely	Likely	Very likely	Absolutely
Confidence levels:		**9**	**8**	**7**	**6**	**5**	**4**	**3**	**2**	**1**
No confidence	**E**	9E	8E	7E	6E	5E	4E	3E	2E	1E
Low confidence	**D**	9D	8D	7D	6D	5D	4D	3D	2D	1D
Some confidence	**C**	9C	8C	7C	6C	5C	4C	3C	2C	1C
High confidence	**B**	9B	8B	7B	6B	5B	4B	3B	2B	1B
Total confidence	**A**	9A	8A	7A	6A	5A	4A	3A	2A	1A

tional Intelligence Model [10]; alternative levels could be empirically obtained from psychological experiments on subjective assessments of likelihood and confidence.

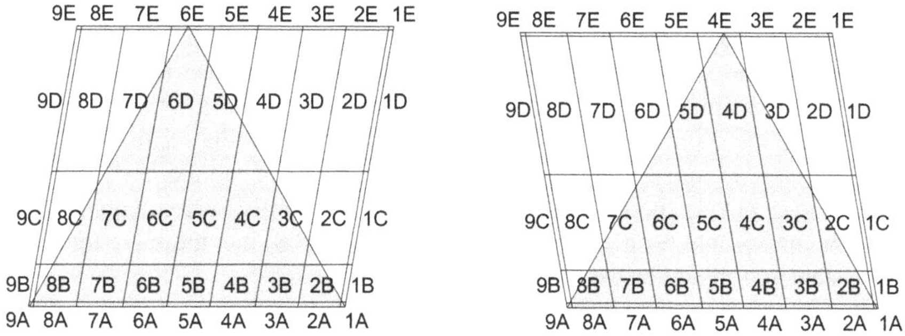

(a) Qualitative mapping with $a = 1/3$ (b) Qualitative mapping with $a = 2/3$

Fig. 3.8 Qualitative parallelogram cells mapped to opinions as a function of the base rate

Figure 3.8 illustrates mappings from qualitative levels to subjective opinions in the case of base rate $a = 1/3$, and in the case of base rate $a = 2/3$. Note that Table 3.4 can be represented as a skewed matrix and that each combination of a qualitative likelihood level and confidence level is represented as a parallelogram-shaped cell inside the matrix. The mapping is determined by the overlap between the qualitative parallelogram cells and the corresponding regions of the opinion triangle. Whenever a qualitative parallelogram cell overlaps, partially or completely, with the opinion triangle, that cell provides a possible mapping.

In the terminology of intelligence analysis the term *analytic confidence* [5] reflects the level of confidence an analyst has in his or her estimates and analyses. Brasfield (2009) gives this characteristic of confidence: *"It is not the same as using words of estimative probability, which indicate likelihood. It is possible for an analyst to suggest an event is virtually certain based on the available evidence, yet have a low amount of confidence in that forecast due to a variety of factors or vice versa."* [5] The difference between likelihood and confidence described by Brasfield is clearly illustrated in Table 3.4.

For binomial and multinomial opinions, the level of confidence can be expressed as the complement of uncertainty mass. Let ω_X be a binomial or multinomial opinions with uncertainty mass u_X, then we define:

$$\text{Confidence}(\omega_X) = c_X = 1 - u_X \;. \tag{3.43}$$

For hyper-opinions, low uncertainty mass does not necessarily indicate high confidence because belief mass can express vagueness, as described in Chapter 4.

Note that the qualitative parallelogram cells overlap with different regions of the opinion triangle depending on the base rate. For example, it can be seen that cell $7D$: 'Unlikely and Very Uncertain' is possible in case $a = 1/3$, but not in case $a = 2/3$. Recall that the projected probability of a state value x is defined as $\mathbf{P}_x = b_x + a_x u_x$. It can then be observed that when $a_x, u_x \longrightarrow 1$ (which expresses a vacuous opinion on a left-skewed matrix), then $\mathbf{P}_x \longrightarrow 1$ (which expresses high likelihood), meaning that e.g. the likelihood level 'Unlikely' is impossible.

Mapping from qualitative levels of likelihood and confidence to a subjective opinion is quite simple. Determine the qualitative levels in Table 3.4, and geometrically locate the approximate middle point of the corresponding qualitative parallelogram cell in Figure 3.8. The middle point overlaps with, and thereby maps to a corresponding opinion point in the opinion triangle. Naturally, some mappings will always be impossible for a given base rate (see Figure 3.8), but these are logically inconsistent and should be excluded from selection.

Although a specific combination of qualitative levels, represented as a parallelogram cell, maps to different geometric areas in the opinion triangle depending on the base rate, it will always correspond to the same range of Beta PDFs. It is simple to visualise ranges of binomial opinions with opinion triangles, but it would be difficult to visualise ranges of Beta PDFs. The mapping between binomial opinions and Beta PDFs therefore provides a very powerful way of interpreting Beta PDFs in terms of qualitative levels, and vice versa.

Chapter 4
Decision Making Under Vagueness and Uncertainty

Decision making is the process of identifying and choosing between alternative options based on beliefs about the different options and their associated utility gains or losses. The decision maker can be the analyst of the situation, or can act on advice produced by an analyst. In the following, we do not distinguish between the decision maker and the analyst, and use the term 'analyst' to cover both.

It is crucial to understand how various aspects of an opinion should (rationally) determine the optimal decision. For this purpose some essential concepts such as *sharp* and *vague* belief mass are needed. These are described next. A summary of decision criteria based on opinions is provided in Section 4.4.

4.1 Aspects of Belief and Uncertainty in Opinions

The previous chapter on the different categories of opinions only distinguishes between belief mass and uncertainty mass. This chapter dissects these two types into more granular types called sharp belief mass, vague belief mass and focal uncertainty mass.

4.1.1 Sharp Belief Mass

Belief mass that only supports a specific value is called *sharp belief mass* because it is non-vague and non-uncertain, and it sharply supports a single value and thereby discriminates between this and other values. Note that belief sharpness is relative to a specific value, so that even belief mass on a composite value (and its subsets) is considered sharp for that composite value because it discriminates between that value and other non-subset values.

Definition 4.1 (Sharp Belief Mass). Let $\mathbb{X}$ be a domain with hyperdomain $\mathscr{R}(\mathbb{X})$ and variable X. Given an opinion ω_X, the sharp belief mass of value $x \in \mathscr{R}(\mathbb{X})$ is the function $\boldsymbol{b}_X^{\mathrm{S}} : \mathscr{R}(\mathbb{X}) \rightarrow [0,1]$ expressed as

$$\text{Sharp belief mass:} \quad \boldsymbol{b}_X^{\mathrm{S}}(x) = \sum_{x_i \subseteq x} \boldsymbol{b}_X(x_i) \,, \quad \forall x \in \mathscr{R}(\mathbb{X}). \tag{4.1}$$

□

It is useful to express sharp belief mass of composite values in order to assist decision making in situations like the Ellsberg paradox described in Section 4.5.

The total belief sharpness denoted b_X^{S} is simply the sum of all belief masses assigned to singletons, defined as follows.

Definition 4.2 (Total Sharp Belief Mass). Let $\mathbb{X}$ be a domain with variable X, and let ω_X be an opinions on $\mathbb{X}$. The total sharp belief mass contained in the opinion ω_X is the function $b_X^{\mathrm{TS}} : \mathbb{X} \rightarrow [0,1]$ expressed as

$$\text{Total sharp belief mass:} \quad b_X^{\mathrm{TS}} = \sum_{x_i \in \mathbb{X}} \boldsymbol{b}_X(x_i) \,. \tag{4.2}$$

□

The total sharp belief mass represents the complement of the sum of uncertainty and total vague belief mass, as described below.

4.1.2 Vague Belief Mass

Recall from Section 2.3 that the composite set, denoted $\mathscr{C}(\mathbb{X})$, is the set of all composite values from the hyperdomain. Belief mass assigned to a composite value represents *vague belief mass* because it expresses cognitive vagueness. It does not discriminate between the singletons in the composite value, and supports the truth of multiple singletons in $\mathbb{X}$ simultaneously. In the case of binary domains, there can be no vague belief mass, because there are no composite values. In the case of hyperdomains, composite values exist, and every singleton $x \in \mathbb{X}$ is a member of multiple composite values. The vague belief mass on a value $x \in \mathscr{R}(\mathbb{X})$ is defined as the weighted sum of belief masses on the composite values of which x is a member, where the weights are determined by the base rate distribution. The total amount of vague belief mass is simply the sum of belief masses on all composite values in the hyperdomain. The formal definitions of these concepts are given next.

Definition 4.3 (Vague Belief Mass).

Let $\mathbb{X}$ be a domain with hyperdomain $\mathscr{R}(\mathbb{X})$ and composite set $\mathscr{C}(\mathbb{X})$. Given an opinion ω_X, the vague belief mass on $x \in \mathscr{R}(\mathbb{X})$ is the function $\boldsymbol{b}_X^{\mathrm{V}} : \mathscr{R}(\mathbb{X}) \rightarrow [0,1]$:

$$\text{Vague belief mass:} \quad \boldsymbol{b}_X^{\mathrm{V}}(x) = \sum_{\substack{x_i \in \mathscr{C}(\mathbb{X}) \\ x_i \not\subseteq x}} \boldsymbol{a}_X(x|x_i)\, \boldsymbol{b}_X(x_i) \,, \quad \forall x \in \mathscr{R}(\mathbb{X}). \tag{4.3}$$

□

Note that Eq.(4.3) not only defines vagueness of singletons $x \in \mathbb{X}$, but also defines vagueness of composite values $x \in \mathscr{C}(\mathbb{X})$, i.e. of all values $x \in \mathscr{R}(\mathbb{X})$.

In case x is a composite value, then the belief mass $\boldsymbol{b}_X(x)$ does not contribute to the vague belief mass of x, despite $\boldsymbol{b}_X(x)$ representing vague belief mass for the whole opinion. In case $x \in \mathscr{C}(\mathbb{X})$ then $\boldsymbol{b}_X(x)$ represents sharp belief mass for x and vague belief mass for the whole opinion.

The total vague belief mass in an opinion ω_X is defined as the sum of belief masses on composite values $x \in \mathscr{C}(\mathbb{X})$, formally defined as follows.

Definition 4.4 (Total Vague Belief Mass). Let $\mathbb{X}$ be a domain with variable X, and let ω_X be an opinions on $\mathbb{X}$. The total vagueness contained in the opinion ω_X is the function $b_X^{\mathrm{TV}} : \mathscr{C}(\mathbb{X}) \rightarrow [0,1]$ expressed as:

$$\text{Total vague belief mass:}\quad b_X^{\mathrm{TV}} = \sum_{x \in \mathscr{C}(\mathbb{X})} \boldsymbol{b}_X(x)\,. \tag{4.4}$$

□

An opinion ω_X is dogmatic and vague when $b_X^{\mathrm{TV}} = 1$, and is partially vague when $0 < b_X^{\mathrm{TV}} < 1$. An opinion has mono-vagueness when only a single composite value has (vague) belief mass assigned to it. On the other hand, an opinion has pluri-vagueness when several composite values have (vague) belief mass assigned to them.

Note the difference between uncertainty and vagueness in subjective logic. Uncertainty reflects vacuity of evidence, whereas vagueness results from evidence that fails to discriminate between specific singletons. A vacuous (totally uncertain) opinion – by definition – does not contain any vagueness. Hyper-opinions can contain vagueness, whereas multinomial and binomial opinions never contain vagueness. The ability to express vagueness is thus the main aspect that makes hyper-opinions different from multinomial opinions.

Under the assumption that collected evidence never decays, uncertainty can only decrease over time, because accumulated evidence is never lost. As the natural complement, sharp and vague belief mass can only increase. At the extreme, a dogmatic opinion where $b_X^{\mathrm{TV}} = 1$ expresses *dogmatic vagueness*. A dogmatic opinion where $b_X^{\mathrm{TS}} = 1$ expresses *dogmatic sharp belief*, which is equivalent to a traditional probability distribution over a random variable.

Under the assumption that evidence decays e.g. as a function of time, uncertainty can increase over time because uncertainty increase is equivalent to the loss of evidence. Vagueness decreases in case new evidence is sharp, i.e. when the new evidence supports singletons, and old vague evidence decays. Vagueness increases in case new evidence is vague, i.e. when the new evidence supports composite values, and the old sharp evidence decays.

4.1.3 Dirichlet Visualisation of Opinion Vagueness

The vagueness of a trinomial opinion can not easily be visualised as such on the opinion tetrahedron. However, it can be visualised in the form of a hyper-Dirichlet PDF. Let us for example consider the ternary domain $\mathbb{X}$ with corresponding hyperdomain $\mathscr{R}(\mathbb{X})$ illustrated in Figure 4.1.

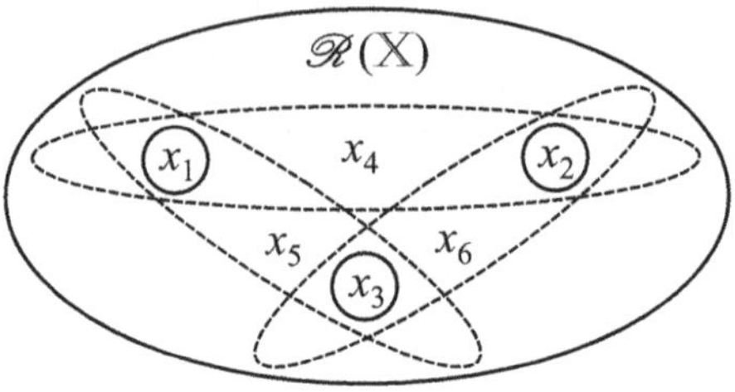

Fig. 4.1 Hyperdomain for the example of vague belief mass

The singletons and composite values of $\mathscr{R}(\mathbb{X})$ are listed below.

$$\begin{cases} \text{Domain:} & \mathbb{X} = \{x_1, x_2, x_3\}, \\ \text{Hyperdomain:} & \mathscr{R}(\mathbb{X}) = \{x_1, x_2, x_3, x_4, x_5, x_6\}, \\ \text{Composite set:} & \mathscr{C}(\mathbb{X}) = \{x_4, x_5, x_6\}, \end{cases} \quad \text{where} \quad \begin{cases} x_4 = \{x_1, x_2\}, \\ x_5 = \{x_1, x_3\}, \\ x_6 = \{x_2, x_3\}. \end{cases} \tag{4.5}$$

Let us further assume a hyper-opinion ω_X with belief mass distribution and base rate distribution specified in Eq.(4.6) below.

$$\text{Belief mass distribution} \begin{cases} \boldsymbol{b}_X(x_6) = 0.8, \\ u_X \quad\;\; = 0.2. \end{cases} \qquad \text{Base rate distribution} \begin{cases} \boldsymbol{a}_X(x_1) = 0.33, \\ \boldsymbol{a}_X(x_2) = 0.33, \\ \boldsymbol{a}_X(x_3) = 0.33. \end{cases} \tag{4.6}$$

Note that this opinion has mono-vagueness, because the vague belief mass is assigned to only one composite value.

The projected probability distribution on X computed with Eq.(3.28), and the vague belief mass computed with Eq.(4.3), are given in Eq.(4.7) below.

$$\text{Projected probability distribution} \begin{cases} \mathbf{P}_X(x_1) = 0.066, \\ \mathbf{P}_X(x_2) = 0.467, \\ \mathbf{P}_X(x_3) = 0.467. \end{cases} \qquad \text{Vague belief mass} \begin{cases} \boldsymbol{b}_X^{\mathrm{V}}(x_1) = 0.0, \\ \boldsymbol{b}_X^{\mathrm{V}}(x_2) = 0.4, \\ \boldsymbol{b}_X^{\mathrm{V}}(x_3) = 0.4. \end{cases} \tag{4.7}$$

The hyper-Dirichlet PDF for this vague opinion is illustrated in Figure 4.2. Note how the probability density is spread out along the edge between the x_2 and x_3 vertices, which precisely indicates that the opinion expresses vagueness between x_2 and x_3. To be mindful of vague belief of this kind can be useful for an analyst, in the sense that it can exclude specific values from being plausible. A non-plausible value in this example is x_1.

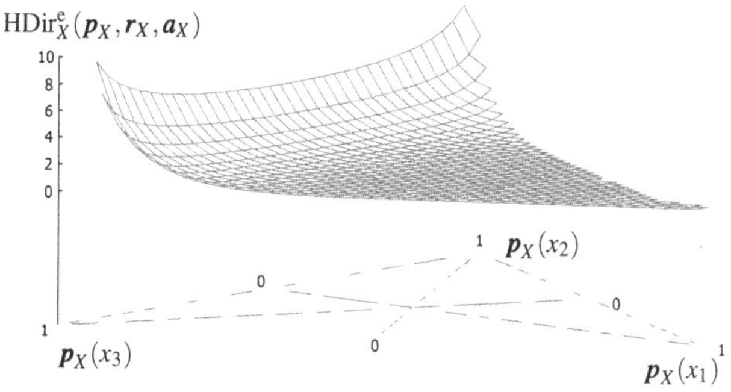

Fig. 4.2 Hyper-Dirichlet PDF with vague belief

In the case of multinomial and hypernomial opinions larger than trinomial, it is challenging to design visualisations. A possible solution in case visualisation is required for opinions over large domains is to use partial visualisation over specific values of the domain that are of interest to the analyst.

4.1.4 Focal Uncertainty Mass

When an opinion contains uncertainty, the simplest interpretation is to consider that the whole uncertainty mass is shared between all the values of the (hyper)domain. However, as indicated by the expressions for projected probability of e.g. Eq.(3.28), the uncertainty mass can be interpreted as being implicitly assigned to (hyper)values of the variable, as a function of the base rate distribution over the variable. This interpretation is captured by the definition of *focal uncertainty mass*.

Definition 4.5 (Focal Uncertainty Mass). Let $\mathbb{X}$ be a domain and $\mathscr{R}(\mathbb{X})$ denote its hyperdomain. Given an opinion ω_X, the focal uncertainty mass of an value $x \in \mathscr{R}(\mathbb{X})$ is computed with the function $\boldsymbol{u}^{\mathrm{F}}_X : \mathscr{R}(\mathbb{X}) \rightarrow [0,1]$ defined as

$$\text{Focal uncertainty mass:} \quad \boldsymbol{u}^{\mathrm{F}}_X(x) = \boldsymbol{a}_X(x)\, u_X \,. \tag{4.8}$$

□

Note that the above definition uses the notation $\boldsymbol{u}_X^{\mathrm{F}}$ in the sense of a distribution of uncertainty mass over values, which is different from total uncertainty mass as a single scalar denoted u_X.

4.2 Mass-Sum

The concepts of sharp belief mass, vague belief mass and focal uncertainty mass of a given value x are representative for the opinion about that value. The concatenation of these masses as a tuple is called the *mass-sum* of a value, as defined below. Similarly, the concepts of total sharp belief mass, total vague belief mass and the uncertainty mass are representative for the whole opinion, where their concatenation represents the total mass-sum of an opinion. Mass-sums and their additivity properties are described next.

4.2.1 Mass-Sum of a Value

The sum of sharp belief mass, vague belief mass and focal uncertainty mass of a value x is equal to the value's projected probability, expressed as

$$\boldsymbol{b}_X^{\mathrm{S}}(x) + \boldsymbol{b}_X^{\mathrm{V}}(x) + \boldsymbol{u}_X^{\mathrm{F}}(x) = \mathbf{P}_X(x). \tag{4.9}$$

Eq.(4.9) shows that the projected probability can be split into three parts which are: i) sharp belief mass, ii) vague belief mass, and iii) focal uncertainty mass. The composition of these three parts, called *mass-sum*, is denoted $\mathbf{M}_X(x)$. The concept of mass-sum is defined next.

Definition 4.6 (Mass-Sum). Let $\mathbb{X}$ be a domain with hyperdomain $\mathscr{R}(\mathbb{X})$, and assume that the opinion ω_X is specified. Consider a value $x \in \mathscr{R}(\mathbb{X})$ with sharp belief mass $\boldsymbol{b}_X^{\mathrm{S}}(x)$, vague belief mass $\boldsymbol{b}_X^{\mathrm{V}}(x)$ and focal uncertainty mass $\boldsymbol{u}_X^{\mathrm{F}}(x)$. The mass-sum function of value x is the triplet denoted $\mathbf{M}_X^{\mathrm{E}}(x)$ expressed as

$$\text{Mass-sum of } x\text{:} \quad \mathbf{M}_X(x) = \left(\boldsymbol{b}_X^{\mathrm{S}}(x), \boldsymbol{b}_X^{\mathrm{V}}(x), \boldsymbol{u}_X^{\mathrm{F}}(x)\right). \tag{4.10}$$

□

Given an opinion ω_X, each value $x \in \mathscr{R}(\mathbb{X})$ has an associated mass-sum $\mathbf{M}_X(x)$ which is a function of the opinion ω_X. The term '*mass-sum*' means that the triplet of sharp belief mass, vague belief mass and focal uncertainty mass has the additivity property of Eq.(4.9).

In order to visualise a mass-sum, consider the ternary domain $\mathbb{X} = \{x_1, x_2, x_3\}$ and hyperdomain $\mathscr{R}(\mathbb{X})$ illustrated in Figure 4.3, where the belief masses and uncertainty mass of opinion ω_X are indicated in the diagram.

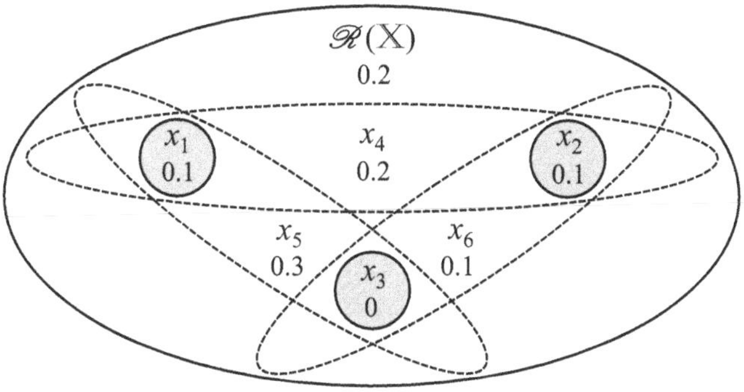

Fig. 4.3 Hyperdomain with belief masses of opinion ω_X

The opinion indicated in Figure 4.3 is specified in more detail in Table 4.1. The table includes the mass-sum components in terms of sharp belief mass, vague belief mass and focal uncertainty mass. The table also shows the projected probability for every value $x \in \mathscr{R}(\mathbb{X})$.

Table 4.1 Example opinion with sharpness, vagueness, focal uncertainty and projected probability.

Value x	Belief mass $\boldsymbol{b}_X(x)$	Base rate $\boldsymbol{a}_X(x)$	Sharp belief mass $\boldsymbol{b}^{\mathrm{S}}_X(x)$	Vague belief mass $\boldsymbol{b}^{\mathrm{V}}_X(x)$	Focal uncertainty mass $\boldsymbol{u}^{\mathrm{F}}_X(x)$	Projected probability $\mathbf{P}_X(x)$
x_1	0.10	0.20	0.10	0.16	0.04	0.30
x_2	0.10	0.30	0.10	0.16	0.06	0.32
x_3	0.00	0.50	0.00	0.28	0.10	0.38
x_4	0.20	0.50	0.40	0.12	0.10	0.62
x_5	0.30	0.70	0.40	0.14	0.14	0.68
x_6	0.10	0.80	0.20	0.34	0.16	0.70
u_X	0.20					

The mass-sums from opinion ω_X listed in Table 4.1 are visualised as a *mass-sum diagram* in Figure 4.4. Mass-sum diagrams are useful for assisting decision making, because the degree of sharp and vague belief mass can be clearly understood.

Visualisation by mass-sum diagrams makes it easy to appreciate the nature of an opinion and to compare opinions as a function of the belief mass distribution in each opinion. Since hyper-opinions can not easily be visualised on simplexes like triangles or tetrahedrons, a mass-sum diagram like the one in Figure 4.4 offers a nice alternative that scales to larger domains.

In Figure 4.4 it can be seen that x_3 has the greatest projected probability among the singletons, expressed as $\mathbf{P}_X(x_3) = 0.38$. However, the mass-sum of x_3 is void of sharp belief mass, so its projected probability is solely based on vagueness and un-

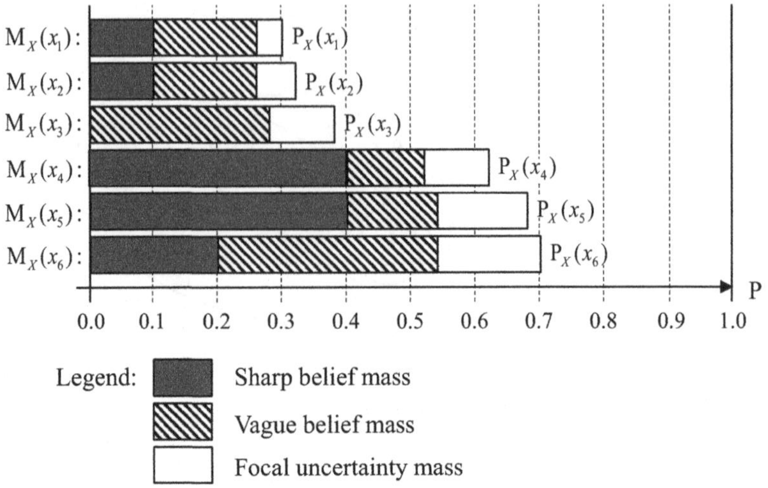

Fig. 4.4 Mass-sum diagram for ω_X

certainty. These aspects are important to consider for decision making, as explained below.

4.2.2 Total Mass-Sum

The belief mass of an opinion as a whole can be decomposed into sharp belief mass which provides distinctive support for singletons, and vague belief mass which provides vague support for singletons. These two belief masses are then complementary to the uncertainty mass. For any opinion ω_X it can be verified that Eq.(4.11) holds:

$$b_X^{\mathrm{TS}} + b_X^{\mathrm{TV}} + u_X = 1\ . \tag{4.11}$$

Eq.(4.11) shows that the belief and uncertainty mass can be split into the three parts of sharp/vague belief mass and uncertainty mass. The composition of these three parts is called *total mass-sum*, denoted $\mathrm{M}_X^{\mathrm{T}}$, and is defined below.

Definition 4.7 (Total Mass-Sum). Let $\mathbb{X}$ be a domain with hyperdomain $\mathscr{R}(\mathbb{X})$, and assume that the opinion ω_X is specified. The total sharp belief mass b_X^{TS}, total vague belief mass b_X^{TV} and uncertainty mass u_X can be combined as a triplet, which is then called the total mass-sum, denoted $\mathrm{M}_X^{\mathrm{T}}$ and expressed as

$$\text{Total mass-sum:}\quad \mathrm{M}_X^{\mathrm{T}} = \left(b_X^{\mathrm{TS}},\, b_X^{\mathrm{TV}},\, u_X\right). \tag{4.12}$$

□

The total mass-sum of opinion ω_X from Figure 4.3 and Table 4.1 is illustrated in Figure 4.5.

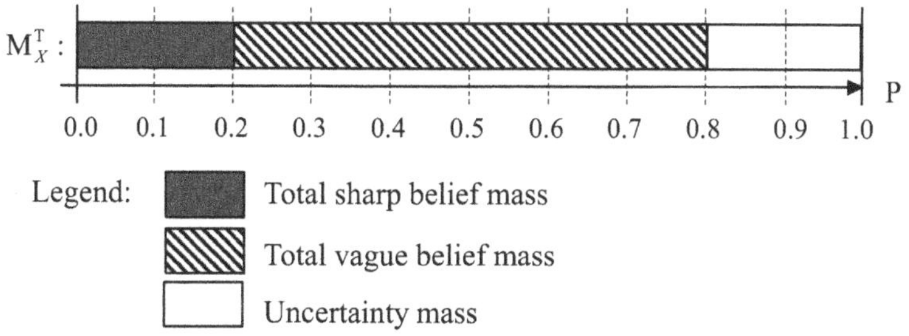

Fig. 4.5 Visualising the total mass-sum of ω_X

4.3 Utility and Normalisation

Assume a random variable X with an associated projected probability distribution $\mathbf{P}_X$. Utility is typically associated with outcomes of a random variable, in the sense that for each outcome x there is an associated utility $\boldsymbol{\lambda}_X(x)$ expressed on some scale such as monetary value, which can be positive or negative. Given utility $\boldsymbol{\lambda}_X(x)$ in case of outcome x, then the expected utility for x is

$$\text{Expected utility:} \quad \mathbf{L}_X(x) = \boldsymbol{\lambda}_X(x)\mathbf{P}_X(x). \tag{4.13}$$

Total expected utility for the variable X is then

$$\text{Total expected utility:} \quad \mathrm{L}_X^{\mathrm{T}} = \sum_{x \in \mathbb{X}} \boldsymbol{\lambda}_X(x)\mathbf{P}_X(x). \tag{4.14}$$

In classical utility theory, decisions are based on expected utility for possible options. It is also possible to eliminate the notion of utility by integrating it into the probabilities for the various options [8], which produces a *utility-normalised probability vector*. This approach greatly simplifies decision-making models, because every option can be represented as a simple utility-probability.

Normalisation is useful when comparing options of variables from different domains, where the different variables have different associated probability distributions and utility vectors. The normalisation factor must be appropriate for all variables, so that the utility-normalised probability vectors are within a given range. Note that in case of negative utility for a specific outcome, the utility-normalised probability for that outcome is also negative. In that sense, utility-normalised probability represents synthetic probability, and not realistic probability.

Given a set of variables, with associated probability distributions and utility vectors, let λ^+ denote the greatest absolute utility of all utilities in all vectors. Thus, if the greatest absolute utility is negative, then λ^+ takes its positive (absolute) value. The utility-normalised probability vector $\mathbf{P}_X^{\mathrm{N}}$ is defined below.

Definition 4.8 (Utility-Normalised Probability Vector). Assume a random variable X with an associated projected probability distribution $\mathbf{P}_X$ and a utility vector $\boldsymbol{\lambda}_X$, which together produce the expected utility distribution $\mathbf{L}_X$. Let λ^+ denote the greatest absolute utility from $\boldsymbol{\lambda}_X$ and from other relevant utility vectors to be considered for comparing different options. The utility-normalised probability vector produced by $\mathbf{P}_X$, $\boldsymbol{\lambda}_X$ and λ^+ is expressed as

$$\mathbf{P}_X^{\mathrm{N}}(x) = \frac{\mathbf{L}_X(x)}{\lambda^+} = \frac{\boldsymbol{\lambda}_X(x)\mathbf{P}_X(x)}{\lambda^+}, \quad \forall x \in \mathbb{X}. \tag{4.15}$$

□

Note that the utility-normalised probability vector $\mathbf{P}_X^{\mathrm{N}}$ does not represent a probability distribution, and in general does not satisfy the additivity requirement of a probability distribution. The vector $\mathbf{P}_X^{\mathrm{N}}$ represents relative probability to be used in comparisons with other vectors of relative probability, for the purpose of choosing between different options.

Similarly to the notion of utility-normalised probability, it is possible to define utility-normalised sharp belief mass, vague belief mass and focal uncertainty mass.

Definition 4.9 (Utility-Normalised Masses). Assume a random variable X with a projected probability distribution $\mathbf{P}_X$. Let $\boldsymbol{b}_X^{\mathrm{S}}(x)$ denote the sharp belief mass of x, let $\boldsymbol{b}_X^{\mathrm{V}}(x)$ denote the vague belief mass of x, and let $\boldsymbol{u}_X^{\mathrm{F}}(x)$ denote the focal uncertainty mass of x. Assume the utility vector $\boldsymbol{\lambda}_X$, as well as λ^+, the greatest absolute utility from $\boldsymbol{\lambda}_X$ and from other relevant utility vectors to be considered for comparing different options. The utility-normalised masses are expressed as

$$\text{Utility-normalised sharp belief mass: } \boldsymbol{b}_X^{\mathrm{NS}}(x) = \frac{\boldsymbol{\lambda}_X(x)\boldsymbol{b}_X^{\mathrm{S}}(x)}{\lambda^+}, \quad \forall x \in \mathbb{X}. \tag{4.16}$$

$$\text{Utility-normalised vague belief mass: } \boldsymbol{b}_X^{\mathrm{NV}}(x) = \frac{\boldsymbol{\lambda}_X(x)\boldsymbol{b}_X^{\mathrm{V}}(x)}{\lambda^+}, \quad \forall x \in \mathbb{X}. \tag{4.17}$$

$$\text{Utility-normalised focal uncertainty mass: } \boldsymbol{u}_X^{\mathrm{NF}}(x) = \frac{\boldsymbol{\lambda}_X(x)\boldsymbol{u}_X^{\mathrm{F}}(x)}{\lambda^+}, \quad \forall x \in \mathbb{X}. \tag{4.18}$$

□

Similarly to the additivity property of sharpness, vague belief mass and focal uncertainty mass of Eq.(4.9), there is additivity of the corresponding utility-normalised masses, which produces *utility-normalised probability*, as expressed in Eq.(4.19):

$$\text{Utility-normalised probability: } \boldsymbol{b}_X^{\mathrm{NS}}(x) + \boldsymbol{b}_X^{\mathrm{NV}}(x) + \boldsymbol{u}_X^{\mathrm{NF}}(x) = \mathbf{P}_X^{\mathrm{N}}(x). \tag{4.19}$$

Having defined utility-normalised probability, it is possible to directly compare options without involving utilities, because utilities are integrated into the utility-normalised probabilities.

Similarly to the mass-sum of Eq.(4.10), it is also possible to describe a corresponding utility-normalised mass-sum, as defined below.

Definition 4.10 (Utility-Normalised Mass-Sum). Let $\mathbb{X}$ be a domain with hyperdomain $\mathscr{R}(\mathbb{X})$, and assume that the opinion ω_X is specified. Also assume that a utility vector $\boldsymbol{\lambda}_X$ is specified. Consider a value $x \in \mathscr{R}(\mathbb{X})$ with the utility normalised masses $\boldsymbol{b}_X^{\mathrm{NS}}(x)$, $\boldsymbol{b}_X^{\mathrm{NV}}(x)$ and $\boldsymbol{u}_X^{\mathrm{NF}}(x)$. The utility-normalised mass-sum function of x is the triplet denoted $\mathbf{M}_X^{\mathrm{N}}(x)$ expressed as

$$\text{Utility-normalised mass-sum:}\quad \mathbf{M}_X^{\mathrm{N}}(x) = \left(\boldsymbol{b}_X^{\mathrm{NS}}(x), \boldsymbol{b}_X^{\mathrm{NV}}(x), \boldsymbol{u}_X^{\mathrm{NF}}(x)\right). \tag{4.20}$$

□

Note that utility-normalised sharp belief mass, vague belief mass and focal uncertainty mass do not represent realistic masses, and must be considered as purely synthetic.

As an example of applying utility-normalised probability, consider two urns named X and Y that both contain 100 red and black balls, where you will be asked to draw a ball at random from one of the urns. The possible outcomes are named $x_1 =$ 'Red' and $x_2 =$ 'Black' for urn X, and are similarly named $y_1 =$ 'Red' and $y_2 =$ 'Black' for urn Y.

You are told that urn X contains 70 red balls, 10 black balls and 20 balls that are either red or black. The corresponding opinion ω_X is expressed as

$$\text{Opinion } \omega_X = \begin{pmatrix} \boldsymbol{b}_X(x_1) = 7/10, & \boldsymbol{a}_X(x_1) = 1/2, \\ \boldsymbol{b}_X(x_2) = 1/10, & \boldsymbol{a}_X(x_2) = 1/2, \\ u_X \quad\;\; = 2/10. & \end{pmatrix} \tag{4.21}$$

You are told that urn Y contains 40 red balls, 20 black balls and 40 balls that are either red or black. The corresponding opinion ω_Y is expressed as

$$\text{Opinion } \omega_Y = \begin{pmatrix} \boldsymbol{b}_Y(y_1) = 4/10, & \boldsymbol{a}_Y(y_1) = 1/2, \\ \boldsymbol{b}_Y(y_2) = 2/10, & \boldsymbol{a}_Y(y_2) = 1/2, \\ u_Y \quad\;\; = 4/10. & \end{pmatrix} \tag{4.22}$$

Imagine that you must select one ball at random, from either urn X or Y, and you are asked to make a choice about which urn to draw it from in a single betting game. With option X, you receive \$1000 if you draw 'Black' from urn X (i.e. if you draw x_2). With option Y, you receive \$500 if you draw 'Black' from urn Y (i.e. if you draw y_2). You receive nothing if you draw 'Red' in either option. Table 4.2 summarises the options in this game.

The mass-sums for drawing 'Black' are different for options X and Y. However, the utility-normalised mass-sums are equal, as illustrated in Figure 4.6. The normalisation factor used in this example is $\lambda^+ = 1000$, since \$1000 is the greatest absolute utility.

Table 4.2 Utilities for betting options X and Y

	Red	Black
Option X, draw from urn X:	0	\$1000
Option Y, draw from urn Y:	0	\$500

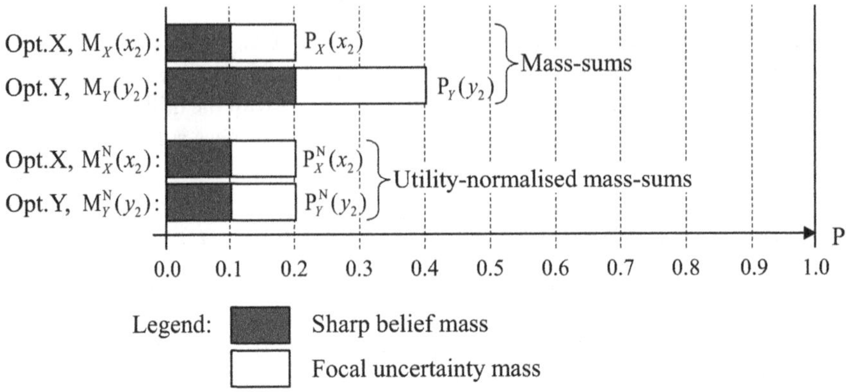

Fig. 4.6 Diagram for mass-sums and utility-normalised mass-sums of options X and Y

It can be mentioned that risk attitudes play a role in a betting situation like this. When options have different probabilities, then a relatively small probability of winning tends to have the effect that participants perceive a *subjective utility* of winning which is smaller than the nominal utility. Since option X has probability $P_X(x_2) = 0.2$ which is smaller than that of option Y with probability $P_Y(y_2) = 0.4$, many people would perceive the subjective utility of winning the bet with option X to be smaller than \$1000. Hence, even though the nominal expected utilities of options X and Y are equal, a risk averse person would typically prefer option Y because its subjective expected utility would be greater than that of option X. However, we do not consider risk attitude and subjective utility here.

In general, the option with the greatest utility-normalised probability should be chosen. Note that the utility-normalised probability is equal for options X and Y, expressed as $\mathbf{P}^N_X(x_2) = \mathbf{P}^N_Y(y_2)$. Hence, utility-normalised probability alone is insufficient for determining the best option in this example. The decision in this case must be based on the sharp belief mass, which is greatest for option Y, expressed as $\boldsymbol{b}^S_Y(y_2) > \boldsymbol{b}^S_X(x_2)$.

Note that it is not meaningful to consider utility-normalised sharp belief mass for choosing between options. This is explained in detail in Section 4.4.

In case of equal utilities for all options, then normalisation is not needed, or it can simply be observed that utility-normalised mass-sums are equal to the corresponding non-normalised mass-sums, as expressed below.

$$\text{When all options have equal utility:} \begin{cases} \text{Projected probability:} & \mathbf{P}_X^{\mathrm{N}} = \mathbf{P}_X, \\ \text{Sharp belief mass:} & \boldsymbol{b}_X^{\mathrm{NS}} = \boldsymbol{b}_X^{\mathrm{S}}, \\ \text{Vague belief mass:} & \boldsymbol{b}_X^{\mathrm{NV}} = \boldsymbol{b}_X^{\mathrm{V}}, \\ \text{Focal uncertainty mass:} & \boldsymbol{u}_X^{\mathrm{NF}} = \boldsymbol{u}_X^{\mathrm{F}}, \\ \text{Mass-sum:} & \mathbf{M}_X^{\mathrm{N}} = \mathbf{M}_X. \end{cases} \quad (4.23)$$

In the examples below, utilities for all options are equal, so for convenience, the diagrams show simple mass-sums, which are equal to the corresponding utility-normalised mass-sums.

4.4 Decision Criteria

We define a set of criteria for making choices of options defined in terms of opinions. The criteria follow the indicated order of priority.

1. The option with the highest utility-normalised probability is the best choice.
2. Given equal maximal utility-normalised probability among multiple options, the option with the greatest sharp belief mass is the best choice.
3. Given equal maximal utility-normalised probability as well as equal maximal sharp belief mass among multiple options, the option with the least focal uncertainty mass (and therefore with the greatest vague belief mass, whenever relevant) is the best option.

The above criteria predict the choice of the majority of participants in the Ellsberg experiment described below, as well as the intuitive best choice in additional examples that combine various degrees of sharpness, vagueness and uncertainty.

A more detailed procedure for making decisions according to these criteria is illustrated in Figure 4.7 below.

The steps of the decision-making process in Figure 4.7 are described in more detail below. We assume uniform utilities for all the options. In case of different utilities, then the expected utilities can be computed by simple product.

(a) The decision maker must have the opinions for the relevant options to be compared. The sharp belief masses, vague belief masses and focal uncertainty masses must be computed, and utility-normalised probabilities must be represented in a normalised form as in the lower part of Figure 4.6.
(b) Compare the utility-normalised probabilities of all relevant options.
(c) In case one option has greatest utility-normalised probability, then that option is the best choice.
(d) Assuming that there are multiple relevant options with the same maximal utility-normalised probability, then compare their sharp belief masses.

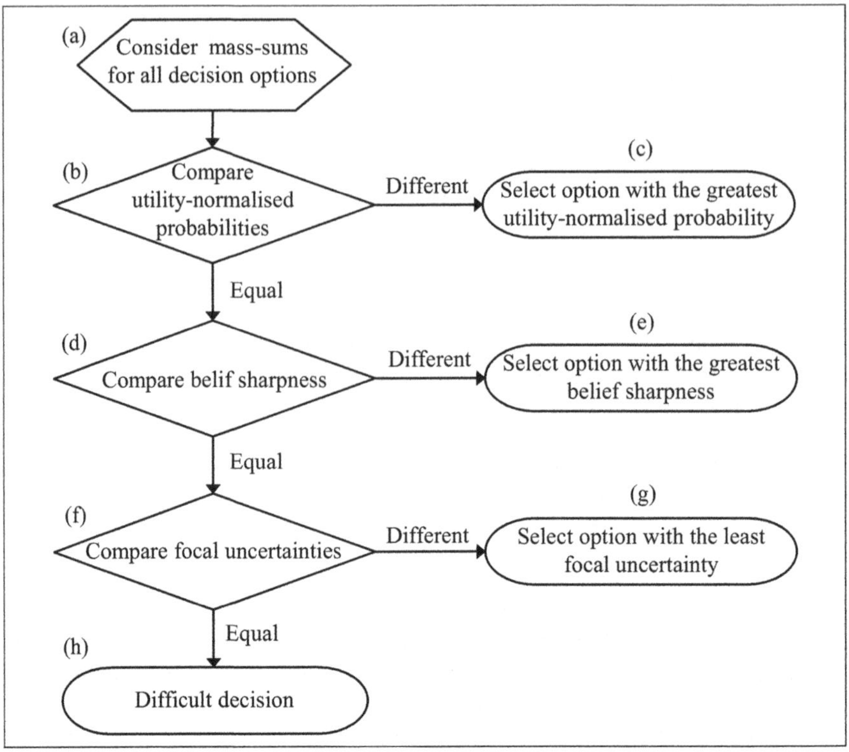

Fig. 4.7 Decision-making process

(e) In case one option has greatest sharp belief mass, then that option is the best choice.
(f) Assuming that there are multiple relevant options with the same maximal utility-normalised probability and the same maximal sharp belief mass, then compare their focal uncertainties.
(g) In case one option has least focal uncertainty mass (i.e. greatest vague belief mass), then that option is the best choice.
(h) Assuming that there are multiple relevant options with the same maximal utility-normalised probability, the same maximal sharp belief mass and the same minimal focal uncertainty mass, then it is challenging to make a decision. However, the composition of each vague belief mass might be different, or the base rates might be different. In addition, it might be meaningful to consider differences between utility-normalised masses. There are thus multiple aspects that could be considered for designing more detailed decision criteria, in addition to those specified above.

The next sections describe examples of decision options where the decision criteria defined above are applied.

4.5 The Ellsberg Paradox

The examples described in this and the next sections apply the decision criteria specified in Section 4.4, showing how sharpness, vagueness and uncertainty in opinions should be used for rational decision making.

The Ellsberg paradox [21] results from an experiment which shows how traditional probability theory is unable to explain typical human decision-making behaviour. Because traditional probability does not express degrees of vagueness and uncertainty, it can not explain the results of the experiment. However, when representing the situation with opinions that do express degrees of vagueness and uncertainty, the results of the experiment become perfectly rational.

In the Ellsberg experiment you are shown an urn with 90 balls in it, and you are told that 30 balls are red, and that the remaining 60 balls are either black or yellow. One ball is going to be selected at random, and you are asked to make a choice in two separate betting games. Figure 4.8 shows the situation of the Ellsberg paradox represented in the form of a hyperdomain with corresponding belief mass distribution.

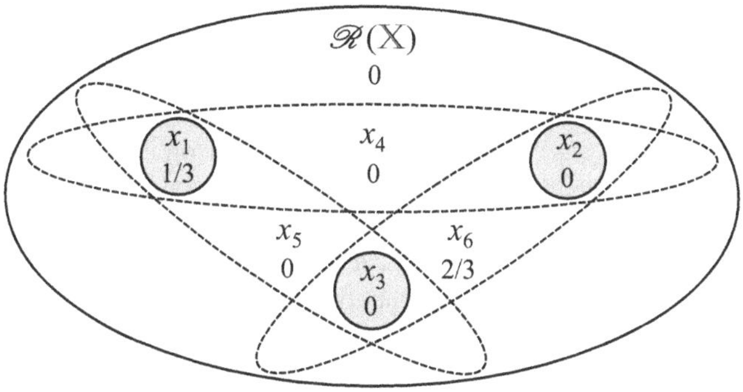

Fig. 4.8 Hyperdomain and belief mass distribution in the Ellsberg paradox

The domain $\mathbb{X}$ and its hyper-opinion are then expressed as

$$\text{Hyperdomain } \mathscr{R}(\mathbb{X}) = \begin{cases} x_1 : \text{Red}, & 30 \text{ balls}, \\ x_2 : \text{Black}, & \\ x_3 : \text{Yellow}, & \\ x_4 : \text{Red or Black}, & \\ x_5 : \text{Red or Yellow}, & \\ x_6 : \text{Black or Yellow}, & 60 \text{ balls}. \end{cases} \tag{4.24}$$

$$\text{Hyper-opinion } \omega_X = \begin{pmatrix} \boldsymbol{b}_X(x_1) = 1/3, & \boldsymbol{a}_X(x_1) = 1/3, \\ \boldsymbol{b}_X(x_2) = 0, & \boldsymbol{a}_X(x_2) = 1/3, \\ \boldsymbol{b}_X(x_3) = 0, & \boldsymbol{a}_X(x_3) = 1/3, \\ \boldsymbol{b}_X(x_4) = 0, & \boldsymbol{a}_X(x_4) = 2/3, \\ \boldsymbol{b}_X(x_5) = 0, & \boldsymbol{a}_X(x_5) = 2/3, \\ \boldsymbol{b}_X(x_6) = 2/3, & \boldsymbol{a}_X(x_6) = 2/3, \\ u_X \quad = 0. & \end{pmatrix} \quad (4.25)$$

A quick look at ω_X reveals that it contains some sharp belief mass, some vague belief mass and no uncertainty mass, so it is a dogmatic and partially vague opinion.

In betting game 1 you must choose between option 1A and 1B. With option 1A you receive \$100 if 'Red' is drawn, and you receive nothing if either 'Black' or 'Yellow' is drawn. With option 1B you receive \$100 if 'Black' is drawn, and you receive nothing if either 'Red' or 'Yellow' is drawn. Table 4.3 summarises the options in game 1.

Table 4.3 Ellsberg game 1: Utilities for betting options 1A and 1B

	Red	Black	Yellow
Option 1A:	\$100	0	0
Option 1B:	0	\$100	0

Make a note of your choice from betting game 1, and then proceed to betting game 2 where you are asked to choose between two new options based on the same random draw of a single ball from the same urn. With option 2A you receive \$100 if either 'Red' or 'Yellow' is drawn, and you receive nothing if 'Black' is drawn. With option 2B you receive \$100 if either 'Black' or 'Yellow' is drawn, and you receive nothing if 'Red' is drawn. Table 4.4 summarises the options in game 2.

Table 4.4 Ellsberg game 2: Utilities for betting options 2A and 2B

	Red	Black	Yellow
Option 2A:	\$100	0	\$100
Option 2B:	0	\$100	\$100

Would you choose option 2A or 2B?

Ellsberg reports that, when presented with these pairs of choices, most people select options 1A and 2B. Adopting the approach of expected utility theory, this reveals a clear inconsistency in probability assessments. On this interpretation, when a person chooses option 1A over option 1B, he or she is revealing a higher subjective probability assessment of picking 'Red' than of picking 'Black'.

However, when the same person prefers option 2B over option 2A, he or she reveals that his or her subjective probability assessment of picking 'Black' or 'Yellow' is higher than of picking 'Red' or 'Yellow', which implies that picking 'Black' has a higher probability assessment than that of picking 'Red'. This seems to contradict the probability assessment of game 1, which therefore represents a paradox.

When explicitly expressing the vagueness of the opinions, the majority's preference for choices 1A and 2B becomes perfectly rational, as explained next.

The utilities for options 1A and 1B are equal (\$100), so there is no difference between the utility-normalised probabilities and the projected probabilities which are used for decision modelling below. Projected probabilities are computed with Eq.(3.28) which for convenience is repeated below:

$$\mathbf{P}_X(x) = \sum_{x_j \in \mathscr{R}(\mathbb{X})} \boldsymbol{a}_X(x|x_j)\, \boldsymbol{b}_X(x_j) + \boldsymbol{a}_X(x)\, u_X . \tag{4.26}$$

Relative base rates are computed with Eq.(2.10) which for convenience is repeated below:

$$\boldsymbol{a}_X(x|x_j) = \frac{\boldsymbol{a}_X(x \cap x_j)}{\boldsymbol{a}_X(x_j)} . \tag{4.27}$$

The projected probabilities of x_1 and x_2 in game 1 are then

$$\begin{aligned} &\text{Option 1A:} \quad \mathbf{P}_X(x_1) = \boldsymbol{a}_X(x_1|x_1)\, \boldsymbol{b}_X(x_1) = 1 \cdot \tfrac{1}{3} = \tfrac{1}{3} . \\ &\text{Option 1B:} \quad \mathbf{P}_X(x_2) = \boldsymbol{a}_X(x_2|x_6)\, \boldsymbol{b}_X(x_2) = \tfrac{1}{2} \cdot \tfrac{2}{3} = \tfrac{1}{3} . \end{aligned} \tag{4.28}$$

Note that $\mathbf{P}_X(x_1) = \mathbf{P}_X(x_2)$, which makes the options equal from a purely first-order probability point of view. However they are affected by different vague belief mass as shown below.

Vague belief mass of x, denoted $\boldsymbol{b}_X^{\mathrm{V}}(x)$, is computed with Eq.(4.3) which for convenience is repeated below:

$$\boldsymbol{b}_X^{\mathrm{V}}(x) = \sum_{\substack{x_j \in \mathscr{C}(\mathbb{X}) \\ x_j \not\subseteq x}} \boldsymbol{a}_X(x|x_j)\, \boldsymbol{b}_X(x_j) . \tag{4.29}$$

The vague belief masses of x_1 and x_2 in game 1 are then

$$\begin{aligned} &\text{Option 1A:} \quad \boldsymbol{b}_X^{\mathrm{V}}(x_1) = 0 , \\ &\text{Option 1B:} \quad \boldsymbol{b}_X^{\mathrm{V}}(x_2) = \boldsymbol{a}_X(x_2|x_6)\, \boldsymbol{b}_X(x_6) = \tfrac{1}{2} \cdot \tfrac{2}{3} = \tfrac{1}{3} . \end{aligned} \tag{4.30}$$

Given the absence of uncertainty, the additivity property of Eq.(4.9) allows us to compute the sharp belief masses as $\boldsymbol{b}_X^{\mathrm{S}}(x_1) = 1/3$ and $\boldsymbol{b}_X^{\mathrm{S}}(x_2) = 0$.

The mass-sum diagram of the options in Ellsberg betting game 1 is illustrated in Figure 4.9.

The difference between options 1A (x_1) and 1B (x_2) emerges with their different sharp and vague belief masses. People clearly prefer choice 1A because it only has sharp belief mass, whereas choice 1B only has vague belief mass.

We now turn to betting game 2, where Option 2A (x_5) and Option 2B (x_6) have the following projected probabilities:

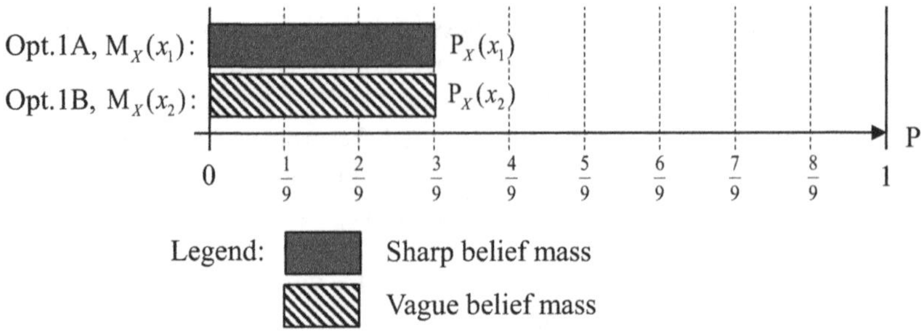

Fig. 4.9 Mass-sum diagram for game 1 in the Ellsberg paradox

$$\begin{aligned} &\text{Option 2A:}\quad \mathbf{P}_X(x_5) = \boldsymbol{a}_X(x_1|x_1)\,\boldsymbol{b}_X(x_1) + \boldsymbol{a}_X(x_3|x_6)\,\boldsymbol{b}_X(x_6) = 1\cdot\tfrac{1}{3} + \tfrac{1}{2}\cdot\tfrac{2}{3} = \tfrac{2}{3},\\ &\text{Option 2B:}\quad \mathbf{P}_X(x_6) = \boldsymbol{a}_X(x_2|x_6)\,\boldsymbol{b}_X(x_6) + \boldsymbol{a}_X(x_3|x_6)\,\boldsymbol{b}_X(x_6) = \tfrac{1}{2}\cdot\tfrac{2}{3} + \tfrac{1}{2}\cdot\tfrac{2}{3} = \tfrac{2}{3}. \end{aligned} \tag{4.31}$$

Note that $\mathbf{P}_X(x_5) = \mathbf{P}_X(x_6)$, which makes the options equal from a first-order probability point of view. However they have different vague belief masses, as shown below. Vague belief mass is computed with Eq.(4.3).

The vague belief masses of x_5 and x_6 in game 2 are

$$\begin{aligned} &\text{Option 2A:}\quad \boldsymbol{b}^{\mathrm{V}}_X(x_5) = \boldsymbol{a}_X(x_3|x_6)\,\boldsymbol{b}_X(x_6) = \tfrac{1}{2}\cdot\tfrac{2}{3} = \tfrac{1}{3}\,,\\ &\text{Option 2B:}\quad \boldsymbol{b}^{\mathrm{V}}_X(x_6) = 0\,. \end{aligned} \tag{4.32}$$

Given the absence of uncertainty, the additivity property of Eq.(4.9) allows us to compute the sharp belief masses as $\boldsymbol{b}^{\mathrm{S}}_X(x_5) = 1/3$ and $\boldsymbol{b}^{\mathrm{S}}_X(x_6) = 2/3$.

The mass-sum diagram of the options in Ellsberg betting game 2 is illustrated in Figure 4.10.

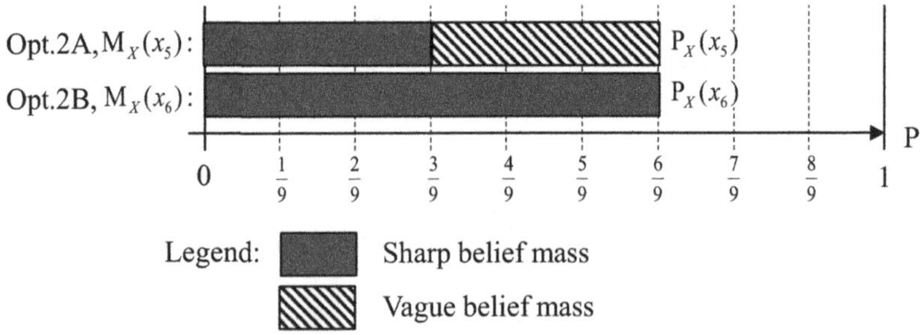

Fig. 4.10 Mass-sum diagram for game 2 in the Ellsberg paradox

The difference between options 2A and 2B emerges with their different sharp and vague belief masses. People clearly prefer choice 2B (x_6), because it has no vagueness, whereas choice 2A (x_5) is affected by its vagueness of $1/3$.

We have shown that preferring option 1A over option 1B, and that preferring option 2B over option 2A, is perfectly rational, and therefore does not represent a paradox within the opinion model.

Other models of uncertain probabilities are also able to explain the Ellsberg paradox, such as e.g. Choquet capacities (Choquet 1953 [14], Chateauneuf 1991 [11]). However, the Ellsberg paradox only involves vagueness, not uncertainty. In fact, the Ellsberg paradox is too simplistic for teasing out the whole spectre of sharp belief, vague belief and uncertainty of opinions. The next section presents examples where all aspects are taken into account.

4.6 Examples of Decision Making

The three examples presented in this section involve sharp belief, vague belief and uncertainty. Different situations of varying degrees of sharp belief, vague belief and uncertainty can be clearly distinguished and compared when represented as subjective opinions. As far as we are aware, no other model of uncertain reasoning is able to distinguish and correctly rank the described situations in the same way.

Each example consist of a game where you are presented with two urns denoted X and Y, both with 90 balls, and you are asked to pick a random ball from one of the two urns, with the chance of winning \$100 if you pick a yellow ball.

4.6.1 Decisions with Difference in Projected Probability

In game 1 you receive the following information. You are told that urn X contains 90 balls that are either red, black or yellow. The corresponding hyper-opinion ω_X is expressed as

$$\text{Hyper-opinion about } X \text{ in game 1} \quad \omega_X = \begin{pmatrix} \boldsymbol{b}_X(x_1) = 0, & \boldsymbol{a}_X(x_1) = 1/3, \\ \boldsymbol{b}_X(x_2) = 0, & \boldsymbol{a}_X(x_2) = 1/3, \\ \boldsymbol{b}_X(x_3) = 0, & \boldsymbol{a}_X(x_3) = 1/3, \\ \boldsymbol{b}_X(x_4) = 0, & \boldsymbol{a}_X(x_4) = 2/3, \\ \boldsymbol{b}_X(x_5) = 0, & \boldsymbol{a}_X(x_5) = 2/3, \\ \boldsymbol{b}_X(x_6) = 0, & \boldsymbol{a}_X(x_6) = 2/3, \\ u_X \quad = 1. & \end{pmatrix} \tag{4.33}$$

You are told that in urn Y, 40 balls are red, 30 balls are black and 20 balls are yellow. The corresponding hyper-opinion ω_Y is expressed as

$$\text{Hyper-opinion about } Y \text{ in game 1} \quad \omega_Y = \begin{pmatrix} \boldsymbol{b}_Y(y_1) = 4/9, & \boldsymbol{a}_Y(y_1) = 1/3, \\ \boldsymbol{b}_Y(y_2) = 3/9, & \boldsymbol{a}_Y(y_2) = 1/3, \\ \boldsymbol{b}_Y(y_3) = 2/9, & \boldsymbol{a}_Y(y_3) = 1/3, \\ \boldsymbol{b}_Y(y_4) = 0, & \boldsymbol{a}_Y(y_4) = 2/3, \\ \boldsymbol{b}_Y(y_5) = 0, & \boldsymbol{a}_Y(y_5) = 2/3, \\ \boldsymbol{b}_Y(y_6) = 0, & \boldsymbol{a}_Y(y_6) = 2/3, \\ u_Y \quad = 0. & \end{pmatrix} \tag{4.34}$$

You must select one ball at random, from either urn X or Y, and you are asked to make a choice about which urn to draw it from in a single betting game. You receive \$100 if 'Yellow' (x_3 or y_3) is drawn, and you receive nothing if either 'Red' or 'Black' is drawn. Table 4.5 summarises the options in this game.

Table 4.5 Game 1: Utilities for betting options 1X and 1Y

	Red	Black	Yellow
Option 1X, draw ball from urn X:	0	0	\$100
Option 1Y, draw ball from urn Y:	0	0	\$100

Without having conducted any experiment, when presented with this pair of choices, it seems obvious to select option 1X. The intuitive reason is that option 1X has the greatest projected probability of picking 'Yellow' and thereby the greatest probability of winning \$100. Eq.(4.35) gives the computed results for projected probability which is computed with Eq.(3.28).

The projected probabilities of x_3 and y_3 in options 1X and 1Y are

$$\begin{aligned} &\text{Option 1X:} \quad \mathbf{P}_X(x_3) = \boldsymbol{a}_X(x_3)u_X = \tfrac{1}{3}\cdot 1 = \tfrac{1}{3}\,, \\ &\text{Option 1Y:} \quad \mathbf{P}_Y(y_3) = \boldsymbol{b}_Y(y_3) \qquad = \tfrac{2}{9}\,. \end{aligned} \tag{4.35}$$

Figure 4.11 shows the mass-sum diagram of $\mathbf{M}_X(x_3)$ and $\mathbf{M}_Y(y_3)$ of options 1X and 1Y respectively. Note that the utility for picking a 'Yellow' is equal for both options, so that $\mathbf{M}_X(x_3) = \mathbf{M}_X^{\mathrm{N}}(x_3)$ and $\mathbf{M}_Y(y_3) = \mathbf{M}_Y^{\mathrm{N}}(y_3)$, i.e. the utility-normalised and the non-normalised mass-sums are equal. So while Figure 4.11 shows mass-sums, the corresponding utility-normalised mass-sums are equal.

It can be seen that $\mathbf{P}_X(x_3) > \mathbf{P}_Y(y_3)$, which indicates that the rational choice is option 1X. Note that option 1X has focal uncertainty mass of $1/3$, in contrast to option 1Y which has no uncertainty. In the case of highly risk-averse participants, option 1Y might be preferred, but this should still be considered 'irrational'. It is worth investigating how risk aversion can be formalised in order to provide an additional decision criterion for situations like this.

Given that the decision must be based on the set of decision criteria specified in Section 4.4, the option with the greatest projected probability is to be preferred. Since option 1X has the greatest projected probability, the preference for option 1X is clear in game 1.

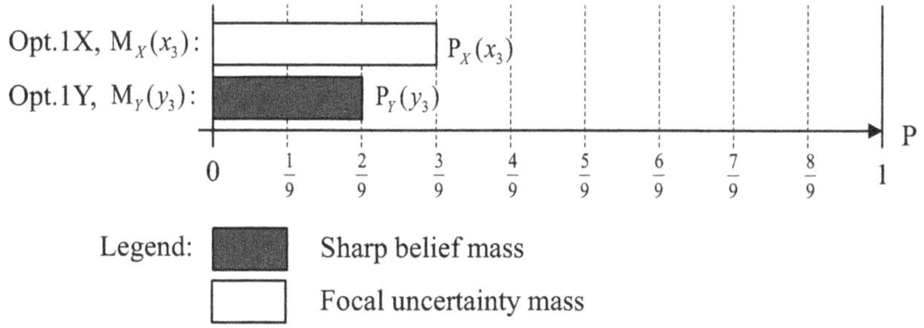

Fig. 4.11 Mass-sum diagram for options 1X and 1Y

4.6.2 Decisions with Difference in Sharpness

In game 2 you receive the following information. You are told that in urn X, 30 balls are red, and 60 balls are either black or yellow. The corresponding hyper-opinion ω_X is expressed as

$$\text{Hyper-opinion about } X \text{ in game 2} \quad \omega_X = \begin{pmatrix} \mathbf{b}_X(x_1) = 1/3, & \mathbf{a}_X(x_1) = 1/3, \\ \mathbf{b}_X(x_2) = 0, & \mathbf{a}_X(x_2) = 1/3, \\ \mathbf{b}_X(x_3) = 0, & \mathbf{a}_X(x_3) = 1/3, \\ \mathbf{b}_X(x_4) = 0, & \mathbf{a}_X(x_4) = 2/3, \\ \mathbf{b}_X(x_5) = 0, & \mathbf{a}_X(x_5) = 2/3, \\ \mathbf{b}_X(x_6) = 2/3, & \mathbf{a}_X(x_6) = 2/3, \\ u_X \quad = 0. & \end{pmatrix} \tag{4.36}$$

You are told that in urn Y, 10 balls are red, 10 balls are black, 10 balls are yellow, and the remaining 60 balls are either red, black or yellow. The corresponding hyper-opinion ω_Y is expressed as

$$\text{Hyper-opinion about } Y \text{ in game 2} \quad \omega_Y = \begin{pmatrix} \mathbf{b}_Y(y_1) = 1/9, & \mathbf{a}_Y(y_1) = 1/3, \\ \mathbf{b}_Y(y_2) = 1/9, & \mathbf{a}_Y(y_2) = 1/3, \\ \mathbf{b}_Y(y_3) = 1/9, & \mathbf{a}_Y(y_3) = 1/3, \\ \mathbf{b}_Y(y_4) = 0, & \mathbf{a}_Y(y_4) = 2/3, \\ \mathbf{b}_Y(y_5) = 0, & \mathbf{a}_Y(y_5) = 2/3, \\ \mathbf{b}_Y(y_6) = 0, & \mathbf{a}_Y(y_6) = 2/3, \\ u_Y \quad = 2/3. & \end{pmatrix} \tag{4.37}$$

One ball is going to be selected at random from either urn X or Y, and you are asked to make a choice about which urn to draw it from in a single betting game. You receive \$100 if 'Yellow' (x_3 or y_3) is drawn, and you receive nothing if either 'Red' or 'Black' is drawn. Table 4.6 summarises the options in this game.

Without having conducted any experiment, when presented with this pair of choices, it appears obvious to select option 2Y. The intuitive reason is that option 2Y includes some sharp belief mass in favour of 'Yellow', whereas with option 2X

Table 4.6 Game 2: Utilities for betting options 2X and 2Y

	Red	Black	Yellow
Option 2X, draw ball from urn X:	0	0	\$100
Option 2Y, draw ball from urn Y:	0	0	\$100

there is none. Below are the expressions for projected probability, sharp belief mass, vague belief mass and focal uncertainty mass.

Projected probabilities are computed with Eq.(3.28), relative base rates are computed with Eq.(2.10), and focal uncertainty mass with Eq.(4.3).

The projected probabilities of x_3 and y_3 in options 2X and 2Y are

$$\begin{aligned} &\text{Option 2X:} \quad \mathbf{P}_X(x_3) = \boldsymbol{a}_X(x_3|x_6)\,\boldsymbol{b}_X(x_6) \;= \tfrac{1}{2}\cdot\tfrac{2}{3} \qquad = \tfrac{1}{3}, \\ &\text{Option 2Y:} \quad \mathbf{P}_Y(y_3) = \boldsymbol{b}_Y(y_3) + \boldsymbol{a}_Y(y_3)\,u_Y = \tfrac{1}{9} + \tfrac{1}{3}\cdot\tfrac{2}{3} = \tfrac{1}{3}. \end{aligned} \tag{4.38}$$

Note that $\mathbf{P}_X(x_3) = \mathbf{P}_Y(y_3)$, which makes options 2X and 2Y equivalent from a purely first-order probability point of view. However they have different sharp belief mass, vague belief mass and focal uncertainty mass as shown below.

The sharp belief masses of x_3 and y_3 are

$$\begin{aligned} &\text{Option 2X:} \quad \boldsymbol{b}^{\mathrm{S}}_X(x_3) = 0, \\ &\text{Option 2Y:} \quad \boldsymbol{b}^{\mathrm{S}}_Y(y_3) = \boldsymbol{b}_Y(y_3) = \tfrac{1}{9}. \end{aligned} \tag{4.39}$$

The vague belief masses of x_3 and y_3 are

$$\begin{aligned} &\text{Option 2X:} \quad \boldsymbol{b}^{\mathrm{V}}_X(x_3) = \boldsymbol{a}_X(x_3|x_6)\,\boldsymbol{b}_X(x_6) = \tfrac{1}{2}\cdot\tfrac{2}{3} = \tfrac{1}{3}, \\ &\text{Option 2Y:} \quad \boldsymbol{b}^{\mathrm{V}}_Y(y_3) = 0. \end{aligned} \tag{4.40}$$

Focal uncertainty masses of x_3 and y_3 are

$$\begin{aligned} &\text{Option 2X:} \quad \boldsymbol{u}^{\mathrm{F}}_X(x_3) = 0, \\ &\text{Option 2Y:} \quad \boldsymbol{u}^{\mathrm{F}}_Y(y_3) = \boldsymbol{a}_Y(y_3)u_Y = \tfrac{1}{3}\cdot\tfrac{6}{9} = \tfrac{2}{9}. \end{aligned} \tag{4.41}$$

Note that the additivity property of Eq.(4.9) holds for x_3 and y_3.

Figure 4.12 shows the mass-sum diagram of $\mathbf{M}_X(x_3)$ and $\mathbf{M}_Y(y_3)$ of options 2X and 2Y respectively.

The difference between options 2X and 2Y emerges with their different sharp belief masses, where the option 2Y has greater sharp belief mass. This also means that option 2Y has lower sum of vague belief mass and uncertainty, and therefore is the preferred option.

Game 2 shows that when projected probabilities are equal, but the sharp belief masses are different, then the option with the greatest sharp belief mass is the best

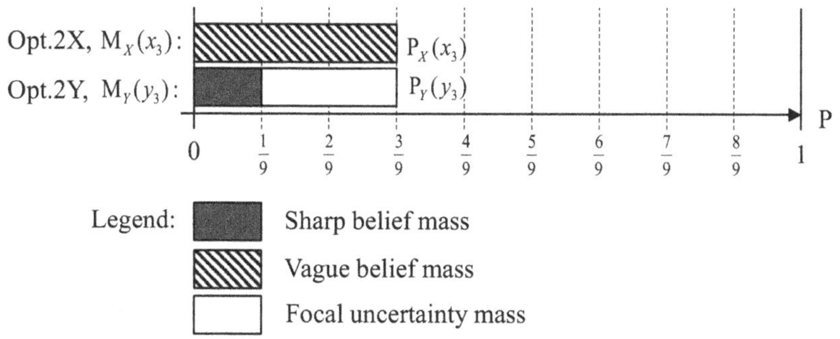

Fig. 4.12 Mass-sum diagram for options 2X and 2Y

choice. Option 2Y is therefore the rational preferred choice because it clearly has the greater sharp belief mass of the two.

4.6.3 Decisions with Difference in Vagueness and Uncertainty

In game 3 you receive the following information. You are told that in urn X, 20 balls are red, 40 balls are either black or yellow, and the remaining 30 balls are either red, black or yellow. For urn Y you are only told that the 90 balls in the urn are either red, black or yellow. The corresponding hyper-opinions are expressed as

$$\text{Hyper-opinion about } X \text{ in game 3} \quad \omega_X = \begin{pmatrix} \boldsymbol{b}_X(x_1) = 2/9, & \boldsymbol{a}_X(x_1) = 1/3, \\ \boldsymbol{b}_X(x_2) = 0, & \boldsymbol{a}_X(x_2) = 1/3, \\ \boldsymbol{b}_X(x_3) = 0, & \boldsymbol{a}_X(x_3) = 1/3, \\ \boldsymbol{b}_X(x_4) = 0, & \boldsymbol{a}_X(x_4) = 2/3, \\ \boldsymbol{b}_X(x_5) = 0, & \boldsymbol{a}_X(x_5) = 2/3, \\ \boldsymbol{b}_X(x_6) = 4/9, & \boldsymbol{a}_X(x_6) = 2/3, \\ u_X \quad = 3/9. & \end{pmatrix} \tag{4.42}$$

$$\text{Hyper-opinion about } Y \text{ in game 3} \quad \omega_Y = \begin{pmatrix} \boldsymbol{b}_Y(y_1) = 0, & \boldsymbol{a}_Y(y_1) = 1/3, \\ \boldsymbol{b}_Y(y_2) = 0, & \boldsymbol{a}_Y(y_2) = 1/3, \\ \boldsymbol{b}_Y(y_3) = 0, & \boldsymbol{a}_Y(y_3) = 1/3, \\ \boldsymbol{b}_Y(y_4) = 0, & \boldsymbol{a}_Y(y_4) = 2/3, \\ \boldsymbol{b}_Y(y_5) = 0, & \boldsymbol{a}_Y(y_5) = 2/3, \\ \boldsymbol{b}_Y(y_6) = 0, & \boldsymbol{a}_Y(y_6) = 2/3, \\ u_Y \quad = 1. & \end{pmatrix} \tag{4.43}$$

One ball is going to be selected at random either from urn X or from urn Y, and you are asked to make a choice about which urn to draw it from in a single betting game. You receive \$100 if 'Yellow' (x_3 or y_3) is drawn, and you receive nothing if either 'Red' or 'Black' is drawn. Table 4.7 summarises the options in this game.

Table 4.7 Game 3: Utilities for betting options 3X and 3Y

	Red	Black	Yellow
Option 3X, draw ball from urn X:	0	0	\$100
Option 3Y, draw ball from urn Y:	0	0	\$100

Without having conducted any experiment, when presented with this pair of choices, it seems obvious to select option 3X. The intuitive reason is that option 3X has less focal uncertainty mass than option 3Y. Below are the expressions for the projected probability and sharp belief mass.

Projected probabilities are computed with Eq.(3.28), relative base rates are computed with Eq.(2.10), and focal uncertainty mass with Eq.(4.3).

The projected probabilities of x_3 and y_3 in options 3X and 3Y are

$$\begin{aligned} \text{Option 3X:}\ \ \mathbf{P}_X(x_3) &= \boldsymbol{a}_X(x_3|x_6)\,\boldsymbol{b}_X(x_6) + \boldsymbol{a}_X(x_3)u_X = \tfrac{1}{2}\cdot\tfrac{4}{9} + \tfrac{1}{3}\cdot\tfrac{3}{9} = \tfrac{1}{3}, \\ \text{Option 3Y:}\ \ \mathbf{P}_Y(y_3) &= \boldsymbol{a}_Y(y_3)\,u_Y = \tfrac{1}{3}\cdot 1 = \tfrac{1}{3}. \end{aligned} \quad (4.44)$$

$$\begin{aligned} \text{Option 3X:}\ \ \boldsymbol{b}^{\mathrm{S}}_X(x_3) &= 0, \\ \text{Option 3Y:}\ \ \boldsymbol{b}^{\mathrm{S}}_Y(y_3) &= 0. \end{aligned} \quad (4.45)$$

Note that $\mathbf{P}_X(x_3) = \mathbf{P}_Y(y_3)$, which makes options 3X and 3Y equal from a purely first-order probability point of view. In addition we have equal sharp belief mass expressed by $\boldsymbol{b}^{\mathrm{S}}_X(x_3) = \boldsymbol{b}^{\mathrm{S}}_Y(y_3)$. However they have different vague belief mass and focal uncertainty mass as shown below. The vague belief masses of x_3 and y_3 are

$$\begin{aligned} \text{Option 3X:}\ \ \boldsymbol{b}^{\mathrm{V}}_X(x_3) &= \boldsymbol{a}_X(x_3|x_6)\,\boldsymbol{b}_X(x_6) = \tfrac{1}{2}\cdot\tfrac{4}{9} = \tfrac{2}{9}, \\ \text{Option 3Y:}\ \ \boldsymbol{b}^{\mathrm{V}}_Y(y_3) &= 0. \end{aligned} \quad (4.46)$$

The focal uncertainty masses of x_3 and y_3 are

$$\begin{aligned} \text{Option 3X:}\ \ \boldsymbol{u}^{\mathrm{F}}_X(x_3) &= \boldsymbol{a}_X(x_3)u_X = \tfrac{1}{3}\cdot\tfrac{3}{9} = \tfrac{1}{9}, \\ \text{Option 3Y:}\ \ \boldsymbol{u}^{\mathrm{F}}_Y(y_3) &= \boldsymbol{a}_Y(y_3)u_Y = \tfrac{1}{3}\cdot 1 = \tfrac{1}{3}. \end{aligned} \quad (4.47)$$

Note that the additivity property of Eq.(4.9) holds for x_3 and y_3.

Figure 4.13 shows the mass-sum diagram of $\mathbf{M}_X(x_3)$ and $\mathbf{M}_Y(y_3)$ of options 3X and 3Y respectively.

An interesting aspect of game 3 is that the respective vague belief masses and focal uncertainty masses of x_3 and y_3 are different. Vagueness is preferable over uncertainty, because vagueness is based on evidence, whereas uncertainty reflects vacuity of evidence. The option with the least uncertainty, and thereby with the greatest vagueness, is therefore preferable.

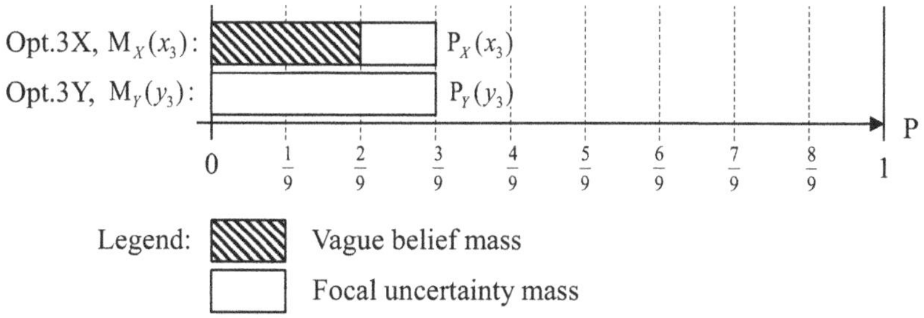

Fig. 4.13 Mass-sum diagram for options 3X and 3Y

Game 3 shows that when projected probabilities are equal, and the sharp belief masses are also equal (zero in this case), but the focal uncertainty masses and vagueness are different, then the option with the least focal uncertainty mass is the best choice. Option 3X is therefore the rationally preferred choice, because it clearly has the lower focal uncertainty mass of the two.

4.7 Entropy in the Opinion Model

Information theory [91] provides a formalism for modelling and measuring first-order uncertainty about the outcome of random events that are governed by probability distributions. The amount of information associated with a random variable is called *entropy*, where high entropy indicates that it is difficult to predict outcomes, and low entropy indicates easy predictions. The amount of information associated with a given outcome is called *surprisal*, where high surprisal indicates an *a priori* unlikely outcome, and low surprisal indicates an *a priori* likely outcome. People tend to be risk-averse [21], so they prefer to make decisions under low entropy and low surprisal. For example, most people prefer the option of receiving $1,000 over the option of an all-or-nothing coin flip for $2,000. The expected utility is $1,000 in both options, but the former option exposes the participant to zero bits surprisal (i.e. no surprisal), and the latter option exposes him or her to one bit surprisal. Given that the expected utility is otherwise equal (as in the example above), people prefer betting with the lowest possible exposure to surprisal.

Belief and uncertainty are intimately linked with regard to information theory in the opinion model. In the sections below, we introduce standard notions of information surprisal and entropy from classical information theory, before extending these notions to opinions. A more detailed discussion and treatment of classical entropy can be found, e.g. in [73].

4.7.1 Outcome Surprisal

Surprisal, aka self-information, is a measure of the information content associated with the outcome of a random variable under a given probability distribution. The measuring unit of surprisal can be bits, nats or hartleys, depending on the base of the logarithm used in its calculation. When logarithm base 2 is used, the unit is bits, which is also used below.

Definition 4.11 (Surprisal). The surprisal (or self-information) of an outcome x of a discrete random variable X with probability distribution $\boldsymbol{p}_X$ is expressed as

$$\mathbf{I}_X(x) = -\log_2(\boldsymbol{p}_X(x)) \,. \tag{4.48}$$

□

Surprisal measures the degree to which an outcome is surprising. An outcome is more surprising the less likely it is to happen. When the base of the logarithm is 2, as in Eq.(4.48), the surprisal is measured in bits. The more surprising an outcome is, the more informative it is, and the more bits it contains.

For example, when considering a fair coin, the probability is 0.5 for both 'heads' and 'tails', so each time the coin lands with 'heads' or 'tails', the observed amount of information is $\mathbf{I}(\text{tossing fair coin}) = -\log_2(0.5) = \log_2(2) = 1$ bit of information.

When considering a fair die, the probability is $1/6$ for each face, so each time the die produces one of its six faces, the observed amount of information is $\mathbf{I}(\text{throwing fair die}) = -\log_2(1/6) = \log_2(6) = 2.585$ bits.

In case of an unfair die where the probability of 'six' is only $1/16$ (as opposed to $1/6$ for a fair die), throwing a 'six' amounts to $\mathbf{I}(\text{'six'}) = -\log_2(1/16) = \log_2(16) = 4$ bits surprisal.

In information theory, the surprisal of an outcome is completely determined by the probability that it happens. Opinion outcome surprisal is defined below.

Definition 4.12 (Opinion Outcome Surprisal). Assume a (hyper-) opinion ω_X where the variable X takes its values from the hyperdomain $\mathscr{R}(\mathbb{X})$. Given that the projected probability of outcome x is $\mathbf{P}_X(x)$, the opinion surprisal of outcome x is

$$\text{Opinion Outcome Surprisal:}\;\; \mathbf{I}^{\mathrm{P}}_X(x) = -\log_2(\mathbf{P}_X(x)) \,. \tag{4.49}$$

□

In the opinion model, the surprisal of an outcome can be partially sharp, vague or uncertain, in any proportion. These concepts are defined below.

Definition 4.13 (Surprisal of Sharpness, Vagueness and Focal Uncertainty). Assume a (hyper-) opinion ω_X where the variable X takes its values from the hyperdomain $\mathscr{R}(\mathbb{X})$. Given that the projected probability of outcome x is $\mathbf{P}_X(x)$, the sharpness, vagueness and focal uncertainty surprisals of outcome x are expressed as

$$\text{Belief sharpness surprisal: } \mathbf{I}_X^{\mathrm{S}}(x) = \frac{\boldsymbol{b}_X^{\mathrm{S}}(x)\mathbf{I}_X^{\mathrm{P}}(x)}{\mathbf{P}_X(x)}, \tag{4.50}$$

$$\text{Belief vagueness surprisal: } \mathbf{I}_X^{\mathrm{V}}(x) = \frac{\boldsymbol{b}_X^{\mathrm{V}}(x)\mathbf{I}_X^{\mathrm{P}}(x)}{\mathbf{P}_X(x)}, \tag{4.51}$$

$$\text{Focal uncertainty surprisal: } \mathbf{I}_X^{\mathrm{U}}(x) = \frac{\boldsymbol{u}_X^{\mathrm{F}}(x)\mathbf{I}_X^{\mathrm{P}}(x)}{\mathbf{P}_X(x)}. \tag{4.52}$$

□

Note that the opinion surprisal of an outcome consists of the sum of the sharpness, vagueness and focal uncertainty surprisal, expressed as

$$\mathbf{I}_X^{\mathrm{S}}(x) + \mathbf{I}_X^{\mathrm{V}}(x) + \mathbf{I}_X^{\mathrm{U}}(x) = \mathbf{I}_X^{\mathrm{P}}(x). \tag{4.53}$$

The decision criteria described in Section 4.4 are expressed in terms of projected probability consisting of sharp belief mass, vague belief mass and focal uncertainty mass. Given that opinion outcome surprisal is a function of the same concepts, the same decision criteria can equivalently be articulated in terms of outcome surprisal consisting of sharpness, vagueness, and focal uncertainty surprisal. However, using projected probability has obvious advantages when including utility in the decision process, because their product then produces the expected utility directly.

4.7.2 Opinion Entropy

Information entropy can be interpreted as expected surprisal, and is the sum over products of surprisal and probability of outcomes, as defined below.

Definition 4.14 (Entropy). The entropy, denoted $\mathrm{H}(X)$, of a random variable X that takes its values from a domain $\mathbb{X}$ is the expected surprisal expressed as

$$\mathrm{H}(X) = \sum_{x \in \mathbb{X}} p_X(x)\,\mathrm{I}_X(x) = -\sum_{x \in \mathbb{X}} p_X(x)\log_2(p_X(x)). \tag{4.54}$$

□

Entropy measures the expected information carried by a random variable. In information theory, the entropy of a random variable is determined by the probability of its outcome in one test. The more evenly the outcome probabilities of a random variable are distributed, the more entropy the random variable carries. If one outcome is absolutely certain, then the variable carries zero entropy.

The *opinion entropy* of a (hyper-) variable X with an associated opinion ω_X is simply the entropy computed over the projected probability distribution $\mathbf{P}_X$, similarly to Eq.(4.54).

Definition 4.15 (Opinion Entropy). Assume a (hyper-) opinion ω_X, where the variable X takes its values from the hyperdomain $\mathscr{R}(\mathbb{X})$. The opinion entropy, denoted $\mathrm{H}^{\mathrm{P}}(\omega_X)$, is the expected surprisal expressed as

$$\mathrm{H}^{\mathrm{P}}(\omega_X) = -\sum_{x\in\mathbb{X}} \mathbf{P}_X(x)\log_2(\mathbf{P}_X(x))\,. \tag{4.55}$$

□

Opinion entropy is insensitive to change in the uncertainty mass of an opinion, as long as the projected probability distribution $\mathbf{P}_X$ remains the same.

Proposition 4.1. *Let ω_X^A and ω_X^B be two opinions, such that $u_X^A > u_X^B$ and $\mathbf{P}_X^A = \mathbf{P}_X^B$, then $\mathrm{H}^{\mathrm{P}}(\omega_X^A) = \mathrm{H}^{\mathrm{P}}(\omega_X^B)$.*

Proof. The proposition's validity follows from the fact that H^{P} is determined by the projected probability distributions, which are equal for ω_X^A and ω_X^B. □

In order to account for difference in uncertainty, as well as in vagueness, it is necessary to introduce *sharpness entropy*, *vagueness entropy* and *uncertainty entropy*. These entropy concepts can be computed based on the sharp belief mass $\boldsymbol{b}_X^{\mathrm{S}}$, vague belief mass $\boldsymbol{b}_X^{\mathrm{V}}$ and focal uncertainty mass $\boldsymbol{u}_X^{\mathrm{F}}$, as defined in Section 4.1.

Definition 4.16 (Sharpness Entropy). Assume a (hyper-) opinion ω_X, where the variable X takes its values from the hyperdomain $\mathscr{R}(\mathbb{X})$. The sharpness entropy, denoted $\mathrm{H}^{\mathrm{S}}(\omega_X)$, is the expected surprisal from sharp belief mass, expressed as

$$\mathrm{H}^{\mathrm{S}}(\omega_X) = -\sum_{x\in\mathbb{X}} \boldsymbol{b}_X^{\mathrm{S}}(x)\log_2(\mathbf{P}_X(x))\,. \tag{4.56}$$

□

Definition 4.17 (Vagueness Entropy). Assume a (hyper-) opinion ω_X where the variable X takes its values from the hyperdomain $\mathscr{R}(\mathbb{X})$. The vagueness entropy, denoted $\mathrm{H}^{\mathrm{V}}(\omega_X)$, is the expected surprisal from vague belief mass, expressed as

$$\mathrm{H}^{\mathrm{V}}(\omega_X) = -\sum_{x\in\mathbb{X}} \boldsymbol{b}_X^{\mathrm{V}}(x)\log_2(\mathbf{P}_X(x))\,. \tag{4.57}$$

□

Definition 4.18 (Uncertainty Entropy). Assume a (hyper-) opinion ω_X where the variable X takes its values from the hyperdomain $\mathscr{R}(\mathbb{X})$. The uncertainty entropy, denoted $\mathrm{H}^{\mathrm{U}}(\omega_X)$, is the expected surprisal from focal uncertainty mass expressed as

$$\mathrm{H}^{\mathrm{U}}(\omega_X) = -\sum_{x\in\mathbb{X}} \boldsymbol{u}_X^{\mathrm{F}}(x)\log_2(\mathbf{P}_X(x))\,. \tag{4.58}$$

□

Note the additivity property of the above defined entropy concepts:

$$\mathrm{H}^{\mathrm{S}}(\omega_X) + \mathrm{H}^{\mathrm{V}}(\omega_X) + \mathrm{H}^{\mathrm{U}}(\omega_X) = \mathrm{H}^{\mathrm{P}}(\omega_X). \tag{4.59}$$

Thus, for a given opinion entropy, there is a continuum of sums of sharpness, vagueness and uncertainty entropy. The structure of the sum reflects the type of evidence on which the entropy is based. In case of an urn of 100 balls where you only know that the balls can be red or black, the entropy for you is one bit with regard to the variable of picking a red or a black ball. This entropy consists solely of one bit of uncertainty entropy. In another case, where you learn that there are exactly 50 red balls and 50 black balls, the entropy for you is still one bit, however in this case this entropy consists solely of one bit of sharpness entropy. In the opinion model, entropy consists of the three different types of entropy as shown in Eq.(4.59), which gives a more informative expression of entropy than classical information entropy.

For decision making, sharpness entropy is preferable over vagueness entropy, which is turn is preferable over uncertainty entropy, as defined in Section 4.4.

In the case of two variables with equal entropy containing the exact same sum of sharpness, vagueness and uncertainty entropy, the two variables might still have different structures of vagueness entropy, and thereby be different in nature. However, this topic is outside of the scope of the current presentation.

The cross entropy of an opinion measures the difference between the projected probability distribution and the base rate distribution.

Definition 4.19 (Base-Rate to Projected-Probability Cross Entropy). The base-rate to projected-probability cross entropy, denoted $H^{\mathrm{BP}}(\omega_X)$, is the base-rate expected projected probability expressed as

$$\mathrm{H}^{\mathrm{BP}}(\omega_X) = -\sum_{x \in \mathbb{X}} \boldsymbol{a}_X(x) \log_2(\mathbf{P}_X(x)) \,. \tag{4.60}$$

□

For a given entropy, the cross entropy is maximum when the projected probability and base rate have equal distributions.

4.8 Conflict Between Opinions

A fundamental assumption behind subjective logic is that different agents can have different opinions about the same variable. This also reflects the subjective reality of how we perceive the world we live in.

For decision making however, having different opinions about the same thing can be problematic, because it can make it difficult to agree on the best course of action.

When it can be assumed that a ground truth exists (without being directly observable), the fact that agents have different opinions can be interpreted as an indicator that one or multiple agents are wrong. In such situations it can be meaningful to apply strategies to revise opinions, such as for trust revision described in Section 14.5.

The *degree of conflict*, abbreviated DC, is a measure of the difference between opinions, and can be used in strategies for dealing with situations of difference between opinions about the same target.

Let B and C be two agents that have their respective opinions ω_X^B and ω_X^C about the same variable X. The most basic measure of conflict between the two opinions ω_X^B and ω_X^C is the *projected distance*, denoted PD, expressed by Eq.(4.61):

$$\text{Projected Distance:} \quad \mathrm{PD}(\omega_X^B, \omega_X^C) = \frac{\sum_{x \in \mathbb{X}} |\mathbf{P}_X^B(x) - \mathbf{P}_X^C(x)|}{2} . \tag{4.61}$$

The property that $\mathrm{PD} \in [0,1]$ can be explained. Obviously $\mathrm{PD} \geq 0$. Furthermore, given that $\sum \mathbf{P}_X^B(x) + \sum \mathbf{P}_X^C(x) = 2$, independently of the cardinality of $\mathbb{X}$, it can be observed that $\mathrm{PD} \leq 1$. The case $\mathrm{PD} = 0$ occurs for equal projected probability distributions, reflecting non-conflicting (but possibly different) opinions. The case $\mathrm{PD} = 1$ occurs for absolute opinions with different projected probability.

A large PD does not necessarily indicate conflict, because the potential conflict is defused in case one (or both) opinions have high uncertainty. The more uncertain one or both opinions are, the more tolerance for a large PD should be given.

Tolerance for a large PD in case of high uncertainty reflects the fact that uncertain opinions carry little weight in a potential fusion operation.

A natural measure of the common certainty between two opinions ω_X^B and ω_X^C is their *conjunctive certainty*, denoted CC:

$$\text{Conjunctive Certainty:} \quad \mathrm{CC}(\omega_X^B, \omega_X^C) = (1 - u_X^B)(1 - u_X^C) . \tag{4.62}$$

Note that $\mathrm{CC} \in [0,1]$, where $\mathrm{CC} = 0$ means that one or both opinions are vacuous, and $\mathrm{CC} = 1$ means that both opinions are dogmatic, i.e. have zero uncertainty mass.

The *degree of conflict* (DC) is simply defined as the product of PD and CC.

Definition 4.20 (Degree of Conflict). Assume two agents B and C with their respective opinions ω_X^B and ω_X^C about the same variable X.

$\mathrm{DC}(\omega_X^B, \omega_X^C)$ denotes the *degree of conflict* between ω_X^B and ω_X^C:

$$\text{Degree of Conflict:} \quad \mathrm{DC}(\omega_X^B, \omega_X^C) = \mathrm{PD}(\omega_X^B, \omega_X^C) \cdot \mathrm{CC}(\omega_X^B, \omega_X^C) . \tag{4.63}$$

□

As as example, consider the two binomial opinions $\omega_{X_1}^B = (0.05, 0.15, 0.80, 0.90)$ and $\omega_{X_1}^C = (0.68, 0.22, 0.10, 0.90)$. Figure 4.14 is a screenshot of the visualisation demonstration applet of subjective logic, showing two example opinions $\omega_{X_1}^B$ and $\omega_{X_1}^C$ as points in the opinion triangle on the left, with their equivalent PDFs on the right. In this case we get $\mathrm{DC}(\omega_{X_1}^B, \omega_{X_1}^C) = 0$, meaning that there is no conflict.

The reason why $\mathrm{DC}(\omega_{X_1}^B, \omega_{X_1}^C) = 0$ is because $\mathrm{PD}(\omega_{X_1}^B, \omega_{X_1}^C) = 0$. In terms of Definition 4.20, there is thus no conflict between these opinions, although their belief masses are quite different.

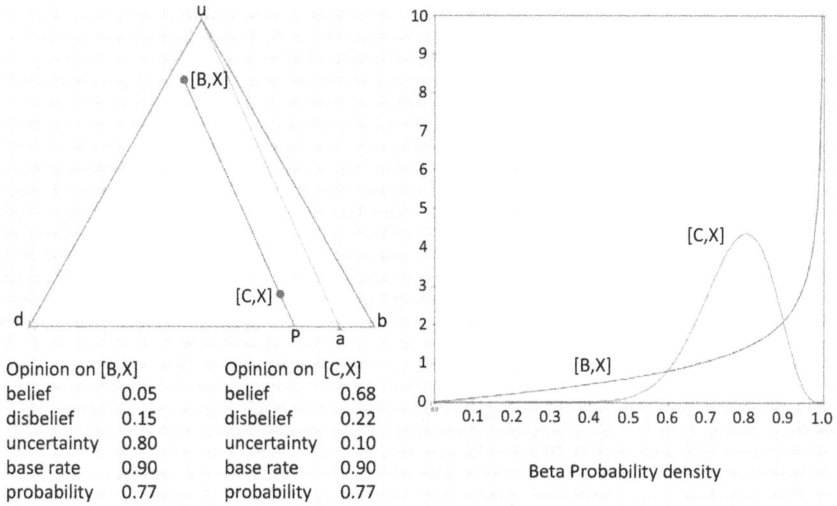

Fig. 4.14 Example of opinions $\omega^B_{X_1}$ and $\omega^C_{X_1}$ where $\mathrm{DC}(\omega^B_{X_1}, \omega^C_{X_1}) = 0.0$

The next example shows two binomial opinions $\omega^B_{X_2} = (0.05, 0.15, 0.80, 0.10)$ and $\omega^C_{X_2} = (0.68, 0.22, 0.10, 0.10)$ with the same belief masses as in the previous example, but with different base rate. In this example, there is some conflict, which shows that the degree of conflict is influenced by base rates.

The degree of conflict can be computed according to Eq.(4.63) as

$$\begin{aligned} \mathrm{DC}(\omega^B_{X_2}, \omega^C_{X_2}) &= \mathrm{PD}(\omega^B_{X_2}, \omega^C_{X_2}) \cdot \mathrm{CC}(\omega^B_{X_2}, \omega^C_{X_2}) \\ &= 0.56 \cdot (1.00 - 0.80)(1.00 - 0.10) = 0.10. \end{aligned} \tag{4.64}$$

Figure 4.15 is a screenshot of the visualisation of the binomial opinions $\omega^B_{X_2}$ and $\omega^C_{X_2}$. The opinion points on the left have equivalent PDFs on the right.

Although the conflict might seem high due to the very different projected probabilities, the fact that $\omega^B_{X_2}$ is highly uncertain defuses the potential conflict, so that the degree of conflict only becomes $\mathrm{DC}(\omega^B_{X_2}, \omega^C_{X_2}) = 0.10$.

The notion of degree of conflict, as described here, only provides a relatively coarse measure of conflict between two opinions. For example, two opinions with very different PDFs can have zero conflict, as shown in Figure 4.14.

Because opinions are multi-dimensional, a more complete expression for conflict would necessarily require multiple parameters. However, this would partially defeat the purpose of having a simple measure of conflict between opinions.

The degree of conflict expressed by Definition 4.20 provides a simple way of assessing conflict between two opinions, which is useful e.g. for trust revision described in Section 14.5.

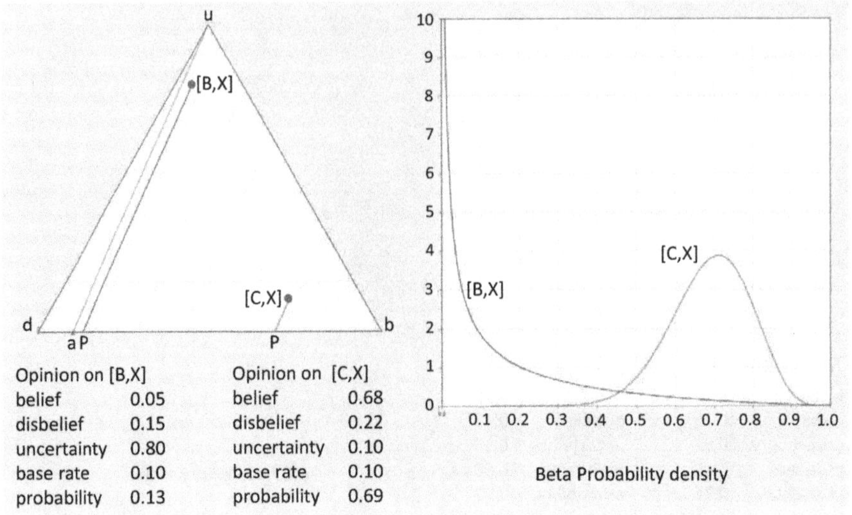

Fig. 4.15 Example of opinions $\omega^{B}_{X_2}$ and $\omega^{C}_{X_2}$ where $\mathrm{DC}(\omega^{B}_{X_2}, \omega^{C}_{X_2}) = 0.1$

4.9 Ambiguity

A statement is normally articulated to carry a specific meaning which is intended to be interpreted in the same way by any recipient of the statement. Ambiguity exists when there is uncertainty about the meaning of the statement, typically because there are several plausible interpretations. Ambiguity is thus an attribute of any statement whose intended meaning can not be definitively resolved [27]. Consider for example the statement: "*He returns from the bank*", which carries (at least) two plausible meanings: i) He has visited a financial institution, presumably to do some financial transaction, and he now returns; ii) he has been down by the river bank, possibly for fishing or swimming, and he now returns.

In contrast, the concept of vagueness is when the interpretation of statements is assumed to be clear, i.e. the analyst understands the meaning of the domain and its values, but can not determine which of the values in particular is true.

In terms of subjective opinions, ambiguity should therefore be seen as uncertainty about the domain and its values, in the sense that the analyst lacks a clear understanding of the domain itself or of the values contained in it.

An analyst who misunderstands the meaning of a domain and its values will obviously not understand what he or she analyses, which may lead to erratic evaluations and decisions. Hence, ambiguity is clearly an important topic for decision making. Nevertheless, a theory of ambiguity is outside of the scope of this book. The exploration of ambiguity, in the sense of domain uncertainty, must therefore be a topic of future research.

Chapter 5
Principles of Subjective Logic

This chapter compares subjective logic with other relevant reasoning frameworks, and gives an overview of the general principles of subjective logic.

5.1 Related Frameworks for Uncertain Reasoning

5.1.1 Comparison with Dempster-Shafer Belief Theory

Dempster-Shafer Belief Theory (DST), also known as evidence theory, has its origin in a model for upper and lower probabilities proposed by Dempster in 1960. Based on Dempster's model, Shafer later proposed a model for expressing beliefs [90]. DST uses the term *'frame of discernment'*, or 'frame' for short, to denote the set of exclusive possible states, which corresponds to a domain in subjective logic. Belief mass can be assigned to any subset of the frame, including the whole frame itself. The main idea behind DST is to abandon the additivity principle of probability theory, i.e. that the sum of probabilities on all pairwise exclusive possibilities must add up to one. The advantage of this approach is e.g. that uncertainty about the probabilities, i.e. the lack of evidence to support any specific probability, can be explicitly expressed by assigning belief mass to the whole frame.

The DST belief model is highly expressive, and extends the notion of probability. By using beliefs it is possible to provide the argument *"I don't know"* as input to a reasoning model, which is not possible with probabilities. This capability has made DST quite popular among researchers and practitioners in the AI (Artificial Intelligence) community.

Consider a domain $\mathbb{X}$ with its hyperdomain $\mathscr{R}(\mathbb{X})$ and powerset $\mathscr{P}(\mathbb{X})$. Recall that $\{\mathbb{X}\} \in \mathscr{P}(\mathbb{X})$. Let x denote a specific value of $\mathscr{R}(\mathbb{X})$ or of $\mathscr{P}(\mathbb{X})$.

In DST, the belief mass on value x is denoted $\boldsymbol{m}(x)$, and the belief mass distribution is called a *basic belief assignment* (bba). It is possible to define a direct bijective mapping between the bba of DST and the belief mass distribution and uncertainty mass of subjective opinions, as expressed by Eq.(5.1):

$$\text{Mapping between the bba of DST and the belief/uncertainty masses of subjective opinions:} \quad \begin{cases} \boldsymbol{m}(x) &= \boldsymbol{b}_X(x)\,, \quad \forall x \in \mathscr{R}(\mathbb{X}), \\ \boldsymbol{m}(\mathbb{X}) &= u_X\,. \end{cases} \tag{5.1}$$

Technically, the bba of DST and the belief/uncertainty representation of subjective opinions are thus equivalent. Their interpretations however are different. Subjective opinions can not assign belief mass to the domain $\mathbb{X}$ itself. This interpretation corresponds to the (hyper-) Dirichlet model, where only observations of values of $\mathbb{X}$ (or $\mathscr{R}(\mathbb{X})$) are counted as evidence. The domain $\mathbb{X}$ itself can not be an observation in the (hyper-) Dirichlet model, and hence can not be counted as evidence. Base rates are not part of DST, so the projected (called *'pignistic'*) probability is computed with default base rates equal to the relative cardinalities.

A typical application of DST in the literature is belief fusion where Dempster's rule is the classical operator [90]. There has been considerable confusion and controversy around the adequacy of belief fusion operators [93], especially regarding Dempster's rule. The confusion started with Zadeh's example from 1984 [101] where Dempster's rule is applied to a situation for which it is unsuitable and therefore produces erratic results. The controversy followed when authors failed to realise that it is not a question of whether Dempster's rule is correct or wrong, but of recognising the type of situations for which Dempster's rule is suitable.

As an analogy of the controversy around Dempster's rule, imagine a world where the swim vest (analogy of Dempster's rule) has been invented as a safety device (analogy of a belief fusion operator). Then somebody demonstrates with an example that swim vests provide very poor protection in a car crash (analogy of Zadeh's example). Some researchers explain this by saying that swim vests perform poorly only in the case of high speed (analogy of high conflict) car crashes, and suggest to reduce the driving speed to make swim vests perform better. Other researchers propose the seat belt as an alternative safety device because it works well in car crashes, but this proposal is met with criticism by people who claim that seat belts provide poor protection in a sinking boat, in which case swim vests provide good protection. Many other safety devices are invented, and each device is promoted with an anecdotal example where it provides relatively good protection. In this confusing discussion nobody seems to understand that different safety hazards require different safety devices for protection, and that there is no single safety device that can provide adequate protection in all situations.

In an analogous fashion, the fact that different belief fusion situations require different belief fusion operators has often been ignored in the belief theory literature, and has been a significant source of confusion for many years [53]. There is nothing wrong with Dempster's rule *per se*; there are situations where it is perfectly appropriate, and there are situations where it is clearly inappropriate. No single belief fusion operator is suitable in every situation.

The corresponding operator for Dempster's rule in subjective logic is the *belief constraint fusion operator* which is described in Chapter 12.

5.1.2 Comparison with Imprecise Probabilities

The Imprecise Dirichlet Model (IDM) [98] for multinomial variables was proposed as a method for determining upper and lower probabilities produced by setting the minimum and maximum base rates in the Beta or Dirichlet PDF for each possible value in the domain. The expected probability resulting from assigning the maximum base rate (i.e. equal to one) to the probability of a value in the domain produces the upper probability, and the expected probability resulting from assigning a zero base rate to a value in the domain produces the lower probability.

The upper and lower probabilities are interpreted as the upper and lower bounds for the relative frequency of the outcome. However, these bounds can not be taken literally, as explained below.

Let $\boldsymbol{r}_X$ represent the evidence for the Dirichlet PDF, and let the non-informative prior weight be $W = 2$. According to the Imprecise Dirichlet Model (IDM) [98], the upper and lower probabilities for a value $x \in \mathbb{X}$ are defined as:

$$\text{IDM upper probability:} \quad \mathrm{E}_X^+(x) = \frac{\boldsymbol{r}_X(x) + W}{W + \sum_{i=1}^k \boldsymbol{r}_X(x_i)}, \quad \forall x \in \mathbb{X}, \tag{5.2}$$

$$\text{IDM lower probability:} \quad \mathrm{E}_X^-(x) = \frac{\boldsymbol{r}_X(x)}{W + \sum_{i=1}^k \boldsymbol{r}_X(x_i)}, \quad \forall x \in \mathbb{X}. \tag{5.3}$$

There is a direct correspondence to the uncertainty mass of subjective opinions:

$$u_X = \mathrm{E}_X^+(x) \; - \; \mathrm{E}_X^-(x). \tag{5.4}$$

The IDM expresses the effect of base rate ignorance on the expected probability, which is to produce an interval of expected probability. More specifically, if the analyst has some evidence about a possible event x but ignores its base rate, it is possible to determine an interval for the possible expected probability $\mathrm{E}_X(x)$. Of course, the IDM upper probability $\mathrm{E}_X^+(x)$ and IDM lower probability $\mathrm{E}_X^-(x)$ can not be literally interpreted as absolute upper and lower bounds for the probability.

For example, assume a bag with nine red marbles and one black marble, meaning that the relative frequencies of red and black marbles are $p(\text{red}) = 0.9$ and $p(\text{black}) = 0.1$. The non-informative prior weight is set to $W = 2$. Assume that you pick one marble which turns out to be black. According to Eq.(5.3) the lower probability is then $\mathrm{E}_X^-(\text{black}) = \frac{1}{3}$. It would be incorrect to literally interpret this value as the lower bound for the probability because obviously it is greater than the actual relative frequency of black balls. In other words, if $\mathrm{E}_X^-(\text{black}) > p(\text{black})$ then $\mathrm{E}_X^-(\text{black})$ can not possibly be the lower bound for $p(\text{black})$.

This case shows that the upper and lower probabilities defined by the IDM should be interpreted as a rough probability interval, because it must accommodate the possibility that actual probabilities (relative frequencies) can be outside the range.

5.1.3 Comparison with Fuzzy Logic

The domains for variables in fuzzy logic consist of terms with vague and partially overlapping semantics. For example, in case the variable is 'Height of a person' then possible values are 'short', 'average' or 'tall'. The fuzziness comes from whether a person of a specific height should be considered short, average or tall. A person measuring 182 cm might be considered to be somewhat average and somewhat tall. In fuzzy logic, this is expressed by *fuzzy membership functions*, whereby a person could be considered to be 0.5 average and 0.5 tall. Note that the height of a person can be measured in an exact and crisp way, whereas variables consist of terms that are fuzzy/vague in nature.

In subjective logic on the other hand, the domains consist of terms that are considered crisp in nature, whereas subjective opinions contain belief mass and uncertainty mass that express uncertainty and vagueness. This difference between fuzzy logic and subjective logic is illustrated in Figure 5.1.

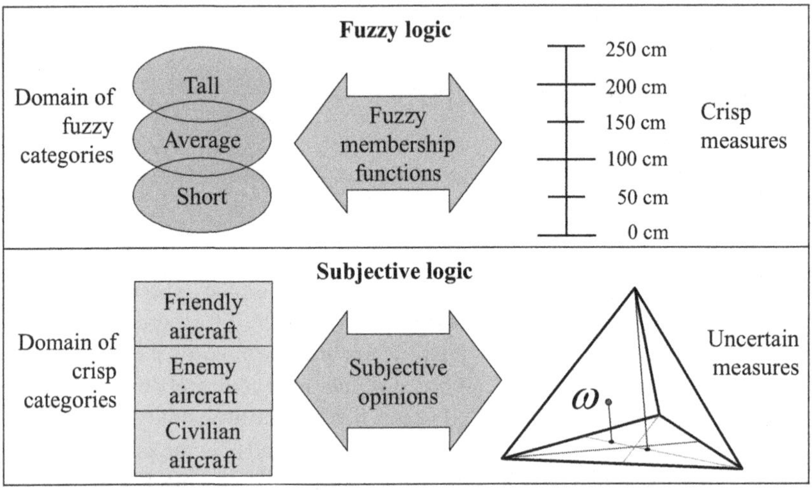

Fig. 5.1 Difference between fuzzy membership functions and subjective opinions.

Fuzzy logic and subjective logic thus handle different aspects of uncertainty and vagueness. A natural idea is to combine these two reasoning frameworks. It is then a question of how this should be done, and whether it would produce a more flexible and powerful reasoning model than either fuzzy logic or subjective logic in isolation.

Without going deeper into this topic, we can simply mention the possibility of combining fuzzy logic and subjective logic, e.g. by expressing fuzzy membership functions in terms of opinions, as described in [61]. If for example the height of a person is only known with imprecision, then this can naturally be reflected by expressing the fuzzy membership function as an uncertain subjective opinion.

5.1.4 Comparison with Kleene's Three-Valued Logic

In Kleene's three-valued logic [25], propositions can be assigned one of three truth-values specified as TRUE, FALSE and UNKNOWN. The first two truth values are interpreted as the traditional TRUE and FALSE in binary logic. The UNKNOWN value can be thought of as neither TRUE nor FALSE. In Kleene logic it is assumed that when the truth value of a particular proposition is UNKNOWN, then it might secretly have the value TRUE or FALSE at any moment in time, but the actual truth value is not available to the analyst.

The logical AND and OR operators in Kleene's three-valued logic are specified in Tables 5.1.a and 5.1.b below.

Table 5.1 Truth tables for Kleene's three-valued AND and OR operators

$x \wedge y$		y F	y U	y T
x	F	F	F	F
	U	F	U	U
	T	F	U	T

(a) Truth table for AND

$x \vee y$		y F	y U	y T
x	F	F	U	T
	U	U	U	T
	T	T	T	T

(b) Truth table for OR

There are obvious problems with Kleene's logic, as explained below.

According to truth table 5.1.a, the truth value of the conjunction $(x \wedge y)$ is specified to be UNKNOWN when the truth values of x and y are both defined as UNKNOWN. However, in the case of an infinitely large number of variables $x, y, \ldots z$ that are all UNKNOWN, Kleene's logic would still dictate the truth of the serial conjunction $(x \wedge y \cdots \wedge z)$ to be UNKNOWN. This result is inconsistent with the intuitive conclusion where the correct value should be FALSE. A simple example illustrates why this is so.

Assume the case of flipping a fair coin multiple times, where each flip is a separate variable. An observer's best guess about whether the next outcome will be *heads* might be expressed as *"I don't know"*, which in three-valued logic would be expressed as UNKNOWN. However, the observer's guess about whether the next n outcomes will all be *heads*, when n is infinite, should intuitively be expressed as FALSE, because the likelihood that an infinite series of outcomes will only produce *heads* becomes infinitesimally small.

In subjective logic, this paradox is easily solved when multiplying a series of vacuous opinions. The product of an arbitrarily long series of vacuous binomial opinions would still be vacuous, but the projected probability would be close to zero because the product base rate shrinks to zero. This result is illustrated with an example below.

Figure 5.2 is a screenshot of the online demonstrator for SL operators. The example shows the product resulting from multiplying the two vacuous binomial opinions $\omega_x = (0, 0, 1, \frac{1}{2})$ and $\omega_y = (0, 0, 1, \frac{1}{2})$.

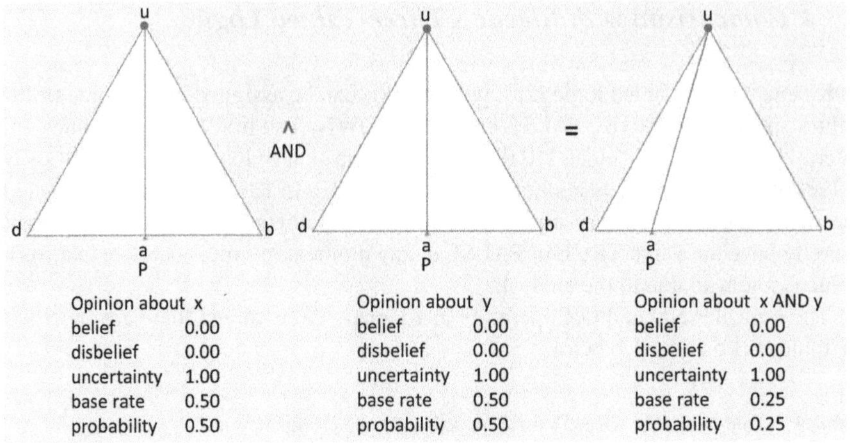

Fig. 5.2 Example multiplication of two vacuous opinions

The method of multiplying two binomial opinions is described in Section 7.1 below, but this trivial example can be directly understood from Figure 5.2.

The product opinion $\omega_{x\wedge y} = (0, 0, 1, \frac{1}{4})$ is still vacuous, but the projected product probability is $\mathrm{P}(x \wedge y) = \frac{1}{4}$. In case the product has n factors that are all the same vacuous opinions, then the product has a projected probability $\mathrm{P}(x \wedge y \wedge \ldots z) = (\frac{1}{2})^n$ which quickly converges towards zero, as would be expected.

At first glance Kleene's three-valued logic might seem to represent a special case of subjective logic. However, as the example above illustrates, applying the truth tables of Kleene's logic to practical situations leads to counter-intuitive results. The corresponding results under subjective logic correspond well with intuition.

5.2 Subjective Logic as a Generalisation of Probabilistic Logic

We define probabilistic logic (PL) as a set of logic operators generalised as probabilistic formulas e.g. as expressed in Table 1.1. PL operators generalise the traditional binary logic (BL) operators AND, OR, XOR, MP etc., in the sense that when the probability arguments are 0 or 1 (equivalent to Boolean FALSE or TRUE), the PL operators correctly populate the traditional truth tables of the corresponding BL operators. It means that PL operators are homomorphic to the truth tables of BL in case probability arguments are 0 or 1, and are generalisations in other cases.

Similarly, subjective logic generalises PL operators in the sense that when opinion arguments are dogmatic (equivalent to probabilities), then they produce dogmatic opinions equivalent to probabilities produced by the corresponding PL operators. This means that SL operators are homomorphic to PL operators in case opinion arguments are dogmatic, and are generalisations in other cases.

In the case of absolute opinion arguments (equivalent to Boolean TRUE or FALSE), SL operators are homomorphic to BL truth tables. The generalisations and homomorphisms are illustrated in Figure 5.3.

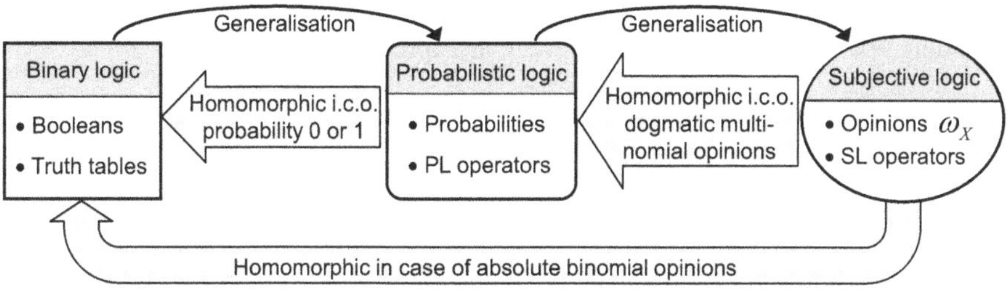

Fig. 5.3 Generalisations and homomorphisms between SL, PL and BL

A *homomorphism* from an algebra denoted [domain A, set of A-operators] to an algebra denoted [domain B, set of B-operators] exists when their respective operator sets e.g. denoted $(\overset{\mathrm{A}}{+}, \overset{\mathrm{A}}{\times}, \ldots)$ and $(\overset{\mathrm{B}}{+}, \overset{\mathrm{B}}{\times}, \ldots)$ satisfy the following properties under the mapping F from variables $x, y, \ldots \in \mathrm{A}$ to variables $F(x), F(y), \ldots \in \mathrm{B}$:

$$\text{Homomorphism:} \quad \begin{cases} F(x \overset{\mathrm{A}}{+} y) = F(x) \overset{\mathrm{B}}{+} F(y), \\ F(x \overset{\mathrm{A}}{\times} y) = F(x) \overset{\mathrm{B}}{\times} F(y). \end{cases} \tag{5.5}$$

Given a homomorphism, we say e.g. that operator $\overset{\mathrm{A}}{+}$ is *homomorphic* to $\overset{\mathrm{B}}{+}$. For example, multiplication of binomial opinions is homomorphic to multiplication of binomial probabilities which in turn is homomorphic to binary logic AND.

An *isomorphism* between an algebra denoted [domain A, set of A-operators] and an algebra denoted [domain B, set of B-operators] exists when in addition to Eq.(5.5) the mapping F is bijective so that the following holds:

$$\text{Isomorphism:} \quad \begin{cases} F^{-1}(F(x) \overset{\mathrm{B}}{+} F(y)) = x \overset{\mathrm{A}}{+} y, \\ F^{-1}(F(x) \overset{\mathrm{B}}{\times} F(y)) = x \overset{\mathrm{A}}{\times} y. \end{cases} \tag{5.6}$$

Given an isomorphism, we say e.g. that operators $\overset{\mathrm{A}}{+}$ and $\overset{\mathrm{B}}{+}$ are *isomorphic*. For example, multiplication with integers and multiplication with Roman numerals are isomorphic, although obviously multiplication with integers is simpler to compute. In case two values are represented in Roman numerals, and we need to compute their product, it is simplest to first map the Roman numerals to integers, do the multiplication and finally map the product back to a Roman numeral.

Subjective logic isomorphisms, illustrated in Figure 5.4, allow effective usage of operators from both the Dirichlet and the belief models.

Different expressions that traditionally are equivalent in binary logic are not necessarily equal in subjective logic. Take for example distributivity of AND over OR:

$$x \wedge (y \vee z) \;\Leftrightarrow\; (x \wedge y) \vee (x \wedge z)\,. \tag{5.7}$$

This equivalence only holds for binary logic, not for subjective logic. The corresponding opinions are in general different, as expressed by Eq.(5.8):

$$\omega_{x\wedge(y\vee z)} \;\neq\; \omega_{(x\wedge y)\vee(x\wedge z)}\,. \tag{5.8}$$

This is no surprise, as the corresponding PL operator for multiplication is also non-distributive over comultiplication, as expressed by Eq.(5.9):

$$p(x)\,(p(y) \sqcup p(z)) \;\neq\; (p(x)\,p(y)) \sqcup (p(x)\,p(z))\,. \tag{5.9}$$

The symbol $\sqcup$ denotes coproduct of independent probabilities, defined as

$$p(x) \sqcup p(y) = (p(x)\,p(y)) - p(x) - p(y)\,. \tag{5.10}$$

Coproduct of probabilities generalises binary logic OR. This means that Eq.(5.10) generates the traditional truth table for binary logic OR when the input probability arguments are either 0 (FALSE) or 1 (TRUE).

Multiplication is distributive over addition in subjective logic, as expressed by

$$\omega_{x\wedge(y\cup z)} = \omega_{(x\wedge y)\cup(x\wedge z)}\,. \tag{5.11}$$

De Morgan's laws are also satisfied in subjective logic as e.g. expressed by:

$$\begin{aligned} &\text{De Morgan 1:} \quad \omega_{\overline{x\wedge y}} = \omega_{\bar{x}\vee\bar{y}}\,, \\ &\text{De Morgan 2:} \quad \omega_{\overline{x\vee y}} = \omega_{\bar{x}\wedge\bar{y}}\,. \end{aligned} \tag{5.12}$$

Note also that Definition 6.3 of complement gives the following equalities:

$$\begin{aligned} \omega_{\overline{x\wedge y}} &= \neg\omega_{x\wedge y}\,, \\ \omega_{\overline{x\vee y}} &= \neg\omega_{x\vee y}\,. \end{aligned} \tag{5.13}$$

Subjective logic provides a rich set of operators, whose input and output arguments are in the form of subjective opinions. Opinions can be applied to domains of any cardinality, but some SL operators are only defined for binomial opinions and not for multinomial opinions, or are defined for binomial and multinomial opinions, but not for hyper-opinions. Opinion operators can be expressed for the belief notation (i.e. traditional opinion notation), for the evidence notation (i.e. as Dirichlet PDFs), or for the probabilistic notation (as defined in Section 3.7.1). We only express SL operators for the belief notation, because it normally produces the simplest and most compact expressions. However, it can be practical to use other notations in specific cases.

Table 5.2 provides equivalent values and interpretations in belief notation, evidence notation and probabilistic notation, as well as their interpretation, for a selection of binomial opinions.

Table 5.2 Examples of equivalent notations for binomial opinions, and their interpretations

Belief notation (b,d,u,a)	Evidence notation (r,s,a)	Probabilistic notation (P,u,a)	Interpretations as binomial opinion, Beta PDF and projected probability
$(1,0,0,a)$	$(\infty,0,a)$	$(1,0,a)$	Absolute positive binomial opinion (Boolean TRUE), Dirac delta function, projected probability $\mathrm{P}=1$
$(0,1,0,a)$	$(0,\infty,a)$	$(0,0,a)$	Absolute negative binomial opinion (Boolean FALSE), Dirac delta function, probability $\mathrm{P}=0$
$(\frac{1}{2},\frac{1}{2},0,a)$	(∞,∞,a)	$(\frac{1}{2},0,a)$	Dogmatic binomial opinion denoted $\underline{\omega}$, Dirac delta function, projected probability $\mathrm{P}=\frac{1}{2}$
$(\frac{1}{4},\frac{1}{4},\frac{1}{2},\frac{1}{2})$	$(1,1,\frac{1}{2})$	$(\frac{1}{2},\frac{1}{2},\frac{1}{2})$	Uncertain binomial opinion, symmetric Beta PDF of one positive and one negative observation, projected probability $\mathrm{P}=\frac{1}{2}$
$(0,0,1,a)$	$(0,0,a)$	$(a,1,a)$	Vacuous binomial opinion denoted $\widehat{\omega}$, prior Beta PDF with base rate a, projected probability $\mathrm{P}=a$
$(0,0,1,\frac{1}{2})$	$(0,0,\frac{1}{2})$	$(\frac{1}{2},1,\frac{1}{2})$	Vacuous binomial opinion denoted $\widehat{\omega}$, uniform Beta PDF, projected probability $\mathrm{P}=\frac{1}{2}$

The various example binomial opinions in Table 5.2 correspond to Booleans, probabilities and Beta PDFs. (Interested readers might want to try the visualisation demonstrator for binomial opinions at `http://folk.uio.no/josang/sl/`.) Hyper-opinions, the most general subjective opinions, correspond to hyper-Dirichlet PDFs. The ability to represent such a wide range of different argument types demonstrates the richness of expression offered by the opinion representation. The ability to use the same range of argument types as input to analytical models demonstrates the flexibility of subjective logic as a general reasoning framework.

Mathematically complex Bayesian computations are efficiently done in subjective logic. However, this efficiency comes at the cost of approximating the variance of products and coproducts. For example, a binomial product of two Beta PDFs in the form of a joint PDF might be tractable in pure Bayesian analysis, but anything more complex soon becomes intractable. The analytically correct binomial product of two Beta PDFs in the formalism of traditional Bayesian analysis is in general not a Beta PDF, and usually involves hypergeometric series. However, subjective logic approximates the product as a binomial opinion that is equivalent to a Beta PDF.

5.3 Overview of Subjective-Logic Operators

Table 5.3 Correspondence between SL operators, binary logic / set operators and SL notation

SL operator (page)	Symbol	BL / set operator	Symbol	SL notation
Addition (p.95)	$+$	Union	$\cup$	$\omega_{x\cup y} = \omega_x + \omega_y$
Subtraction (p.97)	$-$	Difference	$\setminus$	$\omega_{x\setminus y} = \omega_x - \omega_y$
Complement (p.99)	$\neg$	NOT (Negation)	$\overline{x}$	$\omega_{\overline{x}} = \neg\omega_x$
Multiplication (p.102)	$\cdot$	AND (Conjunction)	$\wedge$	$\omega_{x\wedge y} = \omega_x \cdot \omega_y$
Comultiplication (p.103)	$\sqcup$	OR (Disjunction)	$\vee$	$\omega_{x\vee y} = \omega_x \sqcup \omega_y$
Division (p.110)	$/$	UN-AND (Unconjunct.)	$\widetilde{\wedge}$	$\omega_{x\widetilde{\wedge}y} = \omega_x / \omega_y$
Codivision (p.112)	$\widetilde{\sqcup}$	UN-OR (Undisjunction)	$\widetilde{\vee}$	$\omega_{x\widetilde{\vee}y} = \omega_x \,\widetilde{\sqcup}\, \omega_y$
Multinomial product (p.118)	$\cdot$	Cartesian product	$\times$	$\omega_{XY} = \omega_X \cdot \omega_Y$
Deduction (p.133)	$\circledcirc$	MP (Modus Ponens)	$\Vert$	$\omega_{Y\Vert X} = \omega_X \circledcirc \boldsymbol{\omega}_{Y\vert X}$
Abduction (p.171)	$\widetilde{\circledcirc}$	MT (Modus Tollens)	$\widetilde{\Vert}$	$\omega_{X\widetilde{\Vert}Y} = \omega_Y \widetilde{\circledcirc}(\boldsymbol{\omega}_{Y\vert X}, \boldsymbol{a}_X)$
Bayes' theorem (p.187)	$\widetilde{\phi}$	CP (contraposition)	$\widetilde{\vert}$	$\boldsymbol{\omega}_{X\widetilde{\vert}Y} = \widetilde{\phi}(\boldsymbol{\omega}_{Y\vert X}, \boldsymbol{a}_X)$
Joint opinions (p.199)	$\cdot$	Cartesian product	$\times$	$\omega_{YX} = \boldsymbol{\omega}_{Y\vert X} \cdot \omega_X$
Constraint fusion (p.215)	$\odot$	n.a.	$\&$	$\omega_X^{A\&B} = \omega_X^A \odot \omega_X^B$
Cumulative Fusion (p.225)	$\oplus$	n.a.	$\diamond$	$\omega_X^{A\diamond B} = \omega_X^A \oplus \omega_X^B$
Averaging fusion (p.229)	$\underline{\oplus}$	n.a.	$\underline{\diamond}$	$\omega_X^{A\underline{\diamond}B} = \omega_X^A \,\underline{\oplus}\, \omega_X^B$
Weighted fusion (p.231)	$\widehat{\oplus}$	n.a.	$\widehat{\diamond}$	$\omega_X^{A\widehat{\diamond}B} = \omega_X^A \widehat{\oplus} \omega_X^B$
CC-fusion (p.233)	ⓒⓒ	n.a.	$\heartsuit$	$\omega_X^{A\heartsuit B} = \omega_X^A$ ⓒⓒ ω_X^B
Unfusion (p.238)	$\ominus$	n.a.	$\overline{\diamond}$	$\omega_X^{A\overline{\diamond}B} = \omega_X^A \ominus \omega_X^B$
Trust discounting (p.254)	$\otimes$	Trust transitivity	$:$	$\omega_X^{[A;B]} = \omega_B^A \otimes \omega_X^B$

Most of the operators in Table 5.3 correspond to well-known operators from binary logic and probability calculus, while others are specific to subjective logic.

The correspondence between SL operators and traditional operators of BL (binary logic) means that they are related through homomorphisms. The homomorphisms of Figure 5.3 can be illustrated with concrete examples.

Assume two independent binomial opinions ω_x and ω_y. Let $\mathrm{P}(\omega_x)$ denote the projected probability of ω_x, which then is the probability of x. Similarly, the expressions $\mathrm{P}(\omega_y)$ and $\mathrm{P}(\omega_{x\wedge y})$ represent the probabilities of y and $(x \wedge y)$ respectively. The homomorphism from SL to PL illustrated in Figure 5.3 means for example that

$$\text{In case of dogmatic opinions:} \quad \mathrm{P}(\omega_{x\wedge y}) = \mathrm{P}(\omega_x) \cdot \mathrm{P}(\omega_y)\ . \tag{5.14}$$

The homomorphism of Eq.(5.14) is of course also valid in case ω_x and ω_y are absolute opinions.

Assume now two absolute binomial opinions ω_x and ω_y, and let $\mathrm{B}(\omega_x)$ denote the Boolean value of x. Similarly, the expressions $\mathrm{B}(\omega_y)$ and $\mathrm{B}(\omega_{x\wedge y})$ represent the Boolean values of y and $(x \wedge y)$ respectively. The homomorphism from SL to BL illustrated in Figure 5.3 means for example that

$$\text{In case of absolute opinions:} \quad \mathrm{B}(\omega_{x\wedge y}) = \mathrm{B}(\omega_x) \wedge \mathrm{B}(\omega_y)\ . \tag{5.15}$$

In the special case of absolute binomial opinions and with the homomorphisms of Eq.(5.15), distributivity of product over coproduct of opinions holds, in contrast to the general case of Eq.(5.8). This leads to the equality of Eq.(5.16):

$$\text{In the case of absolute opinions:} \quad \mathrm{B}(\omega_{x\wedge(y\vee z)}) \;=\; \mathrm{B}(\omega_{(x\wedge y)\vee(x\wedge z)})\ . \tag{5.16}$$

Recall from Eq.(3.42) the probabilistic notation of binomial opinions:

$$\text{Probabilistic notation:} \quad \pi_x = (\mathrm{P}(x), u_x, a_x), \quad \text{where:} \begin{cases} \mathrm{P}(x): \ \text{probability of } x, \\ u_x: \ \text{uncertainty}, \\ a_x: \ \text{base rate of } x. \end{cases} \tag{5.17}$$

Binary logic AND corresponds to multiplication of opinions [51]. For example, given the pair of probabilistic binomial opinions on the values $x \in \mathbb{X}$ and $y \in \mathbb{Y}$

$$\begin{cases} \pi_x = (1,0,a_x) \\ \pi_y = (0,0,a_y) \end{cases} \quad \text{with respective corresponding Booleans:} \quad \begin{cases} \text{TRUE} \\ \text{FALSE} \end{cases} \tag{5.18}$$

$$\begin{array}{lcccc} \text{Their product is} & \pi_{x\wedge y} & = & \pi_x & \cdot & \pi_y \\ \text{expressed with numerical values} & (0,0,a_x a_y) & = & (1,0,a_x) & \cdot & (0,0,a_y) \\ \text{which corresponds to} & \text{FALSE} & = & \text{TRUE} & \wedge & \text{FALSE}\ . \end{array} \tag{5.19}$$

It is interesting to note that subjective logic represents a calculus for Dirichlet PDFs, because opinions are equivalent to Dirichlet PDFs. In general, analytical manipulation of Dirichlet PDF is complex, and can only be done for simple operations such as joint distribution. However, following a pure analytical method quickly becomes unmanageable when applied to the more complex operators of Table 5.3, such as conditional deduction and abduction. Subjective logic therefore has the advantage of providing advanced operators for Dirichlet PDFs, for which no practical analytical solutions previously existed. It should be mentioned that the simplicity of some SL operators comes at the cost of allowing those operators to be approximations of the analytically correct operators. This is discussed in more detail in Section 7.1.

Subjective opinions can have multiple equivalent representations, as described in Section 3.7. It naturally follows that each SL operator can be expressed for the various opinion representations. Since the different representations of opinions are equivalent, the different expressions of the same operator are isomorphic to each other, as illustrated in Figure 5.4.

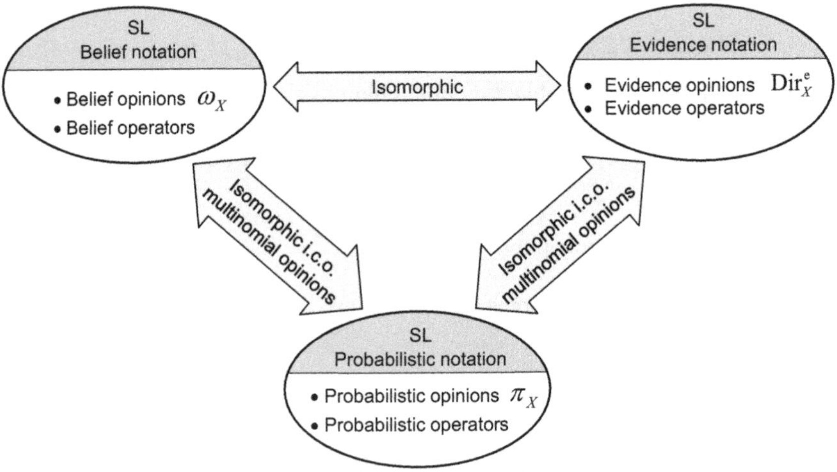

Fig. 5.4 Isomorphisms between the SL operators for different opinion representations

The fact that subjective opinions can be expressed based on the belief notation, the evidence notation or the probabilistic notation also means that SL operators can be expressed in these different notations. Since the different representations of a subjective opinion are equivalent, the operators are isomorphic, as illustrated in Figure 5.4. Throughout this book opinions and operators are generally expressed in the belief notation, because it gives the simplest and most compact expressions.

The next chapters describe the operators listed in Table 5.3. Online demonstrations of some of the subjective-logic operators can be accessed at `http://folk.uio.no/josang/sl/`.

Chapter 6
Addition, Subtraction and Complement

This chapter describes addition, subtraction and complement of subjective opinions, as a generalisation of the corresponding operators for probabilities.

6.1 Addition

Addition of opinions in subjective logic is a binary operator that takes opinions about two mutually exclusive values (i.e. two disjoint subsets of the same domain) as arguments, and outputs an opinion about the union of the values [72]. Consider for example the domain $\mathbb{X} = \{x_1, x_2, x_3\}$ illustrated in Figure 6.1, with the assumed union of x_1 and x_2.

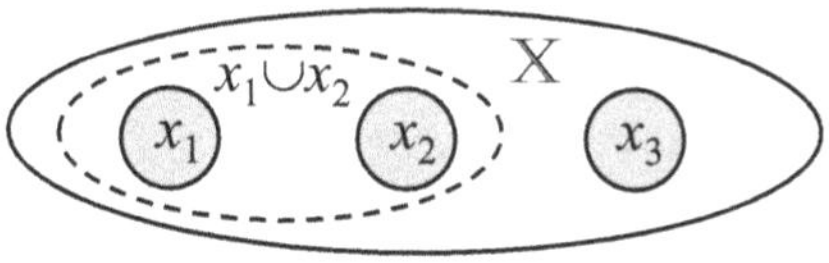

Fig. 6.1 Union of values, corresponding to addition of opinions

Assume that the binomial opinions ω_{x_1} and ω_{x_2} apply to x_1 and x_2 respectively. The addition of ω_{x_1} and ω_{x_2} then consists of computing the opinion about $x_1 \cup x_2$ as a function of the two former opinions. The operator for addition first described in [72] is defined below.

Definition 6.1 (Addition). Assume a domain $\mathbb{X}$ where x_1 and x_2 are two singleton values, or alternatively two disjoint subsets, i.e. $x_1 \cap x_2 = \emptyset$. We require that the two values x_1 and x_2 together do not represent a complete partition of $\mathbb{X}$, in other words we require $x_1 \cup x_2 \subset \mathbb{X}$.

Let $\omega_{x_1} = (b_{x_1}, d_{x_1}, u_{x_1}, a_{x_1})$ and $\omega_{x_2} = (b_{x_2}, d_{x_2}, u_{x_2}, a_{x_2})$ be two binomial opinions that respectively apply to x_1 and x_2. The opinion about $x_1 \cup x_2$ as a function of the opinions about x_1 and x_2 is defined as:

$$\text{Opinion sum} \quad \omega_{(x_1 \cup x_2)}: \begin{cases} b_{(x_1 \cup x_2)} = b_{x_1} + b_{x_2}, \\ d_{(x_1 \cup x_2)} = \dfrac{a_{x_1}(d_{x_1} - b_{x_2}) + a_{x_2}(d_{x_2} - b_{x_1})}{a_{x_1} + a_{x_2}}, \\ u_{(x_1 \cup x_2)} = \dfrac{a_{x_1} u_{x_1} + a_{x_2} u_{x_2}}{a_{x_1} + a_{x_2}}, \\ a_{(x_1 \cup x_2)} = a_{x_1} + a_{x_2}. \end{cases} \tag{6.1}$$

By using the symbol '+' to denote the addition operator for opinions, addition can be expressed as $\omega_{(x_1 \cup x_2)} = \omega_{x_1} + \omega_{x_2}$. □

It can be verified that the addition operator preserves the addition of projected probabilities, as expressed by Eq.(6.2):

$$\text{Addition of projected probabilities:} \quad \mathrm{P}(x_1 \cup x_2) = \mathrm{P}(x_1) + \mathrm{P}(x_2)\,. \tag{6.2}$$

Figure 6.2 is a screenshot of the online demonstrator for SL operators. The example shows addition of the two binomial opinions $\omega_{x_1} = (0.20, 0.40, 0.40, 0.25)$ and $\omega_{x_2} = (0.10, 0.50, 0.40, 0.50)$.

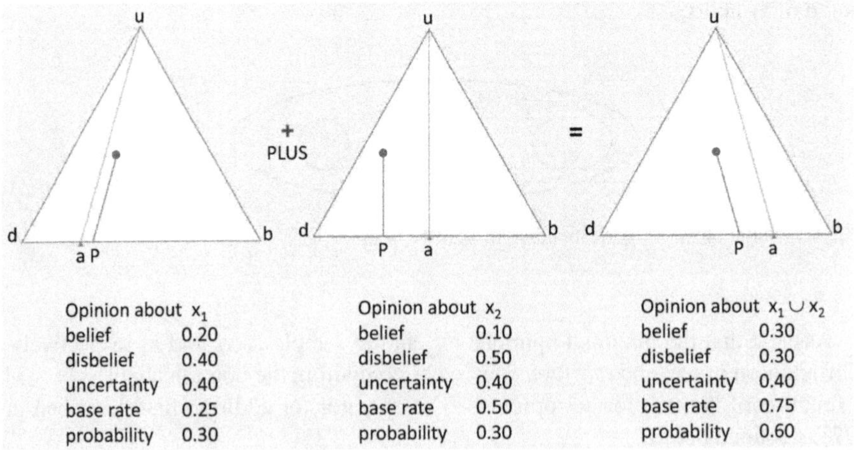

Fig. 6.2 Example addition of two binomial opinions

The sum is simply $\omega_{(x_1 \cup x_2)} = (0.30, 0.30, 0.40, 0.75)$, and it can be verified that $\mathrm{P}(x_1 \cup x_2) = 0.30 + 0.30 = 0.60$.

Opinion addition generates vague belief mass $b_{(x_1 \cup x_2)}$ from the sharp belief masses b_{x_1} and b_{x_2}. Opinion addition might therefore not be as useful as one might intuitively assume. Also, opinion addition does not apply to the case when $\mathbb{X} = (x_1 \cup x_2)$, because the resulting belief mass would be totally vague, so the opinion should be considered vacuous.

The cumulative fusion operator described in Chapter 12 might seem to be related to the addition operator, but these two operators have different interpretations and purposes, so they should not be confused. The cumulative fusion operator is based on addition of evidence in the evidence space, whereas the addition operator is based on addition of belief mass in the belief space. Cumulative fusion does not produce any vagueness when applied to binomial or multinomial opinions, it only accumulates vague evidence when applied to hyper-opinions.

6.2 Subtraction

The inverse operation to opinion addition is opinion subtraction [72]. Since addition of opinions yields the opinion about $x_1 \cup x_2$ from the opinions about disjoint subsets of the domain, then the difference between the opinions about $x_1 \cup x_2$ and x_2 (i.e. the opinion about $(x_1 \cup x_2) \backslash x_2$) can only be defined if $x_2 \subseteq (x_1 \cup x_2)$ where x_2 and $(x_1 \cup x_2)$ are subsets of the domain $\mathbb{X}$, i.e. the system must be in the state $(x_1 \cup x_2)$ whenever it is in the state x_2. The operator for subtraction first described in [72] is defined below:

Definition 6.2 (Subtraction). Let $(x_1 \cup x_2)$ and x_2 be subsets of the same domain $\mathbb{X}$ where $(x_1 \cup x_2) \cap x_2 = x_2$. The opinion about $(x_1 \cup x_2) \backslash x_2$ as a function of the opinions about $(x_1 \cup x_2)$ and x_2 is expressed below.

$$\omega_{((x_1 \cup x_2)\backslash x_2)} : \begin{cases} b_{((x_1 \cup x_2)\backslash x_2)} = b_{(x_1 \cup x_2)} - b_{x_2}, \\[2ex] d_{((x_1 \cup x_2)\backslash x_2)} = \dfrac{a_{(x_1 \cup x_2)}(d_{(x_1 \cup x_2)} + b_{x_2}) - a_{x_2}(1 + b_{x_2} - b_{(x_1 \cup x_2)} - u_{x_2})}{a_{(x_1 \cup x_2)} - a_{x_2}}, \\[2ex] u_{((x_1 \cup x_2)\backslash x_2)} = \dfrac{a_{(x_1 \cup x_2)} u_{(x_1 \cup x_2)} - a_{x_2} u_{x_2}}{a_{(x_1 \cup x_2)} - a_{x_2}}, \\[2ex] a_{((x_1 \cup x_2)\backslash x_2)} = a_{(x_1 \cup x_2)} - a_{x_2}. \end{cases} \tag{6.3}$$

Since both $u_{((x_1 \cup x_2)\backslash x_2)}$ and $d_{((x_1 \cup x_2)\backslash x_2)}$ should be non-negative, the following constraints apply:

$$\begin{cases} (u_{((x_1 \cup x_2)\backslash x_2)} \geq 0) \Rightarrow (a_{x_2} u_{x_2} \leq a_{(x_1 \cup x_2)} u_{(x_1 \cup x_2)}), \\ (d_{((x_1 \cup x_2)\backslash x_2)} \geq 0) \Rightarrow (a_{(x_1 \cup x_2)}(d_{(x_1 \cup x_2)} + b_{x_2}) \geq a_{x_2}(1 + b_{x_2} - b_{(x_1 \cup x_2)} - u_{x_2})). \end{cases} \quad (6.4)$$

By using the symbol '$-$' to denote the subtraction operator for opinions, subtraction can be denoted $\omega_{((x_1 \cup x_2)\backslash x_2)} = \omega_{(x_1 \cup x_2)} - \omega_{x_2}$. □

Given the structure of the example domain $\mathbb{X}$ in Figure 6.1, it is obvious that $\omega_{((x_1 \cup x_2)\backslash x_2)} = \omega_{x_1}$.

The subtraction operator reduces vagueness, and removes vagueness completely if $((x_1 \cup x_2)\backslash x_2)$ is a singleton. Subtraction of opinions is consistent with subtraction of probabilities, as expressed by Eq.(6.5):

$$\text{Subtraction of projected probabilities:} \quad \mathrm{P}(x_1) = \mathrm{P}(x_1 \cup x_2) - \mathrm{P}(x_2). \quad (6.5)$$

Figure 6.3 is a screenshot of the online demonstrator for SL operators. The example shows subtraction from the binomial opinion $\omega_{(x_1 \cup x_2)} = (0.70, 0.10, 0.20, 0.75)$ of the binomial opinion $\omega_{x_2} = (0.50, 0.30, 0.20, 0.25)$.

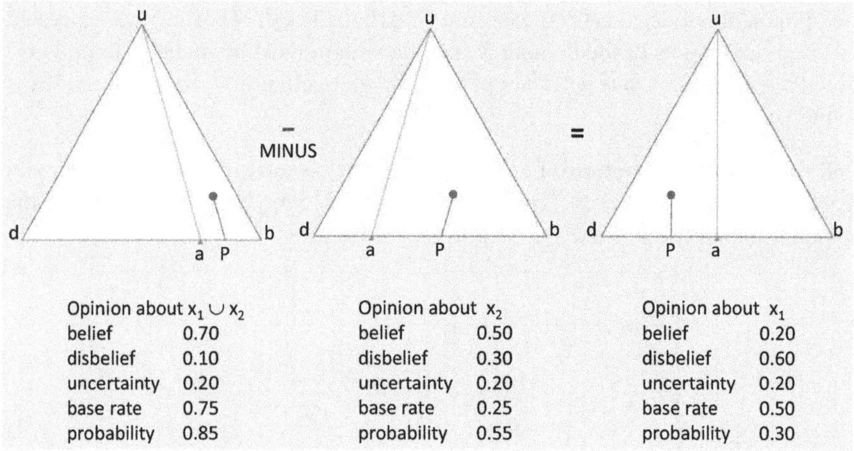

Fig. 6.3 Example subtraction between two binomial opinions

The difference is simply $\omega_{x_1} = (0.20, 0.60, 0.20, 0.50)$, and it can be verified that $\mathrm{P}((x_1 \cup x_2) \setminus x_2) = \mathrm{P}(x_1) = 0.85 - 0.55 = 0.30$.

6.3 Complement

A binomial opinion focuses on a single value x in a binary domain $\mathbb{X} = \{x, \overline{x}\}$, or on a subset x as one of the two halves in a binary partition of a multinomial domain $\mathbb{X}$. The complement of this opinion is simply the opinion about the complement value $\overline{x}$. This is illustrated in Figure 6.4.

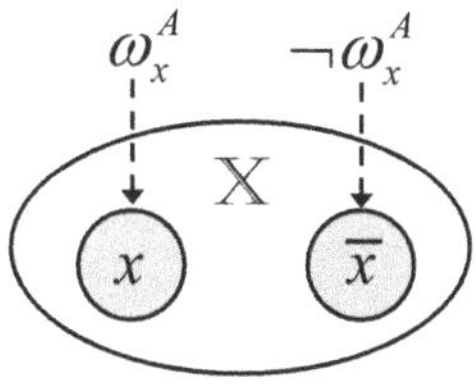

Fig. 6.4 Complement of binomial opinion

Definition 6.3 (Complement). Assume the domain $\mathbb{X} = \{x, \overline{x}\}$ which can be assumed to be binary or to be a binary partition of two subsets, where $\omega_x = (b_x, d_x, u_x, a_x)$ is a binomial opinion about x. Its complement is the binomial opinion $\omega_{\overline{x}}$ expressed as

$$\text{Complement opinion } \omega_{\overline{x}} : \begin{cases} b_{\overline{x}} = d_x, \\ d_{\overline{x}} = b_x, \\ u_{\overline{x}} = u_x, \\ a_{\overline{x}} = 1 - a_x. \end{cases} \tag{6.6}$$

The complement operator denoted '¬' is a unary operator. Applying the complement operator to a binomial opinion is expressed as

$$\neg\omega_x = \omega_{\overline{x}} \, . \tag{6.7}$$

□

The complement operator corresponds to binary logic NOT, and to complement of probabilities. For projected probabilities it can be verified that

$$\mathrm{P}(\neg\omega_x) = 1 - \mathrm{P}(\omega_x) \, . \tag{6.8}$$

Figure 6.5 is a screenshot of the online demonstrator for binomial SL operators, showing the complement of the binomial opinion $\omega_x = (0.50, 0.10, 0.40, 0.25)$.

The complement opinion is simply $\omega_{\overline{x}} = (0.10, 0.50, 0.40, 0.75)$, and it can be verified that $\mathrm{P}(\overline{x}) = 1 - \mathrm{P}(x) = 1.00 - 0.60 = 0.40$.

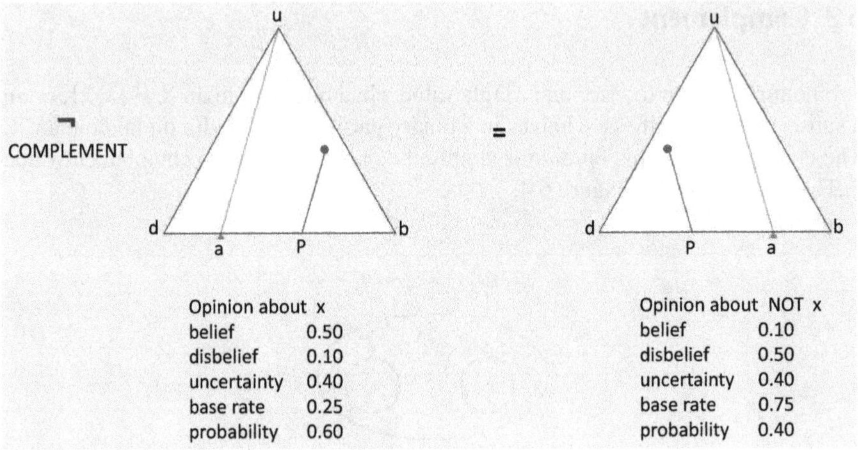

Fig. 6.5 Example complement of binomial opinion

Chapter 7
Binomial Multiplication and Division

This chapter describes the binomial SL operators 'multiplication' and 'comultiplication' [51] that correspond to binary logic AND and OR, as well as their inverse operators 'division' and 'codivision' that correspond to binary logic UN-AND and UN-OR. The operators described here assume independent argument opinions. Conditional multiplication of dependent opinions is described in Section 11.2.

7.1 Binomial Multiplication and Comultiplication

Binomial multiplication and comultiplication in subjective logic take binomial opinions about two values from distinct binary domains as input arguments and produce a binomial opinion as result. The resulting product and coproduct opinions relate to subsets of the Cartesian product of the two binary domains. The Cartesian product of the two binary domains $\mathbb{X} = \{x, \overline{x}\}$ and $\mathbb{Y} = \{y, \overline{y}\}$ produces the quaternary set $\mathbb{X} \times \mathbb{Y} = \{(xy), (x\overline{y}), (\overline{x}y), (\overline{x}\overline{y})\}$ which is illustrated in Figure 7.1 below.

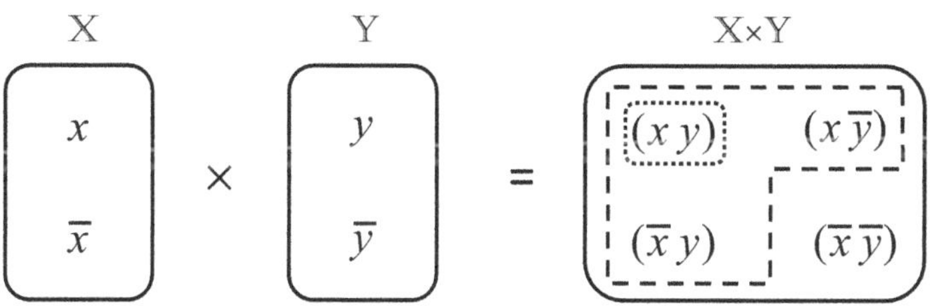

Fig. 7.1 Cartesian product of two binary domains

Theoretically it is possible to compute products of Beta PDFs and Dirichlet PDFs, although closed expressions for the general case might be practically intractable. When assuming that such product PDFs exist, one would expect them to be equivalent to products of opinions in subjective logic. However, in general, products of opinions in subjective logic represent approximations of the analytically correct products of Beta PDFs. The approximation only applies to the variance of the products. The projected probability of the product of binomial opinions is always equal to the corresponding expected probability of the product of Beta PDFs.

The same can be said for coproducts, quotients and co-quotients. There is hardly any work on deriving these results for Beta PDFs in the literature, so subjective logic currently offers the most practical operators for computing products, coproducts, quotients and co-quotients of Beta PDFs.

7.1.1 Binomial Multiplication

Let ω_x and ω_y be opinions about x and y respectively held by the same analyst. Then the product opinion $\omega_{x\wedge y}$ is the analyst's opinion about the conjunction $x \wedge y = \{(xy)\}$ that is represented by the area enclosed by the dotted line in Figure 7.1. The coproduct opinion $\omega_{x\vee y}$ is the opinion about the disjunction $x \vee y = \{(xy),\ (x\bar{y}),\ (\bar{x}y)\}$ that is represented by the area enclosed by the dashed line in Figure 7.1. Obviously $\mathbb{X}\times\mathbb{Y}$ is not binary, and hence coarsening is required in order to determine the product and coproduct opinions as binomial opinions.

Definition 7.1 (Binomial Multiplication). Let $\mathbb{X} = \{x,\bar{x}\}$ and $\mathbb{Y} = \{y,\bar{y}\}$ be two separate domains, and let $\omega_x = (b_x, d_x, u_x, a_x)$ and $\omega_x = (b_y, d_y, u_y, a_y)$ be independent binomial opinions on x and y respectively. Given opinions about independent propositions x and y, the binomial opinion $\omega_{x\wedge y}$ on the conjunction $(x \wedge y)$ is

$$\text{Product } \omega_{x\wedge y}: \begin{cases} b_{x\wedge y} = b_x b_y + \frac{(1-a_x)a_y b_x u_y + a_x(1-a_y)u_x b_y}{1-a_x a_y}, \\ \\ d_{x\wedge y} = d_x + d_y - d_x d_y, \\ \\ u_{x\wedge y} = u_x u_y + \frac{(1-a_y)b_x u_y + (1-a_x)u_x b_y}{1-a_x a_y}, \\ \\ a_{x\wedge y} = a_x a_y. \end{cases} \tag{7.1}$$

By using the symbol '$\cdot$' to denote this operator, multiplication of opinions can be written as $\omega_{x\wedge y} = \omega_x \cdot \omega_y$. □

Figure 7.2 is a screenshot of the online demonstrator for SL operators. The example shows multiplication of the two binomial opinions specified as $\omega_x = (0.75, 0.15, 0.10, 0.50)$ and $\omega_y = (0.10, 0.00, 0.90, 0.20)$.

The product is $\omega_{(x\wedge y)} = (0.15, 0.15, 0.70, 0.10)$, and it can be verified that Eq.(7.2) holds for the product projected probability.

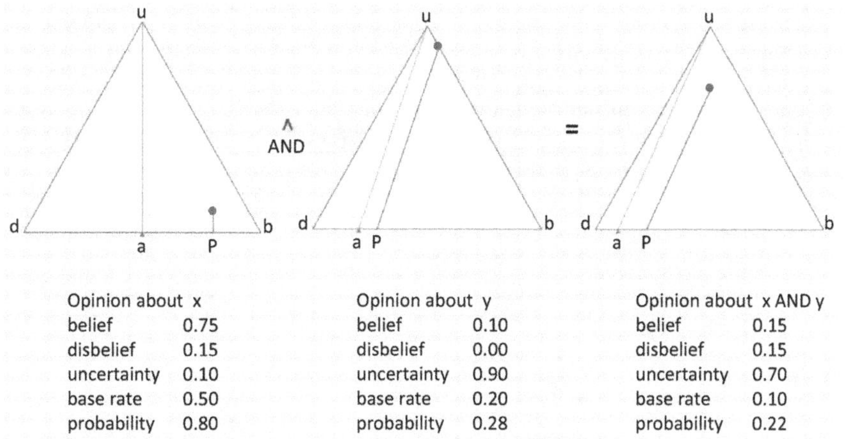

Fig. 7.2 Example multiplication of two binomial opinions

$$\begin{aligned} \mathrm{P}(x \wedge y) &= \mathrm{P}(x) \cdot \mathrm{P}(y) \\ &= 0.80 \cdot 0.28 = 0.22\,. \end{aligned} \tag{7.2}$$

Notice that ω_x has relatively low uncertainty, whereas ω_y has relatively high uncertainty. An interesting property of the multiplication operator, which can be seen in Figure 7.2, is that the product opinion has an uncertainty mass on a level between the uncertainty masses of the factor opinions.

7.1.2 Binomial Comultiplication

Comultiplication of binomial opinions is defined next.

Definition 7.2 (Binomial Comultiplication). Let $\mathbb{X} = \{x,\bar{x}\}$ and $\mathbb{Y} = \{y,\bar{y}\}$ be two separate domains, and let $\omega_x = (b_x, d_x, u_x, a_x)$ and $\omega_x = (b_y, d_y, u_y, a_y)$ be independent binomial opinions on x and y respectively. The binomial opinion $\omega_{x\vee y}$ on the disjunction $x \vee y$ is

$$\text{Coproduct } \omega_{x\vee y}: \begin{cases} b_{x\vee y} = b_x + b_y - b_x b_y\,, \\[2ex] d_{x\vee y} = d_x d_y + \frac{a_x(1-a_y)d_x u_y + (1-a_x)a_y u_x d_y}{a_x + a_y - a_x a_y}\,, \\[2ex] u_{x\vee y} = u_x u_y + \frac{a_y d_x u_y + a_x u_x d_y}{a_x + a_y - a_x a_y}\,, \\[2ex] a_{x\vee y} = a_x + a_y - a_x a_y\,. \end{cases} \tag{7.3}$$

By using the symbol '$\sqcup$' to denote this operator, comultiplication of opinions can be written as $\omega_{x\vee y} = \omega_x \sqcup \omega_y$. □

Figure 7.3 is a screenshot of the online demonstrator for SL operators. The example shows the coproduct of the two binomial opinions $\omega_x = (0.75, 0.15, 0.10, 0.50)$ and $\omega_y = (0.35, 0.00, 0.65, 0.20)$.

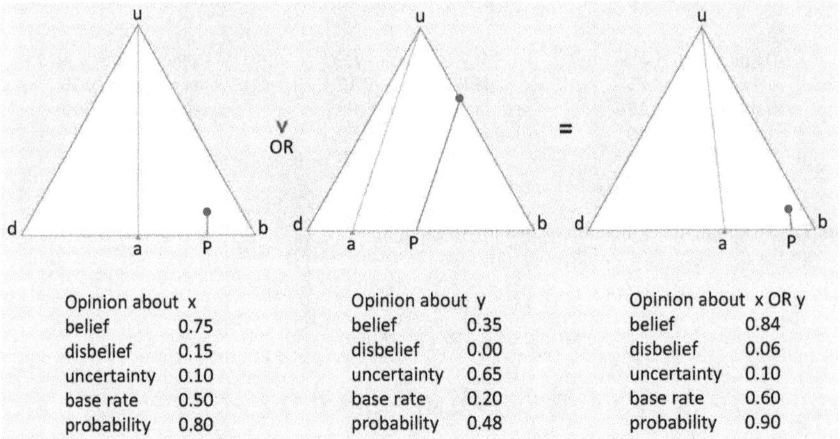

Fig. 7.3 Example comultiplication of two binomial opinions

The coproduct is $\omega_{(x\vee y)} = (0.84, 0.06, 0.10, 0.60)$, and it can be verified that Eq.(7.4) holds for the coproduct projected probability.

$$
\begin{aligned}
\mathrm{P}(x \vee y) &= \mathrm{P}(x) \sqcup \mathrm{P}(y) \\
&= \mathrm{P}(x) + \mathrm{P}(y) - (\mathrm{P}(x) \cdot \mathrm{P}(y)) \\
&= 0.80 + 0.48 - (0.80 \cdot 0.48) = 0.90.
\end{aligned}
\tag{7.4}
$$

Notice that ω_x has relatively low uncertainty whereas ω_y has relatively high uncertainty. Similarly to the case of multiplication above, it can be seen in Figure 7.3 that the coproduct opinion has an uncertainty mass on a level between the uncertainty masses of the factor opinions.

7.1.3 Approximations of Product and Coproduct

The expressions for product in Definition 7.1, and for coproduct in Definition 7.2, might appear ad hoc. However, there is a clear rationale behind their design.

The rationale is that the product and coproduct beliefs and disbeliefs must be at least as large as the raw products of belief and disbelief from the factor opinions; anything else would be irrational. If the product disbelief is $d_{x\wedge y} = d_x + d_y - d_x d_y$, and the coproduct belief is $b_{x\vee y} = b_x + b_y - b_x b_y$, then this requirement is satisfied. The product and coproduct beliefs and disbeliefs could of course be larger than that, but the larger they are, the smaller the uncertainty. The operators are so designed that the maximum uncertainty is preserved in the product and coproduct, which occurs when the disbelief of the product and the belief of the coproduct are exactly as they are defined.

The operators for multiplication and comultiplication are thus conservative, in the sense that they preserve the maximum uncertainty mass possible. The variance of the product and coproduct can easily be computed through Eq.(3.10), where the variance is a function of the uncertainty, as expressed in Eq.(7.5) and Eq.(7.6):

$$\text{Product variance: } \mathrm{Var}(x\wedge y) = \frac{\mathrm{P}(x\wedge y)\,(1-\mathrm{P}(x\wedge y))u_{x\wedge y}}{W + u_{x\wedge y}}, \tag{7.5}$$

$$\text{Coproduct variance: } \mathrm{Var}(x\vee y) = \frac{\mathrm{P}(x\vee y)\,(1-\mathrm{P}(x\vee y))u_{x\vee y}}{W + u_{x\vee y}}, \tag{7.6}$$

where W denotes the non-informative prior weight, which is normally set to $W = 2$. The non-informative prior weight is discussed in Section 3.4.2.

From Eq.(7.5) and Eq.(7.6) it can be seen that when the uncertainty is zero, the variance is also zero, which corresponds to a dogmatic opinion. The case in Eq.(7.5) where $\mathrm{P}(x\wedge y) = 1/2$ and $u_{x\wedge y} = 1$ is a vacuous opinion which corresponds to the uniform Beta PDF, with variance $1/12$. The similar case also exists for Eq.(7.6).

It is interesting to ask how well the level of uncertainty corresponds with the analytically 'correct' level of uncertainty, in the sense of how closely the variance of the product and coproduct follow the analytically correct variance of the product and coproduct.

Multiplication and comultiplication represent a self-dual system represented by $b \leftrightarrow d$, $u \leftrightarrow u$, $a \leftrightarrow (1-a)$, and $\wedge \leftrightarrow \vee$, that is, for example, the expressions for $b_{x\wedge y}$ and $d_{x\vee y}$ are dual to each other, and one determines the other by the correspondence, and similarly for the other expressions. This is equivalent to the observation that the opinions satisfy de Morgan's Laws, *i.e.* $\omega_{x\wedge y} = \omega_{\overline{\overline{x}\vee\overline{y}}}$ and $\omega_{x\vee y} = \omega_{\overline{\overline{x}\wedge\overline{y}}}$. However, it should be noted that multiplication and comultiplication are not distributive over each other, *i.e.* for example that

$$\omega_{x\wedge(y\vee z)} \neq \omega_{(x\wedge y)\vee(x\wedge z)}\ . \tag{7.7}$$

This is to be expected, because if x, y and z are independent, then $x\wedge y$ and $x\wedge z$ are not generally independent in probability calculus, so distributivity does not hold. In fact distributivity of conjunction over disjunction and vice versa only holds in binary logic.

Multiplication and comultiplication produce very good approximations of the analytically correct products and coproducts when the arguments are Beta probability density functions [51]. The difference between the subjective logic product and the analytically correct product of Beta density functions is best illustrated with the example of multiplying two equal vacuous binomial opinions $\omega = (0,0,1,\frac{1}{2})$, which are equivalent to the uniform Beta PDF expressed as $\text{Beta}(p_x,1,1)$.

Theorem 7.1. *Let* $\mathbb{X} = \{x,\overline{x}\}$ *and* $\mathbb{Y} = \{y,\overline{y}\}$ *be two binary domains, and let* $X \in \mathbb{X}$ *and* $Y \in \mathbb{Y}$ *be independent binary random variables with identical uniform probability density functions, which for example can be described as* $\text{Beta}_X(p_x,1,1)$ *and* $\text{Beta}_Y(p_y,1,1)$. *Then the probability density function* $\text{PDF}(p(Z=(x\wedge y)))$ *for the product random variable* $Z = X \cdot Y$ *is given by*

$$\text{PDF}(p(Z=(x\wedge y))) = -\ln p(Z=(x\wedge y)), \quad \textit{for} \;\; 0 < p(Z) < 1\,. \tag{7.8}$$

The proof is given in [51]. This result applies to the case of the independent propositions x and y, where the joint variable Z takes values from the Cartesian product domain $\mathbb{Z} = \{(x\wedge y),(x\wedge\overline{y}),(\overline{x}\wedge y),(\overline{x}\wedge\overline{y})\}$. Specifically, this means that when the probabilities of x and y have uniform distributions, then the probability of the conjunction $x\wedge y$ has the probability density function $\text{PDF}(p(Z=(x\wedge y)))$ with expected probability $\text{E}(Z=(x\wedge y)) = \frac{1}{4}$.

This can be contrasted with the *a priori* non-informative probability density function $\text{Dir}(p_Q,(\frac{1}{2},\frac{1}{2},\frac{1}{2},\frac{1}{2}))$ over the quaternary domain $\mathbb{Q} = \{q_1,q_2,q_3,q_4\}$. The corresponding *a priori* probability density function for the probability of q_1 is $\text{Beta}(p(q_1),(\frac{1}{2},\frac{3}{2}))$ which can be derived directly from $\text{Dir}(p_Q,(\frac{1}{2},\frac{1}{2},\frac{1}{2},\frac{1}{2}))$. Interestingly we get equal expected probabilities: $\text{E}(q_1) = \text{E}(Z=(x\wedge y)) = \frac{1}{4}$.

The difference between $\text{Beta}(p(q_1),(\frac{1}{2},\frac{3}{2}))$ and $\text{PDF}(p(Z=(x\wedge y))) = -\ln p(Z=(x\wedge y))$ is illustrated in Figure 7.4 below.

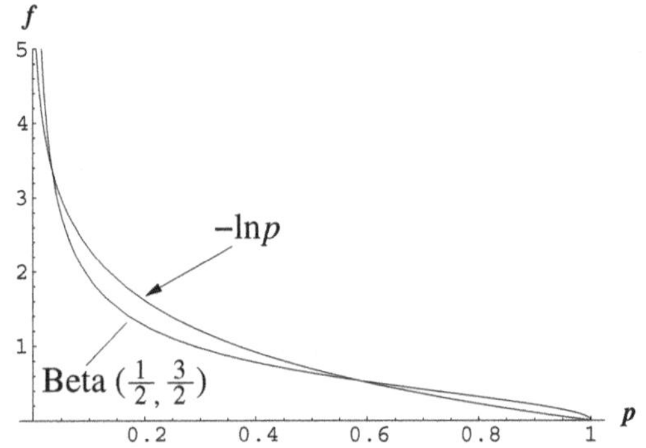

Fig. 7.4 Comparison between $\text{Beta}(p(q_1),(\frac{1}{2},\frac{3}{2}))$ and $\text{PDF}(p(Z=(x\wedge y))) = -\ln p(Z=(x\wedge y))$

The analytically correct product of two uniform distributions is represented by $\mathrm{PDF}(p(Z=(x\wedge y))) = -\ln p$, whereas the product produced by the multiplication operator is $\mathrm{Beta}\left(p(q_1), (\frac{1}{2}, \frac{3}{2})\right)$, which demonstrates that multiplication and comultiplication in subjective logic produce approximate results. More specifically, it can be shown that the projected probability is always exact, and that the variance is approximate. The quality of the variance approximation is analysed in [51], and is very good in general. The discrepancies grow with the amount of uncertainty in the arguments, so Figure 7.4 illustrates the worst case.

The advantage of the multiplication and comultiplication operators of subjective logic is their simplicity, which means that analytical expressions that otherwise would be complex, and sometimes intractable, can be analysed efficiently. The analytical result of products and coproducts of Beta PDFs will in general involve the Gauss hypergeometric function [84]. The analysis of anything but the most basic models based on such functions would soon become unmanageable.

7.2 Reliability Analysis

The modern use of the term 'reliability' originates from the U.S. military in the 1940s, where it meant that a product would operate as expected for a specified period of time. Reliability analysis of systems is now a mature discipline based on a set of well-established modelling techniques. This section describes how subjective logic can be applied to system reliability analysis.

7.2.1 Simple Reliability Networks

For the purpose of reliability analysis, a system consists of components that are represented as edges in a graph. This network of components is not intended to reflect the physical architecture of the system, but only to represent the reliability dependencies of the system. The connection between components in this way represents a semantic relationship which is similar to trust relationships described in Chapter 14.

A serial connection of two components reflects the property that both components must function correctly for the whole system to function correctly. In binary logic this dependency relationship is computed with the AND connective. In probabilistic logic it is computed with the product operator. In subjective logic it is computed with binomial multiplication according to Definition 7.1.

A parallel connection of two components reflects the property that at least one of the components must function correctly for the whole system to function correctly. In binary logic this dependency relationship is computed with the OR connective. In probabilistic logic it is computed with the coproduct operator. In subjective logic it is computed with binomial comultiplication according to Definition 7.2.

Figure 7.5.a illustrates a system S which consists of the components w, x, y and z. From a reliability point of view assume that these components can be considered connected as a reliability network consisting of serial and parallel connections, as illustrated in Figure 7.5.b.

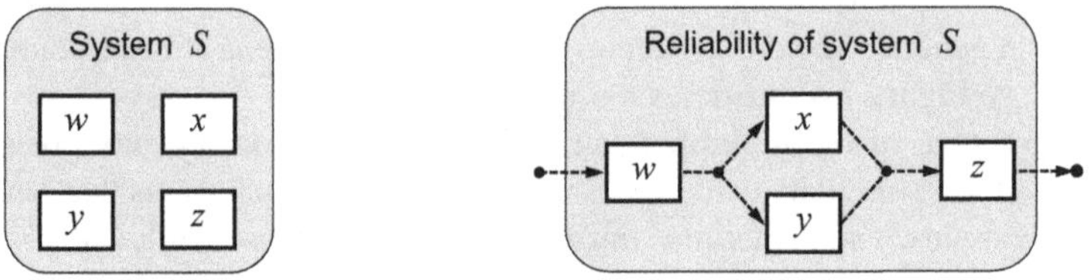

a) System components b) Reliability dependence relationships

Fig. 7.5 System components with series-parallel dependencies

Figure 7.5.b expresses that the correct function of system S requires that both w and z must function correctly, and in addition that either x or y must function correctly.

This reliability network can be formally expressed as

$$S = w \wedge (x \vee y) \wedge z\,. \tag{7.9}$$

The advantage of using subjective logic for reliability analysis is that component reliability can be expressed with degrees of uncertainty. To compute the reliability of system S, the reliability of each component can be expressed as the binomial opinions ω_w, ω_x, ω_y and ω_z. By applying binomial multiplication and comultiplication the reliability of system S can be computed as

$$\omega_S = \omega_{(w \wedge (x \vee y) \wedge z)} = \omega_w \cdot (\omega_x \sqcup \omega_y) \cdot \omega_w\,. \tag{7.10}$$

As an example, Table 7.1 specifies opinions for the reliabilities of components w, x, y and z, as well as the resulting reliability opinion of system S.

Table 7.1 Example reliability analysis of system S

Opinion parameter		Component reliabilities				System reliability
		ω_w	ω_x	ω_y	ω_z	$\omega_{(w\wedge(x\vee y)\wedge z)}$
Belief mass	b	0.90	0.50	0.00	0.00	0.43
Disbelief mass	d	0.10	0.00	0.00	0.00	0.10
Uncertainty mass	u	0.00	0.50	1.00	1.00	0.47
Base rate	a	0.90	0.80	0.80	0.90	0.78
Projected probability	P	0.90	0.90	0.80	0.90	0.80

It can be verified that the following holds, as expected:

$$
\begin{aligned}
P(w \wedge (x \vee y) \wedge z) &= P(w) \cdot (P(x) \sqcup P(y)) \cdot P(z) \\
&= P(w) \cdot P(z) \cdot (P(x) + P(y) \; - \; P(x) \cdot P(y)) \\
&= 0.90 \cdot 0.90 \cdot (0.90 + 0.80 \; - \; 0.90 \cdot 0.80) \\
&= 0.80.
\end{aligned} \tag{7.11}
$$

Thanks to the bijective mapping between belief opinions and evidence opinions in the form of Beta PDFs as defined by Eq.(3.11), it is also possible to conduct reliability analysis where the reliability of individual components is expressed in terms of Beta PDFs.

7.2.2 Reliability Analysis of Complex Systems

System reliability networks can be more complex than that illustrated in the previous section. Consider for example the five-component system S shown in Figure 7.6.a, and assume that its reliability can be modelled in the form of the reliability network of Figure 7.6.b.

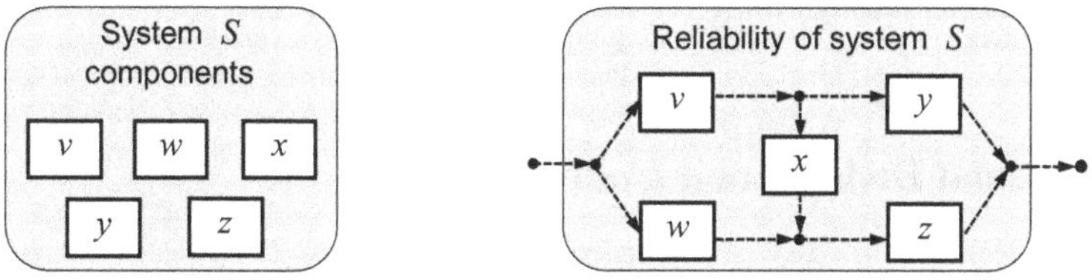

a) System components b) Reliability dependence relationships

Fig. 7.6 System components with complex dependencies

As Figure 7.6.b illustrates, this reliability network can not be broken down into a group of series and parallel edges. This complicates the problem of determining the system's reliability. If the system could be broken down into series-parallel configurations, it would be a relatively simple matter to determine the mathematical or analytical formula that describes the system's reliability. A good description of possible approaches to analysing the reliability of complex systems is presented in [77] (p.161). Some of the methods for analytically obtaining the reliability of a complex system are:

- Decomposition method. The decomposition method applies the law of total probability. It involves choosing a 'key' edge, and then calculating the reliability of the network twice: once as if the key edge failed, and once as if the key

edge succeeded. These two probabilities are then combined to obtain the reliability of the system, since at any given time the key edge will fail or operate.
- Event space method. The event space method applies the mutually exclusive events axiom. All mutually exclusive events are determined, and those which result in system success are considered. The reliability of the system is simply the probability of the union of all mutually exclusive events that yield a system success. Similarly, the unreliability is the probability of the union of all mutually exclusive events that yield a system failure.
- Path-tracing method. This method considers every path from the starting point to the ending point. System success means that at least one path from the beginning to the end of the network is available. In a plumbing metaphor, if an edge in the network fails, the 'water' can no longer flow through it. As long as there is at least one path for the 'water' to flow from the start to the end of the network, the network is successful. This method involves identifying all of the paths the 'water' could take, and calculating the reliability of the path based on the edges that lie along that path. The reliability of the system is simply the probability of the union of these paths.

We refer to [77] for a more detailed description of the above mentioned methods. System reliability analysis of this kind can be conducted with subjective logic to the extent that the relevant probabilistic methods can be generalised to methods of subjective logic. This topic is outside of the scope of this book, and must be the subject of future investigations.

7.3 Binomial Division and Codivision

Division and codivision naturally represent the inverse operations of multiplication and comultiplication. These operations are well defined for probabilities. The operators corresponding to division and codivision in binary logic are called UN-AND and UN-OR respectively [51].

7.3.1 Binomial Division

The inverse operation to binomial multiplication is binomial division. The quotient of opinions about propositions x and y represents the opinion about a proposition z which is independent of y such that $\omega_x = \omega_{y \wedge z}$.

Definition 7.3 (Binomial Division). Let $\mathbb{X} = \{x, \overline{x}\}$ and $\mathbb{Y} = \{y, \overline{y}\}$ be domains, and let $\omega_x = (b_x, d_x, u_x, a_x)$ and $\omega_y = (b_y, d_y, u_y, a_y)$ be binomial opinions on x and y satisfying Eq.(7.13). The division of ω_x by ω_y produces the quotient opinion $\omega_{x \widetilde{\wedge} y} = (b_{x \widetilde{\wedge} y}, d_{x \widetilde{\wedge} y}, u_{x \widetilde{\wedge} y}, a_{x \widetilde{\wedge} y})$ defined by

$$\text{Quotient } \omega_{x\tilde{\wedge}y}: \begin{cases} b_{x\tilde{\wedge}y} = \frac{a_y(b_x+a_x u_x)}{(a_y-a_x)(b_y+a_y u_y)} - \frac{a_x(1-d_x)}{(a_y-a_x)(1-d_y)}, \\ d_{x\tilde{\wedge}y} = \frac{d_x-d_y}{1-d_y}, \\ u_{x\tilde{\wedge}y} = \frac{a_y(1-d_x)}{(a_y-a_x)(1-d_y)} - \frac{a_y(b_x+a_x u_x)}{(a_y-a_x)(b_y+a_y u_y)}, \\ a_{x\tilde{\wedge}y} = \frac{a_x}{a_y}, \end{cases} \tag{7.12}$$

where the following constraints are satisfied:

$$\text{Constraints for binomial division:} \begin{cases} a_x < a_y, \\ d_x \geq d_y, \\ b_x \geq \frac{a_x(1-a_y)(1-d_x)b_y}{(1-a_x)a_y(1-d_y)}, \\ u_x \geq \frac{(1-a_y)(1-d_x)u_y}{(1-a_x)(1-d_y)}. \end{cases} \tag{7.13}$$

By using the symbol '/' to denote this operator, division of opinions can be written as $\omega_{x\tilde{\wedge}y} = \omega_x / \omega_y$. □

Figure 7.7 is a screenshot of the online demonstrator for SL operators. The example shows the division of the binomial opinion $\omega_{(x\wedge y)} = (0.10, 0.80, 0.10, 0.20)$ by the opinion $\omega_y = (0.40, 0.00, 0.60, 0.50)$.

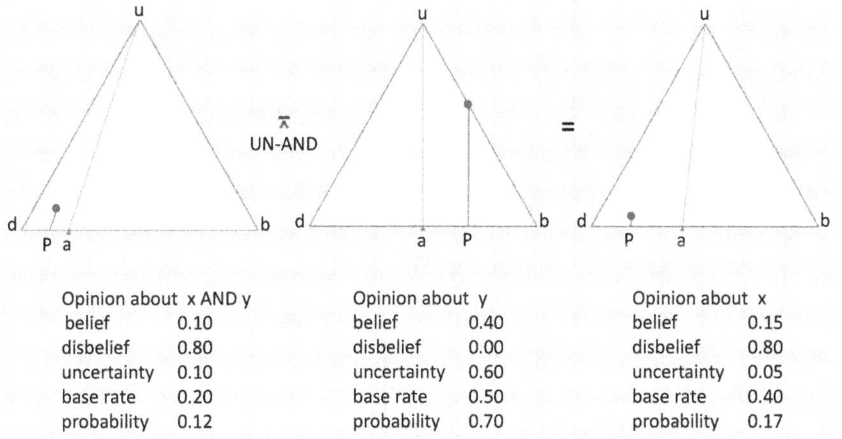

Fig. 7.7 Example division of a binomial opinion by another binomial opinion

The quotient is $\omega_x = \omega_{((x \wedge y) \widetilde{\wedge} y)} = (0.15, 0.80, 0.05, 0.40)$, and it can be verified that Eq.(7.14) holds for the quotient projected probability:

$$\begin{aligned} \mathrm{P}(x) &= \mathrm{P}((x \wedge y) \widetilde{\wedge} y) \\ &= \mathrm{P}(x \wedge y)/\mathrm{P}(y) \\ &= 0.12/0.70 = 0.17. \end{aligned} \tag{7.14}$$

Although probability division is a traditional operation used in probabilistic modelling and analysis, the corresponding binary logic operator 'UN-AND' is rarely or never used.

7.3.2 Binomial Codivision

The inverse operation to comultiplication is codivision. The co-quotient of opinions about propositions x and y represents the opinion about a proposition z which is independent of y such that $\omega_x = \omega_{y \vee z}$.

Definition 7.4 (Binomial Codivision). Let $\mathbb{X} = \{x, \bar{x}\}$ and $\mathbb{Y} = \{y, \bar{y}\}$ be domains, and let $\omega_x = (b_x, d_x, u_x, a_x)$ and $\omega_y = (b_y, d_y, u_y, a_y)$ be binomial opinions on x and y satisfying Eq.(7.16). The codivision of opinion ω_x by opinion ω_y produces the co-quotient opinion $\omega_{x \widetilde{\vee} y} = (b_{x \widetilde{\vee} y}, d_{x \widetilde{\vee} y}, u_{x \widetilde{\vee} y}, a_{x \widetilde{\vee} y})$ defined by

$$\text{Co-quotient } \omega_{x \widetilde{\vee} y}: \begin{cases} b_{x \widetilde{\vee} y} = \frac{b_x - b_y}{1 - b_y}, \\ d_{x \widetilde{\vee} y} = \frac{(1-a_y)(d_x + (1-a_x)u_x)}{(a_x - a_y)(d_y + (1-a_y)u_y)} - \frac{(1-a_x)(1-b_x)}{(a_x - a_y)(1-b_y)}, \\ u_{x \widetilde{\vee} y} = \frac{(1-a_y)(1-b_x)}{(a_x - a_y)(1-b_y)} - \frac{(1-a_y)(d_x + (1-a_x)u_x)}{(a_x - a_y)(d_y + (1-a_y)u_y)}, \\ a_{x \widetilde{\vee} y} = \frac{a_x - a_y}{1 - a_y}, \end{cases} \tag{7.15}$$

where the following constraints are satisfied:

$$\text{Constraints for binomial codivision: } \begin{cases} a_x > a_y, \\ b_x \geq b_y, \\ d_x \geq \frac{(1-a_x)a_y(1-b_x)d_y}{a_x(1-a_y)(1-b_y)}, \\ u_x \geq \frac{a_y(1-b_x)u_y}{a_x(1-b_y)}. \end{cases} \tag{7.16}$$

By using the symbol '$\widetilde{\Box}$' to denote this operator, codivision of opinions can be written as $\omega_{x\widetilde{\vee}y} = \omega_x \,\widetilde{\Box}\, \omega_y$.   □

Figure 7.8 is a screenshot of the online demonstrator for SL operators. The example shows the co-quotient produced by codividing the binomial opinion $\omega_{(x\vee y)} = (0.05, 0.55, 0.40, 0.75)$ by the binomial opinion $\omega_y = (0.00, 0.80, 0.20, 0.50)$.

Opinion about x OR y		Opinion about y		Opinion about x	
belief	0.05	belief	0.00	belief	0.05
disbelief	0.55	disbelief	0.80	disbelief	0.49
uncertainty	0.40	uncertainty	0.20	uncertainty	0.46
base rate	0.75	base rate	0.50	base rate	0.50
probability	0.35	probability	0.10	probability	0.28

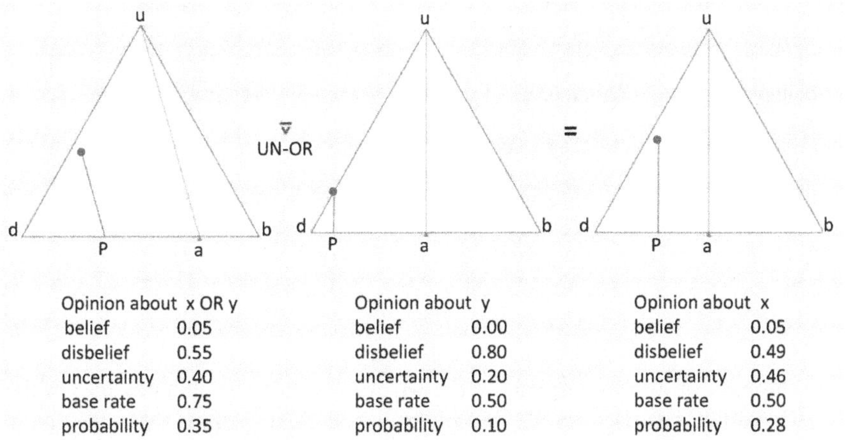

Fig. 7.8 Example codivision of a binomial opinion by another binomial opinion

The co-quotient is $\omega_x = (0.05, 0.49, 0.46, 0.50)$, and it can be verified that Eq.(7.17) holds for the co-quotient projected probability:

$$P(x) = P((x \vee y)\widetilde{\vee}y)$$
$$= P(x \vee y) \,\widetilde{\Box}\, P(y)$$
$$= (P(x \vee y) - P(y))/(1 - P(y)) \tag{7.17}$$
$$= \frac{0.35 - 0.10}{1 - 0.10} = 0.28.$$

Although probability codivision exists in probabilistic modelling and analysis, the corresponding binary logic operator 'UN-OR' introduced in 2004 [51] is rarely or never used.

7.4 Correspondence with Probabilistic Logic

Multiplication, comultiplication, division and codivision of dogmatic opinions are equivalent to the corresponding probabilistic-logic operators in Table 7.2, where independent variables are assumed.

Table 7.2 Probabilistic-logic operators corresponding to subjective-logic operators.

Operator name:	Result name:	Probabilistic-logic operator:
Multiplication	Product	$p(x \wedge y) = p(x)p(y)$
Comultiplication	Coproduct	$p(x \vee y) = p(x) + p(y) - p(x)p(y)$
Division	Quotient	$p(x \widetilde{\wedge} y) = p(x)/p(y)$
Codivision	Co-quotient	$p(x \widetilde{\vee} y) = (p(x) - p(y))/(1 - p(y))$

In the case of absolute opinions, i.e. when the argument opinions have either $b = 1$ (absolute belief) or $d = 1$ (absolute disbelief), then these opinions can be interpreted as Boolean TRUE or FALSE, so the multiplication and comultiplication operators are homomorphic to the binary logic operators AND, OR, UN-AND and UN-OR, as illustrated in Figure 5.3.

Chapter 8
Multinomial Multiplication and Division

This chapter describes multiplication and division involving multinomial opinions, which generalise multiplication and division of binomial opinions described in the previous chapter.

8.1 Multinomial Multiplication

Multinomial (and hypernomial) multiplication is different from binomial multiplication, in the sense that the product opinion on the whole Cartesian product domain is considered, instead of just on one value of the Cartesian product domain. The multiplication operator described here assumes independent factor opinions. The computation of joint opinions is described in Section 11.2.

8.1.1 Elements of Multinomial Multiplication

Figure 8.1 below illustrates the general situation with two domains $\mathbb{X}$ and $\mathbb{Y}$ that form the Cartesian product $\mathbb{X}\times\mathbb{Y}$. The product of two opinions ω_X and ω_Y produces belief masses on singleton values of $\mathbb{X}\times\mathbb{Y}$ as well as on the row and column subsets of $\mathbb{X}\times\mathbb{Y}$.

In order to produce an opinion with only belief mass on each singleton value of $\mathbb{X}\times\mathbb{Y}$ as well as uncertainty mass on $\mathbb{X}\times\mathbb{Y}$, some of the belief mass on the row and column subsets of $\mathbb{X}\times\mathbb{Y}$ must be redistributed to the singleton values in such a way that the projected probability of each singleton value in $\mathbb{X}\times\mathbb{Y}$ equals the product of projected probabilities of pairs of singleton values from $\mathbb{X}$ and $\mathbb{Y}$ respectively.

Evaluating the multinomial product of two separate multinomial opinions involves the Cartesian product of the respective domains to which the opinions apply. Let the factor domains $\mathbb{X}$ and $\mathbb{Y}$ be expressed as

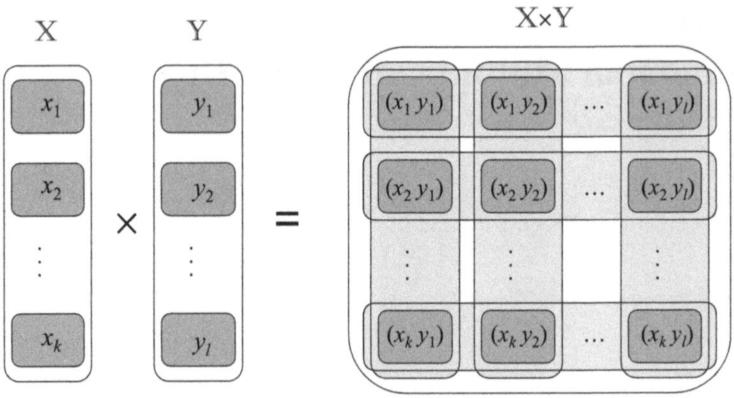

Fig. 8.1 Cartesian product of two domains

$$\text{Factor domains:} \begin{cases} \mathbb{X} = \{x_1, x_2, \dots, x_k\} \text{ with cardinality } k, \\ \\ \mathbb{Y} = \{y_1, y_2, \dots, y_l\} \text{ with cardinality } l. \end{cases} \tag{8.1}$$

The Cartesian product $\mathbb{X}\times\mathbb{Y}$ with cardinality kl is expressed as the matrix

$$\mathbb{X}\times\mathbb{Y} = \begin{pmatrix} (x_1 y_1), & (x_1 y_2), & \cdots, & (x_1 y_l) \\ (x_2 y_1), & (x_2 y_2), & \cdots, & (x_2 y_l) \\ \cdot & \cdot & \cdots, & \cdot \\ \cdot & \cdot & \cdots, & \cdot \\ (x_k y_1), & (x_k y_2), & \cdots, & (x_k y_l) \end{pmatrix}. \tag{8.2}$$

The joint random variable XY takes its values from the Cartesian product domain $\mathbb{X}\times\mathbb{Y}$. The multinomial product of multinomial opinions applies to this variable. The raw product terms between ω_X and ω_Y can be distinguished into four groups.

1. The first group of terms consists of product belief masses on singletons of $\mathbb{X}\times\mathbb{Y}$:

$$\boldsymbol{b}_{XY}^{\text{Singletons}} = \begin{cases} \boldsymbol{b}_X(x_1)\boldsymbol{b}_Y(y_1), \ \boldsymbol{b}_X(x_1)\boldsymbol{b}_Y(y_2), \ \dots, \ \boldsymbol{b}_X(x_1)\boldsymbol{b}_Y(y_l), \\ \boldsymbol{b}_X(x_2)\boldsymbol{b}_Y(y_1), \ \boldsymbol{b}_X(x_2)\boldsymbol{b}_Y(y_2), \ \dots, \ \boldsymbol{b}_X(x_2)\boldsymbol{b}_Y(y_l), \\ \cdot \qquad\qquad\qquad \cdot \qquad\qquad\qquad \dots \ \cdot \\ \cdot \qquad\qquad\qquad \cdot \qquad\qquad\qquad \dots \ \cdot \\ \boldsymbol{b}_X(x_k)\boldsymbol{b}_Y(y_1), \ \boldsymbol{b}_X(x_k)\boldsymbol{b}_Y(y_2), \ \dots, \ \boldsymbol{b}_X(x_k)\boldsymbol{b}_Y(y_l). \end{cases} \tag{8.3}$$

2. The second group of terms consists of belief masses on rows of $\mathbb{X}\times\mathbb{Y}$:

$$\boldsymbol{b}_{XY}^{\text{Rows}} = (\boldsymbol{b}_X(x_1)u_Y, \ \boldsymbol{b}_X(x_2)u_Y, \ \dots, \ \boldsymbol{b}_X(x_k)u_Y) \ . \tag{8.4}$$

3. The third group consists of belief masses on columns of $\mathbb{X}\times\mathbb{Y}$:

$$\boldsymbol{b}_{XY}^{\text{Columns}} = (u_X\boldsymbol{b}_Y(y_1), \ u_X\boldsymbol{b}_Y(y_2), \ \dots, \ u_X\boldsymbol{b}_Y(y_l)) \ . \tag{8.5}$$

4. The last term is simply the uncertainty mass on the whole product domain:

$$u_{XY}^{\text{Domain}} = u_X u_Y \,. \tag{8.6}$$

The computation of product base rates is straightforward according to Eq.(8.7):

$$\boldsymbol{a}_{XY} = \begin{cases} \boldsymbol{a}_X(x_1)\boldsymbol{a}_Y(y_1),\ \boldsymbol{a}_X(x_1)\boldsymbol{a}_Y(y_2),\ \ldots,\ \boldsymbol{a}_X(x_1)\boldsymbol{a}_Y(y_l), \\ \boldsymbol{a}_X(x_2)\boldsymbol{a}_Y(y_1),\ \boldsymbol{a}_X(x_2)\boldsymbol{a}_Y(y_2),\ \ldots,\ \boldsymbol{a}_X(x_2)\boldsymbol{a}_Y(y_l), \\ \quad\cdot \qquad\qquad\qquad \cdot \qquad\qquad \ldots \quad \cdot \\ \boldsymbol{a}_X(x_k)\boldsymbol{a}_Y(y_1),\ \boldsymbol{a}_X(x_k)\boldsymbol{a}_Y(y_2),\ \ldots,\ \boldsymbol{a}_X(x_k)\boldsymbol{a}_Y(y_l). \end{cases} \tag{8.7}$$

The challenge is how to interpret the various types of product belief masses. In the case of hypernomial products, the product belief masses are directly interpreted as part of the hypernomial belief mass distribution, as explained in Section 8.1.6.

In the case of multinomial products, some of the belief mass on the row and column subsets of $\mathbb{X}\times\mathbb{Y}$ must be redistributed to the singleton values in such a way that the projected probability of each singleton value equals the product of projected probabilities of pairs of singleton values from $\mathbb{X}$ and $\mathbb{Y}$ respectively. There are (at least) three different approaches to multinomial opinion products that produce consistent projected probability products, namely *normal multiplication* described in Section 8.1.2, *proportional multiplication* described in Section 8.1.4 and *projected multiplication* described in Section 8.1.5.

Whatever method is used, the projected probability distribution $\mathbf{P}_{XY}$ of the product is always the same:

$$\mathbf{P}_{XY}(xy) = \mathbf{P}_X(x)\mathbf{P}_Y(y) \,. \tag{8.8}$$

The product variance depends on the uncertainty, which in general is different for each method. Based on the Dirichlet PDF of the computed products, the product variance can easily be computed through Eq.(3.18), as expressed in Eq.(8.9):

$$\text{Multinomial product variance: } \text{Var}_{XY}(xy) = \frac{\mathbf{P}_{XY}(xy)(1-\mathbf{P}_{XY}(xy))u_{XY}}{W+u_{XY}}, \tag{8.9}$$

where W denotes the non-informative prior weight, which is normally set to $W = 2$. The non-informative prior weight is discussed in Section 3.4.2.

For example, it can be seen that when the uncertainty is zero, the variance is also zero, which is the case for dogmatic multinomial opinions. In the general case, the product variance of Eq.(8.9) is an approximation of the analytically correct variance, which typically is complex, and for which there is no closed expression.

8.1.2 Normal Multiplication

The singleton terms of Eq.(8.3) and the uncertainty mass on the whole domain of Eq.(8.6) are unproblematic, because they conform with the multinomial opinion representation of having belief mass only on singletons and on the whole domain. In contrast, the sets of terms on rows of Eq.(8.4) and columns of Eq.(8.5) apply to overlapping subsets, which is not compatible with the required format for multinomial opinions, and therefore the belief mass needs to be reassigned. Some belief mass from those terms can be reassigned to belief mass on singletons, and some to uncertainty mass on the whole domain. These principles are formalised in the following two steps.

Step 1: Determining normal uncertainty mass.

Consider the belief masses from Eq.(8.4) and Eq.(8.5) as potential contributors to uncertainty mass, expressed as

$$\begin{aligned}
&\text{Potential uncertainty mass from rows:} && u_{XY}^{\text{Rows}} = \textstyle\sum_{x\in\mathbb{X}} \boldsymbol{b}_{XY}^{\text{Rows}}(x),\\
&\text{Potential uncertainty mass from columns:} && u_{XY}^{\text{Columns}} = \textstyle\sum_{y\in\mathbb{Y}} \boldsymbol{b}_{XY}^{\text{Columns}}(y).
\end{aligned} \tag{8.10}$$

The sum of the uncertainty masses from Eq.(8.6) and Eq.(8.10) represents the maximum possible uncertainty mass u_{XY}^{Max} expressed as

$$u_{XY}^{\text{Max}} = u_{XY}^{\text{Rows}} + u_{XY}^{\text{Columns}} + u_{XY}^{\text{Domain}}. \tag{8.11}$$

The minimum possible uncertainty mass u_{XY}^{Min} is simply

$$u_{XY}^{\text{Min}} = u_{XY}^{\text{Domain}}. \tag{8.12}$$

The projected probability of each singleton in the product domain can easily be computed as the product of the projected probabilities of each pair of values of X and Y according to Eq.(8.13):

$$\mathbf{P}_X(x)\mathbf{P}_Y(y) = (\boldsymbol{b}_X(x) + \boldsymbol{a}_X(x)u_X)(\boldsymbol{b}_Y(y) + \boldsymbol{a}_Y(y)u_Y)\,. \tag{8.13}$$

We also require that the projected probability distribution over the product variable can be computed as a function of the product opinion according to Eq.(8.14):

$$\mathbf{P}_{XY}(xy) = \boldsymbol{b}_{XY}(xy) + \boldsymbol{a}_X(x)\boldsymbol{a}_Y(y)u_{XY}\,. \tag{8.14}$$

Obviously, the quantities of Eq.(8.13) and Eq.(8.14) are equal, so we can write

$$\begin{aligned}
&\mathbf{P}_X(x)\,\mathbf{P}_Y(y) = \mathbf{P}_{XY}(xy)\\
\Leftrightarrow\quad &(\boldsymbol{b}_X(x) + \boldsymbol{a}_X(x)u_X)(\boldsymbol{b}_Y(y) + \boldsymbol{a}_Y(y)u_Y) = \boldsymbol{b}_{XY}(xy) + \boldsymbol{a}_X(x)\boldsymbol{a}_Y(y)u_{XY} \qquad (8.15)\\
\Leftrightarrow\quad &u_{XY} = \frac{(\boldsymbol{b}_X(x)+\boldsymbol{a}_X(x)u_X)(\boldsymbol{b}_Y(y)+\boldsymbol{a}_Y(y)u_Y)-\boldsymbol{b}_{XY}(xy)}{\boldsymbol{a}_X(x)\boldsymbol{a}_Y(y)}\ .
\end{aligned}$$

The task now is to determine u_{XY} and the belief distribution $\boldsymbol{b}_{XY}$ of the multinomial product opinion ω_{XY}. There is at least one product value $(x_i y_j)$ for which the following equation can be satisfied:

$$\boldsymbol{b}_{XY}^{\text{Singletons}}(x_i y_j) = \boldsymbol{b}_{XY}(x_i y_j)\ . \tag{8.16}$$

Based on Eq.(8.15) and Eq.(8.16), there is thus at least one product value $(x_i y_j)$ for which the following equation can be satisfied:

$$\begin{aligned}
u_{XY}^{(i,j)} &= \frac{(\boldsymbol{b}_X(x_i)+\boldsymbol{a}_X(x_i)u_X)(\boldsymbol{b}_Y(y_j)+\boldsymbol{a}_Y(y_j)u_Y)-\boldsymbol{b}_{XY}^{\text{Singletons}}(x_i y_j)}{\boldsymbol{a}_X(x_i)\boldsymbol{a}_Y(y_j)}\\
&= \frac{\mathbf{P}_X(x_i)\mathbf{P}_Y(y_i)-\boldsymbol{b}_{XY}^{\text{Singletons}}(x_i y_j)}{\boldsymbol{a}_X(x_i)\boldsymbol{a}_Y(y_j)}\ ,
\end{aligned} \tag{8.17}$$

where $u_{XY}^{\text{Min}} \leq u_{XY}^{(i,j)} \leq u_{XY}^{\text{Max}}$.

In order to determine the uncertainty mass for the product opinion, each product value $(x_i y_j) \in \mathbb{X}\times\mathbb{Y}$ must be visited in turn to find the smallest uncertainty mass $u_{XY}^{(i,j)}$ that satisfies Eq.(8.17).

The product uncertainty can now be determined as the smallest $u_{XY}^{(i,j)}$ from Eq.(8.17), expressed as

$$u_{XY} = \min_{(xy)\in\mathbb{X}\times\mathbb{Y}} \left[u_{XY}^{(i,j)}\right]\ . \tag{8.18}$$

Step 2: Determining normal belief mass.

Having determined the uncertainty mass u_{XY} according to Eq.(8.18), the expression for the product projected probability of Eq.(8.13) can be used to compute the belief mass on each value in the product domain, as expressed by Eq.(8.19):

$$\begin{aligned}
\boldsymbol{b}_{XY}(xy) &= \mathbf{P}_X(x)\mathbf{P}_Y(y) - \boldsymbol{a}_X(x)\boldsymbol{a}_Y(y)u_{XY}\\
&= (\boldsymbol{b}_X(x) + \boldsymbol{a}_X(x)u_X)(\boldsymbol{b}_Y(y) + \boldsymbol{a}_Y(y)u_Y) - \boldsymbol{a}_X(x)\boldsymbol{a}_Y(y)u_{XY}\ .
\end{aligned} \tag{8.19}$$

It can be shown that the additivity property of Eq.(8.20) is preserved:

$$u_{XY} + \sum_{(xy)\in\mathbb{X}\times\mathbb{Y}} \boldsymbol{b}_{XY}(xy) = 1\ . \tag{8.20}$$

This completes the two-step procedure for normal multinomial multiplication, where the product opinion is expressed by

$$\omega_{XY} = (\boldsymbol{b}_{XY}, u_{XY}, \boldsymbol{a}_{XY}) . \tag{8.21}$$

From Eq.(8.19) it follows directly that the product operator is commutative. It can also be shown that the product operator is associative.

Although not immediately obvious, the normal multinomial product opinion method described here is a generalisation of the binomial product described in Section 7.1.1. Because of the relative simplicity of the binomial product, it can be described as a closed expression. For the normal multinomial product however, the stepwise procedure described above is needed.

8.1.3 Justification for Normal Multinomial Multiplication

The method to determine the product uncertainty in Eq.(8.18) might appear ad hoc. However, there is a clear rationale behind this method.

We define as a requirement that the product belief masses must be at least as large as the product belief masses of Eq.(8.3); anything else would be irrational. Remember that the larger the product uncertainty, the smaller the product belief masses, so this requirement would not be satisfied for all product belief masses if the product uncertainty is too high. The largest uncertainty that still satisfies the requirement is defined as the product uncertainty. The method for determining the product uncertainty in Section 8.1.2 follows exactly this principle.

The operator for normal multinomial multiplication is thus conservative, in the sense that it preserves the maximum uncertainty possible under the constraints that at least one product belief mass is equal to that computed by Eq.(8.3), and the remaining belief masses are greater.

8.1.4 Proportional Multiplication

Given the product projected probability distribution $\mathbf{P}_{XY}$ computed with Eq.(8.8), the question is how to compute an appropriate uncertainty level. Computation of the proportional product follows the two-step procedure below.

Step 1: Determining proportional uncertainty mass.

The proportional method uses u_X and u_Y together with the theoretical maximum uncertainty masses $\ddot{u}_X$ and $\ddot{u}_Y$, and computes the uncertainty mass u_{XY} based on the assumption that u_{XY} is the proportional average of u_X and u_Y, as expressed by Eq.(8.22).

$$\frac{u_{XY}}{\ddot{u}_{XY}} = \frac{u_X + u_Y}{\ddot{u}_X + \ddot{u}_Y} \tag{8.22}$$

$$\Leftrightarrow \quad u_{XY} = \frac{\ddot{u}_{XY}(u_X + u_Y)}{\ddot{u}_X + \ddot{u}_Y} \,. \tag{8.23}$$

The computation of uncertainty-maximised opinions $\ddot{\omega}_X$ with uncertainty $\ddot{u}_X$ is described in Section 3.5.6. The convention for marginal cases of division by zero is that the whole fraction is equal to zero, as e.g. expressed by Eq.(8.24):

$$\text{IF } (\ddot{u}_X + \ddot{u}_Y = 0) \text{ THEN } u_{XY} = 0 \,. \tag{8.24}$$

Eq.(8.24) is sound in all cases, because we always have $(u_X + u_Y) \leq (\ddot{u}_X + \ddot{u}_Y)$. Of course, the uncertainty sum $(u_X + u_Y)$ is strictly limited by the maximum possible uncertainty sum $(\ddot{u}_X + \ddot{u}_Y)$. This property ensures that $u_{XY} \in [0,1]$ in Eq.(8.23).

Step 2: Determining proportional belief mass.

Having computed the uncertainty level u_{XY} in Eq.(8.23), the belief masses are computed according to

$$\boldsymbol{b}_{XY}(xy) = \mathbf{P}_{XY}(xy) - \boldsymbol{a}_{XY}(xy)u_{XY}, \;\; \text{for each } (xy) \in \mathbb{X} \times \mathbb{Y} \,. \tag{8.25}$$

This completes the two-step procedure for computing the proportional product opinion ω_{XY}, expressed as

$$\omega_{XY} = \omega_X \cdot \omega_Y \,. \tag{8.26}$$

Proportional multiplication as described here produces slightly less uncertainty than normal multiplication described in Section 8.1.2, and can therefore be considered as slightly more aggressive. The precise nature of their similarities and differences remains to be analysed.

8.1.5 Projected Multiplication

The belief mass distribution consisting of $\boldsymbol{b}_{XY}^{\text{Singletons}}$ from Eq.(8.3), $\boldsymbol{b}_{XY}^{\text{Rows}}$ from Eq.(8.4) and $\boldsymbol{b}_{XY}^{\text{Columns}}$ from Eq.(8.5) represent a hypernomial opinion. Eq.(8.6) gives the uncertainty is u_{XY}^{Domain} and Eq.(8.7) gives the base rate distribution $\boldsymbol{a}_{XY}$.

Then this hypernomial opinion is projected to a multinomial opinion according to Eq.(3.30) on p.40. The result is the multinomial product opinion ω'_{XY}.

In general the projected multinomial product opinion ω'_{XY} has less uncertainty than the normal product opinion ω_{XY} described in Section 8.1.2 above, although both have the same projected probability distribution.

In case one or both of the factor opinions ω_X and ω_Y contain significant uncertainty it is desirable to let this be reflected in the product opinion. The normal or the proportional multinomial multiplication operator, described in Sections 8.1.2 and 8.1.4, are therefore the preferred methods to be used.

8.1.6 Hypernomial Product

Evaluating the hypernomial product of two separate multinomial or hypernomial (or even binomial) opinions involves the Cartesian product of the respective domains to which the factor opinions apply. Assume the two domains $\mathbb{X}$ of cardinality k and $\mathbb{Y}$ of cardinality l, as well as their hyperdomains $\mathscr{R}(\mathbb{X})$ of cardinality $\kappa = (2^k - 2)$ and $\mathscr{R}(\mathbb{Y})$ of cardinality $\lambda = (2^l - 2)$.

The Cartesian product $\mathbb{X}\times\mathbb{Y}$ with cardinality kl is expressed as the matrix

$$\mathbb{X}\times\mathbb{Y} = \begin{pmatrix} (x_1y_1), & (x_1y_2), & \cdots, & (x_1y_l) \\ (x_2y_1), & (x_2y_2), & \cdots, & (x_2y_l) \\ . & . & \cdots & . \\ . & . & \cdots & . \\ (x_ky_1), & (x_ky_2), & \cdots, & (x_ky_l) \end{pmatrix}. \quad (8.27)$$

The hyperdomain of $\mathbb{X}\times\mathbb{Y}$ is denoted $\mathscr{R}(\mathbb{X}\times\mathbb{Y})$. Let ω_X and ω_Y be two independent hypernomial opinions that apply to the separate domains. The task is to compute the hypernomial product opinion ω_{XY}. Table 8.1 summarises the characteristics of the opinions and domains involved in a hypernomial product.

Table 8.1 Hypernomial product elements

	Dom.	Cardi.	Hyperdom.	Hypercardi.	Var.	Val.	Bel. mass dist.	♯ bel. masses
Factor ω_X	$\mathbb{X}$	k	$\mathscr{R}(\mathbb{X})$	κ	X	x	$\boldsymbol{b}_X$	κ
Factor ω_Y	$\mathbb{Y}$	l	$\mathscr{R}(\mathbb{Y})$	λ	Y	y	$\boldsymbol{b}_Y$	λ
Product ω_{XY}	$\mathbb{X}\times\mathbb{Y}$	kl	$\mathscr{R}(\mathbb{X}\times\mathbb{Y})$	$(2^{kl}-2)$	XY	xy	$\boldsymbol{b}_{XY}$	$(\kappa\lambda+\kappa+\lambda)$

The expression $(\kappa\lambda + \kappa + \lambda)$ represents the number of belief masses of the hypernomial product. This number emerges as follows: the opinion factor ω_X's belief mass distribution $\boldsymbol{b}_X$ can have κ belief masses, and the opinion factor ω_Y's belief mass distribution $\boldsymbol{b}_Y$ can have λ belief masses, so their product produces $\kappa\lambda$ belief masses. In addition, the product between $\boldsymbol{b}_X$ and u_Y produces κ belief masses, and the product between $\boldsymbol{b}_Y$ and u_X produces λ belief masses. Note that $(\kappa\lambda + \kappa + \lambda) \propto 2^{k+l}$.

The expression $(2^{kl} - 2)$ represents the number of hypervalues in $\mathscr{R}(\mathbb{X}\times\mathbb{Y})$. Note that $(2^{kl} - 2) \propto 2^{kl}$.

Because $2^{kl} \gg 2^{k+l}$ with growing k and l, the number $(2^{kl} - 2)$ of possible values in $\mathscr{R}(\mathbb{X}\times\mathbb{Y})$ is in general far superior to the number $(\kappa\lambda + \kappa + \lambda)$ of belief masses of the hypernomial product. A hypernomial opinion product is thus highly constrained with regard to the set of hypervalues that receive belief mass from the multiplication.

The belief product terms produced by $\omega_X \cdot \omega_Y$ can be separated into the four groups described below.

1. The first group of terms consists of belief masses on hypervalues of $\mathscr{R}(\mathbb{X}\times\mathbb{Y})$:

$$\boldsymbol{b}_{XY}^{\text{HValues}} = \begin{cases} \boldsymbol{b}_X(x_1)\boldsymbol{b}_Y(y_1),\ \boldsymbol{b}_X(x_1)\boldsymbol{b}_Y(y_2),\ \ldots,\ \boldsymbol{b}_X(x_1)\boldsymbol{b}_Y(y_\lambda), \\ \boldsymbol{b}_X(x_2)\boldsymbol{b}_Y(y_1),\ \boldsymbol{b}_X(x_2)\boldsymbol{b}_Y(y_2),\ \ldots,\ \boldsymbol{b}_X(x_2)\boldsymbol{b}_Y(y_\lambda), \\ \quad . \qquad\qquad\qquad . \qquad\qquad\qquad \ldots\ . \\ \boldsymbol{b}_X(x_\kappa)\boldsymbol{b}_Y(y_1),\ \boldsymbol{b}_X(x_\kappa)\boldsymbol{b}_Y(y_2),\ \ldots,\ \boldsymbol{b}_X(x_\kappa)\boldsymbol{b}_Y(y_\lambda). \end{cases} \tag{8.28}$$

2. The second group of terms consists of belief masses on hyperrows of $\mathscr{R}(\mathbb{X}\times\mathbb{Y})$:

$$\boldsymbol{b}_{XY}^{\text{HRows}} = (\boldsymbol{b}_X(x_1)u_Y,\ \boldsymbol{b}_X(x_2)u_Y,\ \ldots,\ \boldsymbol{b}_X(x_\kappa)u_Y)\ . \tag{8.29}$$

3. The third group consists of belief masses on hypercolumns of $\mathscr{R}(\mathbb{X}\times\mathbb{Y})$:

$$\boldsymbol{b}_{XY}^{\text{HColumns}} = (u_X\boldsymbol{b}_Y(y_1),\ u_X\boldsymbol{b}_Y(y_2),\ \ldots,\ u_X\boldsymbol{b}_Y(y_\lambda))\ . \tag{8.30}$$

4. The last term is simply the belief mass on the whole product domain:

$$u_{XY}^{\text{HDomain}} = u_X u_Y\ . \tag{8.31}$$

The set of $\kappa\lambda$ belief masses of $\boldsymbol{b}_{XY}^{\text{HValues}}$, the κ belief masses of $\boldsymbol{b}_{XY}^{\text{HRows}}$ and the λ belief masses of $\boldsymbol{b}_{XY}^{\text{HColumns}}$ together form the belief mass distribution $\boldsymbol{b}_{XY}^{\text{Hyper}}$ of ω_{XY}:

$$\boldsymbol{b}_{XY}^{\text{Hyper}} = (\boldsymbol{b}_{XY}^{\text{HValues}},\ \boldsymbol{b}_{XY}^{\text{HRows}},\ \boldsymbol{b}_{XY}^{\text{HColumns}})\ . \tag{8.32}$$

The uncertainty mass is simply u_{XY}^{HDomain}. Finally the base rate distribution $\boldsymbol{a}_{XY}$ is the same as that of multinomial products in Eq.(8.7). The hypernomial product opinion is then defined as

$$\omega_{XY}^{\text{Hyper}} = (\boldsymbol{b}_{XY}^{\text{Hyper}},\ u_{XY}^{\text{HDomain}}, \boldsymbol{a}_{XY})\ . \tag{8.33}$$

If needed, the hypernomial product opinion $\omega_{XY}^{\text{Hyper}}$ can be projected to a multinomial opinion according to Eq.(3.30) on p.40. The result is then a multinomial product opinion ω'_{XY} which has the same projected probability distribution as that of $\omega_{XY}^{\text{Hyper}}$.

8.1.7 Product of Dirichlet Probability Density Functions

Multinomial opinion multiplication can be leveraged to compute products of Dirichlet PDFs (Probability Density Functions) described in Section 3.5.2.

Assume domains $\mathbb{X}$ and $\mathbb{Y}$. The variables X and Y take their values from $\mathbb{X}$ and $\mathbb{Y}$ respectively. In the Dirichlet model the analyst observes occurrences of values $x \in \mathbb{X}$ and values $y \in \mathbb{Y}$, and represents these observations as evidence vectors $\boldsymbol{r}_X$ and $\boldsymbol{r}_Y$, so that e.g. $\boldsymbol{r}_X(x)$ represents the number of observed occurrences of the value x. In addition the analyst must specify the base rate distributions $\boldsymbol{a}_X$ over $\mathbb{X}$ and $\boldsymbol{a}_Y$ over $\mathbb{Y}$. These parameters define the Dirichlet PDFs on X and Y.

Let e.g. $\mathrm{Dir}^{\mathrm{e}}_X$ and $\mathrm{Dir}^{\mathrm{e}}_Y$ denote the evidence-Dirichlet PDFs on variables X and Y respectively, according to Eq.(3.16). Their product can be denoted

$$\mathrm{Dir}^{\mathrm{e}}_{XY} = \mathrm{Dir}^{\mathrm{e}}_X \cdot \mathrm{Dir}^{\mathrm{e}}_Y \,. \tag{8.34}$$

The procedure for computing $\mathrm{Dir}^{\mathrm{e}}_{XY}$ according to Eq.(8.34) is described next and is also illustrated in Figure 8.2.

1. Specify the evidence parameters $(\boldsymbol{r}_X, \boldsymbol{a}_X)$ and $(\boldsymbol{r}_Y, \boldsymbol{a}_Y)$ of the factor Dirichlet PDFs.
2. Derive opinions ω_X and ω_Y from the Dirichlet PDFs according to the mapping of Eq.(3.23).
3. Compute $\omega_{XY} = \omega_X \cdot \omega_Y$ as described in Section 8.1.2 in case of multinomial product.
4. Derive the product Dirichlet PDF $\mathrm{Dir}^{\mathrm{e}}_{XY}$ from the multinomial product opinion ω_{XY} according to the mapping of Eq.(3.23).

Figure 8.2 depicts the procedure just described.

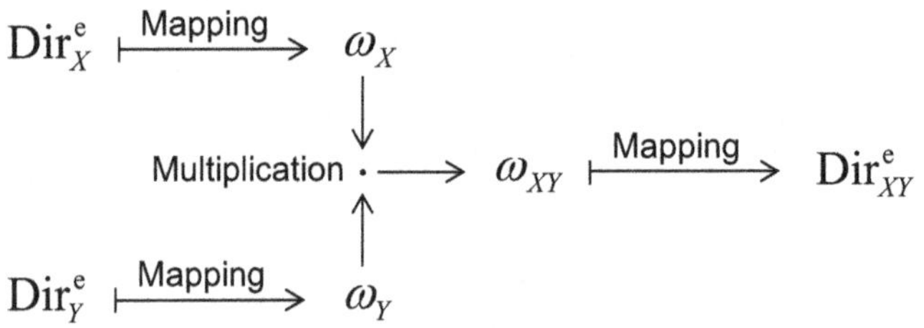

Fig. 8.2 Procedure for computing the product of Dirichlet PDFs

In general, the product of two Dirichlet PDFs can be computed as a Dirichlet PDF. If needed a Dirichlet HPDF can be projected onto a Dirichlet PDF. This is done by first mapping the Dirichlet HPDF to a hyper-opinion according to Eq.(3.35). Then the hyper-opinion is projected onto a multinomial opinion according to Eq.(3.30). Finally the multinomial opinion can be used in the multiplication operation.

The above described method for computing a product Dirichlet PDF from two Dirichlet PDFs is very simple and requires very little computation. Although not equivalent, this result is related to Dirichlet convolution.

8.2 Examples of Multinomial Product Computation

We consider the scenario where a GE (Genetic Engineering) process can produce Male (M) or Female (F) fertilised eggs. In addition, each fertilised egg can have genetic mutation 1 or 2 independently of its gender. This constitutes two binary domains representing gender $\mathbb{X} = \{x_{\mathrm{M}}, x_{\mathrm{F}}\}$ and mutation $\mathbb{Y} = \{y_1, y_2\}$ with variables X and Y, or alternatively the quaternary product domain $\mathbb{X}\times\mathbb{Y} = \{(x_{\mathrm{M}}\, y_1), (x_{\mathrm{M}}\, y_2), (x_{\mathrm{F}}\, y_1), (x_{\mathrm{F}}\, y_2)\}$ with joint variable XY. Sensor G observes whether each egg has gender M or F, and Sensor H whether the egg has mutation 1 or 2.

Sensors G and H thus observe different and orthogonal aspects which are assumed independent, so that opinions derived from their observations can be combined using multiplication. It is assumed that the analyst A has a level of trust in the reliability of the sensors, which can influence the translation of sensor data into opinions according to trust discounting described in Section 14.3. This is illustrated in Figure 8.3.

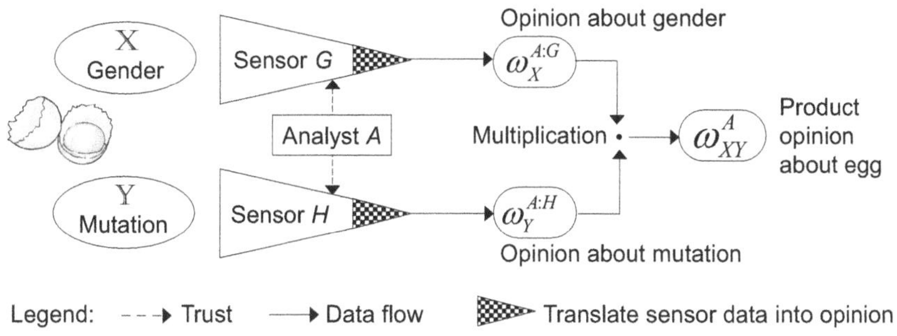

Fig. 8.3 Multiplication of opinions on orthogonal aspects of GE eggs

The result of opinion multiplication in this case can be interpreted as an opinion based on observation by a single sensor which simultaneously detects both aspects.

There can be many different methods for translating sensor data into opinions, and the general topic of analysing sensor data is outside the scope of this book. The example below assumes that the sensors are able to detect gender and mutation with high reliability, and that statistical observations can be made.

Assume that 20 eggs have been produced, with aspects observed for each egg. Table 8.2 summarises the observations and the resulting opinions.

The Cartesian product domain and the projected probabilities are expressed as

$$\mathbb{X}\times\mathbb{Y} = \begin{pmatrix} (x_{\mathrm{M}}\, y_1), & (x_{\mathrm{M}}\, y_2) \\ (x_{\mathrm{F}}\, y_1), & (x_{\mathrm{F}}\, y_2) \end{pmatrix}, \qquad \mathrm{P}(XY) = \begin{pmatrix} 0.49, & 0.16 \\ 0.26, & 0.09 \end{pmatrix}. \tag{8.35}$$

Table 8.2 Observations of egg gender and mutation

	Observations	Opinions	Base Rates	Probabilities
Gender opinion:	$r(x_M) = 12$	$b(x_M) = 0.60$	$a(x_M) = 0.50$	$P(x_M) = 0.65$
	$r(x_F) = 6$	$b(x_F) = 0.30$	$a(x_F) = 0.50$	$P(x_F) = 0.35$
		$u_X = 0.10$		
Mutation opinion:	$r(y_1) = 14$	$b(y_1) = 0.70$	$a(y_1) = 0.50$	$P(y_1) = 0.75$
	$r(y_2) = 4$	$b(y_2) = 0.20$	$a(y_2) = 0.50$	$P(y_2) = 0.25$
		$u_Y = 0.10$		

The next section describes and compares the normal product, the proportional product and the projected product in this example. Then Section 8.2.2 describes the hypernomial product in this example.

8.2.1 Comparing Normal, Proportional and Projected Products

Below are presented the results of multinomial multiplication according to the three multiplication methods presented in Sections 8.1.2 – 8.1.5.

Table 8.3 shows the results of normal multinomial product, proportional product, as well projected multinomial product. Also shown are the Dirichlet PDF parameters that are obtained with the mapping of Eq.(3.23). Table 8.3 therefore accounts for both multinomial opinion product as well as Dirichlet PDF product.

Table 8.3 Multinomial products of egg gender and mutation

	Opinions	Base Rates	Probabilities	Eq. Observations
Normal product:	$b(x_M y_1) = 0.460$	$a(x_M y_1) = 1/4$	$P(x_M y_1) = 0.49$	$r(x_M y_1) = 8.36$
	$b(x_M y_2) = 0.135$	$a(x_M y_2) = 1/4$	$P(x_M y_2) = 0.16$	$r(x_M y_2) = 2.45$
	$b(x_F y_1) = 0.235$	$a(x_F y_1) = 1/4$	$P(x_F y_1) = 0.26$	$r(x_F y_1) = 4.27$
	$b(x_F y_2) = 0.060$	$a(x_F y_2) = 1/4$	$P(x_F y_2) = 0.09$	$r(x_F y_2) = 1.09$
	$u_{XY} = 0.110$			$\sum r = 16.18$
Proportional product:	$b(x_M y_1) = 0.473$	$a(x_M y_1) = 1/4$	$P(x_M y_1) = 0.49$	$r(x_M y_1) = 16.21$
	$b(x_M y_2) = 0.148$	$a(x_M y_2) = 1/4$	$P(x_M y_2) = 0.16$	$r(x_M y_2) = 5.07$
	$b(x_F y_1) = 0.248$	$a(x_F y_1) = 1/4$	$P(x_F y_1) = 0.26$	$r(x_F y_1) = 8.50$
	$b(x_F y_2) = 0.073$	$a(x_F y_2) = 1/4$	$P(x_F y_2) = 0.09$	$r(x_F y_2) = 2.50$
	$u_{XY} = 0.058$			$\sum r = 32.28$
Projected product:	$b(x_M y_1) = 0.485$	$a(x_M y_1) = 1/4$	$P(x_M y_1) = 0.49$	$r(x_M y_1) = 97$
	$b(x_M y_2) = 0.160$	$a(x_M y_2) = 1/4$	$P(x_M y_2) = 0.16$	$r(x_M y_2) = 32$
	$b(x_F y_1) = 0.260$	$a(x_F y_1) = 1/4$	$P(x_F y_1) = 0.26$	$r(x_F y_1) = 52$
	$b(x_F y_2) = 0.085$	$a(x_F y_2) = 1/4$	$P(x_F y_2) = 0.09$	$r(x_F y_2) = 17$
	$u_{XY} = 0.010$			$\sum r = 198$

The normal product preserves the most uncertainty, the proportional product preserves about 50% less uncertainty, and the projected product hardly preserves any uncertainty at all. The normal product therefore represents the most conservative approach, and should normally be used for multinomial product computation in general situations. The analytically correct product of Dirichlet PDFs is computationally complex, and the methods described here represent approximations. Simulations of the binomial product in Section 7.1.3 show that the normal product is a very good approximation of the analytically correct product.

8.2.2 Hypernomial Product Computation

Computation of hypernomial products does not require any synthesis of uncertainty mass, and is therefore much simpler than the computation of multinomial products. We continue the example of observing egg gender and mutation.

Based on the observation parameters of Table 8.2, the hypernomial product can be computed according to the method described in Section 8.1.6.

In the case of hypernomial products, the power-subset denoted $\mathscr{P}^*(\mathbb{X}\times\mathbb{Y})$ expressed in Eq.(8.36) must be used:

$$\mathscr{P}^*(\mathbb{X}\times\mathbb{Y}) = \begin{pmatrix} (x_{\mathrm{M}}\,y_1), & (x_{\mathrm{M}}\,y_2), & (x_{\mathrm{M}}\,Y) \\ (x_{\mathrm{F}}\,y_1), & (x_{\mathrm{F}}\,y_2), & (x_{\mathrm{F}}\,Y) \\ (X\,y_1), & (X\,y_2), & (X\,Y) \end{pmatrix}. \tag{8.36}$$

Table 8.4 shows the hypernomial product ω_{XY}, including the projected probabilities of the joint singleton values.

Table 8.4 Hypernomial product of egg gender and mutation

	Belief/uncertainty mass	Base Rates	Probabilities
	$b(x_{\mathrm{M}}\,y_1) = 0.42$	$a(x_{\mathrm{M}}\,y_1) = 0.25$	$\mathrm{P}(x_{\mathrm{M}}\,y_1) = 0.49$
	$b(x_{\mathrm{M}}\,y_2) = 0.12$	$a(x_{\mathrm{M}}\,y_2) = 0.25$	$\mathrm{P}(x_{\mathrm{M}}\,y_1) = 0.16$
Hypernomial	$b(x_{\mathrm{F}}\,y_1) = 0.21$	$a(x_{\mathrm{F}}\,y_1) = 0.25$	$\mathrm{P}(x_{\mathrm{F}}\,y_1) = 0.26$
product:	$b(x_{\mathrm{F}}\,y_2) = 0.06$	$a(x_{\mathrm{F}}\,y_2) = 0.25$	$\mathrm{P}(x_{\mathrm{F}}\,y_1) = 0.09$
	$b(x_{\mathrm{M}}\,Y) = 0.07$		
	$b(x_{\mathrm{F}}\,Y) = 0.07$		
	$b(X\,y_1) = 0.06$		
	$b(X\,y_2) = 0.03$		
	$u_{XY} = 0.01$		

Note that hypernomial multiplication produces relatively large amounts of vague belief mass.

8.3 Multinomial Division

Multinomial division is the inverse operation of multinomial multiplication described at the beginning of Chapter 8. Similarly to how multinomial multiplication applies to the Cartesian product of two domains, multinomial division applies to the Cartesian quotient of a product domain by one of its factor domains.

8.3.1 Elements of Multinomial Division

Consider the Cartesian product domain $\mathbb{X} \times \mathbb{Y}$, and the factor domain $\mathbb{Y}$. The Cartesian quotient resulting from dividing product domain $\mathbb{X} \times \mathbb{Y}$ by factor domain $\mathbb{Y}$ produces the quotient domain $\mathbb{X}$, as illustrated in Figure 8.4.

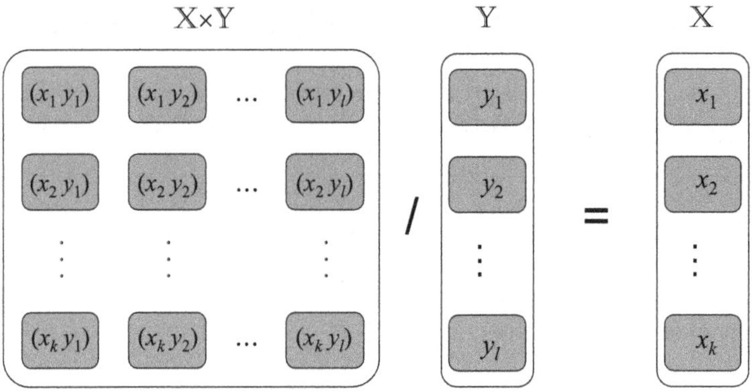

Fig. 8.4 Cartesian quotient of a Cartesian product domain divided by one of its factors

Assume a multinomial opinion $\omega_{XY} = (\boldsymbol{b}_{XY}, u_{XY}, \boldsymbol{a}_{XY})$ on the product domain $\mathbb{XY}$ with the following belief mass distribution and base rate distribution:

$$\boldsymbol{b}_{XY} = \begin{cases} \boldsymbol{b}_{XY}(x_1\,y_1),\ \boldsymbol{b}_X(x_1\,y_2),\ \ldots,\ \boldsymbol{b}_X(x_1\,y_l) \\ \boldsymbol{b}_{XY}(x_2\,y_1),\ \boldsymbol{b}_X(x_2\,y_2),\ \ldots,\ \boldsymbol{b}_X(x_2\,y_l) \\ \cdot \qquad\qquad\quad \cdot \qquad\qquad \ldots,\ \cdot \\ \cdot \qquad\qquad\quad \cdot \qquad\qquad \ldots,\ \cdot \\ \boldsymbol{b}_{XY}(x_k\,y_1),\ \boldsymbol{b}_X(x_k\,y_2),\ \ldots,\ \boldsymbol{b}_X(x_k\,y_l) \end{cases} \tag{8.37}$$

$$\boldsymbol{a}_{XY} = \begin{cases} \boldsymbol{a}_{XY}(x_1\,y_1),\ \boldsymbol{a}_X(x_1\,y_2),\ \ldots,\ \boldsymbol{a}_X(x_1\,y_l) \\ \boldsymbol{a}_{XY}(x_2\,y_1),\ \boldsymbol{a}_X(x_2\,y_2),\ \ldots,\ \boldsymbol{a}_X(x_2\,y_l) \\ \cdot \qquad\qquad\quad \cdot \qquad\qquad \ldots,\ \cdot \\ \cdot \qquad\qquad\quad \cdot \qquad\qquad \ldots,\ \cdot \\ \boldsymbol{a}_{XY}(x_k\,y_1),\ \boldsymbol{a}_X(x_k\,y_2),\ \ldots,\ \boldsymbol{a}_X(x_k\,y_l) \end{cases} \tag{8.38}$$

Assume also the multinomial opinion $\omega_Y = (\boldsymbol{b}_Y, u_Y, \boldsymbol{a}_Y)$ on domain $\mathbb{Y}$. We want to determine ω_X by multinomial division according to

$$\omega_X = \omega_{XY} / \omega_Y \,. \tag{8.39}$$

It can already be mentioned that there is no general solution to this seemingly simple equation. A general solution would have to satisfy the unrealistic requirement of Eq.(8.40):

$$\text{Unrealistic: } \mathbf{P}_X(x_i) = \frac{\mathbf{P}_{XY}(x_i y_1)}{\mathbf{P}_Y(y_1)} = \frac{\mathbf{P}_{XY}(x_i y_2)}{\mathbf{P}_Y(y_2)} = \ldots \frac{\mathbf{P}_{XY}(x_i y_l)}{\mathbf{P}_Y(y_l)}, \text{ for all } x_i \in \mathbb{X}. \tag{8.40}$$

Eq.(8.40) does not hold in general, because there is only one single product opinion ω_{XY} for which Eq.(8.40) always holds, making it impossible to satisfy that requirement in general. Instead, the realistic situation is expressed by Eq.(8.41):

$$\text{Realistic: } \mathbf{P}_X(x_i) \neq \frac{\mathbf{P}_{XY}(x_i y_1)}{\mathbf{P}_Y(y_1)} \neq \frac{\mathbf{P}_{XY}(x_i y_2)}{\mathbf{P}_Y(y_2)} \neq \ldots \frac{\mathbf{P}_{XY}(x_i y_l)}{\mathbf{P}_Y(y_l)}, \text{ for all } x_i \in \mathbb{X}. \tag{8.41}$$

For the base rate distributions $\boldsymbol{a}_X$, $\boldsymbol{a}_Y$ and $\boldsymbol{a}_{XY}$, we assume that the requirement does hold, as expressed by Eq.(8.42):

$$\text{Assumed: } \boldsymbol{a}_X(x_i) = \frac{\boldsymbol{a}_{XY}(x_i y_1)}{\boldsymbol{a}_Y(y_1)} = \frac{\boldsymbol{a}_{XY}(x_i y_2)}{\boldsymbol{a}_Y(y_2)} = \ldots \frac{\boldsymbol{a}_{XY}(x_i y_l)}{\boldsymbol{a}_Y(y_l)}, \text{ for all } x_i \in \mathbb{X}. \tag{8.42}$$

Because there is no general analytical solution to multinomial division, we will instead describe two partial solutions below. Two possible methods are *averaging proportional division* and *selective division*. These are described next.

8.3.2 Averaging Proportional Division

The method for averaging proportional division, denoted '/', is synthetic by nature, in the sense that it produces a solution where there is no real analytical solution in general. The produced solution can not be described as an approximation, because there is not even a correct solution to approximate.

The main principle of averaging proportional division is simply to compute the average of the different projected probabilities from Eq.(8.41). However, potential problems with zero divisors and non-additivity must be addressed, by defining one limit rule and one condition:

$$\text{Limit rule:} \begin{cases} \text{IF} & (\mathbf{P}_{XY}(x_i y_j) = \mathbf{P}_Y(y_j) = 0) \text{ for some } (i,j), \\ \text{THEN} & \frac{\mathbf{P}_{XY}(x_i y_j)}{\mathbf{P}_Y(y_j)} = 0. \end{cases} \tag{8.43}$$

$$\text{Condition:} \begin{cases} \text{IF} & (\mathbf{P}_{XY}(x_i y_j) > 0) \wedge (\mathbf{P}_Y(y_j) = 0) \text{ for some } (i,j), \\ \text{THEN} & \text{no division is possible.} \end{cases} \tag{8.44}$$

Thus, by respecting the limit rule of Eq.(8.43) and the condition of Eq.(8.44), a preliminary quotient projected probability distribution can be computed as

$$\mathbf{P}_X^{\text{Pre}}(x_i) = \frac{1}{l}\left(\sum_{j=1}^{l} \frac{\mathbf{P}_{XY}(x_i y_j)}{\mathbf{P}_Y(y_j)}\right). \tag{8.45}$$

Notice the cardinality $l = |\mathbb{Y}|$ used for computing the preliminary quotient probability distribution. The probability distribution $\mathbf{P}_X^{\text{Pre}}$ is non-additive (i.e. the sum is not equal to 1) in general. Additivity can be restored by simple normalisation through the normalisation factor ν_X^{Ave} expressed as

$$\nu_X^{\text{Ave}} = \sum_{i=1}^{k} \mathbf{P}_X^{\text{Pre}}(x_i). \tag{8.46}$$

The average quotient projected probability distribution $\mathbf{P}_X^{\text{Ave}}$ can then be computed, as expressed in Eq.(8.47):

$$\mathbf{P}_X^{\text{Ave}}(x_i) = \frac{\mathbf{P}_X^{\text{Pre}}(x_i)}{\nu_X^{\text{Ave}}}. \tag{8.47}$$

The average quotient projected probability distribution is then

$$\mathbf{P}_X^{\text{Ave}} = \{\mathbf{P}_X^{\text{Ave}}(x_i), \text{ for } i = 1,\ldots,k\}. \tag{8.48}$$

One disadvantage of $\mathbf{P}_X^{\text{Ave}}$ is obviously that in general, $\mathbf{P}_{XY} \neq \mathbf{P}_X^{\text{Ave}} \cdot \mathbf{P}_Y$. However, it can be noted that the following equality holds:

$$\mathbf{P}_X^{\text{Ave}} = (\mathbf{P}_X^{\text{Ave}} \cdot \mathbf{P}_Y)/\mathbf{P}_Y. \tag{8.49}$$

Given the average quotient projected probability distribution $\mathbf{P}_X^{\text{Ave}}$, the question is how to compute an appropriate level of uncertainty, based on the uncertainties u_{XY} and u_Y. One simple heuristic method is to take the theoretical maximum uncertainty levels $\ddot{u}_{XY}$ and $\ddot{u}_Y$, and define the uncertainty level u_Y based on the assumption that u_{XY} is the proportional average of u_X and u_Y, as expressed by Eq.(8.50). This produces a preliminary uncertainty u_X^{Pre}:

$$\frac{u_{XY}}{\ddot{u}_{XY}} = \frac{u_X^{\text{Pre}} + u_Y}{\ddot{u}_X + \ddot{u}_Y} = \frac{u_X^{\text{Pre}}}{\ddot{u}_X + \ddot{u}_Y} + \frac{u_Y}{\ddot{u}_Y + \ddot{u}_Y} \tag{8.50}$$

$$\Leftrightarrow \quad \frac{u_X^{\text{Pre}}}{\ddot{u}_X + \ddot{u}_Y} = \frac{u_{XY}}{\ddot{u}_{XY}} - \frac{u_Y}{\ddot{u}_X + \ddot{u}_Y} \tag{8.51}$$

$$\Leftrightarrow \quad u_X^{\text{Pre}} = \frac{u_{XY}(\ddot{u}_X + \ddot{u}_Y)}{\ddot{u}_{XY}} - u_Y \,. \tag{8.52}$$

The computation of uncertainty-maximised opinions $\ddot{\omega}_X$ with uncertainty $\ddot{u}_X$ is described in Section 3.5.6. The convention for marginal cases of division by zero is that the whole fraction is equal to zero, as e.g. expressed by

$$\text{IF} \quad (u_{XY} = 0) \wedge (\ddot{u}_{XY} = 0) \quad \text{THEN} \quad \frac{u_{XY}}{\ddot{u}_{XY}} = 0\,. \tag{8.53}$$

Eq.(8.53) is sound in all cases, because we always have $u_{XY} \leq \ddot{u}_{XY}$. Of course, the uncertainty u_{XY} is strictly limited by the maximum possible uncertainty $\ddot{u}_{XY}$.

The uncertainty mass u_X^{Pre} of Eq.(8.52) could theoretically take values greater than 1 or less than 0. Therefore, in order to normalise the situation, it is necessary to complete the computation by constraining its range:

$$\text{Range constraint:} \begin{cases} \text{IF} & (u_X^{\text{Pre}} > 1) \;\; \text{THEN} \;\; u_X = 1, \\ \text{ELSEIF} & (u_X^{\text{Pre}} < 0) \;\; \text{THEN} \;\; u_X = 0, \\ \text{ELSE} & \qquad\qquad\qquad\quad u_X = u_X^{\text{Pre}}. \end{cases} \tag{8.54}$$

With the uncertainty mass u_X, the belief masses are computed as

$$\boldsymbol{b}_X(x) = \mathbf{P}_X(x) - \boldsymbol{a}_X(x) u_X, \;\; \text{for each } x \in \mathbb{X}\,. \tag{8.55}$$

This completes the computation of the averaging proportional quotient opinion:

$$\omega_X^{\text{Ave}} = \omega_{XY} / \omega_Y\,. \tag{8.56}$$

The averaging aspect of this operator stems from the averaging of the projected probabilities in Eq.(8.45). The proportional aspect comes from the computation of uncertainty in Eq.(8.52), proportionally to the uncertainty of the argument opinions.

8.3.3 Selective Division

The method for selective division, denoted $\omega_{XY} \,/\!\!/\, \omega_Y$, assumes that one of the values of Y has been observed, meaning that this value is considered to be absolutely TRUE. Let the specific observed value be y_j, then the belief mass distribution $\boldsymbol{b}_Y$ and projected probability distribution $\mathbf{P}_Y$ are expressed by

$$y_j \text{ is TRUE } \Rightarrow \begin{cases} \boldsymbol{b}_Y(y_j) = 1, \quad \text{and } \mathbf{P}_Y(y_j) = 1, \\ \\ \boldsymbol{b}_Y(y_g) = 0, \quad \text{and } \mathbf{P}_Y(y_g) = 0 \text{ for all other values } y_g \neq y_j\,. \end{cases} \tag{8.57}$$

The quotient projected probability distribution is expressed as:

$$\mathbf{P}_X(x_i) = \frac{\mathbf{P}_{XY}(x_i y_j)}{\mathbf{P}_Y(y_j)} = \mathbf{P}_{XY}(x_i y_j), \text{ for } i = 1, \ldots, k. \tag{8.58}$$

The uncertainty mass can be determined in the same way as for averaging proportional division according to Eq.(8.52), but since it is assumed that $u_Y = 0$ (because some y_j is TRUE), then a simplified version of Eq.(8.52) is expressed as

$$u_X^{\text{Sel}} = \frac{u_{XY}\, \ddot{u}_X}{\ddot{u}_{XY}}\,. \tag{8.59}$$

It can be verified that $u_X^{\text{Sel}} \in [0,1]$, so no constraining is needed. With the uncertainty mass u_X^{Sel}, the quotient belief mass distribution is computed as

$$\boldsymbol{b}_X^{\text{Sel}}(x) = \mathbf{P}_X(x) - \boldsymbol{a}_X(x) u_X^{\text{Sel}}, \text{ for each } x \in \mathbb{X}\,. \tag{8.60}$$

This completes the computation of the selective quotient opinion expressed as

$$\omega_X^{\text{Sel}} = \omega_{XY} \,/\!\!/\, \omega_Y\,. \tag{8.61}$$

The selective aspect of this division method is that one of the divisor values is assumed to be TRUE, which thereby selects one specific quotient term from the candidate projected probability terms, thereby avoiding the complications of unequal terms.

Chapter 9
Conditional Reasoning and Subjective Deduction

This chapter first discusses conditional reasoning in general including Bayes' theorem, and then describes the deduction operator in subjective logic. The subjective Bayes' theorem and the subjective abduction operator are described in Chapter 10.

9.1 Introduction to Conditional Reasoning

Both binary logic and probability calculus have methods for conditional reasoning, where deduction and abduction are essential operators. Reasoning with deduction directly follows the direction of the conditionals, and is e.g. used in predictive reasoning. Reasoning with abduction goes in the opposite direction by using Bayes' theorem to invert the conditionals, and is e.g. used in diagnostic reasoning.

In binary logic the classical operators for conditional inference are *Modus Ponens* (MP) which corresponds to deduction, *contraposition* (CP) which corresponds to Bayes' theorem and *Modus Tollens* (MT) which corresponds to abduction.

Let x and y be propositions where it is believed that the truth of y to a certain degree depends on the truth of x. Deductive reasoning is to derive belief in the truth of proposition y from having belief in the truth of proposition x. In binary logic, this is captured by MP (Modus Ponens) expressed as

$$\text{MP:} \quad \{(x \rightarrow y), x\} \ \vdash \ y \,, \tag{9.1}$$

where '$\vdash$' means 'entails' and $(x \rightarrow y)$ denotes the conditional relationship between cause x and consequence y. A standard interpretation of MP in normal language is: *"I know that whenever x is true, so is y. Since x is asserted to be true, so must y."*

Furthermore, when believing that y to a certain degree depends on x, the inverse is often also, but not necessarily, the case, as formalised by Bayes' theorem. In binary logic, a special case of this principle is captured by the CP rule, expressed as

$$\text{CP:} \quad (x \rightarrow y) \Leftrightarrow (\overline{y} \rightarrow \overline{x}) \,. \tag{9.2}$$

A standard interpretation of CP in normal language is: *"I know that whenever x is true, so is y. As a consequence, whenever y is false, then x must be false too."*

Finally, when believing that the truth of proposition y to a certain degree depends on the truth of proposition x, then abductive reasoning is to derive belief in x from having belief in y, which can be interpreted as deriving an explanation (x) for the observed (y). In binary logic, a specific case of abductive reasoning is captured by MT expressed as

$$\text{MT:} \quad \{(x \rightarrow y), \bar{y}\} \;\vdash\; \bar{x}\,. \tag{9.3}$$

MT emerges directly from the combination of MP and CP. An interpretation of MT in normal language is: *"I know that whenever x is true, so is y. Since y is asserted to be false, then x can not possibly be true, hence x must be false."* Note that reasoning with MT goes in the opposite direction to that of the conditional $(x \rightarrow y)$, which is why it represents a form of abductive reasoning.

Our experience tells us that certain states of the world are related. Consider for example 'weather' and 'umbrella' as the variables X and Y respectively, then we can say that the state of rainy weather and the state of carrying an umbrella are related. This situation can be modelled with the conditional proposition *"If it rains, Bob carries an umbrella"* which is of the form "IF x THEN y". Here x denotes the antecedent proposition/state (aka evidence), and y the consequent proposition/state (aka hypothesis) of the conditional. A causal conditional is when states of the parent (antecedent) variable can cause states of the child (consequent) variable.

There is a causal connection between rain and carrying an umbrella, so for a reasoning model about weather and umbrella it is natural to let the weather variable be the parent, and the umbrella variable be the child, as illustrated in Figure 9.1.

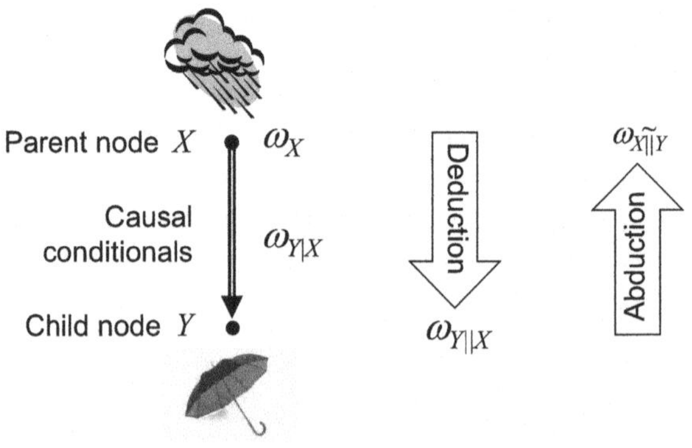

Fig. 9.1 Principles of deduction and abduction (see notation in Section 9.3)

A conditional is a complex proposition consisting of antecedent and consequent sub-propositions, that practically or hypothetically represent states in the real world. The conditional proposition does not represent a state in the same way; rather it represents a relationship between states of the world. Conditionals make it possible to reason from belief about antecedent propositions to infer belief about consequent propositions, which commonly is called deductive reasoning. In addition, conditionals can also be used to reason from belief about consequent propositions to infer belief about antecedent propositions, which commonly is called abductive reasoning. Abductive reasoning involves inversion of conditionals by using Bayes' theorem.

In the case of a *causal conditional*, the parent variable dynamically influences the child variable in space and time. For example, consider the binary parent proposition *"It rains"*, and the binary child proposition *"Bob carries an umbrella"*, which both can be evaluated to TRUE or FALSE. Initially, assume that both propositions are FALSE. Subsequently, assume that the parent proposition becomes TRUE, and that this makes the child proposition also become TRUE. If this dynamic conditional relationship holds in general, then it can be seen as a TRUE conditional.

Note that in the case of a TRUE causal conditional, forcing the child proposition to become TRUE normally does not influence the parent proposition in any way. The above scenario of rain and umbrellas clearly demonstrates this principle, because carrying an umbrella obviously does not bring rain. However, in the case of a TRUE causal conditional, simply knowing that the child is TRUE can nevertheless indicate that the parent might be TRUE, because seeing Bob carrying an umbrella can plausibly indicate that it rains. Hence, in the case of a TRUE causal conditional, to force or to know the child proposition to be TRUE can have very different effects on the parent proposition. However, to force or to know the parent proposition to be TRUE have equal effect on the child proposition.

A *derivative conditional* is an inverse-causal conditional, meaning that forcing the parent proposition to become TRUE does not necessarily make the child proposition become TRUE as well. For example, the conditional *"IF Bob carries an umbrella THEN it must be raining"* is a derivative conditional, because forcing Bob to carry an umbrella does not cause rain.

Conditionals can also be non-causal. For example if two lamps are connected to the same electric switch, then observing one of the lamps being lit gives an indication of the other lamp being lit too, so there is clearly a correlation between them. However neither lamp actually causes the other to light up, rather it is the flipping of the switch which causes both lamps to light up at the same time. It can be challenging to identify causal connections between variables, which is nicely illustrated by the quote: *"Correlation is not causation but it sure is a hint"* [97].

Conditionals are logically directed from the antecedent to the consequent proposition. The idea is that an analyst with belief about the conditional's validity and the antecedent's truth can infer belief about the consequent proposition's truth. However, in case the analyst needs to infer knowledge about the antecedent proposition, then the conditional can not be used directly. What the analyst needs is the opposite conditional, where the propositions have swapped places. For example assume that Alice knows that Bob usually carries an umbrella when it rains, which can be expressed as a causal conditional. If she wants to know whether it rains by observing if Bob picks up his umbrella before going out, then the causal conditional is not directly applicable. Alice might intuitively infer that it probably rains when seeing that he picks up an umbrella, and she then practices abductive reasoning because she applies the inverse of a causal conditional. This is also called derivative reasoning, because she implicitly inverts the initial conditional (whether it is causal or not). Abductive reasoning requires inversion of conditionals using Bayes' theorem, and can be challenging to intuitively understand. The *base-rate fallacy* is a form of flawed intuitive abductive reasoning caused by ignoring or incorrectly applying Bayes' theorem. It is therefore important to apply Bayes' theorem correctly and consistently. The probabilistic Bayes' theorem is described in Section 9.2.1, and the subjective Bayes' theorem in Chapter 10.

The validity of conditionals can be expressed in different ways, e.g. as Boolean TRUE or FALSE, as probabilities, or as subjective opinions. Conditional probabilities are expressed as $p(\text{<consequent>} \mid \text{<antecedent>})$, i.e. with the consequent variable first, and the antecedent variable last. The sections below first describe probabilistic deduction and abduction including Bayes' theorem, and then describes in detail the methods for binomial and multinomial deduction in subjective logic.

9.2 Probabilistic Conditional Inference

With the aim of giving the reader a gentle introduction to the principles of deduction and abduction, this section provides a brief overview of probabilistic deduction and abduction, with a short discussion about the interpretation of Bayes' theorem.

9.2.1 Bayes' Theorem

Bayes' theorem is named after the English statistician and philosopher Thomas Bayes (1701–1761), who formally demonstrated how new evidence can be used to update beliefs. This formalism was further developed by the French mathematician Pierre-Simon Laplace (1749–1827), who first published the traditional formulation of Bayes' theorem in his 1812 *Théorie analytique des probabilités*. Bayes' theorem is traditionally expressed as in Eq.(9.4):

$$\text{Traditional statement of Bayes' theorem:} \quad p(x|y) = \frac{p(x)p(y|x)}{p(y)} \,. \tag{9.4}$$

With Bayes' theorem, the inverted conditional $p(x|y)$ can be computed from the conditional $p(y|x)$. However, this traditional expression of Bayes' theorem hides some subtleties related to base rates, as explained below. People who have a basic knowledge of probability theory, but who are not familiar with Bayes' theorem, can easily get confused when confronted with it for the first time.

Assume for example the case of buying a lottery ticket with a low probability of winning, expressed as the conditional probability $p(y|x) = 0.001$, where the statements are x: 'bought ticket' and y: 'won prize'. Assume further that you actually bought a ticket, so that $p(x) = 1.0$, and actually won, so that $p(y) = 1.0$. An intuitive, but wrong, interpretation of Bayes' theorem would then be that $p(x|y) = (0.001 \times 1.0)/1.0 = 0.001$, i.e. that the probability of having bought a ticket given a win is only 0.001, which clearly is wrong. The obvious correct answer is that if you won a prize then you certainly bought a ticket, expressed by $p(x|y) = 1.0$.

People who are familiar with Bayes' theorem know that $p(x)$ and $p(y)$ are base rates (prior probabilities), but this is typically not mentioned in explanations of Bayes' theorem in text books. It is often only when practical examples are presented that it becomes clear that Bayes' theorem requires base rates (priors) of x and y, and not situation-dependent probabilities of x and y.

In order to avoid confusion between the base rate of x, and the probability of x, we use the term $a(x)$ to denote the base rate of x. Similarly, the term $a(y)$ denotes the base rate of y. With this convention, Bayes' theorem can be formalised more intuitively, as expressed in Theorem 9.1.

Theorem 9.1 (Bayes' Theorem with Base Rates).

$$p(x|y) = \frac{a(x)p(y|x)}{a(y)} \,. \tag{9.5}$$

Proof. Formally, a conditional probability is defined as follows:

$$\text{Conditional probability:}\quad p(y|x) = \frac{p(x \wedge y)}{p(x)} \,. \tag{9.6}$$

Conditionals represent general dependence relationships between statements, so the terms $p(x \wedge y)$ and $p(x)$ on the right-hand side of Eq.(9.6) must necessarily represent general prior probabilities, and not for example probabilities of specific observations. A general prior probability is the same as a base rate, as explained in Section 2.6. Hence, more explicit versions of Eq.(9.6) can be expressed as

$$\text{Conditional probabilities based on base rates:}\quad \begin{cases} p(y|x) = \dfrac{a(x \wedge y)}{a(x)} \,, \\[2ex] p(x|y) = \dfrac{a(x \wedge y)}{a(y)} \,. \end{cases} \tag{9.7}$$

Bayes' theorem can easily be derived from the definition of conditional probability of Eq.(9.7) which expresses the conditional probability of $p(y|x)$ and $p(x|y)$ in terms of base rates:

$$\begin{cases} p(y|x) = \dfrac{a(x \wedge y)}{a(x)} \\[2ex] p(x|y) = \dfrac{a(x \wedge y)}{a(y)} \end{cases} \Rightarrow \quad p(x|y) = \frac{a(x)p(y|x)}{a(y)} \,. \tag{9.8}$$

□

However, Bayes' theorem in the form of Eq.(9.5) hides the fact that the base rate $a(y)$ is a *marginal base rate* (MBR) which must be expressed as a function of the base rate $a(x)$ [56]. This requirement is implemented in Theorem 9.2.

Theorem 9.2 (Bayes' Theorem with Marginal Base Rate).

$$p(x|y) = \frac{a(x)p(y|x)}{a(x)p(y|x) + a(\overline{x})p(y|\overline{x})} \; . \tag{9.9}$$

Proof. The marginal base rate $a(y)$ is derived by expressing the independent Bayes' theorem formulas for $p(y|x)$ and $p(y|\overline{x})$:

$$\begin{cases} p(y|x) = \dfrac{a(y)p(x|y)}{a(x)} \\ p(y|\overline{x}) = \dfrac{a(y)p(\overline{x}|y)}{a(\overline{x})} = \dfrac{a(y)(1-p(x|y))}{a(\overline{x})} \end{cases} \tag{9.10}$$

$$\Longleftrightarrow \begin{cases} p(x|y) = \dfrac{a(x)p(y|x)}{a(y)} \\ p(x|y) = \dfrac{a(y)-a(\overline{x})p(y|\overline{x})}{a(y)} \end{cases} \tag{9.11}$$

$$\Longrightarrow \quad a(y) = a(x)p(y|x) + a(\overline{x})p(y|\overline{x}). \tag{9.12}$$

Eq.(9.9) emerges by inserting Eq.(9.12) in Eq.(9.5). □

Note that Eq.(9.12) simply is an instance of the law of total probability:

$$\text{Law of total probability:} \quad p(y) = p(x)p(y|x) + p(\overline{x})p(y|\overline{x}) \; . \tag{9.13}$$

The traditional formulation of Bayes' theorem of Eq.(9.4) is unnecessarily ambiguous because it does not distinguish between base rates (priors) and probabilities (posteriors), and because it does not show that the base rates of x and y are dependent. Bayes' theorem with MBR expressed in Eq.(9.9) rectifies this problem by expressing the MBR of y denoted $a(y)$ as a function of the base rate $a(x)$.

Let us revisit the example of the lottery, where the probability of a win given the purchase of a ticket is $p(y|x) = 0.001$, and where intuition dictates that the probability of having bought a ticket given a win must be $p(x|y) = 1$. We assume that the probability of winning given no ticket is zero, expressed by $p(y|\overline{x}) = 0$. The correct answer then emerges directly from Eq.(9.9), expressed by

$$\text{Probability of ticket given win:} \quad p(x|y) = \frac{a(x)p(y|x)}{a(x)p(y|x) + a(\overline{x})p(y|\overline{x})} = 1. \tag{9.14}$$

In fact, neither the base rate of winning, nor the base rate of having bought a ticket, have any influence on the result, due to the fact that the probability of winning given no ticket is always zero.

9.2.2 Binomial Probabilistic Deduction and Abduction

The notation $p(y\|x)$ represents the marginal probability of y derived with the law of total probability. Hence, term $p(y\|x)$ represents a derived probability, whereas the term $p(y|x)$ represents an input argument probability. This notational convention is also used for subjective opinions below.

Figure 9.1 shows a deductive and an abductive reasoning situations where X is the parent variable and Y is the child variable. Parent-child reasoning models are typically assumed to be causal, where parent nodes have a causal influence over child nodes. In this situation, conditionals are typically expressed in the same direction as the reasoning, i.e. with parent as antecedent, and child as consequent.

Causal conditional inference, the standard form of *deduction*, is when the analyst has evidence about the parent variable, and the child variable is the query target.

Assume that the values x and $\overline{x}$ are relevant to the value y (and $\overline{y}$) according to the conditional statements $y|x$ and $y|\overline{x}$. Here, x and $\overline{x}$ are parents and y is the child of the conditionals. Let $p(x)$, $p(y|x)$ and $p(y|\overline{x})$ be probability assessments of x, $y|x$ and $y|\overline{x}$ respectively. By using the law of total probability of Eq.(9.13), the conditionally deduced probability $p(y\|x)$ can be computed as

$$\text{Deduced probability:} \quad \begin{aligned} p(y\|x) &= p(x)p(y|x) + p(\overline{x})p(y|\overline{x}) \\ &= p(x)p(y|x) + (1-p(x))p(y|\overline{x}) \, . \end{aligned} \tag{9.15}$$

In case the analyst knows exactly that x is true, i.e. $p(x) = 1$, then from Eq.(9.15) it can immediately be seen that $p(y\|x) = p(y|x)$. Conversely, in case the analyst knows exactly that x is false, i.e. $p(x) = 0$, then from Eq.(9.15) it can immediately be seen that $p(y\|x) = p(y|\overline{x})$.

Derivative conditional inference, called *abduction*, is when the analyst has evidence about the child variable, and the parent variable is the query target of the reasoning. In this case, the available conditionals are directed in the opposite direction to the reasoning, and opposite to what the analyst needs.

Assume that the state values x and $\overline{x}$ are relevant to y according to the conditional statements $y|x$ and $y|\overline{x}$, where x and $\overline{x}$ are parent values, and y and $\overline{y}$ are child values. Let $p(y)$, $p(y|x)$ and $p(y|\overline{x})$ be probability assessments of y, $y|x$ and $y|\overline{x}$ respectively. The required conditionals can be correctly derived by inverting the available conditionals using Bayes' theorem with MBR from Eq.(9.9).

The conditionally abduced probability $p(y\,\widetilde{\|}\,x)$ can then be computed as:

$$\begin{aligned} p(x\,\widetilde{\|}\,y) &= p(y)p(x|y) + p(\overline{y})p(x|\overline{y}) \\ &= p(y)\left(\frac{a(x)p(y|x)}{a(x)p(y|x)+a(\overline{x})p(y|\overline{x})}\right) + p(\overline{y})\left(\frac{a(x)p(\overline{y}|x)}{a(x)p(\overline{y}|x)+a(\overline{x})p(\overline{y}|\overline{x})}\right). \end{aligned} \tag{9.16}$$

Note that Eq.(9.16) simply results from the application of conditional deduction according to Eq.(9.15) with x and y swapped in every term, where the conditionals are determined according to Eq.(9.9).

The terms used in Eq.(9.15) and Eq.(9.16) have the following interpretations:

$$p(y|x)\ :\ \text{the conditional probability of } y \text{ given that } x \text{ is TRUE,}$$

$$p(y|\overline{x})\ :\ \text{the conditional probability of } y \text{ given that } x \text{ is FALSE,}$$

$$p(x|y)\ :\ \text{the conditional probability of } x \text{ given that } y \text{ is TRUE,}$$

$$p(x|\overline{y})\ :\ \text{the conditional probability of } x \text{ given that } y \text{ is FALSE,}$$

$$p(y)\ :\ \text{the probability of } y,$$

$$p(\overline{y})\ :\ \text{the probability of the complement of } y\ (= 1 - p(y)),$$

$$a(x)\ :\ \text{the base rate of } x,$$

$$p(y\|x)\ :\ \text{the marginal probability of } y \text{ deduced from evidence on } x,$$

$$p(x\widetilde{\|}y)\ :\ \text{the marginal probability of } x \text{ abduced from evidence on } y.$$

The binomial expressions for probabilistic deduction of Eq.(9.15) and probabilistic abduction of Eq.(9.16) can be generalised to multinomial expressions as explained below.

9.2.3 Multinomial Probabilistic Deduction and Abduction

Let $\mathbb{X} = \{x_i \mid i = 1, \ldots, k\}$ be the parent domain with random variable X, and let $\mathbb{Y} = \{y_j \mid j = 1, \ldots, l\}$ be the child domain with random variable Y. The conditional relationship between X and Y is then expressed as the set of conditionals $p(Y|X)$ with k specific conditionals $p(Y|x_i)$, each having the l dimensions of Y. This is illustrated in Figure 9.2.

A specific conditional probability distribution $\boldsymbol{p}(Y|x)$ relates the value x to the values of variable Y. The conditional probability distribution $\boldsymbol{p}(Y|x)$ consists of l probabilities expressed as

$$\boldsymbol{p}(Y|x) = \{p(y_j|x),\ \text{for } j = 1, \ldots, l\},\ \text{where} \sum_{j=1}^{l} p(y_j|x) = 1\,. \tag{9.17}$$

The term $\boldsymbol{p}(Y|X)$ denotes the set of probability distributions of the form of Eq.(9.17), which can be expressed as

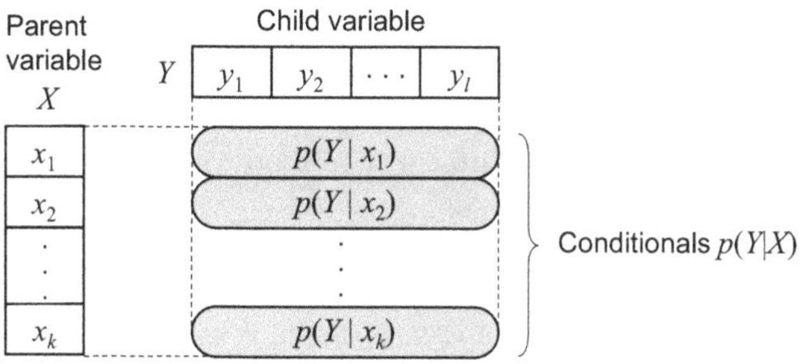

Fig. 9.2 Multinomial conditionals between parent X and child Y

$$\boldsymbol{p}(Y|X) = \{\boldsymbol{p}(Y|x_i),\ \text{for}\ i = 1,\ldots,k\}\ . \tag{9.18}$$

The law of total probability for multinomial probability distributions is

$$\text{Multinomial law of total probability:}\ p(y) = \sum_{i=1}^{k} p(x_i)p(y|x_i)\ . \tag{9.19}$$

The probabilistic expression for multinomial conditional deduction from X to Y is directly derived from the law of total probability of Eq.(9.19). The deduced probability distribution over Y is denoted $\boldsymbol{p}(Y\|X)$, where the deduced probability $p(y\|X)$ of each value y is

$$\text{Deduced probability:}\quad p(y\|X) = \sum_{i=1}^{k} p(x_i)p(y|x_i)\ . \tag{9.20}$$

The deduced probability distribution on Y can be expressed as

$$\boldsymbol{p}(Y\|X) = \{p(y_j\|X)\ \text{for}\ j = 1,\ldots,l\}\ \text{where}\ \sum_{j=1}^{l} p(y_j\|X) = 1\ . \tag{9.21}$$

Note that in case the exact variable value $X = x_i$ is known, i.e. $p(x_i) = 1$, then from Eq.(9.20) it can immediately be seen that the deduced probability distribution becomes $p(Y\|X) = p(Y|x_i)$.

Moving over to multinomial abduction, it is necessary to first compute the inverted conditionals using the multinomial Bayes' theorem with MBR. Let us first repeat Bayes' theorem with base rates:

$$p(x|y) = \frac{a(x)p(y|x)}{a(y)}, \tag{9.22}$$

where $a(x)$ and $a(y)$ are base rates (prior probabilities). Applying the law of total probability to base rates produces the marginal base rate (MBR) for $a(y)$:

$$\text{Multinomial MBR:}\ \ a(y) = \sum_{i=1}^{k} a(x_i)p(y|x_i). \tag{9.23}$$

The expression for inverting probabilistic conditionals, and for Bayes' theorem with MBR likewise, is then

$$\text{General Bayes' theorem with MBR:}\ \ p(x|y) = \frac{a(x)p(y|x)}{\sum_{i=1}^{k} a(x_i)p(y|x_i)}. \tag{9.24}$$

Note that Bayes' theorem must have a MBR in the denominator, like in Eq.(9.24), in order for repeated conditional inversions to produce the same set of conditionals every time. In other words, inconsistent inversion of conditionals would in general result from setting an arbitrary base rate $a(y)$ in Eq.(9.22). It is therefore recommended to always use the MBR distribution when applying Bayes' theorem.

A generalisation of MBRs for conditional opinions is described in Section 9.5.1. MBRs are also used for the subjective Bayes' theorem described in Section 9.32.

By swapping x and y in every term of Eq.(9.20) and substituting the conditionals with inverted multinomial conditionals from Eq.(9.24), the general expression for probabilistic abduction emerges:

$$\text{Abduced probability:}\ \ p(x\widetilde{\|}Y) = \sum_{j=1}^{l} p(y_j)\left(\frac{a(x)p(y_j|x)}{\sum_{i=1}^{k} a(x_i)p(y_j|x_i)}\right). \tag{9.25}$$

The set of abduced probability distributions can be expressed as

$$p(X\widetilde{\|}Y) = \{p(x_i\|Y) \text{ for } i = 1,\ldots,k\}, \text{ where } \sum_{i=1}^{k} p(x_i\|Y) = 1\,. \tag{9.26}$$

The above described formalism is illustrated by a numerical example in Section 10.8.1.

9.3 Notation for Subjective Conditional Inference

This section introduces the notation used for conditional deduction and abduction in subjective logic. The notation is similar to the corresponding notation for probabilistic deduction and abduction. The detailed mathematical description of the deduction operators is provided in subsequent sections below. The operator for abduction is described in Chapter 10. Abduction requires inversion of conditional opinions using the subjective Bayes' theorem, which is also described in Chapter 10.

Notations used in the formalism for subjective conditional inference have the interpretations described next.

ω_X : multinomial opinion $\omega_X = (\boldsymbol{b}_X, u_X, \boldsymbol{a}_X)$ on X,

$\boldsymbol{b}_X(x)$: belief mass of specific value x,

u_X : uncertainty mass on X,

$\boldsymbol{a}_X$: base rate distribution over X,

$\boldsymbol{a}_X(x)$: base rate of specific value x,

$\boldsymbol{\omega}_{Y|X}$: set of multinomial conditional opinions on Y,

$\omega_{Y|x}$: multinomial conditional opinion on Y,

$\boldsymbol{b}_{Y|x}(y)$: conditional belief mass of specific value y,

$\boldsymbol{\omega}_{X\tilde{|}Y}$: set of inverted multinomial conditional opinions on X,

$\omega_{X\tilde{|}y}$: inverted multinomial conditional opinion on X,

$\boldsymbol{b}_{X\tilde{|}y}(x)$: inverted conditional belief mass of specific value x,

$\omega_{Y\|X}$: deduced multinomial opinion on Y,

$\boldsymbol{b}_{Y\|X}(y)$: deduced belief mass of specific value y,

$\omega_{X\tilde{\|}Y}$: abduced multinomial opinion on X,

$\boldsymbol{b}_{X\tilde{\|}Y}(x)$: abduced belief mass of specific value x.

Note that the deduced opinion $\omega_{Y\|X}$ is equal to the *marginal opinion* $\omega_{[\![Y]\!]}$ derived from the *joint opinion* ω_{YX}. Joint opinions are described in Section 11.2.

9.3.1 Notation for Binomial Deduction and Abduction

Let $\mathbb{X} = \{x, \overline{x}\}$ and $\mathbb{Y} = \{y, \overline{y}\}$ be two binary domains with respective variables X and Y, where there is a degree of relevance between X and Y. Let $\omega_x = (b_x, d_x, u_x, a_x)$, $\omega_{y|x} = (b_{y|x}, d_{y|x}, u_{Y|x}, a_{y|x})$ and $\omega_{y|\overline{x}} = (b_{y|\overline{x}}, d_{y|\overline{x}}, u_{Y|\overline{x}}, a_{y|\overline{x}})$ be an agent's respective opinions about x being true, about y being true given that x is true, and finally about y being true given that x is false.

Conditional deduction is computed with the deduction operator denoted '$\circledcirc$', so that the notation for binomial deduction is

$$\text{Binomial deduction:} \quad \omega_{y\|x} = \omega_x \circledcirc (\omega_{y|x},\ \omega_{y|\bar{x}}) \,. \tag{9.27}$$

Conditional abduction is computed with the abduction operator '$\widetilde{\circledcirc}$':

$$\begin{aligned} \text{Binomial abduction:} \quad \omega_{\widetilde{x\|y}} &= \omega_y \,\widetilde{\circledcirc}\, (\omega_{y|x},\ \omega_{y|\bar{x}},\ a_x) \\ &= \omega_y \,\circledcirc\, \widetilde{\phi}(\omega_{y|x},\ \omega_{y|\bar{x}},\ a_x) \\ &= \omega_y \,\circledcirc\, (\omega_{\widetilde{x|y}},\ \omega_{\widetilde{x|\bar{y}}}) \,. \end{aligned} \tag{9.28}$$

The conditionally abduced opinion $\omega_{\widetilde{x\|y}}$ expresses the belief about x being true as a function of the beliefs about y and the two sub-conditionals $y|x$ and $y|\bar{x}$, as well as of the base rate a_x.

In order to compute Eq.(9.28), it is necessary to invert the conditional opinions $\omega_{y|x}$ and $\omega_{y|\bar{x}}$ using the operator for conditional inversion denoted $\widetilde{\phi}$. Conditional inversion is based on the subjective Bayes' theorem described in Section 10.3. The notation for the binomial subjective Bayes' theorem is

$$\text{Binomial subjective Bayes' theorem:} \quad (\omega_{\widetilde{x|y}}, \omega_{\widetilde{x|\bar{y}}}) = \widetilde{\phi}(\omega_{y|x}, \omega_{y|\bar{x}}, a_x) \,. \tag{9.29}$$

9.3.2 Notation for Multinomial Deduction and Abduction

Let domain $\mathbb{X}$ have cardinality $k = |\mathbb{X}|$ and domain $\mathbb{Y}$ have cardinality $l = |\mathbb{Y}|$, where variable X plays the role of parent, and variable Y the role of child.

Assume the set $\boldsymbol{\omega}_{Y|X}$ of conditional opinions of the form $\omega_{Y|x_i}$, where $i = 1, \ldots, k$. There is thus one conditional opinion for each value x_i of the parent variable. Each of these conditionals must be interpreted as the subjective opinion on Y given that x_i is TRUE. The subscript notation on each conditional opinion $\omega_{Y|x_i}$ specifies not only the child variable Y it applies to, but also the value x_i of the parent variable it is conditioned on.

By extending the notation for binomial conditional deduction to the case of multinomial opinions, the general expression for multinomial conditional deduction is written as

$$\text{Multinomial opinion deduction:} \quad \omega_{Y\|X} = \omega_X \circledcirc \boldsymbol{\omega}_{Y|X} \,, \tag{9.30}$$

where the symbol '⊚' denotes the conditional deduction operator for subjective opinions, and where $\boldsymbol{\omega}_{Y|X}$ is a set of $k = |\mathbb{X}|$ different opinions conditioned on each $x_i \in \mathbb{X}$ respectively.

The structure of deductive reasoning is illustrated in Figure 9.3. The conditionals are expressed on the child variable, which is also the target variable for the deductive reasoning. In the example of weather being the parent variable, and carrying an umbrella being the child variable, the evidence is about the weather, and the conclusion is an opinion about carrying an umbrella.

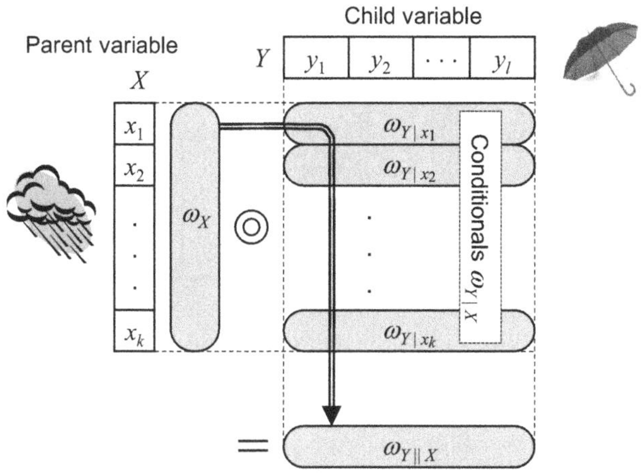

Fig. 9.3 Structure of conditionals for deduction

In the case of abduction, the goal is to reason from the child variable Y to the parent variable X, which involves the conditional inversion operator $\widetilde{\phi}$:

$$\text{Multinomial subjective abduction:} \quad \omega_{X\widetilde{\|}Y} = \omega_Y \,\widetilde{\circledcirc}\, (\boldsymbol{\omega}_{Y|X},\, \boldsymbol{a}_X)$$

$$= \omega_Y \circledcirc \widetilde{\phi}(\boldsymbol{\omega}_{Y|X},\, \boldsymbol{a}_X) \qquad (9.31)$$

$$= \omega_Y \circledcirc \boldsymbol{\omega}_{X\widetilde{|}Y}\,,$$

where the symbol '$\widetilde{\circledcirc}$' denotes the conditional abduction operator for subjective opinions, and $\boldsymbol{\omega}_{Y|X}$ is a set of $k = |\mathbb{X}|$ different multinomial opinions conditioned on each $x_i \in \mathbb{X}$ respectively. The base rate distribution over X is denoted by $\boldsymbol{a}_X$.

In order to compute the abduced opinion according to Eq.(9.31) it is necessary to invert the set of conditional opinions $\boldsymbol{\omega}_{Y|X}$ with the subjective Bayes' theorem described in Section 10.6. The notation is

$$\text{Subjective Bayes' theorem:} \quad \boldsymbol{\omega}_{X\widetilde{|}Y} = \widetilde{\phi}(\boldsymbol{\omega}_{Y|X},\, \boldsymbol{a}_X)\,. \qquad (9.32)$$

The structure of abductive reasoning is illustrated in Figure 9.4. The fact that both the evidence opinion as well as the set of conditional opinions are expressed on the child variable makes this reasoning situation complex. The parent is now the target query variable, so it is a situation of reasoning from child to parent. In the example of weather being the causal parent variable, and carrying an umbrella being the consequent child variable, the evidence is about carrying an umbrella, and the conclusion is an opinion about its possible cause which e.g. is rainy weather.

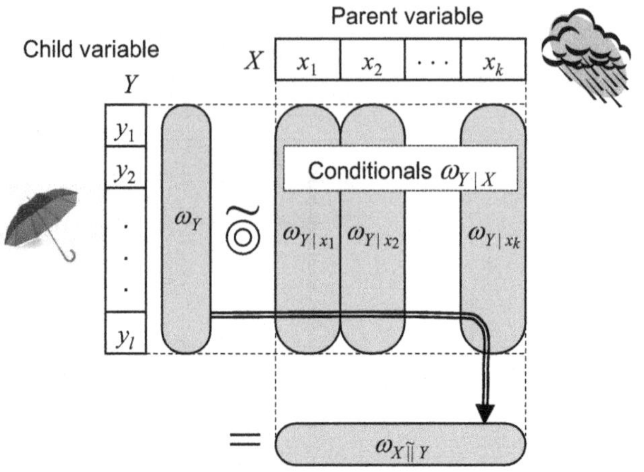

Fig. 9.4 Structure of conditionals for abduction

Note that input conditionals do not necessarily have to be causal, they could just as well be anti-causal. However, for analysts it is typically easier to express conditionals in the causal direction, which is the reason why it is normally assumed that parent variables represent causes of child variables.

In the context of intelligence analysis the term *'derivative reasoning'* is used in the sense of applying anti-causal conditionals, e.g. by inverting causal conditionals (using Bayes' theorem [102]), or by estimating anti-causal conditionals directly.

The above sections presented high level concepts of conditionals, as well as of deductive and abductive reasoning. The next sections describe the binomial and multinomial deduction operators in subjective logic.

The binomial case can be described in the form of closed expressions, whereas the multinomial case requires a series of steps that need to be implemented as an algorithm. For that reason, the cases of binomial and multinomial deduction are presented separately.

9.4 Binomial Deduction

Conditional deduction with binomial opinions has previously been described in [62]. However, that description did not mention the marginal base rate (MBR) of Eq.(9.36) which should be applied for consistency. The MBR is included in Definition 9.1 below which defines binomial deduction.

9.4.1 Marginal Base Rate for Binomial Opinions

In general, the base rate of x and the conditionals on y put constraints on the base rate of y. The base rate consistency requirement is to derive a specific base rate determined by the law of total probability. The expression for the MBR a_y in Eq.(9.40) is derived from the law of total probability:

$$\text{Binomial law of total probability: } a_y = a_x \mathrm{P}(y|x) + a_{\overline{x}} \mathrm{P}(y|\overline{x}) \,. \tag{9.33}$$

Assuming that $\omega_{y|x}$ and $\omega_{y|\overline{x}}$ are not both vacuous, i.e. that $u_{y|x} + u_{y|\overline{x}} < 2$ the simple expression for the MBR a_y can be derived as follows:

$$a_y = a_x \mathrm{P}(y|x) + a_{\overline{x}} \mathrm{P}(y|\overline{x}) \tag{9.34}$$

$$\Leftrightarrow \quad a_y = a_x (b_{y|x} + a_y u_{y|x}) + a_{\overline{x}} (b_{y|\overline{x}} + a_y u_{y|\overline{x}}) \tag{9.35}$$

$$\Leftrightarrow \quad a_y = \frac{a_x b_{y|x} + a_{\overline{x}} b_{y|\overline{x}}}{1 - a_x u_{y|x} - a_{\overline{x}} u_{y|\overline{x}}} \,. \tag{9.36}$$

With the MBR of Eq.(9.36) it is guaranteed that the projected probabilities of binomial conditional opinions do not change after multiple inversions.

In case $\omega_{y|x}$ and $\omega_{y|\overline{x}}$ are both vacuous, i.e. when $u_{y|x} = u_{y|\overline{x}} = 1$, then there is no constraint on the base rate a_y, as in the case of the free base-rate interval described in Section 9.4.2.

Figure 9.5 is a screenshot of binomial deduction, involving the MBR which is equal to the deduced projected probability given a vacuous antecedent $\widehat{\omega}_x$, according to the requirement of Eq.(9.36).

To intuitively see why it is necessary to use the MBR, consider the case of a pair of dogmatic conditional opinions $\omega_{y|x}$ and $\omega_{y|\overline{x}}$, where both projected probabilities are $\mathrm{P}(y|x) = \mathrm{P}(y|\overline{x}) = 1$. In this trivial case we always have $\mathrm{P}(y) = 1$, independently of the projected probability $\mathrm{P}(x)$. It would then be totally inconsistent to e.g. have base rate $a_y = 0.5$ when we always have $\mathrm{P}(y) = 1$. The base rate must reflect reality, so the only consistent base rate in this case is $a_y = 1$, which emerges directly from Eq.(9.36).

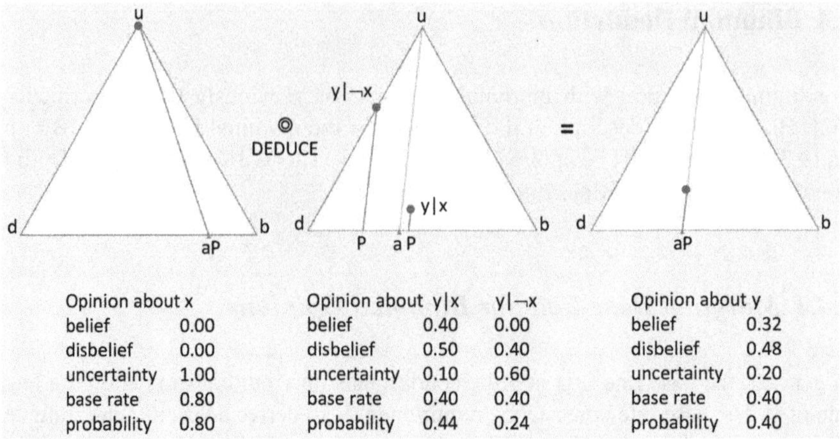

Fig. 9.5 Screenshot of deduction with vacuous antecedent $\widehat{\omega}_x$ and MBR $a_y = 0.40$

9.4.2 Free Base-Rate Interval

A less strict requirement than the MBR for a_y is to allow the base rate to be selected from an interval. This section describes the relatively lax requirement of setting an interval from which a free base rate can be chosen.

The idea is that the base rate a_y in Eq.(9.40) must take its value from the interval defined by a lower base rate limit a_y^- and an upper base rate limit a_y^+ in order to be consistent with the conditionals. In the case of dogmatic conditionals, the free base-rate interval shrinks to a single base rate which in fact is the MBR. The upper and lower limits for free base rates are the projected probabilities of the consequent opinions resulting from first assuming a vacuous antecedent opinion $\widehat{\omega}_x$, and then hypothetically setting maximum (=1) and minimum (=0) base rates for the consequent variable y. The upper and lower base rate limits are

$$\begin{aligned}\text{Upper base rate:} \quad a_y^+ &= \max_{a_y=0}^{1}[a_x \mathrm{P}(y|x) + a_{\overline{x}} \mathrm{P}(y|\overline{x})] \\ &= \max_{a_y=0}^{1}[a_x (b_{y|x} + a_y u_{y|x}) + a_{\overline{x}} (b_{y|\overline{x}} + a_y u_{y|\overline{x}})] \,.\end{aligned} \tag{9.37}$$

$$\begin{aligned}\text{Lower base rate:} \quad a_y^- &= \min_{a_y=0}^{1}[a_x \mathrm{P}(y|x) + a_{\overline{x}} \mathrm{P}(y|\overline{x})] \\ &= \min_{a_y=0}^{1}[a_x (b_{y|x} + a_y u_{y|x}) + a_{\overline{x}} (b_{y|\overline{x}} + a_y u_{y|\overline{x}})] \,.\end{aligned} \tag{9.38}$$

Figure 9.6 is a screenshot of binomial deduction, indicating the upper base rate $a_y^+ = 0.52$, which is equal to the deduced projected probability given a vacuous antecedent $\widehat{\omega}_x$ and a hypothetical base rate $a_y = 1$, according to Eq.(9.37).

Opinion about x		Opinion about $y\|x$		$y\|\neg x$	Opinion about y	
belief	0.00	belief	0.40	0.00	belief	0.32
disbelief	0.00	disbelief	0.50	0.40	disbelief	0.48
uncertainty	1.00	uncertainty	0.10	0.60	uncertainty	0.20
base rate	0.80	base rate	1.00	1.00	base rate	1.00
probability	0.80	probability	0.50	0.60	probability	0.52

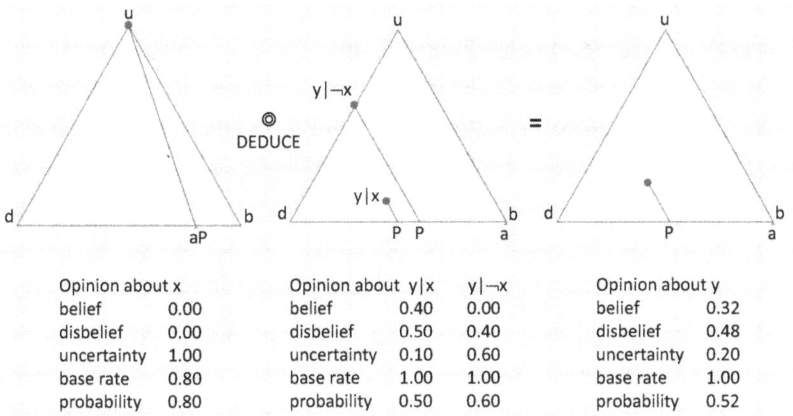

Fig. 9.6 Screenshot of deduction with vacuous antecedent $\widehat{\omega}_x$ and upper base rate $a_y = 0.52$

Figure 9.7 is a screenshot of binomial deduction, indicating the lower base rate $a_y^- = 0.32$, which is equal to the deduced projected probability given a vacuous antecedent $\widehat{\omega}_x$ and a hypothetical zero base rate $a_y = 0$, according to Eq.(9.38).

Opinion about x		Opinion about $y\|x$		$y\|\neg x$	Opinion about y	
belief	0.00	belief	0.40	0.00	belief	0.32
disbelief	0.00	disbelief	0.50	0.40	disbelief	0.48
uncertainty	1.00	uncertainty	0.10	0.60	uncertainty	0.20
base rate	0.80	base rate	0.00	0.00	base rate	0.00
probability	0.80	probability	0.40	0.00	probability	0.32

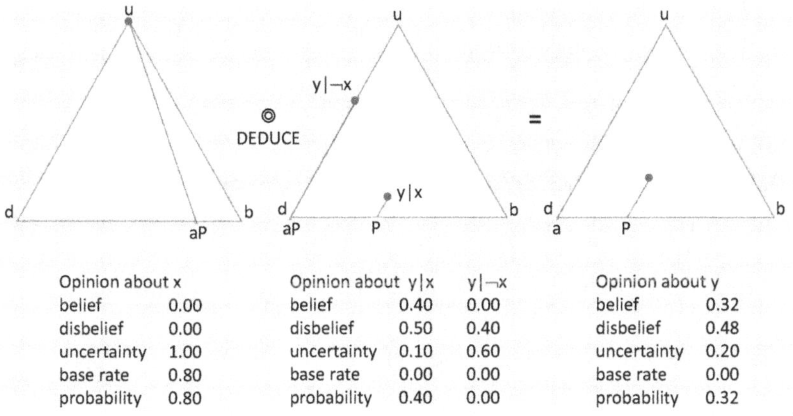

Fig. 9.7 Screenshot of deduction with vacuous antecedent $\widehat{\omega}_x$ and lower free base rate $a_y = 0.32$

Dogmatic conditionals make the base-rate interval collapse to the MBR of Eq.(9.39):

$$a_y = a_x \, P(y|x) + a_{\bar{x}} P(y|\bar{x}) = a_x b_{y|x} + a_{\bar{x}} b_{y|\bar{x}} \, . \qquad (9.39)$$

In case both $\omega_{y|x}$ and $\omega_{y|\bar{x}}$ are vacuous opinions, i.e. when $u_{y|x} = u_{y|\bar{x}} = 1$, then the free base-rate interval for a_y is $[0,1]$, meaning that there is no consistency constraint on the base rate a_y which can be chosen arbitrarily.

9.4.3 Method for Binomial Deduction

Binomial opinion deduction is a generalisation of probabilistic conditional deduction expressed in Eq.(9.15). It is assumed that the analyst has the pair of conditionals $\omega_{y|x}$ and $\omega_{y|\bar{x}}$, applies the MBR a_y (or selects a_y from the free base-rate interval), and has an evidence opinion ω_x.

Definition 9.1 (Conditional Deduction with Binomial Opinions).
Let $\mathbb{X} = \{x, \bar{x}\}$ and $\mathbb{Y} = \{y, \bar{y}\}$ be binary domains where there is a degree of relevance of variable $X \in \mathbb{X}$ to variable $Y \in \mathbb{Y}$. Assume an analyst who has the opinion $\omega_{y|x} = (b_{y|x}, d_{y|x}, u_{Y|x}, a_y)$ about y being true given x, the opinion $\omega_{y|\bar{x}} = (b_{y|\bar{x}}, d_{y|\bar{x}}, u_{y|\bar{x}}, a_y)$ about y being true given NOT x, and finally the opinion $\omega_x = (b_x, d_x, u_x, a_x)$ about x itself. The deduced opinion $\omega_{y\|x} = (b_{y\|x}, d_{y\|x}, u_{y\|x}, a_y)$ is computed as

$$\omega_{y\|x} : \begin{cases} b_{y\|x} = b_y^{\mathrm{I}} - a_y K, \\ d_{y\|x} = d_y^{\mathrm{I}} - (1-a_y)K, \\ u_{y\|x} = u_y^{\mathrm{I}} + K, \\ a_y = \dfrac{a_x b_{y|x} + a_{\bar{x}} b_{y|\bar{x}}}{1 - a_x u_{y|x} - a_{\bar{x}} u_{y|\bar{x}}}, \text{ if } u_{y|x} + u_{y|\bar{x}} < 2, \;\; a_y \in [0,1] \text{ otherwise}, \end{cases} \tag{9.40}$$

$$\text{where} \quad \begin{cases} b_y^{\mathrm{I}} = b_x b_{y|x} + d_x b_{y|\bar{x}} + u_x (b_{y|x} a_x + b_{y|\bar{x}}(1-a_x)), \\ d_y^{\mathrm{I}} = b_x d_{y|x} + d_x d_{y|\bar{x}} + u_x (d_{y|x} a_x + d_{y|\bar{x}}(1-a_x)), \\ u_y^{\mathrm{I}} = b_x u_{y|x} + d_x u_{y|\bar{x}} + u_x (u_{y|x} a_x + u_{y|\bar{x}}(1-a_x)), \end{cases} \tag{9.41}$$

and where K is determined according to the following selection criteria:

$$\textbf{Case I:} \quad ((b_{y|x} > b_{y|\bar{x}}) \wedge (d_{y|x} > d_{y|\bar{x}})) \vee ((b_{y|x} \le b_{y|\bar{x}}) \wedge (d_{y|x} \le d_{y|\bar{x}})) \implies K = 0, \tag{9.42}$$

$$\begin{aligned} \textbf{Case II.A.1:} \quad & ((b_{y|x} > b_{y|\bar{x}}) \wedge (d_{y|x} \le d_{y|\bar{x}})) \\ & \wedge\, (\mathrm{P}(y\|\widehat{x}) \le (b_{y|\bar{x}} + a_y(1 - b_{y|\bar{x}} - d_{y|x}))) \\ & \wedge\, (\mathrm{P}(x) \le a_x) \\ & \implies K = \frac{a_x u_x (b_y^{\mathrm{I}} - b_{y|\bar{x}})}{(b_x + a_x u_x) a_y}, \end{aligned} \tag{9.43}$$

$$\begin{aligned}
\textbf{Case II.A.2:}\quad & ((b_{y|x} > b_{y|\overline{x}}) \wedge (d_{y|x} \leq d_{y|\overline{x}})) \\
& \wedge (\mathrm{P}(y\|\widehat{x}) \leq (b_{y|\overline{x}} + a_y(1 - b_{y|\overline{x}} - d_{y|x}))) \\
& \wedge (\mathrm{P}(x) > a_x) \\
& \Longrightarrow K = \frac{a_x u_x (d_y^{\mathrm{I}} - d_{y|x})(b_{y|x} - b_{y|\overline{x}})}{(d_x + (1 - a_x)u_x) a_y (d_{y|\overline{x}} - d_{y|x})},
\end{aligned} \tag{9.44}$$

$$\begin{aligned}
\textbf{Case II.B.1:}\quad & ((b_{y|x} > b_{y|\overline{x}}) \wedge (d_{y|x} \leq d_{y|\overline{x}})) \\
& \wedge (\mathrm{P}(y\|\widehat{x}) > (b_{y|\overline{x}} + a_y(1 - b_{y|\overline{x}} - d_{y|x}))) \\
& \wedge (\mathrm{P}(x) \leq a_x) \\
& \Longrightarrow K = \frac{(1 - a_x) u_x (b_y^{\mathrm{I}} - b_{y|\overline{x}})(d_{y|\overline{x}} - d_{y|x})}{(b_x + a_x u_x)(1 - a_y)(b_{y|x} - b_{y|\overline{x}})},
\end{aligned} \tag{9.45}$$

$$\begin{aligned}
\textbf{Case II.B.2:}\quad & ((b_{y|x} > b_{y|\overline{x}}) \wedge (d_{y|x} \leq d_{y|\overline{x}})) \\
& \wedge (\mathrm{P}(y\|\widehat{x}) > (b_{y|\overline{x}} + a_y(1 - b_{y|\overline{x}} - d_{y|x}))) \\
& \wedge (\mathrm{P}(x) > a_x) \\
& \Longrightarrow K = \frac{(1 - a_x) u_x (d_y^{\mathrm{I}} - d_{y|x})}{(d_x + (1 - a_x)u_x)(1 - a_y)},
\end{aligned} \tag{9.46}$$

$$\begin{aligned}
\textbf{Case III.A.1:}\quad & ((b_{y|x} \leq b_{y|\overline{x}}) \wedge (d_{y|x} > d_{y|\overline{x}})) \\
& \wedge (\mathrm{P}(y\|\widehat{x}) \leq (b_{y|x} + a_y(1 - b_{y|x} - d_{y|\overline{x}}))) \\
& \wedge (\mathrm{P}(x) \leq a_x) \\
& \Longrightarrow K = \frac{(1 - a_x) u_x (d_y^{\mathrm{I}} - d_{y|\overline{x}})(b_{y|\overline{x}} - b_{y|x})}{(b_x + a_x u_x) a_y (d_{y|x} - d_{y|\overline{x}})},
\end{aligned} \tag{9.47}$$

$$\begin{aligned}
\textbf{Case III.A.2:}\quad & ((b_{y|x} \leq b_{y|\overline{x}}) \wedge (d_{y|x} > d_{y|\overline{x}})) \\
& \wedge (\mathrm{P}(y\|\widehat{x}) \leq (b_{y|x} + a_y(1 - b_{y|x} - d_{y|\overline{x}}))) \\
& \wedge (\mathrm{P}(x) > a_x) \\
& \Longrightarrow K = \frac{(1 - a_x) u_x (b_y^{\mathrm{I}} - b_{y|x})}{(d_x + (1 - a_x)u_x) a_y},
\end{aligned} \tag{9.48}$$

$$\begin{aligned}
\textbf{Case III.B.1:}\quad & ((b_{y|x} \leq b_{y|\overline{x}}) \wedge (d_{y|x} > d_{y|\overline{x}})) \\
& \wedge (\mathrm{P}(y\|\widehat{x}) > (b_{y|x} + a_y(1 - b_{y|x} - d_{y|\overline{x}}))) \\
& \wedge (\mathrm{P}(x) \leq a_x) \\
& \Longrightarrow K = \frac{a_x u_x (d_y^{\mathrm{I}} - d_{y|\overline{x}})}{(b_x + a_x u_x)(1 - a_y)},
\end{aligned} \tag{9.49}$$

$$\begin{aligned}
\textbf{Case III.B.2:}\quad & ((b_{y|x} \leq b_{y|\overline{x}}) \wedge (d_{y|x} > d_{y|\overline{x}})) \\
& \wedge (\mathrm{P}(y\|\widehat{x}) > (b_{y|x} + a_y(1 - b_{y|x} - d_{y|\overline{x}}))) \\
& \wedge (\mathrm{P}(x) > a_x) \\
& \Longrightarrow K = \frac{a_x u_x (b_y^{\mathrm{I}} - b_{y|x})(d_{y|x} - d_{y|\overline{x}})}{(d_x + (1 - a_x)u_x)(1 - a_y)(b_{y|\overline{x}} - b_{y|x})},
\end{aligned} \tag{9.50}$$

$$\text{where} \begin{cases} \mathrm{P}(y\|\widehat{x}) = b_{y|x} a_x + b_{y|\overline{x}}(1 - a_x) + a_y(u_{y|x} a_x + u_{y|\overline{x}}(1 - a_x)), \\ \\ \mathrm{P}(x) \quad\; = b_x + a_x u_x. \end{cases} \tag{9.51}$$

□

The computed $\omega_{y\|x}$ is the conditionally deduced opinion derived from ω_x, $\omega_{y|x}$ and $\omega_{y|\bar{x}}$. It expresses the belief in y being true as a function of the belief in x and of the two sub-conditionals $y|x$ and $y|\bar{x}$. By using the symbol '$\circledcirc$' to designate this operator, we define $\omega_{y\|x} = \omega_x \circledcirc (\omega_{y|x}, \omega_{y|\bar{x}})$. The closed form expression of Definition 9.1 is equivalent to the special case of 2×2 deduction using the multinomial method for conditional deduction of Definition 9.2.

Figure 9.8 is a screenshot of binomial deduction, involving the MBR $a_y = 0.40$. The deduced opinion $\omega_{y\|x} = (0.07, 0.42, 0.51, 0.40)$ lies within the sub-triangle defined by the conditionals $\omega_{y|x}$ and $\omega_{y|\bar{x}}$ at the base, and the sub-triangle apex opinion $\omega_{y\|\hat{x}} = (0.32, 0.48, 0.20, 0.40)$. In this case, the image sub-triangle has collapsed to a line between $\omega_{y|x}$ and $\omega_{y|\bar{x}}$, because the sub-triangle apex opinion $\omega_{y\|\hat{x}}$ is situated on that line.

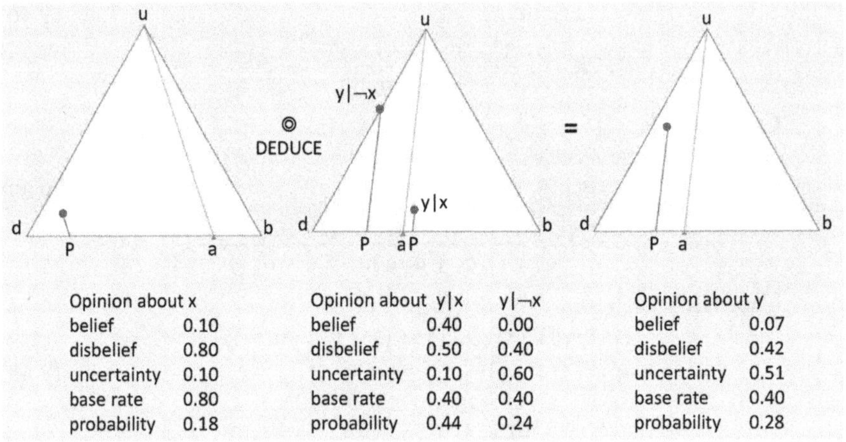

Fig. 9.8 Screenshot of deduction, involving MBR $a_y = 0.40$

Note that in case x is known to be true, i.e. $\omega_x = (1,0,0,a)$ is an absolute positive opinion, then obviously $\omega_{y\|x} = \omega_{y|x}$. Similarly, in case x is known to be false, i.e. $\omega_x = (0,1,0,a)$ is an absolute negative opinion, then obviously $\omega_{y\|x} = \omega_{y|\bar{x}}$.

9.4.4 Justification for the Binomial Deduction Operator

While not particularly complex, the closed-form expression for binomial conditional inference has many cases which can be difficult to understand and interpret. A more direct and intuitive way to understand how the operator works is to look at its geometrical representation in the triangle space. Figure 9.9 illustrates the geometrical structure with the parent triangle to the left and the child triangle to the right.

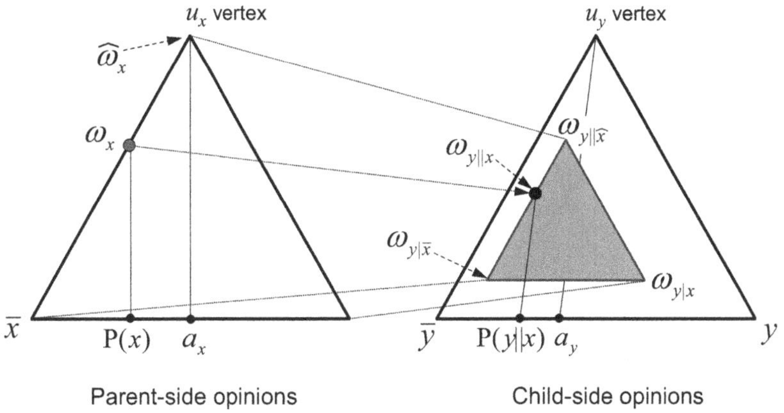

Fig. 9.9 Projection from parent opinion triangle to child opinion sub-triangle

Consider Figure 9.9 where the sub-triangle defined by the conditional opinions inside the child opinion triangle have the vertices $\omega_{y|x}$, $\omega_{y|\overline{x}}$ and $\omega_{y\|\widehat{x}}$. Various parent-side and child-side opinions shown in Figure 9.9 are specified in Eq.(9.52):

Parent-side opinions: Child-side opinions:

$$\begin{cases} \omega_x &= (0.00,\ 0.40,\ 0.60,\ 0.50), \\ \widehat{\omega}_x &= (0.00,\ 0.00,\ 1.00,\ 0.50), \\ \mathrm{P}(x) &= 0.30, \end{cases} \qquad \begin{cases} \omega_{y|x} &= (0.55,\ 0.30,\ 0.15,\ 0.38), \\ \omega_{y|\overline{x}} &= (0.10,\ 0.75,\ 0.15,\ 0.38), \\ \omega_{y\|\widehat{x}} &= (0.19,\ 0.30,\ 0.51,\ 0.38), \\ \omega_{y\|x} &= (0.15,\ 0.48,\ 0.37,\ 0.38), \\ \mathrm{P}(y\|x) &= 0.29. \end{cases} \tag{9.52}$$

The image space of the child opinion is a sub-triangle, where the two sub-conditionals $\omega_{y|x}$ and $\omega_{y|\overline{x}}$ form the two base vertices. The third vertex of the sub-triangle is the child opinion resulting from a vacuous parent opinion $\widehat{\omega}_x$. This particular child opinion, called *sub-triangle apex opinion* denoted $\omega_{y\|\widehat{x}}$, is determined by the base rates of x and y, as well as by the horizontal distance between the sub-conditionals. Through linear mapping, the parent opinion then dictates the actual position of the child opinion within that sub-triangle.

For example, when the parent is believed to be TRUE, i.e. $\omega_x = (1, 0, 0, a_x)$, the child opinion is $\omega_{y\|x} = \omega_{y|x}$; when the parent is believed to be FALSE, i.e. $\omega_x = (0, 1, 0, a_x)$, the child opinion is $\omega_{y\|x} = \omega_{y|\overline{x}}$; and when the parent opinion is vacuous, i.e. $\widehat{\omega}_x = (0, 0, 1, a_x)$, the child opinion is $\omega_{y\|x} = \omega_{y\|\widehat{x}}$. For all other parent opinions the child opinion is determined by a linear mapping from the parent opinion point in the left-hand triangle to the corresponding child opinion point in the right-hand sub-triangle.

Note that when $\omega_{y|x} = \omega_{y|\bar{x}}$, the child sub-triangle is reduced to a single point, so that it is necessary that $\omega_{y\|x} = \omega_{y|x} = \omega_{y|\bar{x}} = \omega_{y\|\hat{x}}$ in this case. This would mean that there is no relevance relationship between parent and child.

In the general case, the child image sub-triangle is not equilateral as in the example above. By setting the base rate of x different from 0.5, and by defining sub-conditionals with different levels of uncertainty, the child image sub-triangle can be skewed, where even the sub-triangle apex opinion $\omega_{y\|\hat{x}}$ can have less uncertainty than $\omega_{y|x}$ or $\omega_{y|\bar{x}}$.

9.5 Multinomial Deduction

Conditional deduction with multinomial opinions has previously been described in [44]. However, the description below has improved clarity [38] and also includes a description of the MBR distribution for child variable Y.

Multinomial opinion deduction is a generalisation of probabilistic conditional deduction, as expressed in Eq.(9.20).

Let $X = \{x_i | i = 1,\ldots,k\}$ and $Y = \{y_j | j = 1,\ldots,l\}$ be random variables, where X is the evidence variable and Y is the target query variable in their respective domains.

Assume an opinion $\omega_X = (\boldsymbol{b}_X, u_X, \boldsymbol{a}_X)$ on X, and a set of conditional opinions $\omega_{Y|x_i}$ on Y, one for each x_i, $i = 1,\ldots,k$. The conditional opinion $\omega_{Y|x_i}$ is a subjective opinion on Y given that X takes the value x_i. Formally, each conditional opinion $\omega_{Y|x_i}$, $i = 1,\ldots,k$, is a tuple

$$\omega_{Y|x_i} = (\boldsymbol{b}_{Y|x_i}, u_{Y|x_i}, \boldsymbol{a}_Y) \,, \tag{9.53}$$

where $\boldsymbol{b}_{Y|x_i} : Y \to [0,1]$ is a belief mass distribution and $u_{Y|x_i} \in [0,1]$ is an uncertainty mass, such that Eq.(2.6) holds, and the base rate distribution $\boldsymbol{a}_Y : Y \to [0,1]$ is a prior probability distribution of Y. We denote by $\boldsymbol{\omega}_{Y|X}$ the set of all conditional opinions on Y given the values of X:

$$\boldsymbol{\omega}_{Y|X} = \left\{ \omega_{Y|x_i} | i = 1,\ldots,k \right\} \,. \tag{9.54}$$

Motivated by the above analysis, we want to *deduce* a subjective opinion on the target variable Y:

$$\omega_{Y\|X} = (\boldsymbol{b}_{Y\|X}, u_{Y\|X}, \boldsymbol{a}_Y) \,, \tag{9.55}$$

where $\boldsymbol{b}_{Y\|X} : Y \to [0,1]$ is a belief mass distribution and $u_{Y\|X} \in [0,1]$ is an uncertainty mass, such that Eq.(2.6) holds.

Note that the base rate distribution $\boldsymbol{a}_Y$ is the same for all of the conditional opinions in $\boldsymbol{\omega}_{Y|X}$, as well as for the deduced opinion $\omega_{Y\|X}$.

9.5.1 Marginal Base Rate Distribution

Similarly to the MBR for binomial conditionals as described in Section 9.4.1, a MBR distribution can be computed for multinomial conditional opinions. This is necessary for general consistency, and in particular if it is required that the set of conditional opinions between nodes X and Y can be inverted multiple times, while preserving their projected probability distributions.

Assume parent node X and child node Y with associated set of conditional opinions $\boldsymbol{\omega}_{Y|X}$. Let $\widehat{\omega}_X$ denote the vacuous opinion on X.

Let $\mathbf{P}_{Y\|\widehat{X}}$ denote the projected probability distribution of the sub-simplex apex opinion $\omega_{Y\|\widehat{X}}$. The constraint on the base rate distribution $\boldsymbol{a}_Y$ is

$$\text{Law of total probability for base rates:}\quad \boldsymbol{a}_Y = \mathbf{P}_{Y\|\widehat{X}}\,. \tag{9.56}$$

Assuming that the conditional opinions $\boldsymbol{\omega}_{Y|X}$ are not all vacuous, formally expressed as $\sum_{x\in\mathbb{X}} u_{Y|x} < k$, the simple expression for the MBR $\boldsymbol{a}_Y(y)$ can be derived from Eq.(9.56) as follows:

$$\begin{aligned} \boldsymbol{a}_Y(y) &= \sum_{x\in\mathbb{X}} \boldsymbol{a}_X(x)\,\mathbf{P}_{Y|x}(y) = \sum_{x\in\mathbb{X}} \boldsymbol{a}_X(x)\,(\boldsymbol{b}_{Y|x}(y)+\boldsymbol{a}_Y(y)\,u_{Y|x}) \\ \Leftrightarrow\quad \boldsymbol{a}_Y(y) &= \frac{\sum_{x\in\mathbb{X}} \boldsymbol{a}_X(x)\,\boldsymbol{b}_{Y|x}(y)}{1-\sum_{x\in\mathbb{X}} \boldsymbol{a}_X(x)\,u_{Y|x}}\,. \end{aligned} \tag{9.57}$$

There can be multiple subjective opinions on the same variable, but the MBR is assumed to be equal for all opinions on the same variable. MBR distributions over multiple conditionally related variables form a network of MBRs, called a base rate network (BRN), described in Section 17.3.

By using the MBR distribution $\boldsymbol{a}_Y$ of Eq.(9.57), it is guaranteed that the multinomial opinion conditionals get the same projected probability distributions after multiple inversions. Note that Eq.(9.57) is a generalisation of the binomial case in Eq.(9.36).

In case all conditionals in the set $\boldsymbol{\omega}_{Y|X}$ are vacuous, i.e. when $\sum_{x\in\mathbb{X}} u_{Y|x} = k$, then there is no constraint on the base rate distribution $\boldsymbol{a}_Y$.

9.5.2 Free Base-Rate Distribution Intervals

Similarly to the free base-rate interval for binomial conditionals as described in Section 9.4.2, there is a set of free base-rate intervals for the base rate distribution of multinomial conditional opinions.

More specifically, the base rate distribution $\boldsymbol{a}_Y$ of the deduced opinion $\omega_{Y\|X}$ in Eq.(9.64) must be constrained by intervals defined by a lower base rate limit $a_Y^-(y)$ and an upper base rate limit $a_Y^+(y)$ for each value $y \in \mathbb{Y}$ in order to be consistent with the set of conditionals $\boldsymbol{\omega}_{Y|X}$.

In the case of dogmatic conditionals, the set of free base-rate intervals is reduced to a MBR distribution. The upper and lower limits for consistent base rates are the projected probabilities of the consequent opinions resulting from first assuming a vacuous antecedent opinion ω_X, and then hypothetically setting maximum (=1) and minimum (=0) base rates for values $y \in \mathbb{Y}$.

Assume parent node X of cardinality k, and child node Y of cardinality l, with associated set of conditional opinions $\boldsymbol{\omega}_{Y|X}$. Let $\widehat{\omega}_X$, where $\widehat{u}_X = 1$, denote the vacuous opinion on X. As before, $\mathbf{P}_{Y\|\widehat{X}}$ denotes the projected probability distribution of the sub-simplex apex opinion $\omega_{Y\|\widehat{X}}$. The free base-rate distribution $\boldsymbol{a}_Y$ is constrained by the following upper and lower limits:

$$\begin{aligned}\text{Upper base rate:}\quad a_Y^+(y) &= \max_{\boldsymbol{a}_Y(y)=0}^{1}[\mathbf{P}_{Y\|\widehat{X}}(y)]\\ &= \max_{\boldsymbol{a}_Y(y)=0}^{1}[\sum_{x\in\mathbb{X}}\boldsymbol{a}_X(x)\,\mathbf{P}_{Y|x}(y)]\\ &= \max_{\boldsymbol{a}_Y(y)=0}^{1}[\sum_{x\in\mathbb{X}}\boldsymbol{a}_X(x)\,(\boldsymbol{b}_{Y|x}(y)+\boldsymbol{a}_Y(y)\,u_{Y|x})],\end{aligned} \tag{9.58}$$

$$\begin{aligned}\text{Lower base rate:}\quad a_Y^-(y) &= \min_{\boldsymbol{a}_Y(y)=0}^{1}[\mathbf{P}_{Y\|\widehat{X}}(y)]\\ &= \min_{\boldsymbol{a}_Y(y)=0}^{1}[\sum_{x\in\mathbb{X}}\boldsymbol{a}_X(x)\,\mathbf{P}_{Y|x}(y)]\\ &= \min_{\boldsymbol{a}_Y(y)=0}^{1}[\sum_{x\in\mathbb{X}}\boldsymbol{a}_X(x)\,(\boldsymbol{b}_{Y|x}(y)+\boldsymbol{a}_Y(y)\,u_{Y|x})].\end{aligned} \tag{9.59}$$

The free base-rate interval for $\boldsymbol{a}_Y(y)$ is then expressed as $[a_Y^-(y), a_Y^+(y)]$, meaning that the base rate $\boldsymbol{a}_Y(y)$ must be within that interval in order to be consistent with the set of conditionals $\boldsymbol{\omega}_{Y|X}$. Note that the free base-rate interval $[a_Y^-(y), a_Y^+(y)]$ is also a function of the base rate distribution $\boldsymbol{a}_X$. In the case of dogmatic conditionals $\boldsymbol{\omega}_{Y|X}$ the set of free base-rate intervals for $\boldsymbol{a}_Y$ collapses to a base rate distribution, where each base rate $\boldsymbol{a}_Y(y)$ is expressed by Eq.(9.60):

$$\boldsymbol{a}_Y(y) = \sum_{x\in\mathbb{X}}\boldsymbol{a}_X(x)\,\mathbf{P}_{Y|x}(y) = \sum_{x\in\mathbb{X}}\boldsymbol{a}_X(x)\,\boldsymbol{b}_{Y|x}(y)\,. \tag{9.60}$$

In case the set of conditional opinions $\boldsymbol{\omega}_{Y|X}$ contains only vacuous opinions, i.e. when $u_{Y|x} = 1$ for all $x \in \mathbb{X}$, then every free base-rate interval is $[0,1]$, meaning that there is no constraint on the base rate distribution $\boldsymbol{a}_Y$ other than the additivity requirement $\sum \boldsymbol{a}_Y(y) = 1$.

9.5.3 Constraints for Multinomial Deduction

The definition of Bayesian deduction for subjective opinions should be compatible with the definition of Bayesian deduction for probability distributions, described in Section 9.2. This requirement leads to the following conclusion: the projected probability of the deduced opinion $\omega_{Y\|X}$ should satisfy the probabilistic deduction relation given in Eq.(9.20):

$$\mathbf{P}_{Y\|X}(y_j) = \sum_{i=1}^{k} \mathbf{P}_X(x_i)\mathbf{P}_{Y|x_i}(y_j) , \tag{9.61}$$

for $j = 1, \ldots, l$, where the factors on the right-hand side of Eq.(9.61) can be computed with Eq.(3.12).

On the other hand, from Eq.(3.12), we have

$$\mathbf{P}_{Y\|X}(y_j) = \boldsymbol{b}_{Y\|X}(y_j) + \boldsymbol{a}_Y(y_j)u_{Y\|X} . \tag{9.62}$$

Eq.(9.61) and Eq.(9.62) together determine l linear equations with the beliefs $\boldsymbol{b}_{Y\|X}(y_j)$, $j = 1, \ldots, l$, and uncertainty $u_{Y\|X}$ as variables. We obtain one more equation over the same variables from the additivity property for the beliefs and uncertainty of the subjective opinion $\omega_{Y\|X}$, by Eq.(2.6):

$$u_{Y\|X} + \sum_{j=1}^{l} \boldsymbol{b}_{Y\|X}(y_j) = 1 . \tag{9.63}$$

This means that we have a system of $l+1$ equations with $l+1$ variables, which might seem to fully determine the deduced opinion $\omega_{Y\|X}$. However, the projected probabilities on the left-hand side of the equations in Eq.(9.62) also add up to 1, which makes this system dependent. Hence, the system has an infinite number of solutions, which means that there are infinitely many subjective opinions on Y with a base rate $\boldsymbol{a}_Y$, the projected probability distribution of which satisfies Eq.(9.61). This is in correspondence with the geometrical representation given in Figure 9.9 and Figure 9.10, namely: once we have an opinion point ω_Y as a solution, then every other point in Ω_Y, lying on the line through ω_Y parallel to the director line, will also be a solution. The question is which one of these points is the most appropriate to represent the deduced opinion on Y from the given input opinions.

The above observation suggests that we need to somehow choose and fix one belief mass (or the uncertainty mass) of the deduced opinion, and determine the rest of the values from the projected probability relations in Eq.(9.62). Since, in general, we do not have a reason to distinguish among belief mass values, the obvious candidate for this is the uncertainty mass. In what follows, we provide a method for determining the most suitable uncertainty mass value for the deduced opinion corresponding to the given input opinions, i.e. we provide a method for fully determining the deduced opinion.

The method of obtaining the deduced opinion $\omega_{Y\|X}$ from the opinions in the set $\boldsymbol{\omega}_{Y|X}$ and an opinion ω_X, i.e. the method of determining a suitable uncertainty mass value of the opinion $\omega_{Y\|X}$ for the given input, is inspired by the geometric analysis of the input opinions and how they are related. The idea is that the conditional opinions in $\boldsymbol{\omega}_{Y|X}$ are input arguments to the *deduction operator* which maps ω_X into $\omega_{Y\|X}$. Multinomial deduction is denoted by

$$\omega_{Y\|X} = \omega_X \circledcirc \boldsymbol{\omega}_{Y|X} \; . \tag{9.64}$$

.

The deduction operator '$\circledcirc$' maps Ω_X, the opinion space of X, into a sub-space of Ω_Y called the *deduction sub-space*. The following intuitive constraints are taken into consideration in providing the definition of the deduction operator: Ω_X,

Constraint 1. The vertices lying on the base of the opinion space Ω_X map correspondingly into the opinion points determined by $\boldsymbol{\omega}_{Y|X}$. This means that the conditional opinions on Y in the set $\boldsymbol{\omega}_{Y|X} = \{\omega_{Y|x_i} | i = 1, \ldots, k\}$, correspond to the *absolute opinions* on X, namely

$$\omega_{Y|x_i} = \omega_X^i \circledcirc \boldsymbol{\omega}_{Y|X} \; , \tag{9.65}$$

for $i = 1, \ldots, k$, where $\omega_X^i = (\boldsymbol{b}_X^i, u_X^i, \boldsymbol{a}_X)$ denotes the absolute opinion on X such that $\boldsymbol{b}_X^i(x_i) = 1$ (and consequently $\boldsymbol{b}_X^i(x_j) = 0$, for $j \neq i$, and $u_X^i = 0$), and $\boldsymbol{a}_X$ is the same as in ω_X.

Constraint 2. The apex of the opinion space Ω_X maps into the apex of the deduction sub-space. The apex of Ω_X corresponds to the *vacuous opinion* on X given as

$$\widehat{\omega}_X = (\boldsymbol{b}_0, 1, \boldsymbol{a}_X) \; , \tag{9.66}$$

where $\boldsymbol{b}_0$ denotes the zero-belief mass distribution that has $\boldsymbol{b}_0(x_i) = 0$, for every $i = 1, \ldots, k$ (and consequently $u_0 = 1$). The sub-simplex apex opinion $\omega_{Y\|\widehat{X}}$ is opinion on Y that corresponds to the apex of the deduction sub-space, corresponding to the deduction of the vacuous opinion $\widehat{\omega}_X$. Then we obtain the following constraint on the operator $\circledcirc$:

$$\omega_{Y\|\widehat{X}} = \widehat{\omega}_X \circledcirc \boldsymbol{\omega}_{Y|X} \; . \tag{9.67}$$

Now, according to Eq.(9.65) and Eq.(9.67), the vertices of the domain opinion space Ω_X are mapped into the opinion points $\omega_{Y|x_i}$, $i = 1, \ldots, k$, and $\omega_{Y\|\widehat{X}}$ by the deduction operator $\circledcirc$. We want the deduction operator to be defined in such a way that the deduction sub-space is the 'convex closure' of these points. In that way, the deduction sub-space, and the deduction itself, can be fully determined by the given conditional opinions in $\boldsymbol{\omega}_{Y|X}$, and the given base rate distribution $\boldsymbol{a}_X$.

Constraint 3. The image of an evidence opinion point ω_X on the evidence variable X is obtained by linear projection of the opinion point of ω_X inside the deduction sub-space, and represents the deduced opinion $\omega_{Y\|X}$ on the target variable Y.

A visualisation of the above in the case of trinomial opinions where the domain simplexes are tetrahedrons, is given in Figure 9.10.

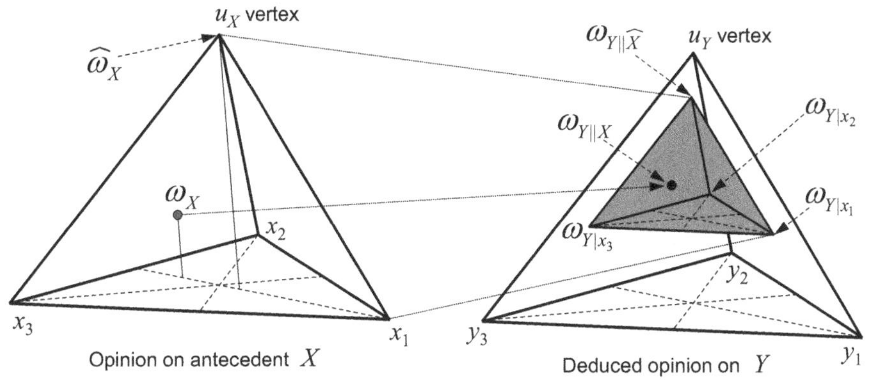

Fig. 9.10 Linear projection of evidence opinion ω_X into the target deduction sub-space

The deduction sub-space is shown as a shaded tetrahedron inside the domain tetrahedron of Y on the right-hand side of Figure 9.10.

Based on the above assumptions, the deduced opinion $\omega_{Y\|X}$ results from first constructing the deduction sub-space, and then projecting the opinion ω_X onto it.

The deduction sub-space is bounded by the k points $\omega_{Y|x_i}$, $i = 1,\ldots,k$, and the point that corresponds to the sub-simplex apex opinion $\omega_{Y\|\widehat{X}}$. While the former are given, the latter needs to be computed, as described in Step 2 in Section 9.5.4 below.

The opinion ω_X is then linearly projected onto this sub-space, which means that its uncertainty mass $u_{Y\|X}$ is determined as a linear transformation of the parameters of ω_X, with the belief masses determined accordingly.

9.5.4 Method for Multinomial Deduction

Deduction for multinomial conditional opinions can be described in three steps. The first step consists of determining the MBR distribution (or set of free base rate intervals) for $\boldsymbol{a}_Y$. The second step consists of determining the image sub-simplex of the deduction space Y. The third step consists of linear mapping of the opinion on X into the sub-simplex of Y to produce the deduced opinion $\omega_{Y\|X}$.

Step 1: Compute the MBR distribution $\boldsymbol{a}_Y$ according to Eq.(9.68), as described in Section 9.5.1:

$$\boldsymbol{a}_Y(y) = \frac{\sum_{x\in\mathbb{X}} \boldsymbol{a}_X(x)\, \boldsymbol{b}_{Y|x}(y)}{1 - \sum_{x\in\mathbb{X}} \boldsymbol{a}_X(x)\, u_{Y|x}}\,, \quad \text{for } \; y \in \mathbb{Y}. \tag{9.68}$$

Alternatively, if the analyst wants to specify the base rate distribution more freely, a set of base rate intervals can be computed as described in Section 9.5.2.

Step 2: The belief masses of the deduced opinion $\omega_{Y\|X}$ should be at least as large as the minimum of the corresponding belief masses in the conditionals, i.e.

$$\boldsymbol{b}_{Y\|X}(y_j) \geq \min_i [\boldsymbol{b}_{Y|x_i}(y_j)], \; \forall j = 1, \ldots, l \,. \tag{9.69}$$

The constraint in Eq.(9.69) is intuitively clear. The same constraint was pointed out by Pearl (1990) as a *principle of plausible reasoning* [82].

Eq.(9.69) holds for the belief masses of every deduced opinion, and in particular for the belief masses of the sub-simplex apex opinion $\omega_{Y\|\widehat{X}}$. In determining $\omega_{Y\|\widehat{X}}$ we need to consider the constraint of the projected probability distribution of Eq.(9.61), and keep track of the condition in Eq.(9.69), while maximizing the uncertainty.

The fact that all deduced opinions should satisfy Eq.(9.69) has the following geometrical interpretation in simplex opinion spaces: all the deduced opinion points must be inside the *auxiliary deduction sub-space* of Ω_Y, that is the sub-space bounded by the planes $\boldsymbol{b}_Y(y_j) = \min_i [\boldsymbol{b}_{Y|x_i}(y_j)]$ (parallel to the sides of Ω_Y).

By applying Eq.(9.61) to the vacuous opinion $\widehat{\omega}_X$, we obtain the following equation for the projected probability distribution of the sub-simplex apex opinion $\omega_{Y\|\widehat{X}}$:

$$\mathbf{P}_{Y\|\widehat{X}}(y_j) = \sum_{i=1}^{k} \boldsymbol{a}_X(x_i) \mathbf{P}_{Y|x_i}(y_j) \,. \tag{9.70}$$

On the other hand, for the projected probability of $\omega_{Y\|\widehat{X}}$, according to the definition of projected probability given in Eq.(3.12), we have the following:

$$\mathbf{P}_{Y\|\widehat{X}}(y_j) = \boldsymbol{b}_{Y\|\widehat{X}}(y_j) \; + \; \boldsymbol{a}_Y(y_j) u_{Y\|\widehat{X}} \,. \tag{9.71}$$

Thus, we need to find the point $\omega_{Y\|\widehat{X}} = (\boldsymbol{b}_{Y\|\widehat{X}}, u_{Y\|\widehat{X}}, \boldsymbol{a}_Y)$ with the greatest possible uncertainty satisfying the requirements in Eq.(9.69) and Eq.(9.71), where $\mathbf{P}_{Y\|\widehat{X}}(y_j)$ is determined by Eq.(9.70). For simplicity we define:

$$u_j \; = \; \frac{\mathbf{P}_{Y\|\widehat{X}}(y_j) \; - \; \min_i [\boldsymbol{b}_{Y|x_i}(y_j)]}{\boldsymbol{a}_Y(y_j)}, \qquad \text{for every } j = 1, \ldots, l. \tag{9.72}$$

Hence we have $u_{Y\|\widehat{X}} \leq u_j$, for every $j = 1, \ldots, l$. (9.73)

The greatest $u_{Y\|\widehat{X}}$ for which Eq.(9.73) holds is $u_{Y\|\widehat{X}} = \min_j [u_j]$. (9.74)

From Eq.(9.69) and Eq.(9.71) it follows that $u_{Y\|\widehat{X}}$ is non-negative. It is also less than or equal to 1 since, if we assume the opposite, it would follow that $u_j > 1$, for every $j = 1, \ldots, l$, which leads to $\mathbf{P}_{Y\|\widehat{X}}(y_j) > \min_i [\boldsymbol{b}_{Y|x_i}(y_j) + \boldsymbol{a}_Y(y_j)]$, for every $j = 1, \ldots, l$. Summing up by j in the last inequality would lead to a contradiction, since both the projected probabilities and the base rates of Y sum up to 1. Hence, $u_{Y\|\widehat{X}}$ determined by Eq.(9.74) is a well-defined uncertainty mass. It is obviously the greatest value satisfying Eq.(9.73), hence also the initial requirements.

Having determined $u_{Y\|\widehat{X}}$, the corresponding belief masses $\boldsymbol{b}_{Y\|\widehat{X}}(y_j)$, $j = 1,\ldots,l$ emerge from Eq.(9.71), and hence determine the sub-simplex apex opinion $\omega_{Y\|\widehat{X}}$.

The opinion point $\omega_{Y\|\widehat{X}}$ can be geometrically determined as the intersection between the surface of the auxiliary deduction sub-space and the *projector line* (line parallel to the director) passing through the point on the base corresponding to the projected probability determined by Eq.(9.70).

Step 3: The vertices of the opinion simplex of X map into the vertices of the deduction sub-space. This leads to the following linear expression for the uncertainty $u_{Y\|X}$ of an opinion $\omega_{Y\|X}$ on Y, deduced from an opinion $\omega_X = (\boldsymbol{b}_X, u_X, \boldsymbol{a}_X)$ on X:

$$u_{Y\|X} = u_X \, u_{Y\|\widehat{X}} \; + \; \sum_{i=1}^{k} u_{Y|x_i} \boldsymbol{b}_X(x_i) \, . \tag{9.75}$$

We obtain the last expression as the weighted average of the sub-simplex apex opinion uncertainty and the input conditional opinion uncertainties.

From the equivalent form of Eq.(9.75) we obtain

$$u_{Y\|X} = u_{Y\|\widehat{X}} \; - \; \sum_{i=1}^{k} (u_{Y\|\widehat{X}} - u_{Y|x_i}) \boldsymbol{b}_X(x_i) \, . \tag{9.76}$$

The interpretation of Eq.(9.76) is that the uncertainty of a deduced opinion $\omega_{Y\|X}$ from an arbitrary opinion ω_X is obtained when the maximum uncertainty of the deduction, $u_{Y\|\widehat{X}}$, is decreased by the weighted average of the beliefs multiplied by the 'uncertainty distance' of the conditional opinions to the maximum uncertainty.

Having deduced the uncertainty $u_{Y\|X}$, we can determine the belief mass distribution, $\boldsymbol{b}_{Y\|X} = \{\boldsymbol{b}_{Y\|X}(y_j),\ j = 1,\ldots,l\}$, of the deduced opinion by rearranging Eq.(9.62) into the following form:

$$\boldsymbol{b}_{Y\|X}(y_j) = \mathbf{P}_{Y\|X}(y_j) - \boldsymbol{a}_Y(y_j) u_{Y\|X} \, . \tag{9.77}$$

The deduced multinomial opinion is then

$$\omega_{Y\|X} = (\boldsymbol{b}_{Y\|X},\ u_{Y\|X},\ \boldsymbol{a}_Y). \tag{9.78}$$

This marks the end of the three-step procedure for multinomial deduction.

Definition 9.2 (Multinomial Conditional Deduction). Let $\boldsymbol{\omega}_{Y|X}$ be a set of multinomial conditional opinions, and let ω_X be an opinion on X. The opinion $\omega_{Y\|X}$ derived through the three-step procedure described above is the deduced opinion derived as a function of $\boldsymbol{\omega}_{Y|X}$ and ω_X. The symbol $\circledcirc$ denotes the operator for conditional deduction which is denoted as

$$\text{Multinomial conditional deduction:} \quad \omega_{Y\|X} = \omega_X \circledcirc \boldsymbol{\omega}_{Y|X} \, . \tag{9.79}$$

□

In the special case of 2×2 deduction, the method described above is equivalent to that of Definition 9.1. Note that in case the analyst knows the exact value of variable $X = x_i$, i.e. $\boldsymbol{b}_X(x_i) = 1$ so that ω_X is an absolute opinion, then obviously $\omega_{Y\|X} = \omega_{Y|x_i}$.

The above described procedure can be applied also in the case when some of the given opinions are hyper-opinions. In that case, we first determine the corresponding projections of the hyper-opinions into multinomial opinions, in the way described in Section 3.6.2, and then deduce an opinion from the projections. The resulting deduced opinion is then multinomial.

9.6 Example: Match-Fixing

In this example a football game is to be played between Team 1 and Team 2. It is generally predicted that Team 1 will win if the game is played in a fair manner. A gambler who plans to bet on the game has received second-hand information indicating possible match-fixing. The source, which can not be absolutely trusted, told the gambler that Team 1 has been paid to lose. Because of the low odds of Team 2 winning there is great profit to be made if one could predict that Team 2 will win. The gambler has an opinion about the outcome of the match in case Team 1 has been paid to lose, and in the absence of match-fixing. The gambler also has an opinion about whether Team 1 actually has been been paid to lose.

Let $\mathbb{X} = \{x_1, x_2\}$ denote the domain representing whether Team 1 has been paid to lose:

$$\text{Domain for variable } X: \quad \mathbb{X} = \begin{cases} x_1: & \text{Team 1 has been paid to lose,} \\ x_2: & \text{No match-fixing.} \end{cases}$$

Let $\mathbb{Y} = \{y_1, y_2, y_3\}$ denote the domain representing which team wins the match:

$$\text{Domain for variable } Y: \quad \mathbb{Y} = \begin{cases} y_1: & \text{Team 1 wins the match,} \\ y_2: & \text{Team 2 wins the match,} \\ y_3: & \text{The match ends in a draw.} \end{cases}$$

The argument opinions are given in Table 9.1.

Table 9.1 Opinion ω_X (match-fixing), and conditional opinions $\boldsymbol{\omega}_{Y|X}$ (which team wins)

Opinion on X		Conditional opinions $\boldsymbol{\omega}_{Y\|X}$	
		y_1 $\quad$ y_2 $\quad$ y_3	
$\boldsymbol{b}_X(x_1) = 0.90$	$\boldsymbol{a}_X(x_1) = 0.1$	$\boldsymbol{b}_{Y\|x_1} = \{0.00,\ 0.80,\ 0.10\}$	$u_{Y\|x_1} = 0.10$
$\boldsymbol{b}_X(x_2) = 0.00$	$\boldsymbol{a}_X(x_2) = 0.9$	$\boldsymbol{b}_{Y\|x_2} = \{0.70,\ 0.00,\ 0.10\}$	$u_{Y\|x_2} = 0.20$
$u_X = 0.10$			

This example involves a two-dimensional evidence domain $\mathbb{X}$ and a three-dimensional hypothesis domain $\mathbb{Y}$. Geometrically seen, the deduction maps a triangular evidence space into a pyramidal hypothesis space as illustrated in Figure 9.11. Note that the shape and placement of the image sub-triangle is meant to be indicative, and not an exact representation of the numerical values in this example.

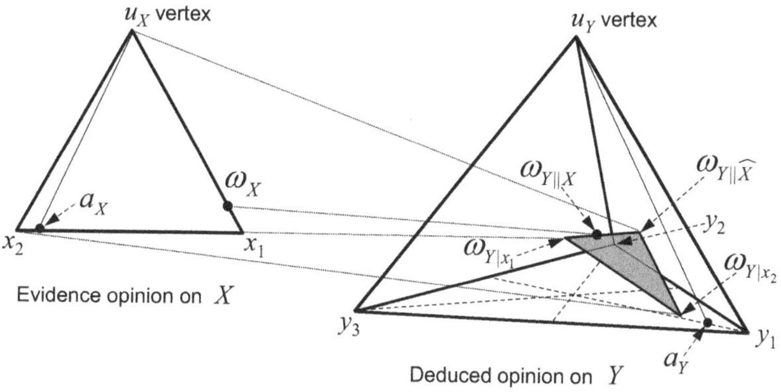

Fig. 9.11 Indicative illustration of deduction in the match-fixing example

The first step in the derivation of $\omega_{Y\|X}$ is to apply Eq.(9.68) to compute the MBR distribution:

$$\text{MBR distribution} \quad \boldsymbol{a}_Y = \begin{cases} \boldsymbol{a}_Y(y_1) = 0.778, \\ \boldsymbol{a}_Y(y_2) = 0.099, \\ \boldsymbol{a}_Y(y_3) = 0.123. \end{cases} \tag{9.80}$$

The second step is to use Eq.(9.74) to compute the sub-simplex apex uncertainty, which produces $u_{Y\|\widehat{X}} = 0.190$.

The third step is to apply Eq.(9.76) and Eq.(9.77) to compute the deduced opinion about which team will win the match, which produces

$$\omega_{Y\|X} = \begin{pmatrix} \boldsymbol{b}_{Y\|X}(y_1) = 0.063, & \boldsymbol{a}_{Y\|X}(y_1) = 0.778, \\ \boldsymbol{b}_{Y\|X}(y_2) = 0.728, & \boldsymbol{a}_{Y\|X}(y_2) = 0.099, \\ \boldsymbol{b}_{Y\|X}(y_3) = 0.100, & \boldsymbol{a}_{Y\|X}(y_3) = 0.123, \\ u_{Y\|X} \quad = 0.109. & \end{pmatrix} \begin{cases} \mathbf{P}_{Y\|X}(y_1) = 0.148, \\ \mathbf{P}_{Y\|X}(y_2) = 0.739, \\ \mathbf{P}_{Y\|X}(y_3) = 0.113. \end{cases} \tag{9.81}$$

Based on the opinion about match-fixing, as well as on the conditional opinions, it appears that Team 1 has a relatively slim chance of winning. Despite the high base rate of winning given by $\boldsymbol{a}_{Y\|X}(y_1) = 0.778$, when the evidence of match fixing is taken into account the projected probability of Team 1 winning the match is only $\mathbf{P}_{Y\|X}(y_1) = 0.148$. The probability of Team 2 winning is $\mathbf{P}_{Y\|X}(y_2) = 0.739$.

Hence, by betting on Team 2 the gambler has the prospect of making a big profit with relatively low risk. This example is continued in Section 11.4.

9.7 Interpretation of Material Implication in Subjective Logic

Material implication is traditionally denoted $(x \rightarrow y)$, where x represents the antecedent and y the consequent of the logical relationship between the propositions x and y. Material implication is a truth-functional connective, meaning that it is defined by its truth table, Table 9.2.

While truth-functional connectives normally have a relatively clear interpretation in normal language, this is not the case for material implication. The implication $(x \rightarrow y)$ could for example be expressed as *"If x is true, then y is true"*. However, this does not say anything about the case when x is false, which is problematic for the interpretation of the corresponding entries in the truth table. In this section we show that material implication is not closed under Boolean truth values, and that it in fact produces uncertainty in the form of a vacuous opinion. When seen in this light, it becomes clear that the traditional definition of material implication is based on the over-simplistic and misleading interpretation of uncertainty as Boolean TRUE. We redefine material implication with subjective logic to preserve the uncertainty that it unavoidably produces in specific cases. We then compare the new definition of material implication with conditional deduction, and show that they reflect the same mathematical equation rearranged in different forms.

9.7.1 Truth-Functional Material Implication

By definition, logical propositions in binary logic can only be evaluated to TRUE or FALSE. A logical proposition can be composed of sub-propositions that are combined with logical connectives. For example, the conjunctive connective $\wedge$ can be used to combine propositions x and y into the conjunctive proposition $(x \wedge y)$. In this case the proposition $(x \wedge y)$ is a complex proposition because it is composed of sub-propositions. The $\wedge$ connective has its natural language interpretation expressed as *"x and y are both TRUE"*. A logical proposition is said to be *truth-functional* when its truth depends on the truth of its sub-propositions alone [6]. Traditionally, it is required that the complex proposition has a defined truth value for all the possible combinations of truth values of the sub-propositions, in order for the truth function to be completely defined.

Defining material implication as truth-functional means that its truth values are determined as a function of the truth values of x and y alone, as shown in Table 9.2.

Table 9.2 Basic cases in truth table for material implication

	x	y	$x \rightarrow y$
Case 1:	F	F	T
Case 2:	F	T	T
Case 3:	T	F	F
Case 4:	T	T	T

The truth table of Table 9.2 happens to be equal to the truth table of $(\bar{x} \vee y)$, which is the reason why the traditional definition of truth-functional material implication leads to the equivalence $(x \to y) \Leftrightarrow (\bar{x} \vee y)$.

However, treating conditionals as truth-functional in this fashion leads to well-known inconsistencies. Truth-functional material implication should therefore not be considered to be a binary logic operator at all. The natural language interpretation assumes that there is a relevance connection between x and y which does not emerge from Table 9.2. The relevance property which intuitively, but mistakenly, is assumed by $(x \to y)$ can be expressed as *"The truth value of x is relevant for the truth value of y"*. For example, connecting a false antecedent proposition with an arbitrary consequent proposition gives a true implication according to material implication, but is quite nonsensical when expressed in normal language such as *"If 2 is odd, then 2 is even"*.

Furthermore, connecting an arbitrary antecedent with a true consequent proposition is true according to material implication, even when the antecedent and consequent have no relevance to each other. An example expressed in normal language is *"If it rains, then 2 is even"*.

The problem is that it takes more than just a truth table to determine whether a proposition x is relevant for another proposition y. In natural language, the term *'relevance'* assumes that when the truth value of the antecedent varies, so does that of the consequent. Correlation of truth variables between antecedent and consequent is thus a necessary element for relevance. Material implication defined in terms of Table 9.2 does not consider any relevance between the propositions, and therefore does not reflect the meaning of the natural language concept of implication. Table 9.2 gives a case-by-case static view of truth values which is insufficient to derive any relevance relationships.

9.7.2 Material Probabilistic Implication

By material probabilistic implication we mean that the probability value of the conditional $p(y|x)$ shall be determined as a function of other probability variables. This then corresponds directly with propositional logic material implication where the truth value of the conditional is determined as a function of the antecedent and the consequent truth values according to the truth table.

Eq.(9.15) on p.139 expresses binomial probabilistic deduction as

$$p(y\|x) = p(x)p(y|x) + p(\bar{x})p(y|\bar{x}) \ . \tag{9.82}$$

The difference between probabilistic conditional deduction and probabilistic material implication is a question of rearranging Eq.(9.82), so $p(y|x)$ is expressed as

$$p(y|x) = \frac{p(y\|x) - p(\bar{x})p(y|\bar{x})}{p(x)} \ . \tag{9.83}$$

Based on Eq.(9.83) and Eq.(9.82), the probability, and thereby the truth value, of the conditional $(y|x)$ can be determined in most cases, but of course not in the cases of zero divisor which are problematic.

- **Cases 1 & 2:** $p(x) = 0$
  The case $p(x) = 0$ in Eq.(9.83) immediately appears problematic. It is therefore necessary to consider Eq.(9.82) instead.

  It can be seen that the term involving $p(y|x)$ disappears from Eq.(9.82) when $p(x) = 0$. As a result $p(y|x)$ can take any value in the range $[0,1]$, so $p(y|x)$ must be expressed as a probability density function. Without any prior information, the density function must be considered to be uniform, which in subjective logic has a specific interpretation as will be explained below.

  A realistic example could for example be when considering the propositions x: *"The switch is on"* and y: *"The light is on"*. Recall that x is FALSE (i.e. *"The switch is off"*) in the cases under consideration here.

  Let us first consider the situation corresponding to Case 1 in Table 9.2 where $y\|x$ is FALSE (i.e. *"The light is off with the given switch position, which happens to be off"*), which would be the case when $y|\overline{x}$ is FALSE. In this situation it is perfectly possible that $y|x$ is FALSE too (i.e. *"The light is off whenever the switch is on"*). It is for example possible that the switch in question is not connected to the lamp in question, or that the bulb is blown.

  Let us now consider the situation corresponding to Case 2 in Table 9.2 where $y\|x$ is TRUE (i.e. *"The light is on with the given switch position, which happens to be off"*), which would be the case when $y|\overline{x}$ is TRUE. In this situation it is also perfectly possible that $y|x$ is FALSE (i.e. *"The light is off whenever the switch is on"*). It is for example possible that the electrical connections have been inverted, so that the light is on when the switch is off, and vice versa.

  These examples are in direct contradiction with Cases 1 & 2 of Table 9.2 which dictates that the corresponding implication $(x \rightarrow y)$ should be TRUE in both cases. The observation of this contradiction proves that the traditional definition of material implication is inconsistent with standard probability calculus.
- **Cases 3 & 4:** $p(x) = 1$
  Necessarily $p(\overline{x}) = 0$, so that Eq.(9.83) is transformed into $p(y|x) = p(y\|x)$. Thus when x is TRUE (i.e. $p(x) = 1$) then necessarily $(x \rightarrow y)$ will have the same truth value as y. This does not necessarily mean that the truth value of x is relevant to the truth value of y. In fact it could be either relevant or irrelevant. For example consider the antecedent proposition x: *"It rains"* combined with the consequent y: *"I carry an umbrella"*, then it is plausibly relevant, but combined with the consequent y: *"I wear glasses"*, then it is plausibly irrelevant. It can be assumed that x and y are TRUE in this example so that the implication is TRUE.

The unclear level of relevance can also be observed in examples where the consequent y is FALSE so that the implication $(x \rightarrow y)$ becomes FALSE. The level of relevance between the antecedent and the consequent is thus independent of the truth value of the implication $(x \to y)$ alone. The criteria for relevance are described in more detail below.

9.7.3 Relevance in Implication

Material implication is in general nonsensical precisely because it ignores any relevance connection between the antecedent x and the consequent y.

A meaningful conditional relationship between x and y requires that the antecedent x is relevant to the consequent y, or in other words that the consequent depends on the antecedent, as expressed in relevance logics [20]. Conditionals that are based on the dependence between consequent and antecedent are considered to be universally valid (and not just truth-functional), and are called *logical conditionals* [18]. Deduction with logical conditionals reflects human intuitive conditional reasoning, and does not lead to any of the paradoxes of material implication.

It is possible to express the relevance between the antecedent variable X and a consequent value y as a function of the conditionals. Since X and Y are binary this is the same as the relevance of x to y (and x to $\bar{y}$). According to Definition 10.1 and Eq.(10.4) this relevance is denoted $\Psi(y|X)$ and is expressed as

$$\Psi(y|X) = |p(y|x) - p(y|\bar{x})| \,. \tag{9.84}$$

Obviously, $\Psi(y|X) \in [0,1]$. In particular, the case $\Psi(y|X) = 0$ expresses total irrelevance of x (or variable X) to y, and the case $\Psi(y|X) = 1$ expresses total relevance of x (or variable X) to y.

To say that x is relevant to y is the same as to say that y is dependent on x. Similarly, to say that x is irrelevant to y is the same as to say that y is independent of x. This interpretation equivalence is further discussed in Section 10.2.

The degree of relevance can not be derived from the traditional truth-functional definition of material implication, because the truth value of $(\bar{x} \to y)$ is missing from the truth table. In order to rectify this problem, an augmented truth table that includes $(\bar{x} \to y)$ is given below.

Table 9.3 Truth and relevance table for material implication

	x	y	$\bar{x} \to y$	$x \to y$	Relevance
Case 1a:	F	F	F	Any	Any
Case 1b:	F	F	T	Undefined	Undefined
Case 2a:	F	T	F	Undefined	Undefined
Case 2b:	F	T	T	Any	Any
Case 3a:	T	F	F	F	None
Case 3b:	T	F	T	F	Total
Case 4a:	T	T	F	T	Total
Case 4b:	T	T	T	T	None

From Table 9.3 it can be seen that the truth table entries in Cases 1 and 2 are either 'Any' (uncertain and unconfident) or 'Undefined'. The term 'Any' is used to indicate that any truth or probability for $(x \rightarrow y)$ is possible in Cases 1a and 2b, not just Boolean TRUE or FALSE. Only in Cases 3 and 4 is the truth table clear about the truth value of $(x \rightarrow y)$. The same applies to the relevance between x and y, where any relevance value is possible in Cases 1a and 2b, and only Cases 3 and 4 define the relevance crisply as either 'no relevance' or 'total relevance'. Total relevance can be interpreted in the sense $x \Leftrightarrow y$ or $x \Leftrightarrow \bar{y}$, i.e. that x and y are either equivalent or complementary/inequivalent.

Our analysis shows that the natural conditional relationship between two propositions can not be meaningfully be described with a simple binary truth table, because other values than Boolean TRUE and FALSE are possible. The immediate conclusion is that material implication is not closed under a Boolean truth value space. Not even by assigning probabilities to $(x \rightarrow y)$ in Table 9.3 can material implication be made meaningful. Below we show that subjective logic with its explicit uncertainty is suitable for defining material implication. However, this does not mean that material implication is useful.

9.7.4 Subjective Interpretation of Material Implication

The discussion in Section 9.7.3 above concluded that any probability is possible in Cases 1 and 2 of the truth table of material implication. The uniform probability density function expressed by $\text{Beta}(p_x, 1, 1)$ which is equivalent to the vacuous opinion $\omega = (0, 0, 1, \frac{1}{2})$ is therefore a meaningful and sound representation of the term *'Any'* in Table 9.3. Similarly to three-valued logics, such as Kleene logic [25], it is possible to define three-valued truth as {TRUE, FALSE, UNCERTAIN}, abbreviated as {T, F, U}, where the truth value UNCERTAIN represents $\omega = (0, 0, 1, \frac{1}{2})$.

Given that material implication is not closed in the binary truth value space, an augmented truth table can be defined that reflects the ternary value space of $(x \rightarrow y)$ as a function of the binary truth values of x and y, as shown in Table 9.4.

Table 9.4 Augmented truth table for material implication

	x	y	$x \rightarrow y$	Opinion
Case 1:	F	F	U:	$\omega_{(x \rightarrow y)} = (0, 0, 1, \frac{1}{2})$
Case 2:	F	T	U:	$\omega_{(x \rightarrow y)} = (0, 0, 1, \frac{1}{2})$
Case 3:	T	F	F:	$\omega_{(x \rightarrow y)} = (0, 1, 0, a_y)$
Case 4:	T	T	T:	$\omega_{(x \rightarrow y)} = (1, 0, 0, a_y)$

Table 9.4 defines material implication as truth-functional, in the sense that it is determined as a function of binary truth values of x and y. Specifying the truth value UNCERTAIN (vacuous opinion) in the column for $(x \rightarrow y)$ in the truth table is a necessary consequence of the analysis in Section 9.7.2, but this means that the truth table is no longer closed under Boolean truth values.

It can be argued that if values other than Boolean TRUE and FALSE are allowed for $(x \rightarrow y)$, then it is natural to also allow the same for x and y. This is indeed possible, and can be expressed in terms of subjective logic as described next.

9.7.5 Comparison with Subjective Logic Deduction

With the mathematical details omitted, the notation for binomial conditional deduction in subjective logic is

$$\omega_{y\|x} = \omega_x \circledcirc (\omega_{y|x}, \omega_{y|\bar{x}}) , \tag{9.85}$$

where the terms are interpreted as follows:

$\omega_{y|x}$: opinion about y given x is TRUE,
$\omega_{y|\bar{x}}$: opinion about y given x is FALSE,
ω_x : opinion about the antecedent x,
$\omega_{y\|x}$: opinion about the consequent y given x.

Figure 9.12 is a demonstrator screenshot showing conditional deduction.

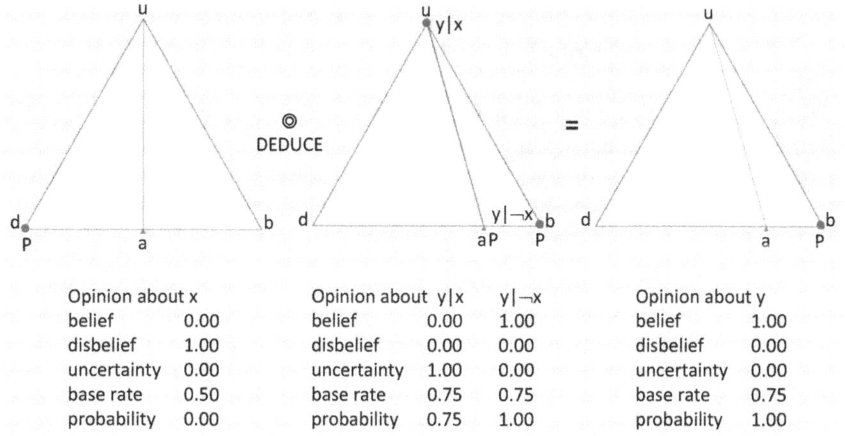

Fig. 9.12 Screenshot of deduction from the subjective logic demonstrator

The input arguments in the example of Figure 9.12 are binomial opinions which can be mapped to Beta PDFs according to Definition 3.3. The leftmost triangle represents the opinion on x, and the rightmost triangle that on y. The middle triangle represents the conditional opinions on $y|x$ and $y|\overline{x}$. The particular example illustrates Case 2b of Table 9.3 and Case 2 of Table 9.4.

Eq.(9.85) corresponds directly to the probabilistic version of Eq.(9.82). While both expressions take three input variables, the difference between them is that the input variables in Eq.(9.82) are scalars, whereas those of Eq.(9.85) are three-dimensional. Given that the base rates of $\omega_{y|x}$ and $\omega_{y|\overline{x}}$ are equal, Eq.(9.85) takes eight scalar input parameters.

9.7.6 How to Interpret Material Implication

We have shown that material implication is inconsistent with traditional probabilistic logic. This is nothing new, e.g. Nute and Cross (2002) pointed out that *"There can be little doubt that neither material implication nor any other truth function can be used by itself to provide an adequate representation of the logical and semantic properties of English conditionals"* [79].

In this section we have presented a redefinition of material implication as a probabilistic material implication. The difference between probabilistic material implication and conditional deduction is a question of rearranging equations, as in the transition from Eq.(9.15) to Eq.(9.83).

The analysis of material implication demonstrates that it is impossible to determine the conditional $p(y|x)$ or the corresponding implication $(x \rightarrow y)$ as a truth function, because the required conditional $p(y|\overline{x})$, or the corresponding implication $(\overline{x} \rightarrow y)$ is missing. Material implication produces an uncertain conclusion precisely because it attempts to determine the conditional relationship without the necessary evidence.

We have shown that when the antecedent is FALSE, then the truth value of the material implication should be 'uncertain', instead of TRUE. Hence, a more general reasoning calculus than binary logic is needed to allow a consistent definition of material implication; subjective logic is one possibility.

Chapter 10
Subjective Abduction

This chapter describes how subjective logic can be used for reasoning in the opposite direction to that of the conditionals, which typically involves the subjective version of Bayes' theorem.

10.1 Introduction to Abductive Reasoning

Abduction is reasoning in the opposite direction to the available conditionals. Since conditionals are typically causal, the abduction process typically consists of reasoning from an observed fact/event to determine (the likelihood of) possible causes of the fact/event. This is a relatively complex reasoning process. However, we constantly do intuitive abductive reasoning, and mostly without much effort. Unfortunately, mental abductive reasoning is often affected by error, because of typical human reasoning fallacies, such as ignoring base rates.

Simple examples of mental abductive reasoning are when we try to find causes for something we observe. Assume for example that you follow the principle of locking the front door when leaving your house for work every morning. Then one evening when you return home, you find the door unlocked. Abductive reasoning then kicks in to explore possible causes for why the door is unlocked, such as the possibility that a burglar picked the lock and robbed the house, or that you forgot to lock the door when you left in the morning.

Another typical example of abductive reasoning is when medical doctors diagnose diseases through tests. A pharmaceutical company that develops a medical test for a specific disease must determine the quality of the test by applying it to a number of persons who certainly do have the disease, as well as to a number of persons who certainly do not have the disease. Let AS (Affected Subjects) denote the number of persons with the disease, and let US (Unaffected Subjects) denote the number of persons who do not have the disease.

The respective numbers of TP (True Positives), TN (True Negatives), FP (False Positives), and FN (False Negatives) can be observed when applying the test. Note that AS = TP + FN, and that US = TN + FP. The quality of the test is then described in terms of its *sensitivity* aka TPR (True Positive Rate) and its *specificity* aka TNR (True Negative Rate), expressed as follows:

$$\begin{aligned} \text{Sensitivity:}\quad \text{TPR} &= \frac{\text{TP}}{\text{TP+FN}} = \frac{\text{TP}}{\text{AS}}, \\ \text{Specificity:}\quad \text{TNR} &= \frac{\text{TN}}{\text{TN+FP}} = \frac{\text{TN}}{\text{US}}. \end{aligned} \tag{10.1}$$

Sensitivity quantifies the test's ability to avoid false negatives, and specificity quantifies the test's ability to avoid false positives. The larger the sensitivity TPR and specificity TNR, the better the quality of the test.

It turns out that the quality aspects of the test can be expressed in terms of the conditional probabilities

$$\begin{aligned} \text{Sensitivity::}\quad & p(\text{'Positive test'} \mid \text{'Affected subject'}) &= \text{TPR}, \\ \text{Unspecificity:}\; & p(\text{'Positive test'} \mid \text{'Unaffected subject'}) &= 1 - \text{TNR}, \end{aligned} \tag{10.2}$$

where 'unspecificity' is the complement of 'specificity'.

The conditionals of Eq.(10.2) are causal, because the presence or absence of the disease causes the test to be positive or negative. The problem with these conditionals is that the medical doctor can not apply them directly to make the diagnosis. What is needed is the opposite pair of conditionals, so that from a positive or negative test, the medical doctor can assess the likelihood that the patient is affected or not affected by the disease. The process of inverting the conditionals of Eq.(10.2) and making a diagnosis in this situation is precisely abductive reasoning which involves Bayes' theorem.

Experiments show that humans are quite bad at intuitive abductive reasoning. For example, the base-rate fallacy [7, 66] in medicine consists of ignoring low base rates and making the erroneous assumption that $p(y|x) = p(x|y)$. While this reasoning error produces relatively good approximations of correct diagnostic probabilities in many situations, it can lead to a completely wrong result and wrong diagnosis in case the base rate of the disease in the population is very low, and the reliability of the test is not perfect.

Medical tests are of course not only used for diseases, but can potentially be designed and used for any medical condition. An extreme example of the base-rate fallacy is to conclude that a male person is pregnant just because he tests positive in a pregnancy test. Obviously, the base rate of male pregnancy is zero, and assuming that no test is absolutely perfect, it would be correct to conclude that the male person is not pregnant, and to see the positive test merely as a false positive.

In legal reasoning, the base-rate fallacy is called the *prosecutor's fallacy* [88], which consists of assigning too high a base rate (prior probability) to finding a true match of e.g. fingerprints or DNA. For example, if a specific fingerprint is found on the murder weapon at a crime scene, and a search is done through a database containing hundreds of millions of samples, then the base rate of a true match is extremely low, so it would be unsafe to interpret a match in the database directly as a true match and thereby as a proof of guilt. Instead, it is more likely to be a false match, i.e. the identified suspect is probably not the person who left the fingerprint, and is therefore probably not guilty, even if the fingerprint matches. In order to correctly assess the fingerprint match as proof, the prosecutors must also consider the quality (sensitivity and specificity) of the matching procedure, as well as the base rate of true matches given demographic and other circumstantial parameters.

The correct reasoning that takes base rates into account can easily be formalised mathematically, which is often needed in order to avoid errors of intuition in medical diagnostics, legal argumentation and other situations of abductive reasoning.

Aspects of abductive reasoning are also mentioned in connection with conditional deduction, described in Chapter 9. We therefore recommend readers to take a look at the introduction to conditional reasoning in Section 9.1, the description of probabilistic conditional inference in Section 9.2, as well as the subjective logic notation for conditional inference in Section 9.3.

In this section we describe the principle of abductive reasoning and its expression in the framework of subjective logic. Before providing the details of binomial and multinomial abduction in subjective logic, the next section first introduces the concept of *relevance*, which is necessary for inverting binomial and multinomial conditionals [63].

10.2 Relevance and Dependence

The concepts of relevance and dependence are closely related. In subjective logic, 'relevance' expresses the conditional relationship between a (parent) variable and a specific value of another (child) variable, whereas 'dependence' expresses the conditional relationship between different (parent and child) variables.

More specifically, relevance between a variable X and a specific value of another variable Y expresses the likelihood of (observing) a change in the specific value of Y given (observations of) a change in the values of X. Relevance is a continuous measure, and hence can express any degree of relevance, not just total relevance or irrelevance.

In the literature on Bayesian networks, the term 'dependence' is typically interpreted in a binary way, in the sense that a variable Y is either dependent or independent on another variable X. It is possible to define a continuous measure of dependence between two variables as a function of the relevance relationships between the same variables. This concept of dependence is used in subjective logic, so that dependence measures can express any degree of dependence, not just total dependence or independence.

10.2.1 Relevance and Irrelevance

This section formally defines the concept of relevance, both for probability distributions and for opinions. The definition of probabilistic relevance is given below.

Definition 10.1 (Probabilistic Relevance).
Given two variables $X = \{x_i | i = 1, \ldots, k\}$ and $Y = \{y_j | j = 1, \ldots, l\}$, and a set of conditional probability distributions $p(Y|x_i)$, $i = 1, \ldots, k$, the relevance of variable X to a value y_j is defined as

$$\Psi(y_j|X) = \max_{x_i \in X}[p(y_j|x_i)] - \min_{x_i \in X}[p(y_j|x_i)] \,. \quad (10.3)$$

□

Relevance expresses the diagnostic power of a set of conditionals, i.e. how strongly, according to the conditionals, the possible values of the random variable X influence the truth/presence of value y_j (Y taking the value y_j or not).

Obviously, $\Psi(y_j|X) \in [0,1]$, for every $j = 1, \ldots, l$. The limit case $\Psi(y_j|X) = 1$ expresses *total relevance* (determination), and $\Psi(y_j|X) = 0$ expresses *total irrelevance* of X to y_j.

In the case of binary probabilistic conditionals $p(y|x)$ and $p(y|\overline{x})$, the expression for relevance is simplified to

$$\Psi(y|X) = |p(y|x) - p(y|\overline{x})| \,. \quad (10.4)$$

The concept of relevance can be extended to conditional subjective opinions, simply by projecting conditional opinions to their corresponding projected probability functions, and applying Eq.(10.3).

Definition 10.2 (Subjective Relevance). Assume a set of conditional opinions $\boldsymbol{\omega}_{Y|X}$, where each conditional opinion $\omega_{Y|x_i}$ has a corresponding projected probability distribution $\mathbf{P}_{Y|x_i}$. The relevance of X to each y_j is expressed as

$$\Psi(y_j|X) = \max_{x_i \in X}[\mathbf{P}_{Y|x_i}(y_j)] - \min_{x_i \in X}[\mathbf{P}_{Y|x_i}(y_j)] \,. \quad (10.5)$$

□

Relevance is equivalent to *diagnosticity* which is a central concept in ACH (analysis om competing hypotheses) [34, 5]. Diagnosticity is the power of influence of a given evidence variable X over the truth of a specific hypothesis y_j. Through inversion of conditionals the same diagnosticity translates into diagnosticity of (symptom) variable Y over the truth of a specific hypothesis x_i.

It is useful to also define *irrelevance*, $\overline{\Psi}(y_j|X)$, as the complement of relevance:

$$\overline{\Psi}(y_j|X) = 1 - \Psi(y_j|X) \,. \quad (10.6)$$

The irrelevance $\overline{\Psi}(y_j|X)$ expresses the lack of diagnostic power of the conditionals $\boldsymbol{\omega}_{Y|X}$ over the value y_j, leading to uncertainty when applying the subjective Bayes' theorem.

Note that in the case of binary variables X and Y, where X takes its values from $\mathbb{X} = \{x, \overline{x}\}$ and Y takes its values from $\mathbb{Y} = \{y, \overline{y}\}$, the above equations give the same relevance and irrelevance values for the two values of Y. For simplicity, we denote relevance of X to y and X to $\overline{y}$ by $\Psi(y|X)$ in both cases.

10.2.2 Dependence and Independence

This section formally defines the concept of dependence and independence.

Definition 10.3 (Dependence). Given two variables X and Y, and a set of relevance measures $\Psi(y_j|X)$, $j = 1, \ldots, l$, the dependence of variable Y on variable X is

$$\delta(Y|X) = \max_{y \in \mathbb{Y}}[\Psi(y|X)] \,. \tag{10.7}$$

□

The dependence expresses how strongly according to the conditionals, the random variable X influences the random variable Y.

Obviously, $\delta(Y|X) \in [0,1]$. The limit case $\delta(Y|X) = 1$ expresses total dependence, and $\delta(Y|X) = 0$ expresses total independence of Y on X.

Independence, denoted $\overline{\delta}(Y|X)$, is the complement of dependence:

$$\overline{\delta}(Y|X) = 1 - \delta(Y|X) \,. \tag{10.8}$$

The independence $\overline{\delta}(Y|X)$ is a factor for uncertainty of the inverted conditional opinions $\boldsymbol{\omega}_{X\tilde{|}Y}$ as described next.

10.3 Binomial Subjective Bayes' Theorem

This section describes the mathematics of inverting binomial conditional opinions which is based on the binomial subjective Bayes' theorem.

10.3.1 Principles for Inverting Binomial Conditional Opinions

Assume that the available conditionals $\omega_{y|x}$ and $\omega_{y|\overline{x}}$ are expressed in the opposite direction to that needed for deducing $\omega_{x\|y}$ expressed as

$$\omega_{x\|y} = \omega_y \circledcirc (\omega_{x|y}, \omega_{x|\overline{y}}) \,. \tag{10.9}$$

Binomial abduction simply consists of first inverting the pair of available conditionals $(\omega_{y|x}, \omega_{y|\bar{x}})$ to produce the opposite pair of conditionals $(\omega_{x\tilde{|}y}, \omega_{x\tilde{|}\bar{y}})$, and subsequently using these as input to binomial deduction described in Section 9.4.

Figure 10.1 illustrates the principle of conditional inversion, in the simple case of the conditionals $\omega_{y|x} = (0.80, 0.20, 0.00, 0.50)$ and $\omega_{y|\bar{x}} = (0.20, 0.80, 0.00, 0.50)$, and where $a_x = 0.50$. The inversion produces the pair of conditional opinions $\omega_{y|x} = (0.72, 0.12, 0.16, 0.50)$ and $\omega_{y|\bar{x}} = (0.16, 0.72, 0.12, 0.50)$, which are computed with the method described below.

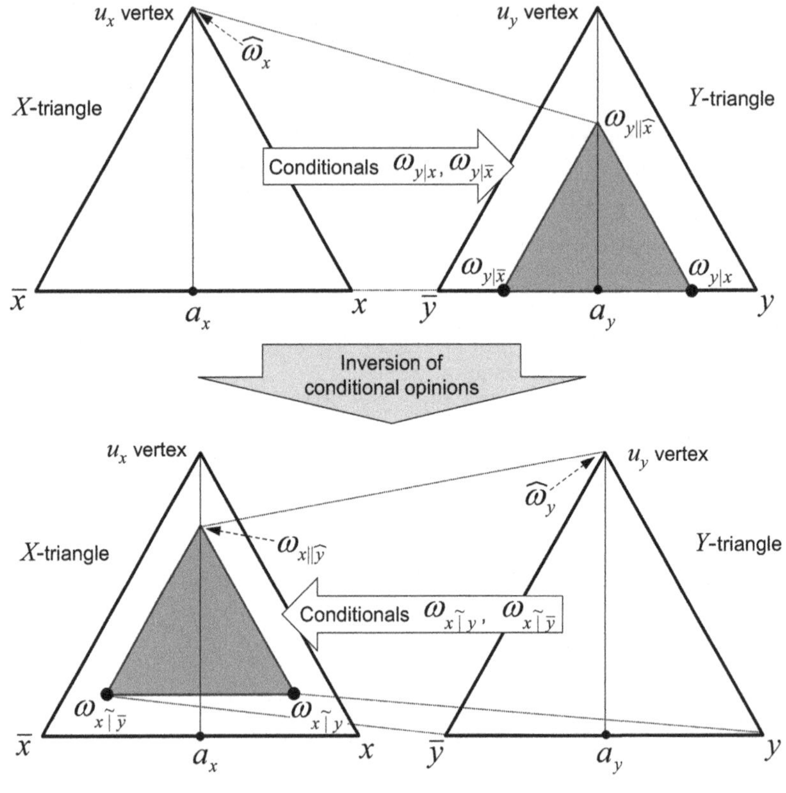

Fig. 10.1 Inversion of binomial conditionals

The top of Figure 10.1 show how the conditionals define the shaded sub-triangle within the Y-triangle, which is the image of possible deduced opinions $\omega_{y\|x}$.

The lower half of Figure 10.1 illustrates how the inverted conditionals define the shaded sub-triangle within the X-sub-triangle, which represents the image area for possible abduced opinions $\omega_{x\tilde{\|}y}$.

Note that in general, inversion produces increased uncertainty mass, as seen by the higher position of the shaded sub-triangle on the lower half of Figure 10.1. Increased uncertainty is a natural consequence of inversion. The ability to explicitly observe this behaviour is an advantage of the subjective Bayes' theorem over the traditional probabilistic Bayes' theorem.

The projected probabilities of the available conditionals $\omega_{y|x}$ and $\omega_{y|\overline{x}}$ are

$$\begin{cases} \mathrm{P}(y|x) = b_{y|x} + a_y u_{y|x} \,, \\ \\ \mathrm{P}(y|\overline{x}) = b_{y|\overline{x}} + a_y u_{y|\overline{x}}, \end{cases} \tag{10.10}$$

where $a(y)$ is the MBR from Eq.(9.36). In line with Bayes' theorem of Eq.(9.9) the projected probabilities of the inverted conditionals $\omega_{\widetilde{x|y}}$ and $\omega_{\widetilde{x|\overline{y}}}$ are computed using the results of Eq.(10.10) and the base rate a_x:

$$\begin{cases} \mathrm{P}(x|y) = \frac{a_x \mathrm{P}(y|x)}{a_x \mathrm{P}(y|x) + a_{\overline{x}} \mathrm{P}(y|\overline{x})}, \\ \\ \mathrm{P}(x|\overline{y}) = \frac{a_x \mathrm{P}(\overline{y}|x)}{a_x \mathrm{P}(\overline{y}|x) + a_{\overline{x}} \mathrm{P}(\overline{y}|\overline{x})}. \end{cases} \tag{10.11}$$

A pair of dogmatic conditional opinions can be synthesised from the projected probabilities of Eq.(10.11):

$$\begin{cases} \underline{\omega}_{x|y} = (\mathrm{P}(x|y), \mathrm{P}(\overline{x}|y), 0, a_x), \\ \\ \underline{\omega}_{x|\overline{y}} = (\mathrm{P}(x|\overline{y}), \mathrm{P}(\overline{x}|\overline{y}), 0, a_x). \end{cases} \tag{10.12}$$

where $\mathrm{P}(\overline{x}|y) = (1 - \mathrm{P}(x|y))$ and $\mathrm{P}(\overline{x}|\overline{y}) = (1 - \mathrm{P}(x|\overline{y}))$.

The pair of dogmatic conditionals $\underline{\omega}_{x|y}$ and $\underline{\omega}_{x|\overline{y}}$ of Eq.(10.12) and the pair of inverted conditional opinions $\omega_{\widetilde{x|y}}$ and $\omega_{\widetilde{x|\overline{y}}}$ have by definition equal projected probabilities. However, $\omega_{\widetilde{x|y}}$ and $\omega_{\widetilde{x|\overline{y}}}$ do in general contain uncertainty, in contrast to $\underline{\omega}_{x|y}$ and $\underline{\omega}_{x|\overline{y}}$ which are void of uncertainty. The inverted conditional opinions $\omega_{\widetilde{x|y}}$ and $\omega_{\widetilde{x|\overline{y}}}$ are derived from the dogmatic opinions of Eq.(10.12) by determining their appropriate amounts of uncertainty mass.

10.3.2 Uncertainty Mass of Inverted Binomial Conditionals

The inverted conditional uncertainty mass is a function of the following factors:

- the theoretical maximum uncertainty masses $\ddot{u}_{x|y}$ and $\ddot{u}_{x|\overline{y}}$,
- the weighted proportional uncertainty $u^{\mathrm{w}}_{y|X}$ based on $u_{y|x}$ and $u_{y|\overline{x}}$,
- the irrelevance $\overline{\Psi}(y|X)$.

These factors are applied in the four-step procedure described below.

Step 1: Theoretical maximum uncertainties $\ddot{u}_{x|y}$ and $\ddot{u}_{x|\bar{y}}$.

Figure 10.2 illustrates the principle for determining the uncertainty-maximised conditional $\ddot{\omega}_{x|y}$. The same principle is used for $\omega_{\widetilde{x|\bar{y}}}$.

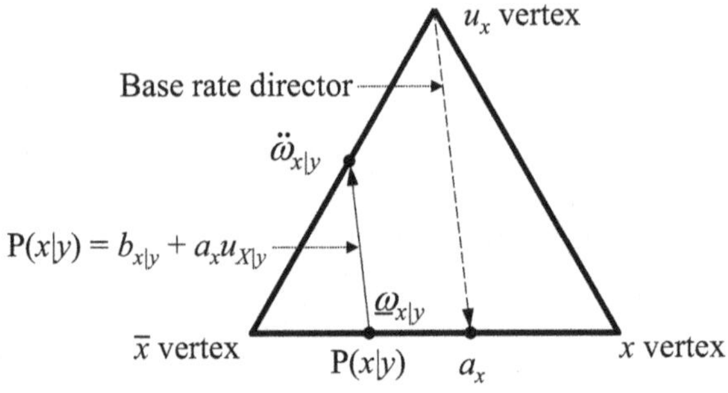

Fig. 10.2 Dogmatic conditional $\underline{\omega}_{x|y}$, and corresponding uncertainty-maximised conditional $\ddot{\omega}_{x|y}$

The theoretical maximum uncertainties, $\ddot{u}_{x|y}$ for $\omega_{\widetilde{x|y}}$, and $\ddot{u}_{x|\bar{y}}$ for $\omega_{\widetilde{x|\bar{y}}}$, are determined by setting either the belief or the disbelief mass to zero, according to the simple IF-THEN-ELSE algorithm below.

$$
\begin{array}{ll}
\multicolumn{2}{l}{\text{Computation of } \ddot{u}_{x|y}} \\
\hline
\text{IF} & \mathrm{P}(x|y) < a_x \\
\text{THEN} & \ddot{u}_{x|y} = \mathrm{P}(x|y)/a_x \\
\text{ELSE} & \ddot{u}_{x|y} = (1-\mathrm{P}(x|y))/(1-a_x)
\end{array}
\tag{10.13}
$$

$$
\begin{array}{ll}
\multicolumn{2}{l}{\text{Computation of } \ddot{u}_{x|\bar{y}}} \\
\hline
\text{IF} & \mathrm{P}(x|\bar{y}) < a_x \\
\text{THEN} & \ddot{u}_{x|\bar{y}} = \mathrm{P}(x|\bar{y})/a_x \\
\text{ELSE} & \ddot{u}_{x|\bar{y}} = (1-\mathrm{P}(x|\bar{y}))/(1-a_x)
\end{array}
\tag{10.14}
$$

Step 2: Weighted proportional uncertainty $u^{\mathrm{W}}_{y|X}$.

We need the sum of conditional uncertainty $u^{\mathrm{S}}_{y|X}$, computed as

$$
u^{\mathrm{S}}_{y|X} = u_{y|x} + u_{y|\bar{x}} \,. \tag{10.15}
$$

The proportional uncertainty weights $\mathrm{w}^{u}_{y|x}$ and $\mathrm{w}^{u}_{y|\bar{x}}$ are computed as

$$
\begin{cases}
\mathrm{w}^{u}_{y|x} = \dfrac{u_{y|x}}{u^{\mathrm{S}}_{y|X}} & \text{for } u^{\mathrm{S}}_{y|X} > 0, \\[2ex]
\mathrm{w}^{u}_{y|x} = 0 & \text{for } u^{\mathrm{S}}_{y|X} = 0,
\end{cases}
\tag{10.16}
$$

$$\begin{cases} \mathrm{w}^{u}_{y|\bar{x}} = \dfrac{u_{y|\bar{x}}}{u^{\mathrm{S}}_{y|X}} & \text{for } u^{\mathrm{S}}_{y|X} > 0, \\ \\ \mathrm{w}^{u}_{y|\bar{x}} = 0. & \text{for } u^{\mathrm{S}}_{y|X} = 0 \end{cases} \tag{10.17}$$

We also need the theoretical maximum uncertainty masses $\ddot{u}_{y|x}$ and $\ddot{u}_{y|\bar{x}}$ which are determined by setting either the belief or the disbelief mass to zero, according to the simple IF-THEN-ELSE algorithm below, where a_y is the MBR.

$$\begin{array}{ll} \multicolumn{2}{l}{\text{Computation of } \ddot{u}_{y|x}} \\ \hline \text{IF} & \mathrm{P}(y|x) < a_y \\ \text{THEN} & \ddot{u}_{y|x} = \mathrm{P}(y|x)/a_y \\ \text{ELSE} & \ddot{u}_{y|x} = (1-\mathrm{P}(y|x))/(1-a_y) \end{array} \tag{10.18}$$

$$\begin{array}{ll} \multicolumn{2}{l}{\text{Computation of } \ddot{u}_{y|\bar{x}}} \\ \hline \text{IF} & \mathrm{P}(y|\bar{x}) < a_y \\ \text{THEN} & \ddot{u}_{y|\bar{x}} = \mathrm{P}(y|\bar{x})/a_y \\ \text{ELSE} & \ddot{u}_{y|\bar{x}} = (1-\mathrm{P}(y|\bar{x}))/(1-a_y) \end{array} \tag{10.19}$$

The weighted proportional uncertainty components $u^{\mathrm{w}}_{y|x}$ and $u^{\mathrm{w}}_{y|\bar{x}}$ are computed as

$$\begin{cases} u^{\mathrm{w}}_{y|x} = \dfrac{\mathrm{w}^{u}_{y|x} u_{y|x}}{\ddot{u}_{y|x}} & \text{for } \ddot{u}_{y|x} > 0, \\ \\ u^{\mathrm{w}}_{y|x} = 0 & \text{for } \ddot{u}_{y|x} = 0, \end{cases} \tag{10.20}$$

$$\begin{cases} u^{\mathrm{w}}_{y|\bar{x}} = \dfrac{\mathrm{w}^{u}_{y|\bar{x}} u_{y|\bar{x}}}{\ddot{u}_{y|\bar{x}}}, & \text{for } \ddot{u}_{y|\bar{x}} > 0, \\ \\ u^{\mathrm{w}}_{y|\bar{x}} = 0 & \text{for } \ddot{u}_{y|\bar{x}} = 0. \end{cases} \tag{10.21}$$

The weighted proportional uncertainty $u^{\mathrm{w}}_{y|X}$ can then be computed as

$$u^{\mathrm{w}}_{y|X} = u^{\mathrm{w}}_{y|x} + u^{\mathrm{w}}_{y|\bar{x}}\,. \tag{10.22}$$

Step 3: Relative uncertainties $\widetilde{u}_{x|y}$ and $\widetilde{u}_{x|\bar{y}}$.

The relative uncertainties $\widetilde{u}_{x|y}$ and $\widetilde{u}_{x|\bar{y}}$ are computed as

$$\begin{aligned} \widetilde{u}_{x|y} = \widetilde{u}_{x|\bar{y}} &= u^{\mathrm{w}}_{y|X} \sqcup \overline{\Psi}(y|X) \\ &= u^{\mathrm{w}}_{y|X} + \overline{\Psi}(y|X) - u^{\mathrm{w}}_{y|X}\,\overline{\Psi}(y|X). \end{aligned} \tag{10.23}$$

The relative uncertainty $\widetilde{u}_{x|y}$ is an increasing function of the weighted proportional uncertainty $u^{\mathrm{w}}_{y|X}$, because uncertainty in the initial conditionals is reflected by uncertainty in the inverted conditionals. A practical example is when Alice is ignorant about whether Bob carries an umbrella in sunny or rainy weather. Then observing Bob carrying an umbrella provides no information about the weather.

$\widetilde{u}_{x|y}$ is also an increasing function of the irrelevance $\overline{\Psi}(y|X)$, because if $\omega_{y|x}$ and $\omega_{y|\bar{x}}$ reflect irrelevance, then there is no basis for deriving belief about the inverted conditionals $\omega_{\widetilde{x|y}}$ and $\omega_{\widetilde{x|\bar{y}}}$, so they must be uncertainty-maximised. A practical example is when Alice knows that Bob always carries an umbrella both in rain and sun. Then observing Bob carrying an umbrella tells her nothing about the weather.

The relative uncertainty $\widetilde{u}_{x|y}$ is thus high in case one or both the weighted proportional uncertainty $u^{\mathrm{w}}_{y|X}$ and the irrelevance $\overline{\Psi}(y|X)$ are high. This principle is modelled by computing $\widetilde{u}_{x|y}$ as the coproduct of $u^{\mathrm{w}}_{y|X}$ and $\overline{\Psi}(y|X)$, denoted by the coproduct operator $\sqcup$ in Eq.(10.23). Note that $\widetilde{u}_{x|\bar{y}} = \widetilde{u}_{x|y}$ in the binomial case.

Step 4: Uncertainty of inverted conditional opinions.

Having computed $\ddot{u}_{x|y}$ and the relative uncertainty $\widetilde{u}_{x|y}$, the uncertainty masses $u_{\widetilde{x|y}}$ and $u_{\widetilde{x|\bar{y}}}$ can finally be computed:

$$\text{Inverted binomial uncertainty:} \begin{cases} u_{\widetilde{x|y}} = \ddot{u}_{x|y}\widetilde{u}_{x|y}, \\ \\ u_{\widetilde{x|\bar{y}}} = \ddot{u}_{x|\bar{y}}\widetilde{u}_{x|\bar{y}}. \end{cases} \tag{10.24}$$

This marks the end of the four-step procedure for the computation of uncertainty.

10.3.3 Deriving Binomial Inverted Conditionals

Having determined $\mathrm{P}(x|y)$ in Eq.(10.11) and the uncertainty levels in the four-step procedure of Section 10.3.2 the computation of the inverted opinions is easy:

$$\omega_{\widetilde{x|y}} = \begin{cases} b_{\widetilde{x|y}} = \mathrm{P}(x|y) - a_x u_{\widetilde{x|y}}\,, \\ d_{\widetilde{x|y}} = 1 - b_{\widetilde{x|y}} - u_{\widetilde{x|y}}\,, \\ u_{\widetilde{x|y}}\,, \\ a_x\,, \end{cases} \tag{10.25}$$

$$\omega_{\widetilde{x|\bar{y}}} = \begin{cases} b_{\widetilde{x|\bar{y}}} = \mathrm{P}(x|\bar{y}) - a_x u_{\widetilde{x|\bar{y}}}\,, \\ d_{\widetilde{x|\bar{y}}} = 1 - b_{\widetilde{x|\bar{y}}} - u_{\widetilde{x|\bar{y}}}\,, \\ u_{\widetilde{x|\bar{y}}}\,, \\ a_x\,. \end{cases} \tag{10.26}$$

The process of inverting conditional opinions as described above is in fact the subjective Bayes' theorem for binomial conditional opinions. This property is articulated in Definition 10.4.

Definition 10.4 (Binomial Subjective Bayes' Theorem). Let $\{\omega_{y|x}, \omega_{y|\overline{x}}\}$ be a pair of binomial conditional opinions, and let a_x be the base rate of x. The pair of inverted conditionals $\{\omega_{x\widetilde{|}y}, \omega_{x\widetilde{|}\overline{y}}\}$ is derived through the procedure for Eq.(10.25) and Eq.(10.26) above. By using the symbol $\widetilde{\phi}$ to denote the operator for inversion of conditional opinions, the binomial Bayes' theorem can be expressed as

$$\text{Binomial subjective Bayes' theorem: } (\omega_{x\widetilde{|}y}, \omega_{x\widetilde{|}\overline{y}}) = \widetilde{\phi}(\omega_{y|x}, \omega_{y|\overline{x}}, a_x). \tag{10.27}$$

□

Note that the binomial subjective Bayes' theorem of Definition 10.4 is equivalent to the multinomial Bayes' theorem of Definition 10.6 in the special case of binary variables X and Y where the set of conditional opinions is reduced to a pair.

Binomial abduction, described in Section 10.4, consists of first inverting the pair of conditionals using the subjective Bayes' theorem, and then applying these for binomial conditional deduction.

10.3.4 Convergence of Repeated Inversions

An interesting question is, what happens when conditionals are repeatedly inverted? With arbitrary base rates applied to Bayes' theorem of Eq.(9.5), the conditionals will in general change after multiple inversions, which can produce inconsistency. However, when applying Bayes' theorem with MBR of Eq.(9.9) the pair of double-inverted conditionals is equal to the original pair of conditionals, formally:

$$\begin{aligned}(p(y|x), p(y|\overline{x})) &= \widetilde{\phi}(p(x|y), p(x|\overline{y}), a(y)) \\ &= \widetilde{\phi}(\widetilde{\phi}(p(y|x), p(y|\overline{x}), a(x)), a(y)) \,.\end{aligned} \tag{10.28}$$

When a pair of conditional opinions have MBRs their projected probabilities are also unchanged after repeated inversions. However, repeated inversion of conditional opinions produces increase uncertainty mass in general.

The increasing uncertainty is of course limited by the theoretical maximum uncertainty mass for each conditional. In general, the uncertainty mass of conditional opinions converges towards their theoretical maximum, as inversions are repeated infinitely many times.

Figure 10.3 illustrates the process of repeated inversion of conditionals, based on the same example as in Figure 10.1, where the initial conditionals are $\omega_{y|x} = (0.80, 0.20, 0.00, 0.50)$ and $\omega_{y|\overline{x}} = (0.20, 0.80, 0.00, 0.50)$, and where the equal base rates are $a_x = a_y = 0.50$.

Table 10.1 lists a selection of the computed conditional opinions $\omega_{y\widetilde{|}x}$ and $\omega_{x\widetilde{|}y}$. The set consists of: i) the convergence conditional opinion, ii) the first eight inverted conditional opinions, and iii) the initial conditional opinion, in that order.

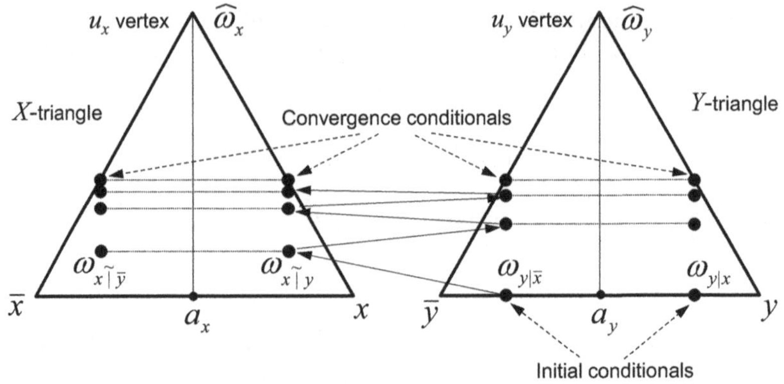

Fig. 10.3 Convergence of repeated inversion of pairs of binomial conditionals

Table 10.1 Series of inverted conditional opinions

	Index	Opinion	Belief	Disbelief	Uncertainty	Base rate
Convergence	∞	$\ddot{\omega}_{\widetilde{y|}x} = \ddot{\omega}_{\widetilde{x|}y}$	= (0.6,	0.0,	0.4,	0.5)
	.		...	...	...	...
	8	$\omega_{\widetilde{y|}^{8}x}$	= (0.603358,	0.003359,	0.393282,	0.5)
	7	$\omega_{\widetilde{x|}^{7}y}$	= (0.605599,	0.005599,	0.388803,	0.5)
	6	$\omega_{\widetilde{y|}^{6}x}$	= (0.609331,	0.009331,	0.381338,	0.5)
	5	$\omega_{\widetilde{x|}^{5}y}$	= (0.615552,	0.015552,	0.368896,	0.5)
	4	$\omega_{\widetilde{y|}^{4}x}$	= (0.62592,	0.02592,	0.34816,	0.5)
	3	$\omega_{\widetilde{x|}^{3}y}$	= (0.6432,	0.0432,	0.3136,	0.5)
	2	$\omega_{\widetilde{y|}^{2}x}$	= (0.672,	0.072,	0.256,	0.5)
	1	$\omega_{\widetilde{x|}y}$	= (0.72,	0.12,	0.16,	0.5)
Initial	0	$\omega_{y|x}$	= (0.8,	0.2,	0.0 ,	0.5)

The increase of uncertainty mass is relative large in the first few inversions, and rapidly becomes smaller. Two convergence conditional opinions are $\omega_{\widetilde{y|}x} = \omega_{\widetilde{x|}y} = (0.60, 0.00, 0.40, 0.50)$. The two others are $\omega_{\widetilde{y|}\overline{x}} = \omega_{\widetilde{x|}\overline{y}} = (0.00, 0.60, 0.40, 0.50)$.

The inverted opinions were computed with an office spreadsheet, which started rounding off results from index 6. The final convergence conditional was not computed with the spreadsheet, but was simply determined as the opinion with the theoretical maximum uncertainty.

The above example is rather simple, with its perfectly symmetrical conditionals and base rates of $1/2$. In general, the two pairs of convergence conditionals are not equal. The equality in our example above is coincidentally due to the symmetric conditionals and base rates. However, the same pattern of increasing uncertainty towards a convergence limit occurs for arbitrary conditionals and base rates. The generation of uncertainty mass reflects a fundamental property of the subjective

Bayes' theorem, which is invisible in the probabilistic Bayes' theorem. A validation of the subjective Bayes' theorem is given as a numerical example in Section 17.2.3.

10.4 Binomial Abduction

Binomial abduction with the conditionals $\omega_{y|x}$ and $\omega_{y|\bar{x}}$ consists of first producing the inverted conditionals $\omega_{x\tilde{|}y}$ and $\omega_{x\tilde{|}\bar{y}}$ as described in Section 10.3, and subsequently applying them in binomial conditional deduction. This is defined below.

Definition 10.5 (Binomial Abduction).
Assume the binary domains $\mathbb{X} = \{x, \bar{x}\}$ and $\mathbb{Y} = \{y, \bar{y}\}$, where the pair of conditionals $(\omega_{y|x}, \omega_{y|\bar{x}})$ is available to the analyst. Assume further that the analyst has the opinion ω_y about y (as well as the complement $\omega_{\bar{y}}$ about $\bar{y}$), and wants to determine an opinion about x. Binomial abduction means to compute the opinion about x in this situation, which consists of the following two-step process:

1. Invert the pair of available conditionals $(\omega_{y|x}, \omega_{y|\bar{x}})$ using the subjective binomial Bayes' theorem to produce the inverted pair of conditionals $(\omega_{x\tilde{|}y}, \omega_{x\tilde{|}\bar{y}})$, as described in Section 10.3.
2. Apply the pair of inverted conditionals $\{\omega_{x\tilde{|}y}, \omega_{x\tilde{|}\bar{y}}\}$ together with the opinion ω_y to compute binomial deduction, as denoted in Eq.(10.31) and described in Section 9.4.

□

Binomial abduction produces the opinion $\omega_{x\tilde{\|}y}$ about x, and is expressed as

$$\text{Binomial abduction: } \omega_{x\tilde{\|}y} = \omega_y \tilde{\circledcirc} (\omega_{y|x}, \omega_{y|\bar{x}}, a_x) \tag{10.29}$$

$$= \omega_y \circledcirc \tilde{\phi}(\omega_{y|x}, \omega_{y|\bar{x}}, a_x) \tag{10.30}$$

$$= \omega_y \circledcirc (\omega_{x\tilde{|}y}, \omega_{x\tilde{|}\bar{y}}) \,. \tag{10.31}$$

□

Conditional abduction according to Eq.(10.29), with the original pair of binomial conditionals $(\omega_{y|x}, \omega_{y|\bar{x}})$, is transformed to binomial conditional deduction according to Eq.(10.31) which takes as argument the pair of inverted conditionals $(\omega_{x\tilde{|}y}, \omega_{x\tilde{|}\bar{y}})$ produced by the binomial subjective Bayes' theorem.

Figure 10.4 is a screenshot of binomial abduction, involving the MBR $a_y = 0.33$.

The abduced opinion $\omega_{x\tilde{\|}y} = (0.17, 0.08, 0.75, 0.20)$ contains considerable uncertainty, which is partially due to the following uncertainty factors that appear in the computation:

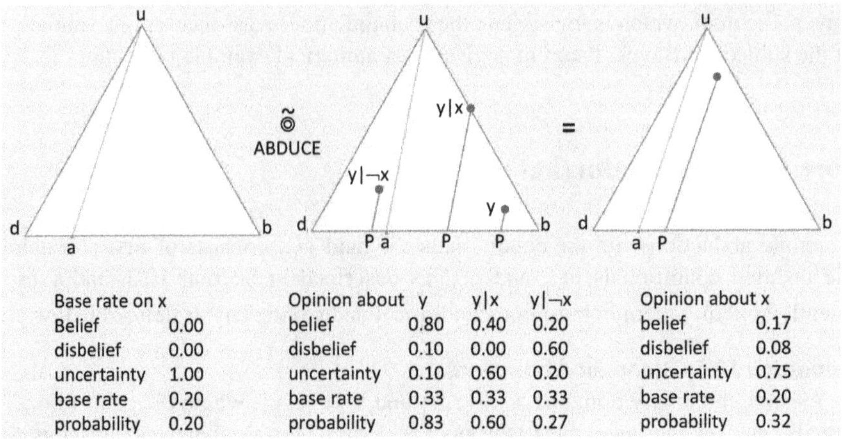

Fig. 10.4 Screenshot of abduction, involving the MBR $a_y = 0.33$

$$\begin{cases} \text{Irrelevance:} & \overline{\Psi}(y|X) = 0.67, \\ \text{Weighted relative uncertainty:} & u^{\mathrm{w}}_{y|X} \quad = 0.81, \\ \text{Apex point uncertainty in } X\text{-sub-triangle:} & u_{x\|\widehat{y}} \quad = 0.95, \\ \text{Argument uncertainty:} & u_Y \quad = 0.10. \end{cases} \tag{10.32}$$

Notice that the difference between deduction and abduction simply depends on which conditionals are available to the analyst. In the case of causal situations, it is normally easier to estimate causal conditionals than the opposite derivative conditionals. Assuming that there is a causal conditional relationship from x to y, the analyst therefore typically has available the pair of conditionals $(\omega_{y|x}, \omega_{y|\overline{x}})$, so that computing an opinion about x would require abduction.

10.5 Illustrating the Base-Rate Fallacy

The base-rate fallacy is briefly discussed in Section 10.1. This section provides simple visualisations of how the base-rate fallacy can materialise, and how it can be avoided. Assume medical tests for diseases A and B, where the sensitivity and specificity for both tests are equal, as expressed by the following conditional opinions:

$$\text{Sensitivity ('Positive test on affected person'):} \quad \omega_{y|x} : \begin{cases} b_{y|x} = 0.90, \\ d_{y|x} = 0.05, \\ u_{y|x} = 0.05, \end{cases}$$
$$\text{Specificity ('Negative test on unaffected person'):} \quad \omega_{\overline{y}|\overline{x}} : \begin{cases} b_{\overline{y}|\overline{x}} = 0.90, \\ d_{\overline{y}|\overline{x}} = 0.05, \\ u_{\overline{y}|\overline{x}} = 0.05. \end{cases} \tag{10.33}$$

Note that the computation in the examples uses the unspecificity opinion $\omega_{y|\overline{x}}$, i.e. the complement of the specificity opinion, expressed as $\omega_{y|\overline{x}} = \neg\omega_{\overline{y}|\overline{x}}$. A good test should have low unspecificity, i.e. the opinion about positive test given unaffected person should have low projected probability.

In the first situation, assume that the base rate for disease A in the population is $a_x = 0.5$, hence the MBR of the test result becomes $a_y = 0.5$ too. Assume further that a patient tests positive for disease A. The abduced opinion about whether the patient has disease A is illustrated in Figure 10.5. The projected probability that the patient has disease A is $\mathrm{P}(x) = 0.93$.

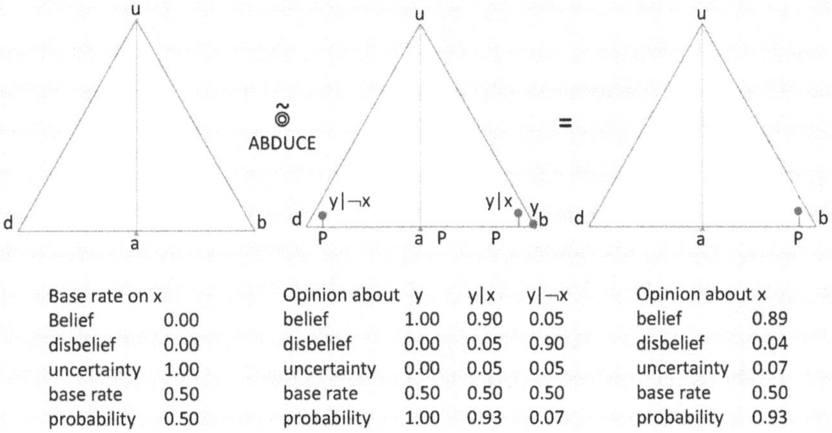

Fig. 10.5 Screenshot of medical test of disease A with base rate $a_x = 0.50$

In the second situation, assume that the base rate for disease B in the population is $a_x = 0.01$, hence the MBR of the test result becomes $a_y = 0.06$. Assume further that a patient tests positive for disease B. The abduced opinion about the patient having disease B is illustrated in Figure 10.6. The projected probability of having disease B is only $\mathrm{P}(x) = 0.15$, and the uncertainty is considerable.

The examples of Figure 10.5 and Figure 10.6 give completely different results regarding the likelihood that that the person is affected by disease A or B.

Note that tests A and B both have the same quality, as expressed by their equal sensitivity and specificity. Despite having equal quality, the diagnostic conclusions

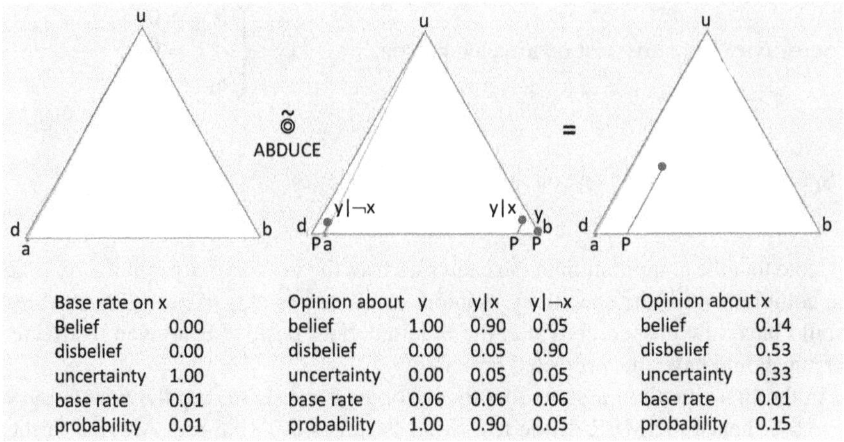

Fig. 10.6 Screenshot of medical test of disease B with base rate $a_x = 0.01$

to be drawn from a positive test A and a positive test B are radically different. This difference is due to the base rate which is very different in the two examples. It is thus not enough to simply consider the quality of tests when making diagnostics, the practitioner must also take into account the base rates of diseases or other medical conditions that are being tested.

The conclusion to be drawn from the examples is that the medical practitioner must always consider the base rate of the condition that a patient is tested for, or else risk falling victim to the base-rate fallacy and making the wrong diagnosis.

The quality of a test can be expressed in terms of the relevance of the disease on the test results. Tests A and B in the example above have relatively high, but not perfect relevance.

In the next example illustrated in Figure 10.7, assume a test C with low quality (high irrelevance) as expressed by the conditionals below.

$$\text{Sensitivity ('Positive test on affected person'):} \quad \omega_{y|x} : \begin{cases} b_{y|x} = 0.90, \\ d_{y|x} = 0.05, \\ u_{y|x} = 0.05, \end{cases}$$

$$\text{Specificity ('Negative test on unaffected person'):} \quad \omega_{\overline{y}|\overline{x}} : \begin{cases} b_{\overline{y}|\overline{x}} = 0.25, \\ d_{\overline{y}|\overline{x}} = 0.70, \\ u_{\overline{y}|\overline{x}} = 0.05. \end{cases} \tag{10.34}$$

Note that the computation again uses the unspecificity opinion $\omega_{y|\overline{x}}$ expressed as $\omega_{y|\overline{x}} = \neg\omega_{\overline{y}|\overline{x}}$.

In this case, assume that the base rate for disease C in the population is $a_x = 0.50$, then the MBR of the test result becomes $a_y = 0.84$.

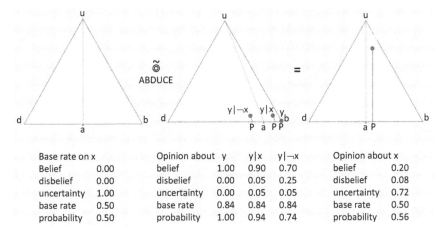

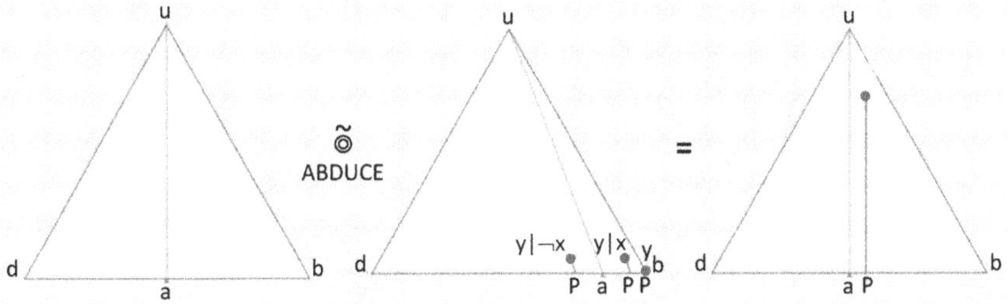

Base rate on x	
Belief	0.00
disbelief	0.00
uncertainty	1.00
base rate	0.50
probability	0.50

Opinion about	y	y|x	y|¬x
belief	1.00	0.90	0.70
disbelief	0.00	0.05	0.25
uncertainty	0.00	0.05	0.05
base rate	0.84	0.84	0.84
probability	1.00	0.94	0.74

Opinion about x	
belief	0.20
disbelief	0.08
uncertainty	0.72
base rate	0.50
probability	0.56

Fig. 10.7 Screenshot of medical test C with poor quality

Note the dramatic increase in uncertainty, which is mainly due to the high irrelevance $\overline{\Psi}(y|X) = 0.80$. The closer together the conditional opinion points are positioned in the opinion triangle (in the opinion simplex in general), the higher the irrelevance. In the extreme case when all conditional opinion points are in exactly the same position, the irrelevance is total, meaning that variable Y is independent of variable X.

10.6 The Multinomial Subjective Bayes' Theorem

10.6.1 Principles for Inverting Multinomial Conditional Opinions

Multinomial abduction in subjective logic requires inversion of conditional opinions of the form $\omega_{Y|x_i}$ into conditional opinions of the form $\omega_{X|y_j}$, analogously to Eq.(10.36) in the case of Bayesian inference. This section describes the principles of multinomial conditional opinion inversion, which in fact represents a generalisation of Bayes' theorem.

Figure 10.8 illustrates the principle of inversion of multinomial conditional opinions. The initial conditionals project the X-simplex (the opinion space of X) onto a sub-simplex within the Y-simplex, as shown in the top part of Figure 10.8, which is the basis for deduction as described in the previous section. The goal of the inversion is to derive conditionals that define a projection from the opinion space of Y onto a sub-space of the opinion space of X (as shown in the bottom part of Figure 10.8), which in turn can support deduction from Y to X. Then an opinion on X can be deduced from an evidence opinion on Y, which completes the abduction process.

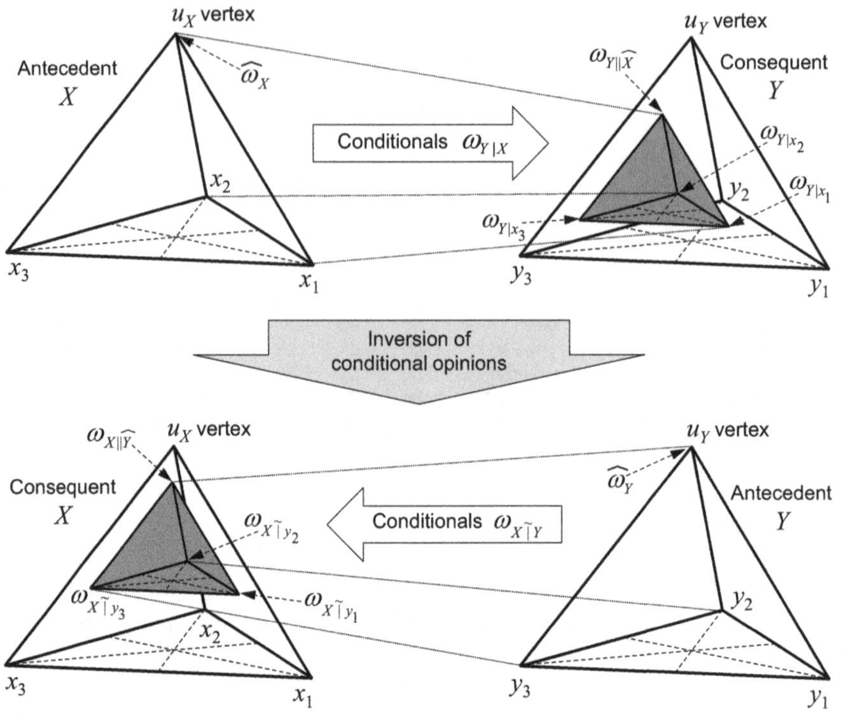

Fig. 10.8 Inversion of multinomial conditional opinions

In case the conditionals are expressed as hyper-opinions, then it is required that they be projected to multinomial opinion arguments that only provide belief support for singleton values. Eq.(3.30) describes the method for projecting hyper-opinions into multinomial opinions.

Now, for the inversion of conditional opinions, assume two random variables X and Y with respective cardinalities $k = |X|$ and $l = |Y|$, with a set of multinomial conditionals $\boldsymbol{\omega}_{Y|X}$, and the base rate distribution $\boldsymbol{a}_X$ on X:

$$\text{Inversion arguments:} \quad \begin{cases} \boldsymbol{\omega}_{Y|X} = \left\{\omega_{Y|x_1}, \ldots, \omega_{Y|x_k}\right\}, \\ \boldsymbol{a}_X. \end{cases} \tag{10.35}$$

Since we want the projected probabilities of the inverted conditional opinions to behave in the same way as when applying Bayes' theorem in traditional Bayesian inference described in Section 9.2, the projected probabilities of each inverted conditional opinion $\omega_{X\tilde{|}y_j}$ are determined according to the following equation, which is analogous to Eq.(9.24):

$$\mathbf{P}_{X|y_j}(x) = \frac{\boldsymbol{a}_X(x)\mathbf{P}_{Y|x}(y_j)}{\sum_{i=1}^{k} \boldsymbol{a}_X(x_i)\mathbf{P}_{Y|x_i}(y_j)}, \quad \text{for } x \in \mathbb{X}. \tag{10.36}$$

The simplest inverted opinions $\omega_{X\tilde{|}y_j}$, $j = 1, \ldots, l$, to satisfy Eq.(10.36) are the dogmatic opinions defined in the following way:

$$\underline{\omega}_{X|y_j} : \begin{cases} \boldsymbol{b}_{X\tilde{|}y_j}(x_i) = \mathbf{P}_{X|y_j}(x_i), \; i = 1, \ldots, k, \\ u_{X\tilde{|}y_j} \quad\quad = 0, \\ \boldsymbol{a}_{X|y_j} \quad\quad = \boldsymbol{a}_X. \end{cases} \tag{10.37}$$

However, the proper inverted conditional opinions $\boldsymbol{\omega}_{X\tilde{|}Y}$ do in general contain uncertainty, in contrast to the dogmatic opinions $\underline{\omega}_{X|Y}$ which are void of uncertainty. The crux is to determine the appropriate uncertainty for each inverted conditional. Then, the corresponding belief masses emerge directly.

10.6.2 Uncertainty Mass of Inverted Multinomial Conditionals

The amount of uncertainty mass to be assigned to the inverted conditional opinions depends on the following factors:

- the *maximum possible uncertainty mass* $\ddot{u}_{X|y_j}$ of the opinions $\omega_{X\tilde{|}y_j}$ satisfying Eq.(10.36), for each $j = 1, \ldots, l$,
- the *weighted proportional uncertainty* $u^{\mathrm{w}}_{Y|X}$ of the uncertainties $u_{Y|x_i}$, and
- the *irrelevance* measures $\overline{\Psi}(y_j|X)$, for $j = 1, \ldots, l$.

The principles of determining uncertainty masses of inverted conditional opinions are concisely formalised by the four-step procedure below.

Step 1: Theoretical maximum uncertainties $\ddot{u}_{X|y_j}$.

First we identify the theoretical maximum uncertainties $\ddot{u}_{X|y_j}$ of the inverted conditionals, by converting as much belief mass as possible into uncertainty mass, while preserving consistent projected probabilities according to Eq.(10.36). This process is illustrated in Figure 10.9.

The line defined by the set of equations

$$\mathbf{P}_{X|y_j}(x_i) = \boldsymbol{b}_{X\tilde{|}y_j}(x_i) + \boldsymbol{a}_X(x_i)u_{X\tilde{|}y_j}, \quad i = 1, \ldots k, \tag{10.38}$$

which by definition is parallel to the base rate director line and which joins $\underline{\omega}_{X|y_j}$ and $\ddot{\omega}_{X|y_j}$ in Figure 10.9, defines possible opinions $\omega_{X\tilde{|}y_j}$ for which the projected probability is consistent with Eq.(10.36). As the illustration shows, an opinion $\ddot{\omega}_{X|y_j}$ is uncertainty-maximised when Eq.(10.38) is satisfied and at least one belief mass of $\ddot{\omega}_{X|y_j}$ is zero, since the corresponding point then lies on a side of the simplex. In general, not all belief masses can be zero simultaneously, except for the vacuous opinion. The example of Figure 10.9 indicates the case when $\boldsymbol{b}_{X\tilde{|}y_j}(x_1) = 0$.

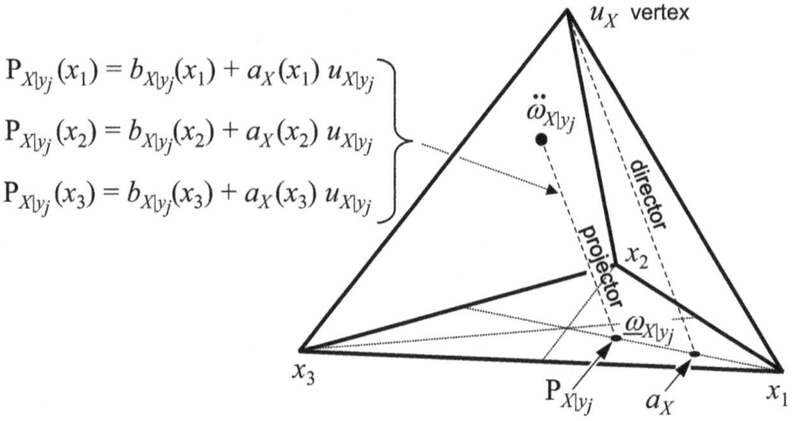

Fig. 10.9 Dogmatic opinion $\underline{\omega}_{X|y_j}$, and corresponding uncertainty-maximised opinion $\ddot{\omega}_{X|y_j}$

The opinion $\ddot{\omega}_{X|y_j}$ should satisfy the following requirements:

$$\ddot{u}_{X|y_j} = \frac{\mathbf{P}_{X|y_j}(x_{i_0})}{\boldsymbol{a}_X(x_{i_0})}, \quad \text{for some } i_0 \in \{1,\ldots,k\}, \text{ and} \tag{10.39}$$

$$\mathbf{P}_{X|y_j}(x_i) \geq \boldsymbol{a}_X(x_i) u_{X\widetilde{|}y_j}, \quad \text{for every } i \in \{1,\ldots,k\}. \tag{10.40}$$

The requirement of Eq.(10.40) ensures that all the belief masses determined according to Eq.(3.12) are non-negative. These requirements lead to the uncertainty maximum for $u_{X\widetilde{|}y_j}$:

$$\ddot{u}_{X|y_j} = \min_i \left[\frac{\mathbf{P}_{X|y_j}(x_i)}{\boldsymbol{a}_X(x_i)} \right] = \min_i \left[\frac{\mathbf{P}_{Y|x_i}(y_j)}{\sum_{g=1}^{k} \boldsymbol{a}_X(x_g)\mathbf{P}_{Y|x_g}(y_j)} \right]. \tag{10.41}$$

Step 2: Weighted proportional uncertainty $u^{\mathrm{w}}_{Y|X}$.

We need the sum of conditional uncertainty $u^{\mathrm{S}}_{Y|X}$, computed as

$$u^{\mathrm{S}}_{Y|X} = \sum_x u_{Y|x}\,. \tag{10.42}$$

The proportional uncertainty weights $\mathrm{w}^u_{Y|x}$ are computed as

$$\begin{cases} \mathrm{w}^u_{Y|x} = \dfrac{u_{Y|x}}{u^{\mathrm{S}}_{Y|X}}, & \text{for } u^{\mathrm{S}}_{Y|X} > 0, \\[2ex] \mathrm{w}^u_{Y|x} = 0 & \text{for } u^{\mathrm{S}}_{Y|X} = 0. \end{cases} \tag{10.43}$$

We also need the theoretical maximum uncertainty $\ddot{u}_{Y|x_i}$ of each conditional $\omega_{Y|x_i}$. The theoretical maximum uncertainty must satisfy the following requirements:

$$\ddot{u}_{Y|x_i} = \frac{\mathbf{P}_{Y|x_i}(y_{j0})}{\boldsymbol{a}_Y(y_{j0})}, \quad \text{for some } j_0 \in \{1,\ldots,l\}, \text{ and} \tag{10.44}$$

$$\mathbf{P}_{Y|x_i}(y_j) \geq \boldsymbol{a}_Y(y_j)u_{Y|x_i}, \quad \text{for every } j \in \{1,\ldots,l\}, \tag{10.45}$$

where $\boldsymbol{a}_Y$ is the marginal base rate distribution from Eq.(9.68). The requirement of Eq.(10.45) ensures that all belief masses determined according to Eq.(3.12) are non-negative. These requirements lead to the uncertainty maximum for $u_{Y|x_i}$:

$$\ddot{u}_{Y|x_i} = \min_j \left[\frac{\mathbf{P}_{Y|x_i}(y_j)}{\boldsymbol{a}_Y(y_j)} \right]. \tag{10.46}$$

The weighted proportional uncertainty components $u^{\mathrm{w}}_{Y|x}$ are computed as

$$\begin{cases} u^{\mathrm{w}}_{Y|x} = \dfrac{w^u_{Y|x} u_{Y|x}}{\ddot{u}_{Y|x}}, & \text{for } \ddot{u}_{Y|x} > 0, \\[2ex] u^{\mathrm{w}}_{Y|x} = 0 & \text{for } \ddot{u}_{Y|x} = 0. \end{cases} \tag{10.47}$$

The weighted proportional uncertainty $u^{\mathrm{w}}_{Y|X}$ can then be computed as

$$u^{\mathrm{w}}_{Y|X} = \sum_{i=1}^{k} u^{\mathrm{w}}_{Y|x_i}. \tag{10.48}$$

Step 3: Relative uncertainties $\widetilde{u}_{x|y}$.

The relative uncertainty, denoted $\widetilde{u}_{X|y_j}$, is computed as the coproduct of the weighted proportional uncertainty $u^{\mathrm{w}}_{Y|X}$ and the irrelevance $\overline{\Psi}(y_j|X)$:

$$\begin{aligned} \widetilde{u}_{X|y_j} &= u^{\mathrm{w}}_{Y|X} \sqcup \overline{\Psi}(y_j|X) \\ &= u^{\mathrm{w}}_{Y|X} + \overline{\Psi}(y_j|X) - u^{\mathrm{w}}_{Y|X}\, \overline{\Psi}(y_i|X). \end{aligned} \tag{10.49}$$

The irrelevance $\overline{\Psi}(y_j|X)$ of the variable X to the particular value y_j of Y, is obviously a factor for determining the uncertainty $u_{X\widetilde{|}y_j}$. For example, if the original conditionals $\boldsymbol{\omega}_{Y|X}$ reflect total irrelevance of the variable X to the value y_j of Y, then there is no basis for deriving belief about the inverted conditionals $\omega_{X\widetilde{|}y_j}$, and the latter must have maximal uncertainty. This is assured by Eq.(10.49) when the irrelevance $\overline{\Psi}(y_j|X) = 1$.

A practical example is when we know that the weather has no influence on the outcome of a football game between two given football teams. Then observing the outcome of a specific game gives no information about the weather, obviously.

The weighted proportional uncertainty $u^{\mathrm{w}}_{Y|X}$ must be taken into account, because uncertainty in one reasoning direction should be reflected by uncertainty in the opposite reasoning direction. A practical example is when the outcome of a given football game *a priori* is totally uncertain, but where information about match-fixing could provide strong evidence for predicting the outcome. But then, if the analyst is ignorant about whether match-fixing is taking place, then the outcome of the game is still uncertain.

According to Eq.(10.48), $u^{\mathrm{w}}_{Y|X}$ represents the proportional expected uncertainty of Y given X, which represents a general uncertainty level for the deductive reasoning, and which must be reflected in the inverted conditionals as well.

The justification for Eq.(10.49) is that the relative uncertainty $\widetilde{u}_{x|y}$ should be an increasing function of both the weighted proportional uncertainty $u^{\mathrm{w}}_{Y|X}$, and the irrelevance $\overline{\Psi}(y_j|X)$. In addition to that, all three values should lie in the interval $[0,1]$. The disjunctive combination of the weighted proportional uncertainty $u^{\mathrm{w}}_{Y|X}$ and the irrelevance $\overline{\Psi}(y|X)$ is an adequate choice because it ensures the following:

- when one of the two operands equals 0, the result equals the other one,
- when one of the two operands equals 1, the result also equals 1.

Step 4: Uncertainty of inverted multinomial conditionals.

The uncertainty mass of each inverted conditional, denoted $u_{X\widetilde{|}y_j}$, is computed by multiplying the theoretical maximum uncertainty $\ddot{u}_{X|y_j}$ by the relative uncertainty $\widetilde{u}_{X|y_j}$, as expressed by Eq.(10.50):

$$u_{X\widetilde{|}y_j} = \ddot{u}_{X|y_j}\,\widetilde{u}_{X|y_j} = \ddot{u}_{X|y_j}\left(u^{\mathrm{w}}_{Y|X} + \overline{\Psi}(y_j|X) - u^{\mathrm{w}}_{Y|X}\,\overline{\Psi}(y_i|X)\right). \tag{10.50}$$

The uncertainty mass $u_{X\widetilde{|}y_j}$ is in the range $[0,\ddot{u}_{X|y_j}]$, because the relative uncertainty $\widetilde{u}_{X|y_j}$ is in the range $[0,1]$.

This marks the end of the four-step procedure for determining uncertainty mass of inverted multinomial conditional opinions.

10.6.3 Deriving Multinomial Inverted Conditionals

Given the uncertainty masses $u_{X\widetilde{|}y_j}$ for $j = 1,\ldots,l$, the inverted conditional opinions are simply determined as

$$\omega_{X\widetilde{|}y_j} = (\boldsymbol{b}_{X\widetilde{|}y_j},\ u_{X\widetilde{|}y_j},\ \boldsymbol{a}_X), \tag{10.51}$$

where $\boldsymbol{b}_{X\widetilde{|}y_j}(x) = \mathbf{P}_{X|y_j}(x) - u_{X\widetilde{|}y_j}\boldsymbol{a}_X(x)$, for $x \in \mathbb{X}$. The projected probabilities $\mathbf{P}_{X|y_j}(x)$ are computed with Eq.(10.36).

Eq.(10.51) determines the set $\boldsymbol{\omega}_{X\tilde{|}Y}$ of inverted conditional opinions of Eq.(10.51). The process of inverting conditional opinions as described above is in fact Bayes' theorem generalised to multinomial conditional opinions. This property is articulated in Definition 10.6:

Definition 10.6 (Multinomial Subjective Bayes' Theorem). Let $\boldsymbol{\omega}_{Y|X}$ be a set of multinomial conditional opinions, and let $\boldsymbol{a}_X$ be the base rate distribution over X. The set of conditional opinions $\boldsymbol{\omega}_{X\tilde{|}Y}$ derived according to Eq.(10.51) described above is the inverted set of conditional opinions of the former set. The symbol $\widetilde{\phi}$ denotes the operator for conditional inversion and thereby for the subjective Bayes' theorem. Hence, inversion of a set of conditional opinions is denoted as

$$\text{Subjective Bayes' theorem:}\quad \boldsymbol{\omega}_{X\tilde{|}Y} = \widetilde{\phi}\left(\boldsymbol{\omega}_{Y|X},\, \boldsymbol{a}_X\right). \tag{10.52}$$

□

A validation of the subjective Bayes' theorem is given as a numerical example in Section 17.2.3. As explained in Section 10.3.4, repeated inversion of conditionals with MBRs preserves the projected probabilities, and produces increased uncertainty masses in general. The increased uncertainty mass, and thereby the reduced confidence, is a natural consequence of conditional inversion. This effect is not visible for probabilistic conditional inversion, and demonstrates the advantage of the subjective Bayes' theorem over the probabilistic Bayes' theorem.

The increase in uncertainty mass is of course limited by the theoretical maximum uncertainty mass for each conditional. Repeated inversion will ultimately make the uncertainty masses converge towards their theoretical maximum.

10.7 Multinomial Abduction

Multinomial abduction is a two-step process, where the first consists of inverting a set of multinomial conditional opinions using the subjective Bayes' theorem as described in Section 10.6, which in the second step are used as arguments for multinomial deduction. The abduced result is denoted $\omega_{X\tilde{\|}Y}$. The abduction operator is concisely defined below.

Definition 10.7 (Multinomial Abduction).

Let $X = \{x_i | i = 1,\dots,k\}$ and $Y = \{y_j | j = 1,\dots,l\}$ be random variables, where now Y is the evidence variable, and X is the target variable.

The symbol '$\widetilde{\circledcirc}$' denotes the conditional abduction operator for subjective opinions. There are three groups of arguments: i) $\boldsymbol{\omega}_{Y|X} = \{\omega_{Y|x_i},\ i = 1,\dots,k\}$, which represents the set of all the $k = |X|$ different conditional opinions over Y; ii) the base rate distribution $\boldsymbol{a}_X$); iii) the evidence opinion ω_Y.

Given the above, assume that the analyst wants to derive a subjective opinion on X. Multinomial abduction means to compute the opinion about X in this situation, which consists of the following two-step process:

1. Invert the set of available conditionals $\boldsymbol{\omega}_{Y|X}$ to produce the set of conditionals $\boldsymbol{\omega}_{X\tilde{|}Y}$, as described in Section 10.6.
2. Apply the set of inverted conditionals $\boldsymbol{\omega}_{X\tilde{|}Y}$ together with the argument opinion ω_Y to compute the abduced opinion $\omega_{X\tilde{\|}Y}$, as described in Section 9.5.4 on multinomial deduction.

Multinomial abduction produces the opinion $\omega_{X\tilde{\|}Y}$ about the variable X expressed as

$$\omega_{X\tilde{\|}Y} = \omega_Y \,\widetilde{\circledcirc}\, (\boldsymbol{\omega}_{Y|X}, \boldsymbol{a}_X)\,. \tag{10.53}$$

□

The difference between inversion and abduction is thus that abduction takes the evidence argument ω_y, whereas inversion does not. Eq.(10.55) makes explicit how abduction involves the subjective Bayes' theorem.

$$\begin{aligned}
\text{Abduction (using Bayes' theorem): } \omega_{X\tilde{\|}Y} &= \omega_Y \,\widetilde{\circledcirc}\, (\boldsymbol{\omega}_{Y|X}, \boldsymbol{a}_X) && (10.54)\\
&= \omega_Y \,\circledcirc\, \widetilde{\phi}(\boldsymbol{\omega}_{Y|X}, \boldsymbol{a}_X) && (10.55)\\
&= \omega_Y \,\circledcirc\, \boldsymbol{\omega}_{X\tilde{|}Y}\,. && (10.56)
\end{aligned}$$

Conditional abduction according to Eq.(10.54), with the original set of multinomial conditionals $\boldsymbol{\omega}_{Y|X}$, is equivalent to multinomial conditional deduction according to Eq.(10.56) which takes as argument the set of inverted conditionals $\boldsymbol{\omega}_{X\tilde{|}Y}$ produced by the subjective Bayes' theorem.

Notice that the difference between deduction and abduction simply depends on which conditionals are initially available to the analyst. In the case of causal situations, it is normally easier to estimate causal conditionals than the opposite derivative conditionals. Assuming that there is a causal conditional relationship from X to Y, the analyst therefore typically has available the set of conditionals $\boldsymbol{\omega}_{Y|X}$. Hence, computing an opinion about X given a set of conditionals $\boldsymbol{\omega}_{Y|X}$ requires abduction.

10.8 Example: Military Intelligence Analysis

This section presents the same example twice, first in the formalism of probability calculus, and second in the formalism of subjective logic.

10.8.1 Example: Intelligence Analysis with Probability Calculus

Two countries A and B are in conflict, and intelligence analysts of country B want to assess whether country A intends to use military aggression. The analysts of country B consider the following possible alternatives regarding country A's plans:

$$\begin{aligned} x_1 &: \text{No military aggression from country } A, \\ x_2 &: \text{Minor military operations by country } A, \\ x_3 &: \text{Full invasion of country } B \text{ by country } A. \end{aligned} \tag{10.57}$$

The analysts of country B want to determine the most likely plan of country A by observing troop movements in country A. For this, assume that they have spies placed inside country A. The analysts of country B consider the following possible movements of troops:

$$\begin{aligned} y_1 &: \text{No movement of country } A\text{'s troops}, \\ y_2 &: \text{Minor movements of country } A\text{'s troops}, \\ y_3 &: \text{Full mobilisation of all country } A\text{'s troops}. \end{aligned} \tag{10.58}$$

The analysts have defined a set of conditional probabilities of troop movements as a function of military plans, as specified by Table 10.2.

Table 10.2 Conditional probabilities $p(Y|X)$: troop movement y_j given military plan x_i

Probability vectors	Troop movements y_1 No movemt.	y_2 Minor movemt.	y_3 Full mob.
$\boldsymbol{p}(Y\|x_1)$:	$p(y_1\|x_1) = 0.50$	$p(y_2\|x_1) = 0.25$	$p(y_3\|x_1) = 0.25$
$\boldsymbol{p}(Y\|x_2)$:	$p(y_1\|x_2) = 0.00$	$p(y_2\|x_2) = 0.50$	$p(y_3\|x_2) = 0.50$
$\boldsymbol{p}(Y\|x_3)$:	$p(y_1\|x_3) = 0.00$	$p(y_2\|x_3) = 0.25$	$p(y_3\|x_3) = 0.75$

The rationale behind the conditionals are as follows. In case country A has no plans of military aggression (x_1), then there is little rational reason for troop movements. However, even without plans of military aggression against country B, it is possible that country A expects military aggression from country B, forcing troop movements by country A. In case country A prepares for minor military operations against country B (x_2), then necessarily troop movements are required. In case country A prepares for a full invasion of country B (x_3), then significant troop movements are required.

Assume that, based on observations by spies of country B, the analysts assess the likelihoods of actual troop movements to be

$$p(y_1) = 0.20\,, \quad p(y_2) = 0.60\,, \quad p(y_3) = 0.20\,. \tag{10.59}$$

The analysts are faced with an abductive reasoning situation, and must first derive the inverted conditionals $p(X|Y)$. Assume that the analysts estimate the base rates (prior probabilities) of military plans to be

$$a(x_1) = 0.70\,, \quad a(x_2) = 0.20\,, \quad a(x_3) = 0.10\,. \tag{10.60}$$

The expression of Eq.(9.24) can now be used to derive the required inverted conditionals, which are given in Table 10.3 below.

Table 10.3 Conditional probabilities $p(X|Y)$: military plan x_i given troop movement y_j

	Probabilities of military plans given troop movement		
	$p(X|y_1)$	$p(X|y_2)$	$p(X|y_3)$
Military plan	No movemt.	Minor movemt.	Full mob.
y_1: No aggr.	$p(x_1|y_1) = 1.00$	$p(x_1|y_2) = 0.58$	$p(x_1|y_3) = 0.50$
y_2: Minor ops.	$p(x_2|y_1) = 0.00$	$p(x_2|y_2) = 0.34$	$p(x_2|y_3) = 0.29$
y_3: Invasion	$p(x_3|y_1) = 0.00$	$p(x_3|y_2) = 0.08$	$p(x_3|y_3) = 0.21$

The expression of Eq.(9.20) can now be used to derive the probabilities of the various military plans of country A, resulting in

$$p(x_1\widetilde{\|}Y) = 0.65\,,\quad p(x_2\widetilde{\|}Y) = 0.26\,,\quad p(x_3\widetilde{\|}Y) = 0.09\,. \tag{10.61}$$

Based on the results of Eq.(10.61), it seems most likely that country A does not plan any military aggression against country B. However, these results hide uncertainty, and can thereby give a misleading estimate of country A's plans. Analysing the same example with subjective logic in Section 10.8.2 gives a more nuanced picture, by explicitly showing the amount of uncertainty affecting the results.

10.8.2 Example: Intelligence Analysis with Subjective Logic

In this example we revisit the intelligence analysis situation of Section 10.8.1, but now with conditionals and evidence represented as subjective opinions. When analysed with subjective logic, the conditionals are affected by uncertainty but still have the same projected probability distributions as before. For the purpose of the example we assign the maximum possible amount of uncertainty to the set of dogmatic opinions that correspond to the probabilistic conditionals of the example in Section 10.8.1. These dogmatic opinions are specified in Table 10.4.

Table 10.4 Dogmatic conditional opinions $\underline{\omega}_{Y|X}$: troop movement y_j given military plan x_i

Opinions	Troop movements			
	y_1 :	y_2 :	y_3 :	Uncertainty
$\underline{\omega}_{Y|X}$	No movemt.	Minor movemt.	Full mob.	Any
$\underline{\omega}_{Y|x_1}$:	$\boldsymbol{b}_{Y|x_1}(y_1) = 0.50$	$\boldsymbol{b}_{Y|x_1}(y_2) = 0.25$	$\boldsymbol{b}_{Y|x_1}(y_3) = 0.25$	$u_{Y|x_1} = 0.00$
$\underline{\omega}_{Y|x_2}$:	$\boldsymbol{b}_{Y|x_2}(y_1) = 0.00$	$\boldsymbol{b}_{Y|x_2}(y_2) = 0.50$	$\boldsymbol{b}_{Y|x_2}(y_3) = 0.50$	$u_{Y|x_2} = 0.00$
$\underline{\omega}_{Y|x_3}$:	$\boldsymbol{b}_{Y|x_3}(y_1) = 0.00$	$\boldsymbol{b}_{Y|x_3}(y_2) = 0.25$	$\boldsymbol{b}_{Y|x_3}(y_3) = 0.75$	$u_{Y|x_3} = 0.00$

To recall, the base rates over the three possible military plans in X that were already specified in Eq.(10.60), are repeated in Eq(10.62) below:

$$\text{Military plan base rates: } \boldsymbol{a}_X(x_1) = 0.70, \quad \boldsymbol{a}_X(x_2) = 0.20, \quad \boldsymbol{a}_X(x_3) = 0.10. \tag{10.62}$$

The opinion conditionals affected by uncertainty specified in Table 10.5 are obtained by uncertainty-maximisation of the dogmatic opinion conditionals of Table 10.4. The uncertainty-maximisation depends on the base rates in Eq.(10.63) over the three possible troop movements in Y. The base rates are MBRs as described in Section 9.5.1.

$$\text{Troop movement base rates: } \boldsymbol{a}_Y(y_1) = 0.35, \quad \boldsymbol{a}_Y(y_2) = 0.30, \quad \boldsymbol{a}_Y(y_3) = 0.35. \tag{10.63}$$

With the base rates over Y, the uncertainty $\ddot{u}_{Y|x_i}$ of the uncertainty-maximised conditional opinions about troop movement of Table 10.5 are obtained according to Eq.(10.64), which is equivalent to Eq.(10.41) described in Section 10.6:

$$\ddot{u}_{Y|x_i} = \min_j \left[\frac{\mathbf{P}_{Y|x_i}(y_j)}{\boldsymbol{a}_Y(y_j)} \right] . \tag{10.64}$$

The belief masses of the uncertainty-maximised opinions are then computed according to Eq.(10.65):

$$\boldsymbol{b}_{Y|x_i}(y_j) = \mathbf{P}_{Y|x_i}(y_j) - \boldsymbol{a}_Y(y_j)\ddot{u}_{Y|x_i} . \tag{10.65}$$

The uncertainty-maximised conditional opinions are given in Table 10.5.

Table 10.5 Uncertain conditional opinions $\boldsymbol{\omega}_{Y|X}$: troop movement y_j given military plan x_i

Opinions	Troop movements			
	y_1:	y_2:	y_3:	Uncertainty
$\boldsymbol{\omega}_{Y\|X}$	No movemt.	Minor movemt.	Full mob.	Any
$\omega_{Y\|x_1}$:	$\boldsymbol{b}_{Y\|x_1}(y_1) = 0.25$	$\boldsymbol{b}_{Y\|x_1}(y_2) = 0.04$	$\boldsymbol{b}_{Y\|x_1}(y_3) = 0.00$	$u_{Y\|x_1} = 0.71$
$\omega_{Y\|x_2}$:	$\boldsymbol{b}_{Y\|x_2}(y_1) = 0.00$	$\boldsymbol{b}_{Y\|x_2}(y_2) = 0.50$	$\boldsymbol{b}_{Y\|x_2}(y_3) = 0.50$	$u_{Y\|x_2} = 0.00$
$\omega_{Y\|x_3}$:	$\boldsymbol{b}_{Y\|x_3}(y_1) = 0.00$	$\boldsymbol{b}_{Y\|x_3}(y_2) = 0.25$	$\boldsymbol{b}_{Y\|x_3}(y_3) = 0.75$	$u_{Y\|x_3} = 0.00$

The opinion about troop movements also needs to be uncertainty-maximised, in accordance with Eq.(10.64) and Eq.(10.65), where the uncertainty-maximised opinion is expressed by Eq.(10.66):

$$\omega_Y = \begin{cases} \boldsymbol{b}_Y(y_1) = 0.00, & \boldsymbol{a}_Y(y_1) = 0.35, \\ \boldsymbol{b}_Y(y_2) = 0.43, & \boldsymbol{a}_Y(y_2) = 0.30, \\ \boldsymbol{b}_Y(y_3) = 0.00, & \boldsymbol{a}_Y(y_3) = 0.35, \\ u_Y \quad\; = 0.57. & \end{cases} \tag{10.66}$$

First, the opinion conditionals must be inverted by taking into account the base rate of military plans expressed in Eq.(10.60). The inversion process produces the inverted conditional expressed in Table 10.6.

Table 10.6 Conditional opinions $\boldsymbol{\omega}_{X\widetilde{|}Y}$: Military plan x_i given Troop movement y_j

	Opinions of military plans given troop movement		
Military plan	$\omega_{X\widetilde{|}y_1}$ No movemt.	$\omega_{X\widetilde{|}y_2}$ Minor movemt.	$\omega_{X\widetilde{|}y_3}$ Full mob.
x_1: No aggression	$\boldsymbol{b}_{X\widetilde{|}y_1}(x_1) = 1.00$	$\boldsymbol{b}_{X\widetilde{|}y_2}(x_1) = 0.00$	$\boldsymbol{b}_{X\widetilde{|}y_3}(x_1) = 0.00$
x_2: Minor ops.	$\boldsymbol{b}_{X\widetilde{|}y_1}(x_2) = 0.00$	$\boldsymbol{b}_{X\widetilde{|}y_2}(x_2) = 0.17$	$\boldsymbol{b}_{X\widetilde{|}y_3}(x_2) = 0.14$
x_3: Invasion	$\boldsymbol{b}_{X\widetilde{|}y_1}(x_3) = 0.00$	$\boldsymbol{b}_{X\widetilde{|}y_2}(x_3) = 0.00$	$\boldsymbol{b}_{X\widetilde{|}y_3}(x_3) = 0.14$
X: Any	$u_{X\widetilde{|}y_1} = 0.00$	$u_{X\widetilde{|}y_2} = 0.83$	$u_{X\widetilde{|}y_3} = 0.72$

Then the likelihoods of country A's plans can be computed as the opinion

$$\omega_{X\widetilde{\|}Y} = \begin{cases} \boldsymbol{b}_{X\widetilde{\|}Y}(x_1) = 0.00, & \boldsymbol{a}_X(x_1) = 0.70, \quad \mathbf{P}_{X\widetilde{\|}Y}(x_1) = 0.65, \\ \boldsymbol{b}_{X\widetilde{\|}Y}(x_2) = 0.07, & \boldsymbol{a}_X(x_2) = 0.20, \quad \mathbf{P}_{X\widetilde{\|}Y}(x_2) = 0.26, \\ \boldsymbol{b}_{X\widetilde{\|}Y}(x_3) = 0.00, & \boldsymbol{a}_X(x_3) = 0.10, \quad \mathbf{P}_{X\widetilde{\|}Y}(x_3) = 0.09, \\ u_{X\widetilde{\|}Y} \quad\quad = 0.93. & \end{cases} \tag{10.67}$$

These results can be compared with those of Eq.(10.61) which were derived with probabilities only, and which are equal to the probability distribution given in the rightmost column of Eq.(10.67).

An important observation is that, although x_3 (full invasion) seems to be country A's least likely plan in probabilistic terms as expressed by $\mathbf{P}_{X\widetilde{\|}Y}(x_3) = 0.09$, there is considerable uncertainty, as expressed by $u_{X\widetilde{\|}Y} = 0.93$. In fact, the probability $\mathbf{P}_X(x_1) = 0.65$ of the most likely plan x_1 has no belief support at all, and is only based on uncertainty, which would be worrisome in a real situation. A likelihood expressed as a scalar probability can thus hide important aspects of the situation, which will only come to light when uncertainty is explicitly expressed, as in the example above.

Due to its relatively large uncertainty mass, the opinion $\omega_{X\widetilde{\|}Y}$ produced by this example expresses low *analytic confidence* when using the terminology from intelligence analysis [5]. The difference between the dimensions of likelihood and confidence in intelligence analysis is equivalent to the difference between projected probability and certainty of subjective opinions, as explained in Section 3.7.2 and visualised by Table 3.4.

The ability of subjective logic to generate conclusions that reflect levels of confidence can be combined with the relatively qualitative process of ACH (analysis of competing hypotheses) [34, 5] to produce a formal and more quantitative framework for intelligence analysis.

Chapter 11
Joint and Marginal Opinions

Joint opinions apply to product variables e.g. denoted XY. Given a joint opinion over XY there are separate marginal opinions on X as well as on Y. In case a conditional relationship between X and Y is expressed as $X \Longrightarrow Y$, i.e. where X is the parent and Y is the child variable, then the joint opinion is typically denoted ω_{YX}. The values of YX form a matrix with rows and columns swapped relative to XY. With regard to the joint opinion ω_{YX} the marginal opinion on Y (denoted $\omega_{[\![Y]\!]}$) and the deduced opinion on Y (denoted $\omega_{Y\|X}$) have equal projected probability distributions so we can write $\mathbf{P}_{[\![Y]\!]} = \mathbf{P}_{Y\|X}$. However, their uncertainty masses are in general different because of the approximate computation of uncertainty mass.

11.1 Joint Probability Distributions

A joint probability distribution over dependent variables is derived through conditionals. If e.g. the conditional probability $p(y|x)$ and the probability $p(x)$ are specified for some state values x and y, then the joint probability of the conjunctive state value (yx) is

$$p(yx) = p(y|x)p(x)\ . \tag{11.1}$$

This principle can be expressed in a more general way. Let $\mathbb{X}$ and $\mathbb{Y}$ be domains with cardinalities $k = |\mathbb{X}|$ and $l = |\mathbb{Y}|$, where X and Y be variables over $\mathbb{X}$ and $\mathbb{Y}$ respectively. Let $\boldsymbol{p}(Y|X)$ denote a set of k conditional probability distributions, each denoted $\boldsymbol{p}(Y|x_i)$. Finally, let $\boldsymbol{p}(X)$ be a probability distributions over X

The probability distribution over the joint variable YX can then be derived through vector multiplication as

$$\text{Joint probability distribution:}\quad \begin{aligned} \boldsymbol{p}(YX) &= \boldsymbol{p}(Y|X)\cdot\boldsymbol{p}(X) \\ &= \{\boldsymbol{p}(Y|x_i)\,p(x_i),\quad \forall x_i \in \mathbb{X}\}\ , \end{aligned} \tag{11.2}$$

where the symbol '$\cdot$' denotes vector multiplication. The vector multiplication which generalises the product of Eq.(11.1) is explicitly expressed as:

$$
\boldsymbol{p}(YX) = \begin{pmatrix} p(y_1|x_1), & p(y_1|x_2), & \cdots, & p(y_1|x_k) \\ p(y_2|x_1), & p(y_2|x_2), & \cdots, & p(y_2|x_k) \\ \cdot & \cdot & \cdots & \cdot \\ \cdot & \cdot & \cdots & \cdot \\ p(y_l|x_1), & p(y_l x_2), & \cdots, & p(y_l|x_k) \end{pmatrix} \cdot \begin{pmatrix} p(x_1) \\ p(x_2) \\ \cdot \\ \cdot \\ p(x_k) \end{pmatrix}
$$

$$
= \begin{pmatrix} p(y_1 x_1), & p(y_1 x_2), & \cdots, & p(y_1 x_k) \\ p(y_2 x_1), & p(y_2 x_2), & \cdots, & p(y_2 x_k) \\ \cdot & \cdot & \cdots & \cdot \\ \cdot & \cdot & \cdots & \cdot \\ p(y_l x_1), & p(y_l x_2), & \cdots, & p(y_l x_k) \end{pmatrix} . \tag{11.3}
$$

Marginalisation of $\boldsymbol{p}(YX)$ on Y produces the marginal probability distribution over Y denoted $\boldsymbol{p}([\![Y]\!])$ where the variable X has been out-marginalised:

$$
\boldsymbol{p}([\![Y]\!]) = \left\{ p(y) = \sum_{x \in \mathbb{X}} p(yx), \quad \forall y \in \mathbb{Y} \right\} . \tag{11.4}
$$

Marginalisation according to to Eq.(11.4) uses the law of total probability of Eq.(9.13). The marginal probability distribution $\boldsymbol{p}([\![Y]\!])$ is equal to the deduced probability distribution of Eq.(9.21) which is denoted $\boldsymbol{p}(Y\|X)$. Hence, we can write

$$
\boldsymbol{p}([\![Y]\!]) = \boldsymbol{p}(Y\|X) . \tag{11.5}
$$

Marginalisation of $\boldsymbol{p}(YX)$ on X is denoted $\boldsymbol{p}([\![X]\!])$, where the variable Y has been out-marginalised. It turns out that this simply produces $\boldsymbol{p}([\![X]\!]) = \boldsymbol{p}(X)$.

As an example of computing a joint probability distribution, assume the domain of weather types $\mathbb{X} = \{x_1, x_2 x_3\}$ where x_1 : '*sunny*', x_2 : '*overcast*' and x_3 : '*rain*', as well as the domain $\mathbb{Y} = \{y_1, y_2\}$ where y_1 : '*umbrella*', y_2 : '*no umbrella*'. Table 11.1 specifies an example of evidence and conditional probabilities.

Table 11.1 Evidence and conditional probabilities

	Weather type evidence:		
	Sunny: x_1	Overcast: x_2	Rain: x_3
	$p(x_1)$	$p(x_2)$	$p(x_3)$
Probabilities:	0.5	0.3	0.2

	Conditional probabilities as a function of:		
	Sunny: x_1	Overcast: x_2	Rain: x_3
	$p(y\|x_1)$	$p(y\|x_2)$	$p(y\|x_3)$
Umbrella: y_1	0.1	0.5	0.9
No umbrella: y_2	0.9	0.5	0.1

The probability distribution over the joint variable YX is then

$$\boldsymbol{p}(YX) = \begin{pmatrix} p(y_1x_1), & p(y_1x_2), & p(y_1x_3) \\ p(y_2x_1), & p(y_2x_2), & p(y_2x_3) \end{pmatrix} = \begin{pmatrix} 0.05, & 0.15, & 0.18 \\ 0.45, & 0.15, & 0.02 \end{pmatrix} . \tag{11.6}$$

The most probable joint state is thus no umbrella in sunny weather, as expressed by $p(y_2x_1) = 0.45$. The least probable joint state is no umbrella in rainy weather, as expressed by $p(y_2x_3) = 0.02$.

11.2 Joint Opinion Computation

Section 8.1 above describes the computation of product opinions ω_{XY} for independent variables. In contrast, this section describes the computation of joint opinions ω_{YX} where Y and X can be dependent in terms of a set of conditional opinions $\boldsymbol{\omega}_{Y|X}$. The general idea of computing joint opinions was originally proposed in [37].

A joint opinion ω_{YX} is required to be consistent with the joint projected probability distribution $\mathbf{P}_{YX}$ according to the principles described in Section 11.1. The generalisation to subjective opinions requires the computation of the joint uncertainty mass u_{YX}. The elements needed for computing joint opinions are described in Sections 11.2.1 – 11.2.3 below.

11.2.1 Joint Base Rate Distribution

The joint base rate distribution $\boldsymbol{a}_{YX}$ is computed according to the same principle as for the joint probability distribution:

$$\boldsymbol{a}_{YX} = \mathbf{P}_{Y|X} \cdot \boldsymbol{a}_X , \tag{11.7}$$

where '·' denotes vector multiplication. Each joint base rate is expressed as

$$\boldsymbol{a}_{YX}(yx) = \mathbf{P}_{Y|x}(y)\, \boldsymbol{a}_X(x) . \tag{11.8}$$

By expanding $\mathbf{P}_{Y|x}(y)$ in Eq.(11.8) we first derive Eq.(11.10). Then, by substituting $\boldsymbol{a}_Y(y)$ in Eq.(11.10) for $\boldsymbol{a}_Y(y)$ from Eq.(9.57) the base rate $\boldsymbol{a}_{YX}(yx)$ emerges in Eq.(11.11):

$$\begin{aligned} \boldsymbol{a}_{YX}(yx) &= \mathbf{P}_{Y|x}(y)\, \boldsymbol{a}_X(x) & (11.9) \\ &= \left(\boldsymbol{b}_{Y|x}(y) + \boldsymbol{a}_y(y)\, u_{Y|x}\right) \boldsymbol{a}_X(x) & (11.10) \\ &= \left(\boldsymbol{b}_{Y|x}(y) + \left(\frac{\sum_{x_i \in \mathbb{X}} \boldsymbol{a}_X(x_i)\, \boldsymbol{b}_{Y|x_i}(y)}{1 - \sum_{x_i \in \mathbb{X}} \boldsymbol{a}_X(x_i)\, u_{Y|x_i}}\right) u_{Y|x}\right) \boldsymbol{a}_X(x) . & (11.11) \end{aligned}$$

It can be verified that Eq.(11.11) behaves correctly. Assume e.g. that $\omega_{Y|x}$ is dogmatic, i.e. that $u_{Y|x} = 0$, in which case $\boldsymbol{b}_{Y|x}(y) = \mathbf{P}_{Y|x}(y)$. Then trivially Eq.(11.11) is reduced to Eq.(11.9) and Eq.(11.8) as expected. Assume now that $\omega_{Y|x}$ is vacuous with $u_{Y|x} = 1$ and $\boldsymbol{b}_{Y|x}(y) = 0$. Then trivially $\boldsymbol{a}_{YX}(yx) = \boldsymbol{a}_Y(y)\,\boldsymbol{a}_X(x)$ as expected because a vacuous conditional expresses independence. It can also be verified that the marginalisation $\boldsymbol{a}_X(x) = \sum_{x \in \mathbb{X}} \boldsymbol{a}_{YX}(yx)$ holds, which gives the MBR distribution.

11.2.2 Joint Uncertainty Mass

The computation of the joint uncertainty mass u_{YX} is based on the proportional average which involves the following three elements:

- the theoretical maximum joint uncertainty mass $\ddot{u}_{YX}$,
- the marginalised uncertainty mass $u_{[\![X]\!]}$ and its theoretical maximum $\ddot{u}_{[\![X]\!]}$, and
- the marginalised uncertainty mass $u_{[\![Y]\!]}$ and its theoretical maximum $\ddot{u}_{[\![Y]\!]}$.

The computation of joint uncertainty mass is concisely formalised by the three-step procedure below. Subsequently, the belief masses emerge directly.

Step 1: Theoretical maximum joint uncertainty $\ddot{u}_{YX}$.

With the projected conditional probability distributions $\mathbf{P}_{Y|X}$ and $\mathbf{P}_X$ it is possible to determine the projected joint probability distribution $\mathbf{P}_{YX}$ according to the method of Section 11.1. The dogmatic joint opinion $\underline{\omega}_{YX} = (\mathbf{P}_{YX}, 0, \boldsymbol{a}_{YX})$ can then be expressed. The goal is now to determine the appropriate uncertainty mass for ω_{YX}. We can determine the maximum possible uncertainty $\ddot{u}_{XY}$ of the joint opinion, by converting as much belief mass in $\underline{\omega}_{YX}$ as possible into uncertainty mass, while preserving consistent projected probability distribution $\mathbf{P}_{YX}$. The method for computing $\ddot{u}_{YX}$ is described in Section 3.5.6.

Step 2: Uncertainty masses $u_{[\![X]\!]}$ **and** $u_{[\![Y]\!]}$ **with their maximums** $\ddot{u}_{[\![X]\!]}$ **and** $\ddot{u}_{[\![Y]\!]}$.

Given the conditional opinions $\boldsymbol{\omega}_{Y|X}$ and the evidence opinion ω_X, the deduced $\omega_{Y\|X}$ provides the required marginal opinions and uncertainty masses:

$$\begin{cases} \omega_{[\![X]\!]} &= \omega_X \, , \\ \mathbf{P}_{[\![Y]\!]} &= \mathbf{P}_{Y\|X} \, , \end{cases} \qquad\qquad \begin{cases} u_{[\![X]\!]} &= u_X \, , \\ u_{[\![Y]\!]} &\simeq u_{Y\|X} \, . \end{cases} \tag{11.12}$$

The opinion ω_X and its uncertainty mass u_X are given, hence we have $u_{[\![X]\!]}$. The deduced opinion $\omega_{Y\|X}$ and its uncertainty mass $u_{Y\|X}$ can be computed with the deduction operator from Section 9.5, which gives an approximate $u_{[\![Y]\!]}$.

The theoretical maximum uncertainty masses $\ddot{u}_{[\![X]\!]}$ and $\ddot{u}_{[\![Y]\!]}$ is computed with the method described in Section 3.5.6.

Step 3: Proportional joint uncertainty mass u_{YX} .

The method for computing the proportional joint uncertainty mass is similar to that used for proportional multiplication described in Section 8.1.4.

The proportional method uses $u_{[\![X]\!]}$ and $u_{[\![Y]\!]}$ together with the theoretical maximum uncertainty masses $\ddot{u}_{[\![X]\!]}$ and $\ddot{u}_{[\![Y]\!]}$, and computes the uncertainty mass u_{YX} based on the assumption that u_{XY} is the proportional average of $u_{[\![X]\!]}$ and $u_{[\![Y]\!]}$, as expressed by Eq.(11.13).

$$\frac{u_{YX}}{\ddot{u}_{YX}} = \frac{u_{[\![X]\!]} + u_{[\![Y]\!]}}{\ddot{u}_{[\![X]\!]} + \ddot{u}_{[\![Y]\!]}} \tag{11.13}$$

$$\Leftrightarrow \quad u_{YX} = \frac{\ddot{u}_{YX}(u_{[\![X]\!]} + u_{[\![Y]\!]})}{\ddot{u}_{[\![X]\!]} + \ddot{u}_{[\![Y]\!]}} \,. \tag{11.14}$$

$$\text{IF } (\ddot{u}_{[\![X]\!]} + \ddot{u}_{[\![Y]\!]} = 0) \text{ THEN } u_{YX} = 0\,. \tag{11.15}$$

Eq.(11.15) is sound in all cases because $(u_{[\![X]\!]} + u_{[\![Y]\!]}) \leq (\ddot{u}_{[\![X]\!]} + \ddot{u}_{[\![Y]\!]})$. This ensures that $u_{YX} \in [0,1]$ in Eq.(11.14).

This marks the end of the three-step procedure for computing u_{YX}.

11.2.3 Assembling the Joint Opinion

Given the joint base rate distribution $\boldsymbol{a}_{YX}$ and the uncertainty mass u_{YX}, the joint opinion ω_{YX} is simply determined as

$$\omega_{YX} = (\boldsymbol{b}_{YX}, u_{YX}, \boldsymbol{a}_{YX}), \tag{11.16}$$

where $\boldsymbol{b}_{YX}((yx)_i) = \mathbf{P}_{YX}((yx)_i) - u_{YX}\boldsymbol{a}_{YX}((yx)_i)$, for $i = 1, \ldots, lk$.

By using the multiplication symbol '$\cdot$' as symbol for the joining operation, the joint product can be expressed as

$$\omega_{YX} = \boldsymbol{\omega}_{Y|X} \cdot \omega_X \,. \tag{11.17}$$

The conditionals can express different degrees of dependence between variables as expressed in Section 10.2. As the dependence decreases towards independence, the joint operation described here converges towards proportional multiplication described in Section 8.1.4.

The computation of joint opinions is a fundamental building block for generalising Bayesian networks into subjective Bayesian networks in Chapter 17. Chaining of joint opinions is described in Section 17.2.4.

11.3 Opinion Marginalisation

Assume the domains $\mathbb{X}$ and $\mathbb{Y}$ with variables X and Y, and let ω_{XY} be a joint multinomial opinion on the Cartesian product domain $\mathbb{X} \times \mathbb{Y}$. This joint opinion can be marginalised on one of the factor variables. The interpretation of this operation is that a marginal opinion represents the opinion on one of the variables without reference to the other, i.e where the other variable has been marginalised out.

11.3.1 Opinion Marginalisation Method

Let $\mathbb{X}$ be a domain of cardinality $k = |\mathbb{X}|$, and let $\mathbb{Y}$ be a domain of cardinality $l = |\mathbb{Y}|$, with X and Y as their respective variables. Let ω_X and ω_Y be two opinions, and let ω_{XY} be a joint opinion on domain $\mathbb{X} \times \mathbb{Y}$. The joint opinion ω_{XY} can be marginalised onto X or Y, where both are described below.

Marginalisation onto X produces the marginal probability distribution $\mathbf{P}_{[\![X]\!]}$ on X where the variable Y has been eliminated, and correspondingly for $\mathbf{P}_{[\![Y]\!]}$:

$$\mathbf{P}_{[\![X]\!]}(x_i) = \sum_{j=1}^{l} \mathbf{P}_{XY}(x_i y_j), \qquad \mathbf{P}_{[\![Y]\!]}(y_j) = \sum_{i=1}^{k} \mathbf{P}_{XY}(x_i y_j). \tag{11.18}$$

Similarly, the marginal base rate distributions $\boldsymbol{a}_{[\![X]\!]}$ and $\boldsymbol{a}_{[\![Y]\!]}$ are computed as

$$\boldsymbol{a}_{[\![X]\!]}(x_i) = \sum_{j=1}^{l} \boldsymbol{a}_{XY}(x_i y_j), \qquad \boldsymbol{a}_{[\![Y]\!]}(y_j) = \sum_{i=1}^{k} \boldsymbol{a}_{XY}(x_i y_j). \tag{11.19}$$

The marginal belief mass distributions $\boldsymbol{b}_{[\![X]\!]}$ and $\boldsymbol{b}_{[\![Y]\!]}$ are computed as

$$\boldsymbol{b}_{[\![X]\!]}(x_i) = \sum_{j=1}^{l} \boldsymbol{b}_{XY}(x_i y_j), \qquad \boldsymbol{b}_{[\![Y]\!]}(y_j) = \sum_{i=1}^{k} \boldsymbol{b}_{XY}(x_i y_j). \tag{11.20}$$

The marginal uncertainty masses are equal to the joint uncertainty mass:

$$u_{[\![X]\!]} \;=\; u_{[\![Y]\!]} \;=\; u_{YX}\,. \tag{11.21}$$

All the elements are then in place so that we can express the marginal opinions $\omega_{[\![X]\!]} = (\boldsymbol{b}_{[\![X]\!]}, u_{[\![X]\!]}, \boldsymbol{a}_{[\![X]\!]})$ and $\omega_{[\![Y]\!]} = (\boldsymbol{b}_{[\![Y]\!]}, u_{[\![Y]\!]}, \boldsymbol{a}_{[\![Y]\!]})$.

It is also possible to derive marginal conditionals based on ω_{YX}, i.e. to derive a set of conditional opinions $\boldsymbol{\omega}_{[\![Y|X]\!]}$ that together with ω_X would generate joint opinion ω'_{YX}. The marginal projected conditional probabilities are given by Eq.(11.22):

$$\mathbf{P}_{[\![Y|x]\!]}(y) = \frac{\mathbf{P}_{YX}(yx)}{\sum_{y_j \in \mathbb{Y}} \mathbf{P}_{YX}(y_j x)}\,. \tag{11.22}$$

The uncertainty mass for each marginal conditional opinion $\omega_{[\![Y|x]\!]}$ is defined as

$$u_{[\![Y|x]\!]} = \frac{u_{YX}\,\ddot{u}_{Y|x}}{\ddot{u}_{YX}}. \tag{11.23}$$

The marginal conditional belief mass distributions $\boldsymbol{b}_{[\![Y|x]\!]}$ are then computed with Eq.(3.12), which completes the derivation of the set of marginal conditional opinions $\boldsymbol{\omega}_{[\![Y|X]\!]}$. Note that the derivation of a marginal conditional opinion generates increased uncertainty in general because it is based on less evidence than the whole joint opinion. This effect is of course not visible for probabilistic marginal conditionals, which is a limitation of the purely probabilistic approach.

11.4 Example: Match-Fixing Revisited

We revisit the example of match-fixing from Section 9.6. The scenario is a football match between Team 1 and Team 2, where it is generally predicted that Team 1 will win. A gambler who plans to bet on the match has received second-hand information indicating possible match-fixing whereby Team 1 has been paid to lose. The gambler has an opinion about the outcome of the match in case Team 1 has been paid to lose, and in the absence of match-fixing. The gambler also has an opinion about whether Team 1 actually has been paid to lose.

As before, variable X represents whether Team 1 has been paid to lose:

$$\text{Domain for variable } X: \quad \mathbb{X} = \begin{cases} x_1: & \text{Team 1 has been paid to lose,} \\ x_2: & \text{No match-fixing.} \end{cases}$$

Variable Y represents which team wins the game:

$$\text{Domain for variable } Y: \quad \mathbb{Y} = \begin{cases} y_1: & \text{Team 1 wins the match,} \\ y_2: & \text{Team 2 wins the match,} \\ y_3: & \text{The match ends in a draw.} \end{cases}$$

For convenience, Table 11.2 repeats the example opinions from Section 9.6.

Table 11.2 Opinion ω_X (match-fixing), and conditional opinions $\boldsymbol{\omega}_{Y|X}$ (which team wins)

Opinion on X		Conditional opinions $\boldsymbol{\omega}_{Y\|X}$ y_1 y_2 y_3	
$\boldsymbol{b}_X(x_1) = 0.90$	$\boldsymbol{a}_X(x_1) = 0.1$	$\boldsymbol{b}_{Y\|x_1} = \{0.00,\ 0.80,\ 0.10\}$	$u_{Y\|x_1} = 0.10$
$\boldsymbol{b}_X(x_2) = 0.00$	$\boldsymbol{a}_X(x_2) = 0.9$	$\boldsymbol{b}_{Y\|x_2} = \{0.70,\ 0.00,\ 0.10\}$	$u_{Y\|x_2} = 0.20$
$u_X = 0.10$			

Since the evidence domain $\mathbb{X}$ is binary and the hypothesis domain $\mathbb{Y}$ is ternary, the joint opinion ω_{YX} applies to the 6-dimensional domain $\mathbb{Y}\times\mathbb{X}$.

11.4.1 Computing the Join Opinion

The joint projected probabilities can be computed according to Eq.(11.3):

The first step in deriving the joint opinion ω_{YX} is to compute the joint projected probability distribution according to Eq.(11.3) and the joint base rate distribution using Eq.(11.11), which produces

$$\mathbf{P}_{YX} = \begin{pmatrix} 0.071, & 0.077 \\ 0.737, & 0.002 \\ 0.011, & 0.011 \end{pmatrix}, \quad \boldsymbol{a}_{YX} = \begin{pmatrix} 0.008, & 0.770 \\ 0.081, & 0.178 \\ 0.011, & 0.112 \end{pmatrix}. \tag{11.24}$$

The second step is to compute the joint uncertainty mass using Eq.(11.14), as well as the belief mass distribution using Eq.(3.12). Required input argument $u_{[\![X]\!]} = u_X$ is given, and we set $u_{[\![Y]\!]} = u_{Y\|X}$ from Eq.(9.81). The arguments $\ddot{u}_{[\![X]\!]}$, $\ddot{u}_{[\![Y]\!]}$ and $\ddot{u}_{YX}$ are computed with Eq.(3.27). The belief mass distribution and the joint uncertainty mass are then

$$\boldsymbol{b}_{YX} = \begin{pmatrix} 0.070, & 0.022, \\ 0.731, & 0.001, \\ 0.101, & 0.003. \end{pmatrix}, \quad u_{YX} = 0.072\,. \tag{11.25}$$

11.4.2 Computing Marginal Opinions

The evidence opinion ω_X from Table 11.2 and the deduced opinion $\omega_{Y\|X}$ from Eq.(9.81) can be compared with the marginal opinions $\omega_{[\![X]\!]}$ and $\omega_{[\![Y]\!]}$. Table 11.3 summarises the latter opinions.

Table 11.3 Marginal opinions $\omega_{[\![X]\!]}$ and $\omega_{[\![Y]\!]}$

	Opinions	Base Rates	Probabilities
	$\boldsymbol{b}_{[\![X]\!]}(x_1) = 0.903$	$\boldsymbol{a}_{[\![X]\!]}(x_1) = 0.1$	$\mathbf{P}_{[\![X]\!]}(x_1) = 0.91$
Marginalisation on X:	$\boldsymbol{b}_{[\![X]\!]}(x_2) = 0.025$	$\boldsymbol{a}_{[\![X]\!]}(x_2) = 0.9$	$\mathbf{P}_{[\![X]\!]}(x_2) = 0.09$
	$u_{[\![X]\!]} = 0.072$		
	$\boldsymbol{b}_{[\![Y]\!]}(y_1) = 0.092$	$\boldsymbol{a}_{[\![Y]\!]}(y_1) = 0.778$	$\mathbf{P}_{[\![Y]\!]}(y_1) = 0.148$
Marginalisation on Y:	$\boldsymbol{b}_{[\![Y]\!]}(y_2) = 0.732$	$\boldsymbol{a}_{[\![Y]\!]}(y_2) = 0.099$	$\mathbf{P}_{[\![Y]\!]}(y_2) = 0.739$
	$\boldsymbol{b}_{[\![Y]\!]}(y_3) = 0.104$	$\boldsymbol{a}_{[\![Y]\!]}(y_3) = 0.123$	$\mathbf{P}_{[\![Y]\!]}(y_3) = 0.113$
	$u_{[\![Y]\!]} = 0.072$		

It can be seen that the marginal base rate distributions and marginal projected probability distributions are equal to those of Table 11.2 and Eq.(9.81), as expected. In contrast, the marginal uncertainty mass $u_{[\![X]\!]} = u_{[\![Y]\!]} = 0.072$ is not exactly the same as in Table 11.2 and Eq.(9.81). This is due to the approximate nature of uncertainty mass in the computation of deduction and joint opinions in subjective logic.

The marginal conditional opinions are given in Table 11.4.

Table 11.4 Marginal conditional opinions

Marginal conditional opinion $\omega_{[\![Y\|x_1]\!]}$	Marginal conditional opinion $\omega_{[\![Y\|x_2]\!]}$
$\boldsymbol{b}_{[\![Y\|x_1]\!]} = \{0.022, 0.803, 0.103\}$ (y_1, y_2, y_3), $u_{[\![Y\|x_1]\!]} = 0.072$	$\boldsymbol{b}_{[\![Y\|x_2]\!]} = \{0.743, 0.006, 0.107\}$ (y_1, y_2, y_3), $u_{[\![Y\|x_2]\!]} = 0.144$

Again, the uncertainty masses, as well as the belief mass distributions, are approximate. The exact nature of this approximation needs further investigation.

Chapter 12
Belief Fusion

Belief fusion is a central concept in subjective logic. It allows evidence and opinions from different source agents about the same domain of interest to be merged, in order to provide an opinion about the domain representing the combination of the different source agents.

12.1 Interpretation of Belief Fusion

In many situations, there are multiple sources of evidence about a domain of interest, and in these there can be significant differences between the argument opinions. It is often useful to combine the evidence from different sources, in order to produce an opinion that better reflects the collection of different opinions, or that is closer to the ground truth than each opinion in isolation. Belief fusion means precisely to merge multiple opinions, in order to produce a single opinion that is more correct (according to some criteria) than each opinion in isolation. The principle of opinion fusion is illustrated in Figure 12.1.

In general, the source of an opinion can e.g. be a human agent's judgement or a sensor producing data which can be translated into an opinion. Separate sources, e.g. denoted A and B, can produce opinions about the same variable X. In this situation belief fusion consists of merging the different sources into a single source that can be denoted $(A \diamond B)$, and mathematically combining their opinions into a single opinion which then represents the opinion of the merged source $(A \diamond B)$.

Different belief fusion situations can vary significantly and semantically depending on the purpose and nature of the fusion process, and hence require different fusion operators. However, it can be challenging to identify the correct fusion operator for a specific situation. In general, a given fusion operator is inadequate when it produces wrong results in some instances of a situation, even if it produces correct results in most instances of the situation. A fusion operator should produce adequate results in all realistic instances of the situation to be modelled.

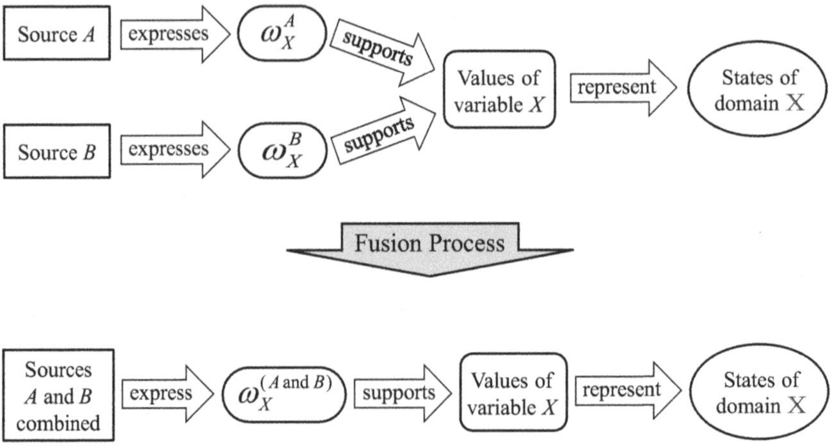

Fig. 12.1 Fusion process principle

In order to see the importance of using the correct belief fusion model in a given fusion situation let us look at other situation types where the effect of applying the correct or incorrect formal model is more obvious. First, consider the situation of predicting the physical strength of a steel chain, where the classical and correct model is that of the weakest link. Then, consider the situation of determining the competitive strength of a relay swimming team, for which an adequate model is the average strength of each swimmer on the team.

Applying the weakest link model to assess the competitive strength of the relay swimming team is an approximation which might give good predictions in most instances of high-level swimming championships. However, it is obviously a poor model and would produce unreliable predictions in general.

Similarly, applying the average strength model for assessing the physical strength of the chain represents an approximation which would produce satisfactory strength predictions in most instances of high-quality steel chains where the link strength is highly uniform. However, it is obviously a very poor model which would be unreliable in general, and which could be fatal if life depended on it.

These examples illustrate that it is insufficient to simply use a few anecdotal examples to test whether the weakest link principle is an adequate model for predicting the strength of relay swimming teams. Similarly it is insufficient to simply use a few anecdotal examples to test whether the averaging principle is adequate for modelling the strength of steel chains. Without a clear understanding of the situation to be modelled, the analyst does not have a basis for selecting the correct and appropriate model. The selection of appropriate models might be obvious for the simple examples above, but it can be challenging to judge whether a fusion operator is adequate for an arbitrary situation of belief fusion [58].

The conclusion to be drawn from this discussion is that the analyst must first understand the dynamics of the situation at hand in order to find the best model for analysing it. The next section focuses on the correctness of belief fusion models.

12.1.1 Correctness and Consistency Criteria for Fusion Models

We argue that meaningful and reliable belief fusion depends on the fusion operator's ability to produce correct results for the practical or hypothetical situation that is being analysed. This calls for a definition of what it means for results to be 'correct'.

Definition 12.1 (Correctness of Results). In general the correctness of the results produced by an analytic model is the degree to which the results represent the true state of the real situation that is being modelled. □

To clarify this definition, it is useful to distinguish between three types of truth: 1) ground truth, 2) consensus truth, and 3) subjective truth, as described below, where ground truth is the strongest and subjective truth is the weakest form of truth.

- **Ground truth** about a given situation is its objectively observable state.
- **Consensus truth** about a given situation is the state that is identified to be the actual state by a commonly shared opinion, or the state that is identified to be the actual state according to commonly accepted norms or standards.
- **Subjective truth** about a given situation is the state identified to be the actual state by the analyst's own subjective opinion about the situation.

The term *'true state'* can also be used in the sense that the state is satisfactory or preferred. For example when a group of people want to choose a movie to watch at the cinema together, it would seem strange to say that one specific movie is more 'true' than another. Instead, one specific movie (the true state) can be considered to be the most satisfactory for all the group members to watch together.

Fusion models, when applied to analyse fusion situations, produce fused output results. Three different types of result correctness emerge from the three different types of truth, where objective correctness is the strongest, and subjective correctness is the weakest.

- **Objective result correctness** is the degree to which the result represents the ground truth of the situation.
- **Consensus result correctness** is the degree to which the result represents the consensus truth of the situation.
- **Subjective result correctness** is the degree to which the result represents the subjective truth of the situation.

Depending on whether ground truth, consensus truth or subjective truth is available, the strongest form of correctness should be required for assessing the results. For example, assume a weather forecast model with all its various input parameters and their complex relationships. Weather forecasts can be compared with the actual weather when the time of the forecast arrives a day or two later, hence it is reasonable to require objective correctness when assessing weather forecasting models.

The case of predicting global warming might seem similar to that of forecasting the weather, because models for global warming are also based on many different input parameters with complex relationships. Although predicting global warming to occur over the next 100 years can be objectively verified or refuted, the time scale makes it impossible to objectively assess the correctness of the models in the short term. Instead, practical assessment of model correctness must be based on consensus among experts. So with no ground truth as benchmark, it is only possible to require consensus correctness in the short term. Unfortunately, in 100 years (e.g. after year 2100), when the ground truth about global warming predicted for the next 100 years finally becomes available, there will probably no longer be any interest in assessing the correctness of the models used to make the predictions today, and the individuals who designed the models will be long gone. Designers of global-warming models will thus never be confronted with the ground truth about their models and predictions, which is worrisome, because it removes an important incentive for the analysts to be thorough and objective.

Despite the lack of objective basis, consensus correctness as a criterion is often used for selecting specific models, and for determining whether or not the results they produce are to be used in planning and decision making.

In situations where ground truth can not be observed, and consensus truth is impossible to obtain, only subjective criteria for truth can be used. Models for which subjective correctness criteria can be used include e.g. models for making personal decisions about which career path to follow, or which partner to live with. In theory, such decision are made based on multiple forms of evidence that must be fused to form an opinion. People normally do not use formal models to analyse such situations, and instead use their intuition. Models assessed under subjective correctness criteria are often only used for practical decisions made by individuals, so statistical evidence can be difficult to obtain. However there are expert systems for e.g. career path choice and partner matching. In case these services include a feedback system, as described in Chapter 16, it could be possible to determine statistically whether a particular model predicts 'good' career choices and 'happy' unions in the long term.

With regard to Definition 12.1, when something has been observed once or a small number of times it may be unclear whether the observations are representative of the true state of the situation. Although a model produces correct results in some instances, there might be other instances where the results are clearly wrong, in which case the model must be considered inadequate in general.

For example, assume a rather naïve analyst who misinterprets the situation of adding apples from two baskets, and erroneously thinks that the product rule of integer multiplication is an appropriate model for apple addition. Assume further that the analyst tries a specific example with two apples in each basket, and computes the sum with the product rule, which gives four apples. When observing a real example of two baskets of two apples each, it turns out that adding them together also produces four apples. This result could mistakenly be interpreted as a confirmation that the product rule is a correct model, simply because the computed result is the same as the ground truth in this particular instance. It is of course wrong to conclude that a model is correct just because it produces results that (perhaps by coincidence) correspond to the ground truth in a single instance. In order for a model to be correct, it is natural to require that results produced by it are generally correct, and not just in anecdotal instances of a situation. In order to distinguish between anecdotally correct results and generally correct results, it is necessary to also consider consistency, which leads to the following definition.

Definition 12.2 (Model Correctness). A model is correct for a specific situation when it consistently produces correct results in all instances of the situation. □

On a high level of abstraction, a correct reasoning model according to Definition 12.2 must faithfully reflect the (class of) situations that are being modelled. A precise way of expressing this principle is that for a given class of situations, there is one correct model. Note that it is possible to articulate three types of model correctness according to the three types of result correctness.

- **Objective model correctness** for a specific class of situations is the model's ability to consistently produce objectively correct results for all possible situations in the class.
- **Consensus model correctness** for a specific class of situations is the model's ability to consistently produce consensus-correct results for all possible situations in the class.
- **Subjective model correctness** for a specific class of situations is the model's ability to consistently produce subjectively correct results for all possible situations in the class.

Depending on whether ground truth, consensus truth or subjective truth is available, the strongest form of model correctness should be required for practical analysis. Observing result correctness in one instance is not sufficient to conclude that a model is correct. It can be theoretically impossible to verify that all possible results are consistently correct, so proving that a model is correct in general can be challenging. On the other hand, if a single false result is observed it can be concluded that the model is inadequate for the situation in general. In such cases it might be meaningful to indicate the range of validity of the model, which limits the range of input arguments, or possibly the range of output results.

The next two sections described interpretations of fusion operators defined in subjective logic, and selection criteria that analysts can use when deciding which fusion operator to use for a specific situation.

12.1.2 Classes of Fusion Situations

Situations of belief fusion involve belief arguments from multiple sources that must be fused in some way to produce a single belief argument. More specifically, the situation is characterised by a domain consisting of two or more state values, accompanied by a set of different belief arguments about these values. It is assumed that each belief argument supports one or several state values. The purpose of belief fusion is to produce a new belief that identifies the most 'correct' state value(s) in the domain. The meaning of 'most correct state value' can also be that it is the most acceptable or most preferred value.

Different beliefs can be fused in various ways, each reflecting how the specific fusion situation is modelled. It is often challenging to determine the correct or the most appropriate fusion operator for a specific situation. One way of addressing this challenge is to classify types of similar situations according to their typical characteristics, which then allows to determine which fusion operator is most adequate for each class. Four distinct classes as well as one hybrid class of fusion situations are described below.

- **Belief Constraint Fusion** (BCF) is when it is assumed that: 1) each belief argument can dictate which state values are the most correct, and 2) there is no room for compromise in case of totally conflicting arguments, hence the fusion result is not defined in that case. In some situations this property is desirable. An example is when two persons try to agree on seeing a movie at the cinema. If their preferences include some common movies they can decide to watch one of them. Yet, if their preferences do not have any movies in common then there is no solution, so the rational consequence is that they will not watch any movie together. Constraint fusion is described in Section 12.2.
- **Cumulative Belief Fusion** (CBF) is when it is assumed that the amount of independent evidence increases by including more and more sources. Two forms of CBF exist: 1) *aleatory* (A-CBF) which applies to statistical evidence and 2) *epistemic* (E-CBF) which applies to epistemic opinions. For example, a mobile network operator could fuse the observed location of a subscriber over time with A-CBF, which produces an aleatory opinion with decreasing uncertainty about the typical locations of that subscriber. Another example is when witnesses express their opinions about who shot Kennedy, which when fused with E-CBF produces an epistemic opinion about who shot him. Cumulative fusion is described in Section 12.3.
- **Averaging Belief Fusion** (ABF) is when dependence between sources is assumed. In other words, including more sources does not mean that more evidence is supporting the conclusion. An example of this type of situation is when a jury tries to reach a verdict after having observed the court proceedings. ABF is idempotent but does not have a neutral element, because every opinion, also a vacuous one, carries the same weight. Averaging fusion is described in Section 12.4.
- **Weighted Belief Fusion** (WBF) can be used when the source argument opinions should be weighted as a function of the confidence of the opinions. In case of equally confident argument opinions the fusion is averaging. In case one of the opinions is confident and the other is uncertain, then the confident opinion carries the highest weight, but the overall confidence does not increase. WBF is idempotent, commutative and has the vacuous opinion as neutral element. The type of situations when WBF is suitable is when experts (e.g. medical doctors) express multinomial opinions about a set of hypothesis (e.g. diagnoses). PCF is described in Section 12.5. CCF does not identify shared (vague) belief on overlapping (composite) values in the domain, and simply computes the weighted average of such belief masses.

- **Consensus & Compromise Fusion** (CCF) can be used when the analyst naturally wants to preserve shared beliefs from each source, and to transform conflicting beliefs into vague belief. In this way consensus belief is preserved when it exists, and compromise vague belief is formed when necessary. In the case of totally conflicting beliefs, then the resulting fused belief is vague or uncertain. CCF is idempotent, commutative and has the vacuous opinion as neutral element. The type of situations when CCF is suitable is when experts (e.g. medical doctors) express hyper-opinions about a set of hypothesis (e.g. diagnoses). CCF takes into account shared (vague) belief on overlapping (composite) values, and is therefore suitable for fusing hyper-opinions. CCF is described in Section 12.6.

The subtle differences between the fusion situations above illustrate the challenge of modelling them correctly. For instance, consider the task of determining the location of a mobile phone subscriber at a specific point in time by collecting location evidence from a base station, in which case it seems natural to use belief constraint fusion. If two adjacent base stations detect the subscriber, then the belief constraint operator can be used to locate the subscriber within the overlapping region of the respective radio cells. However, if two base stations far apart detect the subscriber at the same time, then the result of belief constraint fusion is not defined so there is no conclusion. With additional assumptions, it would still be reasonable to think that the subscriber is probably located in one of the two cells, but not which one in particular, and that the case needs further investigation because the inconsistent signals might be caused by an error in the system. The method of trust revision described in Section 14.5 can be applied in this situation.

12.1.3 Criteria for Fusion Operator Selection

While having multiple fusion classes can help in scoping the solution space, there is still the issue of determining which class a specific situation belongs to. The approach we propose is to specify a set of test assumptions about a fusion situation, where each assumption can be tested to be either valid or invalid for the situation. In other words, we decompose the classification problem so it now becomes a matter of judging whether specific assumptions apply to the situation.

In order to select the correct or most adequate fusion model the analyst must consider the set of assumptions about the fusion situation to be analysed and for each assumption judge whether it is applicable. The most adequate fusion model is then identified as a function of the set of assumptions that applies to the situation to be analysed. This procedure for identifying and selecting the most appropriate fusion operator is illustrated in Figure 12.2. The steps in the selection procedure are further described below.

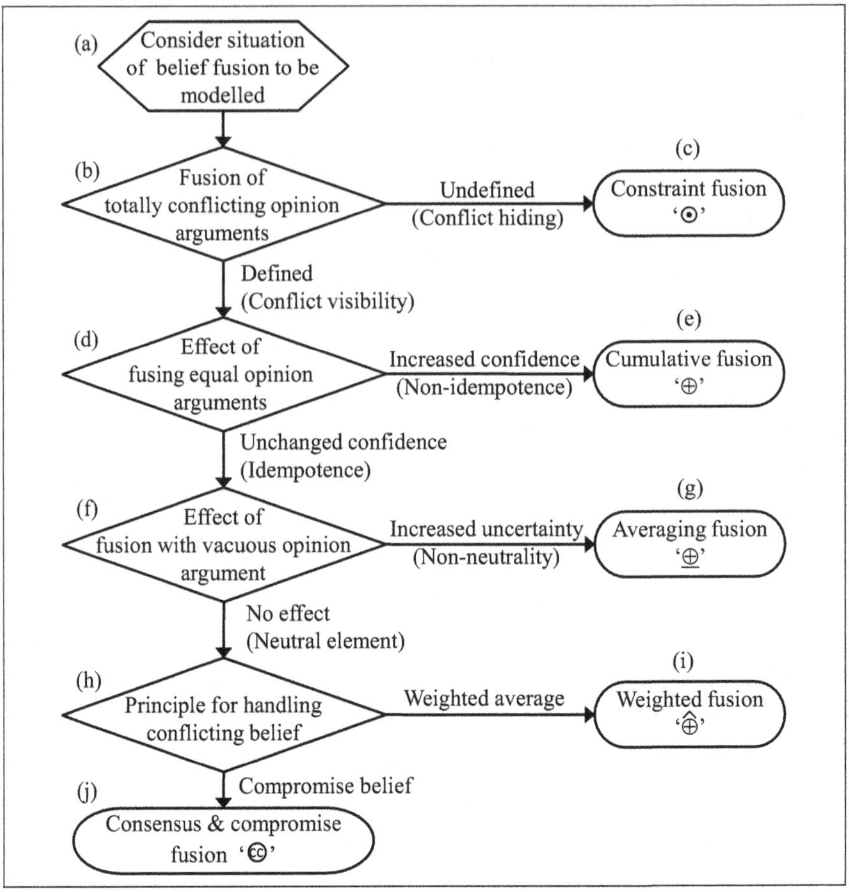

Fig. 12.2 Procedure for selecting the most adequate fusion operator

(a) The analyst first needs a good understanding of the situation to be modelled in order to select the most suitable fusion operator. This includes being able to make the binary choices of (b), (d), (f) and (h) below.
(b) Does it make sense to fuse two totally conflicting opinion arguments?
(c) In case no compromise can be imagined between two totally conflicting arguments, then it is probably adequate to apply the belief constraint fusion operator. This fusion operator is not defined in case of totally conflicting arguments, which reflects the assumption that there is no compromise solution for totally conflicting arguments.
(d) Should two equal opinion arguments produce a fused opinion which is equal to the arguments?
(e) In case it is not assumed that two equal arguments should produce an equal fusion result, then it is probably adequate to apply the cumulative fusion operator. This means that equal arguments are considered as independent support for

specific values of the variable, so that two equal arguments produce reduced uncertainty. In other words the operator should be non-idempotent, as is the case for cumulative fusion. This operator can also handle totally conflicting opinions.

(f) Should a vacuous opinion have any influence on the fusion result?

(g) In case it is assumed that a vacuous opinion has an influence on the fused result, then there is no neutral element so it is probably adequate to apply the averaging fusion operator. This can be meaningful e.g. for making a survey of opinions where the lack of opinions (uncertainty) shall also be visible.

(h) How should conflicting belief be handled?

(i) The simplest belief conflict management principle is to compute the confidence-weighted average (conflict) belief. The weighted belief fusion operator is adequate for fusing multinomial opinions, but less so for fusing hyper-opinions because the operator is blind to common belief between two vague belief arguments on partially overlapping composite values.

(j) In case it is assumed that conflicting belief should be transformed into compromise (vague) belief then it is probably adequate to apply consensus & compromise fusion which is also well suited for fusing hyper-opinions. This operator takes into account common belief between two vague belief arguments, and is thereby 'smarter' than weighted belief fusion.

The fusion operators from Figure 12.2 are described in the next sections.

12.2 Belief Constraint Fusion

Situations where agents with different preferences try to agree on a single choice occur frequently. This must not be confused with fusion of evidence from different agents to determine the most likely correct hypothesis or actual event. Multi-agent preference combination assumes that each agent has already made up her mind, and then that they together want to determine the most acceptable decision or choice for all. Preferences over a variable can be expressed in the form of subjective opinions. The constraint fusion operator of subjective logic can be applied as a method for merging preferences of multiple agents into a single preference for the whole group. This model is expressive and flexible, and produces perfectly intuitive results. Preference can be represented as belief mass, and indifference can be represented as uncertainty mass. Positive and negative preferences are considered as symmetric concepts, so they can be represented in the same way and combined using the same operator. A vacuous opinion has no influence, and thereby represents the neutral element.

12.2.1 Method of Constraint Fusion

The belief constraint fusion operator described here is an extension of Dempster's rule, which in Dempster-Shafer belief theory is often presented as a method for (cumulative) fusion of beliefs from different independent sources [90] with the purpose of identifying the most correct hypothesis value from the domain. However, many authors have demonstrated that Dempster's rule is not an appropriate operator for this type of fusion [101], and argue that it is better suited as a method for belief constraint fusion [53, 55], as we do too.

Definition 12.3 (The Constraint Fusion Operator). Assume the domain $\mathbb{X}$ and its hyperdomain $\mathscr{R}(\mathbb{X})$, and assume the hypervariable X which takes its values from $\mathscr{R}(\mathbb{X})$. Let agent A hold opinion ω_X^A and agent B hold opinion ω_X^B. The superscripts A and B are attributes that identify the respective belief sources or belief owners. These two opinions can be mathematically merged using the belief constraint fusion operator denoted '$\odot$' which can be expressed as

$$\text{Belief Constraint Fusion:} \quad \omega_X^{(A\&B)} = \omega_X^A \odot \omega_X^B \,. \tag{12.1}$$

Source combination denoted '&' thus corresponds to belief fusion with '$\odot$'. The algebraic expression for the belief constraint fusion operator is given by Eq.(12.2):

$$\forall\, x \in \mathscr{R}(\mathbb{X}) \quad \omega_X^{(A\&B)}: \begin{cases} \boldsymbol{b}_X^{(A\&B)}(x) = \frac{\text{Har}(x)}{(1-\text{Con})}, \\ u_X^{(A\&B)} \quad = \frac{u_X^A u_X^B}{(1-\text{Con})}, \\ \boldsymbol{a}^{(A\&B)}(x) = \frac{\boldsymbol{a}_X^A(x)(1-u_X^A)+\boldsymbol{a}_X^B(x)(1-u_X^B)}{2-u_X^A-u_X^B}, & \text{for } u_X^A + u_X^B < 2\,, \\ \boldsymbol{a}^{(A\&B)}(x) = \frac{\boldsymbol{a}_X^A(x)+\boldsymbol{a}_X^B(x)}{2}, & \text{for } u_X^A = u_X^B = 1\,. \end{cases} \tag{12.2}$$

The term $\text{Har}(x)$ represents the relative *harmony* between constraints (in terms of overlapping belief mass) on x. The term Con represents the relative *conflict* between constraints (in terms of non-overlapping belief mass) between ω_X^A and ω_X^B. These parameters are defined below:

$$\text{Har}(x) = \boldsymbol{b}_X^A(x)u_X^B + \boldsymbol{b}_X^B(x)u_X^A + \sum_{(x^A \cap x^B)=x} \boldsymbol{b}_X^A(x^A)\boldsymbol{b}_X^B(x^B), \tag{12.3}$$

$$\text{Con} = \sum_{(x^A \cap x^B)=\emptyset} \boldsymbol{b}_X^A(x^A)\boldsymbol{b}_X^B(x^B). \tag{12.4}$$

□

The divisor $(1-\mathrm{Con})$ in Eq.(12.2) normalises the belief mass and uncertainty; it ensures their additivity. The use of the constraint fusion operator is mathematically possible only if ω_X^A and ω_X^B are not totally conflicting, i.e., if $\mathrm{Con} \neq 1$.

The constraint fusion operator is commutative and non-idempotent. Associativity is preserved when the base rate is equal for all agents. Associativity in case of different base rates requires that all preference opinions be combined in a single operation which requires a generalisation of Eq.(12.2) for multiple agents, i.e. for multiple input arguments, which is relatively trivial.

The base rates of the two arguments are normally equal, expressed by $a_X^A = a_X^B$, but different base rates can be used in case of base rate disagreement between agents A and B, in which case the fused base rate distribution is the confidence-weighted average base rate.

Associativity in case of different base rates requires that all preference opinions be combined in a single operation which generalises Definition 12.3 for more that two sources, which is relatively trivial. A totally indifferent opinion acts as the neutral element for constraint fusion, formally expressed as

$$\text{IF } (\omega_X^A \text{ is totally indifferent, i.e. with } u_X^A = 1) \text{ THEN } (\omega_X^A \odot \omega_X^B = \omega_X^B)\,. \quad (12.5)$$

Having a neutral element in the form of the totally indifferent opinion can be useful when modelling situations of preference combination.

The rich format of subjective opinions makes it simple to express positive and negative preferences within the same framework, as well as indifference/uncertainty. Because preferences can be expressed over arbitrary subsets of the domain, this is in fact a multi-polar model for expressing and combining preferences. Even in the case of totally conflicting dogmatic opinions the belief constraint fusion operator produces meaningful results, namely that the preferences are incompatible. Examples in Sections 12.2.3 – 12.2.6 demonstrates the usefulness of this property.

12.2.2 Frequentist Interpretation of Constraint Fusion

The nature of the constraint fusion operator can be challenging to understand. However, it has a very clear frequentist interpretation which is described next.

Assume a domain $\mathbb{X}$ with its hyperdomain $\mathscr{R}(\mathbb{X})$and powerset $\mathscr{P}(\mathbb{X})$. Recall from Eq.(2.1) that $\mathscr{P}(\mathbb{X}) = \mathscr{R}(\mathbb{X}) \cup \{\{\mathbb{X}\}, \{\emptyset\}\}$. Let x denote a specific value of the hyperdomain $\mathscr{R}(\mathbb{X})$ or of the powerset $\mathscr{P}(\mathbb{X})$.

Let X be a hypervariable in $\mathscr{R}(\mathbb{X})$, and let χ (Greek letter 'chi') be a random variable which takes its values from the powerset $\mathscr{P}(\mathbb{X})$. We consider a repetitive process denoted U which generates unconstrained instances of the variable χ, which in turn gets constrained through serially arranged stages A and B, to produce a constrained output value of the variable denoted χ''. To be unconstrained means that $\chi = \{\mathbb{X}\}$. To constrain χ by e.g. x^A is to produce a new χ' so that $\chi' := \chi \cap x^A$. This means that χ' has been modified to take a value in $\mathscr{P}(\mathbb{X})$ with smaller or equal cardinality, i.e. that χ' typically has a value consisting of fewer singleton values than χ. Repeated constraining produces the final constrained value χ''

Assume the opinions $\omega_X^A = (\boldsymbol{b}_X^A, u_X^A, \boldsymbol{a}_X^A)$ and $\omega_X^B = (\boldsymbol{b}_X^B, u_X^B, \boldsymbol{a}_X^B)$. Let $\boldsymbol{p}_\chi^A$ be a probability distribution over χ where $\boldsymbol{p}_\chi^A(x) = \boldsymbol{b}_X^A(x)$ for $x \in \mathscr{R}(\mathbb{X})$, and where $\boldsymbol{p}_\chi^A(\mathbb{X}) = u_X^A$. Similarly, let $\boldsymbol{p}_\chi^B$ be a probability distribution over χ based on ω_X^B in the same way.

The serial constraining configuration is determined by the probability distributions $\boldsymbol{p}_\chi^A$ and $\boldsymbol{p}_\chi^B$ in the following way. At stage A, a specific value $x^A \in \mathscr{P}(\mathbb{X})$ is selected with probability $\boldsymbol{p}_\chi^A(x^A)$. At stage B, a specific value $x^B \in \mathscr{P}(\mathbb{X})$ is selected with probability $\boldsymbol{p}_\chi^B(x^B)$. The unconstrained variable χ produced at stage U is first constrained at stage A by computing $\chi' := (\chi \cap x^A) = x^A$, which in turn is constrained at stage B to produce $\chi'' := (\chi' \cap x^B) = x^C$. The final constrained values $x^C = (x^A \cap x^B)$ are collected at stage C. This is illustrated in Figure 12.3.

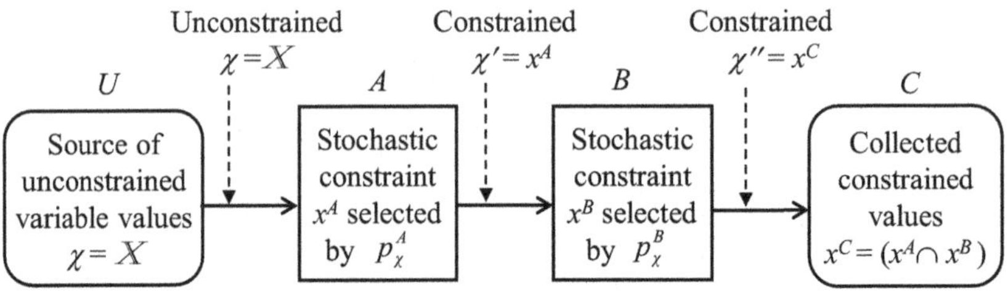

Fig. 12.3 Frequentist interpretation of constraint fusion

Assume that a series of unconstrained variable instances χ are generated at source U, and that the resulting constrained values are collected at stage C.

If e.g. for a specific instance i of the process in Figure 12.3, the constraints are such that $(x_i^A \cap x_i^B) = x_i^C \neq \emptyset$, then a non-empty value x_i^C is collected. If for another instance j the constraints are such that $(x_j^A \cap x_j^B) = x_j^C = \emptyset$, then the collected value is $\emptyset$. If for yet another instance k the constraints are $x_k^A = x_k^B = \mathbb{X}$ so that $(x_k^A \cap x_k^B) = \mathbb{X}$, then the collected value is $\mathbb{X}$.

Relative to the total number of collected values (including $\{\mathbb{X}\}$ and $\{\emptyset\}$), the relative proportions of each type of collected values can be expressed by a relative frequency probability distribution $\boldsymbol{p}_\chi^C$.

Let n denote the total number of collected values, and let T denote the Boolean truth function such that T(TRUE) $= 1$ and T(FALSE) $= 0$. Then the convergence probability distribution of $\boldsymbol{p}_\chi^C$ when n approaches infinity is expressed as:

$$\boldsymbol{p}_\chi^C(x) = \lim_{n \to \infty} \left(\frac{\sum_{i=1}^n \mathrm{T}(x_i^C = x)}{n - \sum_{i=1}^n \mathrm{T}(x_i^C = \emptyset)} \right), \qquad \forall x \in \mathscr{P}(\mathbb{X}). \tag{12.6}$$

The stochastic constraint opinion ω_X^C is derived from the probability distribution $\boldsymbol{p}_\chi^C$ according to Definition 12.4.

Definition 12.4 (Stochastic Constraint Opinion).

Given the convergent constrained relative frequency distribution $\boldsymbol{p}_X^C$ of Eq.(12.6) the stochastic constraint opinion is expressed as

$$\omega_X^C : \begin{cases} \boldsymbol{b}_X^C(x) = \boldsymbol{p}_X^C(x), \text{ for } x \in \mathscr{R}(\mathbb{X}), \\ u_X^C \quad = \boldsymbol{p}_X^C(\mathbb{X}), \\ \boldsymbol{a}_X^C \quad = \boldsymbol{a}_X \,. \end{cases} \tag{12.7}$$

□

The stochastically constrained opinion ω_X^C is equal to $\omega_X^{(A\&B)}$ produced by the belief constraint fusion operator of Definition 12.3, hence the following theorem can be stated.

Theorem 12.1 (Equivalence Between Stochastic and Belief Constraint Fusion). *Stochastic constraint fusion of Definition 12.3 is equivalent to the belief constraint fusion of Definition 12.4. This can be expressed as*

$$\omega_X^{(A\&B)} \equiv \omega_X^C \,. \tag{12.8}$$

Proof.
The stepwise transformation of $\boldsymbol{b}_X^C(x)$ into $\boldsymbol{b}_X^{(A\&B)}(x)$, as well as of u_X^C into $u_X^{(A\&B)}$, demonstrates the equivalence. The transformation of belief mass is outlined first.

Transformation $\boldsymbol{b}_X^C \longrightarrow \boldsymbol{b}_X^{(A\&B)}$:

$$
\begin{aligned}
1:\ \boldsymbol{b}_X^C(x) &= \boldsymbol{p}_X^C(x)\,, && \forall\, x \in \mathscr{R}(\mathbb{X}) \\
2: \quad &= \lim_{n\to\infty}\left(\frac{\sum_{i=1}^{n}\mathrm{T}((x_i^A \cap x_i^B)=x)}{n-\sum_{i=1}^{n}\mathrm{T}((x_i^A \cap x_i^B)=\emptyset)}\right), && \forall\, x \in \mathscr{R}(\mathbb{X}),\ x_i^A, x_i^B \in \mathscr{P}(\mathbb{X}) \\
3: \quad &= \frac{n\left(\sum\limits_{(x^A\cap x^B)=x} \boldsymbol{p}_X^A(x^A)\boldsymbol{p}_X^B(x^B)\right)}{n\left(1-\sum\limits_{(x^A\cap x^B)=\emptyset} \boldsymbol{p}_X^A(x^A)\boldsymbol{p}_X^B(x^B)\right)}, && \forall\, x \in \mathscr{R}(\mathbb{X}),\ x^A, x^B \in \mathscr{P}(\mathbb{X}) \\
4: \quad &= \frac{\sum\limits_{(x^A\cap x^B)=x} \boldsymbol{p}_X^A(x^A)\boldsymbol{p}_X^B(x^B)}{1-\sum\limits_{(x^A\cap x^B)=\emptyset} \boldsymbol{p}_X^A(x^A)\boldsymbol{p}_X^B(x^B)}, && \forall\, x \in \mathscr{R}(\mathbb{X}),\ x^A, x^B \in \mathscr{P}(\mathbb{X}) \\
5: \quad &= \frac{\boldsymbol{b}_X^A(x)u_X^B+\boldsymbol{b}_X^B(x)u_X^A + \sum\limits_{(x^A\cap x^B)=x} \boldsymbol{b}_X^A(x^A)\boldsymbol{b}_X^B(x^B)}{1-\sum\limits_{(x^A\cap x^B)=\emptyset} \boldsymbol{b}_X^A(x^A)\boldsymbol{b}_X^B(x^B)}, && \forall\, x \in \mathscr{R}(\mathbb{X}),\ x^A, x^B \in \mathscr{R}(\mathbb{X}) \\
6: \quad &= \frac{\mathrm{Har}(x)}{(1-\mathrm{Con})} \quad = \quad \boldsymbol{b}_X^{(A\&B)}(x)\,, && \forall\, x \in \mathscr{R}(\mathbb{X}).
\end{aligned}
\tag{12.9}
$$

The crucial point is the transformation from step 2 to step 3. The validity of this transformation is evident, because at every instance i the following probability equalities hold:

$$
\begin{aligned}
p((x_i^A \cap x_i^B) = x) &= \sum_{(x_i^A\cap x_i^B)=x} \boldsymbol{p}_X^A(x_i^A)\boldsymbol{p}_X^B(x_j^B), \\
p((x_i^A \cap x_i^B) = \emptyset) &= \sum_{(x_i^A\cap x_i^B)=\emptyset} \boldsymbol{p}_X^A(x_i^A)\boldsymbol{p}_X^B(x_i^B).
\end{aligned}
\tag{12.10}
$$

Hence, the probabilities of the two Boolean truth functions in step 2 above are given by Eq.(12.10). The transformation from step 2 to step 3 above simply consists of rewriting these probabilities.

The transformation of the uncertainty mass from being based on stochastic constraints to being based on belief constraints follows next.

Simplified transformation $u^C_X \longrightarrow u^{(A\&B)}_X$:

$$\begin{aligned}
1:\ u^C_X &= \boldsymbol{p}^C_X(\mathbb{X}) \\
2:\ &= \lim_{n\to\infty}\left(\frac{\sum_{i=1}^n \mathrm{T}((x^A_i \cap x^B_i)=\mathbb{X})}{n-\sum_{i=1}^n \mathrm{T}((x^A_i \cap x^B_i)=\emptyset)}\right), && x^A_i, x^B_i \in \mathscr{P}(\mathbb{X}) \\
3:\ &= \frac{\boldsymbol{p}^A_X(\mathbb{X})\boldsymbol{p}^B_X(\mathbb{X})}{1-\sum\limits_{(x^A\cap x^B)=\emptyset} \boldsymbol{p}^A_X(x^A)\boldsymbol{p}^B_X(x^B)}, && x^A, x^B \in \mathscr{P}(\mathbb{X}) \\
4:\ &= \frac{u^A_X u^B_X}{1-\sum\limits_{(x^A\cap x^B)=\emptyset} \boldsymbol{b}^A_X(x^A)\boldsymbol{b}^B_X(x^B)}, && x^A, x^B \in \mathscr{R}(\mathbb{X}) \\
5:\ &= \frac{u^A_X u^B_X}{(1-\mathrm{Con})} = u^{(A\&B)}_X .
\end{aligned} \tag{12.11}$$

□

While Theorem 12.1 is based on long-term frequentist situations, the same result can be extended to the combination of subjective opinions in the same way that frequentist probability calculus can be extended to subjective probability and non-frequentist situations. According to de Finetti [17], a frequentist probability is no more objective than a subjective (non-frequentist) probability, because even if observations are objective, their translation into probabilities is always subjective.

de Finetti [16] provides further justification for this view by explaining that subjective knowledge of a system often carries more weight when estimating probabilities of future events than purely objective observations of the past. The only case where probability estimates can be purely based on frequentist information is in abstract examples from textbooks. Frequentist information is thus just another form of evidence used to estimate probabilities.

Because a subjective opinion is simply a probability distribution over a hyperdomain, de Finetti's view can obviously be extended to subjective opinions. Hence, there is not only a mathematical equivalence, but also an interpretational equivalence between stochastic constraint fusion and belief constraint fusion.

12.2.3 Expressing Preferences with Subjective Opinions

Preferences can be expressed as soft or hard constraints, qualitative or quantitative, ordered or partially ordered, etc. It is possible to specify a mapping between qualitative verbal tags and subjective opinions, which enables easy solicitation of preferences [83]. Table 12.1 describes examples of how preferences can be expressed.

All the preference types of Table 12.1 can be interpreted in terms of subjective opinions, and further combined by considering them as constraints expressed by different sources/agents. The examples which comprise two binary domains could

Table 12.1 Example preferences and corresponding subjective opinions

Example & Type	**Opinion Expression**	
"Ingredient x is mandatory" Hard positive	Binary domain Binomial opinion	$\mathbb{X} = \{x, \bar{x}\}$ $\omega_x : (1, 0, 0, 1/2)$
"Ingredient x is totally out of the question" Hard negative	Binary domain Binomial opinion	$\mathbb{X} = \{x, \bar{x}\}$ $\omega_x : (0,\ 1,\ 0,\ 1/2)$
"My preference rating for x is 3 out of 10" Quantitative	Binary domain Binomial opinion	$\mathbb{X} = \{x, \bar{x}\}$ $\omega_x : (0.3,\ 0.7,\ 0.0,\ 1/2)$
"I prefer x or y, but z is also acceptable" Qualitative	Ternary domain Trinomial opinion	$\Theta = \{x, y, z\}$ $\omega_\Theta : (b(x,y) = 0.6,\ b(z) = 0.3,$ $u = 0.1,\ a(x,y,z) = 1/3)$
"I like x, but I like y even more" Positive rank	Two binary domains Binomial opinions	$\mathbb{X} = \{x, \bar{x}\}$ and $\mathbb{Y} = \{y, \bar{y}\}$ $\omega_x : (0.6,\ 0.3,\ 0.1,\ 1/2)$, $\omega_y : (0.7,\ 0.2,\ 0.1,\ 1/2)$
"I don't like x, and I dislike y even more" Negative rank	Two binary domains Binomial opinions	$\mathbb{X} = \{x, \bar{x}\}$ and $\mathbb{Y} = \{y, \bar{y}\}$ $\omega_x : (0.3,\ 0.6,\ 0.1,\ 1/2)$, $\omega_y : (0.2,\ 0.7,\ 0.1,\ 1/2)$
"I'm indifferent about x, y and z" Neutral	Ternary domain Trinomial opinion	$\Theta = \{x, y, z\}$ $\omega_\Theta : (u_\Theta = 1.0,\ a(x,y,z) = 1/3)$
"I'm indifferent but most people prefer x" Neutral with bias	Ternary domain Trinomial opinion	$\Theta = \{x, y, z\}$ $\omega_\Theta : (u_\Theta = 1.0,\ a(x) = 0.6,$ $a(y) = 0.2, a(z) = 0.2)$

equally well have been modelled with a quaternary product domain with a corresponding quatronomial product opinion. In fact, to compute product opinions over product domains is an alternative approach of simultaneously considering preferences over multiple variables.

Default base rates are specified in all but the last example, which indicates total indifference, but with a bias that expresses the average preference in the population. Base rates are useful in many situations, such as for default reasoning. Base rates influence the computed results only in case of significant indifference or uncertainty.

12.2.4 Example: Going to the Cinema, First Attempt

Assume three friends, Alice, Bob and Clark, who want to see a film together at the cinema one evening, and that the only films showing are *Black Dust* (BD), *Grey Matter* (GM) and *White Powder* (WP), represented as the ternary domain $X = \{\text{BD, GM, WP}\}$. Assume that the friends express their preferences in the form of the opinions of Table 12.2.

Table 12.2 Fusion of film preferences

	Preferences of:			Results of preference combinations:	
	Alice	Bob	Clark	(Alice & Bob)	(Alice & Bob & Clark)
	ω_X^A	ω_X^B	ω_X^C	$\omega_X^{A\&B}$	$\omega_X^{A\&B\&C}$
$b(\text{BD}) =$	0.99	0.00	0.00	0.00	0.00
$b(\text{GM}) =$	0.01	0.01	0.00	1.00	1.00
$b(\text{WP}) =$	0.00	0.99	0.00	0.00	0.00
$b(\text{GM} \cup \text{WP}) =$	0.00	0.00	1.00	0.00	0.00

Alice and Bob have strong and conflicting preferences. Clark, who strictly does not want to watch *Black Dust*, and who is indifferent about the two other films, is not sure whether he wants to come along, so Table 12.2 shows the results of applying the belief/preference constraint fusion operator, first without him, and then when including him in the party.

By applying belief constraint fusion, Alice and Bob conclude that the only film they are both interested in seeing is *Grey Matter*. Including Clark in the party does not change that result because he is indifferent to *Grey Matter* and *White Powder* anyway, he just does not want to watch *Black Dust*.

The belief mass values of Alice and Bob in the above example are in fact equal to those that Zadeh [101] used to demonstrate the unsuitability of Dempster's rule for fusing beliefs, because it produces counter-intuitive results. Zadeh's example describes a medical case where two medical doctors express their expert opinions about possible diagnoses, which typically should have been modelled with the weighted belief fusion (WBF) operator, or alternatively with the consensus & compromise fusion (CCF) operator [58], not with Dempster's rule. In order to select the appropriate operator, it is crucial to fully understand the nature of the situation to be modelled. The failure to understand that Dempster's rule does not represent an operator for cumulative or averaging belief fusion, combined with the unavailability of the general cumulative, averaging, weighted and consensus & compromise fusion operators during that period (1976 [90] – 2013 [58]), has often led to inappropriate applications of Dempster's rule to cases of belief fusion [53]. However, when specifying the same numerical values as in [101] in a case of preference constraints such as in the example above, the belief constraint fusion operator (which is a simple extension of Dempster's rule) is the correct fusion operator which produces perfectly intuitive results.

12.2.5 Example: Going to the Cinema, Second Attempt

In this example Alice and Bob soften their preference with some indifference in the form of $u = 0.01$, as specified by Table 12.3. Clark has the same opinion as in the previous example, and is still not sure whether he wants to come along, so Table 12.3 shows the results both without him, and with his preference included.

Table 12.3 Fusion of film preferences with indifference and non-default base rates

		Preferences of:			Results of preference combinations:	
		Alice	Bob	Clark	(Alice & Bob)	(Alice & Bob & Clark)
		ω_X^A	ω_X^B	ω_X^C	$\omega_X^{A\&B}$	$\omega_X^{A\&B\&C}$
$\boldsymbol{b}(\text{BD})$	=	0.98	0.00	0.00	0.490	0.000
$\boldsymbol{b}(\text{GM})$	=	0.01	0.01	0.00	0.015	0.029
$\boldsymbol{b}(\text{WP})$	=	0.00	0.98	0.00	0.490	0.961
$\boldsymbol{b}(\text{GM} \cup \text{WP})$	=	0.00	0.00	1.00	0.000	0.010
u	=	0.01	0.01	0.00	0.005	0.000
$\boldsymbol{a}(\text{BD})$	=	0.6	0.6	0.6	0.6	0.6
$\boldsymbol{a}(\text{GM}) = a(\text{WP})$	=	0.2	0.2	0.2	0.2	0.2

The expected effect of specifying some indifference in the preferences is that Alice and Bob should pick film *Black Dust* or *White Powder*, because in both cases, one of them actually prefers one of the films, and the other finds it acceptable. Neither Alice nor Bob prefers *Grey Matter*, they only find it acceptable, so it turns out to be a bad choice for both of them. When taking into consideration that the base rate $a(\text{BD}) = 0.6$ and the base rate $a(\text{WP}) = 0.2$, the expected preference levels according to Eq.(3.28) are such that

$$\mathbf{P}_X^{A\&B}(\text{BD}) > \mathbf{P}_X^{A\&B}(\text{WP}) . \tag{12.12}$$

More precisely, the expected preference levels according to Eq.(3.28) are

$$\mathbf{P}_X^{A\&B}(\text{BD}) = 0.493 , \qquad \mathbf{P}_X^{A\&B}(\text{WP}) = 0.491 . \tag{12.13}$$

Because of the higher base rate, *Black Dust* also has a higher expected preference than *White Powder*, so the rational choice would be to watch *Black Dust*.

However, when including Clark, who does not want to watch *Black Dust*, the base rates no longer dictate the result. In this case constraint fusion with Eq.(3.28) produces $\mathbf{P}^{A\&B\&C}(\text{WP}) = 0.966$ so the obvious choice is to watch *White Powder*.

12.2.6 Example: Not Going to the Cinema

Assume now that Alice and Bob have totally conflicting preferences as specified in Table 12.4, i.e. Alice has a hard preference for *Black Dust* and Bob has a hard preference for *White Powder*. Clark still has the same preference as before, i.e. he does not want to watch *Black Dust*, and is indifferent about the other two films.

Table 12.4 Combination of film preferences with hard and conflicting preferences

		Preferences of:			Results of preference combinations:	
		Alice	Bob	Clark	(Alice & Bob)	(Alice & Bob & Clark)
		ω_X^A	ω_X^B	ω_X^C	$\omega_X^{A\&B}$	$\omega_X^{A\&B\&C}$
$b(\text{BD})$	=	1.00	0.00	0.00	Undefined	Undefined
$b(\text{GM})$	=	0.00	0.00	0.00	Undefined	Undefined
$b(\text{WP})$	=	0.00	1.00	0.00	Undefined	Undefined
$b(\text{GM} \cup \text{WP})$	=	0.00	0.00	1.00	Undefined	Undefined

In this case, the belief constraint fusion operator can not be applied because Eq.(12.2) involves a division by zero. The conclusion is that the friends will not go to the cinema to see a film together that evening. The test for detecting this situation is to observe $Con = 1$ in Eq.(12.4). It makes no difference to include Clark in the party, because a conflict can not be resolved by including additional preferences. However it would have been possible for Bob and Clark to watch *White Powder* together without Alice.

12.3 Cumulative Fusion

Cumulative belief fusion is equivalent to simply adding up the evidence parameters of the evidence notation of opinions seen in Figure 5.4. The cumulative fusion operator for belief opinions is then obtained through the bijective mapping between belief opinions and evidence opinions, as described by Definition 3.9. It is meaningful to distinguish between aleatory and epistemic opinions, described in Section 3.3, with regard to cumulative fusion. The two case are therefore presented separately.

12.3.1 Aleatory Cumulative Fusion

Assume a domain $\mathbb{X}$ and its hyperdomain $\mathscr{R}(\mathbb{X})$. Assume a process where variable X takes values from $\mathbb{X}$ resulting from the process. Consider two agents A and B who observe the outcomes of the process over two separate time periods. Their observations can be vague, meaning that sometimes they observe an outcome which might be one of multiple possible singletons in $\mathbb{X}$, but they are unable to identify the observed outcome uniquely.

For example, assume that persons A and B are observing coloured balls being picked from an urn, where the balls can have one of four colours: black, white, red or green. Assume further that the observers are colour-blind, which means that sometimes they are unable see the difference between red and green balls, although they can always tell the other colour combinations apart. As a result, their observations can be vague, meaning that sometimes they perceive a specific ball to be either red or green, but are unable to identify the ball's colour precisely. This corresponds to the situation where X is a hypervariable which takes its values from $\mathscr{R}(\mathbb{X})$.

The symbol '$\diamond$' denotes the fusion of two observers A and B into a single imaginary observer denoted $(A \diamond B)$.

Definition 12.5 (The Cumulative Fusion Operator).
Let ω^A and ω^B be source A and B's respective opinions over the same (hyper)variable X on domain $\mathbb{X}$. Let $\omega_X^{(A\diamond B)}$ be the opinion such that

$$\text{Case I: For } u_X^A \neq 0 \lor u_X^B \neq 0:$$

$$\begin{cases} \boldsymbol{b}_X^{(A\diamond B)}(x) = \frac{\boldsymbol{b}_X^A(x)u_X^B + \boldsymbol{b}_X^B(x)u_X^A}{u_X^A + u_X^B - u_X^A u_X^B}, \\ u_X^{(A\diamond B)} = \frac{u_X^A u_X^B}{u_X^A + u_X^B - u_X^A u_X^B}, \\ \boldsymbol{a}_X^{A\diamond B}(x) = \frac{\boldsymbol{a}_X^A(x)u_X^B + \boldsymbol{a}_X^B(x)u_X^A - (\boldsymbol{a}_X^A(x) + \boldsymbol{a}_X^B(x))u_X^A u_X^B}{u_X^A + u_X^B - 2u_X^A u_X^B} & \text{if } u_X^A \neq 1 \lor u_X^B \neq 1, \\ \boldsymbol{a}_X^{A\diamond B}(x) = \frac{\boldsymbol{a}_X^A(x) + \boldsymbol{a}_X^B(x)}{2} & \text{if } u_X^A = u_X^B = 1, \end{cases} \tag{12.14}$$

$$\text{Case II: For } u_X^A = u_X^B = 0:$$

$$\begin{cases} \boldsymbol{b}_X^{(A\diamond B)}(x) = \gamma_X^A \boldsymbol{b}_X^A(x) + \gamma_X^B \boldsymbol{b}^B(x), \\ u_X^{(A\diamond B)} = 0, \\ \boldsymbol{a}_X^{A\diamond B}(x) = \gamma_X^A \boldsymbol{a}_X^A(x) + \gamma_X^B \boldsymbol{a}^B(x), \end{cases} \text{where} \begin{cases} \gamma^A = \lim_{\substack{u_X^A \to 0 \\ u_X^B \to 0}} \frac{u_X^B}{u_X^A + u_X^B}, \\ \gamma_X^B = \lim_{\substack{u_X^A \to 0 \\ u_X^B \to 0}} \frac{u_X^A}{u_X^A + u_X^B}. \end{cases} \tag{12.15}$$

Then $\omega_X^{(A\diamond B)}$ is called the cumulatively fused opinion of ω_X^A and ω_X^B, representing the combination of the independent opinions of sources A and B. By using the symbol '$\oplus$' to denote this operator, aleatory cumulative belief fusion can be expressed as $\omega_X^{(A\diamond B)} = \omega_X^A \oplus \omega_X^B$. □

It can be verified that the cumulative fusion operator is commutative, associative and non-idempotent. In Case II of Definition 12.5, the associativity depends on the preservation of relative weights of intermediate results, which requires the additional weight parameter γ. In this case, the cumulative fusion operator is equivalent to the weighted average of probabilities.

The argument base rate distributions are normally equal. When that is not the case the fused base rate distribution over X is specified to be the evidence-weighted average base rate.

In case of dogmatic arguments it can be assumed that the limits in Eq.(12.15) are defined as $\gamma_X^A = \gamma_X^B = 0.5$.

The cumulative fusion operator is equivalent to updating prior Dirichlet PDFs by adding new evidence to produce posterior Dirichlet PDFs. Deriving the cumulative belief fusion operator is based on the bijective mapping between belief opinions and evidence opinions. The mapping is expressed in Definition 3.9.

Theorem 12.2. *The cumulative fusion operator of Definition 12.5 is equivalent to simple addition of the evidence parameters of evidence opinions, as expressed in Eq.(3.33).*

Proof. The cumulative belief fusion operator of Definition 12.5 is derived by mapping the argument belief opinions to evidence opinions through the bijective mapping of Definition 3.9. Cumulative fusion of evidence opinions simply consists of evidence parameter addition. The fused evidence opinion is then mapped back to a belief opinion through the bijective mapping of Definition 3.9. This explanation is in essence the proof of Theorem 12.2.

Let the two observers' respective hyper-opinions be expressed as ω_X^A and ω_X^B. The corresponding evidence opinions $\mathrm{Dir}_X^{\mathrm{eH}}(\boldsymbol{p}_X^{\mathrm{H}}, \boldsymbol{r}_X^A, \boldsymbol{a}_X^A)$ and $\mathrm{Dir}_X^{\mathrm{eH}}(\boldsymbol{p}_X^{\mathrm{H}}, \boldsymbol{r}_X^B, \boldsymbol{a}_X^B)$ contain the respective evidence parameters $\boldsymbol{r}_X^A$ and $\boldsymbol{r}_X^B$.

The cumulative fusion of these two bodies of evidence simply consists of vector addition of $\mathrm{Dir}_X^{\mathrm{eH}}(\boldsymbol{p}_X^{\mathrm{H}}, \boldsymbol{r}_X^A, \boldsymbol{a}_X^A)$ and $\mathrm{Dir}_X^{\mathrm{eH}}(\boldsymbol{p}_X^{\mathrm{H}}, \boldsymbol{r}_X^B, \boldsymbol{a}_X^B)$, expressed as

$$\begin{aligned} \mathrm{Dir}_X^{\mathrm{eH}}(\boldsymbol{p}_X^{\mathrm{H}}, \boldsymbol{r}_X^{(A\diamond B)}, \boldsymbol{a}_X^{A\diamond B}) &= \mathrm{Dir}_X^{\mathrm{eH}}(\boldsymbol{p}_X^{\mathrm{H}}, \boldsymbol{r}_X^A, \boldsymbol{a}_X^A) \oplus \mathrm{Dir}_X^{\mathrm{eH}}(\boldsymbol{p}_X^{\mathrm{H}}, \boldsymbol{r}_X^B, \boldsymbol{a}_X^B) \\ &= \mathrm{Dir}_X^{\mathrm{eH}}(\boldsymbol{p}_X^{\mathrm{H}}, (\boldsymbol{r}_X^A + \boldsymbol{r}_X^B), \boldsymbol{a}_X^{A\diamond B}) . \end{aligned} \tag{12.16}$$

More specifically, for each value $x \in \mathscr{R}(\mathbb{X})$ the accumulated source evidence $\boldsymbol{r}_X^{(A\diamond B)}$ is computed as:

$$\boldsymbol{r}_X^{(A\diamond B)}(x) = \boldsymbol{r}_X^A(x) + \boldsymbol{r}_X^B(x) , \quad \forall x \in \mathscr{R}(\mathbb{X}). \tag{12.17}$$

The cumulative fused belief opinion $\omega_X^{A\diamond B}$ of Definition 12.5 results from mapping the fused evidence of Eq.(12.16) back to a belief opinion of Definition 12.5 by applying the bijective mapping of Definition 3.9. □

Figure 12.4 is a screenshot of the online demonstrator for aleatory cumulative belief fusion.

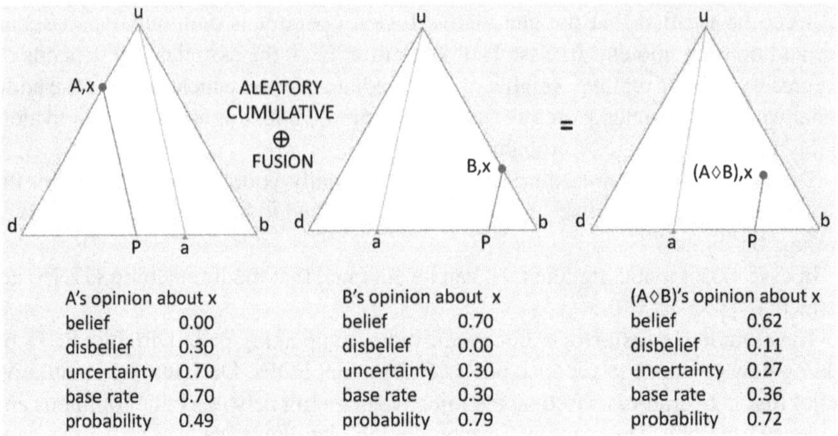

Fig. 12.4 Example aleatory cumulative fusion

The aleatory cumulative fusion operator has been called the consensus operator in the literature [42, 43], but 'cumulative fusion' is more descriptive.

12.3.2 Epistemic Cumulative Fusion

Epistemic opinions, described in Section 3.3, apply to variables that not governed by frequentist processes, so that it is not meaningful to have a model for reducing uncertainty mass through accumulation of statistical sampling. Nevertheless, we think it is meaningful to have an operator for cumulative fusion of epistemic opinions.

Definition 12.6. The method for epistemic cumulative fusion has two steps:

1. Apply aleatory cumulative fusion as described in Section 12.3.1, to fuse the epistemic opinion arguments as described in Section 3.3.
2. Apply uncertainty-maximisation, as described in Section 3.5.6, to the result of the fusion operation.

By using the symbol '$\ddot{\oplus}$' to designate this operator, epistemic cumulative belief fusion can be expressed as $\omega_X^{(A \ddot{\diamond} B)} = \omega_X^A \ddot{\oplus} \omega_X^B$. □

Epistemic cumulative belief fusion can e.g. fuse witness observations. In case two witnesses make mutually contradictory statements, then these statements can not be interpreted as statistical samples and be fused in a cumulative fashion. It would therefore be meaningful to uncertainty-maximise the output result after cumulative fusion, in order to reflect that the result represents an epistemic opinion.

Figure 12.5 is a screenshot of the online demonstrator for epistemic cumulative belief fusion.

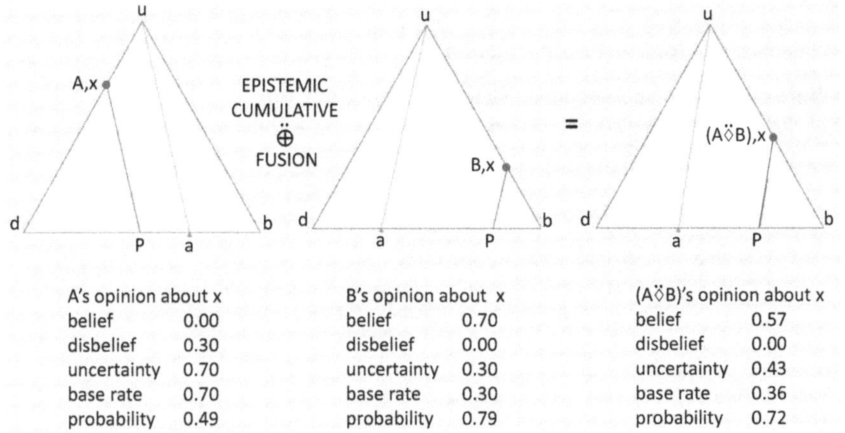

Fig. 12.5 Example epistemic cumulative fusion

Note that the fused opinion $\omega_X^{A\ddot{\diamond}B} = \ddot{\omega}_X^{A\diamond B}$, where $\ddot{\omega}_X^{A\diamond B}$ can be computed from $\omega_X^{A\diamond B}$ according to the uncertainty-maximisation described in Section 3.5.6.

The effect of epistemic cumulative fusion is for example that two contradicting testimonies cancel each other out, when assuming that the two witnesses are equally trusted by the analyst. As a result, the analyst is not more informed about the truth of the case after receiving the contradicting testimonies, and therefore should consider trust revision, or obtaining additional testimonies, as possible strategies to gain more certainty about the case.

12.4 Averaging Belief Fusion

Assume that agents A and B observe the same outcomes of the same process over the same time period, so their opinions are necessarily dependent. Still, their perceptions might be different, e.g. because their cognitive capabilities are different. For example, let A and B observing coloured balls being picked from an urn, where the balls can have one of four colours: black, white, red or green. Assume that observer B is colour-blind, which means that sometimes he has trouble distinguishing between red and green balls, although he can always distinguish between the other colour combinations. Observer A has perfect colour vision, and normally can always tell the correct colour when a ball is picked. As a result, when a red ball is picked, observer A normally identifies it as red, but observer B might identify it as green. This can lead to A and B having conflicting opinions about the same variable, although their observations and opinions are totally dependent. Assume that *a priori* it is unknown whether one of the observers is colour-blind, so that their opinions are considered equally reliable. The averaging belief fusion operator provides an adequate model for this fusion situation.

Definition 12.7 (The Averaging Belief Fusion Operator).
Let ω_X^A and ω_X^B be source A and B's respective opinions over the same (hyper)variable X on domain $\mathbb{X}$. Let $\omega_X^{(A\underline{\diamond}B)}$ be the opinion such that

Case I: For $u_X^A \neq 0 \vee u_X^B \neq 0$:

$$\begin{cases} \boldsymbol{b}_X^{(A\underline{\diamond}B)}(x) = \dfrac{\boldsymbol{b}_X^A(x)u_X^B + \boldsymbol{b}_X^B(x)u_X^A}{u_X^A + u_X^B}, \\ u_X^{(A\underline{\diamond}B)} = \dfrac{2u_X^A u_X^B}{u_X^A + u_X^B}, \\ \boldsymbol{a}_X^{A\underline{\diamond}B}(x) = \dfrac{\boldsymbol{a}_X^A(x) + \boldsymbol{a}_X^B(x)}{2}, \end{cases} \tag{12.18}$$

Case II: For $u_X^A = 0 \wedge u_X^B = 0$:

$$\begin{cases} \boldsymbol{b}_X^{(A\underline{\diamond}B)}(x) = \gamma_X^A \boldsymbol{b}_X^A(x) + \gamma_X^B \boldsymbol{b}_X^B(x), \\ u_X^{A\underline{\diamond}B} = 0, \\ \boldsymbol{a}_X^{A\underline{\diamond}B}(x) = \gamma_X^A \boldsymbol{a}_X^A(x) + \gamma_X^B \boldsymbol{a}^B(x), \end{cases} \quad \text{where} \quad \begin{cases} \gamma_X^A = \lim\limits_{\substack{u_X^A \to 0 \\ u_X^B \to 0}} \dfrac{u_X^B}{u_X^A + u_X^B}, \\ \gamma_X^B = \lim\limits_{\substack{u_X^A \to 0 \\ u_X^B \to 0}} \dfrac{u_X^A}{u_X^A + u_X^B}. \end{cases} \tag{12.19}$$

Then $\omega_X^{A\underline{\diamond}B}$ is called the averaged opinion of ω_X^A and ω_X^B, representing the combination of the dependent opinions of A and B. By using the symbol '$\underline{\oplus}$' to designate this belief operator, we define $\omega_X^{(A\underline{\diamond}B)} \equiv \omega_X^A \underline{\oplus} \omega_X^B$. □

It can be verified that the averaging belief fusion operator is commutative and idempotent, but not associative.

The argument base rate distributions are normally equal. When that is not the case the fused base rate distribution is specified to be the average base rate distribution. In case of dogmatic arguments the limits in Eq.(12.19) can be set to $\gamma_X^A = \gamma_X^B = 0.5$.

The averaging belief fusion operator is equivalent to updating Dirichlet PDFs as the average of source agents' evidence to produce posterior Dirichlet PDFs. The derivation of the averaging belief fusion operator is based on the bijective mapping between the belief and evidence notations described in Definition 3.9.

Theorem 12.3. *The averaging fusion operator of Definition 12.7 is equivalent to simple averaging of the evidence parameters of the Dirichlet HPDF in Eq.(3.33).*

Proof. The averaging belief fusion operator of Definition 12.7 is derived by mapping the argument belief opinions to evidence opinions through the bijective mapping of Definition 3.9. Averaging fusion of evidence opinions simply consists of computing the average of the evidence parameters. The fused evidence opinion is then mapped back to a belief opinion through the bijective mapping of Definition 3.9. This explanation is in essence the proof of Theorem 12.3. A more detailed explanation is provided below.

Let the two observers' respective belief opinions be expressed as ω_X^A and ω_X^B. The corresponding evidence opinions $\mathrm{Dir}_X^{\mathrm{eH}}(\boldsymbol{p}_X^{\mathrm{H}}, \boldsymbol{r}_X^A, \boldsymbol{a}_X^A)$ and $\mathrm{Dir}_X^{\mathrm{eH}}(\boldsymbol{p}_X^{\mathrm{H}}, \boldsymbol{r}_X^B, \boldsymbol{a}_X^B)$ contain the respective evidence parameters $\boldsymbol{r}_X^A$ and $\boldsymbol{r}_X^B$.

The averaging fusion of these two bodies of evidence simply consists of vector averaging of $\mathrm{Dir}_X^{\mathrm{eH}}(\boldsymbol{p}_X^{\mathrm{H}}, \boldsymbol{r}_X^A, \boldsymbol{a}_X^A)$ and $\mathrm{Dir}_X^{\mathrm{eH}}(\boldsymbol{p}_X^{\mathrm{H}}, \boldsymbol{r}_X^B, \boldsymbol{a}_X^B)$, expressed as

$$\begin{aligned} \mathrm{Dir}_X^{\mathrm{eH}}(\boldsymbol{p}_X^{\mathrm{H}}, \boldsymbol{r}_X^{(A\underline{\diamond}B)}, \boldsymbol{a}_X^{A\underline{\diamond}B}) &= \mathrm{Dir}_X^{\mathrm{eH}}(\boldsymbol{p}_X^{\mathrm{H}}, \boldsymbol{r}_X^A, \boldsymbol{a}_X^A) \,\underline{\oplus}\, \mathrm{Dir}_X^{\mathrm{eH}}(\boldsymbol{p}_X^{\mathrm{H}}, \boldsymbol{r}_X^B, \boldsymbol{a}_X^B) \\ &= \mathrm{Dir}_X^{\mathrm{eH}}(\boldsymbol{p}_X^{\mathrm{H}}, (\boldsymbol{r}_X^A + \boldsymbol{r}_X^B)/2, \boldsymbol{a}_X^{A\underline{\diamond}B}) \,. \end{aligned} \tag{12.20}$$

More specifically, for each value $x \in \mathscr{R}(\mathbb{X})$ the average evidence $\boldsymbol{r}_X^{(A\underline{\diamond}B)}$ is

$$\boldsymbol{r}_X^{(A\underline{\diamond}B)}(x) = \frac{\boldsymbol{r}_X^A(x) + \boldsymbol{r}_X^B(x)}{2}. \tag{12.21}$$

The averaging fused belief opinion $\omega_X^{A\underline{\diamond}B}$ of Definition 12.7 results from mapping the fused evidence belief mass of Eq.(12.20) back to a belief opinion as defined in Definition 12.7 by applying the bijective mapping of Definition 3.9. □

The averaging fusion operator represents a generalisation of the dependent consensus operator proposed in [49]. It is possible to combine cumulative and averaging fusion in a hybrid fusion operator, as described in [54].

12.5 Weighted Belief Fusion

The weighted belief fusion (WBF) operator produces averaging beliefs weighted by the opinion confidences. WBF is suitable for fusing (expert) agent opinions in situations where the source agent's confidence should determine the opinion weight in the fusion process. Recall from Eq.(3.43) that the confidence c_X of an opinion ω_X is computed as $c_X = 1 - u_X$.

WBF does not leverage shared belief on partially overlapping composite values, which can be seen as a disadvantage. However, when the arguments are multinomial opinions the fused result will also be a multinomial opinion. The same principle is valid for hyper-opinions.

Definition 12.8 (The Weighted Belief Fusion Operator).
Let ω_X^A and ω_X^B be source A and B's respective opinions over the same (hyper)variable X on domain $\mathbb{X}$. Let $\omega_X^{(A\widehat{\diamond}B)}$ be the opinion such that

$$\omega_X^{A\hat{\diamond}B} = (\boldsymbol{b}_X^{A\hat{\diamond}B},\, u_X^{A\hat{\diamond}B},\, \boldsymbol{a}_X^{A\hat{\diamond}B})\,, \quad \text{where} \tag{12.22}$$

Case I: For $(u_X^A \neq 0 \;\vee\; u_X^B \neq 0) \;\wedge\; (u_X^A \neq 1 \;\vee\; u_X^B \neq 1):$

$$\begin{cases} \boldsymbol{b}_X^{(A\hat{\diamond}B)}(x) = \frac{\boldsymbol{b}_X^A(x)(1-u_X^A)u_X^B + \boldsymbol{b}_X^B(x)(1-u_X^B)u_X^A}{u_X^A + u_X^B - 2u_X^A u_X^B}\,, \\[2ex] u_X^{(A\hat{\diamond}B)} \quad\;\; = \frac{(2-u_X^A-u_X^B)u_X^A u_X^B}{u_X^A + u_X^B - 2u_X^A u_X^B}\,, \\[2ex] \boldsymbol{a}_X^{A\hat{\diamond}B}(x) \;\; = \frac{\boldsymbol{a}_X^A(x)(1-u_X^A) + \boldsymbol{a}_X^B(x)(1-u_X^B)}{2-u_X^A-u_X^B}\,, \end{cases} \tag{12.23}$$

Case II: For $u_X^A = 0 \;\wedge\; u_X^B = 0:$

$$\begin{cases} \boldsymbol{b}_X^{(A\hat{\diamond}B)}(x) = \gamma_X^A\, \boldsymbol{b}_X^A(x) + \gamma_X^B \boldsymbol{b}_X^B(x), \\[2ex] u_X^{A\hat{\diamond}B} \qquad = 0, \\[2ex] \boldsymbol{a}_X^{A\hat{\diamond}B}(x) \;\; = \gamma_X^A\, \boldsymbol{a}_X^A(x) + \gamma_X^B \boldsymbol{a}^B(x), \end{cases} \quad \text{where} \quad \begin{cases} \gamma_X^A = \lim\limits_{\substack{u_X^A \to 0 \\ u_X^B \to 0}} \frac{u_X^B}{u_X^A + u_X^B}\,, \\[4ex] \gamma_X^B = \lim\limits_{\substack{u_X^A \to 0 \\ u_X^B \to 0}} \frac{u_X^A}{u_X^A + u_X^B}\,. \end{cases} \tag{12.24}$$

Case III: For $u_X^A = 1 \;\wedge\; u_X^B = 1:$

$$\begin{cases} \boldsymbol{b}_X^{(A\hat{\diamond}B)}(x) = 0\,, \\[2ex] u_X^{(A\hat{\diamond}B)} \qquad = 1\,, \\[2ex] \boldsymbol{a}_X^{A\hat{\diamond}B}(x) \;\; = \frac{\boldsymbol{a}_X^A(x) + \boldsymbol{a}_X^B(x)}{2}\,, \end{cases} \tag{12.25}$$

Then $\omega_X^{A\hat{\diamond}B}$ is called the weighted fusion opinion of ω_X^A and ω_X^B. By using the symbol '$\widehat{\oplus}$' to denote this belief operator, we define $\omega_X^{(A\hat{\diamond}B)} \equiv \omega_X^A \widehat{\oplus} \omega_X^B$. □

It can be verified that WBF is commutative, idempotent and has the vacuous opinion as neutral element. Semi-associativity requires that three or more arguments must first be combined together in the same operation.

The argument base rate distributions are normally equal. When that is not the case the fused base rate distribution over X is specified to be the confidence-weighted average base rate distribution. In case of dogmatic arguments assume the limits in Eq.(12.24) to be $\gamma_X^A = \gamma_X^B = 0.5$.

The weighted belief fusion operator is equivalent to updating Dirichlet PDFs as the confidence-weighted average of source agents' evidence to produce posterior

Dirichlet PDFs. The derivation of the confidence-weighted fusion operator is based on the bijective mapping between the belief and evidence notations described in Definition 3.9.

Theorem 12.4. *The weighted belief fusion operator of Definition 12.8 is equivalent to confidence-weighted averaging of the evidence parameters of the Dirichlet HPDF in Eq.(3.33).*

Proof. The weighted belief fusion operator of Definition 12.8 is derived by mapping the argument belief opinions to evidence opinions through the bijective mapping of Definition 3.9. Weighted belief fusion of evidence opinions simply consists of computing the confidence-weighted average of the evidence parameters. The fused evidence opinion is then mapped back to a belief opinion through the bijective mapping of Definition 3.9. This explanation is in essence the proof of Theorem 12.4. A more detailed explanation is provided below.

Let the two observers' respective belief opinions be expressed as ω_X^A and ω_X^B. The corresponding evidence opinions $\mathrm{Dir}_X^{\mathrm{eH}}(\boldsymbol{p}_X^{\mathrm{H}}, \boldsymbol{r}_X^A, \boldsymbol{a}_X^A)$ and $\mathrm{Dir}_X^{\mathrm{eH}}(\boldsymbol{p}_X^{\mathrm{H}}, \boldsymbol{r}_X^B, \boldsymbol{a}_X^B)$ contain the respective evidence parameters $\boldsymbol{r}_X^A$ and $\boldsymbol{r}_X^B$.

The weighted fusion of these two bodies of evidence simply consists of weighted vector averaging of $\mathrm{Dir}_X^{\mathrm{eH}}(\boldsymbol{p}_X^{\mathrm{H}}, \boldsymbol{r}_X^A, \boldsymbol{a}_X^A)$ and $\mathrm{Dir}_X^{\mathrm{eH}}(\boldsymbol{p}_X^{\mathrm{H}}, \boldsymbol{r}_X^B, \boldsymbol{a}_X^B)$:

$$\begin{aligned}\mathrm{Dir}_X^{\mathrm{eH}}(\boldsymbol{p}_X^{\mathrm{H}}, \boldsymbol{r}_X^{(A\widehat{\diamond}B)}, \boldsymbol{a}_X^{A\widehat{\diamond}B}) &= \mathrm{Dir}_X^{\mathrm{eH}}(\boldsymbol{p}_X^{\mathrm{H}}, \boldsymbol{r}_X^A, \boldsymbol{a}_X^A) \ \widehat{\oplus}\ \mathrm{Dir}_X^{\mathrm{eH}}(\boldsymbol{p}_X^{\mathrm{H}}, \boldsymbol{r}_X^B, \boldsymbol{a}_X^B) \\ &= \mathrm{Dir}_X^{\mathrm{eH}}(\boldsymbol{p}_X^{\mathrm{H}}, ((\boldsymbol{r}_X^A c_X^A + \boldsymbol{r}_X^B c_X^B)/(c_X^A + c_X^B)), \boldsymbol{a}_X^{A\widehat{\diamond}B}).\end{aligned} \tag{12.26}$$

More specifically, for each value $x \in \mathscr{R}(\mathbb{X})$ the confidence-weighted fusion evidence $\boldsymbol{r}_X^{(A\widehat{\diamond}B)}$ is computed as

$$\boldsymbol{r}_X^{(A\widehat{\diamond}B)}(x) = \frac{\boldsymbol{r}_X^A(x)c_X^A + \boldsymbol{r}_X^B(x)c_X^B}{c_X^A + c_X^B} = \frac{\boldsymbol{r}_X^A(x)(1-u_X^A) + \boldsymbol{r}_X^B(x)(1-c_X^B)}{2 - u_X^A - u_X^B}. \tag{12.27}$$

The weighted fusion opinion $\omega_X^{A\widehat{\diamond}B}$ of Definition 12.8 results from mapping the fused evidence belief mass of Eq.(12.26) back to a belief opinion as defined in Definition 12.8 by applying the bijective mapping of Definition 3.9. □

12.6 Consensus & Compromise Fusion

CC-fusion fusion is specifically designed to be idempotent, having a neutral element, and to transform conflicting beliefs into compromise vague beliefs.

Assume two opinions ω_X^A and ω_X^B over the variable X which takes its values from the hyperdomain $\mathscr{R}(\mathbb{X})$. The superscripts A and B are attributes that identify the respective belief sources or belief owners. These two opinions can be mathematically merged using the CC-fusion operator denoted '$\circledcirc$' which can be expressed as

$$\text{Consensus \& Compromise Fusion: } \omega_X^{A \heartsuit B} = \omega_X^A \circledcirc \omega_X^B \,. \tag{12.28}$$

Belief source combination denoted '$\heartsuit$' thus corresponds to opinion fusion with the CC-operator '$\circledcirc$'. The CC-operator consists of the following three-step process: 1) the consensus step; 2) the compromise step; 3) the merger step. These steps are formally described next.

Step 1: Consensus step.

The consensus step simply consists of determining shared belief mass between the two arguments, which is stored as the belief vector $\boldsymbol{b}_X^{\text{cons}}$ expressed by Eq.(12.29):

$$\boldsymbol{b}_X^{\text{cons}}(x) = \min\left(\boldsymbol{b}_X^A(x),\, \boldsymbol{b}_X^B(x)\right) . \tag{12.29}$$

The sum of consensus belief denoted b_X^{cons} is expressed as:

$$b_X^{\text{cons}} = \sum_{x \in \mathscr{R}(X)} \boldsymbol{b}_X^{\text{cons}}(x) \,. \tag{12.30}$$

The residue belief masses of the arguments are

$$\begin{cases} \boldsymbol{b}_X^{\text{res}A}(x) = \boldsymbol{b}_X^A(x) - \boldsymbol{b}_X^{\text{cons}}(x), \\ \boldsymbol{b}_X^{\text{res}B}(x) = \boldsymbol{b}_X^B(x) - \boldsymbol{b}_X^{\text{cons}}(x). \end{cases} \tag{12.31}$$

Step 2: Compromise step.

The compromise step redistributes conflicting residue belief mass to produce compromise belief mass, stored in $\boldsymbol{b}_X^{\text{comp}}$ expressed by Eq.(12.32):

$$\begin{aligned} \boldsymbol{b}_X^{\text{comp}}(x) = \quad & \boldsymbol{b}^{\text{res}A}(x) u_X^B + \boldsymbol{b}^{\text{res}B}(x) u_X^A \\ + & \sum_{\{y \cap z\} = x} \boldsymbol{a}_X(y|z)\, \boldsymbol{a}_X(z|y)\, \boldsymbol{b}^{\text{res}A}(y)\, \boldsymbol{b}^{\text{res}B}(z) \\ + & \sum_{\substack{\{y \cup z\} = x \\ \{y \cap z\} \neq \emptyset}} (1 - \boldsymbol{a}_X(y|z)\, \boldsymbol{a}_X(z|y))\, \boldsymbol{b}^{\text{res}A}(y)\, \boldsymbol{b}^{\text{res}B}(z) \\ + & \sum_{\substack{\{y \cup z\} = x \\ \{y \cap z\} = \emptyset}} \boldsymbol{b}^{\text{res}A}(y)\, \boldsymbol{b}^{\text{res}B}(z) \,, \quad \text{where } x \in \mathscr{P}(X) \,. \end{aligned} \tag{12.32}$$

Then the following quantities are computed:

$$\text{Preliminary uncertainty mass: } u_X^{\text{pre}} = u_X^A\, u_X^B \,, \tag{12.33}$$

$$\text{Sum of compromise belief: } b_X^{\text{comp}} = \sum_{x \in \mathscr{P}(\mathbb{X})} \boldsymbol{b}_X^{\text{comp}}(x) \,. \tag{12.34}$$

In general, $b_X^{\text{cons}} + b_X^{\text{comp}} + u_X^{\text{pre}} < 1$, hence normalisation of $\boldsymbol{b}_X^{\text{comp}}$ is required:

$$\text{Normalisation factor:} \quad \eta = \frac{1 - b_X^{\text{cons}} - u_X^{\text{pre}}}{b_X^{\text{comp}}} \,. \tag{12.35}$$

Because belief on X represents uncertainty mass, the fused uncertainty is

$$u_X^{A\heartsuit B} = u_X^{\text{pre}} + \eta\, \boldsymbol{b}_X^{\text{comp}}(X) \,. \tag{12.36}$$

The compromise belief mass on X must then be set to zero, i.e. $\boldsymbol{b}_X^{\text{comp}}(X) = 0$.

Step 3: Merging consensus and compromise belief.

After normalisation, the resulting CC-fused belief is

$$\boldsymbol{b}_X^{A\heartsuit B}(x) = \boldsymbol{b}_X^{\text{cons}}(x) + \eta\, \boldsymbol{b}_X^{\text{comp}}(x) \,, \quad \forall x \in \mathscr{R}(X) \,. \tag{12.37}$$

The CC-fused opinion is then expressed as $\omega_X^{A\heartsuit B} = (\boldsymbol{b}_X^{A\heartsuit B},\, u_X^{A\heartsuit B},\, \boldsymbol{a}_X)$.

This marks the end of the three-step process for consensus & compromise fusion.

Definition 12.9 (Consensus & Compromise Fusion). Let ω_X^A and ω_X^B be two separate opinions from sources A and B about variable X. The opinion $\omega_X^{A\heartsuit B}$ derived through the three-step procedure described above is the CC-fused opinion. The symbol '$\copyright$' denotes the CCF-operator, hence CC-fusion can be expressed as

$$\omega_X^{A\heartsuit B} = \omega_X^A \copyright\, \omega_X^B \,. \tag{12.38}$$

□

The CCF-operator is commutative, idempotent and semi-associative, with the vacuous opinion as neutral element. Semi-associativity requires that three or more arguments must first be combined together in the consensus step, and then combined together again in the compromise step before the merging step.

CCF can applicable in a situation where (possibly non-expert) agents have dependent opinions about the same variable, such as when they are asked to give their opinions in a survey.

12.7 Example Comparison of Fusion Operators

The fusion example in Table 12.5 takes as input arguments the numerical belief masses from Zadeh's example [101]. In the original Zadeh's example, the sources are two medical doctors who each have an opinion on the hypothesis space of three possible diseases, for which Dempster's rule (which is called belief constraint fusion (BCF) in subjective logic) is applied. The counter-intuitive results produced by Dempster's rule demonstrate that it is inadequate for this particular class of situations. A more adequate operator for the situation of the two doctors would be weighted belief fusion (WBF) or consensus & compromise fusion (CCF).

The same pair of numerical argument opinions can of course occur in other fusion situations as well. Table 12.5 shows the results of fusion with the operators described in the previous sections. Section 12.1.2 describes types of situations for which each operator is suitable.

On an abstract level, sources A and B provide opinions about the hypothesis space $\mathbb{X} = \{x_1, x_2, x_3\}$ with variable X. The base rate distributions are assumed to be equal and uniform, expressed as $\boldsymbol{a}_X^A = \boldsymbol{a}_X^B = \{1/3,\ 1/3,\ 1/3\}$.

Table 12.5 Zadeh's numerical example applied to belief constraint fusion (BCF), aleatory cumulative belief fusion (A-CBF), epistemic cumulative belief fusion (E-CBF), averaging belief fusion (ABF), weighted belief fusion (WBF) and consensus & compromise fusion (CCF)

	Source opinions:		Fused opinions resulting from applying:					
	A	B	BCF	A-CBF	E-CBF	ABF	WBF	CCF
$b_X(x_1)$ =	0.99	0.00	0.00	0.495	0.485	0.495	0.495	0.000
$b_X(x_2)$ =	0.01	0.01	1.00	0.010	0.000	0.010	0.010	0.010
$b_X(x_3)$ =	0.00	0.99	0.00	0.495	0.485	0.495	0.495	0.000
$b_X(x_1, x_2)$ =	0.00	0.00	0.00	0.000	0.000	0.000	0.000	0.000
$b_X(x_1, x_3)$ =	0.00	0.00	0.00	0.000	0.000	0.000	0.000	0.990
$b_X(x_2, x_3)$ =	0.00	0.00	0.00	0.000	0.000	0.000	0.000	0.000
u_X =	0.00	0.00	0.00	0.000	0.030	0.000	0.000	0.000

Each operator produces intuitive results given respective relevant situations. For example, in the medical situation of the original Zadeh's example where two medical doctors A and B have conflicting opinions about the diagnosis of a patient, CCF produces vague belief in the form of $\boldsymbol{b}_X^{A \heartsuit B}(x_1, x_3) = 0.99$ which seems natural until the doctors can agree on a single diagnosis for the patient.

Zadeh's example does not clearly expose the difference between the various belief fusion operator because many fusion operators produce equal results in Table 12.5. The modified example in Table 12.6 brings greater differentiation in the fusion results by introducing some uncertainty in the argument opinions.

Table 12.6 A variation of Zadeh's example applied to belief constraint fusion (BCF), aleatory cumulative belief fusion (A-CBF), epistemic cumulative belief fusion (E-CBF), averaging belief fusion (ABF), weighted belief fusion (WBF) and consensus & compromise fusion (CCF)

	Source opinions:		Fused opinions resulting from applying:					
	A	B	BCF	A-CBF	E-CBF	ABF	WBF	CCF
$b_X(x_1)$ =	0.98	0.00	0.889	0.890	0.880	0.882	0.889	0.089
$b_X(x_2)$ =	0.01	0.01	0.011	0.010	0.000	0.010	0.010	0.010
$b_X(x_3)$ =	0.00	0.90	0.091	0.091	0.081	0.090	0.083	0.009
$b_X(x_1, x_2)$ =	0.00	0.00	0.000	0.000	0.000	0.000	0.000	0.000
$b_X(x_1, x_3)$ =	0.00	0.00	0.000	0.000	0.000	0.000	0.000	0.891
$b_X(x_2, x_3)$ =	0.00	0.00	0.000	0.000	0.000	0.000	0.000	0.000
u_X =	0.01	0.09	0.009	0.009	0.039	0.018	0.018	0.001

Chapter 13
Unfusion and Fission of Subjective Opinions

Given belief fusion as a principle for merging evidence about a domain of interest, it is natural to think of its opposite. However, it is not immediately clear what the opposite of belief fusion might be. From a purely linguistic and semantic point of view, *fission* naturally appears to be the opposite of fusion. As a consequence we define belief fission for subjective opinions below. In addition, we also define *unfusion* for subjective opinions. The two concepts are related but still clearly different. Their interpretations are explained in their respective sections below.

13.1 Unfusion of Opinions

The principle of unfusion [45] is the opposite of fusion, namely to eliminate the contribution of a specific opinion from an already fused opinion, with the purpose of deriving the remaining opinion. This chapter describes cumulative unfusion, as well as averaging unfusion opinions. These operators can for example be applied to remove the contribution of a given real or hypothetical evidence source in order to determine the result of analysing what the situation would have been in the absence of that evidence source. Figure 13.1 illustrates the principle of unfusion.

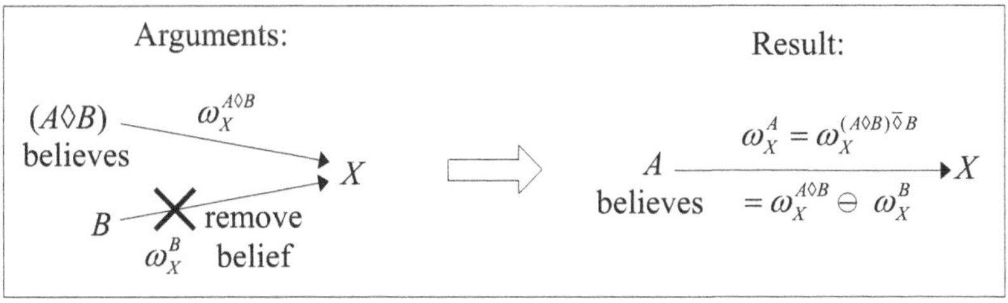

Fig. 13.1 Unfusion operator principle

To divide a fused belief into its contributing belief components is called belief unfusion. This requires the already fused opinion and one of its contributing arguments as input arguments, and produces the complementary contributing argument as output. Unfusion is basically the opposite of fusion, and the formal expressions for unfusion are derived by rearranging the expressions for fusion.

13.1.1 Cumulative Unfusion

Assume a domain $\mathbb{X}$ of cardinality k with hyperdomain $\mathscr{R}(\mathbb{X})$ and associated variable X. Assume two observers A and B who have observed the outcomes of a process over two separate time periods. Assume that the observers' beliefs have been cumulatively fused into $\omega_X^{A \diamond B} = \omega_X^C = (\boldsymbol{b}_X^C, u_X^C, \boldsymbol{a}_X)$, and assume that entity B's contributing opinion $\omega_X^B = (\boldsymbol{b}_X^B, u_X^B, \boldsymbol{a}_X)$ is known.

The cumulative unfusion of these two bodies of evidence is denoted $\omega_X^{C \bar{\diamond} B} = \omega_X^A = \omega_X^C \ominus \omega_X^B$, which represents entity A's contributing opinion. The mathematical expressions for cumulative unfusion are described below.

Definition 13.1 (The Cumulative Unfusion Operator). Let $\omega_X^C = \omega_X^{A \diamond B}$ be the cumulatively fused opinion of ω_X^B and the unknown opinion ω_X^A over the variable X. Let $\omega_X^A = \omega_X^{C \bar{\diamond} B}$ be the opinion such that

$$\text{Case I: For } u_X^C \neq 0 \ \vee \ u_X^B \neq 0:$$

$$\begin{cases} \boldsymbol{b}_X^A(x) = \boldsymbol{b}_X^{C \bar{\diamond} B}(x) = \dfrac{\boldsymbol{b}_X^C(x) u_X^B - \boldsymbol{b}_X^B(x) u_X^C}{u_X^B - u_X^C + u_X^B u_X^C}, \\[2ex] u_X^A = u_X^{C \bar{\diamond} B} = \dfrac{u_X^B u_X^C}{u_X^B - u_X^C + u_X^B u_X^C}, \end{cases} \tag{13.1}$$

$$\text{Case II: For } u_X^C = 0 \ \wedge \ u_X^B = 0:$$

$$\begin{cases} \boldsymbol{b}_X^A(x) = \boldsymbol{b}_X^{C \bar{\diamond} B}(x) = \gamma^B \boldsymbol{b}_X^C(x) - \gamma^C \boldsymbol{b}_X^B(x), \\[1ex] u_X^A = u_X^{C \bar{\diamond} B} = 0, \end{cases} \text{where} \begin{cases} \gamma^B = \displaystyle\lim_{\substack{u_X^C \to 0 \\ u_X^B \to 0}} \dfrac{u_X^B}{u_X^B - u_X^C + u_X^B u_X^C}, \\[2ex] \gamma^C = \displaystyle\lim_{\substack{u_X^C \to 0 \\ u_X^B \to 0}} \dfrac{u_X^C}{u_X^B - u_X^C + u_X^B u_X^C}. \end{cases} \tag{13.2}$$

Then $\omega_X^{C \bar{\diamond} B}$ is called the cumulatively unfused opinion of ω_X^C and ω_X^B, representing the result of eliminating the opinion of B from that of C. By using the symbol '$\ominus$' to designate this belief operator, we define

$$\text{Cumulative unfusion: } \omega_X^{C \bar{\diamond} B} \equiv \omega_X^C \ominus \omega_X^B. \tag{13.3}$$

□

Cumulative unfusion is the inverse of cumulative fusion. The proof and derivation of this is based on rearranging the mathematical expressions of Definition 12.5.

It can be verified that cumulative unfusion is non-commutative, non-associative and non-idempotent. In Case II of Definition 13.1, the unfusion operator is equivalent to the weighted subtraction of probabilities.

13.1.2 Averaging Unfusion

Assume two observers A and B who have observed the same outcomes of a process over the same time period. Assume that the observers' beliefs have been averagely fused into $\omega_X^C = \omega_X^{A \underline{\diamond} B} = (\boldsymbol{b}_X^C, u_X^C, \boldsymbol{a}_X^C)$, and assume that entity B's contributing opinion $\omega_X^B = (\boldsymbol{b}_X^B, u_X^B, \boldsymbol{a}_X^B)$ is known.

The averaging unfusion of these two bodies of evidence is denoted $\omega_X^A = \omega_X^{C \underline{\bar{\diamond}} B} = \omega_X^C \underline{\ominus} \omega_X^B$, which represents entity A's contributing opinion. The mathematical expressions for averaging unfusion are described below.

Definition 13.2 (Averaging Unfusion Operator). Let $\omega_X^C = \omega_X^{A \underline{\diamond} B}$ be the fused average opinion of ω_X^B and the unknown opinion ω_X^A over the variable X. Let $\omega_X^A = \omega_X^{C \underline{\bar{\diamond}} B}$ be the opinion such that

$$\text{Case I: For } u_X^C \neq 0 \ \vee \ u_X^B \neq 0:$$

$$\begin{cases} \boldsymbol{b}_X^A(x) = \boldsymbol{b}_X^{C \underline{\bar{\diamond}} B}(x) = \dfrac{2\boldsymbol{b}_X^C(x) u_X^B - \boldsymbol{b}_X^B(x) u_X^C}{2u_X^B - u_X^C}, \\ u_X^A = u_X^{C \underline{\bar{\diamond}} B} = \dfrac{u_X^B u_X^C}{2u_X^B - u_X^C}, \end{cases} \tag{13.4}$$

$$\text{Case II: For } u_X^C = 0 \ \wedge \ u_X^B = 0:$$

$$\begin{cases} \boldsymbol{b}_x^A = \boldsymbol{b}_X^{C \underline{\bar{\diamond}} B}(x) = \gamma^B \boldsymbol{b}_X^C(x) - \gamma^C \boldsymbol{b}_X^B(x), \\ u_X^A = u_X^{C \underline{\bar{\diamond}} B} = 0, \end{cases} \quad \text{where} \begin{cases} \gamma^B = \lim\limits_{\substack{u_X^C \to 0 \\ u_X^B \to 0}} \dfrac{2u_X^B}{2u_X^B - u_X^C}, \\ \gamma^C = \lim\limits_{\substack{u_X^C \to 0 \\ u_X^B \to 0}} \dfrac{u_X^C}{2u_X^B - u_X^C}. \end{cases} \tag{13.5}$$

(13.6)

Then, $\omega_X^{C \underline{\bar{\diamond}} B}$ is called the average unfused opinion of ω_X^C and ω_X^B, representing the result of eliminating the opinion of B from that of C. By using the symbol '$\underline{\ominus}$' to designate this belief operator, we define

$$\text{Averaging unfusion:} \quad \omega_X^{C \underline{\bar{\diamond}} B} \equiv \omega_X^C \underline{\ominus} \omega_X^B. \tag{13.7}$$

□

Averaging unfusion is the inverse of averaging fusion. The proof and derivation of this is based on rearranging the mathematical expressions of Definition 12.7

It can be verified that the averaging unfusion operator is idempotent, non-commutative and non-associative.

13.1.3 Example: Cumulative Unfusion of Binomial Opinions

Assume that A has an unknown binomial opinion about x. Let B's opinion and the cumulatively fused opinion between A's and B's opinions be specified as

$$\omega_x^{A \diamond B} = (0.90,\ 0.05,\ 0.05,\ 0.50) \text{ and}$$

$$\omega_x^{B} = (0.70,\ 0.10,\ 0.20,\ 0.50)\ .$$

The cumulative unfusion operator can be used to derive A's opinion. By applying the argument opinions to Eq.(13.1) the contributing opinion from A is derived as

$$\omega_x^{A} = (0.91,\ 0.03,\ 0.06,\ 0.50)\ .$$

13.2 Fission of Opinions

Assuming that an opinion can be considered as the actual or virtual result of fusion, there are situations where it could be useful to split it into two separate opinions, and this process is called opinion fission. This operator, which requires an opinion and a fission parameter as input arguments, produces two separate opinions as output. Fission is a form of inverse operation to fusion. The mathematical formulation of fission is described in the following sections.

13.2.1 Cumulative Fission

The principle of opinion fission is a form of opposite operation to opinion fusion. This section describes the fission operator as an opposite form of the cumulative fusion operator described above.

There are an infinite number of ways to split an opinion. The principle followed here is to require an auxiliary fission parameter ϕ to determine how the argument opinion shall be split. As such, opinion fission is a binary operator, i.e. it takes two input arguments, which are the fission parameter and the opinion to be split.

Assume that the opinion $\omega_X^C = (\boldsymbol{b}_X, u_X, \boldsymbol{a}_X)$ over X is held by a real or imaginary entity C.

The fission of ω_X^C consists of splitting ω_X^C into two opinions $\omega_X^{C_1}$ and $\omega_X^{C_2}$ assigned to the (real or imaginary) agents C_1 and C_2, so that $\omega_X^C = \omega_X^{C_1} \oplus \omega_X^{C_2}$. The parameter ϕ determines the relative proportion of belief mass that each new opinion gets. Fission of ω_X^C produces two opinions denoted $\phi \,\mathbb{O}\, \omega_X^C = \omega_X^{C_1}$ and $\overline{\phi} \,\mathbb{O}\, \omega_X^C = \omega_X^{C_2}$. The mathematical expressions for cumulative fission are:

First we map the argument opinion $\omega_X^C = (\boldsymbol{b}_X^C, u_X^C, \boldsymbol{a}_X)$ to the Dirichlet HPDF $\mathrm{Dir}_X^{\mathrm{eH}}(\boldsymbol{p}_X^{\mathrm{H}}, \boldsymbol{r}_X^C, \boldsymbol{a}_X)$ according to the mapping of Definition 3.9. The parameters of this Dirichlet HPDF are linearly split into two parts $\mathrm{Dir}_X^{\mathrm{eH}}(\boldsymbol{p}_X^{\mathrm{H}}, \boldsymbol{r}_X^{C_1}, \boldsymbol{a}_X)$ and $\mathrm{Dir}_X^{\mathrm{eH}}(\boldsymbol{p}_X^{\mathrm{H}}, \boldsymbol{r}_X^{C_2}, \boldsymbol{a}_X)$ as a function of the fission parameter ϕ. These steps produce

$$\mathrm{Dir}_X^{\mathrm{eH}}(\boldsymbol{p}_X^{\mathrm{H}}, \boldsymbol{r}_X^{C_1}, \boldsymbol{a}_X):\begin{cases}\boldsymbol{r}_X^{C_1} = \frac{\phi W \boldsymbol{b}_X^C}{u_X^C}, \\ \\ \boldsymbol{a}_X^{C_1} = \boldsymbol{a}_X\,,\end{cases} \quad \mathrm{Dir}_X^{\mathrm{eH}}(\boldsymbol{p}_X^{\mathrm{H}}, \boldsymbol{r}_X^{C_2}, \boldsymbol{a}_X):\begin{cases}\boldsymbol{r}_X^{C_2} = \frac{(1-\phi) W \boldsymbol{b}_X^C}{u_X^C}, \\ \\ \boldsymbol{a}_X^{C_2} = \boldsymbol{a}_X\,.\end{cases} \tag{13.8}$$

where W denotes the non-informative prior weight.

The reverse mapping of these evidence parameters into two separate opinions according to Definition 3.9 produces the expressions of Definition 13.3 below. As would be expected, the base rate is not affected by fission.

Definition 13.3 (Cumulative Fission Operator).
Cumulative fission of an opinion ω_X^C based on the fission parameter ϕ where $0 < \phi < 1$ produces two opinions $\omega_X^{C_1}$ and $\omega_X^{C_2}$ defined by

$$\omega_X^{C_1}:\begin{cases}\boldsymbol{b}_X^{C_1} = \frac{\phi \boldsymbol{b}_X^C}{u_X^C + \phi \sum_{i=1}^k \boldsymbol{b}_X^C(x_i)}, \\ \\ u_X^{C_1} = \frac{u_X^C}{u_X^C + \phi \sum_{i=1}^k \boldsymbol{b}_X^C(x_i)}, \\ \\ \boldsymbol{a}_X^{C_1} = \boldsymbol{a}_X\,,\end{cases} \quad \omega_X^{C_2}:\begin{cases}\boldsymbol{b}_X^{C_2} = \frac{(1-\phi) \boldsymbol{b}_X^C}{u_X^C + (1-\phi) \sum_{i=1}^k \boldsymbol{b}_X^C(x_i)}, \\ \\ u_X^{C_2} = \frac{u_X^C}{u_X^C + (1-\phi) \sum_{i=1}^k \boldsymbol{b}_X^C(x_i)}, \\ \\ \boldsymbol{a}_X^{C_2} = \boldsymbol{a}_X\,.\end{cases} \tag{13.9}$$

By using the symbol '$\mathbb{O}$' to designate this operator, we define

$$\omega_X^{C_1} = \phi \,\mathbb{O}\, \omega_X^C\,, \tag{13.10}$$

$$\omega_X^{C_2} = \overline{\phi} \,\mathbb{O}\, \omega_X^C\,. \tag{13.11}$$

□

It can be verified that $\omega_X^{C_1} \oplus \omega_X^{C_2} = \omega_X^C$, as expected. In case $\phi = 0$ or $\phi = 1$, one of the resulting opinions will be vacuous, and the other equal to the argument opinion.

13.2.2 Example Fission of Opinion

Consider a ternary domain $\mathbb{X}$ with corresponding variable X and a hyper-opinion ω_X. An analyst wants to split the opinion based on the fission parameter $\phi = 0.75$. Table 13.1 shows the argument opinion as well as the result of the fission operation.

Table 13.1 Example cumulative opinion fission with $\phi = 0.75$

Parameters:		Argument opinion: ω_C^A	Fission result: $\omega_{C_1}^A$	$\omega_{C_2}^A$
belief mass of x_1:	$\boldsymbol{b}(x_1)$	0.20	0.194	0.154
belief mass of x_2:	$\boldsymbol{b}(x_2)$	0.30	0.290	0.230
belief mass of x_3:	$\boldsymbol{b}(x_3)$	0.40	0.387	0.308
uncertainty mass:	u_X	0.10	0.129	0.308
base rate of x_1:	$\boldsymbol{a}(x_1)$	0.10		
base rate of x_2:	$\boldsymbol{a}(x_2)$	0.20		
base rate of x_3:	$\boldsymbol{a}(x_3)$	0.70		
projected prob. of x_1:	$\mathbf{P}(x_1)$	0.21	0.207	0.185
projected prob. of x_2:	$\mathbf{P}(x_1)$	0.32	0.316	0.292
projected prob. of x_3:	$\mathbf{P}(x_1)$	0.47	0.477	0.523

It can be seen that the derived opinion $\omega_{C_1}^A$ contains significantly less uncertainty than $\omega_{C_2}^A$, which means that $\omega_{C_1}^A$ represents the larger evidence base. This is due to the fission parameter $\phi = 0.75$, which dictates the relative proportion of evidence between $\omega_{C_1}^A$ and $\omega_{C_2}^A$ to be 3 : 1.

13.2.3 Averaging Fission

Assume a domain $\mathbb{X}$ and the corresponding variable X. Then assume that the opinion $\omega_X^A = (\boldsymbol{b}_X^A, u_X^A, \boldsymbol{a}_X)$ over X is held by a real or imaginary entity A.

Averaging fission of ω_X^A consists of splitting ω_X^A into two opinions $\omega_X^{A_1}$ and $\omega_X^{A_2}$ assigned to the (real or imaginary) agents A_1 and A_2 so that $\omega_X^A = \omega_X^{A_1} \underline{\oplus} \omega_X^{A_2}$.

It turns out that averaging fission of an opinion trivially produces two opinions that are equal to the argument opinion. This is because the averaging fusion of two equal opinions necessarily produces the same opinion. It would be meaningless to define this operator formally because it is trivial, and because it does not provide a useful model for any interesting practical situation.

Chapter 14
Computational Trust

Subjective logic was originally developed for the purpose of reasoning about trust in information security, such as when analysing trust structures of a PKI (Public-Key Infrastructure) [41]. Subjective logic and its application to this type of computational trust was first proposed in 1997 [40]. The idea of computational trust was originally proposed by Marsh in 1994 [71]. A survey on trust modelling is provided in [12].

The concept of trust is to a large extent a mental and psychological phenomenon which does not correspond to a physical process that can be objectively observed and analysed. For this reason, formal trust models do not have any natural benchmark against which they can be compared and validated. There is thus no single correct formalism for computational trust, so that any formal trust model to a certain extent becomes *ad hoc*. Using subjective logic as a basis for computational trust is therefore just one of several possible approaches.

Computational trust with subjective logic has been a thriving research topic since the first publication in 1997, with subsequent contributions by many different authors. It has the advantage of being intuitively sound and relatively simple, which is important when making practical implementations.

The main SL operators used for computational trust are fusion and trust discounting. Fusion operators are described in Chapter 12. The operator for trust discounting is described in Section 14.3. Trust discounting is the operator for deriving trust or belief from transitive trust paths. Before diving into the mathematical details of trust discounting, the next section introduces the concept of trust from a philosophical perspective.

14.1 The Notion of Trust

Trust is a directional relationship between two parties that can be called *trustor* and *trustee*. One must assume the trustor to be a 'thinking entity' in some form, meaning that it has the ability to make assessments and decisions based on received information and past experience. The trustee can be anything from a person, organisation or physical entity, to abstract notions such as information, propositions or a cryptographic key [39].

A trust relationship has a *scope*, meaning that it applies to a specific purpose or domain of action, such as 'being authentic' in the case of an agent's trust in a cryptographic key, or 'providing reliable information' in the case of a person's trust in the correctness of an entry in Wikipedia. The concept of *trust goal* is sometimes used in the literature [9] with the same meaning as trust scope.

Mutual trust is when both parties trust each other with the same scope, but this is obviously only possible when both parties are cognitive entities capable of doing some form of reliability, risk and policy assessment.

Trust influences the trustor's attitudes and actions, but can also have effects on the trustee and other elements in the environment, for example, by stimulating reciprocal trust [22]. The literature uses the term trust with a variety of different meanings, which often is a source of confusion [74].

Two main interpretations are i) to view trust as the perceived reliability of something or somebody, called *reliability trust*, and ii) to view trust as a decision to enter into a situation of dependence on something or somebody, called *decision trust.* These two different interpretations of trust are explained in the following sections. It can already be mentioned that the notion of trust opinions in subjective logic assumes trust to have the meaning of reliability trust.

14.1.1 Reliability Trust

As the name suggest, reliability trust can be interpreted as the estimated reliability of something or somebody, independently of any actual commitment or decision. The definition by Gambetta (1988) [29] articulates this interpretation.

Definition 14.1 (Reliability Trust). Reliability trust is the subjective belief with which an entity, A, expects that another entity, B, performs a given action on which A's welfare depends. □

In Definition 14.1, trust is interpreted as the trustor's belief regarding the trustee's reliability, in the context of the trustor's potential *dependence* on the trustee. More specifically, the trustor can express the trustee's reliability in terms of a subjective opinion, which thereby becomes a trust opinion.

Assume that an agent A holds a certain belief about an arbitrary variable X, which then represents a belief relationship formally expressed as $[A,X]$, and that agent A also has a level of trust in entity E, which then represents a trust relationship formally expressed as $[A,E]$. A crucial semantic difference between holding a belief about a variable X and having a level of trust in an entity E, is that the trust relationship $[A,E]$ assumes that trustor A potentially or actually is in a situation of dependence on E, whereas the belief relationship $[A,X]$ makes no assumption about dependence.

By *dependence* is meant that the welfare of agent A depends on the performance of E, which A can not accurately predict or control. This uncertainty on the objectives of A means that in case E does not perform as assumed by A, then A would suffer some harm. In general, an agent's uncertainty about reaching objectives is defined as *risk* [36].

The dependence aspect of trust thus creates risk, which is a function of the potential damage resulting from the possible failure of entity E to meet its trust expectations.

Trust opinions are binomial opinions, because they apply to binary variables which naturally can take two values. A general trust domain can be denoted $\mathbb{T} = \{t, \bar{t}\}$, so that a binary random trust variable T can be assumed to take one of these two values with the general meanings:

$$\text{Trust domain } \mathbb{T}: \begin{cases} t: & \text{"The action is performed as expected."} \\ \bar{t}: & \text{"The action is not performed as expected."} \end{cases}$$

Assume that an entity E is trusted to perform a specific action. A binomial trust opinion about E can thus be denoted ω_{t_E}. However, in order to have more direct expressions for trust opinions, we normally use the notation ω_E with the same meaning. This convention is expressed in Eq.(14.1):

$$\text{Equivalent opinion notations for trust in } E\text{:} \quad \omega_E \equiv \omega_{t_E}\,. \tag{14.1}$$

For example, when bank B provides credit to E, it puts itself in a situation of dependence on E, and hence becomes exposed to risk in case E is unable to repay its debt. Trust in target E's creditworthiness can be represented as an opinion on a trust variable T_E which can take values with the following meanings:

$$\text{Trust domain } \mathbb{T}_E: \begin{cases} t_E: & \text{"Entity } E \text{ will pay its debt."} \\ \bar{t}_E: & \text{"Entity } E \text{ will default on its debt."} \end{cases}$$

A binomial opinion about the value t_E is then a trust opinion about E with regard to E's creditworthiness. Bank B's binomial trust opinion about entity E can thus be denoted $\omega^B_{t_E}$. However, for ease of expression, we use the simplified notation ω^B_E according to the notational equivalence of Eq.(14.1).

Subjective opinions about reliability trust fit nicely into the reasoning framework of subjective logic, either as input arguments or as output results. Applying subjective logic to reasoning with trust opinions represents *computational trust*, which is a powerful way of taking subjective aspects of belief reasoning into account. Some SL operators are essential for computational trust, in particular trust discounting described in Section 14.3, and (trust) fusion described in Chapter 12. Trust discounting is used for deriving opinions from transitive trust paths, and trust fusion is used for merging multiple trust paths. In combination, trust discounting and trust fusion form the main building blocks for subjective trust networks, as described in Chapter 15.

14.1.2 Decision Trust

Trust can be interpreted with a more complex meaning than that of reliability trust according to Gambetta's definition. For example, Falcone & Castelfranchi (2001) [23] note that having high (reliability) trust in a person is not necessarily sufficient for deciding to enter into a situation of dependence on that person. They write:

> *"For example it is possible that the value of the damage per se (in case of failure) is too high to choose a given decision branch, and this independently either from the probability of the failure (even if it is very low) or from the possible payoff (even if it is very high). In other words, that danger might seem to the agent an intolerable risk."* [23]

To illustrate the difference between reliability trust and decision trust with a practical example, first consider the situation of a fire drill, where participants are asked to abseil from the third-floor window of a house using a rope. Assume that during the fire drill, the participants find the rope to be in a state of severe deterioration. In this situation, the participants would naturally assess the probability that the rope will hold them while abseiling to be relatively low.

Let R denote the rope, and assume the binary trust domain $\mathbb{T}_R = \{t_R, \bar{t}_R\}$ where the values have the following meanings:

$$\text{Trust domain } \mathbb{T}_R : \begin{cases} t_R : & \text{“The rope will hold me while I'm abseiling down.”} \\ \bar{t}_R : & \text{“The rope will break if I try to abseil down.”} \end{cases}$$

Person A's reliability trust in the rope can then be expressed as the binomial opinion $\omega^A_{t_R}$, but the simplified notation ω^A_R is normally used according to Eq.(14.1).

If person A thinks that the rope will break, she will express this in the form of a binomial opinion ω^A_R with a disbelief parameter d^A_R close to 1.0, to express distrust in the rope R, and will most likely refuse to use it for abseiling. The fire drill situation is illustrated on the left side of Figure 14.1.

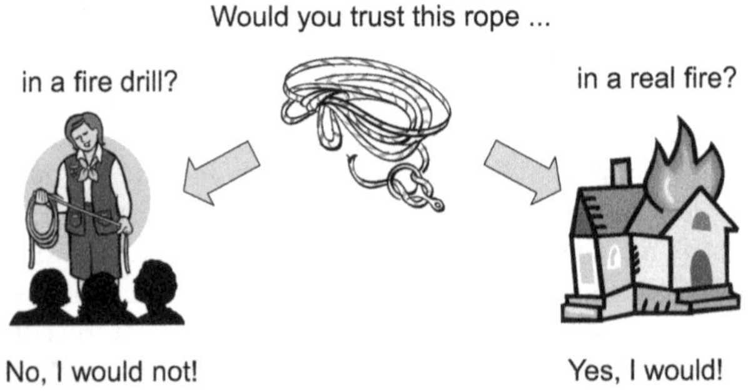

Would you trust this rope ...
in a fire drill?
in a real fire?
No, I would not!
Yes, I would!

Fig. 14.1 Same reliability trust, but different decision trust

Imagine now that the same person is trapped in a real fire, and that the only escape is to abseil from the third-floor window using the same old rope. It is assumed that the trust opinion ω_R^A is the same as before. However, in this situation it is likely that person A would decide to 'trust' the rope for abseiling down, even if she thinks it is possible that it could break. The trust decision has thus changed, even though the reliability trust opinion is unchanged. This paradox is easily explained by the fact that here we are talking about two different types of trust, namely *reliability trust* and *decision trust*.

The change in trust decision is perfectly rational because the likelihood of injury or death while abseiling is assessed against the likelihood of smoke suffocation and death by fire. Although the reliability trust in the rope is the same in both situations, the decision trust changes as a function of the comparatively different utility values associated with the different courses of action in the two situations. This decision situation could be modelled with the formalism of Chapter 4. The following definition captures the concept of decision trust.

Definition 14.2 (Decision Trust). Decision trust is the commitment to depend on something or somebody in a given situation with a feeling of relative security, even though negative consequences are possible (inspired by McKnight and Chervany (1996) [74]). □

In Definition 14.2, trust is primarily interpreted as the commitment to actually rely on a given object, and specifically includes the notions of *dependence* on the trustee, and its *reliability* and *risk*. In addition, Definition 14.2 implicitly also covers situational elements such as *utility* (of possible outcomes), *environmental factors* (law enforcement, contracts, security mechanisms etc.) and *risk attitude* (risk-taking, risk-averse etc.).

Both reliability trust and decision trust reflect a positive belief about something on which the trustor depends for its welfare. Reliability trust is most naturally measured as a probability or opinion about reliability, whereas decision trust is most naturally measured in terms of a binary decision based on multiple factors [50]. While most trust and reputation models assume reliability trust, decision trust can also modelled. Systems based on decision trust models should also be considered as decision support tools.

The difficulty of capturing the notion of trust in formal models in a meaningful way has led some economists to reject it as a computational concept. The strongest expression of this view has been given by Williamson (1993) [99] who argues that the notion of trust should be avoided when modelling economic interactions, because it adds nothing new, and that well-studied notions such as reliability, utility and risk are adequate and sufficient for that purpose. Personal trust is the only type of trust that can be meaningful for describing interactions, according to Williamson. He argues that personal trust applies to emotional and personal interactions such as love relationships, where mutual performance is not always monitored and where failures are forgiven rather than sanctioned. In that sense, traditional computational models would be inadequate, e.g. because of insufficient data and inadequate sanctioning, but also because it would be detrimental to the relationships if the involved parties were to take a computational approach. Non-computational models for trust can be meaningful for studying such relationships according to Williamson, but developing such models should be done within the domains of sociology and psychology, rather than in economics.

In the light of Williamson's view on modelling trust, it becomes important to judge the purpose and merit of computational trust itself. Can computational trust add anything new and valuable to the Internet technology and economy? The answer, in our opinion, is definitely yes. The value of computational trust lies in the architectures and mechanisms for collecting trust-relevant information, for efficient, reliable and secure processing, for distribution of derived trust and reputation scores, and for taking this information into account when navigating the Internet and making decisions about online activities and transactions. Economic models for risk taking and decision making are abstract, and do not address how to build trust networks and reputation systems. Computational trust specifically addresses how to build such systems, and can be combined with economic modelling whenever relevant and useful.

14.1.3 Reputation and Trust

The concept of reputation is closely linked to that of trustworthiness, but it is evident that there is a clear and important difference. For the purpose of this study, we define reputation according to Merriam-Webster's online dictionary [75].

Definition 14.3 (Reputation). The common opinion that people have about someone or something: the way in which people think of someone or something. □

This definition corresponds well with the view of social network researchers [28, 70] that reputation is a quantity derived from the underlying social network which is globally visible to all members of the network. The difference between trust and reputation can be illustrated by the following perfectly normal and plausible statements:

1. *"I trust you because of your good reputation."*

2. *"I trust you despite your bad reputation."*

Assuming that both statements relate to the same trust scope, statement 1) reflects that the relying party is aware of the trustee's reputation, and bases his trust on that. Statement 2) reflects that the relying party has some private knowledge about the trustee, e.g. through direct experience or intimate relationship, and that these factors overrule any (negative) reputation that the person might have. This observation reflects that trust ultimately is a personal and subjective phenomenon that is based on various factors or evidence, and that some of these carry more weight than others. Personal experience typically carries more weight than second-hand trust referrals or reputation, but in the absence of personal experience, trust often has to be based on referrals from others.

Reputation can be considered as a collective measure of trustworthiness (in the sense of reliability) based on the referrals or ratings from members in a community. An individual's subjective trust can be derived from a combination of received referrals and personal experience.

Reputation can relate to a group or to an individual. A group's reputation can for example be modelled as the average of all its members' individual reputations, or as the average of how the group is perceived as a whole by external parties. Tadelis' (2001) [96] study shows that an individual belonging to a given group will inherit an *a priori* reputation based on that group's reputation. If the group is reputable, all its individual members will *a priori* be perceived as reputable, and vice versa.

Reputation systems are automated systems for generating reputation scores about products or services. Reputation systems are based on receiving feedback and ratings from users about their satisfaction with products or services with which they have had direct experience, and uses the ratings and the feedback to derive reputation scores. Reputation systems are widely used on e-commerce platforms, online social networks and in Web 2.0 applications in general.

Evidence opinions, where the number of observations are explicitly represented, are well suited as the basis for computation in reputation systems. Feedback can be represented as an observation, and can be merged using the cumulative fusion operator described in Section 12.3. This type of reputation computation engine is called a *Bayesian reputation system* because it is based on Bayesian statistics through Beta and Dirichlet PDFs. Chapter 16 describes the principles and building blocks of Bayesian reputation systems.

14.2 Trust Transitivity

The formalism for computational trust described in the following sections assumes that trust is interpreted as *reliability trust* according to Definition 14.1. Based on the assumption that reliability trust is a form of belief, degrees of trust can be expressed as trust opinions.

14.2.1 Motivating Example for Transitive Trust

We constantly make choices and decisions based on trust. As a motivating example, let us assume that Alice has trouble with her car, so she needs to get it fixed by a car mechanic. Assume further that Alice has recently moved to the town, and therefore has no experience with having her car serviced in that town. Bob, who is one of her colleagues at work, has lived in the town for many years. When Alice's car broke down, Bob gave her a lift with his car. Alice noticed that Bob's car was well maintained, so she intuitively trusts Bob in matters of car maintenance. Bob tells her that he usually gets his car serviced by a car mechanic named Eric, and that based on direct experience, Eric seems to be a very skilled car mechanic. As a result, Bob has direct trust in Eric. Bob advices her to get her car fixed at Eric's garage. Based on her trust in Bob in matters of car maintenance, and on Bob's advice, Alice develops trust in Eric too. Alice's newly derived trust in Eric is *indirect*, because it is not based on direct experience. Still, it is genuine trust that helps Alice to make a decision about where to get her car fixed.

This example represents trust transitivity, in the sense that Alice trusts Bob who trusts Eric, so that Alice also trusts Eric. This assumes that Bob actually tells Alice that he trusts Eric, which from Alice's perspective is a received *advice opinion* or recommendation. This is illustrated in Figure 14.2, where the indexes indicate the order in which the trust relationships and advices are formed.

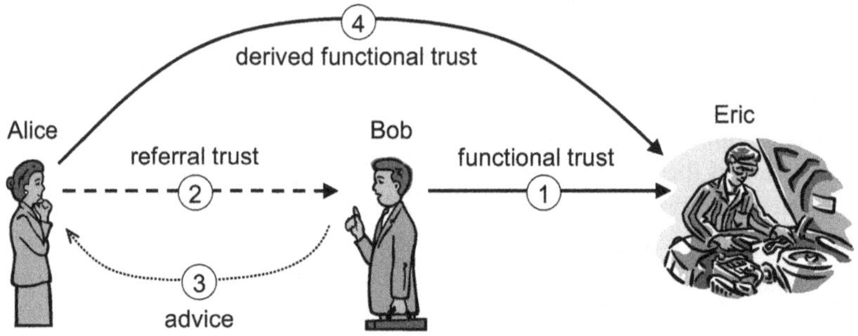

Fig. 14.2 Transitive trust principle

Trust is not always transitive [15]. For example, assume that Alice would trust Bob to look after her child, and that Bob trusts Eric to fix his car, then this does not imply that Alice trusts Eric to look after her child. However, when certain semantic requirements are satisfied [52], trust can be transitive, and a trust system can be used to derive trust. For example, every trust edge along a transitive chain must share the same trust scope. When trying to combine trust about baby-sitting and car mechanics, trust transitivity collapses because the trust scopes are non-overlapping. These semantic requirements for trust transitivity are described in Section 14.2.5 below.

The example above seems to indicate some sort of binary trust between the agents in the transitive chain. In realistic situations reliability trust is usually not just binary, and many researchers have proposed to measure trust in terms of multiple discrete levels (e.g. verbal statements), probabilities or other continuous scales. When applying computation to such trust measures, intuition dictates that trust should be weakened or less confident through transitivity. Revisiting the above example, this means that Alice's derived trust in the car mechanic Eric through the advisor Bob can be at most as strong or confident as Bob's trust in Eric. How trust strength and confidence should be formally represented depends on the particular formalism used.

In some situations it is reasonable to argue that negative trust in an advisor can have the paradoxical effect of strengthening the derived trust in the target entity. This model is based on the principle that *the enemy of my enemy is my friend*. Take for example the case where Alice distrusts Bob, and Bob says that he distrusts Eric. In this situation, it might be reasonable for Alice to derive positive trust in Eric, because she might think: *"In reality Bob thinks that Eric is a good mechanic, but he doesn't want me to know it. Bob is trying to trick me, that's why he gives me a negative recommendation about Eric."*

The question of how transitivity of distrust should be interpreted can quickly become very complex, because it can involve multiple levels of deception. Models based on this type of reasoning have received little attention in the trust and reputation systems literature, and it might be argued that the study of such models belongs to the intelligence analysis discipline, rather than online trust management. However, the fundamental issues and problems are the same in both disciplines.

The safe and conservative approach to trust transitivity is to assume that distrust in a node that forms part of a transitive trust path should contribute to reduced confidence in the opinion about the target entity or variable. This is also the approach taken by the trust-discounting operator described in Section 14.3.

14.2.2 Referral Trust and Functional Trust

With reference to the previous example, it is important to distinguish between trust in the ability to give advice about a good car mechanic, which represents *referral trust*, and trust in actually being a good car mechanic, which represents *functional trust*. The scope of the trust is nevertheless the same, namely "to be a good car mechanic". Assuming that Bob has demonstrated to Alice that he is knowledgeable in matters relating to car maintenance, Alice's referral trust in Bob for the purpose of recommending a good car mechanic can be considered to be *direct*. Assuming that Eric on several occasions has proven to Bob that he is a good mechanic, Bob's functional trust in Eric can also be considered to be direct. Thanks to Bob's advice, Alice also trusts Eric to actually be a good mechanic. However, this functional trust must be considered to be *indirect*, because Alice has not directly observed or experienced Eric's skills in servicing and repairing cars.

The concept of 'referral trust' represents a type of belief/trust relationships that comes in addition to belief relationships and functional trust relationships. The list of all three types of belief/trust relationships is given in Table 14.1, which extends Table 3.1 on p.19.

Table 14.1 Notation for belief, functional trust and referral trust relationships

Nr.	Relationship type	Formal notation	Graph edge notation	Interpretation
1	Belief	$[A,X]$	$A \longrightarrow X$	A has an opinion on variable X
2	Functional trust	$[A,E]$	$A \longrightarrow E$	A has a functional trust opinion on entity E
3	Referral trust	$[A;B]$	$A \dashrightarrow B$	A has a referral trust opinion on entity B

14.2.3 Notation for Transitive Trust

Table 14.1 specifies the notation for representing simple belief and trust relationships, where each relationship is represented by an edge. Transitive trust paths are formed by joining adjacent edges with the transitivity symbol ':', which e.g. can be interpreted as a linked chain. For example the transitive trust path of Figure 14.2 can be formally expressed as

$$\text{Notation for transitive trust in Figure 14.2}: \quad [A,E] = [A;B] : [B,E]. \qquad (14.2)$$

The referral trust edge from A to B is thus denoted $[A;B]$ where the semicolon ';' represents a referral trust relationship. The functional trust edge from B to E is denoted $[B,E]$ where the comma ',' represents a belief or functional trust relationship. The serial/transitive connection of the two trust edges produces the derived functional trust edge $[A,E]$.

The mathematics for computing derived trust opinions resulting from subjective trust networks such as in Figure 14.2 and expressed by Eq.(14.2) is given by the trust-discounting operator described in Section 14.3 below.

Let us slightly extend the example, wherein Bob does not actually know any car mechanics himself, but he trusts Claire, whom he believes knows a good car mechanic. As it happens, Claire is happy to give a positive advice about Eric to Bob, which Bob passes on as an advice to Alice. As a result of transitivity, Alice is able to derive trust in Eric, as illustrated in Figure 14.3.

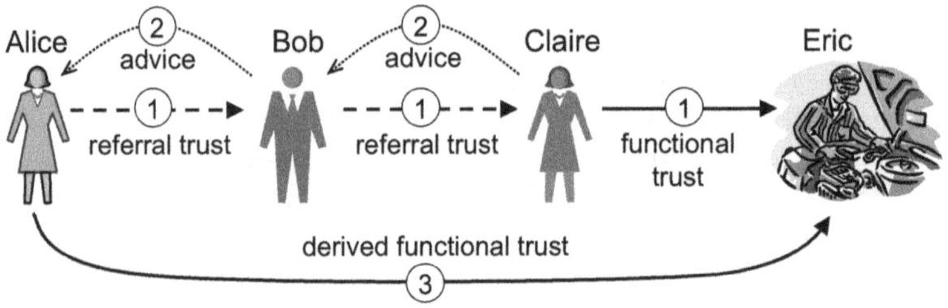

Fig. 14.3 Trust derived through transitivity

This clearly illustrates that referral trust in this example is about the ability to give advice about mechanics who can fix cars, and that functional trust in this example is about the ability to actually fix cars. *"To be skilled at fixing cars"* represents the scope of the trust relationships in this example.

Formal notation of the graph of Figure 14.3 is given in Eq.(14.3):

$$\text{Transitive trust path notation:} \quad [A,E] = [A;B] : [B;C] : [C,E]. \tag{14.3}$$

The functional trust for the example of Figure 14.3 can be represented by the binomial opinion ω^C_E, which then expresses C's level of functional trust in entity E. The equivalent notation $\omega^C_{t_E}$ makes explicit the belief in the trustworthiness of E expressed as the variable value t_E, where high belief mass assigned to t_E means that C has high trust in E.

Similarly, the opinion ω^A_B expresses A's referral trust in B, with equivalent notation $\omega^A_{t_B}$, where the statement t_B e.g. is interpreted as t_B : *"Entity B can provide good advice about car mechanics"*.

14.2.4 Compact Notation for Transitive Trust Paths

A transitive trust path consists of a set of trust edges representing chained trust relationships. Note that two adjacent trust edges repeat the name of a node connecting the two edges together. For example, the node name B appears twice in the notation of the trust path $[A;B] : [B;C]$.

This notation can be simplified by omitting repeated naming of nodes, and by representing consecutive edges as a single multi-edge path. By using this principle, the compact notation for the transitive trust path of Figure 14.3 emerges, as given in Eq.(14.4), which also shows the corresponding equivalent full notation:

$$\text{Equivalent trust path notations:} \quad \underset{\text{Compact:}}{\overline{[A;B;C,E]}} \equiv \underset{\text{Full:}}{\overline{[A;B] : [B;C] : [C,E]}}. \tag{14.4}$$

The advantage of the compact notation is precisely that it is more compact than the full notation, resulting in simpler expressions. We sometimes use the compact notation in our description of trust networks below.

14.2.5 Semantic Requirements for Trust Transitivity

The difference between functional and referral trust might seem subtle. The interpretation of referral trust is that Alice trusts Bob to give advice about somebody (who can give advice about somebody etc.) who can give advice about car mechanics. At the same time, referral trust always assumes the existence of functional trust or belief at the end of the transitive path, which in this example is about being a good car mechanic.

The 'referral' variant of a trust can be considered to be recursive, so that any transitive trust chain, with arbitrary length, can be expressed. This principle is captured by the following criterion.

Definition 14.4 (Functional Trust Derivation Criterion). Derivation of functional trust through referral trust requires that the last trust edge represents functional trust/belief, and all previous trust edges represent referral trust. □

In practical situations, a trust scope can be characterised by being general or specific. For example, knowing how to change wheels on a car is more specific than being a good car mechanic; the former scope is a subset of the latter. Whenever the functional trust scope is equal to, or a subset of the referral trust scopes, it is possible to form transitive paths. This can be expressed with the following consistency criterion.

Definition 14.5 (Trust Scope Consistency Criterion). A valid transitive trust path requires that the trust scope of the functional (and thereby the last) trust/belief edge in the path is in the intersection of the scopes of all previous referral trust edges in the path. □

Trivially, every trust edge can have the same trust scope. Transitive trust propagation is thus possible with functional and referral trust edges based on a single trust scope.

A transitive trust path stops at the first functional trust edge encountered. It is, of course, possible for a principal to have both functional and referral trust in another principal, but that should be expressed as two separate trust edges. The existence of both a functional and a referral trust edge, e.g. from Claire to Eric, should be interpreted as Claire having trust in Eric, not only to be a good car mechanic, but also to give advice about other car mechanics.

14.3 The Trust-Discounting Operator

Trust can be considered to be a particular kind of belief. In that sense, trust can be modelled as an opinion that can be used as an input argument, or that can be the output results, in reasoning models based on subjective logic. We use the term *trust opinion* to denote trust represented as a subjective opinion.

14.3.1 Principle of Trust Discounting

The general idea behind trust discounting is to express degrees of trust in an information source and then to discount information provided by that source as a function of the trust in the source. We represent both the trust and the provided information in the form of subjective opinions, and then define an appropriate operation on these opinions to find the trust-discounted opinion.

Let agent A denote the relying party and agent B denote an information source which can be an agent providing an advice opinion or a sensor producing data which can be translated into an opinion. Assume that source B provides information to agent A about the state of a variable X expressed as a subjective opinion on X. Assume further that agent A has an opinion on the trustworthiness of B with regard to providing information about X, i.e. the trust scope is to provide information about X. Based on the combination of A's trust in B, as well as on B's opinion about X received by A, it is possible for A to derive an opinion about X. This process is illustrated in Figure 14.4.

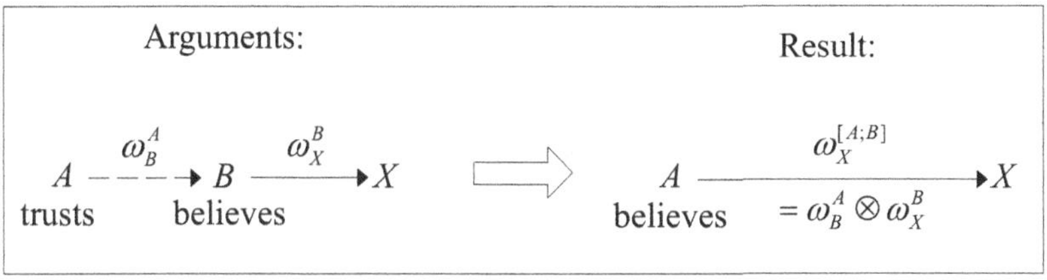

Fig. 14.4 Trust discounting of opinions

Several trust-discounting operators for subjective logic are described in the literature [54, 57]. The general representation of trust discounting is through conditionals [57], while special cases can be expressed with specific trust-discounting operators. In this book we describe *probability-sensitive trust discounting*, which causes the uncertainty in A's derived opinion about X to increase as a function of the projected *distrust* in the source/advisor B. The probability-sensitive trust-discounting operator is described next.

14.3.2 Trust Discounting with Two-Edge Paths

Agent A's referral trust in B can be formally expressed as a binomial opinion on domain $\mathbb{T}_B = \{t_B, \bar{t}_B\}$, where the values t_B and $\bar{t}_B$ denote *trusted* and *distrusted* respectively. We simply denote this opinion by $\omega_B^A = (b_B^A, d_B^A, u_B^A, a_B^A)$. Recall that according to Eq.(14.1), an equivalent notation for this opinion is $\omega_{t_B}^A = (b_{t_B}^A, d_{t_B}^A, u_{t_B}^A, a_{t_B}^A)$, but for practical reasons we use the simplified notation here. The parameters b_B^A, d_B^A and u_B^A express the degrees to which A trusts, does not trust or is uncertain about the trustworthiness of B in the current instance, while a_B^A is a base rate probability that A would assign to the trustworthiness of B *a priori*, before receiving the opinion ω_X^B from B.

Definition 14.6 (Probability-Sensitive Trust Discounting for Two-Edge Path). Assume agents A and B, where A has referral trust in B for a trust scope represented by domain $\mathbb{X}$. Let X denote a variable on domain $\mathbb{X}$, and let $\omega_X^B = (\boldsymbol{b}_X^B, u_X^B, \boldsymbol{a}_X^B)$ be agent B's general opinion on X as advised by B to A. Assume further that agent A's referral trust in B, with respect to advising belief about X, is expressed as ω_B^A. The notation for trust discounting is given by

$$\omega_X^{[A;B]} = \omega_B^A \otimes \omega_X^B \,. \tag{14.5}$$

The trust-discounting operator combines agent A's referral trust opinion about agent B, denoted ω_B^A, to discount B's opinion about variable X, denoted ω_X^B, to produce A's derived opinion about X, denoted $\omega_X^{[A;B]}$. The parameters of the derived opinion $\omega_X^{[A;B]}$ are defined in the following way:

$$\omega_X^{[A;B]}: \begin{cases} \boldsymbol{b}_X^{[A;B]}(x) &= \mathbf{P}_B^A\, \boldsymbol{b}_X^B(x), \\ u_X^{[A;B]} &= 1 - \mathbf{P}_B^A \sum\limits_{x\in\mathscr{R}(\mathbb{X})} \boldsymbol{b}_X^B(x), \\ \boldsymbol{a}_X^{[A;B]}(x) &= \boldsymbol{a}_X^B(x). \end{cases} \tag{14.6}$$

□

Figure 14.5 illustrates the effect of the trust-discounting operator. The example analyses the simple trust network of Eq.(14.7):

$$A \dashrightarrow B \longrightarrow X \,, \tag{14.7}$$

where agent A trusts agent B who in turn has an opinion about X. Let A's trust in B be denoted ω_B^A and let B's opinion about X be denoted ω_X^B. With ω_B^A and ω_X^B as input arguments Eq.(14.6) produces A's derived opinion about X denoted $\omega_X^{[A;B]}$.

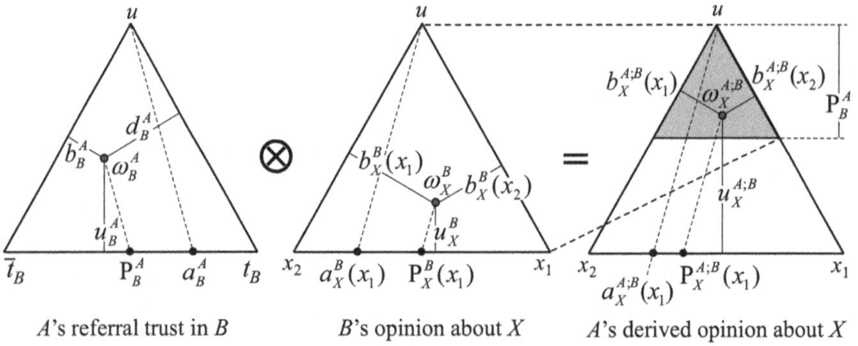

Fig. 14.5 Probability-sensitive trust discounting

The numerical opinions are summarised in Eq.(14.8):

$$\omega_B^A : \begin{cases} b_B^A = 0.20, \\ d_B^A = 0.40, \\ u_B^A = 0.40, \\ a_B^A = 0.75, \\ \mathrm{P}_B^A = 0.50, \end{cases} \quad \omega_X^B : \begin{cases} \boldsymbol{b}_X^B(x_1) = 0.45, \\ \boldsymbol{b}_X^B(x_2) = 0.35, \\ u_X^B \quad = 0.20, \\ \boldsymbol{a}_X^B(x_1) = 0.25, \\ \mathbf{P}_X^B(x_1) = 0.50, \end{cases} \quad \omega_X^{[A;B]} : \begin{cases} \boldsymbol{b}_X^{[A;B]}(x_1) = 0.225, \\ \boldsymbol{b}_X^{[A;B]}(x_2) = 0.175, \\ u_X^{[A;B]} \quad = 0.600, \\ \boldsymbol{a}_X^{[A;B]}(x_1) = 0.250, \\ \mathbf{P}_X^{[A;B]}(x_1) = 0.375. \end{cases} \tag{14.8}$$

The trust-discounted opinion $\omega_X^{[A;B]}$ typically gets increased uncertainty mass, compared to the original opinion advised by B, where the increase of uncertainty mass is dictated by the projected probability of the referral trust opinion ω_B^A. Trust discounting follows the principle that the smaller the projected probability P_B^A, the greater the uncertainty mass of the derived opinion ω_B^A.

Figure 14.5 illustrates the general behaviour of the probability-sensitive trust-discounting operator, where the derived opinion is constrained to the shaded sub-triangle at the top of the right-most triangle. The height of the shaded sub-triangle corresponds to the projected probability of trust in the trust opinion. The effect of this is that the barycentric representation of ω_X^B is shrunk proportionally to P_B^A, to become a barycentric opinion representation inside the shaded sub-triangle.

Some special cases are worth mentioning. In case the projected trust probability equals one, which means complete trust in the source, the relying party fully accepts the received trust/belief opinion, meaning that the derived opinion is equal to the received opinion. In case the projected trust probability equals zero, which means complete distrust in the source, the received opinion is discounted to become a vacuous opinion, meaning that the received opinion is completely discarded.

It can be mentioned that the trust-discounting operator described above is a special case of the general trust-discounting operator for deriving opinions from arbitrarily long trust paths, as expressed by Definition 14.7 below.

14.3.3 Example: Trust Discounting of Restaurant Advice

The following example illustrates how trust discounting is applied intuitively in real situations.

Let us assume that Alice goes on holiday to a city in foreign country, and that she would like to have dinner at a restaurant where the locals go, because she wants to avoid places overrun by tourists. Alice's impression is that it is hard to find a good restaurant, and guesses that only about 20% of the restaurants could be characterised as good. She would of course like to find the best one, as seen by the locals. While walking around the city she meets a local called Bob, who tells her that restaurant Xylo is the favourite place of locals.

We assume that Bob is a stranger to Alice, so that *a priori* her trust in Bob is affected by high uncertainty. However, it is enough for Alice to assume that locals in general give good advice, which translates into a high base rate for her trust in the advice from locals. Even if her trust in Bob is vacuous, a high base rate will result in a strong projected probability of trust. Assuming that Bob gives a very positive advice about Xylo, Alice will derive a positive opinion about the restaurant based on Bob's advice.

This example situation can be translated into numbers. Figure 14.6 is a screenshot of the online demonstrator for subjective logic trust discounting, with arguments that are plausible for the example of the restaurant advice.

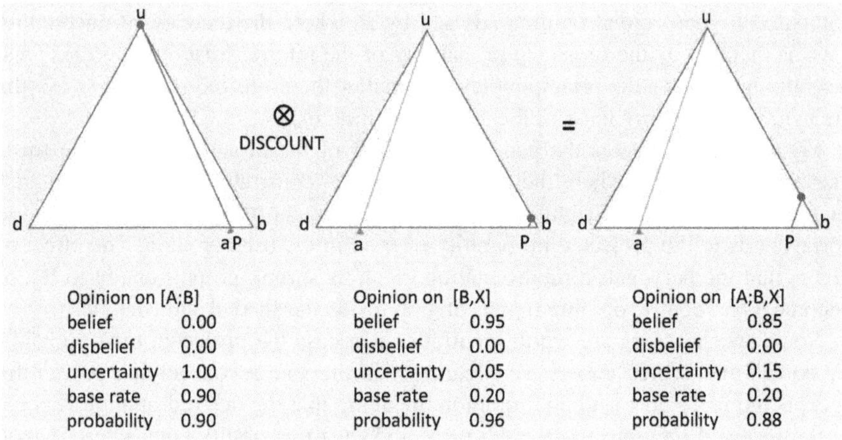

Fig. 14.6 Example trust discounting of restaurant advice

As a result of the advice, Alice becomes quite convinced that Xylo is the right place to go, and intends to have dinner at Xylo in the evening.

However, if Alice receives a second and contradictory piece of advice, her trust in Xylo could drop dramatically, so she might change her mind. This scenario is described in an extended version of this example in Section 14.5.3 below.

The next section describes how transitive trust paths longer that two edges can be analysed.

14.3.4 Trust Discounting for Multi-edge Path

Trust discounting described in Definition 14.6 describes how trust discounting is performed for a trust path consisting of only two adjacent edges, but does not say how it should be computed for longer trust paths. The method for computing transitive trust in case three or more edges are chained is described below.

Consider the graph of Eq.(14.9) which expresses a trust path from node A_1 to node X via an arbitrary number of intermediate nodes $A_2, \ldots A_n$:

$$\text{Multi-edge trust graph: } (A_1 \longrightarrow X) = (A_1 \dashrightarrow A_2 \dashrightarrow \ldots A_n \longrightarrow X)\,. \tag{14.9}$$

The derived functional belief edge $[A_1,X]$ of Eq.(14.9) can be formally expressed in different equivalent forms:

$$\begin{aligned}
&\text{Full formal notation:} && [A_1,X] = [A_1;A_2] : [A_2;A_3] : \ \ldots\ [A_n,X],\\
&\text{Compact trust path notation:} && [A_1,X] = [A_1;A_2;\ \ldots\ A_n,X],\\
&\text{Separate referral and functional:} && [A_1,X] = [A_1;\ \ldots\ A_n] : [A_n,X],\\
&\text{Short notation with separation:} && [A_1,X] = [A_1;A_n] : [A_n,X].
\end{aligned} \tag{14.10}$$

The multi-edge transitive trust path of Eq.(14.9) consists of a leading *referral trust path* and a terminating *functional trust/belief edge* which can be expressed as

$$\text{Referral trust path: } [A_1;\ \ldots\ A_n], \tag{14.11}$$

$$\text{Functional trust/belief edge: } [A_n,X]. \tag{14.12}$$

Let each edge have assigned an opinion, where the inter-agent trust opinions are denoted $\omega^{A_i}_{A_{(i+1)}}$, and the functional opinion at the end of the path is denoted $\omega^{A_n}_X$. All inter-agent opinions represent referral trust, whereas the opinion on the terminating edge represents functional belief.

The projected probability of the referral trust path $[A_1;A_n]$ is computed as

$$\text{Referral Trust Projected Probability: } \mathrm{P}^{A_1}_{A_n} = \prod_{i=1}^{n-1} \mathrm{P}^{A_i}_{A_{i+1}}\,. \tag{14.13}$$

Trust discounting with an arbitrarily long referral trust path is defined as a function of the referral trust projected probability of Eq.(14.13).

Definition 14.7 (Trust Discounting for Multi-edge Paths).

Assume a transitive trust path consisting of chained trust edges between n agents denoted $A_1,\ldots,A_n$, followed by a terminal trust/belief edge between the last agent A_n and the target node X, where the goal is to derive an opinion on the edge between the first agent A_1 and the target X. The parameters of the derived opinion $\omega_X^{A_1}$ are defined in the following way:

$$\omega_X^{A_1} : \begin{cases} \boldsymbol{b}_X^{A_1}(x) & = \mathrm{P}_{A_n}^{A_1} \boldsymbol{b}_X^{A_n}(x), \\ u_X^{A_1} & = 1 - \mathrm{P}_{A_n}^{A_1} \sum\limits_{x \in \mathscr{R}(\mathbb{X})} \boldsymbol{b}_X^{A_n}(x), \\ \boldsymbol{a}_X^{A_1}(x) & = \boldsymbol{a}_X^{B}(x) \end{cases} \tag{14.14}$$

□

The principle of multi-edge trust discounting is to take the projected probabilities of the referral trust part expressed by Eq.(14.13) as a measure of the trust network reliability. This reliability measure is then used to discount the advised functional opinion $\omega_X^{A_n}$ of the final belief edge $[A_n, X]$.

Note that transitive referral trust computation described here is computed similarly to serial reliability of components in a system, as described in Section 7.2. The difference is that in the case of serial reliability analysis, the subjective logic multiplication operator described in Chapter 7 is used, whereas for subjective trust networks, the simple product of projected probabilities is used. More precisely, the trust-discounting operator uses the serial product of projected probabilities as one of the input arguments.

In case every referral trust opinion has projected probability $\mathrm{P}_{A_{i+1}}^{A_i} = 1$, then the product referral trust projected probability also equals 1, so that the derived opinion $\omega_X^{A_1}$ is equal to the received advice opinion $\omega_X^{A_n}$. In case any of the referral trust relationships has projected probability $\mathrm{P}_{A_{i+1}}^{A_i} = 0$, then the product referral trust projected probability is also zero, hence the derived opinion $\omega_X^{A_1}$ becomes vacuous.

Note that the operator for deriving opinions from arbitrarily long trust paths described here is a generalisation of the two-edge trust-discounting operator described by Definition 14.6 above.

As an example consider the trust network expressed as

$$\begin{aligned} [A,X] &= [A;B] : [B;C] : [C;D] : [D,X] \\ &= [A;B;C;D,X] \\ &= [A;B;C;D] : [D,X] = [A;D] : [D,X]. \end{aligned} \tag{14.15}$$

Table 14.2 provides example opinions for the trust path of Eq.(14.15), and shows the result of the trust-discounting computation. It is assumed that X is binary and that ω_X is expressed in the binomial form.

Table 14.2 Example trust discounting in multi-edge path

Parameters:		Argument opinions: ω^A_B	ω^B_C	ω^C_D	ω^D_X	Product: P^A_D	Derived: $\omega_X^{[A;D]}$
belief:	b	0.20	0.20	0.20	0.80		0.35
disbelief:	d	0.10	0.10	0.10	0.20		0.09
uncertainty:	u	0.70	0.70	0.70	0.00		0.56
base rate:	a	0.80	0.80	0.80	0.10		0.10
projected prob.:	P	0.76	0.76	0.76	0.80	0.44	0.41

Although each referral trust edge has relatively high projected probability, their product quickly drops to a relatively low value as expressed by $\mathrm{P}^A_D = 0.44$. The trust-discounted opinion $\omega_X^{[A;D]}$ therefore becomes highly uncertain.

This result reflects the intuition that a long path of indirect trust quickly becomes useless, because functional trust derived from it becomes too uncertain.

It is worth asking the question whether a trust path longer than a few edges can be practical. In everyday contexts, we rarely rely on trust paths longer than a couple of edges. For example, few people would put much faith in an advice delivered like this: *"A colleague of mine told me that his sister has a friend who knows a good car mechanic, so why don't you take your car to his garage?!"*

People naturally become suspicious about the veracity of information or advice in situations with a high degree of separation between themselves and the original source of information about the target X, because we often see how information gets distorted when passed from person to person through many hops. This is because we humans are quite unreliable agents, with regard to truthful representation and forwarding of information that we receive.

However, computer systems are able to correctly propagate information through multiple nodes with high reliability. The application of trust transitivity through long chains therefore seems to be better suited for computer networks than for human social networks.

MANETs (Mobile Ad-Hoc Networks) and sensor networks represent a type of computer networks in which multiple nodes depend on each other for service provision. A typical characteristic of such networks is the uncertain reliability of each node, as well as the lack of control by one node over other nodes. Transitive trust computation with subjective logic is therefore highly relevant for MANETs and sensor networks, even in case of long trust paths.

14.4 Trust Fusion

It is common to collect information from several sources in order to be better informed, e.g when making decisions. In case of opinions this can be called *trust fusion*, meaning that the derived opinions resulting from separate trust paths are fused into one.

Let us continue the example of Alice who needs to have her car serviced, where she has received an advice from Bob to use the car mechanic Eric. This time we assume that Alice has doubts about Bob's advice, so she would like to get a second opinion. She therefore asks her other colleague Claire for her opinion about Eric. The trust graph which includes both pieces of advice is illustrated in Figure 14.7.

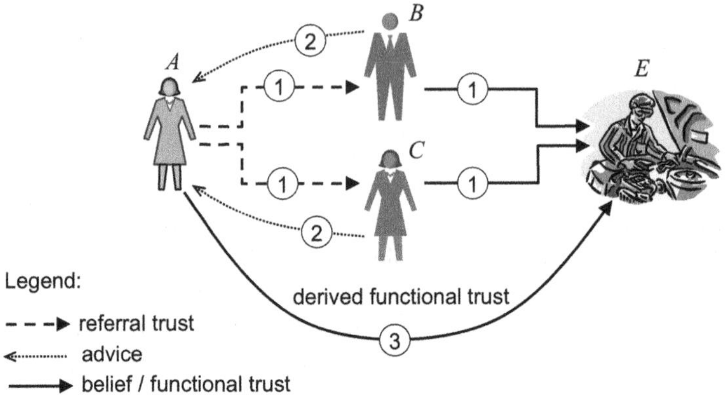

Fig. 14.7 Example of trust fusion

Formal notation of the graph of Figure 14.7 is shown in Eq.(14.16). This trust network also involves trust transitivity which is computed with trust discounting:

$$\text{Trust fusion formal notation:} \quad [A,E] = ([A;B] : [B,E]) \diamond ([A;C] : [C,E]),$$
$$\text{Compact notation:} \quad [A,E] = [A;B,E] \diamond [A;C,E]. \tag{14.16}$$

The computation of trust fusion involves both trust discounting and belief fusion, because what is actually fused is a pair of trust-discounted opinions. The binary variable $X = \{$"E is reliable", "E is unreliable"$\}$ can represent the trust target E in Figure 14.7, so that analyst A in fact derives an opinion about the variable X. The general principle of trust fusion of two opinions about a variable X is illustrated in Figure 14.8.

The symbol $\diamond$ denotes fusion between the two trust paths $[A;B,X]$ and $[A;C,X]$ (in compact notation). The choice of this symbol was motivated by the resemblance between the diamond shape and the graph of a typical trust fusion network, such as

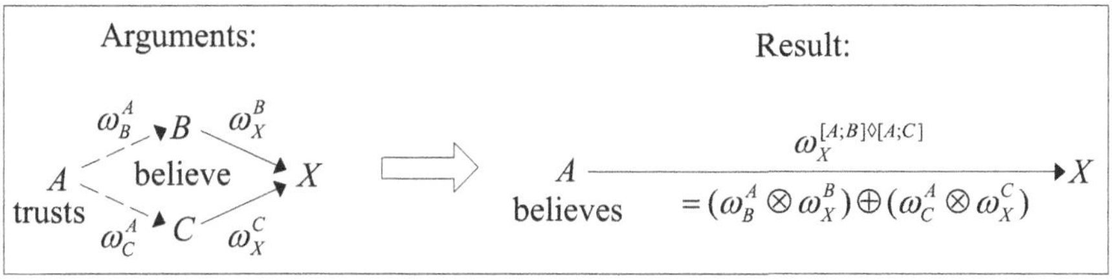

Fig. 14.8 Fusion of trust-discounted opinions

on the left side of Figure 14.8. The expression for A's derived opinion about X as a function of trust fusion is given by Eq.(14.17):

$$\text{Trust fusion computation: } \omega_X^{[A;B]\diamond[A;C]} = (\omega_B^A \otimes \omega_X^B) \oplus (\omega_C^A \otimes \omega_X^C)\,. \qquad (14.17)$$

In the example of Figure 14.8 it is assumed that analyst A receives opinions about X from the sources B and C, and that A has referral trust in both B and C. In general, the opinions that an analyst receives from other sources are *source opinions*.

More specifically, in case the source is an (intelligent) agent the source opinion is an *advice opinion* because it represents the agent's explicit advice. An advice opinion can represent referral trust in another source node/entity or it can be a belief opinion about a target variable.

In case the source is a sensor node the source opinion is a *sensor opinion* because it is derived from data collected by a sensor. Sensor opinions are derived from (low level) sensor data produced by a sensor. The fusion of multiple sensor opinions represents *opinion level sensor fusion*, because the derived opinions are fused, not the (low level) sensor data. Sensor fusion can also be done e.g. at the data level or at the decision level, but these types of sensor fusion are not discussed here.

The operator for fusing multiple trust paths must be selected from the set of belief fusion operators described in Chapter 12, according to the selection criteria described in Figure 12.2. As an example, Eq.(14.17) expresses trust fusion using the cumulative fusion operator '$\oplus$'.

Table 14.3 provides a numerical example, showing the result of cumulative trust fusion in the example of Alice and the car mechanic of Figure 14.7. The trust opinions derived from each path are first computed with the trust-discounting operator of Definition 14.6 (which is a special case of Definition 14.7). Then the two derived trust opinions are fused with the cumulative fusion operator of Definition 12.5.

In this example, both Bob and Claire offer relatively strong recommendations about Eric, so that Alice's first derived trust in Eric is strengthened by asking Claire for a second piece of advice.

Figure 14.9 is a screenshot of the online demonstrator for subjective trust networks based on the input arguments in the example of Table 14.3.

Note that Figure 14.9 shows the same trust network as that of Figure 14.7, but where the opinion triangle for each edge is placed on the edge. The input arguments

Table 14.3 Example trust fusion for the car mechanic situation of Figure 14.7

Parameters:		Argument opinions: ω^A_B	ω^B_E	ω^A_C	ω^C_E	Intermediate: $\omega^{[A;B]}_E$	$\omega^{[A;C]}_E$	Derived: $\omega^{[A;B]\diamond[A;C]}_E$
belief:	b	0.40	0.90	0.50	0.80	0.630	0.600	0.743
disbelief:	d	0.10	0.00	0.00	0.10	0.000	0.075	0.048
uncertainty:	u	0.50	0.10	0.50	0.10	0.370	0.325	0.209
base rate:	a	0.60	0.40	0.50	0.40	0.400	0.400	0.400
projected prob.:	P	0.70	0.94	0.75	0.84	0.778	0.730	0.826

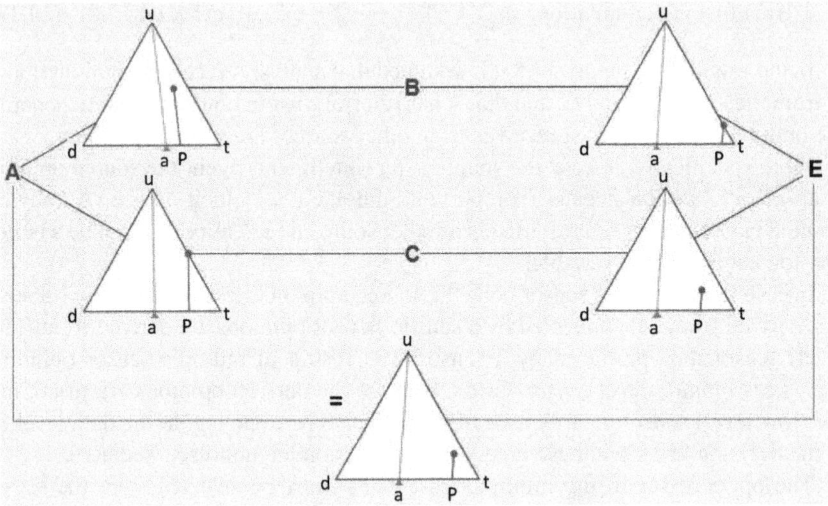

Fig. 14.9 Example trust fusion based on the numbers from Table 14.3

are represented as the four opinion triangles at the top of the figure, and the derived trust opinion is represented as the opinion triangle at the bottom of the figure.

This trust fusion example uses a combination of trust discounting and fusion. By combining fusion and trust discounting, complex trust networks can be modelled and analysed, as described in the following sections, and in Chapter 15.

14.5 Trust Revision

14.5.1 Motivation for Trust Revision

A complicating element in the case of trust fusion appears when multiple sources provide highly conflicting opinions, which might indicate that one or both sources are unreliable. In this situation, a strategy is needed for dealing with the conflict. The chosen strategy must be suitable for the specific situation.

A simplistic strategy for fusing conflicting opinions would be to consider the fused trust opinions as static, and not to revise trust at all. With this strategy the relying party only needs to determine the most suitable fusion operator for the situation to be analysed. For example, if cumulative fusion is considered suitable, then a simple model would be to derive A's opinion about X according to the principle of cumulative trust fusion of Eq.(14.16) as follows:

$$\text{Simple cumulative fusion: } \omega_X^{(A;B)\diamond(A;C)} = (\omega_B^A \otimes \omega_X^B) \oplus (\omega_C^A \otimes \omega_X^C)\,. \qquad (14.18)$$

Fusion of highly conflicting opinions in this way might be appropriate, such as in case of short samples of processes where different types of events might be observed in different periods.

However, there are situations where simple fusion might be inadequate, and where it would be natural to revise one or several argument trust opinions. One such situation is when the opinions ω_X^B and ω_X^C are highly conflicting in terms of their projected probability distributions on X.

For example, if the sources A and B have observed the same evidence or event, possibly at the same time, but still express different opinions, then it is likely that one or both sources are unreliable, so that trust revision should be considered.

Another situation that calls for trust revision is when the relying party A learns that the ground truth about X is radically different from the received source opinions. Hence, the analyst has good reasons to distrust a source that provides a very different opinion.

Since high conflict indicates that one or several sources might be unreliable, the strategy should aim at reducing the influence of unreliable sources, in order to derive the most reliable belief in the target.

A reduction of the influence of unreliable sources typically involves some form of trust revision, i.e. the analyst's trust in some sources can be reduced as a function of their degree of conflict. This section describes a strategy for doing precisely this. A similar approach has been proposed in [89].

14.5.2 Trust Revision Method

Trust revision is based on the degree of conflict between the opinions derived through trust discounting in two different paths. The rationale is that conflict indicates that one or both sources are unreliable, so that the referral trust in the sources should be revised as a function of the degree of conflict.

Recall from Section 4.8 and Definition 4.20 that DC (degree of conflict) is the product of PD (projected probability distance) and CC (conjunctive certainty) expressed as

$$\text{Degree of conflict:} \quad \mathrm{DC} = \mathrm{PD} \cdot \mathrm{CC}\,. \tag{14.19}$$

When applied to the two trust-discounted opinions $\omega_X^{[A;B]}$ and $\omega_X^{[A;C]}$, the projected probability distance PD is expressed as

$$\mathrm{PD}(\omega_X^{[A;B]}, \omega_X^{[A;C]}) = \frac{\sum\limits_{x \in \mathbb{X}} |\mathbf{P}_X^{[A;B]}(x) - \mathbf{P}_X^{[A;C]}(x)|}{2}\,. \tag{14.20}$$

Similarly, when applied to the two trust-discounted opinions $\omega_X^{[A;B]}$ and $\omega_X^{[A;C]}$ the conjunctive certainty CC is expressed as

$$\mathrm{CC}(\omega_X^{[A;B]}, \omega_X^{[A;C]}) = (1 - u_X^{[A;B]})(1 - u_X^{[A;C]})\,. \tag{14.21}$$

The degree of conflict between the two trust-discounted opinions is then:

$$\mathrm{DC}(\omega_X^{[A;B]}, \omega_X^{[A;C]}) = \mathrm{PD}(\omega_X^{[A;B]}, \omega_X^{[A;C]}) \cdot \mathrm{CC}(\omega_X^{[A;B]}, \omega_X^{[A;C]})\,. \tag{14.22}$$

Knowing the degree of conflict is only one of the factors for determining the magnitude of revision for the referral trust opinions ω_B^A and ω_C^A. It is natural to let the magnitude of trust revision also be determined by the relative degree of uncertainty in the referral trust opinions, so that the most uncertain opinion gets revised the most. The rationale is that if the analyst has uncertain referral trust in another agent, then the level of trust could easily change.

The *uncertainty differential* (UD) is a measure of the relative uncertainty between two referral trust opinions. There is one UD for each opinion relative to the other.

$$\text{Uncertainty Differentials:} \begin{cases} \mathrm{UD}(\omega_B^A | \omega_C^A) = \frac{u_B^A}{u_B^A + u_C^A}\,, \\[2ex] \mathrm{UD}(\omega_C^A | \omega_B^A) = \frac{u_C^A}{u_B^A + u_C^A}\,. \end{cases} \tag{14.23}$$

It can be seen that $\mathrm{UD} \in [0,1]$, where $\mathrm{UD} = 0.5$ means that both referral trust opinions have equal uncertainty, and therefore should get their equal share of revision. The case where $\mathrm{UD} = 1$ means that the first referral trust opinion is infinitely more uncertain than the other, and therefore should get all the revision. The case where UD $= 0$ means that the other referral trust opinion is infinitely more uncertain than the first, so that the other opinion should get all the revision.

In summary, the UD factors dictate the relative share of trust revision for each referral trust opinion. The magnitude of trust revision is determined by the *revision factor* RF which is a product of DC and UD:

$$\text{Revision Factors:} \quad \begin{cases} \text{RF}(\omega_B^A) = \text{UD}(\omega_B^A|\omega_C^A) \cdot \text{DC}(\omega_X^{[A;B]}, \omega_X^{[A;C]}), \\ \\ \text{RF}(\omega_C^A) = \text{UD}(\omega_C^A|\omega_B^A) \cdot \text{DC}(\omega_X^{[A;B]}, \omega_X^{[A;C]}). \end{cases} \tag{14.24}$$

Trust revision consists of modifying the referral trust opinions by increasing distrust mass at the cost of trust mass and uncertainty mass. The idea is that sources found to be unreliable should be distrusted more. A source found to be completely unreliable should be absolutely distrusted.

In terms of the opinion triangle, trust revision consists of moving the opinion point towards the $\bar{t}$-vertex, as shown in Figure 14.10. Given the argument referral trust opinion $\omega_B^A = (b_B^A, d_B^A, u_B^A, a_B^A)$, the revised referral trust opinion denoted $\breve{\omega}_B^A$ is expressed as

$$\text{Revised opinion } \breve{\omega}_B^A: \begin{cases} \breve{b}_B^A = b_B^A - b_B^A \cdot \text{RF}(\omega_B^A), \\ \\ \breve{d}_B^A = d_B^A + (1 - d_B^A) \cdot \text{RF}(\omega_B^A), \\ \\ \breve{u}_B^A = u_B^A - u_B^A \cdot \text{RF}(\omega_B^A), \\ \\ \breve{a}_B^A = a_B^A. \end{cases} \tag{14.25}$$

Similarly, given the argument referral trust opinion $\omega_C^A = (b_C^A, d_C^A, u_C^A, a_C^A)$, the revised referral trust opinion denoted $\breve{\omega}_C^A$ is expressed as

$$\text{Revised opinion } \breve{\omega}_C^A: \begin{cases} \breve{b}_C^A = b_C^A - b_C^A \cdot \text{RF}(\omega_C^A), \\ \\ \breve{d}_C^A = d_C^A + (1 - d_C^A) \cdot \text{RF}(\omega_C^A), \\ \\ \breve{u}_C^A = u_C^A - u_C^A \cdot \text{RF}(\omega_C^A), \\ \\ \breve{a}_C^A = a_C^A. \end{cases} \tag{14.26}$$

Figure 14.10 illustrates the effect of trust revision on ω_B^A, which consists of making the referral trust opinion more distrusting.

After trust revision has been applied to produce $\breve{\omega}_B^A$ and $\breve{\omega}_C^A$, trust fusion according to Eq.(14.18) can be repeated, with reduced conflict. Trust-revised averaging fusion is given by the expression in Eq.(14.27) below:

$$\text{Revised trust fusion: } \breve{\omega}_X^{(A;B)\underline{\diamond}(A;C)} = (\breve{\omega}_B^A \otimes \omega_X^B) \underline{\oplus} (\breve{\omega}_C^A \otimes \omega_X^C)\,. \tag{14.27}$$

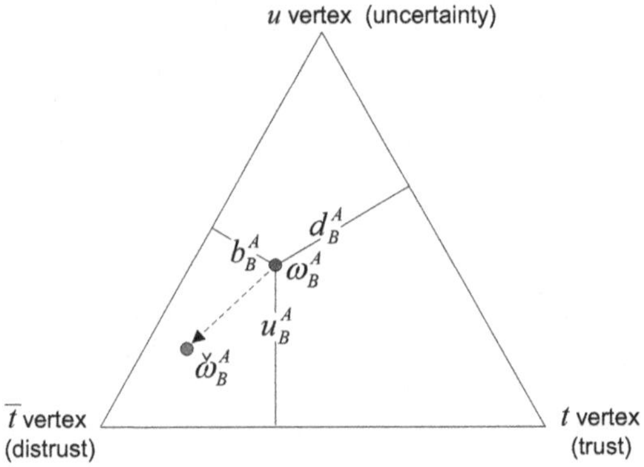

Fig. 14.10 Revision of referral trust opinion ω_B^A to produce $\breve{\omega}_B^A$

Trust revision offers a strategy to handle situations where potentially unreliable sources produce conflicting opinions, presumably because one or both of them give opinions that are wrong or significantly different from the ground truth. Based on the degree of conflict, and also on the prior uncertainty in the referral trust opinions, trust revision determines the degree by which the referral trust opinions should be considered unreliable, and therefore be revised in order to have less influence on the derived fused belief. This process leads to more conservative results that take into account that the information sources might be unreliable.

14.5.3 Example: Conflicting Restaurant Recommendations

We continue the example from Section 14.3.3 about the recommended restaurant Xylo, where this time we assume that Alice stays in a hostel with another traveller named Claire who tells her that she already tried the recommended restaurant, and that she was very disappointed, because the food was average, and that there were no locals there.

Let us assume that Alice has spoken with Claire a few times, and judges her to be an experienced traveller, so she intuitively develops a relatively high trust in Claire. Alice has now received a second piece of advice about the restaurant Xylo. This gives her a basis and a reason to revise her initial trust in Bob, which potentially could translate into distrusting Bob, and which could trigger a change in her initial belief about the restaurant Xylo.

This example situation can be translated into numbers, where ω_B^A, ω_X^B, ω_C^A and ω_X^C are the argument opinions.

Let us first show the result of trust fusion without trust revision, where the derived opinion $\omega_X^{[A;B]\diamond[A;C]}$ is computed with simple trust fusion as

$$\text{Simple trust fusion: } \omega_X^{[A;B]\diamond[A;C]} = (\omega_B^A \otimes \omega_X^B) \oplus (\omega_C^A \otimes \omega_X^C)\,. \tag{14.28}$$

It is assumed that X is binary so that opinions ω_X are expressed as binomial opinions. The argument opinions, as well as the derived opinion, are shown in Table 14.4.

Table 14.4 Simple trust fusion of conflicting advice about restaurant

Parameters:		Argument opinions: ω_B^A	ω_X^B	ω_C^A	ω_X^C	Intermediate: $\omega_X^{[A;B]}$	$\omega_X^{[A;C]}$	Derived: $\omega_X^{[A;B]\diamond[A;C]}$
belief:	b	0.00	0.95	0.90	0.10	0.855	0.099	0.452
disbelief:	d	0.00	0.00	0.00	0.80	0.000	0.792	0.482
uncertainty:	u	1.00	0.05	0.10	0.10	0.145	0.109	0.066
base rate:	a	0.90	0.20	0.90	0.20	0.200	0.200	0.200
projected prob.:	P	0.90	0.96	0.99	0.12	0.884	0.121	0.465

The application of trust fusion to the situation where Alice receives advice from both Bob and Claire produces a derived opinion with projected probability $\mathrm{P}_X^A = 0.465$, which indicates that the chances of Xylo being a good or bad restaurant are about even. This result seems counter-intuitive. Although the projected probabilities $\mathrm{P}_B^A = 0.90$ and $\mathrm{P}_C^A = 0.99$ are relatively close, Alice's referral trust belief $b_C^A = 0.90$ in Claire is much stronger than her referral trust belief $b_B^A = 0.00$ in Bob. It would therefore seem natural to let Claire's advice carry significantly more weight, but in the case of simple trust fusion as expressed in Table 14.4, it does not.

From an intuitive perspective, Alice's natural reaction in this situation would be to revise her referral trust in Bob, because his advice conflicts with that of Claire whom she trusts with more certainty, i.e. with more belief mass. Alice would typically start to distrust Bob, because apparently his advice is unreliable. As a result of this trust revision, Claire's advice would carry more weight.

The application of the trust revision method described in Section 14.5.2 produces the following intermediate values:

$$\text{Conflict: } \begin{cases} \text{Projected distance:} & \mathrm{PD}(\omega_X^{[A;B]}, \omega_X^{[A;C]}) = 0.763, \\ \text{Conjunctive Certainty:} & \mathrm{CC}(\omega_X^{[A;B]}, \omega_X^{[A;C]}) = 0.762, \\ \text{Degree of Conflict:} & \mathrm{DC}(\omega_X^{[A;B]}, \omega_X^{[A;C]}) = 0.581, \end{cases} \tag{14.29}$$

$$\text{Revision:}\begin{cases}\text{Uncertainty Differential for } B: & \mathrm{UD}(\omega^A_B|\omega^A_C) = 0.909,\\ \text{Uncertainty Differential for } C: & \mathrm{UD}(\omega^A_C|\omega^A_B) = 0.091,\\ \text{Revision Factor for } B: & \mathrm{RF}(\omega^A_B) = 0.529,\\ \text{Revision Factor for } C: & \mathrm{RF}(\omega^A_C) = 0.053.\end{cases} \tag{14.30}$$

These intermediate parameters of Eq.(14.29) and Eq.(14.30) determine the trust-revised referral trust opinions $\breve{\omega}^A_B$ and $\breve{\omega}^A_C$ that are specified in Table 14.5. The table also shows the result of applying trust fusion based on the revised referral trust opinions.

Table 14.5 Trust revision of conflicting advice about restaurant

Parameters:		Argument opinions: $\breve{\omega}^A_B$	ω^B_X	$\breve{\omega}^A_C$	ω^C_X	Intermediate: $\breve{\omega}^{[A;B]}_X$	$\breve{\omega}^{[A;C]}_X$	Derived: $\breve{\omega}^{[A;B]\diamond[A;C]}_X$
belief:	b	0.00	0.95	0.85	0.10	0.403	0.094	0.180
disbelief:	d	0.53	0.00	0.05	0.80	0.000	0.750	0.679
uncertainty:	u	0.47	0.05	0.10	0.10	0.597	0.156	0.141
base rate:	a	0.90	0.20	0.90	0.20	0.200	0.200	0.200
projected prob.:	P	0.42	0.96	0.94	0.12	0.522	0.125	0.208

Note that Alice's revised referral trust in Bob has been reduced significantly, whereas her referral trust in Claire has been kept more or less unchanged. This reflects the intuitive reaction we would have in a similar situation.

Trust revision must be considered to be an *ad hoc* method, because there is no parallel in physical processes that can be objectively observed and analysed. Especially the expression for the revision factor RF is affected by the design choice of mirroring intuitive human judgment. There might be different design choices for the revision factor that better reflect human intuition, and that also can be shown to produce sound results under specific criteria. We invite the reader to reflect on these issues, and maybe come up with an alternative and improved design for the revision factor.

Chapter 15
Subjective Trust Networks

A subjective trust network (STN) represents trust and belief relationships from agents, via other agents and sensors to target entities/variables, where each trust and belief relationship is expressed as a subjective opinion. The trust network is typically represented as a graph. Simple STNs have already been described in Chapter 14 on computational trust, including computation of transitive trust paths, and the computation of simple trust fusion networks.

In the case of more complex trust networks, it is necessary to take an algorithmic approach to modelling and analysis. This chapter describes how to deal with trust networks that are more complex than those described in Chapter 14. A study on the propagation of opinions in social networks is provided in [13].

The operators for fusion, trust discounting and trust revision can be applied to trust and belief relationships represented as a DSPG (Directed Series-Parallel Graph). The next section therefore gives a brief introduction to such graphs.

15.1 Graphs for Trust Networks

15.1.1 Directed Series-Parallel Graphs

Series-parallel graphs, called SP-graphs for short, represent a specific type of graphs that have a pair of distinguished vertices called the *source* and *sink*.

The following definition of SP-graphs is taken from [19].

Definition 15.1 (Series-Parallel Graph). A graph is an SP-graph, if it may be turned into a single edge connecting a source node s and a sink node t by a sequence of the following operations:

(i) Replacement of a pair of edges incident to a vertex of degree 2 other than the source or sink with a single edge.
(ii) Replacement of a pair of parallel edges with a single edge that connects their common endpoint vertices.

□

For example, Figure 15.1 illustrates how the SP-graph to the left can be stepwise transformed using the operations of Definition 15.1.

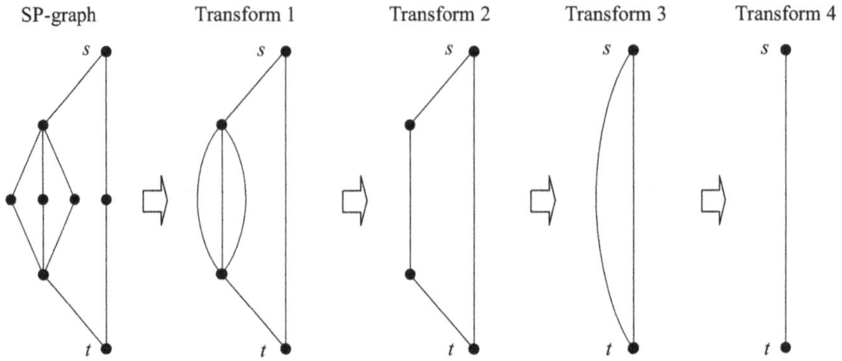

Fig. 15.1 Procedure for transforming an SP-graph into a single edge.

Transform 1 results from applying procedure (i) four times. Transform 2 results from applying procedure (ii) twice. Transform 3 results from applying procedure (i) twice. Transform 4, which is a single edge, results from applying procedure (ii) once. The fact that the graph transforms into a single edge in this way proves that it is an SP-graph.

Trust networks are represented as directed graphs. We therefore assume that an SP-graph representing a trust network is directed from the source to the sink, in which case it is called a *directed series-parallel graph* or DSPG for short [26].

Definition 15.2 (Directed Series-Parallel Graph). A graph is a DSPG (Directed Series-Parallel Graph) iff it is an SP-graph according to Definition 15.1, and it only consists of directed edges that form paths without loops from the source to the sink. □

In the context of trust networks the source node of a DSPG is the analyst agent, aka the relying party, which is typically represented by the label A. In general, the sink node of a DSPG is the target variable, which is typically represented by the label X, but which can also be a trusted entity represented e.g. by the label E.

15.2 Outbound-Inbound Set

A DSPG can consist of multiple subnetworks which themselves are sub-DSPGs. A *parallel-path subnetwork* (PPS) is a subnetwork that consists of parallel paths in a sub-DSPG.

A node can be part of one or multiple edges. In general, the *degree of a node* represents the number of edges that node is part of. Since a DSPG is directed it is possible to distinguish between *inbound degree* (ID) and *outbound degree* (OD) for a node. The inbound degree of a node is the number of inbound edges to that node. Similarly, the outbound degree of a node is the number of outbound edges from that node. Consider for example the following referral trust network:

$$A \dashrightarrow B \dashrightarrow C\,. \tag{15.1}$$

Node B has degree 2, denoted $\mathrm{Deg}(B) = 2$, because it is connected to the two edges $[A;B]$ and $[B;C]$. At the same time, node B has inbound degree $\mathrm{ID}(B) = 1$ because its only inbound edge is $[A;B]$, and has outbound degree $\mathrm{OD}(B) = 1$ because its only outbound edge is $[B;C]$. Node A has $\mathrm{ID}(A) = 0$ and $\mathrm{OD}(A) = 1$. Obviously, for any node V in a DSPG, its degree is represented as $\mathrm{Deg}(V) = \mathrm{ID}(V) + \mathrm{OD}(V)$.

An ordered pair of nodes (V_s, V_t) in a DSPG is said to be *connected* if the second node V_t can be reached by departing from the first node V_s. For example, it can easily be seen that (A, C) in Eq.(15.1) is a connected pair of nodes.

Consider a node in a DSPG. The node's *outbound set* is defined as the set of edges that can be traversed after departing from that node. Similarly, the node's *inbound set* is the set of edges that can be traversed before reaching the node.

Definition 15.3 (OIS: Outbound-Inbound Set). Consider an ordered pair of nodes (V_s, V_t) in a DSPG. We define the *outbound-inbound set* (OIS) of the ordered pair to be the intersection of the outbound set of the first node V_s and the inbound set of the second node V_t. □

Some simple properties of an OIS can be stated.

Theorem 15.1. *A pair of nodes (V_s, V_t) in a DSPG are connected iff their OIS (Outbound-Inbound Set) is non-empty.*

Proof. If OIS $\neq \emptyset$, then the OIS contains at least one edge that can be traversed after departing from the first node V_s and before reaching the second node V_t, which means that it is possible to reach the second node V_t by departing from the first node V_s, so they must be connected. If OIS $= \emptyset$, then the OIS contains no path connecting the two nodes, which means that they are not connected. □

15.2.1 Parallel-Path Subnetworks

A DSPG can in general consist of multiple subnetworks that themselves are DSPGs that can contain parallel paths. We are interested in identifying subnetworks within a DSPG that contain parallel paths. A *parallel-path subnetwork* (PPS) in a DSPG is the set of multiple paths between a pair of connected nodes, as defined next.

Definition 15.4 (Parallel-Path Subnetwork). Select an ordered pair (V_s, V_t) of connected nodes in a DSPG. The subnetwork consisting of the pair's OIS is a parallel-path subnetwork (PPS) iff both the outbound degree of the first node V_s in the OIS satisfies $\text{OD}(V_s) \geq 2$, and the inbound degree of the second node V_t in the OIS satisfies $\text{ID}(V_t) \geq 2$.

The node V_s is called the source of the PPS, and V_t is called the sink of the PPS.

□

Consider for example the OIS of the node pair (C,J) in Figure 15.2. Within that particular OIS we have $\text{OD}(C) = 2$ and $\text{ID}(J) = 3$, which satisfies the requirements of Definition 15.4, hence the OIS is a PPS (parallel-path subnetwork).

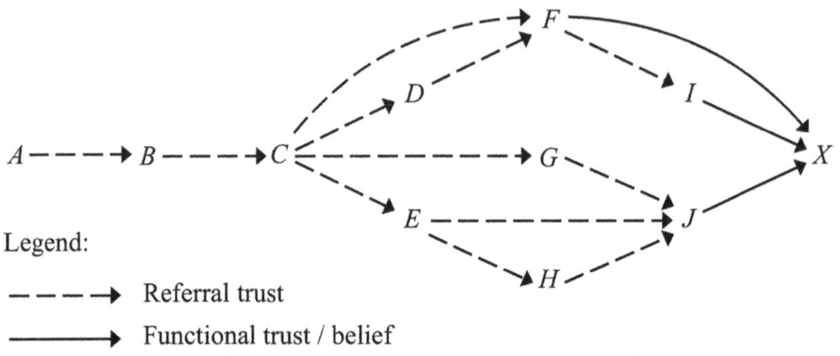

Fig. 15.2 DSPG with five PPSs (parallel-path subnetworks)

It can also be verified that the respective OISs of the node pairs (E,J), (C,F), (F,X) and (C,X) are also PPSs, which means that the DSPG of Figure 15.2 contains five PPSs in total.

However, the subnetwork between the connected node pair (E,X) is not a PPS, because $\text{ID}(X) = 1$ within that OIS (outbound-inbound set), which does not satisfy the requirements of Definition 15.4.

15.2.2 Nesting Level

The concept of *nesting level* is important for analysing trust networks represented as a DSPG. In general, the nesting level of an edge reflects how many PPSs it is part of in the DSPG. Each edge has a specific nesting level greater or equal to 0. For example, a trust network consisting of a single trust path, has trust edges with nesting level 0, because the edges are not part of any subnetwork of parallel paths. The nesting level of an edge in a DSPG is defined next.

Definition 15.5 (Nesting Level). Assume a DSPG consisting of multiple nodes connected via directed edges. The nesting level of an edge in the DSPG is equal to the number of PPSs (parallel-path subnetworks) that the edge is a part of.

Let e.g. $[V_m;V_n]$ be an edge in a DSPG. The nesting level of the edge $[V_m;V_n]$ is formally denoted $\mathrm{NL}([V_m;V_n])$. Nesting levels can be zero or greater. □

In Figure 15.3, the nesting level of edges is indicated by the numbered diamonds on the edges.

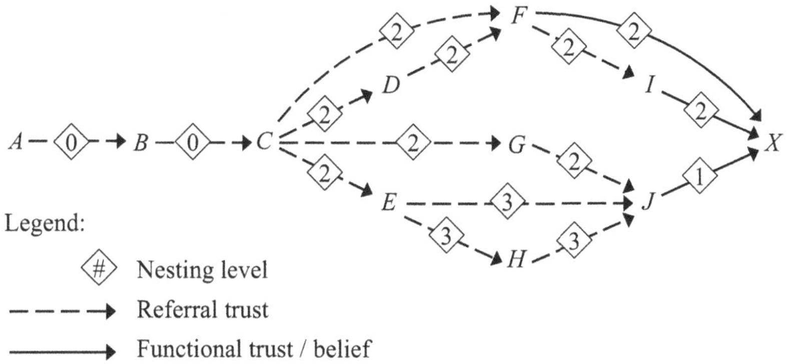

Fig. 15.3 Nesting levels of edges in a DSPG

It can be seen that the edge $[A;B]$ is not part of any PPS, so $\mathrm{NL}([A;B]) = 0$. It can also be seen that the edge $[H;J]$ is part of three PPSs belonging to the node pairs (E,J), (C,J) and (C,X), so $\mathrm{NL}([H;J]) = 3$.

The nesting level determines the order of computation of trust in a DSPG trust network, as described next.

15.3 Analysis of DSPG Trust Networks

We assume that the trust network to be analysed is represented in the form of a DSPG. It can be verified that the trust network of Figure 15.4 represents a DSPG (Directed Series-Parallel Graph) according to Definition 15.2.

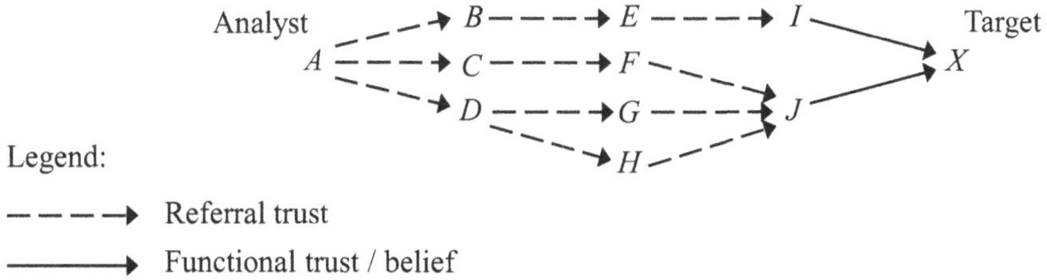

Fig. 15.4 Trust network in the form of a DSPG

It can also be seen that the DSPG of Figure 15.4 consists of three PPSs (parallel-path subnetworks), represented by the source-sink pairs (D,J), (A,J) and (A,X).

The compact formal expression for the trust network of Figure 15.4 is given in Eq.(15.2):

$$[A,X] = [A;B;E;I,X] \diamond (([A;C;F;J] \diamond ([A;D] : ([D;G;J] \diamond [D;H;J]))) : [J,X]). \tag{15.2}$$

Next we describe a simple algorithm for analysing and deriving belief/trust from a DSPG trust network like that of Figure 15.4.

15.3.1 Algorithm for Analysis of DSPG

The procedure for computing derived trust in a trust network represented as a DSPG is illustrated in the form of the flowchart algorithm of Figure 15.5 and explained below. The procedure can e.g. be applied for computing the trust opinion ω_X^A in Figure 15.4. The procedure corresponds well to the operations of graph simplification of Definition 15.1. For the purpose of the computation principles defined here, agents and target are called *nodes*.

The steps of the flowchart algorithm in Figure 15.5 are described below.

(a) Prepare for analysing the trust network. This includes representing the trust network as a set of directed edges with pairs of nodes. Verify that the trust network is indeed a DSPG.
(b) Identify each PPS (Parallel Path Subnetwork) with its pair of source and target nodes (V_s, V_t). Determine the nesting level of every edge as a function of the number of PPSs it is part of.
(c) Select the PPS where all edges have the highest nesting level, and proceed to (d). In case no PPS remains, proceed to (g).
(d) For the selected PPS, compute two-edge or multi-edge trust discounting of every path between V_s and V_t, where the node V_t is considered as the target node of the analysis. As a result, every path is transformed into an edge.
(e) For the selected PPS, compute trust fusion of all edges. As a result, the PPS is transformed into a single edge.
(f) Determine the nesting level of the edge that now replaces the selected PPS.
(g) When no PPS exists, the trust network might still consist of a series of edges. In that case, compute two-edge or multi-edge trust discounting. In case the resulting network consists of a single edge, nothing needs to be done.
(h) The trust network has now been transformed into a single edge between the analyst and the final target, hence the computation is completed.

A parser that implements the computational algorithm of Figure 15.5 is able to analyse the graph of e.g. Figure 15.4, and derive the opinion ω_X^A.

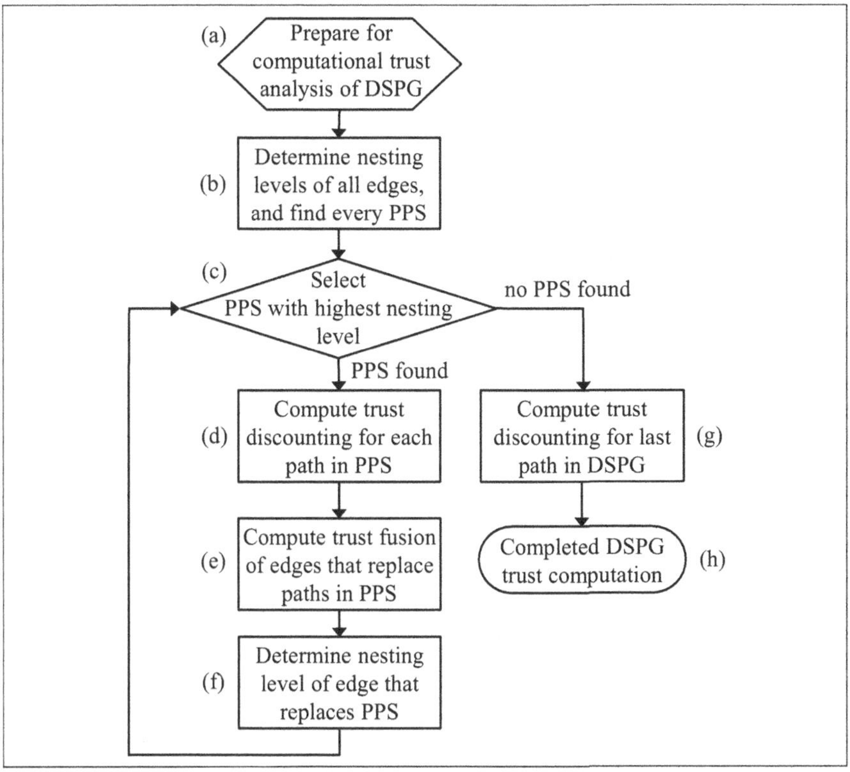

Fig. 15.5 Flowchart algorithm for computational trust analysis of DSPG network

15.3.2 Soundness Requirements for Receiving Advice Opinions

The analyst should receive a source opinion in its original form from the source, and not in the form of an indirect derived opinion. The reason for this is explained below. Figure 15.6 shows an example of how source opinions should not be received.

In Figure 15.6, the trust and advice arrows are indexed according to the order in which they are formed, whereas the initial trust relationships have no index. In the scenario of Figure 15.6, D passes his advice about X to B and C (index 2), so that B and C are able to derive their opinions about X (index 3). Now B and C pass their derived opinions about X to A (index 4), so that she can derive her opinion about X (index 5).

As a result, A perceives the topology to be $([A;B,X] \diamond [A;C,X])$. Note that we use the compact notation presented in Section 14.2.4.

The problem with the scenario of Figure 15.6 is that A ignores the presence of D, so that A in fact derives a hidden topology that is different from the perceived topology, which are both different from the real topology. The three different topologies are given in Table 15.1.

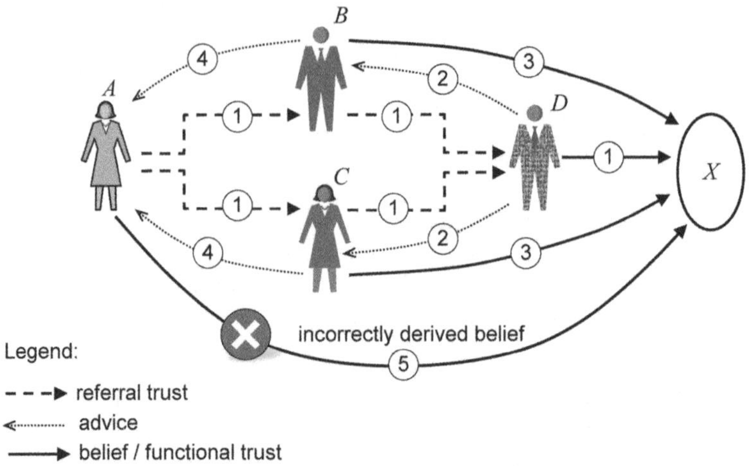

Fig. 15.6 Incorrect way of receiving advice opinions

Table 15.1 Inconsistency of trust network topologies

Perceived topology:	Hidden topology:	Real topology:
$([A;B,X] \diamond [A;C,X])$	$([A;B;D,X] \diamond [A;C;D,X])$	$([A;B;D] \diamond [A;C;D]) : [D,X]$

The reason for this inconsistency is that B's belief relationship $[B,X]$ is derived from $[B;D,X]$, and C's belief relationship $[C,X]$ is derived from $[C;D,X]$. So when B gives the advice opinion ω_X^B, he implicitly gives the advice $\omega_X^{[B;D]}$, and when C gives the advice opinion ω_X^C she implicitly gives the advice $\omega_X^{[C;D]}$, but A ignores the influence of D in the received advice opinions [41]. It can easily be seen that neither the perceived nor the hidden topology is equal to the real topology, which demonstrates that this way of receiving advice opinions can produce inconsistent results.

The sound way of receiving advice opinions is that A receives from B and C the advice opinions they receive from D without modification, as well as their respective trust opinions about D. This principle is certainly possible to follow, but it also requires that A is convinced that B and C have not altered the recommendations from D; precisely this is part of A's referral trust in B and C.

It is thus necessary that A receives all the advice opinions unaltered and as expressed by the original sources. An example of correctly received advice opinions is indicated in Figure 15.7.

In the scenario of Figure 15.7, the perceived topology is equal to the real topology, which can be expressed as

$$[A,X] = ([A;B;D] \diamond [A;C;D]) : [D,X] \,. \tag{15.3}$$

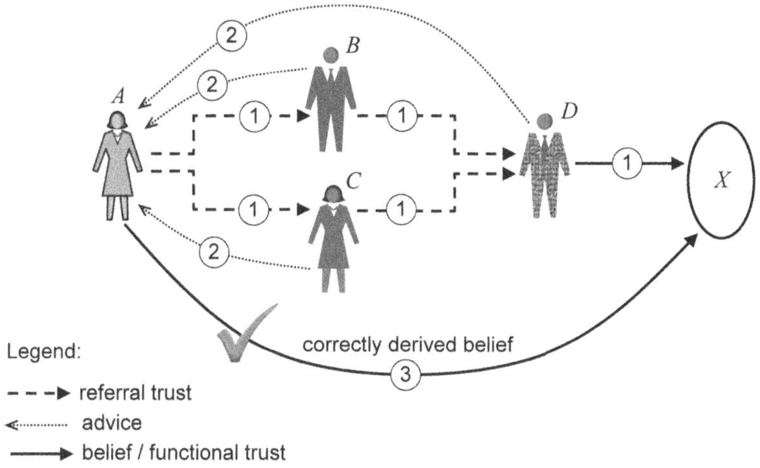

Fig. 15.7 Correct way of receiving advice opinions

The lesson to be learned from the scenarios of Figure 15.6 and Figure 15.7 is that there is a crucial difference between receiving a source opinion that is based on the source's direct observation/evidence, and a receiving a source opinion that is based on the source's indirectly received evidence such as referral trust or belief opinions that the source has received from other sources.

The morale is that analysts should be aware of the difference between receiving direct and indirect source opinions. Figure 15.6 illustrates how problems can occur when received indirect belief opinions are misinterpreted as direct belief opinions, so the golden rule is to only accept sources that can provide direct trust/belief opinions[41]. However, it is not always possible to follow this principle, but to simply be aware of the potential inconsistencies is useful when assessing the results of an analysis, or when considering mitigation strategies against inconsistencies.

If B and C were unreliable, they might want to change the source opinion provided by D. Not only that, a malicious party could intercept and modify the source opinions provided by sources B, C or D before they reach A, so A might require evidence of the authenticity and integrity of the received trust/advice opinions. Cryptographic security mechanisms can typically be used to solve this problem.

15.4 Analysing Complex Non-DSPG Trust Networks

An analyst might be confronted with a trust network that appears more complex than a DSPG. It is desirable not to put any restrictions on the possible trust network topology that can be analysed, except that it should not be cyclic. This means that the set of possible trust paths from the analyst agent A to the target X can contain paths that are inconsistent with a DSPG. The question then arises how such a trust network should be analysed.

A complex non-DSPG trust network is one that is not an SP-graph according to Definition 15.1. In many cases it can be challenging to recognise which referral trust components are in series, and which are in parallel, in a complex network. Figure 15.8 illustrates an example of a complex trust network. The trust network only consists of the edges from A to E and from A to F. The trust network thus consists of referral trust edges only.

The last edges from E and F to the target X represent functional belief relationships which could also be considered to be functional trust relationships according to Figure 14.2. However, for the purpose of trust network analysis described below, only the referral trust network from A to E and F is relevant.

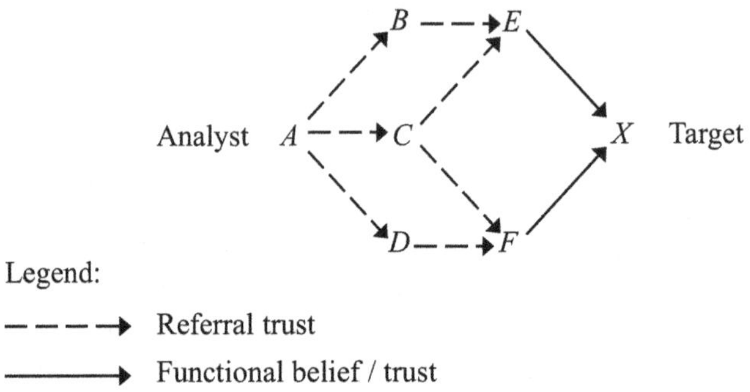

Fig. 15.8 Non-DSPG trust network

Simply by looking at Figure 15.8, it becomes obvious that this trust network can not be broken down into groups of series-parallel paths, which complicates the problem of computing trust from the network. In the case of a DSPG, which can be split into series-parallel configurations, it is simple to determine the mathematical or analytical formula that describes the network's derived trust. However, for a complex non-DSPG network, trust computation requires more involved methods.

Subjective trust networks can be digitally represented and stored in the form of a list of directed trust edges with additional attributes such as trust scope σ, time of collection, trust variant (referral or functional) and trust opinion. Based on the list of edges, an automated parser can establish valid DSPGs between two nodes depending on the need. The trust edges of the non-DSPG trust network of Figure 15.8 can for example be listed as in Table 15.2.

There can be multiple approaches to analysing complex (i.e. non-DSPG) subjective trust networks. This task might appear similar to the case of reliability analysis of complex systems, described in Section 7.2. However, the case of complex STNs is different. The main differences are that trust networks involve possible deception, which system reliability networks do not, and that trust networks involve fusion, which is not an ingredient of system reliability analysis. Hence, the principles for

Table 15.2 Trust edges of the complex trust network in Figure 15.8

Source V_s	Target V_t	Scope	Variant	Opinion
A	B	σ	referral	ω_B^A
A	C	σ	referral	ω_C^A
A	D	σ	referral	ω_D^A
B	E	σ	referral	ω_E^B
C	E	σ	referral	ω_E^C
C	F	σ	referral	ω_F^C
D	F	σ	referral	ω_F^D
E	X	σ	functional	ω_X^E
F	X	σ	functional	ω_X^F

analysing complex reliability networks can not be applied to complex STNs. A different approach is therefore needed for analysing complex STNs.

The simplification of a complex STN removes paths that prevent consistent trust computation, and produces a DSPG trust network which can easily be analysed.

The optimal derived DSPG trust network produces a derived opinion with the highest confidence. The goal is to maximise confidence in the derived opinion, and not e.g. to derive the opinion with the highest projected probability of some value of the variable X. There is a trade-off between the time it takes to find the optimal DSPG, and how close to the optimal DSPG a simplified graph can be. Below we describe an *exhaustive* method that is guaranteed to find the optimal DSPG, and a *heuristic* method that will find a DSPG close to, or equal to the optimal DSPG.

- **Exhaustive Discovery of Optimal DSPG Trust Network**
  The exhaustive method of finding the optimal DSPG trust network consists of determining all possible DSPGs and their derived target opinions, and finally selecting the DSPG and the corresponding canonical expression that produces the trust value with the highest confidence (certainty) level, i.e. with the lowest uncertainty. The computational complexity of this method is $\text{Comp} = lm(2^n - 1)$, where n is the number of possible paths, m is the average number of paths in the DSPGs, and l is the average number of edges in the paths.
- **Heuristic Discovery of Near-Optimal DSPG Trust Network**
  The heuristic method of finding a near-optimal DSPG trust network consists of synthesising the graph by including new paths one by one in decreasing order of confidence. Each new path that would turn the graph into a non-DSPG is excluded. This method only requires the computation of the trust value for a single DSPG and canonical expression, with computational complexity $\text{Comp} = lm$, where m is the average number of paths in the DSPGs, and l is the average number of edges in the paths.

The heuristic method produces a DSPG where the derived opinion's confidence level is equal or close to that of the optimal DSPG. The reason why this method is not guaranteed to produce the optimal DSPG is that it could exclude multiple trust paths with relatively low certainty levels because of incompatibility with a previously included path with higher certainty level. It is possible that the low-certainty paths together could provide higher certainty than the previous high-certainty path alone. In such cases, it would be optimal to exclude the high-certainty path, and instead include the set of low-certainty paths. However, only the exhaustive method described above is guaranteed to find the optimal DSPG in such cases [80].

The next section describes a heuristic method for transforming a complex trust network into a DSPG trust network. The method is heuristic in the sense that it does not necessarily synthesise the optimal DSPC in the sens of maximum certainty of the derived trust. The advantage of the method is to be efficient.

An alternative approach to constructing efficient networks from a potentially large and complex network has been described in [69], where it is called discovery of small worlds. However, we do not follow that approach here.

15.4.1 Synthesis of DSPG Trust Network

Below, we describe an algorithm which is able to simplify a complex trust network like the one in Figure 15.8 in order to synthesise a DSPG trust network.

Simplification of a non-DSPG trust network is a two-step process. First, the complex trust network is analysed to identify all possible trust paths from the analyst A to the target X. Second, a new DSPG trust network is synthesised from scratch by only including those trust paths from the complex trust network that do not break the DSPG property of the synthesised trust network. The final synthesised graph between the source analyst A and the target node X is then a DSPG trust network.

A DSPG can be constructed by sequences of serial and parallel compositions that are defined as follows [26]:

Definition 15.6 (Directed Series and Parallel Composition).

- A *directed series* composition consists of replacing an edge $[A;C]$ with two edges $[A;B]$ and $[B;C]$ where B is a new node.
- A *directed parallel* composition consists of replacing an edge $[A;C]$ with two edges $[A;C]_1$ and $[A;C]_2$.

The principle of directed series-parallel composition is illustrated in Figure 15.9.

a) Serial composition b) Parallel composition

Fig. 15.9 Principles of directed series and parallel composition

Figure 15.10 shows a flowchart algorithm for synthesising a DSPG trust network from a complex trust network according to the heuristic method.

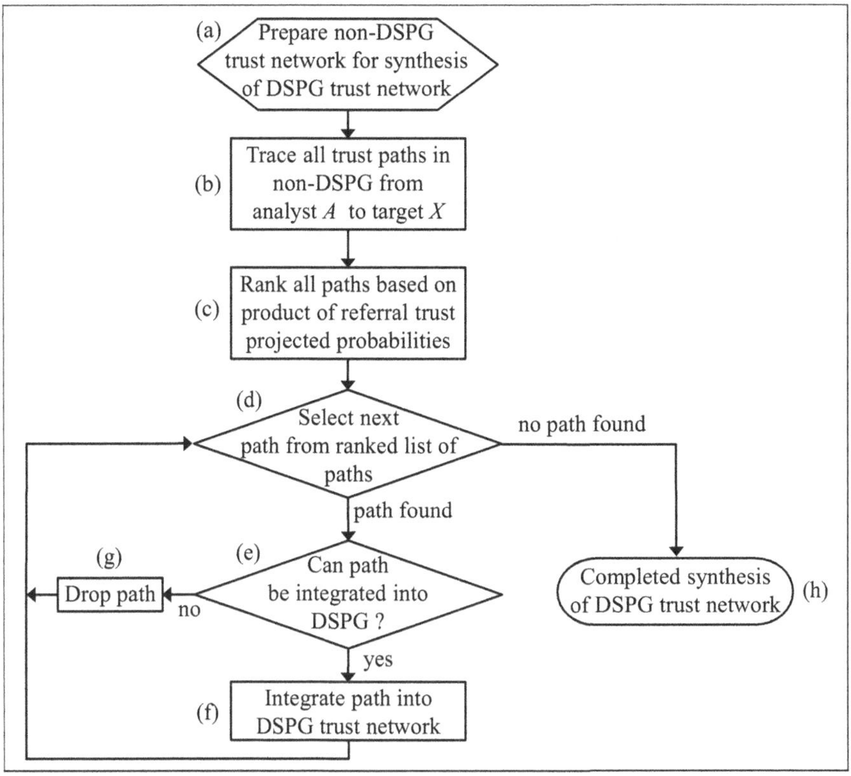

Fig. 15.10 Flowchart algorithm for synthesising a DSPG from a complex non-DSPG

Each step in the flowchart algorithm of Figure 15.10 is described below.

(a) Prepare for simplification of complex trust network. This includes representing the complex trust network as a set of directed edges with pairs of nodes. Set a threshold p_{T} for the lowest relevant reliability of trust paths. Create an empty DSPG trust network to be synthesised.
(b) Identify each trust path from the analyst A to the target node X. For each path, compute the product of the projected probabilities of referral trust edges. The last functional belief/trust edge to the target X is not included in the product.
(c) Create a ranked list of paths according to the products computed in the previous step, i.e. where the path with the highest product has index 1. Include path 1 so that the initial network consists of a single path. Set the index pointer to 1.
(d) Increment the index pointer to select the next path from the ranked list of paths. Exit to termination if there is no path left, or if the path's product referral trust is

smaller than the threshold p_{T}. Continue in case the path's product referral trust greater or equal to the threshold p_{T}.

(e) Check whether the selected trust path can be added and integrated into the DSPG trust network. Use the criteria described in Section 15.4.2.

(f) Add the selected trust path in case it fits into the DSPG. Existing trust edges are not duplicated, only new trust edges are added to the DSPG.

(g) Drop the selected trust path in case it does not fit into the DSPG.

(h) The synthesised DSPG can be analysed according to the algorithm described in Section 15.3.

15.4.2 Criteria for DSPG Synthesis

Ideally, all the possible paths discovered by the algorithm of Figure 15.10 should be taken into account when deriving the opinion/trust value. A general directed graph will often contain loops and dependencies. This can be avoided by excluding certain paths, but this can also cause information loss. Specific selection criteria are needed in order to find the optimal subset of paths to include. With n possible paths, there are $(2^n - 1)$ different combinations for constructing graphs, of which not all are necessarily DSPGs. The algorithm of Figure 15.10 aims at synthesising a DSPG trust network with the least information loss relative to the original complex trust network.

Figure 15.11 illustrates an simple non-DSPG trust graph, where it is assumed that A is the source analyst and X is the target. The two heuristic rules used to discard paths are 1) when a path is inconsistent with a DSPG, and 2) when the product of projected probabilities drops below a predefined threshold.

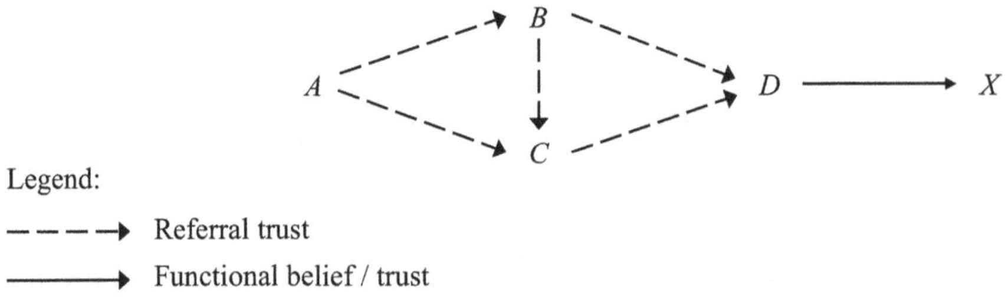

Fig. 15.11 Example complex trust network

In the algorithm of Figure 15.10, it can be noted that step (d) enforces the rule that the product projected probability of the referral trust edges in the graph is greater than or equal to threshold p_{T}. A low product value indicates low certainty in the trust path. By removing paths with low certainty, the number of paths to consider is reduced while the information loss is kept to an insignificant level. The subsequent step (e) checks that the path can be included consistently with the DSPG.

In the complex trust network of Figure 15.11 there are three possible paths between A and X, as expressed by Eq.(15.4) below:

$$\begin{aligned} \phi_1 &= ([A;B] : [B;D] : [D,X]), \\ \phi_2 &= ([A;C] : [C;D] : [D,X]), \\ \phi_3 &= ([A;B] : [B;C] : [C;D] : [D,X]). \end{aligned} \tag{15.4}$$

The three paths can generate the following seven potential combinations/graphs:

$$\begin{aligned} &\gamma_1 = \phi_1, &\quad &\gamma_4 = \phi_1 \diamond \phi_2, &\quad &\gamma_7 = \phi_1 \diamond \phi_2 \diamond \phi_3. \\ &\gamma_2 = \phi_2, & &\gamma_5 = \phi_1 \diamond \phi_3, & & \\ &\gamma_3 = \phi_3, & &\gamma_6 = \phi_2 \diamond \phi_3, & & \end{aligned} \tag{15.5}$$

The expression γ_7 represents a trust network which contains all possible paths between A and X. The problem with γ_7 is that it is a non-DSPG so that it can not be represented in the form of a canonical expression, i.e. where each edge only appears once. In this example, one path must must be removed from the graph in order to have a canonical expression. The expressions γ_4, γ_5 and γ_6 can be canonicalised, and the expressions γ_1, γ_2 and γ_3 are already canonical, which means that all the expressions except γ_7 can be used as a basis for constructing a DSPG and for deriving A's opinion/trust in X.

The synthesis of DSPG starts with by initially selecting the path having the greatest projected probability of referral trust computed from the original source agent to a node which is an immediate neighbour to the ultimate target (i.e. which has a direct functional edge to the ultimate target). Then additional paths are added one by one according to the algorithm of Figure 15.7. When adding new paths, the whole path from the original source to the ultimate target is considered, but sub-paths that already exist in the synthesised graph are ignored, so only non-existing sub-paths are added by bifurcation. Each new sub-path to be included must satisfy the DSPG-synthesis criteria of Definition 15.7.

The criteria of Definition 15.7 refer to the source and target nodes of each new sub-path considered for addition to the existing graph, not to the original source and the ultimate target of the graph. Note that each new sub-path can consist of two or more nodes.

Definition 15.7 (DSPG-Synthesis Criteria for Sub-Path Addition).

1. The target node must be reachable from the source node in the existing graph.
2. The source and target nodes must have equal nesting levels in the existing graph.
3. The nesting level of the source and target nodes must be equal to or less than the nesting level of all intermediate nodes in the existing graph.

□

These criteria are applied in the examples below. Figure 15.12, Figure 15.13 and Figure 15.14 illustrate how new sub-paths can be included in a way that preserves the DSPG property. It is assumed that new sub-paths can contain more than two nodes, but the examples only show addition of sub-paths consisting of single edge between a source and a target.

In the figures, the nesting levels of nodes and edges are indicated as an integer. A bifurcation is when a node has two or more incoming or outgoing edges, and is indicated by brackets in the shaded node boxes. The opening bracket '(' increments the nesting level by 1, and the closing bracket ')' decrements the nesting level by 1. A sub-path is a section of a path without bifurcations. The equal sign '=' means that the node is part of a sub-path, in which case the nesting level of the edge on the side of the '=' symbol is equal to the nesting level of the node. Each time a new path is added to the old graph, some sub-path sections may already exist in the old graph, in which case they are not added, whereas other sub-path sections that do not already exist must be added by bifurcations to the old graph.

- **Illustrating DSPG Synthesis Criterion 1.**
  Figure 15.12 illustrates Criterion 1 of Definition 15.7. The new edge $[B;C]$ is rejected because C is not reachable from B in the existing graph. In contrast, the new edge $[A;D]$ can be included because D is reachable from A.

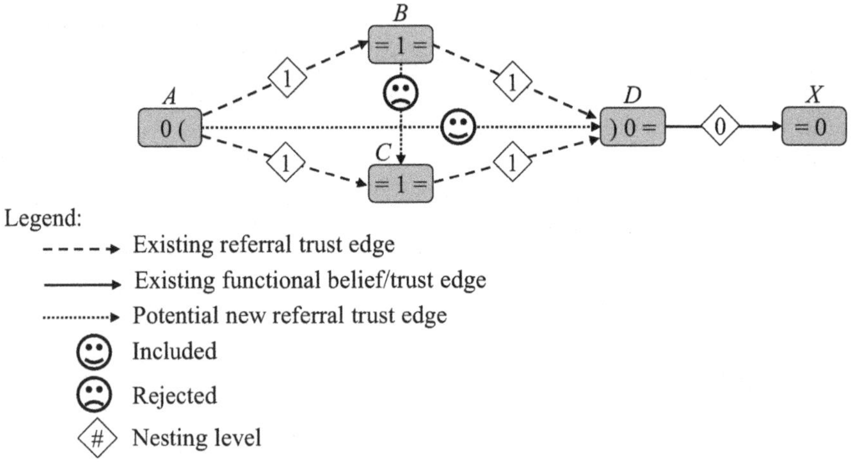

Fig. 15.12 Visualising the criterion that the target must be reachable from the source

The edge $[A;D]$ is included with same nesting level as the sub-paths $([A;B] : [B;D])$ and $([A;C] : [C;D])$. The existing and new updated graphs of Figure 15.12 are expressed below. Note that the brackets around sub-paths, e.g. $([A;B] : [B;D])$, are not reflected in Figure 15.12 because these brackets do not represent nesting, but simply grouping of edges belonging to the same sub-path.

$$\begin{aligned}
&\text{Existing graph: } ((([A;B] : [B;D]) \diamond ([A;C] : [C;D])) : [D;X]), \\
&\text{Updated graph: } ((([A;B] : [B;D]) \diamond ([A;C] : [C;D]) \diamond [A;D]) : [D;X]).
\end{aligned} \tag{15.6}$$

- **Illustrating DSPG Synthesis Criterion 2.**
  Criterion 2 from Definition 15.7 is illustrated in Figure 15.13. The new edge $[B;D]$ is rejected because B and D have different nesting levels, whereas the new edge $[A;D]$ is included because A and D have equal nesting levels. Node A in fact has have nesting levels 0, 1 and 2 simultaneously because it is the source node, and also connects two separate bifurcations with nesting levels 1 and 2 which start from A.

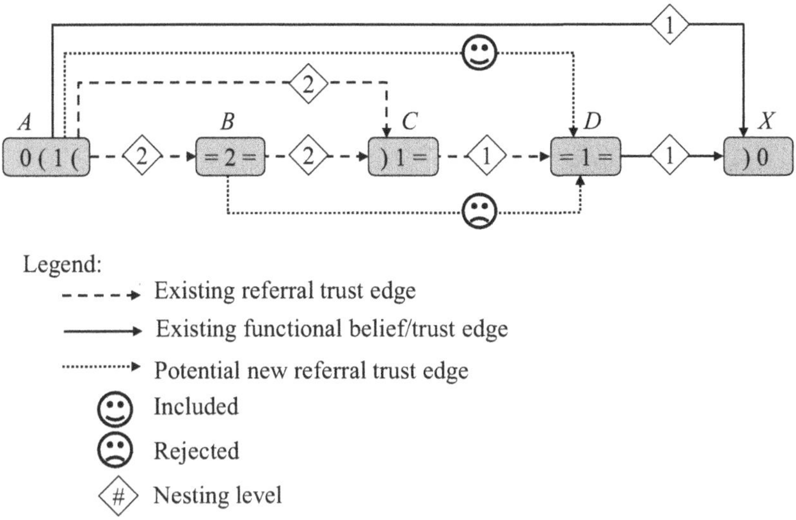

Fig. 15.13 Visualising the criterion that the source and target must have equal nesting levels

Including the new edge $[A;D]$ creates an additional nesting level which also causes the nesting levels of the sub-paths $([A;B] : [B;C])$ and $[A;C]$ to increment to nesting level 3. Also, the edge $[C;D]$ increments to nesting level 2. The existing and updated graphs of Figure 15.13 can then be expressed as

$$\text{Existing graph: } ((((([A;B] : [B;C]) \diamond [A;C]) : [C;D] : [D,X]) \diamond [A,X]),$$

$$\text{Updated graph: } (((((([A;B] : [B;C]) \diamond [A;C]) : [C;D]) \diamond [A;D]) : [D,X]) \diamond [A,X]). \tag{15.7}$$

- **Illustrating DSPG Synthesis Criterion 3.**
  Criterion 3 from Definition 15.7 is illustrated in Figure 15.14. The new edge $[B;D]$ is rejected because the node C has a nesting level that is inferior to that of B and D, whereas the new edge $[A,X]$ is included because the nesting level of C is equal to that of A and X.
  Including the new edge $[A,X]$ creates an additional nesting level which also causes the nesting levels of the existing sub-paths to increment. The existing and new graphs of Figure 15.14 can then be expressed as

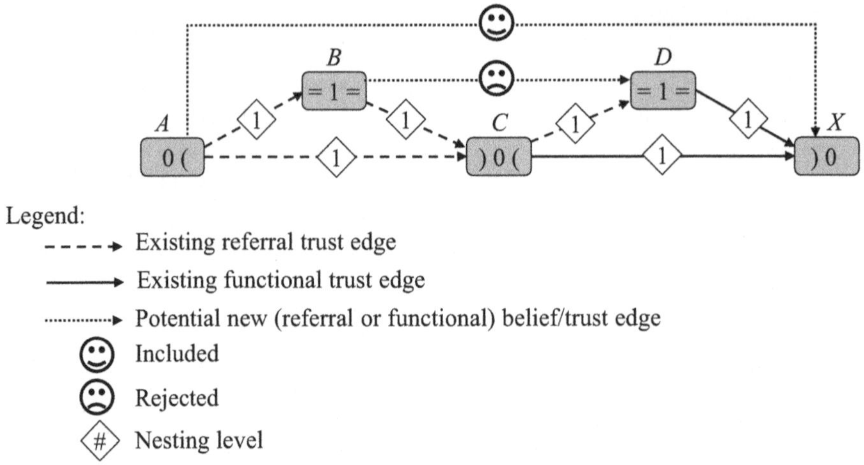

Fig. 15.14 Visualising the criterion that nesting levels of intermediate nodes must be equal to, or greater than that of the source and target

$$\text{Existing graph: } ((([A;B]:[B;C])\diamond[A;C]):(([C;D]:[D,X])\diamond[C,X])),$$

$$\text{Updated graph: } (((([A;B]:[B;C])\diamond[A;C]):(([C;D]:[D,X])\diamond[C,X]))\diamond[A,X]). \tag{15.8}$$

Recall that new sub-paths can have an arbitrary number of nodes, although the examples above only show new sub-paths represented as a single edge between a source and a target. By using the DSPG-synthesis algorithm of Figure 15.10 combined with the DSPG-consistency criteria of Definition 15.7, a canonical trust network can be synthesised. In turn, this canonical trust network can be easily analysed with the operators for trust fusion and trust transitivity.

Chapter 16
Bayesian Reputation Systems

Reputation systems are used to collect and analyse feedback about the performance and quality of products, services and service entities, which we simply call *service objects*. The received feedback can be used to derive reputation scores, which in turn can be published to potential future users. The feedback can also be used internally by the service provider, in order to improve the quality of service objects.

Figure 16.1 illustrates how a reputation system is typically integrated into online service provision. The figure indicates the cyclic sequence of steps, including request and provision of services, in addition to the exchange and processing of feedback ratings and reputation scores. Reputation systems are normally integrated with the service provision function, so that steps related to reputation are linked to the steps of service provision. Feedback from service users is highly valuable to service providers, but there is typically no obvious incentive for service users to provide ratings. In order to increase the amount of feedback, it is common that the service provider explicitly requests feedback from the service users, after a service has been provided and consumed.

From the user's point of view, it is assumed that reputation scores can help predict the future performance of service objects, and thereby reduce uncertainty about making decisions to rely on those service objects [85]. The idea is that transactions with reputable service objects or service providers are likely to result in more favourable outcomes than transactions with disreputable service objects and service providers.

Reputation scores are not only useful for service consumer decision making. Reputation scores can also be used internally by a service provider in order to tune and configure the service provision system, and in general to increase quality and performance.

Reputation systems are typically centralised, meaning that ratings are centrally aggregated, as illustrated in Figure 16.1. Distributed reputation systems have been proposed, and could e.g. be implemented in conjunction with peer-to-peer (P2P) networks [3], where a user must discover and request private reputation ratings from other users in the P2P-network. Distributed reputation systems are not discussed here.

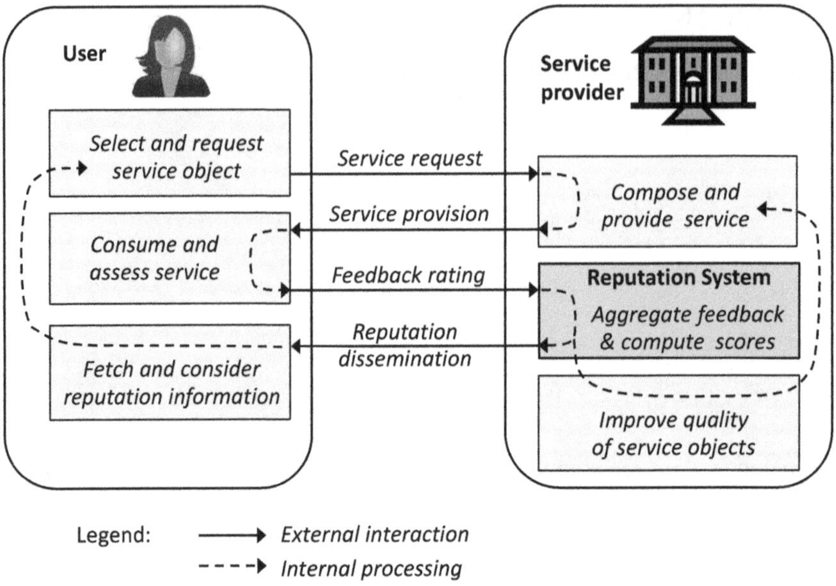

Fig. 16.1 Integration of reputation systems in service architectures

Two fundamental elements of reputation systems are

1. *A collection network* which allows the reputation system to receive and aggregate feedback ratings about service objects from users, as well as quality indicators from other sources.
2. *A reputation score computation engine* used by the reputation system to derive reputation scores for each participant, based on received ratings, and possibly also on other information.

Many different reputation systems, including reputation score computation methods, have been proposed in the literature, and we do not intend to provide a complete survey or comparison here. We refer to [24, 48, 68, 86, 92] as general literature on reputation systems.

The most common approach to computing the reputation score in commercial systems is probably to use some form of weighted mean. Computation methods based on weights distributed around the median rating (i.e. the middle rating in a ranked list of ratings) [1, 2, 30] can provide more stable reputation scores than scores based on the simple mean. It is also possible to compute scores bases on fuzzy logic [4], for example. User-trust and time-related factors can be incorporated into any of the above-mentioned reputation computation methods.

This chapter focuses on reputation score computation methods, and in particular on Bayesian computational methods. Binomial and multinomial Bayesian reputation systems have been proposed and studied e.g. in [47, 46, 61, 100]. The purpose of this chapter is to concisely describe basic features of Bayesian reputation systems.

16.1 Computing Reputation Scores

Binomial reputation systems allow ratings to be expressed with two values, either positive (e.g. *Good*) or negative (e.g. *Bad*). Multinomial reputation systems allow the possibility of providing ratings in different discrete levels such as e.g. *Bad - Mediocre - Average - Good - Excellent.*

16.1.1 Binomial Reputation Score

Binomial Bayesian reputation systems apply to the binary state space {Bad, Good} which reflects the corresponding performance of a service object. The evidence notation of the Beta PDF of Eq.(3.8) takes the two parameters r and s that represent the number of received positive and negative ratings respectively.

Binomial reputation is computed by statistical updating of the Beta PDF. More specifically, the posterior (i.e. updated) reputation is continuously computed by combining the prior (i.e. previous) reputation with every new rating. The expected probability of Eq.(3.9) is used, directly or indirectly, to represent the reputation score. The Beta PDF itself only provides the underlying statistical foundation, and is otherwise not used in the reputation system.

Before receiving any ratings, the prior distribution is the Beta PDF with $r = 0$ and $s = 0$, which with the default base rate $a = 0.5$ produces a uniform prior distribution. Then after observing r 'Good' and s 'Bad' outcomes, the *a posteriori* Beta PDF gives a reputation score S that can be computed with the expression for expected probability of Eq.(3.9), which in terms of reputation score is repeated below:

$$S = (r + Wa)/(r + s + W) . \tag{16.1}$$

This score should be interpreted as the probability that the next experience with the service object will be 'Good'. Recall that W denotes the non-informative prior weight, where $W = 2$ is normally used.

16.1.2 Multinomial Reputation Scores

Multinomial Bayesian reputation systems allow ratings to be provided over k different levels, which can be considered as a set of k disjoint values in a domain. Let this set be denoted $\Lambda = \{L_1, \ldots, L_k\}$, and assume that ratings are provided as votes on the values of Λ. This leads to a Dirichlet PDF (probability density function) over the k-component random probability variable $\boldsymbol{p}(L_i)$, $i = 1, \ldots, k$ with sample space $[0,1]^k$, subject to the simple additivity requirement $\sum_{i=1}^{k} \boldsymbol{p}(L_i) = 1$. The evidence representation of the Dirichlet PDF is given in Eq.(3.16). The Dirichlet PDF itself only provides the underlying statistical foundation, and is otherwise not used in the reputation system.

The Dirichlet PDF with prior captures a sequence of observations of the k possible outcomes with k positive real rating parameters $\boldsymbol{r}(L_i)$, $i = 1,\ldots,k$, each corresponding to one of the possible levels. In order to have a compact notation we define a vector $\boldsymbol{p} = \{\boldsymbol{p}(L_i) \mid 1 \leq i \leq k\}$ to denote the k-component probability variable, and a vector $\boldsymbol{r} = \{r_i \mid 1 \leq i \leq k\}$ to denote the k-component rating variable.

In order to distinguish between the prior default base rate and the posterior ratings, the Dirichlet PDF must be expressed with prior information represented as a base rate distribution $\boldsymbol{a}$ over the rating levels L.

Similarly to the binomial case, the multinomial reputation score $\boldsymbol{S}$ is the distribution of expected probabilities of the k random probability variables, which can be computed with the expression for expected probability distribution of Eq.(3.17), which in terms of score distribution is expressed as

$$\boldsymbol{S}(L_i) = \mathrm{E}(\boldsymbol{p}(L_i) \mid \boldsymbol{r},\boldsymbol{a}) = \frac{\boldsymbol{r}(L_i) + W\boldsymbol{a}(L_i)}{W + \sum_{i=1}^{k} \boldsymbol{r}(L_i)} \; . \tag{16.2}$$

The non-informative prior weight W is normally set to $W = 2$ when a uniform distribution over binary state spaces is assumed. Selecting a larger value for W would result in new observations having less influence over the Dirichlet PDF, and can in fact represent specific prior information provided by a domain expert or by another reputation system.

16.2 Collecting and Aggregating Ratings

Before computing reputation scores, the ratings must be collected and aggregated in some way. This includes taking time decay into account, for example.

16.2.1 Collecting Ratings

Assume k different discrete rating levels L. This translates into having a domain of cardinality k. For binomial reputation systems $k = 2$, and the rating levels are 'Bad' and 'Good'. For a multinomial reputation system $k > 2$ and any corresponding set of suitable rating levels can be used. Let the rating level be indexed by i. The aggregate ratings for a particular service object y are stored as the cumulative vector $\boldsymbol{R}_y$:

$$\boldsymbol{R}_y = (\boldsymbol{R}_y(L_i) \mid i = 1,\ldots,k) \; . \tag{16.3}$$

The simplest way of updating a rating vector as a result of a new rating is by adding the newly received rating vector $\boldsymbol{r}$ to the previously stored vector $\boldsymbol{R}$. The case when old ratings are aged is described in Section 16.2.2.

Each new discrete rating of service object y by an agent A takes the form of a trivial vector $\boldsymbol{r}_y^A$, where only one vector value has rating 1, and all other vector values have rating 0. The index i of the vector value with rating 1 refers to the specific rating level.

16.2.2 Aggregating Ratings with Ageing

Ratings are typically aggregated by simple addition of the components (vector addition). However, service objects may change their quality over time, so it is desirable to give relatively greater weight to more recent ratings. This principle is called *time decay*, which can be taken into account by introducing a *longevity factor* $\lambda \in [0,1]$ for ratings, which controls the rapidity with which old ratings are aged and discounted as a function of time. With $\lambda = 0$, ratings are completely forgotten after a single time period. With $\lambda = 1$, ratings are never forgotten.

Let new ratings be collected in discrete time periods. Let the sum of the ratings of a particular service object y in period τ be denoted by the vector $\boldsymbol{r}_{y,\tau}$. More specifically, it is the sum of all ratings $\boldsymbol{r}_y^A$ of service object y by rating agents A during that period, expressed by

$$\boldsymbol{r}_{y,\tau} = \sum_{A \in M_{y,\tau}} \boldsymbol{r}_y^A\,, \tag{16.4}$$

where $M_{y,\tau}$ is the set of all rating agents who rated service object y during period τ.

Let the total accumulated ratings (with ageing) of service object y after the time period τ be denoted by $\boldsymbol{R}_{y,\tau}$. Then the new accumulated rating after time period $\tau+1$ can be expressed as

$$\boldsymbol{R}_{y,(\tau+1)} = \lambda \cdot \boldsymbol{R}_{y,\tau} + \boldsymbol{r}_{y,(\tau+1)}\,, \quad \text{where } 0 \leq \lambda \leq 1\,. \tag{16.5}$$

Eq.(16.5) represents a recursive updating algorithm that can be executed once every period for all service objects, or alternatively in a discrete fashion for each service object for example after each new rating. Assuming that new ratings are received between time τ and time $\tau+n$, then the updated rating vector can be computed as

$$\boldsymbol{R}_{y,(\tau+n)} = \lambda^n \cdot \boldsymbol{R}_{y,\tau} + \boldsymbol{r}_{y,(\tau+n)}\,, \quad 0 \leq \lambda \leq 1. \tag{16.6}$$

16.2.3 Reputation Score Convergence with Time Decay

The recursive algorithm of Eq.(16.5) makes it possible to compute convergence values for the rating vectors, as well as for reputation scores. Assuming that a particular service object receives the same ratings every period, then Eq.(16.5) defines a geometric series. We use the well-known result for geometric series

$$\sum_{j=0}^{\infty} \lambda^j = \frac{1}{1-\lambda}\,, \qquad \text{for } -1 < \lambda < 1\,. \tag{16.7}$$

Let $\boldsymbol{e}_y$ represent a constant rating vector of service object y for each period. The total accumulated rating vector after an infinite number of periods is then

$$\boldsymbol{R}_{y,\infty} = \frac{\boldsymbol{e}_y}{1-\lambda}\,, \qquad \text{where } 0 \le \lambda < 1\,. \tag{16.8}$$

Eq.(16.8) shows that the longevity factor λ determines the convergence values for the accumulated rating vector according to Eq.(16.5). In general, the components of the accumulated rating vector will never reach infinity, which makes it impossible for the score vector components to cover the whole range $[0,1]$. However, service objects that provide maximum quality services over a long time period might naturally expect to get the highest possible reputation score. An intuitive interpretation of this expectation is that each long-standing service object should have its own individual base rate, which is determined as a function of the service object's total history, or at least a large part of it. This approach is used in the next section to include individual base rates.

16.3 Base Rates for Ratings

The cold-start problem in reputation systems occurs when a service object has not received any ratings, or too few ratings to produce a reliable reputation score. This problem can be solved by basing reputation scores on base rates, which can be individual or community based.

16.3.1 Individual Base Rates

A base rate normally expresses the average in a population or domain. Here we will compute individual base rates from a 'population' consisting of individual performances over a series of time periods. The individual base rate for service object y at time τ is denoted $\boldsymbol{a}_{y,\tau}$, and is based on individual evidence vectors denoted $\boldsymbol{Q}_{y,\tau}$.

Let $\boldsymbol{a}$ denote the community base rate as usual. Then the individual base rate for service object y at time τ can be computed similarly to Eq.(3.17) as

$$\boldsymbol{a}_{y,\tau}(L_i) = \frac{\boldsymbol{Q}_{y,\tau}(L_i) + W\boldsymbol{a}(L_i)}{W + \sum_{i=1}^{k} \boldsymbol{Q}_{y,\tau}(L_i)}\,. \tag{16.9}$$

Reputation scores can be computed as normal with Eq.(16.2), except that the community base rate $\boldsymbol{a}$ is replaced with the individual base rate $\boldsymbol{a}_{y,\tau}$ of Eq.(16.9). It can be noted that the individual base rate $\boldsymbol{a}_{y,\tau}$ is partially a function of the community base rate $\boldsymbol{a}$; this therefore constitutes a two-layered base-rate model.

The components of the reputation score vector computed with Eq.(16.2) based on the individual base rate of Eq.(16.9) can theoretically be arbitrarily close to 0 or 1, with any longevity factor and any community base rate.

The simplest alternative to consider is to let the individual base rate for each service object be a function of the service object's total history. A second similar alternative is to let the individual base rate be computed as a function of a service object's performance over a very long sliding time window. A third alternative is to define an additional high longevity factor for base rates that is much closer to 1 than the common longevity factor λ. The formalisms for these three alternatives are briefly described below.

16.3.2 Total History Base Rate

The total evidence vector $\boldsymbol{Q}_{y,\tau}$ for service object y used to compute the individual base rate at time period τ is expressed as

$$\boldsymbol{Q}_{y,\tau} = \sum_{j=1}^{\tau} \boldsymbol{R}_{y,j} \,. \tag{16.10}$$

16.3.3 Sliding Time Window Base Rate

The evidence vector $\boldsymbol{Q}_{y,\tau}$ for computing a service object y's individual base rate at time period τ is expressed as

$$\boldsymbol{Q}_{y,\tau} = \sum_{j=u}^{\tau} \boldsymbol{R}_{y,j} \quad \text{where Window Size } = (\tau - u) \,. \tag{16.11}$$

The Window Size would normally be a constant, but could also be dynamic. In case e.g. $u = 1$, the Window Size would be increasing and equal to τ, which also would make this alternative equivalent to the total history alternative described above.

16.3.4 High Longevity Factor Base Rate

Let λ denote the normal longevity factor. A high longevity factor λ_{H} can be defined, where $\lambda_{\mathrm{H}} > \lambda$. The evidence vector $\boldsymbol{Q}_{y,\tau}$ for computing a service object y's individual base rate at time period τ is computed as

$$\boldsymbol{Q}_{y,\tau} = \lambda_{\mathrm{H}} \cdot \boldsymbol{Q}_{y,(\tau-1)} + \boldsymbol{r}_{y,\tau}, \text{ where } \lambda < \lambda_{\mathrm{H}} \leq 1 \,. \tag{16.12}$$

In case $\lambda_{\mathrm{H}} = 1$, this alternative would be equivalent to the total history alternative described above. The high longevity factor makes ratings age much more slowly than with the regular longevity factor.

16.3.5 Dynamic Community Base Rate

Bootstrapping a reputation system to a stable and conservative state is important. In the framework described above, the base rate distribution $\boldsymbol{a}$ defines an initial default reputation for all service objects. The base rate can for example be evenly distributed, or biased towards either a negative or a positive reputation. This must be defined by the designers of the reputation system in a specific market or community.

Service objects will come and go during the lifetime of a market, and it is important to be able to assign a reasonable base rate reputation to new service objects. In the simplest case, this can be the same as the initial default reputation used during bootstrap.

However, it is possible to track the average reputation score of the whole community of service objects, and this can be used to set the base rate for new service objects, either directly or with a certain additional bias.

Not only new service objects, but also existing service objects with a standing track record can get the dynamic base rate. After all, a dynamic community base rate reflects the whole community, and should therefore be applied to all service object members of that community. The aggregate reputation vector for the whole community at time τ can be computed as

$$\boldsymbol{R}_{M,\tau} = \sum_{y_j \in M} \boldsymbol{R}_{y,\tau} \,. \tag{16.13}$$

This vector then needs to be normalised to a base rate vector as follows.

Definition 16.1 (Community Base Rate). Let $\boldsymbol{R}_{M,\tau}$ be an aggregate reputation vector for a whole community, and let $\boldsymbol{S}_{M,\tau}$ be the corresponding multinomial probability reputation vector which can be computed with Eq.(16.2). The community base rate as a function of existing reputations at time $\tau+1$ is then simply expressed as the community score at time τ:

$$\boldsymbol{a}_{M,(\tau+1)} = \boldsymbol{S}_{M,\tau} \,. \tag{16.14}$$

The base rate vector of Eq.(16.14) can be given to every new service object that joins the community. In addition, the community base rate vector can be used for every service object every time their reputation score is computed. In this way, the base rate will dynamically reflect the quality of the market at any one time.

If desirable, the base rate for new service objects can be biased in either a negative or a positive direction in order to make it harder or easier to enter the market.

When base rates are a function of the community reputation, the expressions for convergence values with constant ratings can no longer be defined with Eq.(16.8), and will instead converge towards the average score from all the ratings.

16.4 Reputation Representation

Reputation can be represented in different forms. In this section we illustrate reputation as *multinomial probability scores*, and as *point estimates*. Each form is described in turn below.

16.4.1 Multinomial Probability Representation

The most natural approach is to define the reputation score as a function of the expected probability of each score level. The expected probability for each rating level can be computed with Eq.(16.2).

Let $\boldsymbol{R}$ represent the service object's aggregate ratings. The vector $\boldsymbol{S}$ defined by

$$\boldsymbol{S}_y : \left(\boldsymbol{S}_y(L_i) = \frac{\boldsymbol{R}^*_y(L_i) + W\boldsymbol{a}(L_i)}{W + \sum_{j=1}^{k} \boldsymbol{R}^*_y(L_j)}, \quad \text{for } i = 1, \ldots, k \right) \tag{16.15}$$

is the corresponding multinomial probability reputation score. As already stated, $W = 2$ is the value of choice, but a larger value for the constant W can be chosen if a reduced influence of new evidence over the base rate is required.

The reputation score $\boldsymbol{S}$ can be interpreted like a multinomial probability measure as an indication of how a particular service object is expected to perform in future transactions. It can easily be verified that

$$\sum_{i=1}^{k} S(L_i) = 1 \ . \tag{16.16}$$

The multinomial reputation score can for example be visualised as columns, which clearly indicate whether ratings are polarised. Assume for example the five rating levels in Eq.(16.17):

$$\text{Discrete rating levels:} \begin{cases} L_1 : \text{Bad}, \\ L_2 : \text{Mediocre}, \\ L_3 : \text{Average}, \\ L_4 : \text{Good}, \\ L_5 : \text{Excellent}. \end{cases} \tag{16.17}$$

We assume a default base rate distribution. Before any ratings have been received, the multinomial probability reputation score is equal to $1/5$ for all levels. Let us assume that 10 ratings are received. In the first case, 10 *average* ratings are received, which translates into the multinomial probability reputation score of Figure 16.2.a. In the second case, five bad and five excellent ratings are received, which translates into the multinomial probability reputation score of Figure 16.2.b.

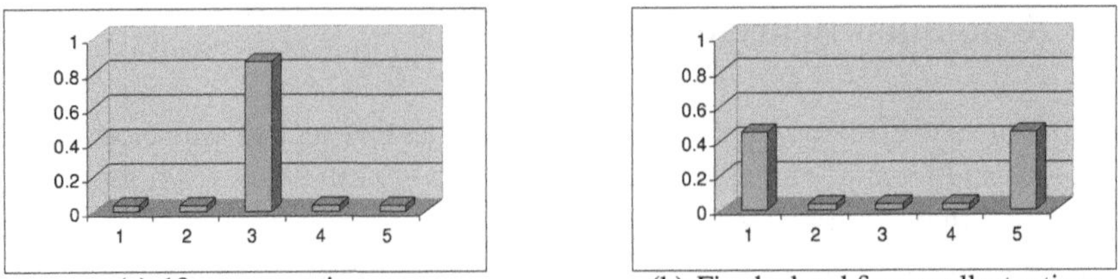

(a) 10 average ratings

(b) Five bad and five excellent ratings

Fig. 16.2 Illustrating score difference resulting from average and polarised ratings

One advantage of multinomial rating systems is the ability to see the difference between the scenarios of Figure 16.2.a and Figure 16.2.b. With a binomial reputation system, the difference between these two rating scenarios would not have been visible.

16.4.2 Point Estimate Representation

While informative, the multinomial probability representation can require considerable space to be displayed on a computer screen. A more compact form can be to express the reputation score as a single value in some predefined interval. This can be done by assigning a point value v to each rating level i, and computing the normalised weighted point estimate score σ.

Assume e.g. k different rating levels with point values evenly distributed in the range [0,1], so that $v(L_i) = \frac{i-1}{k-1}$. The point estimate reputation score is then

$$\sigma = \sum_{i=1}^{k} v(L_i) S(L_i) . \tag{16.18}$$

However, this point estimate removes information, so that for example the difference between the average ratings and the polarised ratings of Figure 16.2.a and Figure 16.2.b is no longer visible. The point estimates of the reputation scores of Figure 16.2.a and Figure 16.2.b are both 0.5, although the ratings in fact are quite different. A point estimate in the range [0,1] can be mapped to any range, such as one-to-five stars, a percentage or a probability.

It is possible to convert multinomial ratings to binomial ratings, as explained below. Let the multinomial reputation model have k rating levels L_i, $i = 1, \ldots, k$, where $\boldsymbol{R}(L_i)$ represents the ratings on each level L_i, and let σ represent the point estimate reputation score from Eq.(16.18). Let the binomial reputation model have positive and negative ratings r and s respectively. The derived converted binomial rating parameters (r,s) are given by

$$\begin{cases} r = \sigma \sum_{i=1}^{k} \boldsymbol{R}_y(L_i)\ , \\ s = \sum_{i=1}^{k} \boldsymbol{R}_y(L_i) - r\ . \end{cases} \tag{16.19}$$

16.4.3 Continuous Ratings

It is common that the rating and scores of service objects are measured on a continuous scale, such as time, throughput or relative ranking, to name a few examples. Even when it is natural to provide discrete ratings, it may be inaccurate to express that something is strictly good or average, so that combinations of discrete ratings, such as *'average-to-good'* would better reflect the rater's opinion. Such ratings can then be considered continuous. To handle this, it is possible to use a fuzzy membership function to convert a continuous rating into a binomial or multinomial rating. For example, with five rating levels the sliding-window function can be illustrated as in Figure 16.3. The continuous q-value determines the r-values for that level.

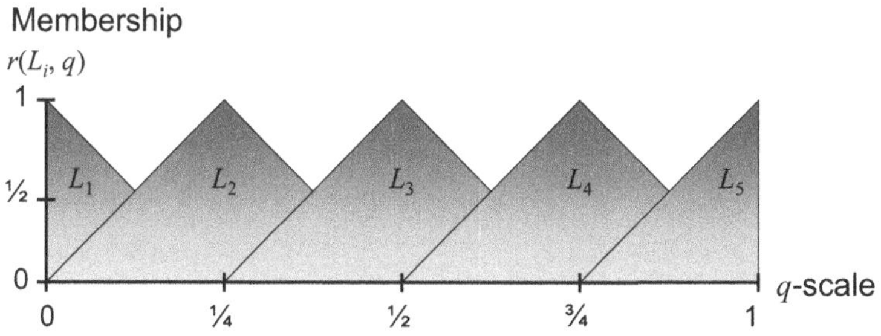

Fig. 16.3 Fuzzy triangular membership functions

16.5 Simple Scenario Simulation

A simple scenario can be used to illustrate the performance of a multinomial reputation system that uses some of the features described above. Let us assume that service objects y and z receive a sequence of ratings over 70 time periods as specified in Table 16.1. The time periods are divided into five groups, where the ratings are the same during the sequence of periods within the same group.

Table 16.1 Sequence of ratings

Group	Sequence	Service object y	Service object z
1	Periods 1 - 10	$10 \times L_1$ ratings in each period	$1 \times L_1$ rating in each period
2	Periods 11-20	$10 \times L_2$ ratings in each period	$1 \times L_2$ rating in each period
3	Periods 21-30	$10 \times L_3$ ratings in each period	$1 \times L_3$ rating in each period
4	Periods 31-40	$10 \times L_4$ ratings in each period	$1 \times L_4$ rating in each period
5	Periods 41-70	$30 \times L_5$ ratings in each period	$3 \times L_5$ ratings in each period

The longevity of ratings is set to $\lambda = 0.9$ and the individual base rate is computed with the high-longevity approach described in Section 16.3.4 with high longevity factor for the base rate set to $\lambda_{\mathrm{H}} = 0.999$. For simplicity in this example the community base rate is assumed to be fixed during the 70 rounds, expressed by $a(L_1) = a(L_2) = a(L_3) = a(L_4) = a(L_5) = 0.2$. Figure 16.4 illustrates the evolution of the scores of service objects y and z during the period.

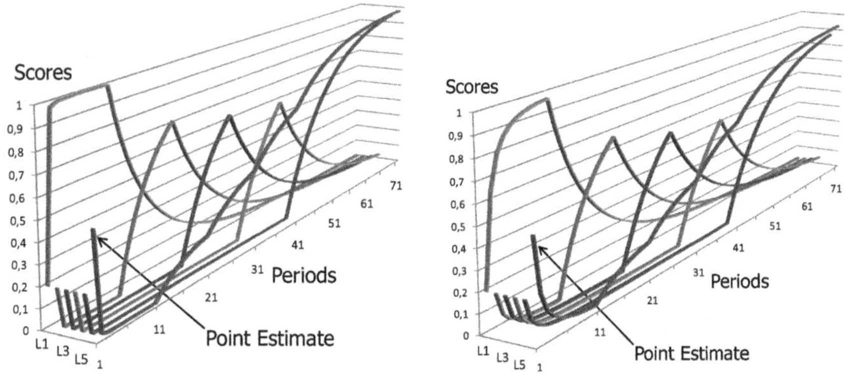

(a) Scores for service object y (b) Scores for service object z

Fig. 16.4 Score evolution for service objects y and z

The scores for both service objects are initially based on the community base rate, and then vary as a function of the received ratings. Both service objects have an initial point estimate of 0.5.

The scores for service object z in Figure 16.4.b are similar in trend, but less articulated than those of service object y in Figure 16.4.a, because service object z receives equal but less frequent ratings. The final score of service object z is visibly lower than 1, because the relatively low number of ratings is insufficient for driving the individual base rate very close to 1. Thanks to the community base rate, all new service objects in a community get a meaningful initial score. In the case of rating scarcity, a service object's score will initially be determined by the community base rate, with the individual base rate dominating as soon as some ratings have been received.

16.6 Combining Trust and Reputation

The multinomial Bayesian reputation systems described above use the same representation as multinomial evidence opinions described in Eq.(3.16), which can be mapped to multinomial opinions according to Definition 3.6. Furthermore, the projection from multinomial ratings to binomial ratings of Eq.(16.19) combined with the binomial mapping of Definition 3.3 makes it possible to represent reputation scores as binomial opinions, which in turn can be applied in computational trust models as described in Chapter 14.

Figure 16.5 illustrates a scenario involving a reputation system that publishes reputation scores about agents in a network. We assume that agent A needs to derive a measure of trust in agent F, and that only agent B has knowledge about F. Assume furthermore that agent A has no direct trust in B, but that A trusts the Reputation System RS and that RS has published a reputation score about B.

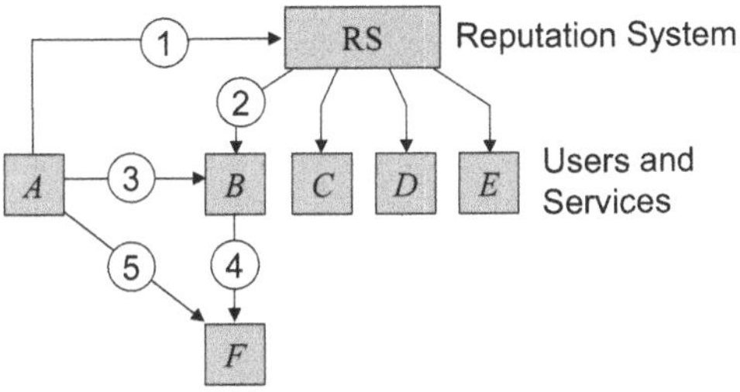

Fig. 16.5 Combining trust and reputation

Agent A has trust ω^A_{RS} in the Reputation System (arrow 1), and agent B has reputation score $\boldsymbol{R}^{\text{RS}}_B$ (arrow 2). The binomial reputation score $\boldsymbol{R}^{\text{RS}}_B$ is a Beta PDF denoted $\text{Beta}^{\text{e}}(p_x, r_x, s_x, a_x)$ as expressed in Eq.(3.8), and which can be mapped to a binomial opinion according to the mapping of Definition 3.3. The binomial opinion derived from the reputation score of B produced by the Reputation System RS is then denoted ω^{RS}_B.

Agent A can then derive a measure of trust in B (arrow 3) based on A's trust in RS and the reputation opinion ω^{RS}_B. Agent B trusts F (arrow 4) with opinion ω^B_F, where it is assumed that B passes this trust advice to A, so that A can derive a degree of trust in F (arrow 5). The trust path is expressed as

$$[A,F] = [A;\text{RS}] : [\text{RS};B] : [B,F]\,. \tag{16.20}$$

The trust edges $[A;\text{RS}]$ and $[\text{RS};B]$ represent referral trust, whereas the trust edge $[B,F]$ represents functional trust.

In the notation of subjective logic, A's derived trust in F can be expressed as

$$\omega^A_F = \omega^A_{\text{RS}} \otimes \omega^{\text{RS}}_B \otimes \omega^B_F\,. \tag{16.21}$$

The computation of ω_F^A is done according to the method for multi-node trust transitivity described in Section 14.3.4.

The compatibility between Bayesian reputation systems and subjective logic provides a flexible framework for analysing trust networks consisting of both reputation scores and private trust values.

Chapter 17
Subjective Networks

This chapter provides an introduction to the concept of *subjective networks* (SN) as graph-based structures of agents and variables combined with conditional opinions and trust opinions [60]. SNs generalise Bayesian network modelling and analysis in two ways: 1) by applying subjective logic instead of probabilistic reasoning, and 2) by integrating subjective trust networks (STNs) which allows different agents to have different opinions about the same variables.

A Bayesian network (BN) [81] is a compact representation of a joint probability distribution of random variables in the form of DAG (directed acyclic graph) and a set of conditional probability distributions associated with each node.

The goal of inference in BNs is to derive a conditional probability distribution of any set of (target) variables in the network, given that the values of any other set of (evidence) variables have been observed. This is done by propagating the probabilistic information through the graph, from the evidence to the target.

One notable limitation of traditional Bayesian network reasoning is that input arguments must be assigned precise probabilities in order for the inference algorithms to work, and for the model to be analysed. This is problematic in situations where probabilities can not be reliably elicited and one needs to do inference with uncertain or incomplete probabilistic information. A natural approach to remedy this limitation is to represent the probabilistic conditionals of BNs with conditional subjective opinions since they can express uncertain probabilities.

A subjective-logic based generalisation of BNs retains the network structure and replaces conditional probability distributions with conditional subjective opinions at every node of the network. This generalisation leads to the concept of *subjective Bayesian network* (SBN) with which conditional inference is done with the operators of subjective logic. The goal of reasoning with SBNs is to derive subjective opinions on the target nodes given a set of conditional and evidence opinions. The input evidence can be direct observations of specific values expressed as absolute opinions, or it can be relatively unclear observations expressed as uncertain opinions.

An additional generalisation of BNs is the integration with STNs, whereby different agents can express different conditional and evidence opinions on the same conditionals and the same variables in the network. This generalisation leads to the concept of SNs (subjective networks) where trust relationships between agents and evidence sources are taken into account when analysing realistic situations. Figure 17.1 illustrates the general idea of SNs which consists of combining SBNs and STNs to produce SNs.

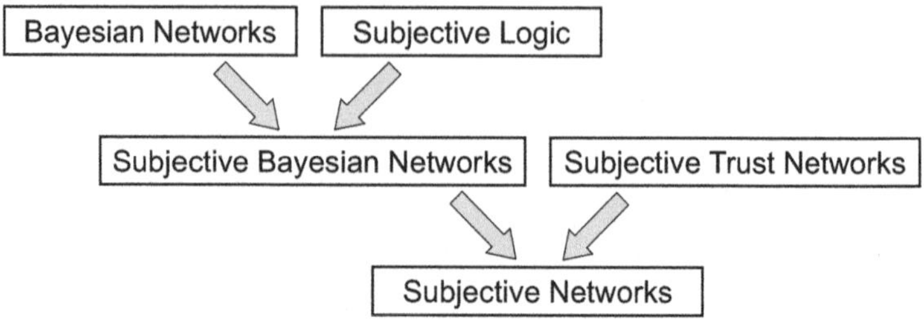

Fig. 17.1 The general idea of subjective networks

The capacity of subjective logic for reasoning in the presence of uncertainty and for reasoning with trust, combined with the power of BNs for modelling conditional knowledge structures, is a very potent combination. This chapter is meant as a brief and high-level introduction to SNs. A separate book is required to properly and thoroughly cover this topic. This is obviously a promising and fertile field of research and development.

In order to set the background for SNs the next section gives a brief introduction to BNs. For a general description BNs, see e.g. [67]. After the introduction, we describe some properties and aspects resulting from the generalisation to SBNs, how it can be applied. Finally, we describe aspects of the generalisation to SNs.

17.1 Bayesian Networks

When events and states are related in time and space, they are conditionally dependent. For example, the state of carrying an umbrella is typically influenced by the state of rain. The principle of BNs is to model these conditional relationships in the form of graphs, consisting of nodes connected with directed edges. To be practical, the graphs must be acyclic to prevent loops, so that the graph is a DAG, to be precise. The nodes are variables that represent possible states or events. The directed edges represent the (causal) relationships between the nodes.

Associated with a Bayesian network graph are various (conditional) probability distributions, which formally specify selected local (conditional) relationships between nodes. Missing probability distributions for query target nodes can be derived through various algorithms that take as input arguments the existing known probability distributions and the structure of the Bayesian network graph.

Initially proposed by Pearl in 1988 [81], Bayesian networks are currently being applied in numerous areas such as medical diagnostics, forensics, financial analysis, marketing, military planning, risk management, artificial intelligence etc.

Figure 17.2 illustrates typical reasoning situations supported by BNs [67], where the arrows $\Longrightarrow$ represent conditional relationships between variables/nodes.

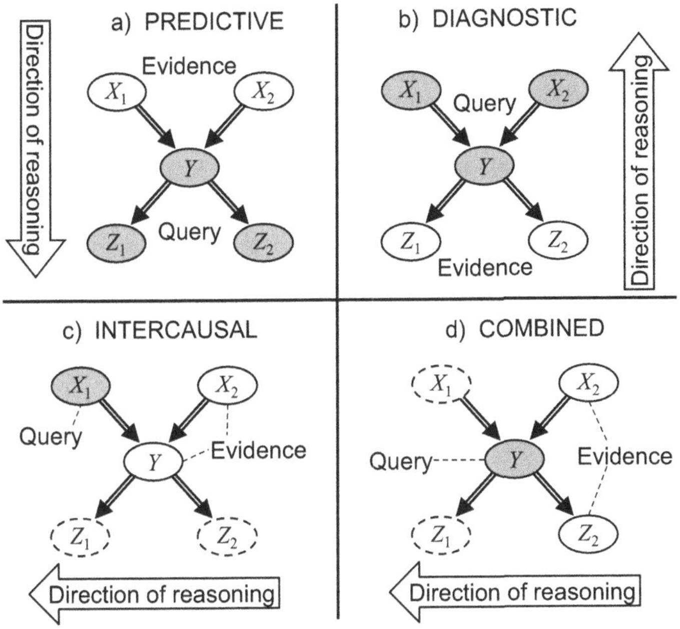

Fig. 17.2 Categories of Bayesian reasoning

Note that the situations illustrated in Figure 17.2 do not represent situations of belief fusion described in Chapter 12. For example in the predictive situation of Figure 17.2.a, the probability distribution over the variable Y should be computed with the set of conditional probability distributions $\boldsymbol{p}(Y|X_1 X_2)$ which are conditioned on the values of the joint variable $(X_1 X_2)$. Attempting to model this situation with any of the belief fusion operators described in Chapter 12 would be an approximation at best but would be incorrect in general. Only a model based on joint conditional probabilities is suitable for expressing the whole range of possible conditional relationships between the parent variable pair $\{X_1\ X_2\}$ and the child variable Y. Models for the situations in Figure 17.2 are sometimes called Bayesian fusion models, but they are not belief fusion models. Bayesian fusion models are based on Bayesian networks and Bayesian classifiers.

The next sections describe models for the reasoning situations of Figure 17.2, first based on probabilistic BNs (Bayesian networks), and then on SBNs (subjective Bayesian networks).

17.1.1 Example: Lung Cancer Situation

A classical Bayesian network example is the case of lung cancer, which on the one hand can have various causes, and on the other hand can cause observable effects [67]. In the example, it is assumed that breathing polluted air, denoted P, and cigarette smoking, denoted S, are the most relevant causes. The estimated likelihood of getting lung cancer is specified as a table with conditional probabilities corresponding to all possible combinations of causes. In addition, assuming that a person has lung cancer (or not), the estimated likelihood of positive cancer detection on an X-ray image, denoted X, and the estimated likelihood of shortness of breath (medical term: *'dyspnoea'*), denoted D, are also specified as probability tables. Figure 17.3 illustrates this particular BN.

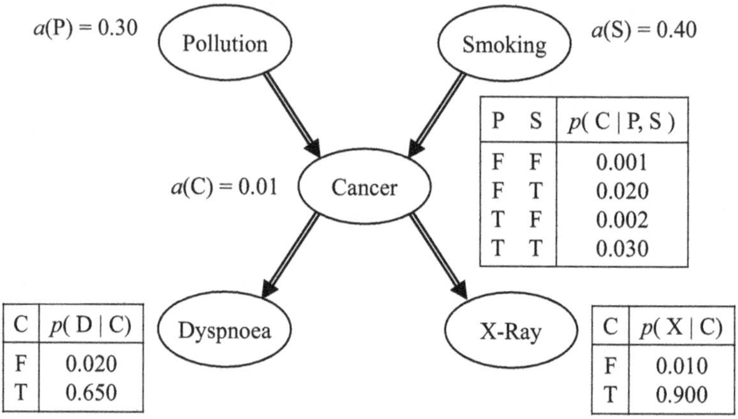

Fig. 17.3 Simple Bayesian network for the lung cancer situation

Once the graph has been drawn and populated with conditional probabilities, the BN becomes a basis for reasoning. In particular, when the value of one or several variables has been observed (or guessed), we can make inferences from the new information. This process is sometimes called probability propagation or belief updating, and consists of applying Bayes' theorem and other laws of probability, with the observed evidence and the probability tables as input parameters, to determine the probability distribution of specific variables of interest.

For example, assume a person who consults his GP because of shortness of breath. From this evidence alone, the GP can estimate the likelihood that the person suffers from lung cancer. The computation applies Bayes' theorem from Eq.(9.9), and requires a base rate (prior probability) of lung cancer in the population (expressed as $a(x)$ in Eq.(9.9)). Assume that the prior probability for lung cancer is $a(\mathrm{C}) = 0.01$. The probability of lung cancer given dyspnoea is then

$$
\begin{aligned}
p(\mathrm{C}|\mathrm{D}) &= \frac{a(\mathrm{C})p(\mathrm{D}|\mathrm{C})}{a(\mathrm{C})p(\mathrm{D}|\mathrm{C})+a(\overline{\mathrm{C}})p(\mathrm{D}|\overline{\mathrm{C}})} \\
&= \frac{0.01\cdot 0.65}{(0.01\cdot 0.65)+(0.99\cdot 0.02)} = 0.25.
\end{aligned} \tag{17.1}
$$

However, assuming that the evidence is not very conclusive, and that many other conditions can also cause shortness of breath, the GP can decide to request an X-ray image of the person's lungs in order to have more firm evidence. Based on indications of lung cancer found on the X-ray image, combined with the evidence of dyspnoea, the GP can update her belief in the likelihood of lung cancer by reapplying Bayes' theorem. The expression for the probability of lung cancer in Eq.(17.2) is conditioned on the joint variables (D,X):

$$
p(\mathrm{C}\,|\,\mathrm{D},\mathrm{X}) = \frac{a(\mathrm{C})p(\mathrm{D},\mathrm{X}\,|\,\mathrm{C})}{a(\mathrm{C})p(\mathrm{D},\mathrm{X}\,|\,\mathrm{C})+a(\overline{\mathrm{C}})p(\mathrm{D},\mathrm{X}\,|\,\overline{\mathrm{C}})}\,. \tag{17.2}
$$

However, there is no available probability table for $p(\mathrm{D},\mathrm{X}\,|\,\mathrm{C})$, so Eq.(17.2) can not be computed directly. Of course, medical authorities could establish a specific probability table for $p(\mathrm{D},\mathrm{X}\,|\,\mathrm{C})$, but because there can be many different indicators for a given diagnosis, it is typically impractical to produce ready-made probability tables for every possible combination of indicators.

Eq.(17.2) can be approximated with the *naïve Bayes* classifier, where separate conditional probability tables for different variables are combined as if they were one single probability table for a joint variable. This simplification is based on the independence assumption of the separate variables, which in many cases is a reasonable assumption. Eq.(17.3) gives the result of the naïve Bayes classifier in the example of diagnosing lung cancer based on both dyspnoea and X-ray. The result shows significantly larger likelihood of cancer than when only based on dyspnoea.

$$
\begin{aligned}
p(\mathrm{C}\,|\,\mathrm{D},\mathrm{X}) &\simeq \frac{a(\mathrm{C})p(\mathrm{D}|\mathrm{C})p(\mathrm{X}|\mathrm{C})}{a(\mathrm{C})p(\mathrm{D}|\mathrm{C})p(\mathrm{X}|\mathrm{C})+a(\overline{\mathrm{C}})p(\mathrm{D}|\overline{\mathrm{C}})p(\mathrm{X}|\overline{\mathrm{C}})} \\
&\simeq \frac{0.01\cdot 0.65\cdot 0.90}{(0.01\cdot 0.65\cdot 0.90)+(0.99\cdot 0.02\cdot 0.01)} = 0.97.
\end{aligned} \tag{17.3}
$$

The BN of Figure 17.3 can also be used for making predictions. Assume for example that according to statistics, the base rate of the population exposed to significant pollution is $a(\mathrm{P}) = 0.30$, and the base rate of smokers is $a(\mathrm{S}) = 0.40$. Assuming independence, the combined base rates of smokers and exposure to pollution are given in Table 17.1.

Table 17.1 Base rates of people exposed to pollution and being smokers

Pollution	Smoker	Probability
F	F	0.42
F	T	0.28
T	F	0.18
T	T	0.12

From the statistics of Table 17.1 and the conditional probability table in Figure 17.3, the base rate of lung cancer in the population can be computed with the deduction operator of Eq.(9.20) to produce $a(\mathrm{C}) = 0.01$.

The BN can also be used to formulate policy targets for public health. Assume that the health authorities want to reduce the base rate of lung cancer to $a(\mathrm{C}) = 0.005$. Then they would have various options, where one option could be to reduce the base rate exposure to pollution to $a(\mathrm{P}) = 0.1$, and the base rate of smokers to $a(\mathrm{S}) = 0.20$. According to this BN, that would give a base rate of lung cancer of $a(\mathrm{C}) = 0.005$.

17.1.2 Variable Structures

BNs typically have many variables, which each can take a different set of values. The sheer number of different variables and values can make the notation daunting. In order to make the formalism as accessible as possible and to avoid confusion, practitioners must try to use a notation that is tidy, concise, consistent and complete. Hopefully, this goal is achieved with the notation used below and elsewhere in this book.

Figure 17.4 illustrates a generalised version of the BN of the above example. In this general case, we assume that there is a central variable Y of cardinality l, a set of K different parent variables X_I with unspecified cardinalities, and a set of M different child variables Z_T with unspecified cardinalities. It is assumed that a given variable X_I takes its values from domain $\mathbb{X}_I$, that variable Y takes its values from domain $\mathbb{Y}$, and that a given variable Z_T takes its values from the domain $\mathbb{Z}_T$.

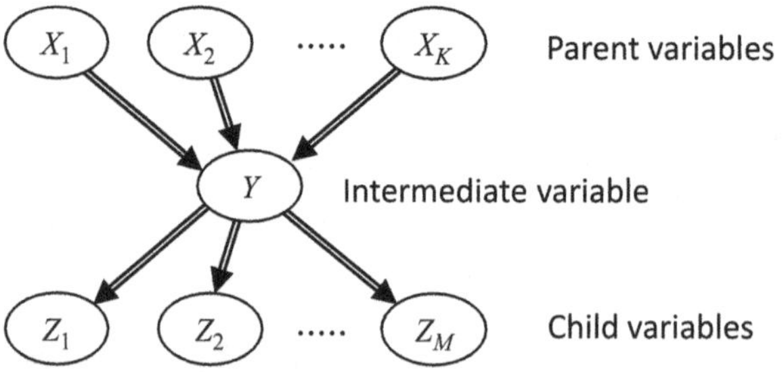

Fig. 17.4 General Bayesian network for intermediate variable with sets of parents and children

A given parent variable X_I can have index $I = 1,\ldots,K$. Now, a specific value of variable X_I can have index $i = 1,\ldots,k$. The value with index i, of the variable with index I, is then denoted $x_{I,i}$. We write $X_I = x_{I,i}$ to denote that variable X_I takes the particular value $x_{I,i}$. Similarly we write $Z_T = x_{T,t}$ for a child variable Z_T which takes a particular value $x_{T,t}$.

As a shorthand, $x_{I:}$ denotes a non-specific value of variable X_I, thereby omitting its explicit value index. Thus, a colon ':' after the index of the variable acts as a placeholder for the missing value index. This convention is summarised as

$$\begin{aligned} x_{I,i} &: \text{Specific value with index } i \text{ of specific variable } X_I \ , \\ x_{I:} &: \text{Some value with non-specific index of specific variable } X_I \ , \\ x &: \text{Some value with non-specific index of variable } X \ . \end{aligned}$$

Similarly, the notation $z_{T:}$ means some value of variable Z_T by omitting its explicit value index. Because there is only one variable Y, we can write y (without subscript and colon ':') to denote some none-specific value of variable Y.

The set of joint variables X_I is denoted $\widehat{X}$, and similarly for the set $\widehat{Z}$ of joint variables Z_T, which are respectively expressed as

$$\begin{aligned} \widehat{X} &= \{X_1, X_2, \ldots, X_K\}, \\ \widehat{Z} &= \{Z_1, Z_2, \ldots, Z_M\}. \end{aligned} \tag{17.4}$$

With these notational conventions, the basic formalism of BNs is expressed in the next sections.

17.1.3 The Chain Rule of Conditional Probability

Consider a BN containing K nodes/variables, X_1 to X_K, and a joint probability distribution over all the variables.

A particular joint probability is denoted $p(X_1 = x_{1:},\ X_2 = x_{2:}, \ldots, X_K = x_{K:})$, which can be expressed more concisely as $p(x_{1:}, x_{2:}, \ldots, x_{K:})$, where $x_{1:}$ simply means a non-specific value of the variable X_1, and similarly for $x_{2:}$ and so forth.

The chain rule of conditional probability reasoning expresses the joint probability in terms of factorisation of conditional probabilities as

$$\begin{aligned} p(x_{K:}, x_{(K-1):}, \ldots, x_{1:}) &= p(x_{1:}, x_{2:}, \ldots, x_{K:}) \quad \text{(due to commutativity of factors)} \\ &= p(x_{K:}|(x_{(K-1):}, \ldots, x_{1:})) \ldots, p(x_{2:}|x_{1:})p(x_{1:}) \\ &= \prod_{I=1}^{K} p(x_{I:}|(x_{(I-1):}, \ldots, x_{1:})) \ . \end{aligned} \tag{17.5}$$

The application of Eq.(17.5) together with Bayes' theorem of Eq.(9.24), a set of independence properties, as well as various computation algorithms, provide the basis for analysing complex BNs. The chain rule of Eq.(17.5) has a generalised expression in subjective logic as described in Section 17.2.4.

17.1.4 Naïve Bayes Classifier

Assume variable Y of cardinality $l = |Y|$, and a single child variable Z of cardinality $m = |Z|$. Recall from Eq.(9.24) on p.142 the extended expression of Bayes' theorem which here can be expressed as:

$$\text{Bayes' theorem with MBR: } p(y|z) = \frac{a(y)p(z|y)}{\sum_{g=1}^{l} a(y_g)p(z|y_g)}\,. \tag{17.6}$$

The prior probability distribution, called the base rate distribution in subjective logic, is denoted $\boldsymbol{a}$, so that e.g. $\boldsymbol{a}(y_j)$ denotes the prior probability of value $y_j \in \mathbb{Y}$. Eq.(17.6) is also called a *Bayesian classifier*, because it gives the probability of a class, which in fact is a value, of Y, based on observing a value of Z.

In the case of multiple child variables Z_T, the general Bayes classifier gives the expression for the probability distribution over Y, given evidence variables with specific values $Z_1 = z_{1:}, Z_2 = z_{2:}, \ldots, Z_M = z_{M:}$:

$$p(y|(z_{1:},\ldots,z_{M:})) = \frac{\boldsymbol{a}(y)p((z_{1:},\ldots,z_{M:})\,|\,y)}{\sum_{g=1}^{l} \boldsymbol{a}(y_g)\boldsymbol{p}((z_{1:},\ldots,z_{M:})\,|\,y_g)}\,. \tag{17.7}$$

Assuming that there is no available multivariate probability table for conditional probability distributions over Y based on joint variables, and that there are only probability tables for conditional probability distributions based on single variables, then it is impossible to apply Eq.(17.7). In practice, this is often the case.

However, if it can be assumed that the variables Z_1, Z_2,..., Z_M are reasonably independent, it is possible to apply the naïve Bayes classifier of Eq.(17.8):

$$p(y|z_{1:},\ldots,z_{M:}) \simeq \frac{a(y)\prod_{T=1}^{M} p(z_{T:}\,|\,y)}{\sum_{g=1}^{l}\left[a(y_g)\prod_{T=1}^{M} p(z_{T:}\,|\,y_g)\right]}\,. \tag{17.8}$$

Eq.(17.8) is the fundamental naïve Bayes classifier which is used in a wide range of applications, such as spam filtering, natural language text classification, medical diagnostics, customer profiling and marketing, just to name a few.

17.1.5 Independence and Separation

A BN is assumed to represent the significant dependencies of all relevant variables of the situation to be analysed. This is expressed by the *Markov property* which states that there are no direct dependencies in the system being modelled which are not already explicitly shown via edges. In the example of lung cancer, there is no way for smoking to influence dyspnoea except by causing cancer.

BNs that have the Markov property are often called *independence-maps* (or I-maps for short), since every independence implicitly indicated by the lack of an edge is real in the situation.

If every edge in a BN corresponds to a *direct* dependence in the situation, then the network is said to be a *dependence-map* (or D-map for short). A BN which is both an I-map and a D-map is called a *perfect map*.

BNs with the Markov property are I-maps by definition, and explicitly express conditional *independencies* between probability distributions of variables in the causal chain. Figure 17.5 illustrates three different graphs which can be assumed to be perfect maps.

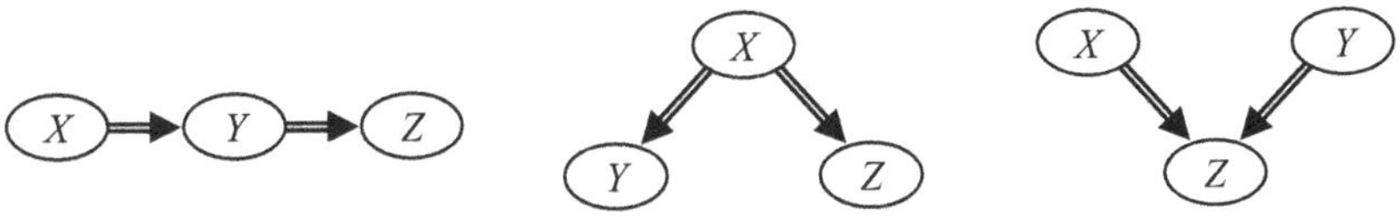

(a) Causal chain (b) Common cause (c) Common effect

Fig. 17.5 Different topologies of causality

Consider a causal chain of the three nodes X, Y and Z, as shown in Figure 17.5.a, which in the case of lung cancer could be expressed as

$$\text{'smoking'} \Longrightarrow \text{'cancer'} \Longrightarrow \text{'dyspnoea'} .$$

Causal chains give rise to conditional independence, which for Figure 17.5.a is reflected by Eq.(17.9):

$$\text{Independence property of Figure 17.5.a}: \quad p(Z|X,Y) = p(Z|Y) . \tag{17.9}$$

With reference to Figure 17.5.a, the probability of dyspnoea (Z) directly depends only on the condition of lung cancer (Y). If we only know that someone is a smoker (X), then that increases the likelihood of both the person having lung cancer (Y) and suffering from shortness of breath (Z). However, if we already know that the person has lung cancer (Y), then knowing that he is a smoker (X) is irrelevant to the probability of dyspnoea (Z). Concisely articulated, dyspnoea is conditionally independent of smoking given lung cancer.

Consider now Figure 17.5.b, where two variables Y and Z have the common cause X. With reference to the same example, lung cancer (X) is the common cause of both symptoms, which are dyspnoea (Y) and positive indication on X-ray (Z). Common causes have the same conditional independence properties as causal chains, as expressed by Eq.(17.10):

$$\text{Independence property of Figure 17.5.b}: \quad p(Z|X,Y) = p(Z|X) . \tag{17.10}$$

With reference to Eq.(17.10), if we already know that the person suffers from lung cancer (X), it is assumed that an additional positive observation of dyspnoea (Y) does not change the likelihood of finding a positive indication on the X-ray image (Z).

Finally, consider Figure 17.5.c, where two variables X and Y have the common effect Z. Common effect situations have the opposite conditional independence structure to that of causal chains and common causes, as expressed by Eq.(17.11):

$$\text{Dependence property Figure 17.5.c}: \quad p(X\,|\,Y,Z) \neq p(X|Z)\,. \tag{17.11}$$

Thus, if the effect Z (e.g., lung cancer) is observed, and we know that one of the causes is absent, e.g. the patient does not smoke (Y), then that evidence increases the likelihood of presence of the other cause, e.g. that he lives in a polluted area (X).

Similarly, if one of the causes has been observed, e.g. that the person lives in a polluted area (X), then the additional observation that the person smokes (Y) would increase the likelihood of lung cancer (Z), as expressed by Eq.(17.12):

$$\text{Dependence property of Figure 17.5.c}: \quad p(Z\,|\,X,Y) \neq p(Z|X)\,. \tag{17.12}$$

As shown by these examples, different graph structures reflect specific dependencies and independencies between node variables.

17.2 Chain Rules for Subjective Bayesian Networks

Paths in a network graph consist of chained conditional links. It is therefore natural to express the chained conditional relationships instead of isolated relationships between just two nodes. Subjective logic defines three types of chained relationships called: i) *chained conditional opinions*, ii) *chained inverted conditionals* and iii) *chained joint opinions*. These are described in the sections below.

17.2.1 Chained Conditional Opinions

The chain rule of subjective conditionals specifies how chained conditionals are combined in terms of iterative deduction of conditional opinions, expressed as

$$\begin{aligned}\boldsymbol{\omega}_{X_K|X_1} &= (\cdots((\boldsymbol{\omega}_{X_2|X_1} \circledcirc \boldsymbol{\omega}_{X_3|X_2}) \circledcirc \boldsymbol{\omega}_{X_4|X_3})\cdots) \circledcirc \boldsymbol{\omega}_{X_K|X_{(K-1)}} \\ &= \Cap_{I=2}^{K} (\boldsymbol{\omega}_{X_I|X_{(I-1)}})\,,\end{aligned} \tag{17.13}$$

where '⋒' denotes chained conditionals with the ⊚-operator for conditional deduction described in Section 9.3.

Figure 17.6 illustrates the chaining of the conditionals.

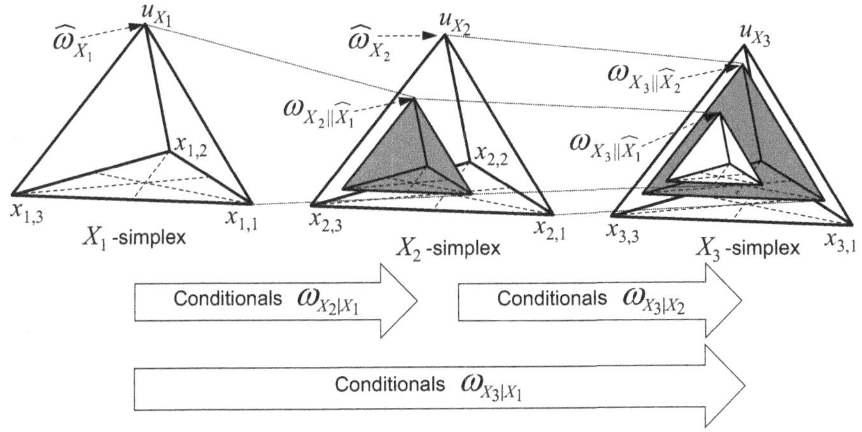

Fig. 17.6 Serially chained conditional opinions

Deduction with the serial conditional $\omega_{X_K|X_1}$ is expressed as

$$\omega_{X_K\|X_1} = \omega_{X_1} \circledcirc \boldsymbol{\omega}_{X_K|X_1} \,. \tag{17.14}$$

Eq.(17.13) provides a basis for generalising chained deduction in subjective BNs.

The irrelevance between the last variable X_K and first variable X_1 is monotonously increasing because each conditional sub-space inside the consecutive simplexes is smaller than the previous conditional sub-space. Only totally dependent variables preserve the size of the conditional sub-space. Assuming that the variables are not totally dependent, the irrelevance between X_K and X_1 increases as a function of K, and hence an infinitely long chain produces a totally irrelevant serial conditional.

17.2.2 Chained Inverted Opinions

The chain rule for inverted conditional opinions is given by Eq.(17.15):

$$\begin{aligned}
\boldsymbol{\omega}_{X_1\widetilde{|}X_K} &= (\cdots((\widetilde{\Phi}(\boldsymbol{\omega}_{X_K|X_{(K-1)}}, \boldsymbol{a}_{X_{(K-1)}})\widetilde{\circledcirc}(\boldsymbol{\omega}_{X_{(K-1)}|X_{(K-2)}}, \boldsymbol{a}_{X_{(K-2)}}))\\
&\quad \widetilde{\circledcirc}(\boldsymbol{\omega}_{X_{(K-2)}|X_{(K-3)}}, \boldsymbol{a}_{X_{(K-3)}}))\cdots)\widetilde{\circledcirc}(\boldsymbol{\omega}_{X_2|X_1}, \boldsymbol{a}_{X_1})\\
&= (\cdots((\widetilde{\Phi}(\boldsymbol{\omega}_{X_K|X_{(K-1)}}, \boldsymbol{a}_{X_{(K-1)}}) \circledcirc \widetilde{\Phi}(\boldsymbol{\omega}_{X_{(K-1)}|X_{(K-2)}}, \boldsymbol{a}_{X_{(K-2)}}))\\
&\quad \circledcirc \widetilde{\Phi}(\boldsymbol{\omega}_{X_{(K-2)}|X_{(K-3)}}, \boldsymbol{a}_{X_{(K-3)}}))\cdots) \circledcirc \widetilde{\Phi}(\boldsymbol{\omega}_{X_2|X_1}, \boldsymbol{a}_{X_1})\\
&= (\cdots((\boldsymbol{\omega}_{X_{(K-1)}\widetilde{|}X_K} \circledcirc \boldsymbol{\omega}_{X_{(K-2)}\widetilde{|}X_{(K-1)}}) \circledcirc \boldsymbol{\omega}_{X_{(K-3)}\widetilde{|}X_{(K-2)}})\cdots) \circledcirc \boldsymbol{\omega}_{X_1\widetilde{|}X_2}\\
&= \Cap_{I=K}^{2} (\boldsymbol{\omega}_{X_{(I-1)}\widetilde{|}X_I}) \,.
\end{aligned} \tag{17.15}$$

Figure 17.7 illustrates the chaining of inverted conditionals according to Eq.(17.15).

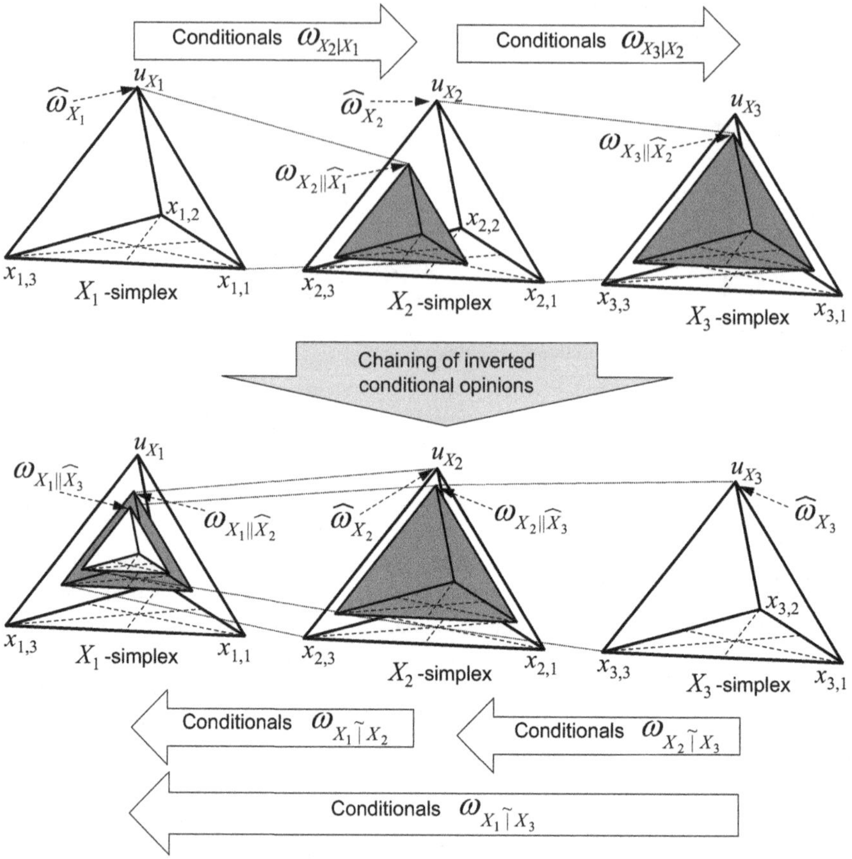

Fig. 17.7 Serially chaining of the subjective Bayes' theorem

Eq.(17.15) is relatively complex, because every conditional is inverted before chaining. A much simpler method to compute the same result as in Eq.(17.15) is to invert the result of serially chained conditionals, as expressed by Eq.(17.16), which only requires one inversion operation using the subjective Bayes' theorem:

$$\boldsymbol{\omega}_{X_1\tilde{|}X_K} = \widetilde{\phi}(\boldsymbol{\omega}_{X_K|X_1}, \boldsymbol{a}_{X_1}) = \widetilde{\phi}\left(\Cap_{I=2}^{K}(\boldsymbol{\omega}_{X_I|X_{(I-1)}}), \boldsymbol{a}_{X_1}\right) . \tag{17.16}$$

Abduction with the serial inverted conditionals $\boldsymbol{\omega}_{X_1\tilde{|}X_K}$ is expressed as

$$\omega_{X_1\tilde{\|}X_K} = \omega_{X_K} \circledcirc \boldsymbol{\omega}_{X_1\tilde{|}X_K} . \tag{17.17}$$

Eq.(17.16) and Eq.(17.17) generalise chained abduction in SBNs, where the abduced opinion $\omega_{X_1 \tilde{\|} X_K}$ is a function of all the intermediate sets of conditionals $\boldsymbol{\omega}_{X_2|X_1}, \ldots, \boldsymbol{\omega}_{X_K|X_{(K-1)}}$.

Serial abduction also assumes that the MBR distributions $\boldsymbol{a}_{X_2}, \ldots, \boldsymbol{a}_{X_K}$ are computed. This is done by serially applying the formula for MBRs of Eq.(9.57) while computing serial deduction according to Eq.(17.14).

17.2.3 Validation of the Subjective Bayes' Theorem

This heuristic validation consists of verifying, with a numerical example, that the two different methods for computing inverted chained conditionals, as expressed by Eq.(17.15) and Eq.(17.16), produce conditional opinions with equal projected probabilities and approximately equal uncertainty masses, as expressed by:

$$\widetilde{\phi}\left(⋒_{I=2}^{K}\left(\boldsymbol{\omega}_{X_I|X_{(I-1)}}\right), \boldsymbol{a}_{X_1}\right) \simeq ⋒_{I=K}^{2}\left(\boldsymbol{\omega}_{X_{(I-1)} \tilde{|} X_I}\right). \tag{17.18}$$

The projected probabilities of $\boldsymbol{\omega}_{X_1 \tilde{|} X_K}$ produced by Eq.(17.15) and Eq.(17.16) respectively are equal by definition. However, the uncertainty masses of $\boldsymbol{\omega}_{X_1 \tilde{|} X_K}$ are in general only approximately equal because conditional inversion with the subjective Bayes' theorem is applied differently in Eq.(17.15) and Eq.(17.16).

The following numerical example illustrates the approximate nature of Eq.(17.18). Assume three binary variables X, Y and Z with the chained conditional relationships $X \Longrightarrow Y \Longrightarrow Z$ and where the base rate distributions over X, Y and Z are

$$\boldsymbol{a}_X = (0.700, 0.300), \quad \boldsymbol{a}_Y = (0.732, 0.268), \quad \boldsymbol{a}_Z = (0.717, 0.282). \tag{17.19}$$

Table 17.2 shows example input conditionals as well as the results of applying Eq.(17.15) and Eq.(17.16) to them. Note that Eq.(17.15) produces $u_{X\tilde{|}z_1} = 0.205$ and $u_{X\tilde{|}z_2} = 0.158$ whereas Eq.(17.16) produces $u_{X\tilde{|}z_1} = 0.184$ and $u_{X\tilde{|}z_2} = 0.151$.

Table 17.2 Chained conditionals

$\boldsymbol{\omega}_{Y\|X}$		$\boldsymbol{\omega}_{Z\|Y}$	
$\omega_{Y\|x_1}$:	$\omega_{Y\|x_2}$:	$\omega_{Z\|y_1}$:	$\omega_{Z\|y_2}$:
$\boldsymbol{b}_{Y\|x_1}(y_1) = 0.950$	$\boldsymbol{b}_{Y\|x_2}(y_1) = 0.100$	$\boldsymbol{b}_{Z\|y_1}(z_1) = 0.900$	$\boldsymbol{b}_{Z\|y_2}(z_1) = 0.050$
$\boldsymbol{b}_{Y\|x_1}(y_2) = 0.000$	$\boldsymbol{b}_{Y\|x_2}(y_2) = 0.850$	$\boldsymbol{b}_{Z\|y_1}(z_2) = 0.050$	$\boldsymbol{b}_{Z\|y_2}(z_2) = 0.850$
$u_{Y\|x_1} = 0.050$	$u_{Y\|x_2} = 0.050$	$u_{Z\|y_1} = 0.050$	$u_{Z\|y_2} = 0.100$

$\boldsymbol{\omega}_{X\tilde{\|}Z} = \boldsymbol{\omega}_{Y\tilde{\|}Z} \circledcirc \boldsymbol{\omega}_{X\tilde{\|}Y}$		$\boldsymbol{\omega}_{X\tilde{\|}Z} = \widetilde{\phi}((\boldsymbol{\omega}_{Y\|X} \circledcirc \boldsymbol{\omega}_{Z\|Y}), \boldsymbol{a}_X)$	
$\omega_{X\tilde{\|}z_1}$:	$\omega_{X\tilde{\|}z_2}$:	$\omega_{X\tilde{\|}z_1}$:	$\omega_{X\tilde{\|}z_2}$:
$\boldsymbol{b}_{X\tilde{\|}z_1}(x_1) = 0.759$	$\boldsymbol{b}_{X\tilde{\|}z_2}(x_1) = 0.075$	$\boldsymbol{b}_{X\tilde{\|}z_1}(x_1) = 0.774$	$\boldsymbol{b}_{X\tilde{\|}z_2}(x_1) = 0.080$
$\boldsymbol{b}_{X\tilde{\|}z_1}(x_2) = 0.036$	$\boldsymbol{b}_{X\tilde{\|}z_2}(x_2) = 0.767$	$\boldsymbol{b}_{X\tilde{\|}z_1}(x_2) = 0.042$	$\boldsymbol{b}_{X\tilde{\|}z_2}(x_2) = 0.769$
$u_{X\tilde{\|}z_1} = 0.205$	$u_{X\tilde{\|}z_2} = 0.158$	$u_{X\tilde{\|}z_1} = 0.184$	$u_{X\tilde{\|}z_2} = 0.151$

17.2.4 Chained Joint Opinions

Similarly to the chain rule for conditional probability deduction of Eq.(17.5) which produces joint probabilities, the computation of joint opinions can also be chained:

$$\begin{aligned}\omega_{(X_K X_{(K-1)} \dots X_1)} &= \boldsymbol{\omega}_{X_K|(X_{(K-1)} \dots X_1)} \cdot \ \dots \ \cdot \boldsymbol{\omega}_{X_3|(X_2 X_1)} \cdot \boldsymbol{\omega}_{X_2|X_1} \cdot \omega_{X_1} \\ &= \prod_{I=1}^{K} \boldsymbol{\omega}_{X_I|(X_{(I-1)} \dots X_1)} \ .\end{aligned} \quad (17.20)$$

The chain rule for joint opinions repeatedly applies the computation of joint opinions which is described in Chapter 11.

Consider a SBN containing a set $\widehat{X}$ of K nodes/variables $X_1, \dots, X_K$ with chained conditional relationships as in Eq.(17.21):

$$X_1 \Longrightarrow X_2 \Longrightarrow \ \dots \ \Longrightarrow X_K \ . \quad (17.21)$$

The joint opinion expressed by $\omega_{\widehat{X}} = \omega_{(X_K \dots X_1)}$ can then be computed with the chain rule of Eq.(17.20).

17.3 Subjective Bayesian Networks

A subjective Bayesian network (SBN) models the random variables of nodes, and their conditional dependencies in the form of a DAG, in the same way as a traditional Bayesian network. The difference is that conditional relationships are represented by conditional opinions in SBNs, whereas they are represented by probability tables and priors in traditional BNs. Given the opinions about the conditional relationships and the opinions about the evidence nodes, it is possible to compute opinions about a set of query nodes.

SBN modelling and analysis generalises traditional BN modelling and analysis, by including the uncertainty dimension, which necessarily involves additional complexity. The advantage of SBNs is that they explicitly express the inherent uncertainty of realistic situations during the formal modelling, thereby producing results that better reflect the situation as seen by the analysts. In other words, the inherent uncertainty of situations no longer has to be 'hidden under the carpet', which is good news for analysts and decision makers.

Since probability distributions over a set of variables are affected by the variables' conditional probabilities, it is natural to assume that the base rate distributions over the same variables are affected by the same conditional probabilities, as reflected by the MBR distribution of Eq.9.57. In that sense there exists an underlying *base rate network* (BRN) which is derived by setting vacuous input argument opinions on parent nodes in the network DAG. The resulting base rate distributions can then be used when deriving opinions from the SBN.

In the sections below, the four reasoning categories of Figure 17.2 are described within the framework of subjective logic.

17.3.1 Subjective Predictive Reasoning

The predictive reasoning category was described as part of the presentation of traditional BNs above. Predictive reasoning is simply the application of deduction, as described in Section 9.5 above.

Let $\widehat{\mathbb{X}}$ denote a set of K domains, let $\widehat{X}$ denote the corresponding joint variable, and let the specific node Y of cardinality $l = |Y|$ represent a consequent variable of interest to the analyst, expressed as

$$\begin{array}{ll} \text{Set of cause variables:} & \widehat{X} = \{X_1, X_2, \ldots, X_K\}\,, \\ \text{Consequent variable:} & Y \end{array} \tag{17.22}$$

Figure 17.8 illustrates the general situation of Bayesian predictive modelling, involving the mentioned variables.

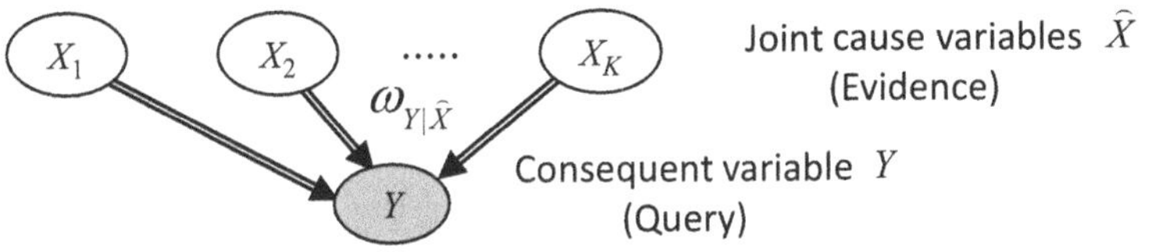

Fig. 17.8 Situation of Bayesian prediction

Assume that there exists a joint set of conditional opinion $\omega_{Y|\widehat{X}}$ which for every combination of values in $\widehat{X}$ specifies an opinion on Y. Assume also that there is a joint parent opinion $\omega_{\widehat{X}}$, then the deduced opinion is expressed as

$$\omega_{Y\|\widehat{X}} = \omega_{\widehat{X}} \circledcirc \boldsymbol{\omega}_{Y|\widehat{X}}\,. \tag{17.23}$$

In case the variables in $\widehat{X}$ can be assumed to be independent, the opinion on the joint variable $\widehat{X}$ can be generated by multinomial multiplication described in Chapter 8, which is expressed by

$$\omega_{\widehat{X}} = \prod_{I=1}^{K} \omega_{X_I}\,. \tag{17.24}$$

Of the two alternative operators for multinomial multiplication for computing Eq.(17.24), proportional multiplication is simply a special case of computing the joint opinion.

17.3.2 Subjective Diagnostic Reasoning

This section briefly describes how the reasoning category of diagnostic reasoning can be handled with subjective logic.

A specific class domain $\mathbb{X}$ with variable X represents the set of classes of interest to the analyst. The classes can e.g. be a set of medical diagnoses, or types of email messages such as 'spam' or 'ham'. Let $\widehat{Y}$ denote a joint set of $L = |\widehat{Y}|$ variables that represent spam indicators, such as the presence of word combinations like *'inheritance'* and *'president'*, because that specific combination typically is an indicator for Nigerian scam emails. The variables are expressed as

$$\begin{aligned} &\text{Class variable:} && X, \\ &\text{Set of indicator variables:} && \widehat{Y} = \{Y_1, Y_2, \ldots, Y_L\}. \end{aligned} \tag{17.25}$$

Figure 17.9 illustrates the situation of Bayesian classifiers, where states of variable X cause states of the joint variable $\widehat{Y}$.

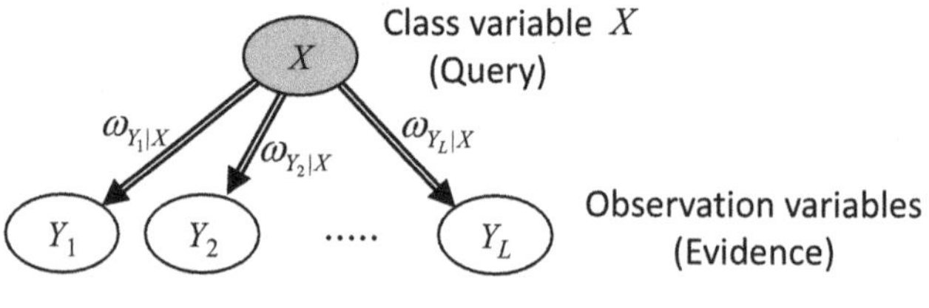

Fig. 17.9 Situation of Bayes classifier

Eq.(17.26) expresses the general subjective Bayes classifier, which gives the conditional opinions on X given the values of the joint evidence variable $\widehat{Y}$. It is based on the subjective Bayes' theorem of Definition 10.6.

$$\boldsymbol{\omega}_{X\widetilde{|}\widehat{Y}} = \widetilde{\phi}(\boldsymbol{\omega}_{\widehat{Y}|X}, \boldsymbol{a}_X) \,. \tag{17.26}$$

In practical situations, the joint conditional opinion $\omega_{\widehat{Y}|X}$ is typically not available, in which case Eq.(17.26) can not be applied directly. It is typically more practical to obtain conditional opinions for single Y-variables. In case it can reasonably be assumed that the Y-variables are independent, the naïve Bayes classifier for subjective logic, expressed in Eq.(17.27), can be used:

$$\boldsymbol{\omega}_{X\,\widetilde{|}\,\widehat{Y}} \simeq \widetilde{\Phi}\left(\left(\prod_{J=1}^{L}\boldsymbol{\omega}_{Y_J|X}\right), \boldsymbol{a}_X\right). \quad (17.27)$$

Eq.(17.27) expresses the general naïve Bayes classifier for subjective logic. The product of conditional opinions $\boldsymbol{\omega}_{(Y_J|X)}$ can be computed by multinomial multiplication described in Chapter 8.

In case an evidence opinion on $\widehat{Y}$ is provided the deduced opinion on X is computed with the deduction operator described in Section 9.5:

$$\omega_{X\|\widehat{Y}} = \omega_{\widehat{Y}} \circledcirc \boldsymbol{\omega}_{X|\widehat{Y}}. \quad (17.28)$$

It will be interesting to see how the subjective naïve classifier performs in fields such as spam filtering, natural language text classification, medical diagnostics, customer profiling and security incident classification.

17.3.3 Subjective Intercausal Reasoning

Situations of intercausal reasoning occur frequently. With reference to the lung cancer example, assume that a non-smoker has been diagnosed with lung cancer, which intuitively would indicate that pollution is a likely cause of the cancer.

Alternatively, if the person is a smoker, then the derived probability of exposure to pollution is typically low, which would indicate that this (low) exposure not is the cause of the cancer.

Let $\widehat{X}$ denote a set of $K = |\,\widehat{\mathbb{X}}\,|$ joint variables, let $\widehat{Y}$ denote a set of $L = |\,\widehat{\mathbb{Y}}\,|$ joint variables, and let Z denote a specific consequent variable, where the three variables are respectively expressed as

$$\begin{aligned} &\text{Set of cause variables:} && \widehat{X} = \{X_1, X_2, \ldots, X_K\},\\ &\text{Set of cause variables:} && \widehat{Y} = \{Y_1, Y_2, \ldots, Y_L\},\\ &\text{Consequent variable:} && Z. \end{aligned} \quad (17.29)$$

Figure 17.10 illustrates the general situation of intercausal reasoning, where the two sets of variables $\widehat{X}$ and $\widehat{Y}$ are causes of the consequent variable Z.

In Figure 17.10 it is assumed that there is evidence on the set of variables $\widehat{Y}$ as well as on Z, and that the query targets the set of variables $\widehat{X}$.

Intercausal reasoning takes place in two steps: 1) Abduction, and 2) Division. More specifically, it is assumed that the analyst has an opinion ω_Z about the consequent variable Z, and that there exists a joint set of conditional opinions $\omega_{Z|(\widehat{X},\widehat{Y})}$. With multinomial abduction, it is possible to compute the opinion $\omega_{(\widehat{X},\widehat{Y})\widetilde{\|}Z}$ expressed as

$$\omega_{(\widehat{X},\widehat{Y})\widetilde{\|}Z} = \omega_Z \,\widetilde{\circledcirc}\, (\boldsymbol{\omega}_{Z|(\widehat{X},\widehat{Y})}, \boldsymbol{a}_{(\widehat{X},\widehat{Y})}). \quad (17.30)$$

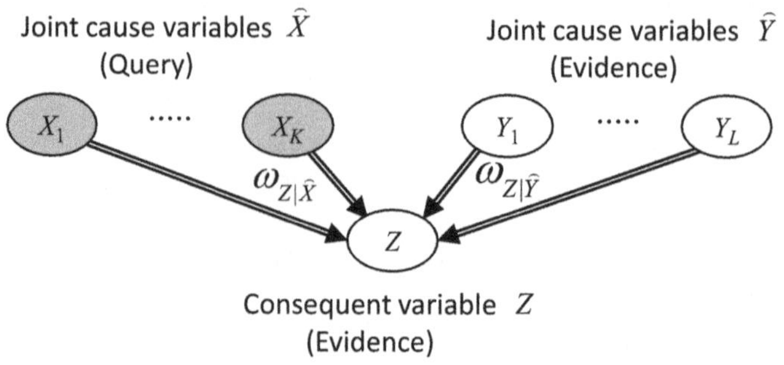

Fig. 17.10 Intercausal reasoning

Having computed the abduced opinion on the joint set of joint variables $(\widehat{X}, \widehat{Y})$, we can proceed to the second step. Assume that the analyst has an opinion $\omega_{\widehat{Y}}$ on the set of joint variables $\widehat{Y}$, then it is possible to derive an opinion $\omega_{\widehat{X}}$ about the set of joint variables $\widehat{X}$ through multinomial division, as expressed by

$$\omega_{\widehat{X}} = \boldsymbol{\omega}_{(\widehat{X},\widehat{Y})\widetilde{\|}Z} \,/\, \omega_{\widehat{Y}} \,. \tag{17.31}$$

Multinomial division is described in Chapter 8. There are two optional division operators. In case the evidence on $\widehat{Y}$ is an absolute (product) opinion, then selective division described in Section 8.3.3 should be used. In case the evidence on $\widehat{Y}$ is a partially uncertain (product) opinion, then proportional division described in Section 8.3.2 should be used.

17.3.4 Subjective Combined Reasoning

The last reasoning category to be described is called combined reasoning because it combines predictive and diagnostic reasoning.

Let $\widehat{X}$ denote a set of $K = |\widehat{X}|$ variables, let $\widehat{Z}$ denote a set of $M = |\widehat{Z}|$ variables, and let Y be an intermediate consequent variable, where all three are expressed as

$$\begin{array}{lll} \text{Set of cause variables:} & \widehat{X} & = \{X_1, X_2, \ldots, X_K\}, \\ \text{Consequent variable:} & Y, & \\ \text{Set of indicator variables:} & \widehat{Z} & = \{Z_1, Z_2, \ldots, Z_M\}. \end{array} \tag{17.32}$$

Figure 17.11 illustrates the general situation of combined reasoning, where the two sets of variables $\widehat{X}$ and $\widehat{Z}$ represent the evidence, and variable Y represents the query variable.

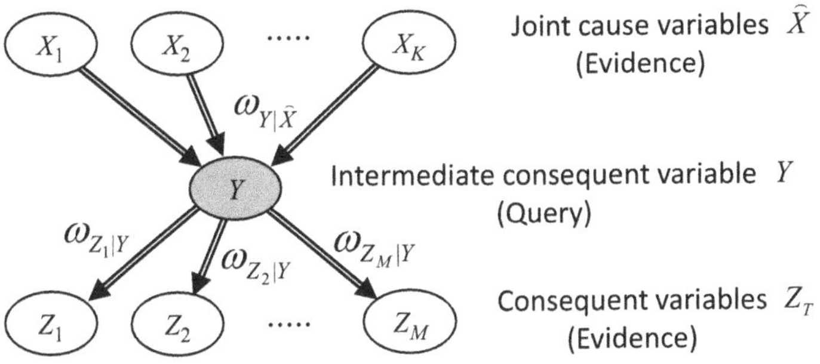

Fig. 17.11 Combined reasoning

The situation of Figure 17.11 can be handled by first computing the inverted conditional opinion $\omega_{\widetilde{\widehat{X}}|Y}$ by using the subjective Bayes' theorem, and subsequently by deriving a naïve Bayes classifier for the variable Y based on both $\omega_{\widetilde{\widehat{X}}|Y}$ and $\omega_{\widehat{Z}|Y}$. The naïve Bayes classifier is expressed by Eq.(17.33):

$$\boldsymbol{\omega}_{Y\widetilde{|}(\widehat{X},\widehat{Z})} \simeq \widetilde{\Phi}\left(\left(\boldsymbol{\omega}_{\widetilde{\widehat{X}}|Y} \cdot \prod_{T=1}^{M} \boldsymbol{\omega}_{Z_T|Y}\right), \boldsymbol{a}_Y\right) . \tag{17.33}$$

In the example of lung cancer, the GP can thus use all the evidence about air pollution, smoking, X-ray and dyspnoea to compute an opinion about whether the person suffers from lung cancer.

17.4 Independence Properties in Subjective Bayesian Networks

The concept of conditional independence in traditional BNs, discussed in Section 17.1.5, can be expressed in a similar way in the context of SBNs. First, consider the criterion for conditional independence in BNs which can be concisely expressed as follows.

Definition 17.1 (Bayesian Conditional Independence).
Variables X and Z are conditionally independent given a value of Y if and only if, given the value of Y, knowledge of the value of X provides no information on the likelihood of values of Z, and knowledge of the value of Z provides no information on the likelihood of values of X. □

In case the criterion of Definition 17.1 is satisfied, then the graph of Eq.(17.34) satisfies the Markov property, which means that it is an I-map:

$$X \Longrightarrow Y \Longrightarrow Z\,. \tag{17.34}$$

In Bayesian theory, a probability distribution (not the base rate distribution) of variable Y is typically known conditionally on another variable, e.g. X, whereas variable X typically is known unconditionally. Knowing the value of a variable, say $X = x$, is equivalent to assigning a probability $p(X = x) = 1$, which is just a limit case of knowing its general probability distribution, where $p(X = x)$ is an arbitrary probability. It is of course a philosophical question whether something can be known unconditionally, but if it can, then there is in principle no difference between knowing a probability distribution over a variable, and knowing the value of a variable, because knowing the value of a variable is equivalent to knowing that its probability is 1.

The independence criterion of Definition 17.1 can be expressed in terms of subjective opinions where 'knowing the value' e.g of intermediate variable Y, is equivalent to having an absolute opinion about that variable.

Definition 17.2 (Subjective Conditional Independence). Variable X and Z are conditionally independent given an opinion on Y iff, given an absolute opinion on Y, any opinion on X provides no information on the likelihood of values of Z, and any opinion on Z provides no information on the likelihood of values of X. □

Variable Z in Eq.(17.34) would be dependent on variable X given a relatively uncertain opinion, or given an uncertainty-maximised opinion about variable Y in Eq.(17.34), because an opinion on X could then influence the opinion on Y, which in turn could influence the opinion on Z. A relatively uncertain but non-uncertainty-maximised opinion is necessarily an aleatory opinion. An uncertainty-maximised opinion can be aleatory or epistemic.

Assume that the Bayesian graph of Eq.(17.34) represents an epistemic situation, i.e. that the variables represent specific instances. Then the input argument opinions should also be epistemic, and therefore uncertainty-maximised. An absolute opinion on Y produces independence between X and Z, i.e. Z is independent of X given an absolute opinion on Y. However, an epistemic non-absolute opinion on Y does not produce independence, i.e. Z is dependent to some degree on X, given the relatively uncertain epistemic opinion on Y.

As an example, consider the practical situation of variable $X = \{x,\bar{x}\}$, where x represents a weather forecast for rain, variable $Y = \{y,\bar{y}\}$, where y represents that Bob carries an umbrella when leaving from home in the morning, and variable $Z = \{z,\bar{z}\}$, where z represents that Bob forgets the umbrella on the train. Assume that Bob usually carries an umbrella when the weather forecast for the day says rain, expressed by the pair of conditional opinions $\boldsymbol{\omega}_{Y|X} = \{\omega_{Y|x}, \omega_{Y|\bar{x}}\}$. Assume further that Bob is rather forgetful, so he often forgets his umbrella on the train, expressed by the pair of conditional opinions $\boldsymbol{\omega}_{Z|Y} = \{\omega_{Z|y}, \omega_{Z|\bar{y}}\}$. Then, if the analyst wants to infer whether Bob will forget the umbrella on the train from the absolute opinion that he carries an umbrella, it can be assumed that the opinion on Z is independent of any opinion on X, because knowing the weather forecast does not change his likelihood of forgetting the umbrella. However, if the observer is uncertain about whether Bob carries an umbrella, expressed by a relatively uncertain epistemic opinion $\omega_Y(y)$, then the opinion on Z is not independent of the opinion on X. If the analyst wants to infer whether Bob will forget his umbrella on the train from an uncertain opinion about whether he carries an umbrella, then knowing the weather forecast will make the opinion about actually carrying an umbrella more certain, which influences the opinion about whether he will forget his umbrella on the train.

The extreme case would be that the analyst has a vacuous opinion on node Y, which would have no effect of reducing the dependence of Z on X. In general, the degree of dependence between X and Y is a function of the uncertainty in the opinion on Y. The dependence is also a function of the (ir)relevance in the pair sets of conditionals $\boldsymbol{\omega}_{Y|X}$ and $\boldsymbol{\omega}_{Z|Y}$.

One way of satisfying the subjective conditional independence requirement of Definition 17.2 is to have variables that are irrelevant to each other, as described in Section 10.2. The BN of Eq.(17.34) has total irrelevance between X and Z either if the set of conditional opinions $\boldsymbol{\omega}_{Y|X}$ makes X totally irrelevant to Y, or if the set of conditional opinions $\boldsymbol{\omega}_{Z|Y}$ makes Y totally irrelevant to Z. In case X is irrelevant to Y, then no opinion on X can influence the opinion on Y. In case Y is irrelevant to Z, then no opinion on Y can influence the opinion on Z.

17.5 Subjective Network Modelling

Different people commonly have different opinions about the same evidence variables and conditionals of a model. Similarly, different sensors can produce different data for the same observed target, which can translate into conflicting opinions about a corresponding target variable. It is also common that no single analyst has first hand opinions about all input conditionals and variables of a model. Traditional Bayesian network modelling can not directly be applied to such situations because they assume a single analyst with a complete view of the whole model. In contrast, subjective networks are perfectly suited to model situations where different agents have different opinions about the conditionals and evidence variables of a model. In such situations the analyst must use possibly conflicting second-hand evidence as input evidence.

The concept of subjective networks is simply the combination of a SBN and a STN. This represents a holistic approach to Bayesian network modelling and analysis by taking uncertainty and subjectivity into account. The SBN models the random variables of nodes and their conditional dependencies represented as a DAG, where the conditional relationships between nodes are represented as subjective opinions. The analyst derives subjective opinions about conditionals and variables either directly through observations or indirectly from other agents through the STN.

Whenever multiple (conflicting) opinions are provided for a specific variable, trust fusion can be applied. In case input opinions are missing for some conditionals or evidence nodes, vacuous opinions can be used as input instead. In this way, the analysis of a model can be done incrementally as more evidence is gathered.

17.5.1 Subjective Network with Source Opinions

Consider the example SN of Figure 17.12 where agent A has a level of trust in agents B, C and D, who in turn have opinions about the evidence variable X, and about the conditional relationships $X \Longrightarrow Y$ and $Y \Longrightarrow Z$. It is implicitly assumed that A receives the source opinions ω_X^B, $\boldsymbol{\omega}_{Y|X}^C$ and $\boldsymbol{\omega}_{Z|Y}^D$ from B, C and D respectively. Analyst A can then derive an opinion about variable Z based on the received opinions.

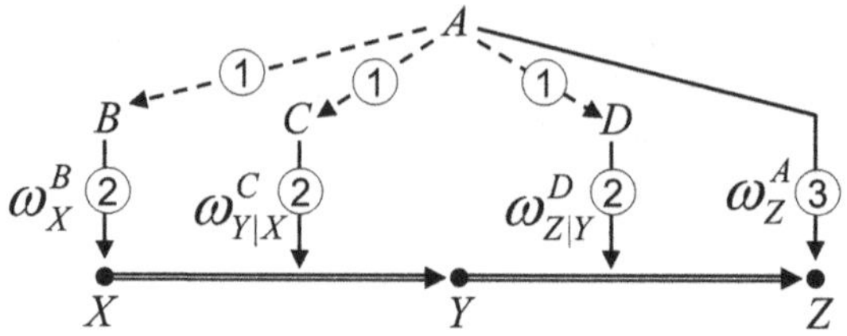

Fig. 17.12 Combining a subjective Bayesian network with transitive trust

The indexed arrows indicate the order the opinions are formed. The derived opinion is indicated with index 3. The expression for A's derived opinion about Z is

$$\begin{aligned}\omega_Z^A &= ((\omega_B^A \otimes \omega_X^B) \circledcirc (\omega_C^A \otimes \boldsymbol{\omega}_{Y|X}^C)) \circledcirc (\omega_D^A \otimes \boldsymbol{\omega}_{Z|Y}^D) \\ &= (\omega_X^{[A;B]} \circledcirc \boldsymbol{\omega}_{Y|X}^{[A;C]}) \circledcirc \boldsymbol{\omega}_{Z|Y}^{[A;D]} \,.\end{aligned} \tag{17.35}$$

17.5.2 Subjective Network with Trust Fusion

In the SN of Figure 17.13 it can be assumed that analyst A has referral trust opinions about agents B and C, who give advice opinions about variable X. At the same time, analyst A has opinions about the conditional relationships $X \Longrightarrow Y$ and $Y \Longrightarrow Z$. Analyst A is then able to derive the opinion ω_Z^A about variable Z.

It is also possible to consider B and C as sensors producing data which can be translated into the opinions ω_X^B and ω_X^C. The expression for A's derived opinion about Z as a function of the other opinions in Figure 17.13 is given by Eq.(17.36):

$$\begin{aligned}\omega_Z^A &= (((\omega_B^A \otimes \omega_X^B) \oplus (\omega_C^A \otimes \omega_X^C)) \circledcirc \boldsymbol{\omega}_{Y|X}^A) \circledcirc \boldsymbol{\omega}_{Z|Y}^A \\ &= (\omega_X^{([A;B]\diamond[A;C])} \circledcirc \boldsymbol{\omega}_{Y|X}^A) \circledcirc \boldsymbol{\omega}_{Z|Y}^A \,.\end{aligned} \tag{17.36}$$

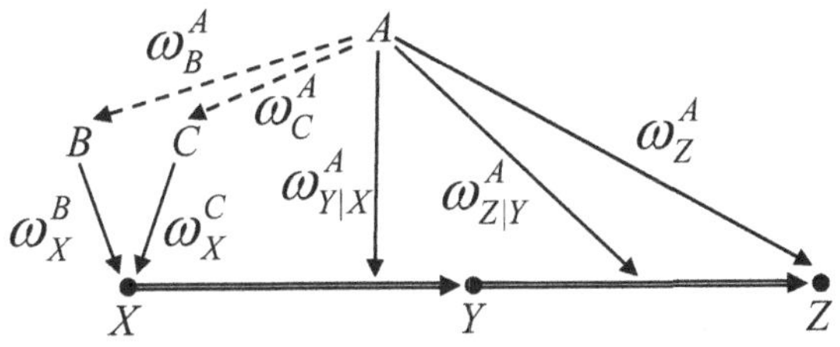

Fig. 17.13 Combining a subjective Bayesian network with trust fusion

17.6 Perspectives on Subjective Networks

With SNs it is possible to model situations where an analyst not only has opinions about about variables but also about sources (agents and sensors) which in turn produce opinions about other sources and variables. In a SN there is a clear distinction between the frame of sources (agents and sensors) which can be modelled with STNs and the frame of variables which can be modelled with SBNs. Figure 17.14 illustrates with an example the integration of STNs and SBNs to form SNs.

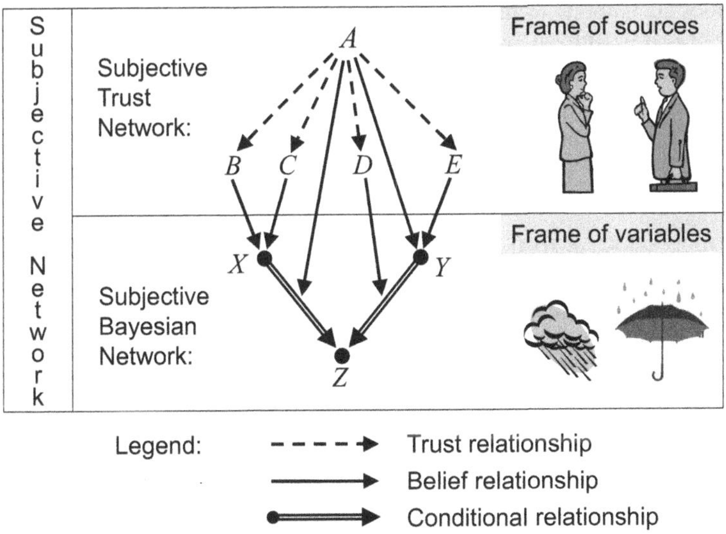

Fig. 17.14 Components of a subjective network

In the STN the belief fusion of $\omega_X^{[A;B]}$ and $\omega_X^{[A;C]}$ produces $\omega_X^{[A;B]\diamond[A;C]}$, and the belief fusion of ω_Y^A and $\omega_Y^{[A;E]}$ produces $\omega_Y^{A\diamond[A;E]}$, as intermediate results. Assuming independence the product opinion ω_{XY}^A can be computed. In the SBN the analyst can not directly use separate sets of conditionals $\boldsymbol{\omega}_{Z|X}$ and $\boldsymbol{\omega}_{Z|Y}$ but must learn the set of joint conditionals $\boldsymbol{\omega}_{Z|XY}$. Analyst A can then apply subjective deduction to derive the opinion $\omega^{A}_{Z\|XY}$ about the target variable Z which subsequently can be used for decision making based on the criteria from Chapter 4.

Note that belief fusion only applies to the fusion of sources in the STN, not to the fusion of variables or Bayesian classifiers in the SBN.

There are multiple advantages of SNs over traditional BNs, some of which are:

- The analyst's trust in the sources is explicitly included in the formal modelling of STNs, but is often ignored or treated in an *ad hoc* manner in traditional BNs.
- Degrees of confidence in probabilities can be explicitly included in SBNs, whereas traditional BNs typically can only handle simple probabilities.
- SNs are flexible in the sense that the analyst can decide how best to combine the frame of sources modelled as a STN and the frame of variables modelled as a SBN. For example, a STN can be used alone when the situation to be analysed does not involve conditional relationships, a SBN can be used alone when all the input evidence for the variables is directly and objectively available, a STN can be combined with a traditional BN if the confidence dimension is not needed for the frame of variables, or a full SN can be used when subjective models of both the frame of sources and the frame of variables are needed.
- The expressions of base rates (prior probabilities) and derived marginal probabilities are ambiguous in traditional Bayesian modelling because the same symbol $p(x)$ is used for both. This practice makes it seem as if the prior probability somehow is replaced by the derived marginal probability, which is not the case. Base rates do not go away just because the analyst derives marginal probabilities for the same variables. This confusion is eliminated in subjective logic by using the symbol $a(x)$ for base rates and the symbol $\mathrm{P}(x)$ for probabilities, which is helpful for learning and practicing Bayesian analysis.

The wide range of methods for reasoning under uncertainty presented in this book makes subjective logic a mature formalism, but more investigation into its theoretical foundations and practical applications with SNs can advance it even further. This will hopefully be a fertile field of research and innovation for many years.

References

1. Ahmad Abdel-Hafez, Yue Xu, and Audun Jøsang. A normal-distribution based rating aggregation method for generating product reputations. *Web Intelligence*, 13(1):43–51, 2015.
2. Ahmad Abdel-Hafez, Yue Xu, and Audun Jøsang. An accurate rating aggregation method for generating item reputation. In *Proceedings of the International Conference on Data Science and Advanced Analytics (DSAA 2015)*, Paris, 2015. IEEE, Los Alamitos.
3. K. Aberer and Z. Despotovic. Managing trust in a peer-2-peer information system. In Henrique Paques, Ling Liu, and David Grossman, editors, *Proceedings of the Tenth International Conference on Information and Knowledge Management (CIKM01)*, pages 10–317. ACM Press, New York, 2001.
4. K.K. Bharadwaj and M.Y.H. Al-Shamri. Fuzzy computational models for trust and reputation systems. *Electronic Commerce Research and Applications*, 8(1):37–47, 2009.
5. Andrew D. Brasfield. Forecasting accuracy and cognitive bias in the analysis of competing hypotheses. Master's thesis, Mercyhurst College, Erie, Pennesylvania, 2009.
6. F.M. Brown. *Boolean Reasoning: The Logic of Boolean Equations*. 1st edition, Kluwer Academic Publishers, 2nd edition, Dover Publications, Mineola, 2003.
7. W. Casscells, A. Schoenberger, and T.B. Graboys. Interpretation by physicians of clinical laboratory results. *New England Journal of Medicine*, 299(18):999–1001, 1978.
8. E. Castagnoli and M. LiCalzi. Expected utility without utility. *Theory and Decision*, 41(3):281–301, November 1996.
9. Christiano Castelfranchi and Rino Falcone. *Trust Theory: A Socio-cognitive and Computational Model*. Wiley Series in Agent Technology. Wiley, New York, 2010.
10. ACPO Centrex. *Guidance on the National Intelligence Model*. National Centre for Policing Excellence, UK, 2005. https://whereismydata.files.wordpress.com/2009/01/national-intelligence-model-20051.pdf (retrieved 05.12.2015).
11. A. Chateauneuf. On the use of capacities in modelling uncertainty aversion and risk aversion. *Journal of Mathematical Economics*, 20(4):343–369, 1991.
12. Jin-Hee Cho, Kevin Chan, and Sibel Adali. A survey on trust modeling. *ACM Computing Surveys*, 48(2):1–40, October 2015.
13. Jin-Hee Cho and Ananthram Swami. Dynamics of uncertain opinions in social networks. In *Proceedings of the 2014 IEEE Military Communications Conference*, MILCOM '14, pages 1627–1632, Washington, DC, USA, 2014. IEEE Computer Society.
14. G. Choquet. Theory of capacities. *Annales de l'Institut Fourier*, 5:131–295, 1953.
15. B. Christianson and W. S. Harbison. Why isn't trust transitive? In M. Lomas, editor, *Proceedings of the Security Protocols International Workshop*, volume 1189 of *LNCS*, pages 171–176. Springer, Berlin, 1996.

16. Bruno de Finetti. The true subjective probability problem. In Carl-Axel Staël von Holstein, editor, *The Concept of Probability in Psychological Experiments*, pages 15–23. D. Reidel, Dordrecht, 1974.
17. Bruno de Finetti. The value of studying subjective evaluations of probability. In Carl-Axel Staël von Holstein, editor, *The Concept of Probability in Psychological Experiments*, pages 1–14. D. Reidel, Dordrecht, 1974.
18. M.R. Diaz. *Topics in the Logic of Relevance*. Philosophia Verlag, München, 1981.
19. R. J. Duffin. Topology of series-parallel networks. *Journal of Mathematical Analysis and Applications*, 10(2):303–313, 1965.
20. J.K. Dunn and G. Restall. Relevance logic. In D. Gabbay and F. Guenthner, editors, *Handbook of Philosophical Logic, 2nd Edition*, volume 6, pages 1–128. Kluwer, Dordrecht, 2002.
21. Daniel Ellsberg. Risk, ambiguity, and the Savage axioms. *Quarterly Journal of Ecomonics*, 75:643–669, 1961.
22. R. Falcone and C. Castelfranchi. How trust enhances and spread trust. In *Proceedings of the 4th Int. Workshop on Deception, Fraud and Trust in Agent Societies, in the 5th International Conference on Autonomous Agents (AGENTS'01)*, May 2001.
23. R. Falcone and C. Castelfranchi. Social trust: A cognitive approach. In C. Castelfranchi and Y.H. Tan, editors, *Trust and Deception in Virtual Societies*, pages 55–99. Kluwer, Dordrecht, 2001.
24. Randy Farmer and Bryce Glass. *Building Web Reputation Systems*. O'Reilly Media / Yahoo Press, Sebastopol, 2010.
25. M. Fitting. Kleene's three-valued logics and their children. *Fundamenta Informaticae*, 20:113–131, 1994.
26. P. Flocchini and F.L. Luccio. Routing in series parallel networks. *Theory of Computing Systems*, 36(2):137–157, 2003.
27. M. Frappier, D. Brown, and R. DiSalle. *Analysis and Interpretation in the Exact Sciences: Essays in Honour of William Demopoulos*. The Western Ontario Series in Philosophy of Science. Springer Netherlands, 2012.
28. L.C. Freeman. Centrality in social networks. *Social Networks*, 1:215–239, 1979.
29. D. Gambetta. Can we trust trust? In D. Gambetta, editor, *Trust: Making and Breaking Cooperative Relations*, pages 213–238. Basil Blackwell. Oxford, 1990.
30. F. Garcin, B. Faltings, and R. Jurca. Aggregating reputation feedback. In *Proceedings of the First International Conference on Reputation: Theory and Technology*, pages 62–74. Italian National Research Council, 2009.
31. P. Gärdenfors and N.-E. Sahlin. Unreliable probabilities, risk taking, and decision making. *Synthese*, 53(3):361–386, 1982.
32. A. Gelman et al. *Bayesian Data Analysis, 2nd ed.* Chapman and Hall/CRC, Boca Raton, 2004.
33. Robin K.S. Hankin. A generalization of the Dirichlet distribution. *Journal of Statistical Software*, 33(11):1–18, February 2010.
34. Richard J. Heuer. *Psychology of Intelligence Analysis*. Central Intelligence Agency, Center for the Study of Intelligence, Washington, D.C., 1999.
35. U. Hoffrage, S. Lindsey, R. Hertwig, and G. Gigerenzer. Communicating statistical information. *Science*, 290(5500):2261–2262, December 2000.
36. ISO. *ISO 31000:2009 - Risk Management Principles and Guidelines*. International Organization for Standardization, 2009.
37. Magdalena Ivanovska, Audun Jøsang, and Francesco Sambo. Subjective networks: Prospectives and challenges. In *Graph Structures for Knowledge Representation and Reasoning, Third International Workshop (GKR@IJCAI 2015)*, Buenos Aires, July 2015.
38. Magdalena Ivanovska, Audun Jøsang, and Francesco Sambo. Bayesian deduction with subjective opinions. In J. Delgrande, F. Wolter, and C. Baral, editors, *15th International Conference on Principles of Knowledge Representation and Reasoning (KR 2016)*. AAAI Press, Palo Alto, 2016.
39. A. Jøsang. The right type of trust for distributed systems. In C. Meadows, editor, *Proc. of the 1996 New Security Paradigms Workshop*. ACM, New York, 1996.

40. A. Jøsang. Artificial reasoning with subjective logic. In Abhaya Nayak and Maurice Pagnucco, editors, *Proceedings of the 2nd Australian Workshop on Commonsense Reasoning*, Perth, December 1997. Australian Computer Society.
41. A. Jøsang. An algebra for assessing trust in certification chains. In J. Kochmar, editor, *Proceedings of the Network and Distributed Systems Security Symposium (NDSS'99)*. The Internet Society, 1999.
42. A. Jøsang. A logic for uncertain probabilities. *International Journal of Uncertainty, Fuzziness and Knowledge-Based Systems*, 9(3):279–311, June 2001.
43. A. Jøsang. The consensus operator for combining beliefs. *Artificial Intelligence*, 142(1–2):157–170, October 2002.
44. A. Jøsang. Conditional reasoning with subjective logic. *Journal of Multiple-Valued Logic and Soft Computing*, 15(1):5–38, 2008.
45. A. Jøsang. Cumulative and averaging unfusion of beliefs. In *The Proceedings of the International Conference on Information Processing and Management of Uncertainty (IPMU2008)*, Malaga, June 2008.
46. A. Jøsang and J. Haller. Dirichlet reputation systems. In *The Proceedings of the International Conference on Availability, Reliability and Security (ARES 2007)*, Vienna, Austria, April 2007.
47. A. Jøsang and R. Ismail. The beta reputation system. In *Proceedings of the 15th Bled Electronic Commerce Conference*, June 2002.
48. A. Jøsang, R. Ismail, and C. Boyd. A survey of trust and reputation systems for online service provision. *Decision Support Systems*, 43(2):618–644, 2007.
49. A. Jøsang and S.J. Knapskog. A metric for trusted systems (full paper). In *Proceedings of the 21st National Information Systems Security Conference*. NSA, October 1998.
50. A. Jøsang and S. Lo Presti. Analysing the relationship between risk and trust. In T. Dimitrakos, editor, *Proceedings of the Second International Conference on Trust Management (iTrust)*, volume 2295 of *LNCS*, pages 135–145. Springer, Berlin, 2004.
51. A. Jøsang and D. McAnally. Multiplication and comultiplication of beliefs. *International Journal of Approximate Reasoning*, 38(1):19–51, 2004.
52. A. Jøsang and S. Pope. Semantic constraints for trust transitivity. In S. Hartmann and M. Stumptner, editors, *Proceedings of the Asia-Pacific Conference of Conceptual Modelling (APCCM) (Volume 43 of Conferences in Research and Practice in Information Technology)*, Newcastle, Australia, February 2005.
53. A. Jøsang and S. Pope. Dempster's rule as seen by little colored balls. *Computational Intelligence*, 28(4):453–474, November 2012.
54. A. Jøsang, S. Pope, and S. Marsh. Exploring different types of trust propagation. In K. Stølen, W.H. Winsborough, F. Martinelli, and F. Massacci, editors, *Proceedings of the 4th International Conference on Trust Management (iTrust)*, volume 3986 of *LNCS*, pages 179–192. Springer, Berlin, 2006.
55. Audun Jøsang. Multi-agent preference combination using subjective logic. In *International Workshop on Preferences and Soft Constraints (Soft'11)*, pages 61–75, Perugia, Italy, 2011.
56. Audun Jøsang. Generalising Bayes' Theorem in Subjective Logic. In *International Conference on Multisensor Fusion and Integration for Intelligent Systems (MFI 2016)*. IEEE, Los Alamitos, 2016.
57. Audun Jøsang, Tanja Ažderska, and Stephen Marsh. Trust transitivity and conditional belief reasoning. In T. Dimitrakos, R. Moona, D. Patel, and D.H. McKnight, editors, *Proceedings of the 6th IFIP International Conference on Trust Management (IFIPTM 2012)*, volume 374 of *IFIP Advances in Information and Communication Technology*, pages 68–83. Springer, Berlin, 2012.
58. Audun Jøsang, Paulo C.G. Costa, and Erik Blash. Determining model correctness for situations of belief fusion. In *Proceedings of the 16th International Conference on Information Fusion (FUSION 2013)*, pages 1225–1232. IEEE, Los Alamitos, 2013.
59. Audun Jøsang and Robin Hankin. Interpretation and fusion of hyper-opinions in subjective logic. In *Proceedings of the 15th International Conference on Information Fusion (FUSION 2012)*. IEEE, Los Alamitos, Singapore, July 2012.

60. Audun Jøsang and Kaplan. Lance. Principles of subjective networks. In *Proceedings of the 19th International Conference on Information Fusion (FUSION 2016)*. IEEE, Los Alamitos, 2016.
61. Audun Jøsang, Xixi Luo, and Xiaowu Chen. Continuous ratings in discrete Bayesian reputation systems. In Y. Karabulut, J.C. Mitchell, P. Herrmann, and C. Damsgaard Jensen, editors, *The Proceedings of the Joint iTrust and PST Conferences on Privacy, Trust Management and Security (Trust Management II / IFIPTM 2008)*, volume 263 of *IFIP International Federation for Information Processing*, pages 151–166, Trondheim, June 2008.
62. Audun Jøsang, Simon Pope, and Milan Daniel. Conditional deduction under uncertainty. In L. Godo, editor, *Proceedings of the 8th European Conference on Symbolic and Quantitative Approaches to Reasoning with Uncertainty (ECSQARU 2005)*, volume 3572 of *LNAI*, pages 824–835. Springer, 2005.
63. Audun Jøsang and Francesco Sambo. Inverting conditional opinions in subjective logic. In *Proceedings of the 20th International Conference on Soft Computing (MENDEL 2014)*, Brno, 2014.
64. Immanuel Kant. *Kritik der praktischen Vernunft*. 1788. Translated and edited by Lewis W. Beck, *Critique of Practical Reason and Other Writings in Moral Philosophy*. The University of Chicago Press, Chicago, 1949.
65. Sherman Kent. Words of estimated probability. In Donald P. Steury, editor, *Sherman Kent and the Board of National Estimates: Collected Essays*. CIA, Center for the Study of Intelligence, 1994.
66. Jonathan Koehler. The base rate fallacy reconsidered: Descriptive, normative and methodological challenges. *Behavioral and Brain Sciences*, 19(1):1–17, 1996.
67. Kevin B. Korb and Ann E. Nicholson. *Bayesian Artificial Intelligence, Second Edition*. CRC, Boca Raton, 2nd edition, 2010.
68. Robert E. Kraut and Paul Resnick. *Building Successful Online Communities: Evidence-Based Social Design*. MIT Press, Cambridge, 2012.
69. V. Latora and M. Marchiori. Economic small-world behavior in weighted networks. *The European Physical Journal B*, 32(2):249–263, 2003.
70. P.V. Marsden and N. Lin, editors. *Social Structure and Network Analysis*. Sage Publications, Beverly Hills, 1982.
71. Stephen Marsh. *Formalising Trust as a Computational Concept*. PhD thesis, University of Stirling, 1994.
72. D. McAnally and A. Jøsang. Addition and subtraction of beliefs. In *Proceedings of Information Processing and Management of Uncertainty in Knowledge-Based Systems (IPMU 2004)*, Perugia, July 2004.
73. Robert J. McEliece. *Theory of Information and Coding*. Cambridge University Press, New York, 2nd edition, 2001.
74. D.H. McKnight and N.L. Chervany. The Meanings of Trust. Technical Report MISRC Working Paper Series 96-04, University of Minnesota, Management Information Systems Reseach Center, 1996.
75. Merriam-Webster. *Merriam-Webster Online*. Available from http://www.m-w.com/, accessed October 2015.
76. August Ferdinand Möbius. *Der barycentrische Calcul*. Leipzig, 1827. Re-published by Georg Olms Verlag, Hildesheim, New York, 1976.
77. Mohammad Modarres, Mark P. Kaminskiy, and Vasiliy Krivtsov. *Reliability Engineering and Risk Analysis: A Practical Guide, Second Edition*. CRC Press, 2002.
78. N. J. Nilsson. Probabilistic logic. *Artificial Intelligence*, 28(1):71–87, 1986.
79. Donald Nute and Charles B. Cross. Conditional Logic. In Dov M. Gabbay and Franz Guenthner, editors, *Handbook of Philosophical Logic, 2nd Edition*. Kluwer, 2002.
80. Yongsu Park. On the optimality of trust network analysis with subjective logic. *Advances in Electrical and Computer Engineering*, 14(3):49–54, 2014.
81. Judea Pearl. *Probabilistic Reasoning in Intelligent Systems*. Morgan Kaufmann Publishers, 1988.

82. Judea Pearl. Reasoning with belief functions: An analysis of compatibility. *International Journal of Approximate Reasoning*, 4:363–389, 1990.
83. Simon Pope and Audun Jøsang. Analsysis of Competing Hypotheses using Subjective Logic. In *Proceedings of the 10th International Command and Control Research and Technology Symposium (ICCRTS)*. United States Department of Defense Command and Control Research Program (DoDCCRP), 2005.
84. A.P. Prudnikov, Yu.A. Brychkov, and O.I. Marichev. *Integrals and Series* (translated from Russian), volume 1–3. Gordon and Breach Science Publishers, Amsterdam, New York, 1986.
85. W. Quattrociocchi, M. Paolucci, and R. Conte. Dealing with Uncertainty: Simulating Reputation in an Ideal Marketplace. In *Proceedings of the 2008 Trust Workshop, at the 7th Int. Joint Conference on Autonomous Agents & Multiagent Systems (AAMAS)*, 2008.
86. P. Resnick, R. Zeckhauser, R. Friedman, and K. Kuwabara. Reputation Systems. *Communications of the ACM*, 43(12):45–48, December 2000.
87. Sebastian Ries, Sheikh Mahbub Habib, Max Mühlhäuser, and Vijay Varadharajan. CertainLogic: A logic for modeling trust and uncertainty. Technical Report TUD-CS-2011-0104, Technische Universität Darmstadt, Darmstadt, Germany, April 2011.
88. B. Robertson and G.A. Vignaux. *Interpreting evidence: Evaluating forensic evidence in the courtroom*. John Wiley & Sons, Chichester, 1995.
89. Murat Sensoy, Jeff Z. Pan, Achille Fokoue, Mudhakar Srivatsa, and Felipe Meneguzzi. Using subjective logic to handle uncertainty and conflicts. In *Proceedings of the 2012 IEEE 11th International Conference on Trust, Security and Privacy in Computing and Communications*, TRUSTCOM '12, pages 1323–1326, Washington, DC, USA, 2012. IEEE Computer Society.
90. G. Shafer. *A Mathematical Theory of Evidence*. Princeton University Press, 1976.
91. C.E. Shannon. A mathematical theory of communication. *Bell System Technical Journal*, 27:379–423, 623–656, July and October 1948.
92. C. Shapiro. Consumer Information, Product Quality, and Seller Reputation. *The Bell Journal of Economics*, 13(1):20–35, 1982.
93. Florentin Smarandache. An In-Depth Look at Information Fusion Rules & the Unification of Fusion Theories. *Computing Research Repository (CoRR), Cornell University arXiv*, cs.OH/0410033, 2004.
94. M. Smithson. *Ignorance and Uncertainty: Emerging Paradigms*. Springer, 1988.
95. David Sundgren and Alexander Karlsson. Uncertainty levels of second-order probability. *Polibits*, 48:5–11, 2013.
96. S. Tadelis. Firm Reputation with Hidden Information. *Economic Theory*, 21(2):635–651, 2003.
97. Edward R. Tufte. *The Cognitive Style of PowerPoint: Pitching Out Corrupts Within*. Graphics Press, Cheshire, Connecticut, 2 edition, 2006.
98. P. Walley. Inferences from Multinomial Data: Learning about a Bag of Marbles. *Journal of the Royal Statistical Society*, 58(1):3–57, 1996.
99. O.E. Williamson. Calculativeness, Trust and Economic Organization. *Journal of Law and Economics*, 36:453–486, April 1993.
100. A. Withby, A. Jøsang, and J. Indulska. Filtering out unfair ratings in Bayesian reputation systems. In *Proceedings of the 7th Int. Workshop on Trust in Agent Societies (at AAMAS'04)*. ACM, 2004.
101. Lotfi A. Zadeh. Review of Shafer's 'A Mathematical Theory of Evidence'. *AI Magazine*, 5:81–83, 1984.
102. Jack Zlotnick. Bayes' theorem for intelligence analysis. *Studies in Intelligence*, 16(2), Spring 1972.

Acronyms

ACH Analysis of competing hypotheses

AS Affected subjects (number of)

BRN Base rate network

BL Binary logic

BN Bayesian network

CP Contraposition

DAG Directed acyclic graph

DSPG Directed series-parallel graph

DST Dempster-Shafer theory

EQU Equivalence

FN False negatives (number of)

FP False-positives (number of)

ID Inbound degree

IDM Imprecise Dirichlet model

MBR Marginal base rate

MP Modus Ponens

MT Modus Tollens

PDF Probability density function

PKI Public-key infrastructure

PL Probabilistic logic

PPS Parallel-path subnetwork

OD Outbound degree

OIS Outbound-inbound set

SBN Subjective Bayesian network

SL Subjective logic

SN Subjective network

STN Subjective trust network

TN True negatives (number of)

TNR True-negative rate

TP True positives (number of)

TPR True-positive rate

US Unaffected subjects (number of)

XOR Exclusive OR (inequivalence)

Index

Printed in the United States
By Bookmasters